Compton's Encyclopedia

and Fact-Index

1986 EDITION COMPTON'S ENCYCLOPEDIA

COPYRIGHT © 1986 by COMPTON'S LEARNING COMPANY
DIVISION OF ENCYCLOPAEDIA BRITANNICA, INC.

Library of Congress Catalog Card Number: 85-71612
International Standard Book Number: 0-85229-435-2
Printed in U.S.A.

THE UNIVERSITY OF CHICAGO
COMPTON'S ENCYCLOPEDIA IS PUBLISHED WITH THE EDITORIAL ADVICE
OF THE FACULTIES OF THE UNIVERSITY OF CHICAGO

"Let knowledge grow from more to more and thus be human life enriched"

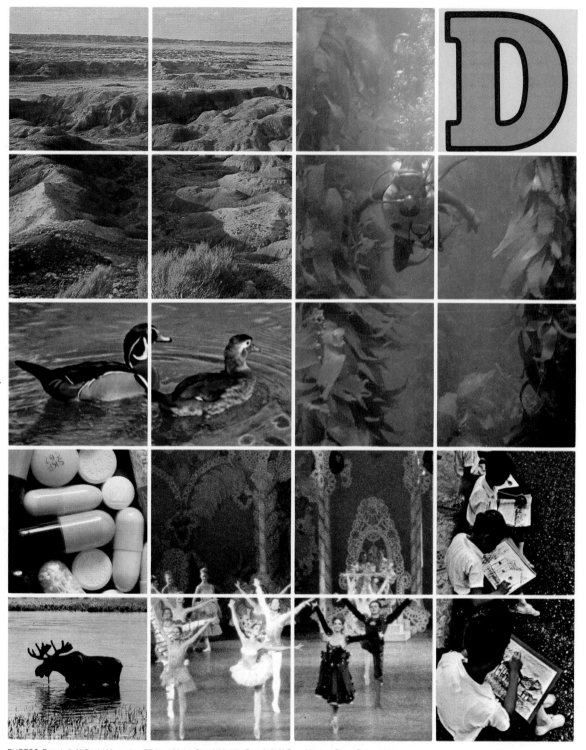

PHOTOS: Row 1: (left) David Muench—EB Inc.; (right) Chuck Nicklin. Row 3: (left) Russ Kinne—Photo Researchers. Row 4: (far left) R. S. Mandelkorn—Stock, Boston; (center) Martha Swope; (far right) Tom Sennett—World Bank. Row 5: (far left) Anita S. Este—Photo Researchers.

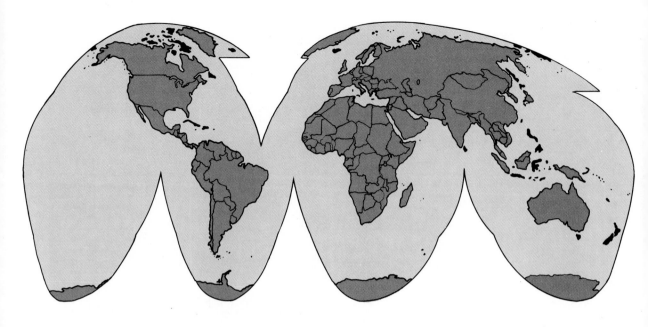

HERE AND THERE IN VOLUME 6

From the A-1 satellite to the zygote cell, thousands of subjects are gathered together in Compton's Encyclopedia and Fact-Index. Organized alphabetically, they are drawn from every field of knowledge. Readers who want to explore their favorite fields in this volume can use this subject-area outline. While it may serve as a study guide, a specialized learning experience, or simply a key for browsing, it is not a complete table of contents.

EXPLORING VOLUME 6

How many languages have been used
on the sound tracks of cartoonist Walt
Disney's animated films?   185.

Why did a French poet use the term orphism for
Robert Delaunay's variation of cubism?   69.

The 18th-century ballerina Camargo revolutionized dance costume
when she shortened her skirts. What was her reason?   27.

What is a "sleeping mouse"?   231.

How did a shepherd make "the greatest manuscript discovery of modern times" in a desert cave on the Dead Sea's shore? 46.

Name the city whose most prominent landmarks are a 13th- to 14th- century church tower and Germany's first skyscraper. 293.

What Mexican flower, brought to Europe by Spaniards, was named for a Swedish botanist? 3.

Which six-legged insect can curve its legs to form a basket for scooping other insects from the air? 238.

Russian Matreshka dolls, which nest inside each other, are fashioned from wood. What other materials have dolls been made of ? 216.

Dave Woodward—CLICK/Chicago

From the article UNDERWATER DIVING

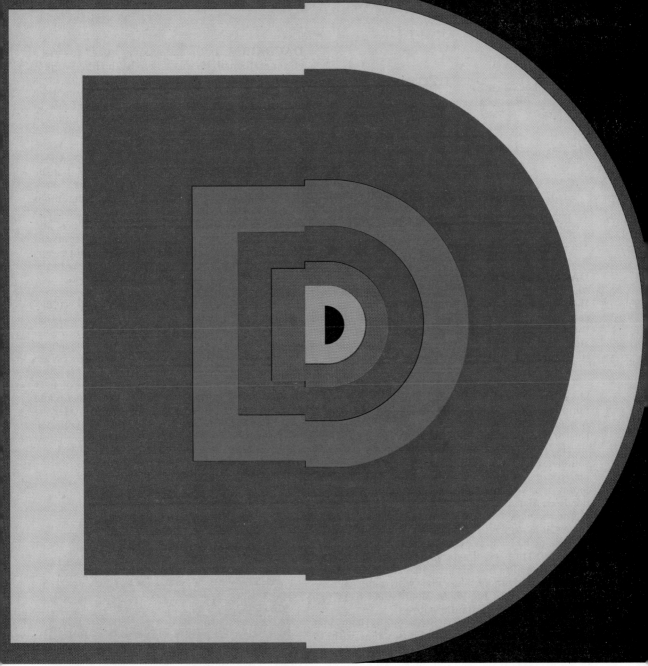

The letter D

may have started as a picture sign of a door, as in Egyptian hieroglyphic writing (1). The earliest form of the sign in the Semitic writings is unknown. About 1000 B.C., in Byblos and in other Phoenician and Canaanite centers, the sign was given a linear form (2), the source of all later forms. In the Semitic languages the sign was called *daleth,* meaning ''door.''

The Greeks changed the Semitic name to *delta.* They retained the Phoenician form of the sign (3). In an Italian colony of Greeks from Khalkis (or Chalcis), the letter was made with a slight curve (4). This shape led to the rounded form found in the Latin writing (5). From Latin the capital letter came unchanged into English. In Greek handwriting the triangle of the capital letter was given a projection upward. During Roman times the triangle was gradually rounded (6).

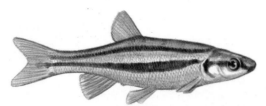

The southern redbelly dace lives in springs and clear streams.

The cutlips minnow occurs in the northeastern United States.

DACE AND MINNOW.

The most abundant of all freshwater fishes are the small minnows called dace. Many species seldom reach a length of 2 inches (5 centimeters). Dace have remarkable lips, which they thrust forward to seize their food—chiefly insects and crustaceans. The young of other fishes feed on these fish that seem never to grow up. Man's supply of edible fish, therefore, depends upon them.

The commonest American variety is known as the black-nosed, or striped, dace, also called the brook minnow. It is about 4 inches (10 centimeters) long. A black stripe runs from the tip of its nose to the base of its tail. The back is olive green; the underside, silvery white. At spawning time, in spring or early summer, the male's fins are tinged with red and the black stripe is bordered with bronze. This dace is found from New England to Minnesota and south to northern Alabama and Virginia.

The common shiner is a favorite bait of bass fishermen. It has a deep, flat body with silvery sides and an olive-green back. It reaches a length of from 5 to 8 inches (13 to 20 centimeters). During the spawning season the male's fins turn red, its back becomes an iridescent blue, and its sides glow with many colors. It is found east of the Rocky Mountains except in Texas and the south Atlantic states.

The adult creek chub measures from 7 to 10 inches (18 to 25 centimeters) long. It is dusky blue with a black spot at the base of the tail. This spot is bordered with red in the male. In the spawning season the male's head turns orange and shows hornlike growths. This dace is found from Maine to Wyoming and south as far as Alabama.

Dace belong to the carp family Cyprinidae (*see* Carp). Members of this family have jaws without teeth, smooth-edged scales, and hairlike ribs that extend the length of the body. The scientific name of the black-nosed dace is *Rhinichthys atratulus;* of the common shiner, *Notropis cornutus;* of the creek chub, *Semotilus atromaculatus.*

The name minnow is also given to the mudminnow, a hardy fish of the family Umbridae that is found in Europe and North America. Mudminnows are about 3 to 6 inches (7.5 to 15 centimeters) long.

DAEDALUS.

In Greek mythology Daedalus was a clever craftsman. He was said to be the first sculptor to make statues having open eyes and with arms standing out from the body. He was also credited with inventing the awl, the bevel, and other tools. In ancient times many wooden temples and statues in Greece and Italy were believed to be his work.

A pupil of Daedalus was his nephew Perdix. When the boy invented the saw and the potter's wheel, Daedalus supposedly became so jealous that he pushed Perdix from the Acropolis in Athens.

After Daedalus fled to Crete, where King Minos ruled, he built the mazelike labyrinth to enclose the Minotaur. Daedalus later offended King Minos, and he and his son Icarus were imprisoned. Daedalus made wings of feathers and wax so they could escape by flying over the sea. Icarus soared too near to the sun. Its heat melted the wax and he drowned.

DAGUERRE, Louis-Jacques-Mandé (1789–1851).

The first practical photographic process that produced lasting pictures was invented by Louis-Jacques-Mandé Daguerre, a French painter and physicist. The photographs that result from his process are called daguerreotypes.

Daguerre was born in Cormeilles, France, near Paris, in 1789. He worked first as a tax collector and then became a successful stage-scene painter for the opera. In 1822 he opened the Diorama, an exhibition

Daguerre perfected the photographic process with which a daguerreotype was made of him in 1848.

of enormous pictorial views that changed in effect as the lighting was altered. He opened a Diorama in London, as well, but it was destroyed by fire.

Daguerre began experimenting, hoping to discover a practical photographic process. The French inventor J.-N. Niepce had been working toward the same end since 1814, and from 1829 the two combined their efforts. After Niepce died in 1833, Daguerre continued refining their techniques and on Jan. 9, 1839, announced the daguerreotype process at a meeting of the Academy of Sciences. For his discovery he was appointed an officer of the Legion of Honor, and the French government published his process and granted him 6,000 francs annually. Daguerre improved his invention and then returned to painting. He died on July 10, 1851, at Bry-sur-Marne, France.

Although Daguerre preferred landscapes for his subjects, daguerreotypes were also used to shoot still lifes, and they made portrait photography a prosperous industry. It was especially popular in the United States. (*See also* Photography.)

Sven Samelius

The common, or garden, dahlia is one of many popular varieties.

DAHLIA. The Aztecs cultivated the dahlia, which grows wild in Central America and Mexico, and Spanish explorers brought the flower to Europe. It was named for Anders Dahl, a Swedish botanist.

Wild dahlias are flat, with a yellow center and eight single scarlet rays. Modern varieties may be globe-shaped and double, or with many petals. Their color may be white, yellow, orange, red, or purple. The plants grow from 18 inches to 20 feet (46 centimeters to 6 meters) high. They bloom in late summer or autumn.

Dahlias may be grown from seed or cuttings, by grafting (to perpetuate rare varieties), or by division of the tuberous roots. Amateur gardeners commonly use the last method. After frost kills the tops, the tubers should be divided and then stored in a cellar.

Dahlias form a genus of the family Compositae. Thousands of varieties of dahlias have been developed from hybrids of *Dahlia pinnata* and *D. coccinea*.

DAIRY INDUSTRY. Milk and milk products, such as butter, cheese, and ice cream, are processed and distributed to the public by dairy plants. The production of milk on dairy farms and the processing of milk and dairy products make up the dairy industry. Plants where butter and cheese or milk and cream are prepared for sale may also be called creameries.

Dairying begins on the farms that raise the milk cows. A typical dairy farm in the midwestern United States may have 60 cows, but a dairy farm in Florida or California may have 500 or more animals. Most milk in the United States is marketed through farmer-owned cooperatives. The milk that is produced on dairy farms is collected at county receiving stations for shipment to dairy plants (*see* Milk).

Milk must meet quality standards and must be produced, processed, and handled in an approved manner in approved facilities and equipment. Dairy farms operate under the rules of sanitation imposed by the health boards of the cities and states they supply. Grade A milk, milk intended to be consumed as fluid milk or cream, is approved for interstate shipment through a voluntary program called the Interstate Milk Shippers Agreement, which is supervised by the Food and Drug Administration (FDA).

Milk and milk products make up about an eighth of all the food eaten by the people of the United States. The annual production is about 140 billion pounds. There are more than 300,000 farms with dairy cows in the United States, but only about 200,000 of these sell milk; the remainder use the milk as animal feed and for their own domestic consumption. There are about 150,000 people employed in the processing and delivery of dairy products (*see also* Cattle).

How Fluid Milk is Processed

Milk must be moved rapidly from the farm to the consumer and kept cold so that it will not spoil. On the dairy farm, milk is collected and quickly refrigerated in stainless steel bulk tanks. It is transported to the processing plant by refrigerated tank trucks where it is automatically pumped into temporary holding tanks. It is then weighed, and samples are sent to the laboratory where tests are made for odor and flavor, bacteria, sediment, and milk protein and fat content. Milk of inferior quality may be rejected. Although dairy farms are routinely inspected by health officials, a farm from which any substandard milk came will be examined at once.

In order to determine the constituents of milk, it is necessary to test for milkfat, protein, and nonfat solids in the milk sample. Milkfat, or butterfat, was formerly determined using the Babcock test, developed at the University of Wisconsin in 1890. More recently, milk constituents are measured automatically by sensitive infrared equipment.

This article was contributed by W.R. Gomes, Professor of Dairy Science, University of Illinois at Urbana-Champaign, College of Agriculture, Urbana.

Grant Heilman

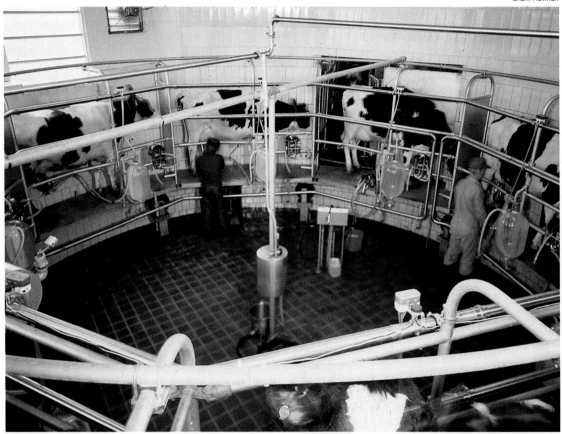

Dairy workers fit milking machines onto milk cows. After the milk is taken from the cows it is transported to county receiving stations for shipment to dairy plants.

Pasteurized and Homogenized Milk

From the temporary holding tanks the milk flows through stainless steel pipes to clarifiers, or filters, and then into pasteurizers. It may be homogenized before or after pasteurization. Pasteurization kills harmful bacteria with heat. The process is named for the French scientist Louis Pasteur, who first developed it to prevent spoilage of other food products (*see* Pasteur). Several methods are available for pasteurization of milk. The batch method involves the heating of milk or milk product in a vat for 30 minutes at 145° F (63° C). The most widely used method for pasteurizing milk is the high-temperature, short-time (HTST) method. In the HTST procedure the milk is heated to 161° F (71.6° C) for 15 seconds. If products are to be stored under refrigeration for long periods of time, as with half-and-half used for coffee, the product may be processed by ultra-high temperature (UHT) pasteurization at 280° F (138° C) for 2 seconds. UHT pasteurization can be used to sterilize milk that is to be stored for a long time at room temperature. In each type of pasteurization, the milk is rapidly cooled to preserve its flavor.

Almost all of the milk sold today is pasteurized. Pasteurizing does not affect milk's nutritive value.

Pasteurizing reduces two vitamins, thiamine and ascorbic acid, but these can readily be obtained in other foods. Cream used in making butter is pasteurized before churning, the process that produces the butter. Ice cream is always pasteurized. Much of the cheese produced is made from pasteurized milk.

In the homogenizer the milk is forced under high pressure through many tiny holes. This breaks up the fat globules into minute particles measuring about 1 micron (about 0.00004 in) in diameter. They do not rise to the top as cream, making the shaking of milk, as was once common, unnecessary.

Cream and Skim Milk

A dairy company may separate cream from whole milk and bottle it at the milk-processing plant. Or it may separate the cream at one plant and ship it to the milk plant for pasteurization. Milk remaining after

The manufacture of milk products (opposite page) begins in the milking parlors of dairy farms. After the milk is collected from the cows, it is quickly refrigerated and transported by refrigerated trucks to receiving stations. The milk is tested for disease organisms and stored briefly before being shipped by refrigerated tank trucks to a processing plant. At the plant the milk is tested for odor and flavor, bacteria, sediment, and milk protein and fat content. The milk is then filtered and pasteurized. Then, depending on the desired product, the milk is processed in various ways.

MILK PROCESSING

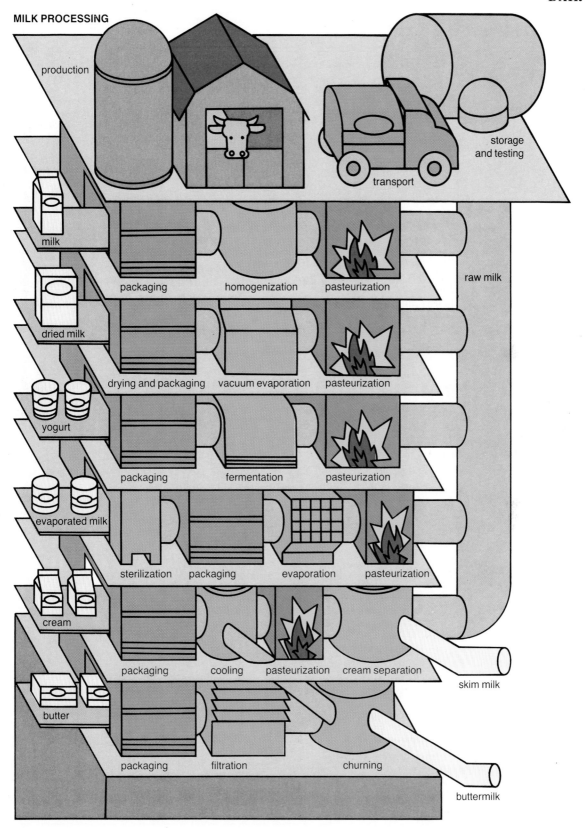

production

storage
and testing

transport

milk

packaging   homogenization   pasteurization

raw milk

dried milk

drying and packaging   vacuum evaporation   pasteurization

yogurt

packaging   fermentation   pasteurization

evaporated milk

sterilization   packaging   evaporation   pasteurization

cream

packaging   cooling   pasteurization   cream separation

skim milk

butter

packaging   filtration   churning

buttermilk

What Does The Label Mean?

Fresh Milk

Raw milk is milk as it comes from the cow. When sold as whole milk, the United States Public Health Service Milk Code states that it must contain at least 8.25 percent milk solids other than fat and 3.25 percent milk fat.

Pasteurized milk has been heated to kill bacteria that might cause disease.

Homogenized milk has been especially treated so that the cream will not rise.

Lowfat milk contains not more than 2.0 percent milk fat and at least 8.25 percent milk solids other than fat. Some lowfat milk is supplemented with 0.5 to 1.5 percent additional nonfat milk solids.

Skim milk has had the milk fat removed. No more than 0.5 percent milk fat is allowed. Nonfat milk solids range from 8.25 to 10.0 percent.

Sterile milk is homogenized, sterilized, and packaged as ultra-high temperature (UHT) milk or canned whole milk. Canned whole milk is produced chiefly for export.

Cultured Milk

Cultured milk has been fermented by harmless bacteria that produce lactic acid during the process. The bacteria may be allowed to develop naturally or may be cultivated ("cultured") artificially and then introduced into the milk. The milk has the same food value it had before souring; it may be slightly more digestible to persons with delicate digestive systems.

Sour milk has been fermented by lactic acid bacilli.

Buttermilk is fresh milk soured by lactic acid bacilli. Butter granules are sometimes added.

Acidophilus milk has been fermented by the bacteria strain called *Lactobacillus acidophilus*.

Yogurt is milk fermented chiefly by *Lactobacillus bulgaricus*.

Concentrated Milk

Concentrated milk is homogenized, pasteurized milk with about two thirds of the water removed. It is reconstituted with water. Lowfat milk and skim milk may also be concentrated.

Frozen milk concentrate is concentrated milk quickly frozen and held at −10° to −20° F (−23° to −29° C) until ready for use.

Evaporated milk is homogenized whole milk with about 60 percent of its water removed by heating in a vacuum cooker. Its food value is about the same as that of fresh whole milk.

Sweetened condensed milk is evaporated milk with 42 percent sucrose, or table sugar, added. Since the sugar acts as a preservative, the milk, when sealed in cans, can be stored without further heat treatment.

Dry milk is milk evaporated to a powder. Whole milk powder has had only the water removed. Nonfat milk solids have had both water and fat removed.

Fortified Milk

Fortified lowfat milk has 0.5 to 1.5 percent nonfat milk solids added.

Vitamin D milk has 400 units of this vitamin added to each quart.

Flavored Milk

Chocolate milk is made by adding chocolate syrup or cocoa powder to whole milk.

Chocolate drink is made by adding chocolate syrup or cocoa powder to partially skim milk.

Fruit flavored dairy drinks are made by adding artificial fruit flavors to partially skim milk.

Cream

Light cream contains 18–30 percent milk fat. It may also be called coffee cream or table cream.

Whipping cream is either light (30–36 percent milk fat) or heavy (36 percent or more milk fat).

Half-and-half has about 10–12 percent milk fat.

Sour cream is cultured homogenized cream ripened or cultured until it is thick, smooth, and pleasant tasting.

This list tells what dairy companies mean by the labels they put on bottled or packaged milk and cream. Today milk is marketed in many forms. Dairies protect the public health, improve the keeping quality of dairy products, and make maximum use of milk by-products. They also preserve surpluses and facilitate distribution and storage.

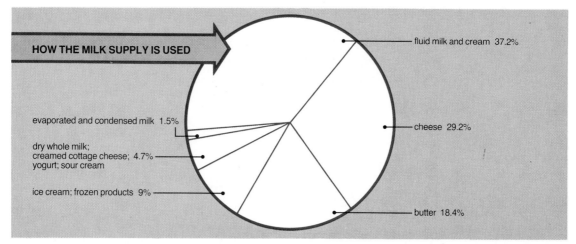

HOW THE MILK SUPPLY IS USED

fluid milk and cream 37.2%

cheese 29.2%

butter 18.4%

evaporated and condensed milk 1.5%

dry whole milk;
creamed cottage cheese; 4.7%
yogurt; sour cream

ice cream; frozen products 9%

the cream has been removed is skim milk. The dairy may sell it for cattle feed, convert it into powdered skim milk, or package it for sale for human use as liquid skim milk.

Before the power cream separator came into use, between 1880 and 1890, the gravity method of cream separation was used. Pans of milk stood on the shelves of the dairy house for 24 to 36 hours until the cream rose and could be skimmed off by hand. This method left from 10 to 20 percent of the fat in the skim milk. Centrifugal cream separators today leave less than 0.01 percent fat.

The cream separator works on the principle that the heavier a whirling body, the greater the force acting on it to move it from the center. From a tank at the top of the cream separator the milk flows down into a large bowl, or drum, making from 5,000 to 9,000 rotations per minute. The cream, being lighter, stays in the center and is drawn off through a tube. The heavier skim milk, forced to the outside, is carried through another tube to a pasteurizer.

Packaging and Delivering Milk

From the coolers the milk flows to the packaging machine. Milk may be packaged in plastic containers or in cardboard cartons that are coated with paraffin wax to make them leakproof. Filled containers then go to a refrigerated room to remain until the delivery trucks pick them up. Every day workers in the dairy plant sterilize the stainless steel and glass piping and all the machines through which the milk has flowed. About one third of the labor time in a dairy plant may be spent in cleaning the equipment. Modern distributors prepare many products in addition to milk, lowfat milk, cream, and skim milk. Dairies also make butter, ice cream, and cheese (see Butter; Cheese; Ice Cream).

By-Products

Some by-products of dairying have industrial uses. Lactose, or milk sugar, is used in the fermentation process that produces penicillin. Lactose is also a base for pills and is used in infant foods.

The milk protein called casein is produced from skim milk. Much of the total production of casein goes into the coating of fine book and magazine papers. This page, for example, has been sprayed with a casein solution. Casein glue is important in woodworking, and casein paints have special uses. A small amount of casein is used to make plastic buttons and costume jewelry.

History of Dairying

Sanskrit records mentioned milk 6,000 years ago. The Bible describes the Promised Land as "a land flowing with milk and honey." The Greek physician Hippocrates recommended milk as a medicine some 2,300 years ago. Christopher Columbus brought cattle to the New World on his second voyage. It has been said that one reason for the high death rate among those who traveled to the New World on the Mayflower was that they had no fresh milk to drink. Cows were brought from Europe to the Jamestown colony in 1611 and to the Plymouth colony in 1624.

Cheese was an important item in the diet of the Vikings, who from about the 8th to the 10th century sailed the seas on long voyages. Cheese was an article of commerce in ancient Rome. Monks developed the art of cheesemaking in Europe in the Middle Ages.

The modern large-scale dairy industry developed with the growth of cities and fast, refrigerated transportation. In 1841 Thomas Selleck, a New York and Erie Railroad stationmaster, asked a farmer to try shipping milk by rail 60 miles (97 kilometers) to New York City. On the day of the "big haul," 60 gallons (227 liters) in a wooden churn were successfully shipped to the city.

A few years later wooden containers for shipment were replaced by metal cans. Sometimes the cans were packed in ice to keep the milk cool. Mechanical refrigeration began to be used between 1880 and 1890. In 1892 Nathan Straus established the first infant milk depot in the United States. He offered sterilized milk for sale at five cents a quart or one cent a glass. The glass milk bottle was invented by Hervey D. Thatcher in 1880.

One of the most common varieties of daisy has white petals surrounding a yellow center.

The mosaic-covered library building at Dakar University is one of the newer buildings in Dakar.

DAISY. The "day's eye," as the daisy was known in Old English, is like a tiny sun surrounded by white rays. The common field, or oxeye, daisy is a species of chrysanthemum native to Europe. Its scientific name is *Chrysanthemum leucanthemum.* Tradition says that it was carried to America in hay brought to feed the horses of General John Burgoyne's army during the Revolutionary War. The painted daisy (*Chrysanthemum coccineum*) has white, crimson, or lilac flowers. These two daisies are related to pyrethrum, from which an insecticide is made.

The petals of the English daisy (*Bellis perennis*) are white tinged with pink. The black-eyed Susan, also known as the yellow daisy (*Rudbeckia hirta*), is a common wild flower. The striking white Shasta daisy is a hybrid developed by Luther Burbank. (*See also* Chrysanthemum.) Michaelmas daisies are species of asters. All daisies are members of the family of plants called Compositae.

DAKAR, Senegal. The capital of Senegal and one of the chief seaports on the West African coast, Dakar is near Africa's most westerly point and is one of tropical Africa's leading industrial and service centers. Its industries include peanut oil, fish canning, flour milling, brewing, truck assembly, and petroleum refining. The city's business activities are international in their range. Peanut cultivation was stimulated in Dakar in 1885 with the opening of West Africa's first railway, which ran from Saint-Louis to Dakar. Peanuts were grown near the railroad's right-of-way. Peanut oil refining became an important industry during World War II because of local and North African needs for vegetable oil, a product that had previously been refined mostly in France.

There are sea and history museums on the islet of Gorée, near Dakar Point, and archaeology and ethnography museums in Dakar. There is also a village of working craftsmen. The only park and zoo are in Hann. Along a road cut into the cliff around Cape Manuel there are excellent views of the harbor and islands. Dakar has some good beaches.

Since World War II Dakar has undergone much urban expansion. The city has several contrasting districts. In the southern district are public buildings, hospitals, the Pasteur Institute, and embassies. The business district is to the north and is focused on the central Place de l'Independence. North and east are the port, the naval arsenal, the fishing harbor, and facilities for shipping peanuts. Industry, markets, and sports stadiums were built in the central business district and its northwestern fringes after 1939. Yoff Airport is north of the city and is an important stopping point for flights between Europe and South America.

European settlement of the area began in 1617 when the Dutch occupied Gorée. The French captured the islet in 1677 but did not occupy the mainland until 1857. In 1866 French steamships began to call there to take on coal. In 1904 Dakar replaced Saint-Louis as the federal capital of French West Africa. During World War I the port grew in importance and volume of trade, and by the 1930s Dakar had replaced Rufisque, to the east, as a peanut-shipping port. Population (1979 estimate), 978,553.

DALEY, Richard J. (1902–76). As the mayor of Chicago from 1955 until his death in 1976 and as chairman of Chicago's Cook County Democratic Central Committee from 1953 to 1976, Richard Joseph Daley was one of the most powerful politicians in the United States. He easily won re-election to office in five successive campaigns from 1959 to 1975, and during his mayoralty Chicago was the scene of an unprecedented building boom, improvement in city services, and urban renewal programs.

Daley was born in the Bridgeport area of Chicago on May 15, 1902. He was graduated from De La Salle Institute in 1918 and worked in the stockyards for several years before studying law. While studying, he worked as a clerk in the Cook County Controller's office. He passed his law examinations, becoming a lawyer, in 1933. In 1936 Daley married Eleanor Guilfoyle, and the couple had three daughters and four sons. One son, Richard M. Daley, served in the Illinois Senate and as Cook County state's attorney.

Daley held several elected posts before becoming mayor: state representative from 1936 to 1938, state senator (1939–46), county deputy controller (1946–49), and county clerk (1950–55). He served as state revenue director, an appointed position, under Governor Adlai Stevenson.

Although Daley remained popular and influential during his several terms, his administration was marred by a number of political scandals, by civil rights disturbances, and by a riot at the 1968 Democratic convention. He died in Chicago of a heart attack on Dec. 20, 1976.

DALI, Salvador (born 1904). Despite all that has been written by and about him, Spanish surrealist artist Salvador Dali remains a mystery as a man and as an artist. A curious blend of reality and fantasy characterized both his life and his works.

In the Catalan town of Figueras, near Barcelona, Dali was born on May 11, 1904. His family encouraged his early interest in art; a room in the family home was the young artist's first studio. In 1921 Dali enrolled at the San Fernando Royal Academy of Fine Arts in Madrid. There he joined an avant-garde circle of students that included filmmaker Luis Buñuel and poet-dramatist Federico García Lorca. Although Dali did very well in his studies, he was expelled from school because of his eccentric dress and behavior.

It was at this time that Dali came under the influence of two forces that shaped his philosophy and his art. The first was Sigmund Freud's theory of the unconscious (*see* Freud). The second was his association with the French surrealists, a group of artists and writers led by the French poet André Breton. In 1928, with the help of the Spanish painter Joan Miró, Dali visited Paris for the first time and was intro-

'Dali Atomicus', a surrealistic photograph of Dali in his studio, was taken by Philippe Halsman.

© Philippe Halsman

duced to the leading surrealists. The following year he settled there, becoming in a short time one of the best-known members of the group. During the 1930s his paintings were included in surrealist shows in most major European cities and in the United States.

Under the influence of the surrealist movement, Dali's artistic style crystallized into the disturbing blend of precise realism and dreamlike fantasy that became his hallmark. Against desolate landscapes he painted unrelated and often bizarre objects. These pictures, described by Dali as "hand-painted dream photographs," are inspired by dreams, hallucinations, and other unconscious forces that the artist is unable to explain; they are produced by a creative method he calls "paranoiac-critical activity." Dali's most characteristic works show the influence not only of the surrealists but also of the Italian Renaissance masters, the mannerists, and the Italian metaphysical painters Carlo Carrà and Giorgio de Chirico.

During World War II Dali and his wife, Gala, took refuge in the United States, returning after the war's end to Spain. His international reputation continued to grow, based as much on his showy life-style and flair for publicity as on his prodigious output of paintings, graphic works, book illustrations, and designs for jewelry, textiles, clothing, costumes, shop interiors, and stage sets. His wife died in 1982.

Dali produced two films—'An Andalusian Dog', released in 1928, and 'The Golden Age' (1930)—with Buñuel. Considered surrealist classics, they are filled with grotesque images. His writings include poetry, fiction, and a controversial autobiography, 'The Secret Life of Salvador Dali'. 'The Persistence of Memory', painted in 1931, is perhaps the most widely recognized surrealist painting in the world (*see* Painting).

DALLAS, Tex. Founded as a simple frontier trading post in 1841, Dallas is now the nucleus of a thriving cosmopolitan area. A far cry from the dusty cattle town often portrayed in popular film and folklore, it is one of the fastest growing cities in the United States. Amer-

icans have flocked to "Big D," doubling the population in little more than the last 30 years. Its main attractions are its sunbelt climate (an average of 237 sunny days per year), one of the lowest unemployment rates in the nation, and a relatively low cost of living.

Situated on a rolling prairie in north central Texas, Dallas is located about 70 miles (110 kilometers) south of the Oklahoma border and about 30 miles (50 kilometers) east of Fort Worth. The downtown area is near the point where three forks of the Trinity

This article was contributed by Susan Krasnow, Senior Editor, *Dallas Observer.*

River merge. The altitude of the city ranges from 450 to 750 feet (140 to 230 meters) above sea level. Normally Dallas has mild winters and hot summers. The average temperature is 65.7° F (18.7° C).

Population

In 1850, when New York City had a population of 600,000, only 430 people lived in Dallas. By 1983, however, Dallas was the second largest city in Texas and the seventh largest in the United States. With an area of 378 square miles (979 square kilometers), the city of Dallas covers about two fifths of Dallas County. In addition to the city, the county is comprised of 27 other municipalities; among the largest are Garland, Irving, Mesquite, Richardson, Grand Prairie, Farmers Branch, Carrollton, Highland Park, and University Park.

Both the city and county are part of a sprawling metropolitan area that covers 8,360 square miles (21,652 square kilometers) and includes 11 counties. The Dallas–Fort Worth area, often called "the Metroplex," is the second fastest growing metropolitan area in the United States.

The median age of Dallas residents is 28.7 years. In 1980 about 61 percent of the city's residents were white and about one third black. About 12 percent were of Hispanic descent. Native Indians and a growing number of Orientals and Europeans are also part of the Dallas community. Religion is an important aspect of Dallas culture. There are more than 1,300 churches. Dallas has the largest Southern Baptist, Presbyterian, and Episcopal congregations in the United States.

The Modern City

Dallas' tourist attractions, historic sites, and cultural organizations draw visitors from around the world. The city is the third most popular tourist destination in the United States. The Dallas Market Center and World Trade Center make up the largest wholesale merchandise mart in the world and one of three principal fashion centers in the United States. The restored John Neely Bryan log cabin, named for Dallas' first white settler, is located on a downtown plaza. The Biblical Arts Center, Dallas Zoo, Dallas Museum of Art, Old City Park, and the observation platform of the 50-story Reunion Tower are other points of interest in the city. State Fair Park is the site of the largest annual state fair in the country and home of the Cotton Bowl, an aquarium, museums of natural history and science, a garden center, a coliseum, a concert hall, and the Age of Steam Railroad Museum. The Dallas Cowboys football team plays at Texas Stadium in suburban Irving. The city has 38 radio stations, nine television stations, and two daily newspapers.

The city's cultural arts organizations include the Dallas Theater Center housed in a building designed by architect Frank Lloyd Wright, symphony orchestra, opera, ballet, summer musicals, black dance theater, Shakespeare festival, civic chorus, and a number of professional and community theater groups.

Balthazar Korab

The 50-story Reunion Tower with its geodesic dome overlooks the gleaming Hyatt Regency Dallas Hotel.

Among the more popular tourist destinations are Kennedy Plaza and Dealey Plaza, the site of the assassination of United States President John F. Kennedy. The Kennedy memorial, an open concrete box on legs, was dedicated in June 1970. The former Texas School Book Depository building, from which Kennedy's assassin is believed to have fired his rifle, was acquired by Dallas County in 1977. The Dallas Public Library has an extensive collection of books and documents relating to the life and to the assassination of President Kennedy.

Dallas' 288 parks cover a total of nearly 47,000 acres (19,000 hectares). Fifty reservoirs and lakes, most of them man-made, provide ample opportunities for water sports and also supply water to Dallas area residents.

Transportation. A major transportation center, Dallas is connected to seven interstate highways. Dallas–Fort Worth International Airport, which opened in 1974, is the largest airport in the United States and one of the busiest. In an effort to solve growing traffic problems within the city, Dallas citizens approved an $8.75 billion mass transit plan in August 1983.

Education. There are 37 degree-granting colleges, universities, and professional schools in Dallas and its surrounding counties. Institutions located within Dallas County include Southern Methodist University, the University of Texas Health Science Center, Baylor University College of Dentistry, University of Dallas (in Irving), Bishop College, Dallas Theological Seminary, University of Texas at Dallas (in Richardson), Dallas Baptist College, and seven two-year colleges that make up the Dallas County Community College District.

In 1970 the Dallas Independent School District opened the Skyline Career Development Center, a model high school, advanced career training center, and community service center. Six magnet high schools offer special career training in business, health, public administration law, transportation, human services, and the arts.

Economy

Dallas is an important financial center in the Southwest and is the home of the Eleventh District Federal Reserve Bank. More petroleum and petroleum-related corporations are headquartered in Dallas than in any other city, though no oil fields exist in the immediate Dallas area. Dallas is one of the world's largest international cotton markets and has the second highest number of insurance company headquarters (more than 250) in the nation.

One reason for Dallas' popularity as a business center is that there are no state or local personal or corporate income taxes. A varied industrial base has contributed to the stability of Dallas' economy. In the Dallas–Fort Worth area, approximately 20 percent of workers are employed in manufacturing trades; 20 percent in service industries; 28 percent in wholesale and retail trade; 12 percent in government; 8 percent in finance, real estate, and insurance; 6 percent in transportation and public utilities; 5 percent in construction; and 1 percent in mining.

Since World War II Dallas has been one of the nation's major manufacturing centers for aircraft and missile parts. In recent years the growth in manufacturing has shifted toward electronics and technology-based industries.

Government and History

Dallas adopted a council–manager form of municipal government in 1931. There are ten council members elected for two-year terms. The city manager, who acts as chief executive officer of the city, handles administrative responsibilities.

Dallas was founded in 1841 when John Neely Bryan, a Tennessee lawyer, set up a trading post and mapped out a half-mile square townsite on "free land" near a shallow crossing on the east bank of the Trinity River. The foresighted Bryan, who saw opportunity in a land that offered no special natural resources, began trading with Indians and westbound wagon trains.

During the city's early years Dallas residents were primarily farmers, tradesmen, and artisans. Because the first railroads initially planned to bypass Dallas, the city might have remained a rural town for a long time. But a persistent campaign by community leaders, combining political pressure and gifts of land and money, persuaded railroad officials to change their minds. The foundation was laid for the city's development as a business center when a north–south line of the Houston & Texas Central Railroad was extended from Houston to Dallas in 1872. In 1873

the east–west line of the Texas & Pacific Railroad was completed through Dallas, making the city the first railroad crossing town in Texas and, soon after, a major distribution center in the Southwest.

Dallas was incorporated as a town in 1856 and as a city in 1871. A fire destroyed most of Dallas' business district in 1860, and floodwaters reached the center of the city before a levee system was built in the 1920s. A prolonged drought in the 1950s created a severe water shortage.

International attention was focused on Dallas on Nov. 22, 1963, when President Kennedy was assassinated there. But the city has since received much more favorable worldwide publicity through the popular, long-running television show 'Dallas'. Southfork Ranch, the home of the show's wealthy Ewing family, has become a major tourist attraction. Population (1980 census), city, 904,078; metropolitan area, 2,974,878.

DAM. People from the beginning of recorded history have constructed barriers across rivers and other water courses to store or divert water. The earliest of these dams were used to water farms. For example, the ancient Egyptians built earth dams that raised the river level and diverted water into canals to irrigate fields above the river. The Moors carried a knowledge of irrigation from Egypt and Babylonia to Spain. Soon after the Pilgrims came to the New World, they too built dams. By 1682 pent-up water from dams turned their waterwheels to grind corn and saw timber.

One of the mightiest man-made structures in the world is Grand Coulee Dam on the Columbia River in Washington. Completed in 1942 by the United States Bureau of Reclamation, it towers 550 feet (170 meters) and is 4,173 feet (1,272 meters) long. All three of the great pyramids of Egypt could be put inside of it. The dam contains enough concrete to build a highway across the United States and back. Its spectacular waterfall is twice as high as Niagara Falls. Behind the dam, the waters of the Columbia River pile up to form a lake 151 miles (243 kilometers) long.

The artificial lake backed up by a dam is called a reservoir. That part of a dam over which the flood waters flow to the river below the dam is the spillway. Water may pass over the crest of the dam itself, or near the dam in chutes, tunnels, or shafts. A sluice is a passage through the dam itself for lowering the water level of the reservoir. Pipes for conducting water to the power turbines are called penstocks. The flow of water through spillways, sluices, and penstocks is regulated by control gates.

Why People Build Dams

Dams are built primarily for irrigation, water supply, flood control, electric power, and improvement of navigation. Many modern dams are multipurpose.

Irrigation dams store water to equalize the water supply for crops throughout the year. Irrigation is a primary purpose, for example, of Hoover Dam (Boulder Dam from 1933 to 1947) on the Colorado

SOLID GRAVITY DAM

Fontana Dam on the Little Tennessee River in North Carolina rises 480 feet, the highest dam of the TVA. Made of solid concrete it holds back the water by its own weight. It is thicker at the base than at the crest. This is the most common type of all concrete dams. It is also the most permanent type of dam and requires the least maintenance.

HOLLOW GRAVITY OR BUTTRESS (MULTIPLE ARCH) DAM

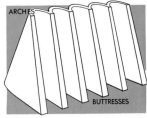

Bartlett Dam, 287 feet high, on the Verde River in Arizona is an example of a concrete multiple-arch dam. It resists water pressure more by its design than by its weight and requires less material than the solid gravity dam. The small view shows the reinforced concrete arches, shaped like half cylinders, resting against triangular buttresses.

HOLLOW GRAVITY OR BUTTRESS (FLAT SLAB) DAM

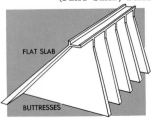

Stony Gorge Dam is on Stony Creek, a tributary of the Sacramento, in California. It requires less concrete and is less costly than the solid gravity type. It depends upon its structure more than its weight to withstand the force of the water. Its relatively thin facing is supported by buttresses. The slab and buttresses are reinforced concrete.

12

ARCHED DAM

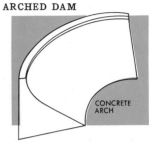

Hungry Horse Dam stands across a deep, narrow canyon on the South Fork of Flathead River in Montana. It is of the arch-gravity type, relying upon its weight and its arch form for strength. Its great concrete arch curves upstream to transfer the tremendous water load of its reservoir to the canyon walls.

EARTH DAM

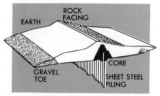

Fort Peck Dam on the Missouri River in Montana is the world's third largest dam, in volume. It is an earth dam of the hydraulic fill type. Sand, gravel, silt, and clay were delivered and distributed at the dam by water in 28-inch pipes. A cut-off wall of sheet steel piling and a watertight core of fine material prevent seepage under and through the dam. Gravel toes give stability to the slopes. A heavy layer of rock on the upstream face protects the dam against water and ice erosion.

ROCK DAM

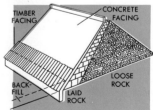

Salt Springs Dam on the North Fork of the Mokelumne River in California is 328 feet high. First, rock was dumped across the river. Then rock was laid on the upstream side to equalize settlement and to act as a cushion for the facing. This watertight facing was built of reinforced concrete slabs. The timber facing nailed to the concrete prevents leaks if the concrete cracks.

13

River. Before the dam was built, the Colorado flooded the Imperial Valley in California and the Yuma Valley in Arizona when the mountain snows melted, and it became a sluggish stream in summer. Now the dam saves the floodwaters and provides a steady supply of water for irrigation (*see* Colorado River).

Dams are used for irrigation also when a river has cut its bed below land to be irrigated. Grand Coulee Dam serves such a purpose. A huge plateau, almost as large as Delaware, lies hundreds of feet above the Columbia River. From the reservoir created by the dam, the world's largest pumps lift water to another man-made lake on the plateau. From there water flows in canals to farms (*see* Columbia River).

Some dams divert rivers into irrigation canals or pipelines. Imperial Dam across the Colorado River is an example. It diverts water from the river into the All-American Canal for irrigation of the Imperial Valley in California and into the Gila Canal for irrigating the Gila Valley in Arizona many miles away (*see* Irrigation).

Dams for Many Other Purposes

Water supply dams collect water for domestic, industrial, and municipal uses for cities such as New York, Los Angeles, San Francisco, and Boston. These cities do not have suitable lakes or rivers nearby for a water supply (*see* Aqueducts; Water).

Flood control dams impound floodwaters of rivers and release them under control to the river below the dam. Examples are the five dams in the Miami River valley. They were built to protect Dayton, Ohio, after a serious flood in 1913 (*see* Flood Control).

Navigation dams are built to maintain a minimum depth of water for ships. To illustrate, the Ohio River formerly was too low for navigation six months of the year. Now a stairlike series of dams and locks on the river maintain a uniform water depth.

Shipping may be blocked by a waterfall or rapids. A dam with a lock can "drown" the obstruction. Such a dam at Louisville, Ky., permits passage around the Falls of the Ohio River.

Hydroelectric power dams are built to generate electric power by directing water in penstocks through *turbines*, wheels with curved blades as spokes. The falling water spins the blades of the turbines connected to generators (*see* Turbine).

Power dams are expected to generate power to repay the cost of construction. The output depends, first, upon the *head* of water, or height of stored water above the turbines. The higher the water the more weight and pressure bear upon the turbine blades. A second factor is the volume of water throughout the year. The minimum flow in dry months fixes the amount of *firm power* which customers can rely upon to receive regularly. Sometimes extra power, or *run-of-stream power*, generated in flood seasons can be sold, usually at lower rates (*see* Waterpower).

Benefits and Problems

These are the main purposes of dams, but there are other benefits. Their reservoirs provide recreation, such as fishing and swimming. They become refuges for fish and birds. Dams conserve soil by preventing erosion. They slow down streams so that the water does not carry away soil (*see* Conservation).

Dams also create problems. Their reservoirs may cover towns or historic and scenic places. Dams may impair fishing. At Bonneville Dam, fishways help the salmon around the dam as they swim upstream to spawn. In *fish ladders*, the fish jump from one ascending pool to another. *Fish locks* lift the fish like locks

Bonneville Dam on the Columbia River typifies the modern multipurpose dam. The powerhouse generates electricity. The dam and lock raise the water level and improve navigation. The huge reservoir retains floodwaters to control floods. To aid conservation of fishing, fish ladders, or steplike pools, and fish locks, which work like ship locks, help salmon get upstream to spawn.

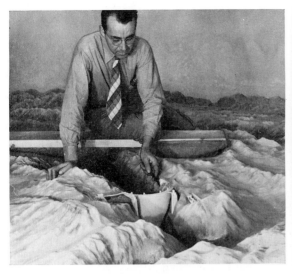

Here (left) is a model of Hoover Dam on the Colorado River. Much preliminary work must be done before actual construction begins. An early step is testing in the laboratory with numerous scale models of plaster, rubber, and concrete. This (right) is the site of Hoover Dam before construction began, looking upstream through Black Canyon. It was finally selected from 70 sites that had been explored. The broken line shows approximately where the dam was to be built.

lift ships. Another problem of dams is silting. Some rivers pick up clay and sand and deposit them behind the dam, thereby lessening its usefulness.

There are structures related to dams. *Cofferdams* are temporary dams built to hold water back so that work can be done. *Dikes* keep the sea off land that is below sea level. *Levees* are artificial riverbanks constructed high enough to prevent flooding. A dam across a river intended to permit flow, once a certain depth of water has been reached, may be called a *barrage*. A small dam that forms a millpond or fishpond is called a *weir*.

Main Types of Dams

Dams are classified into types depending upon their materials, design, and method of construction. The usual types are concrete or masonry, earth, rock, steel, timber, and movable dams. Plain or reinforced concrete is more often used than masonry. Concrete dams are either solid gravity, hollow gravity, or arched.

Solid gravity dams are made of solid concrete. They withstand the pressure or push of water by their weight. In cross section, they are like a triangle, broad at the base and narrow at the crest. They are built in this shape because water pressure becomes greater with the depth of water. Whether a dam backs up water one mile or a hundred miles is not important. Pressure depends not upon how far water is backed upstream but upon its depth at the dam.

Hollow gravity dams are made of less concrete than solid gravity dams. They rely more on their structure than their weight to resist the force of the water. They have a thin facing supported at an incline by a series of triangular buttresses, or piers. Hollow gravity dams may be of three types. The *multiple arch dam* consists of a number of arches supported on buttresses, while the *flat slab dam* is a straight wall resting against buttresses. Similar to the multiple arch dam is the *multiple dome dam*, which has domes instead of arches. Coolidge Dam on the Gila River in Arizona is an outstanding example.

Arched dams consist of a horizontal curve using the principle of the arch for strength against water pressure. They are curved upstream. The force of the water is transmitted to the canyon walls.

Earth and Rock Dams

Earth dams are made by building an embankment of gravel, sand, and clay across a river. To prevent leakage, often a *core*, or inner wall, of concrete or

Cofferdams upstream and downstream block the river and it flows around the dam site in tunnels (such as at lower left). Buckets suspended from cableways place concrete in the forms. A plant for cooling concrete is in front of the dam.

other watertight materials is used. In a *rolled-fill dam*, earth is hauled by vehicles onto the dam and rolled tight with heavy machinery. In the *hydraulic fill dam*, earth is carried to the dam by water in pipes or flumes and also deposited by the water. The placing of the earth is so controlled that the finer, watertight materials form the core. In the *semi-hydraulic fill dam*, trucks bring the earth to the dam and jets of water distribute the materials.

Rock dams are made by dumping rocks across the river. A wall of rocks is then laid on the upstream side and over this is built a waterproof facing of reinforced concrete, timber, or steel.

How Dams Are Built

The methods of building dams may be seen by following the construction of Hoover Dam, built between 1930 and 1935. The engineers constructed a concrete arch-gravity dam at an approved cost of $174,000,000. It is as tall as a 60-story skyscraper. Its crest is 45 feet thick and its base, 660 feet. It stores the entire flow of the Colorado River for two years.

Much preliminary work had to be done. The engineers made geologic and topographic surveys to select the site. They made maps of 70 locations, bored holes to test the rock for a sound foundation, and studied the river's speed, high water level, and silting.

Once the location was chosen, designers made their plans. They then made models to test their design. Where once had been burning desert, engineers built Boulder City to house about 5,000 workers. Construction gangs built railroads and highways for transporting great quantities of equipment and materials.

Workmen strung cables across the canyon from pairs of towers, which travel on tracks along opposite sides of the site. Each of the five cableways could carry 25 tons. Two of them had spans of nearly half a mile.

Construction crews also built a great gravel screening plant and two huge concrete mixing plants.

River Bypasses Dam Site

On each side of the river two tunnels, each 50 feet in diameter, were drilled and blasted from the rock of the canyon walls. They were used to divert the river around the site. Later the tunnels became spillway outlets and penstocks for the power plant.

Next, cofferdams of earth and rock were built upstream and downstream from the dam site to block the river. "High scalers" stripped tons of loose and projecting rock from canyon walls. The *overburden*, or loose rock and muck, was dug out to expose the bedrock. *Grout*, a thin mortar of cement and water, was next forced into the foundation to fill seams and holes.

Forms were made for building the dam in enormous blocks. Concrete was poured into the forms from eight-cubic-yard buckets traveling on the cableways. As each block of concrete dried, grout was pumped between the blocks, making the dam one solid piece.

Allowing so gigantic a structure to cool naturally would have taken a century because of the heat given off by the setting cement. In addition the concrete would have shrunk and cracked. Cold water circulating through 528 miles of one-inch pipes embedded in the concrete carried off the heat.

Refrigerating pipes were also used to freeze landslides of wet earth at Grand Coulee Dam. Another problem was the freezing of control gates in winter. A huge electrical heating apparatus was installed in the spillway and gates.

Famous Dams of the United States

On the great rivers and lesser streams of the United States, many dams have been built by private industry as well as by federal, state, or local govern-

Hoover Dam was built in enormous blocks (left). Water in hundreds of miles of pipes buried in the concrete removed the heat of the setting cement. Grout (cement and water) forced between the blocks made the dam one solid piece. Here (right) the dam rises to near the top of the canyon. In the background are intake towers for the penstocks of the power plant. The concrete blocks are locked together by vertical keys.

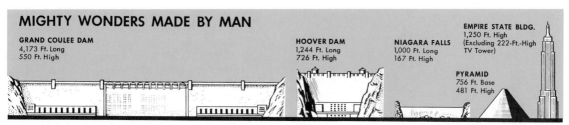

MIGHTY WONDERS MADE BY MAN

GRAND COULEE DAM
4,173 Ft. Long
550 Ft. High

HOOVER DAM
1,244 Ft. Long
726 Ft. High

NIAGARA FALLS
1,000 Ft. Long
167 Ft. High

EMPIRE STATE BLDG.
1,250 Ft. High
(Excluding 222-Ft.-High
TV Tower)

PYRAMID
756 Ft. Base
481 Ft. High

Here Grand Coulee and Hoover dams are compared with other man-made structures and with Niagara Falls. Grand Coulee's spillway is more than twice as high as Niagara Falls. Hoover Dam is half the height of the Empire State Building.

ments. Federal dams usually are constructed by United States Army engineers if navigation is involved and by the Bureau of Reclamation for irrigation projects.

A modern development is the planning of entire river basins as regional units. Multipurpose dams are built on main streams and tributaries.

On the Columbia River are Grand Coulee, Chief Joseph, Rock Island, Priest Rapids, McNary, and Bonneville dams. On its tributaries are Anderson Ranch Dam, on the South Fork of the Boise River in Idaho; and Hungry Horse Dam, on the South Fork of the Flathead River in Montana.

Key structures of California's Central Valley Project and State Water Project are Shasta Dam, on the Sacramento River; Friant Dam, on the San Joaquin; Folsom Dam, on the American; Oroville Dam, on the Feather; and Trinity Dam, on the Trinity.

On the Colorado are Glen Canyon, Hoover, Parker, Imperial, and Davis dams. Chief dams on the Rio Grande are Elephant Butte and Caballo, in New Mexico; and Falcon Dam, which is located between Texas and Mexico.

On the Missouri are Fort Peck Dam, in Montana; Oahe and Fort Randall dams, in South Dakota; Garrison Dam, in North Dakota; and Gavins Point Dam, in South Dakota and Nebraska.

In the Tennessee Valley project (TVA) there are 31 major dams. Nine dams on the Tennessee River constitute the heart of the TVA. The largest of them is Kentucky Dam. (*See also* Tennessee Valley Authority, and articles on individual rivers.)

The highest dam in the United States is the 770-foot (235-meter) earth-fill Oroville Dam. Other dams of great height are Hoover, Dworshak, Glen Canyon, New Bullard's Bar, and New Melones.

The world's largest dams by volume are earth dams. Greatest in the United States is New Cornelia Tailings, with 274,026,000 cubic yards (209,508,000 cubic meters) of material. Then come Fort Peck, Oahe, Oroville, San Luis, Garrison, Cochiti, and Mission Tailings #2.

Some of the greatest reservoirs in volume are Lake Mead, formed by Hoover Dam, and the reservoirs of Garrison, Glen Canyon, Oahe, Fort Peck, and Grand Coulee dams.

The drawing shows how the completed Hoover Dam works. The Nevada wall of the Black Canyon is shown solid, but the Arizona wall has been cut away to reveal construction inside. The fluted cylinders behind the dam are intake towers, and pipes leading from them are penstocks. These convey water to the turbines in the powerhouse at the foot of the dam. While the dam was being built, the four large tunnels, two on each side of the river, diverted the river around the dam site. The upstream ends of these tunnels have been plugged. They serve as penstocks and spillway outlets.

Compton's Encyclopedia

Other Notable Dams

Among the world's highest dams are Grande Dixence and Mauvoisin, in Switzerland; Chicoasén, in Mexico; Vaiont, in Italy; Sayano-Shushenskaya and Chirkeyskaya, in the Soviet Union; Mica, in Canada; and Chivor, in Colombia. Still under construction in the Soviet Union are the world's highest dams—Rogun and Nurek, at more than 1,000 feet (300 meters). Leading foreign dams in volume of materials are Tarbela and Mangla, in Pakistan; Gardiner, in Canada; and Afsluitdijk, in The Netherlands. Dams that form the largest reservoirs in capacity are Owen Falls (Lake Victoria), in Uganda; Bratsk, in the Soviet Union; Aswan High, in Egypt; and Kariba Gorge, bordering Zambia and Zimbabwe.

One of the oldest great dams is Egypt's Aswan for irrigation on the Nile, finished in 1902. The Dneper, completed in 1932, was one of the earliest major Soviet dams. Another historical dam is Mettur, on the Cauvery River in India. The world's first dam to furnish hydroelectric power from ocean tides was completed in 1966. It is located on the Rance River, near Saint-Malo, in France. (*See also* in Fact-Index dams by name and Dam table.)

17

Carl Frank—Photo Researchers

The city of Damascus is viewed here from the Omayyad Mosque, the grandest building in the old section of the city. It has been restored several times after fires and conquest.

DAMASCUS, Syria. The capital of Syria is Damascus, one of the oldest cities in the world. It was an important desert trade center before the days of Christ.

Damascus is located on a fertile plain at the foot of the Anti-Lebanon Range. A system of canals from the Barada River irrigates this rich, green oasis on the edge of the Syrian Desert. The nearest seaport is Beirut, Lebanon, on the Mediterranean, about 70 miles away. A railroad joins the two cities.

New and Old Damascus

Damascus is an interesting mixture of old and new. In the modern part of the city there are up-to-date homes, hotels, and government buildings. There are also factories in this area. These include textile, tanning, canning, match, and glass plants.

The Arabs in old Damascus live much as they did in Biblical times. This part of the city is a center of Moslem life. Rising above the many single-story Arab houses are the graceful minarets and domes of more than 200 mosques.

There was once a wall around Damascus. It is now in ruins. Beyond the ruins of this ancient wall are many new suburbs. Outside the suburbs stretches the irrigated plain. Here grow olives, grapes, oranges, citrons, pomegranates, figs, pears, and other fruits. Nuts, wheat, barley, and tobacco are also important local crops.

The Khans and the Bazaars

The life of this merchant city of the desert centers in its khans (walled camel caravan headquarters) and its bazaars. The "great Khan" is a beautiful building. It has a Moorish gate and a black and white marble cupola supported by marble pillars. In this and other lesser khans important trading is carried on.

The bazaars are simply streets lined with shops, stalls, and cafés. Some of these shops have space for only three or four people. There is a great deal of noise in the bazaars as men bargain back and forth. Each kind of goods has a street or a part of a street to itself—Street of the Saddlers, Street of the Slipper Merchants, Street of the Water-Pipe Makers, Street of the Spice Men, Street of the Dyers, and many others. The longest and busiest thoroughfare of all is the famous Street Which Is Called Straight. It is mentioned in the Bible in connection with St. Paul's conversion to Christianity.

Famous Damasks and Damascus Blades

The looms of Damascus have been famous for centuries. In this city many things are still done in the most primitive way. One may still see, for example, the hand looms worked by a weaver and his draw boy. On these looms are made the beautiful damasks that were known throughout Europe and Asia as early as the time of the Crusades.

Damascus was also noted in the Middle Ages for its Damascus blades. However, these have not been forged here since the 14th century. Then Timur Leng, the terrible Tatar conqueror, raided the city and carried off all the great swordmakers to his own capital. These blades were said to be so keen they could cut a floating web. They were so hard they could cut an iron spear in two as if it were a reed. They were also so elastic they could be bent to a right angle and

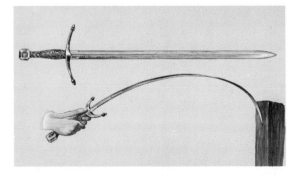

Damascus swords have been celebrated the world over for their superb workmanship, razor-sharp edges, and perfect temper. Many of the handles were inlaid with gold and silver.

spring back as straight as before. The careful twisting and welding of two grades of iron or steel gave them their cutting properties. It also produced a beautiful watermark pattern. To make the swords and scimitars still more attractive, the handles were inlaid with gold and silver in beautiful designs. Damascus is still famed for fine inlay and filigree work.

History of Damascus

There are no records of when Damascus was founded. It is said to be the oldest continuously inhabited city in the world. The first mention of Damascus is in Egyptian records of four thousand years ago. After 1200 BC the kingdom of Damascus became a powerful state that long defied Assyria. In 732 BC, however, Tiglath-Pileser III, king of Assyria, conquered the city. The Old Testament in the Bible tells of David's conquest of Damascus. In 333 BC the city was conquered by Alexander and in AD 63 by the Romans.

From 635, when it fell to Muslim Arabs, until World War I, Damascus was in Arab and Turkish hands except for a brief period in the 12th century when it was held by Crusaders. The sultan Saladin, foe of the Crusaders, died and was buried in Damascus. From 661 until 750 the city was the capital of the Ummayad Dynasty (*see* Caliphate). Over the next centuries Damascus changed hands several times until it was captured by the Ottoman Sultan in 1516. From that time on it was a relatively insignificant outpost in the large Ottoman Empire. By the end of World War I, however, the Ottoman Empire was breaking up. The first Syrian government was set up in 1919 with Damascus as its capital. From then until World War II, Syria was a mandate of France, and much modernization occurred.

During World War II the city was occupied by British and Free French forces. Syria became a republic. It joined Egypt in the United Arab Republic in 1958 but withdrew in 1961 and regained independence. Damascus again became a national capital. Population (1984 estimate), 1,202,000.

DAMON AND PYTHIAS.

The story of Damon and Pythias is a story of friendship. Pythias was condemned to death because he opposed Dionysius, the tyrant of Syracuse, in Sicily. He begged to be allowed to return home to say good-bye to his wife and child. Damon came forward and said he would die in place of Pythias if Pythias did not come back in time.

Pythias had not returned when Damon was brought to the place of execution. Suddenly Pythias rushed through the crowd into Damon's arms. Pythias' horse had been killed, and it was only through great effort that he was able to arrive on time. Then each of the friends pleaded to be allowed to die for the other. Dionysius was so moved that he pardoned them both and begged to share in their friendship. The Knights of Pythias, a fraternal society that was founded at Washington, D.C., in 1864, takes its name from the Pythias of this story.

DAMROSCH, Walter (1862–1950).

Classical music was popularized in the United States through the radio concerts of Walter Damrosch. He was also noted for his support of unknown composers.

Walter Johannes Damrosch was born in Breslau, Silesia, on Jan. 30, 1862. His father, Leopold, was one of the foremost European conductors of his day, and his mother was an opera singer. In 1871 the elder Damrosch became conductor of a New York City choral group.

Young Damrosch made rapid progress. At 16 he was accompanist to a concert violinist. At 18 he was elected permanent conductor of the Newark Harmonic Society. When his father died in 1885, Walter succeeded him as conductor of both the Oratorio Society and the New York Symphony Society. His father also had contracted with the Metropolitan Opera to conduct a season of German opera. Walter Damrosch finished the season and took the company on tour. The next year he was appointed second conductor of the Metropolitan under Anton Seidl.

The composer of six operas, Damrosch founded the Damrosch Opera Company in 1895. Eight years later he reorganized the New York Symphony Society into a permanent orchestra. During his 24 years as its conductor, Damrosch made many tours to cities that had never heard symphonic music. In 1925 he broadcast the first radio concert. Later he began a radio series for children. Damrosch died in New York City on Dec. 22, 1950.

DANA, James Dwight (1813–95).

One of the best-informed men of science in the 19th century, James Dwight Dana greatly influenced the development of geology into a mature science. He also made significant contributions to the subjects of mineralogy and zoology.

Born on Feb. 12, 1813, in Utica, N.Y., Dana was educated at Yale College. As a student of Benjamin Silliman, a leading scientist of the day, Dana turned energetically to the study of natural science and geology. In 1837 he published 'A System of Mineralogy', which became the standard work in its field for more than a century. From 1838 to 1842 Dana was part of an expedition to the South Seas led by the American explorer, Charles Wilkes. He served as geologist and collected much zoological data as well. His writings on the expedition were published in three works: 'Zoophytes' (1846), describing coral-forming animals; 'Geology' (1849); and 'Crustacea' (two volumes, 1852–54), on invertebrate animals.

In 1856 Dana became professor of natural history at Yale. In 1862 he published his 'Manual of Geology', one of the major texts in the field; in 1872 he completed his work on coral reefs by issuing 'Corals and Coral Islands'.

In the last years of his life, Dana concentrated on zoological studies. He was particularly interested in and finally accepted the theory of evolution proposed by Charles Darwin. Dana died at New Haven on April 14, 1895.

Martha Swope

Members of the Paul Taylor Dance Company used more of a
classical style than modern in 'Mercurial Tidings'.

DANCE

DANCE. It is the wedding of movement to music. It
spans culture from soaring ballet leaps to the simple
swaying at a high school prom. It is dance, a means of
recreation, of communication—perhaps the oldest,
yet the most incompletely preserved, of the arts. Its
origins are lost in prehistoric times, but, from the
study of the most primitive peoples, it is known that
men and women have always danced.

There are many kinds of dance. It can be a popular craze, like break dancing, or ballets that feature
superstar performers such as Mikhail Baryshnikov
and Suzanne Farrell. It can be folk dances that have
been handed down through generations, such as the
square dance, or ethnic dances that are primarily associated with a particular country. It can be modern
dance or musical comedy dancing, both fields that
were pioneered by American men and women.

Dances in primitive cultures all had as their subject
matter the changes experienced by people throughout their lives, changes that occurred as people grew
from childhood to old age, those they experienced as
the seasons moved from winter to summer and back
again, changes that came about as tribes won their
wars or suffered defeats.

Two sorts of dance evolved as cultures developed:
social dances on occasions that celebrated births,
commemorated deaths, and marked special events in
between; and magical or religious dances to ask the

gods to end a famine, to provide rain, or to cure the
sick. The medicine men of primitive cultures, whose
powers to invoke the assistance of a god were feared
and respected, are considered by many to be the first
choreographers, or composers of formal dances.

Originally rhythmic sound accompaniment was
provided by the dancers themselves. Eventually a
separate rhythmic accompaniment evolved, probably played on animal skins stretched over wooden
frames and made into drums. Later, melodies were
added; these might have imitated birdcalls or other
sounds of nature, or they might have been a vocal
expression of the dancers' or musicians' state of
mind. The rhythmic beat, however, was the most
important element. This pulsation let all the dancers
keep time together, and it helped them to remember
their movements too. By controlling the rhythm, the
leader of a communal dance could regulate the pace
of the movement.

Primitive dancers also shared certain gestures and
movements, which were drawn from their everyday
lives. People planting seeds swing their arms with
unvarying regularity. People who are hungry rub a

This article was contributed by George Gelles, Consulting
Editor, 'Britannica Book of Music'; former lecturer on dance,
the Smithsonian Institution; and former dance critic, *The
Washington Star*.

hand on their empty bellies. People who want to show respect or admiration bend down or bow before another individual. These gestures, and others like them, were part of the earliest dances.

There is also a large vocabulary of gestures that originated as a means of expressing bodily needs. Caresses are universally taken to signify tender feelings. Clenched fists mean anger. Hopping up and down indicates excitement. Primitive dancers used all of these movements in both their social and religious or magical dances. These dances were not created and performed for entertainment, as many dances are today. One of the major reasons for them was to help tribes survive. Long before the written word could guarantee that traditions would be passed on and respected, it was dance that helped the tribe preserve its continuity.

SOCIAL DANCING

As known today, social dancing is an activity that can be traced back to three sources: the courts of Europe, international society, and primitive cultures. Among noblemen and women of 16th- and 17th-century Europe, ballroom dancing was a popular diversion. After the political upheavals of the 18th and 19th centuries, dances once performed by the aristocracy alone became popular among ordinary people as well. In America, too, dances that were once confined to the gentry who first led the republic passed to the common folk. By the mid-19th century, popular dances attracted many participants who performed minuets, quadrilles, polkas, and waltzes—all of European origin.

None of these dances grew more popular than the waltz, which was first introduced to the Austrian court in the 17th century. Its gliding, whirling movements immediately became the rage throughout the entire population. Some people, however, found waltzing undignified, and in 1760 the performance of waltzes was banned by the church in parts of Germany. Nevertheless, the mania continued, and by the late 18th century waltzing was common in the cosmopolitan cities of London and Paris. People felt the same spirit in the dance that they perceived in the great political events of the day—the French and the American revolutions. The waltz stood for freedom of expression and freedom of movement. Unlike more courtly dances, with their restricted steps and predetermined poses, the waltz allowed the performers to sweep around the dance floor, setting their own boundaries and responsible to nobody but their partners. By the early 20th century the waltz as an art form was exhausted. It found a final admirer in the French composer Maurice Ravel, whose orchestral piece 'The Waltz' both celebrates the dance's traditions and mourns its passing out of fashion.

Around the time of World War I, when America's attention was fixed on other lands around the globe, a dance craze developed that had strong international influence. From South America came the tango and the maxixe. European dances inspired the American

couple Irene and Vernon Castle to develop many new sophisticated dances that won vast popularity and that were performed nationwide.

As the 20th century evolved, African and Caribbean rhythms and movements increasingly influenced social dancing. Swing, the jitterbug, the twist, boogie, and disco dancing all share a free and improvised movement style and a repetitive, percussive rhythm that can be traced to more primitive sources.

Another important influence was felt from Ireland, whose clog dances were first brought to America in the 1840s. After being adapted by local performers, clog dance steps became the tap dances done by generations of minstrels and music hall performers. Tap dancing was originally performed as an accompaniment to song. With costume, makeup, and scenery, it was another of the entertainer's accessories, its percussive and rhythmic patterns heightening a song's effectiveness.

Modern dancers, however, made tap an art form of its own. Rhythms grew more intricate, and movements became larger. Greater emphasis was placed on elements of dance composition and design, and greater value was shown to the music made by the taps themselves. Among the greatest tap dance artists are Bill "Bojangles" Robinson, who refined the minstrel tradition, and Fred Astaire, whose performances are unsurpassed for their musicality and grace (*see* Astaire).

Folk dancing preserved its own identity as these popular dances developed. By folk dance is meant a dance that originated in a particular country or locality and has become closely identified with its nation of origin. The czardas, for example, is unmistakably Hungarian, and the hora is linked to Israel. These dances are often performed by dedicated groups of amateurs who want either to preserve the dance tradition of their ancestors or to share in another country's culture. (*See also* Folk Dance.)

DANCE AS AN ART FORM

Ancient Egypt

The first great culture to infuse its entire society with the magic of dance was that of Egypt. Far more than mere pastime, dancing became an integral part of Egyptian life. It evolved from the most simple rituals used by hunters to find their prey. Performing the dances was believed to help in later hunts. A leader, called a priest–dancer, was responsible for seeing that the dances were performed correctly so that the hunt would be successful.

Eventually these dances were separated from their ritual and became an art of their own. This development paralleled the emergence of Osiris as the Egyptians' most important god. With his mythical sister and wife, Isis, he was a symbol of a more developed civilization on Earth, and belief in him guaranteed everlasting life. Dance was a crucial element in the festivals held for Isis and Osiris. These occurred throughout the year—in the summer, for

Ancient dances were depicted on an Egyptian tomb from the Old Kingdom, 3rd millennium BC (left top), on an Etruscan tomb from northern Italy (left), and in a Greek vase painting from the 5th century BC (above).

instance, when the Nile River began to rise and the corn was ripening, and in the fall on All Souls' Night—the ancient ancestor of Halloween. Dance was also important in the festivals dedicated to Apis, the bull associated with fertility rituals, and also in a ceremony in which priests portrayed the stars in celebration of the cosmos, or harmonious universe.

As was true in more primitive cultures, music was a part of these celebrations but not as important as the dancing itself. Egyptians had developed stringed, wind, and percussion instruments as well as different sorts of whistles and harps.

Dance figured, too, in private life. Professional performers entertained at social events, and traveling troupes gave performances in public squares of great cities such as Thebes and Alexandria.

Movements of Egyptian dances were named after the motion they imitated. For instance, there were "the leading along of an animal," "the taking of gold," and "the successful capture of the boat." Probably many of the poses and motions were highly acrobatic, though in certain instances Egyptian dance steps look remarkably like steps in classical ballet.

Ancient Greece

Myths associated with the Greek god Dionysus are remarkably similar to those that surround the Egyptians' Osiris, suggesting that the early culture of Greece was influenced by that of Egypt. According to the philosopher Aristotle, Greek tragedy originated in the myth of Dionysus' birth. He relates that the poet Arion was responsible for establishing the basic theatrical form, one that incorporated dance, music, spoken words, and costumes. There was always a chief dancer who was the leader of these presentations.

As the form evolved, the leader became something close to what would now be considered a combination choreographer and performer, while other participants assumed the role of an audience. By the 6th century BC, the basic form of theater as known today was established.

No matter how far Greek theater moved from its original ritual sources, it was always connected with the myths of Dionysus. Participation in dance and drama festivals was a religious exercise, not merely an amusement. In Greek plays dance was of major importance, and the three greatest dramatists of the era—Aeschylus, Sophocles, and Euripides—were familiar with dance in both theory and practice. Sophocles, for example, studied both music and dance as a child, and, after the defeat of the Persians in the 5th century BC, he danced in the triumphal celebration. In his childhood Euripides had been affiliated with a troupe of dancers, and in plays such as 'The Bacchae', his last great work, a dancing choir plays a role of major importance.

Even in earlier times dancing was popular among the Greek people. It was thought to promote physical health and to influence one's education positively. These attitudes were passed on from generation to generation. For instance, in Homer's epics, which date from the 11th to 10th century BC, dance is portrayed as a kind of social pastime, not as an activity associated with religious observances. By the end of the 4th century BC, dancing had become a professional activity. Dances were performed by groups, and the motion of most dances was circular. In tragic dances—where mimed expression, or wordless action, was important—the dancers would not touch one another. Generally, in fact, Greek dances were not based on

Louis XIV of France and his queen (left) dance the minuet, a popular dance of the late 17th century. In England the cotillion was depicted (right) in a 1771 engraving by James Caldwall.

the relationship between men and women. Most were performed by either one sex or the other.

Greek dance can be divided into large and small motions—movements and gestures. Movements were closely related to gymnastic exercises; schoolchildren had to master series of harmonious physical exercises that resembled dance. Gestures imitated poses and postures found in everyday life and conveyed all the emotions ranging from anger to joy. For musical accompaniment the Greeks used stringed instruments such as the lyre, flutes such as the panpipe, and a wide variety of percussion instruments, including tambourines, cymbals, and castanets.

Altogether there were more than 200 Greek dances designed for every mood and purpose. There were comic pieces, warlike works, and dances for athletes,

spectacles, and religious worship. For purely social purposes there were dances for weddings, funerals, and seasonal celebrations connected with harvesttime. Yet these dances were not as important as those connected with the theater. By the 5th century BC, dancing had become recognized as an art.

Roman Empire

As early as 364 BC entertainers from Greece were imported to Rome to perform theatrical pieces in honor of the gods and to amuse a population weary from a plague. These performers inspired the local population to develop plays of their own—mimes and bawdy farces that included elements of dance.

Roman culture, which eclipsed the Greek in approximately the 3rd century BC, was in many ways

In Vienna, Austria, the waltz (left) originated in the 19th century. During the "Roaring 20s" in the United States the Charleston (right), illustrated on *Life* magazine's cover, was a high-kicking dance.

SOME MAJOR FIGURES IN DANCE

Some prominent persons are not included below because they are covered in the main text of this article or in other articles in Compton's Encyclopedia (see Fact-Index).

Ailey, Alvin (born 1931). Born in Rogers, Tex. Modern dancer best known for choreography using Lester Horton and ethnic African techniques. In 1958 he founded his own dance company.

Arbeau, Thoinot (1519–95). Born Jehan Tabouret in Dijon, France. Priest and writer known for his dance manual 'Orchésographie' published in 1589. The manual included both court and popular dances and is noted for the simplicity of its instructions.

Béjart, Maurice (born 1927). Born in Marseilles, France. Ballet dancer and choreographer highly influential and extremely popular in Europe. He considered dance to be a way of communicating ideas, and the choreography for his company, the Ballet of the 20th Century, often conveys a message.

Blasis, Carlo (1797?–1878). Born in Naples, Italy. Ballet dancer, choreographer, and teacher associated with La Scala in Milan. His choreography was one of the most influential until at least the end of the 19th century. Ballet steps from his books and manuals are standards.

Camargo, Marie (1710–70). Born in Brussels, Belgium. Ballet dancer noted for innovations that included shortening her costume so that her unusually difficult footwork could be seen by the audience. She was mainly associated with the Paris Opéra.

Cerrito, Fanny (1817–1909). Born Francesca Cerrito in Naples, Italy. Ballerina of the romantic period, and one of the few 19th-century women to excel as a choreographer. Her greatest role was 'Ondine'.

Champion, Gower (1921–80). Born in Geneva, Ill. Dancer and choreographer noted for his successful Broadway musical comedies. Champion and his wife Marge were a popular team in films and in television, and his choreography for plays like 'Hello, Dolly' and '42nd Street' earned Tony awards.

Cunningham, Merce (born 1919). Born in Centralia, Wash. Modern and postmodern dancer and influential choreographer. He was a soloist in Martha Graham's troupe before forming his own company. His most frequently performed works are called "events," made up of pieces of other works. Cunningham frequently collaborated with modern artists and composers.

De Valois, Dame Ninette (born 1898). Born Edris Stannus in Baltiboys, Ireland. Irish dancer and choreographer who founded Britain's national ballet, the Royal Ballet. In 1926 she opened an Academy of Dancing in London and later founded the Vic-Wells Ballet, which ultimately became the Royal Ballet.

Fosse, Bob (born 1923). Born in Chicago. Theater and film dancer, choreographer, and director who began his career in vaudeville and nightclub acts. He then moved to Broadway shows and films and became known for his novel ideas as a dance director. His direction of plays such as 'Pippin' and movies such as 'Cabaret' has earned numerous awards.

Greco, José (born 1918). Born in Montorio nei Frentani, Italy. Dancer and choreographer who became the best-known Spanish dancer outside Spain. He began his career in New York City, where he was discovered by and became the partner of famed dancer La Argentinita. After her death he returned to Spain and formed the José Greco Dance Company. He appeared in several films and in 1971 formed the Foundation for Hispanic Dance.

Joffrey, Robert (born 1930). Born Abdullah Jaffa Bey Khan in Seattle, Wash. Choreographer and ballet dancer who founded the Joffrey Ballet. His earliest company gave its first performance in 1954. He choreographed many operas, including several for the New York City Opera. His best-known ballet is 'Astarte'.

Karsavina, Tamara (1885–1978). Born in St. Petersburg, Russia. One of the greatest dancers of the early 20th century, she was the first modern ballerina. She is famed for the roles she created in ballets such as 'The Firebird' and 'Petrushka' with Diaghilev's Ballets Russes.

Limón, José (1908–72). Born in Culiacán, Mexico. Choreographer and modern dancer considered one of the greatest of modern dancers. He performed on Broadway with the Humphrey/Weidman Group and formed his own company in 1945.

Martins, Peter (born 1946). Born in Copenhagen, Denmark. Ballet dancer and choreographer who became director of the New York City Ballet in 1983. He began his career with the Royal Danish Ballet and received praise for his dancing in the Bournonville repertoire. He became a permanent member of the New York City Ballet in 1970.

Massine, Léonide (1895–1979). Born in Moscow. Ballet dancer who for many years was the principal choreographer for Diaghilev's Ballets Russes. His pieces are still performed in Europe and the United States, and he also appeared in films.

Mitchell, Arthur (born 1934). Born in New York City. Ballet dancer and choreographer who was the first full-time, full-contract black dancer of the New York City Ballet. He was a co-founder of the Dance Theatre of Harlem and its school.

Mordkin, Mikhail (1880–1944). Born in Moscow. Ballet dancer and choreographer whose best choreography was considered equal to that of Fokine and Balanchine. After dancing in the Bolshoi Ballet, he toured the United States with Anna Pavlova. In New York City during the 1920s and 1930s, he founded ballet companies, the second becoming the basis of the American Ballet Theatre.

Page, Ruth (born 1905). Born in Indianapolis, Ind. Ballet dancer and choreographer who was one of the first to create ballets on American themes. Based in Chicago since the 1930s, Page was a constant force in the development of dance in that city and was especially known for her opera choreography.

Robinson, Bill "Bojangles" (1878–1949). Born Luther Robinson in Richmond, Va. Theatrical dancer called "The King of Tapology." He claimed to have no formal training but began performing as a child. He later danced in films and on Broadway and earned a reputation as the greatest tap dancer of all time.

St. Denis, Ruth (1877?–1968). Born Ruth Dennis in Newark, N.J. Concert and interpretive dancer known for her exotic themes for dance pieces based on mythology and Oriental cultures and for her "music visualizations" based on classical music, especially piano pieces. She formed the Denishawn style and schools with her dancer–husband, Ted Shawn.

Sallé, Marie (1707–56). Probably born in France. Ballet dancer and choreographer noted for her efforts in developing *ballet d'action*, or story-telling, movements. She danced in the Paris Opéra and London theaters and was a favorite at the French court.

Shawn, Ted (1891–1972). Born in Kansas City. Concert dancer and choreographer who teamed with Ruth St. Denis to form the Denishawn style of modern dance, abstract works with Oriental and Greek undertones. He later worked in the German modern dance movement and in 1933 formed a company of all-male dancers with the intent of lessening public disapproval of dancing by men. He opened a school called Jacob's Pillow that remains a favorite performance spot for dancers and choreographers.

Taylor, Paul (born 1930). Born in Allegheny County, Penn. Modern dancer and choreographer who used a more classical style than most modern dance choreographers. He danced in Martha Graham's company before the debut of his Paul Taylor Dance Company in 1954.

Tharp, Twyla (born 1942). Born in Portland, Ind. Modern dancer and choreographer whose rapid, seemingly off-balance style achieved great popularity. Tharp used classical and popular music for the dance company she formed in 1965. She also choreographed for films, including 'Amadeus' and 'Hair'.

Vestris, Gaetano (1729–1808). Born in Florence, Italy. Ballet dancer and choreographer known for his technical ability and creativity. He worked for the Paris Opéra from 1748 to 1782, serving as ballet master part of the time, and was ballet master at the King's Theatre in London from 1791 to 1793.

Members of the American Ballet Theatre (above) perform 'The Nutcracker', a popular Christmas ballet. Cynthia Gregory and Eric Bruhn (right) perform José Limón's acclaimed 'The Moor's Pavane'.

influenced by Grecian models. In dance, however, the Romans distorted the balance and harmony that characterized the Greeks, putting the most emphasis on spectacle and mime. Dancing itself almost disappeared.

Roman theater had originated in 240 BC, when public games were held after the victory in the first Punic Wars. As part of these celebrations comedy and tragedy were performed, including drama, music, and dance. According to the writer Plutarch, dance included three elements: motion, posture, and indication, the last a gesture that pointed out some object near the performer.

Performances such as these fed the Romans' love of spectacle. Their desire to see a bustling stage full of people led to performances that took place in ever-larger spaces. Conventional theaters were replaced by the circus and the arena. To get his meaning across to such a large audience, a performer's gestures had to become cruder and coarser. Eventually the artist's skill was blunted, and with this loss of craftsmanship came a loss of social prestige. Dancers, who were honored and respected by the Greeks, became little more than slaves to the Romans.

Though spectacles provided the Roman population with most of its dancing, social and domestic dances were also performed to a limited extent. Most of these had a religious or ritualistic nature. They prophesied events or appeased the gods. Dances were also designed for entertainment, with battle pieces the most common.

In general, however, dancing was not highly thought of. The famous orator Cicero said in a speech that "no man, one may almost say, ever dances when sober, unless perhaps he be a madman; nor in solitude, nor in a moderate and sober party; dancing is the last companion of prolonged feasting, of luxurious situation, and of many refinements."

As the Roman Empire expanded, secular dances showed exotic influences. People from Africa to Britain fell under Roman rule, but their strange, foreign movements and gestures were never truly integrated into a style of dance the Romans could call their own. Like the artworks among their plunder, the dances were merely novelties and curiosities.

While dance itself was diminished by the Romans, pantomime became an art form worthy of respect in itself. Under the reign of Caesar Augustus in about 22 BC, the pantomime dance–drama became an independent form of artistic expression. Most of the pieces were tragedies, and dancers made liberal use of costumes and masks. According to the writings of the 2nd-century Greek satirist Lucian of Samosata, Roman pantomime was a highly developed art form that made lavish and creative use of dance. Though the Romans showed little use for the dance as developed by the Greeks, they excelled in this new form of pantomime dance–drama.

Christian Era

With the rise of Christianity throughout the first millennium, dramatic rituals developed for use during prayer. The Latin mass is the best-known of these rites. Originally dance movements were part of these pieces as well as music and a dramatic dialogue. By the Middle Ages these works moved from inside the churches to the out-of-doors. On cathedral porches, church squares, and marketplaces, miracle plays, mystery plays, and morality plays that taught the church's lessons were enacted in a theatrical way. Rather than being part of the ritual, however, these pieces had become a form of entertainment.

Dance was also observed in two other sorts of activity. In dramatic ritual games with dance movement the passing of the seasons was celebrated, even as it had been by primitive tribes; and in the works of

25

Jack Mitchell   Martha Swope   Martha Swope

Three innovative modern American dancers and choreographers were Merce Cunningham (left), Martha Graham (center), and Twyla Tharp, whose 'Catherine Wheel' was performed by Sara Redner (right).

troubadours and other wandering minstrels, dance and song were used to express the range of human emotions.

Another important rite of the Middle Ages was known as the dance of death. A ritual procession performed throughout Europe from the 14th to the 16th century, it was a sort of danced parade that was led by a figure representing death. It was performed perhaps with the most intensity in the years of the Black Death, a bubonic plague that swept across Europe beginning in 1373. At once grotesque and graceful, the piece expressed the anguish of a diseased civilization.

The dance of death reflected the rituals performed by primitive peoples, who had also danced to acknowledge the passing of the seasons of the year and of a human life on Earth. Other dances in the Middle Ages did the same. During the annual May games, for example, dances were performed that celebrated the greening of the countryside and the fertility of the land. During saints' days, which echoed the rites dedicated to Dionysus, large groups of women danced in churches. Similar to earlier pieces associated with battles, sword dances were performed in Germany, Scotland, and elsewhere in Europe. Similar to the sword dance is the Morris dance, which was performed at secular festivals from Scotland to Spain.

Development of Ballet—Italy

Out of the many styles in the late Middle Ages— religious dancing, folk dancing, and performances by minstrels—emerged the art form now known as ballet. An early pioneer whose work led in this direction was Guglielmo Ebreo, better known as William the Jew, from the Italian town of Pesaro. A teacher of dance to the nobility, he also wrote a study of dance that includes one of the first examples of recorded choreography. These dance steps were not designed for the stage or for professional dancers but for amateurs to perform at festive balls.

At the same time when William was active, dancing was on the move. First performed as part of feasts and then in ballrooms, dances finally found a home in theaters. Performed between the acts of classical comedies, tragedies, or operas, they became known as intermezzos. Gradually the word *balletti,* which originally referred to dances performed in ballrooms, was used for the dramatic works in theaters. Ballet as it is known now was just around the corner.

'Circe', a work created in 1581, is said to be the first ballet. Original in its mixture of theatrical elements that had been found for more than a decade in Italy and France, 'Circe' was the work of an Italian who became a Frenchman, Balthasar de Beaujoyeulx.

His work was the inspiration of the Ballet Comique de la Reine, a sort of grand theatrical presentation that entertained the nobles at court in the last two decades of the 16th century. These rich pieces brought together in a unified way the separate elements of tournament presentations, masquerade, and dramatic pastorals, or rural scenes.

In 1588, a few years after 'Circe', a book crucial in the development of ballet, 'Orchesographie' by Thoinot Arbeau, was published. It set forth the dance steps and rhythms that became the ballet postures and movements in the 17th and 18th centuries.

The next great pioneer was another Italian-born Frenchman, Jean-Baptiste Lully, who was born in Florence and served Louis XIV at Versailles. Though best known as an opera composer, his influence on dance was profound. In 1661 he established a department of dance in the Royal Academy of Music, and he played an important role in making ballets more coherent and unified. He also improved the musical scores to which dancers performed as well as the scenic designs and the librettos, or texts, on which the dances were based. In 1664 Lully began to work with the playwright Molière. They produced many works that had a major effect on both music and dance. In his opera–ballets Lully expanded the scope of dance.

There was greater use made of dancers' arms and legs and a more adventurous attitude toward the space on the stage. (*See also* Lully.)

Growth of Ballet—France

By the 18th century the center of dance activity had moved from Italy to France. For this period the best guide is Pierre Rameau, whose book 'The Dancing Master' is primarily a guide to social dances performed not just in France but throughout all of Europe. As with earlier treatises, 'The Dancing Master' also describes stage presentations, for both social and stage dancing shared the same steps.

In the decades preceding Rameau's book, the public's appetite for dancing had been stimulated. This hunger was satisfied by the opera–ballets that flourished in the first half of the 18th century. These works were operas of a sort, but dancing and orchestral music overshadowed the dramatic elements. The balance that Lully had established between drama, dance, and music had been destroyed. Now, in the opera–ballets, dance was the main element, with music of next importance and drama far behind.

Choreographers of the time tried to avoid an old-fashioned style of movement and aimed instead for a new sort of expressive gesture. Dancing became highly personal and creative. Individual performers often added steps and gestures of their own, and it was during this time that the first great soloists were recognized.

Among the most beloved dancers during the first half of the 18th century was Marie Anne de Dupis, called Camargo, who was brilliant technically and daring; she is credited with shortening her skirt a few inches to allow audience members to better see and appreciate her intricate footwork. Marie Sallé

was also a great favorite and brought a new freedom to the dance through her expressive use of costume and masterful use of gestures. Gaetano Vestris was the first among male dancers, known for his elegance and delicacy.

All of the advances made by these and other artists, and by choreographers of the time, were classified and recorded by the writer Jean-Georges Noverre, whose 'Letters on the Dance' became the authority for succeeding generations. The 'Letters' also proposed to reform dance of the day by getting rid of all movements and gestures not justified by the drama. Like the opera reformer–composer Christoph Willibald Gluck, with whom he was associated, Noverre wanted to purify his art form and make it even more effective for the audience. Noverre's reforms would be remembered and applied into the 20th century.

Salvatore Viganò was another dancer who ultimately changed the course of his art. After performing in his youth in Italy and Spain, he went to Vienna, where he collaborated with Beethoven, among others. The dances he created were notable for their innovative use of groups and their fine attention to detail. More than any of his peers, Viganò made works that recalled the art of sculpture.

Romantic Ballet and Beyond

An Italian master was also responsible for some of the 19th century's most important creations. Carlo Blasis, who was schooled in the ideas of Noverre, published in 1830 his 'Code of Terpsichore', a book of ballet instructions that became the standard manual through all of Europe and even in Russia.

It was Blasis' technique that formed the great ballerinas of the era: Maria Taglioni, Fanny Elssler, Fanny Cerrito, Carlotta Grisi, and Lucille Grahn. Each

Alvin Ailey, kneeling, and a member of his company perform his 'Blues Suite'.

Susan Cook

embodied a different aspect of the romantic ideal for the period. Taglioni thrilled audiences with her virtuoso technique, for example, and Elssler excelled in character dances that evoked exotic lands.

The choreographer who developed and defined romantic ballet was Marius Petipa. He arrived in Saint Petersburg from Italy in 1847, and during his reign as ballet master the Russian school eclipsed all others in theatrical splendor and brilliant dancing. With his assistant Lev Ivanov, he created the core repertoire of the Russian ballet—works such as 'Don Quixote', 'Swan Lake', and 'The Nutcracker'—and his influence is still felt.

It was not a choreographer or even a dancer who spread the Russian ballet through Europe and the Americas but an impresario, or promoter–manager. Sergei Diaghilev's genius was in bringing together some of the foremost artists of his time (*see* Diaghilev). His Ballets Russes, formed in 1909, drew on talents that had been formed at the Maryinsky Theater in St. Petersburg. Michel Fokine, trained as a dancer, developed into a choreographer of great distinction. A work such as 'Les Sylphides' brought to the romantic ballet a new purity. A piece like 'Sheherazade' brought a colorful and exotic strain to the ballet stage (*see* Fokine). Collaborating with him, under

In her choreography for 'Oklahoma!', Agnes de Mille made dance an integral part of American musical comedy. Members of the company (left) are doing a takeoff on the hoedown, a square dance. 'A Chorus Line' (below), Broadway's longest-running musical, was choreographed and directed by Michael Bennett.

Photos, Martha Swope

Diaghilev's watchful eye, were superb designers such as Léon Bakst; musicians such as Igor Stravinsky; dancers such as Vaslav Nijinsky, Tamara Karsavina, and Anna Pavlova (*see* Pavlova); and choreographers Leonide Massine and George Balanchine.

Although America had seen ballet dancers as early as the late 18th century, it was not until the 20th century that the art form took root. Spurred by visits of Diaghilev's troupe, local performers showed a new interest in the art. After the Ballets Russes was dissolved in 1929, many of its dancers found new homes in Europe and America.

Around these performers—artists such as Alexandra Danilova, Alicia Markova, and Massine—companies such as the Ballet Russe de Monte Carlo and the Original Ballet Russe were formed. In the 1930s they toured the United States from coast to coast, sparking still further interest. The first major American company to be established was the Ballet Theatre (now the American Ballet Theatre), founded in 1940. Conceived of as a repository of great works from differing dance styles, Ballet Theatre had difficulty in establishing an identity of its own, even though it often presented significant productions with world-class artists such as Alicia Alonso, Nora Kaye, and Cynthia Gregory. Among its finest choreographers were Antony Tudor, Jerome Robbins, and Twyla Tharp. Most recently the company has been led by the Russian-trained superstar Mikhail Baryshnikov.

The New York City Ballet, which was founded in 1948 with George Balanchine as its principal choreographer, set new standards for the world of ballet. As developed by Balanchine, ballet technique became even more virtuosic and gestures more economical. In the more than 150 works that he created for the company, Balanchine devised some of the century's most profound and beautiful productions. Among his masterpieces are 'Agon' and 'Orpheus', both to music of Igor Stravinsky; 'Serenade', to Tchaikovsky; and 'Concerto Barocco', to Bach. Jerome Robbins, who also worked with the American Ballet Theatre, became a ballet master with the company in 1969 and created two of his finest works for its dancers—'Dances at a Gathering' and 'The Goldberg Variations'. Among the company's best dancers were Diana Adams, Violette Verdy, Suzanne Farrell, Jacques D'Amboise, Edward Villella, and Peter Martins, who took over the company after Balanchine's death in 1983. (*See also* Balanchine.)

Arthur Mitchell, the first black dancer to perform with the New York City Ballet, founded his own Dance Theatre of Harlem in 1971. The first all-black ballet company, it won a new audience for ballet with its energetic and skillful performances and opened new opportunities for young black dancers. Another pioneer was Alvin Ailey, whose American Dance Theater performed a stylistically wide variety of works—from modern dance classics by Ted Shawn to ballet-influenced works by Ailey himself.

In the mid-20th century interest in dance increased not only in America. In England the Royal Ballet

Martha Swope

The Pilobolus Dance Company of New York incorporates acrobatics and gymnastics into its performances.

evolved under choreographer Frederick Ashton into a company of impeccable style and feeling. The pieces Ashton created made perfect use of his dancers, among whom were Margot Fonteyn and, after his defection from the Soviet Union, Rudolf Nureyev.

Even though the center of creativity in ballet shifted to America, the Soviet Union still maintains two venerable companies—the Bolshoi in Moscow and the Kirov, known to Petipa and Diaghilev as the Maryinsky, in Leningrad, formerly St. Petersburg. (*See also* Ballet.)

Modern Dance

At about the same time that Fokine was reforming the traditional ballet in St. Petersburg, an American woman was developing a revolutionary concept of dance. Isadora Duncan was trained in ballet but later found that these movements did not allow her as much expression of herself as she desired. Rather than modifying the conventional postures and steps, Duncan threw them out. Her new form of dance was spontaneous and highly personal and let her feel that her spirit had been liberated (*see* Duncan).

Because it was so personal, this new kind of dance was an art form that could not be passed on to the next generation. Duncan, however, inspired younger people also to express themselves through dance. This was the beginning of the form now called modern dance. Among those included with Duncan as modern-dance pioneers are Ruth St. Denis and Ted Shawn, who specialized in highly theatrical and exotic tableaux, or stage pictures. Like the opera–ballets of the 18th century, their pieces satisfied an audience's hunger for a glimpse of foreign people and places, even though these glimpses were rarely accurate.

Though dancers such as the German Mary Wigman, a highly dramatic performer, had a wide following both in America and Europe, no modern dancer was as influential as the American Martha Graham. A pupil of St. Denis and Shawn, she invented a style of dance that did not just ignore traditional ballet steps but contradicted them completely. Graham's revolutionary technique denied the primary importance of the classical positions of ballet. For her the source of interest and energy was the center of the body, not its extremities. Through her company and her school, which trained successive generations of disciples, Graham influenced every modern dancer of importance—titans such as José Limón, Paul Taylor, Merce Cunningham, and Twyla Tharp are included on this list—and made America the center of creativity for modern dance.

Dance in Musical Comedy

Americans also created the most vital forms of theatrical dancing. The first musical stage performance seen in the United States was a ballad opera called 'Flora', produced in Charleston, S.C., in 1735. More than a century later, 'The Black Crook' (1866) also scored an enormous success. It was not until the 20th century, however, that dancing and drama became truly integrated. Credit for this breakthrough goes to Agnes de Mille, whose 'Oklahoma!' (1943) made dancing an integral part of the story. Performed by dancers who had studied ballet, the dances in 'Oklahoma!' included not just ballet steps but folk dance and modern dance as well (see De Mille). Equally successful were the dances choreographed by Jerome Robbins for 'West Side Story', which brought a new vitality to the musical theater. Robbins, in his turn, influenced other choreographers such as Bob Fosse and Michael Bennett.

ETHNIC DANCE

Older than folk dances are dances performed and preserved by ethnic groups throughout the world. Every culture has developed its own means of expression through movement. These dances were part of tribal rituals, designed to be performed at crucial moments in the life of both the individual and the tribe.

American Indians

Despite similarities in purpose among all tribal dances, differences existed from culture to culture. American Indians, for example, had separate dances for men and for women and others in which men, women, and children took part. These dances emphasized various movements for the feet and postures for the head. Arms were not considered as important. As in many other tribal cultures, drums beat out an accompaniment.

Far East

Dancing in the Orient is different in important ways from that in Western cultures. In Eastern dance every movement has a specific meaning. Each gesture of the hands, the head, the arms, and the feet conveys a specific message that unschooled Western observers can only guess at.

India. In India, as in Western cultures, dances celebrate various festivals and rites of passage. The most important is the Hindu classical dance–drama bharata natya, which comes from the southeast. Performed by one woman, this dance has a great variety of bodily movement and is accompanied by rhythms stamped out by the performer's feet. Kathakali, from southwestern India, is performed only by men and young boys. The movements of these highly theatrical dances are extremely energetic, and drums and other percussion instruments accompany the performers.

Japan. Traditional dances in Japan have been performed for centuries. Among the best-known forms are No and Kabuki, both dance–dramas that combine mime and dance steps. Unlike dancing in the Western world, Japanese dancing is very formal and moves at a slow and stately pace.

China. Chinese dancing was developed thousands of years ago, when formal dances were performed at the ancient Chinese court. Dancing was also an important part of Chinese religion and philosophy.

Traditional Chinese dances are once more being performed in parts of China (left). Mexico's Ballet Folklórico (below) performs a native dance at the Houston Festival in 1985.

Photos, Janice Rubin

Through the ages these dances were largely forgotten and abandoned. Chinese dancing today is most often performed as a part of Chinese opera.

Indonesia. In Indonesia, however, the people have kept their dances alive and infused them through the years with new steps and movements. Instead of clinging to ancient traditions, the Indonesian people have adapted and modernized their dances.

Spain

Native dances from Spain are older than any others found in Europe. Some of the traditional pieces can be traced back to Greek times. When the Romans ruled, Spanish dancers were known throughout the empire for their artistry. During the Renaissance, dances such as the sarabande and the pavane were developed and performed by the ruling classes, while in the provinces the common people made dances of their own such as the fandango, bolero, and cachucha.

Perhaps the best-known Spanish dance is the flamenco, a Gypsy dance thought to be of Indian or Persian origin. A dance of great exuberance and intensity, a flamenco is improvised, the performer working within traditional forms according to his mood. A guitarist follows the rhythms, and friends clap, stamp, and shout their encouragement and approval.

Africa

The origins of African dance are lost in antiquity, but it is known that tribal peoples throughout Africa relied on dance to a remarkable degree. An integral part of everyday life, dances were used to express both joy and grief, to invoke prosperity and avoid disaster, as part of religious rituals, and purely as pastimes.

Though traditional African dance all but vanished as the continent developed in Western ways, several dances survived. Fertility dances in Ivory Coast are done in the shape of a circle. Performers move rhythmically to the beat of drums, and many of the participants wear masks depicting birds and beasts.

Also found in Ivory Coast is a highly dramatic hunting dance. With vivid pantomimed gestures, two men carrying bows and arrows pursue a boy who wears an antelope mask. In a totem dance in Upper Volta, a dozen men wearing animal masks take turns doing acrobatic leaps and jumps to the beating of drums until all but their leader is exhausted.

BIBLIOGRAPHY FOR DANCE

Amberg, George. Ballet: the Emergence of an American Art (Mentor Books, 1949).
Beaumont, C.W. Complete Book of Ballets (Grosset, 1938).
Buckle, Richard. Nijinsky (Simon & Schuster, 1971).
Chujoy, Anatole and Manchester, P.W., eds. The Dance Encyclopedia (Simon & Schuster, 1967).
De Mille, Agnes. Dance to the Piper (Little, 1952).
Duncan, Isadora. My Life (Universal, 1968).
Kerensky, Oleg. Anna Pavlova (Dutton, 1973).
Kirstein, Lincoln. The New York City Ballet (Knopf, 1973).
Money, Keith. Fonteyn: the Making of a Legend (Collins, 1973).
St. Denis, Ruth. An Unfinished Life (Harper, 1939).
Sorell, Walter. The Dance Through the Ages (Grosset, 1967).
Taper, Bernard. Balanchine (Harper, 1963).
Terry, Walter. Miss Ruth (Dodd, 1969).

(Above) Charles Moore—Black Star; (below) Marc and Evelyne Bernheim—Woodfin Camp

A *Makishi* dancer in Zambia (above) dances to the rhythm of drums and to bells attached to his legs. Two young girls in lavish costumes (below) perform the *Legong*, a religious pantomime dance of the island of Bali.

DANDELION

Dandelion blossom

DANDELION. One of the most familiar wild plants is the dandelion. Children have always liked to whistle through its hollow stem, make braided necklaces of its golden yellow blossoms, or blow on a head that has gone to seed and become a so-called "blowball" of fluff. It is, however, a troublesome plant that is a weed in lawns and gardens.

The dandelion lives throughout the temperate zones. It is a perennial, surviving winter and regrowing in early spring. It blooms in spring and summer. The roots may be up to five feet (1.5 meters) deep. The deeply lobed leaves grow out from center close to the ground. The best way to get rid of dandelions in a lawn is to use a weed killer (*see* Weeds). They also may be pulled, but it is necessary to loosen the plant so that the entire root comes out.

Dandelions belong to the composite family of plants. The blossom is actually a bouquet of about 150 to 200 tiny flowers set in a solid head on a receptacle. Each flower is a perfect seed-producing floret. As the small, dry, one-seeded fruits mature, they push up a feathery structure called a pappus on a threadlike stalk. All the pappi together make up the blowball. The wind takes the seeds and scatters them far and wide. (*See also* Flower.)

Dandelion greens are a delicacy in the spring when the leaves are tender and fresh. They can be boiled or eaten raw in salads. The word dandelion comes from the French *dent de lion,* meaning "lion's tooth." The scientific name is *Taraxacum officinale.*

DANTE (1265–1321). The greatest of Italian poets, Dante Alighieri is generally considered with Shakespeare and Goethe as one of the three universal masters in Western literature. His masterpiece, 'The Divine Comedy', is the most important Christian poem. Dante's use of the Italian language in place of Latin in the poem influenced the course of European literature.

Dante was born in Florence between May 15 and June 15, 1265, to a family of lesser nobility. The essential facts of his early life are told in his 'The New Life', written in about 1293. He met the Beatrice of his later poems when he was 9. Although it is unlikely that they ever exchanged more than a few words, Dante's love for her never died. His marriage to Gemma di Manetto Donati had been arranged as early as 1277, and they had three sons and one daughter.

Dante's education gave him a mastery of the Latin learning of the day. As a citizen of one of the chief city-republics he played a part in the violent political and military conflicts that engulfed Italy (*see* Guelfs and Ghibellines). A leader of the White Guelfs, he rose to high office in Florence and was sent as an ambassador to the pope in Rome in 1301.

The victory of the more extreme party in Florence, the Black Guelfs, resulted in the banishment of the leaders of the opposite party, the White Guelfs. Dante was among those sent into exile in 1302. He lived in various places in Italy until at length he settled in Ravenna, where he died on Sept. 14, 1321. A small tomb in Ravenna holds the poet's remains.

Dante's true monument is his immortal poem, 'The Divine Comedy'. It was probably written during his exile, though the dates are uncertain. He titled it 'Comedy'. The word "divine" was not added until sometime in the 16th century. A descriptive narrative of an imaginary journey through hell, purgatory, and heaven, the poem begins on Good Friday of the year 1300 and ends on the Sunday after Easter. The poet pictures himself journeying these ten days through the abyss of hell, up the mount of purgatory, and on through all but the highest circles of heaven. The Roman poet Virgil serves as his guide in hell and purgatory, the "divine Beatrice" in heaven. The poem is crowded with hundreds of persons whom Dante meets along the way. Most are actual persons from the past and from the poet's own time.

It is written in *terza rima,* consisting of stanzas of three lines rhyming *aba, bcb, cdc,* and so on. In its wealth of imagery and in the power of its language, the poem has never been surpassed.

In 'Dante and His Work', an imaginative painting by Domenico di Michelino, the writer stands, book in hand, with scenes from Florence and the 'Divine Comedy' around him.

Georges Danton

J.E. Bulloz

DANTON, Georges (1759–94). One of the leaders of the French Revolution, who had helped send thousands to the guillotine, died on the scaffold himself. His name was Danton.

Georges-Jacques Danton was born on Oct. 26, 1759, at Arcis-sur-Aube. His father was an attorney. The boy was a gifted speaker, and he went to Paris in 1780 to study law.

Danton's appearance was strikingly unattractive. He had an enormously large body and a big head with heavy, coarse features. His face was pitted with smallpox scars, his nose broken and misshapen by an early accident, his eyes small and deep-set. Nevertheless, his powerful voice, eloquent oratory, courage, and forcefulness made him a leader. He rose swiftly in his profession and by 1787 was able to buy a position as advocate of the Royal Council.

Danton realized that the revolution was inevitable. In 1790 he was a founder of the Cordeliers Club, a group of extreme revolutionists. In 1791 he was forced to flee to England to escape arrest. The successful attack on the Tuileries on Aug. 10, 1792, was largely due to his leadership. He became minister of justice in the new provisional government. When Prussian invaders threatened France, his fiery speech before the Assembly inspired the people to resist and to drive out the enemy.

Danton was among those who voted to execute the king and queen of France. In 1793 he became president of the Committee of Public Safety. With Jean Marat and Maximilien Robespierre he helped begin the Reign of Terror.

Apparently Danton's aim was to restore a stable government. The goal of the other committee members was to make themselves all-powerful. When invasion was repelled and the royalist uprisings put down, Danton was the first to urge moderation.

Robespierre decided that Danton should be brought before the Revolutionary Tribunal and condemned. He was formally accused of conspiring to restore the monarchy and died on the guillotine on April 5, 1794. He is still considered one of the ablest and most unselfish leaders of the revolution that overthrew the monarchy in France. (*See also* French Revolution; Jacobins; Marat; Robespierre.)

DANUBE RIVER. The most important river of central and southeastern Europe is the Danube. Rising in the Black Forest mountains of southwestern West Germany near the little city of Donaueschingen, it flows 1,750 miles (2,816 kilometers) to the Black Sea. The river gathers the waters of more than 300 tributaries and drains one twelfth of Europe.

The Europa Canal, 108 miles (174 kilometers) long, joins the Danube to its sister river, the Rhine, by connecting its tributary, the Altmühl, with the Main River. The headwaters of the Danube and the Rhine are very close. The Rhine empties into the North Sea. (*See also* Rhine River.)

Since early history the Danube has been a great water highway. It was once a Roman frontier. Down through the centuries it has been the highway of westward-moving Huns, Slavs, and Magyars. The river has been a barrier and a goal for Russian, Austrian, German, Bulgarian, Turkish, and Romanian armies. It has also been the channel of eastward- and southward-flowing German culture and influence.

In a pleasant little valley of the Black Forest—a northern spur of the Alps—a tiny stream tumbles down the rocks. Gathering volume and strength from many springs and brooks, it cuts a channel across the slopes and spreading hayfields of southern West Germany. This little stream, the Brege, with its twin, the Brigach, is the source of the Danube.

In its course across West Germany the river is not yet the "beautiful blue Danube" of song. It is a rushing stream hurrying along wooded hills and fertile meadows past picturesque Bavarian towns. At Regensburg (historic Ratisbon), its northernmost point, the Danube is alive with towboats, barges, and rafts carrying products from grain-growing Bavaria. Soon the Bohemian hills deflect its course southeastward to Vienna. To the east 30 miles (48 kilometers) is Bratislava and the edge of the rich plain (Alfold) of Hungary, checkered with growing crops. In fertile valleys stand white-walled villages among fields of ripening grain. The people are generally dark skinned, suggesting a warmer sun, a longer summer, and habitual out-of-door life.

Through Hungary and Yugoslavia

After passing through Bratislava, the Danube flows almost 100 miles (160 kilometers) eastward into Hungary. Then the river makes a great bend and begins its 500-mile (800-kilometer) journey into the south.

At Budapest imposing bridges span the Danube's course. Below the city there are tree-shaded villages at the foot of vineyard-covered slopes. Here and there is a group of fishermen's huts and miles of nets drying in the sun. Numerous canals contribute their burden of huge cargoes of grain and lumber from the Hungarian plains.

Just past the junction of the Danube with the eastward-flowing Drava and Sava rivers and the great southward-flowing Tisza (or Theiss) river is Belgrade, Yugoslavia's capital. Here the river, again heading eastward, spreads out like a wide lake.

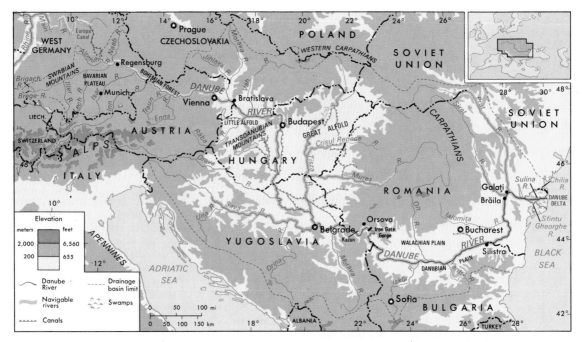

Kazan Narrows and the Iron Gate

A hundred miles (160 kilometers) farther on are the black cliffs of the Kazan passageway. Here the Danube narrows to 160 yards (146 meters), and there is almost a twilight gloom. A long gash in the face of the nearly perpendicular rock walls shows where the Roman emperor Trajan's warriors built a road in the 2nd century on the way to found the colony of Dacia, which today is Romania.

Just below, the river gathers all its force. It batters its way between the Balkan and Carpathian ranges through the historic gorge known as the Iron Gate, which is near Orsova. The commercial importance of the Danube necessitated the blasting of a channel deep enough to allow river steamers to pass the mile and a half (2.4 kilometers) of rapids at all seasons.

The Danube from Orsova on winds sleepily through a peaceful countryside, separating Romania from Bulgaria. Its monotony is broken only by an occasional fishing hamlet or straggling part-Turk, part-Bulgarian, or part-Romanian town. Beyond Silistra the river turns abruptly to the north to the important ports of Brăila and Galaţi. Here, 125 miles (201 kilometers) from the mouth, is the head of navigation for seagoing vessels. These cities, with docks and grain elevators, are the shipping centers for agricultural Romania and other Danubian regions. Forty-five miles (72 kilometers) below Galaţi the river divides into three arms that wander across the flat, swampy delta.

Importance to Europe's Commerce

The Danube serves as a channel for local trade among the nations along its banks. It is also the main route by which the cereals, ores, and petroleum of southeastern Europe are exchanged for manufactured products. The right to enjoy free commerce on the river is vital to the economy of every country in the Danube Valley. Europe recognized this in the Peace of Paris in 1856, which declared that Danube navigation would be free to all nations. Two international commissions governed the river until the years 1938 to 1940, when Germany won control. After World War II the Allies agreed to internationalize the river, but the Eastern-bloc nations of southeastern Europe gained control of the section that flows eastward from Austria into Hungary and beyond.

Bridges that cross the Danube River join the two parts of Budapest, the capital and largest city of Hungary.

Art Resource/EB Inc.

DARDANELLES.

A ribbon of water, only 42 miles (68 kilometers) long and from one to 5 miles (1.6 to 8 kilometers) wide, separates the continent of Europe from the westernmost tip of Asia Minor. This strategically important strait is the Dardanelles. It leads

from the Aegean Sea to the Sea of Marmara and then through the Bosporus strait to the Black Sea. Thus the Dardanelles is the outer gateway to a great productive area. The world's ships must pass through here to reach the grain ports of the Ukraine and the oil ports of Romania and the Caucasus region. The western side of the strait is formed by the Gallipoli peninsula. Major ports along its shores are Gallipoli, Eceabat, and Canakkale; and many famous castles stand along its banks.

The strait is rich with history and legend. In ancient times it was called Hellespont, meaning Helle's Sea, in memory of Helle, a mythical Boetian princess. She was drowned in its swift waters after falling from the back of the legendary ram with the golden fleece. Across the Hellespont from the eastern side, Leander swam nightly to visit Hero, a priestess of Aphrodite. In 480 BC Persia's king Xerxes sent his army across the strait on a bridge of boats to invade Greece. In 334 BC Alexander the Great similarly crossed from Greece to invade Persia. The strait takes its name from the old town of Dardanus.

The Dardanelles passed into Turkey's control in 1453. In later years Turkish control was supported by British diplomacy, which sought to bar Russia from the Mediterranean. But in World War I Turkey was allied with Germany. The British, wanting to get aid to Russia through the Black Sea, tried to capture the Gallipoli peninsula in 1915–16. They were thrown back and the Dardanelles remained unconquered (see World War I).

After Turkey's defeat in 1917 the Dardanelles became part of a neutral "zone of straits," which was under the League of Nations. In 1923 the Treaty of Lausanne returned the region to Turkey. At first Turkey was denied the right to fortify the straits, but in 1936 another treaty restored this right and also permitted Turkey to close the straits to belligerent ships in wartime.

Since Turkey was neutral until the closing days of World War II, the Dardanelles route to the Soviet Union was closed to Great Britain and the United States. With this sea route barred, the Allies were forced to build roads through Iran to get supplies to the Soviets. The Soviet Union became determined to get part control of the Dardanelles after the war. Turkey refused formal demands for a share in the control in 1946 and again in 1947. As the threat of Soviet aggression increased during the Cold War, the United States and Britain encouraged Turkey to stand firm on sole control.

DAR ES-SALAAM, Tanzania.

The headquarters of Dar es-Salaam region, the port city of Dar es-Salaam is also Tanzania's seat of government and largest city as well as an industrial center. Located on the Indian Ocean, Dar es-Salaam is hot and humid with an annual rainfall of 43 inches (109 centimeters).

The city is the last stop of the railroad that goes west to Kigoma on Lake Tanganyika and north to Mwanza on Lake Victoria. The Tanzam Railway, completed in 1975, connects the port with Zambia. Local products include soap, paint, cigarettes, food products, metal- and glasswares, textiles, wood carvings, and shoes. Dar es-Salaam's natural harbor is well sheltered by land and is the outlet for most of mainland Tanzania's agricultural and mineral exports. There is also an international airport.

Modern multistoried buildings sprang up after World War II; a hospital complex and high court were part of the expansion. Educational facilities include the University of Dar es-Salaam, founded in 1961, Ardhi Institute, and several libraries and other research institutes. The National Museum of Tanzania is also in the city.

Dar es-Salaam was founded in 1862 by the sultan of Zanzibar on the site of the village of Mzizima. Its name comes from the Arabic *dar salaam,* meaning "haven of peace." It remained only a small port until the German East Africa Company established a station there in 1887. Since 1907 Dar es-Salaam has been the starting point for the Central Line railroad. It served as the capital of German East Africa from 1891 to 1916 and of Tanganyika from 1961 to 1964. Since that time it has been the capital of Tanzania. In 1974 Dodoma was declared the new capital, though moving all government functions there could take until the 1990s. Population (1978 preliminary census), city, 769,445; region, 851,522.

DARÍO, Rubén

(1867–1916). Rubén Darío was considered by many to be the best poet writing in modern Spanish. He was also one of the major literary innovators of his time.

Born Félix Rubén García Sarmiento on Jan. 18, 1867, in Metapa (now Ciudad Darío), Nicaragua, he began using the pseudonym Rubén Darío at age 14 to sign his poems and stories. In 1886 he left Nicaragua and spent the rest of his life as a world traveler and writer. While living in Chile, Darío published his first major work in 1888, a collection of verse and prose. Entitled 'Blue', the book was soon heralded in South America and Europe as the start of a literary movement called Modernism.

He was Colombian consul in Buenos Aires in the 1890s. In his next significant work, 'Profane Hymns and Other Poems', published in 1896, he continued the innovative style of 'Blue' but placed its main emphasis on the type of Symbolism developed in France. Symbolism was an attempt to formulate new rules and usages of language in poetry—a move away from the objective or representational portrayal to one revealing the intangible.

From 1898 to 1914 Darío lived in Europe as correspondent for a Buenos Aires newspaper. While there he executed his best work, 'Songs of Life and Hope', published in 1905. In this book he was more concerned with matters outside the realm of art—issues such as the defeat of Spain in the Spanish-American War, North American imperialism, and the solidarity of Spanish-speaking peoples.

Darío returned from Europe ill and on the brink of poverty. He died at León, Nicaragua, on Feb. 6, 1916.

Courtesy of the Oriental Institute, the University of Chicago

Darius I, in a bas-relief at Persepolis, gives audience to a dignitary while seated before two incense burners.

DARIUS I (550–486 BC). One of the most powerful monarchs of ancient times was Darius the Great. He ruled over the vast Persian Empire that ranged from the Aegean Sea to the Indus River.

Darius was born in the reign of the great conqueror King Cyrus I. His father was Hystaspes, a satrap (governor of a satrapy, or province) under Cyrus and a distant relative of the king. Darius grew up at the court. When Cyrus' son and successor, Cambyses I, died, the throne was seized by a pretended heir, Gaumata. With the help of six Persian nobles, Darius assassinated the pretender and established himself as king.

The sudden change of rulers encouraged rebellions. Darius spent six years putting down the revolt. To maintain control, he devised a strong uniform system of government (*see* Persian History). He fixed tax rates, set up a standard coinage, and wrote a code of laws. He declared, ". . . I love justice, I hate iniquity. It is not my pleasure that the lower suffer injustice because of the higher."

To encourage trade, Darius dredged the old Egyptian canal connecting the Nile and the Red Sea. He built roads and set up post houses to aid travelers. Under him, slaves completed building the magnificent palaces at Susa and Persepolis. To extend the empire, Darius' generals conquered Thrace and Macedonia in the west and the Punjab and much of the Indus

Valley in the east. Libya became a satrapy in 512 BC. Five years later Darius made an alliance with Athens, but about 500 BC the Ionian Greeks began an uprising against Persian rule (*see* Persian Wars).

For 14 years Darius waged wars with the Greeks. In 486 BC, while preparing a campaign against the Egyptians, he became ill and died. His tomb was built into a cliff near Persepolis. He left a record of his reign chiseled on the side of a rocky cliff overlooking the village of Behistun, in Iran.

DARROW, Clarence (1857–1938). Probably the most celebrated American lawyer of the 20th century, Clarence Darrow worked as defense counsel in many widely publicized trials, earning a permanent place in the annals of legal history. His fame did not decline over the years: in the 1970s his life was the subject of a one-man stage production starring Henry Fonda.

Darrow was born on April 18, 1857, near Kinsman, Ohio. He attended Allegheny College and the University of Michigan briefly before being admitted to the Ohio bar in 1878. In 1887 he moved to Chicago, where he soon was appointed city corporation counsel and later the general attorney for the Chicago and Northwestern Railroad. He resigned this position in 1895 to defend Eugene V. Debs, president of the American Railway Union, and other union leaders who had been arrested on a federal charge of contempt of court over difficulties arising out of the Pullman strike of 1894. Through this trial Darrow established a national reputation as a labor and criminal lawyer.

In 1902 President Theodore Roosevelt appointed him an arbitrator in the Pennsylvania anthracite coal strike. In 1907 he secured the acquittal of labor organizer William D. "Big Bill" Haywood for the murder of former Idaho governor Frank Steunenberg. After World War I he defended war protesters charged with violating state sedition laws.

The two most famous trials in which he participated took place in the 1920s. The first was the notorious Leopold–Loeb murder case of 1924. He saved Nathan Leopold and Richard Loeb from execution—but not from prison—for the murder of 14-year-old Robert Franks. In 1925 Darrow defended high school teacher John T. Scopes, who was charged with violating Ten-

Clarence Darrow

Courtesy of the Chicago Historical Society

nessee law by teaching evolution. The prosecuting attorney in this famous "monkey trial" was William Jennings Bryan.

In his writings and speeches Darrow promoted freedom of expression and the closed shop for unions. He opposed capital punishment and Prohibition. He died in Chicago on March 13, 1938.

DARTS. One of England's oldest sports, the game called darts is played by throwing darts at a circular, numbered board. The game is most popular in English pubs, or public houses, and the similar American neighborhood taverns as a friendly competition between individuals or teams.

The dart board is a circle that is 18 inches (45.72 centimeters) in diameter. It is mounted on a wall so that its center is about 5 feet 8 inches (172.72 centimeters) above the floor. The board is normally made of cork, bristle, elm, or some other material that the darts can easily stick into. The board is divided like a sliced cake or pie into 20 sectors. The sectors are separated by thin wires or other dividers. Each sector is marked with a point value ranging from 1 to 20, but the numbers are not in consecutive order.

A narrow outer ring, which runs through all sectors, doubles the value of the sector for all darts thrown into it. Closer to the center is another narrow ring. This one triples the value of darts in it. In the center of the board are an inner bull's-eye, with a value of 50 points, and a ring surrounding it, also called a bull's-eye, worth 25 points.

The darts themselves are about 6 inches (15 centimeters) long. They are weighted and are feathered much like an arrow at one end and have a needlelike point at the other. Each player takes turns throwing three darts from a distance of 8 feet, in the United States, or 9 feet, in Great Britain (2.44 or 2.74 meters).

In the standard game, the scoring proceeds backward from 301 to zero. Each player must get a dart in the narrow outer ring to begin scoring. This and all subsequent scores are subtracted from 301.

To win, a player must reach exactly zero with a final shot in the narrow outer ring again. If, for instance, only 20 points are needed to reach zero, the player would have to aim for and hit the 10 sector in the double ring. If the throw reduces the score to only one point or takes the total below zero, the score reverts to the total of the previous turn.

In some places different kinds of dart boards are used. For example, certain Yorkshire and Irish boards have a single bull (bull is short for bull's-eye) and no triple rings. Outside of tournament play, the rules of the game, too, may vary.

The game of darts may go back as far as the 12th century. It began as butts, an indoor form of archery, with the butts, or rounded ends, of barrels as targets. It had become a tournament pastime by the 16th century. The Pilgrim Fathers who came to North America aboard the *Mayflower* in 1620 played darts on the journey. In Britain today there are about 7,000 dart clubs in the National Darts Association.

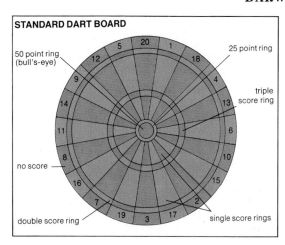

STANDARD DART BOARD

50 point ring (bull's-eye) · 25 point ring · triple score ring · no score · double score ring · single score rings

Other groups that oversee dart-playing contests are the British Darts Organization and the Scottish Darts Association. In addition to a million registered players, there are more than 5 million players who are not affiliated with clubs.

The American Dart Association was formed in 1933. The United States Darting Association, which was organized in 1969, conducts an annual national open tournament.

DARWIN, Charles (1809–82). Although Darwin has been dead for more than a century, people are still interpreting, defending, or criticizing his theories of evolution. Before he became England's greatest biologist, he was such an indifferent student that his father declared, "You care for nothing but shooting, dogs, and rat-catching, and you will be a disgrace to yourself and all your family."

Charles Robert Darwin was born in Shrewsbury on Feb. 12, 1809. Darwin's father was a successful and wealthy physician; his mother was a daughter of Josiah Wedgwood, the famous British potter. She died when Charles was 8 years old, and the boy was reared by three older sisters, who constantly found fault with him.

At school young Charles had no interest in classical languages and ancient history. He liked best to collect shells, birds' eggs, and coins. He also watched birds and insects and helped his brother make chemical experiments at home. These activities, he said in later years, were the best part of his education.

At the age of 16, Darwin began to study medicine at the University of Edinburgh. Here too he found the courses dull, and watching operations made him ill. In 1828 he transferred to Cambridge, intending to become a clergyman. Instead, he devoted most of his time to studying plants and animals and later to geology. He received his bachelor's degree in 1831.

Then came the event that shaped his life—an appointment as unpaid naturalist on the exploring ship *Beagle*. It left England on Dec. 27, 1831, to make astronomical observations, chart the southern coasts of South America, and sail around the world. The voyage, with many side trips on land, lasted until October 1836. During those five years Darwin examined geologic formations, collected fossils, and studied plants and animals. He also began to doubt that the many species of living things had come into being at one moment. In 1837, soon after returning to England, he began to collect information on the subject now called evolution (*see* Evolution).

Early Ideas of Evolution

Evolution was not a new idea, even in Darwin's day. Long before the time of Christ, philosophers had explained the great variety of plants and animals by proposing "natural" ways they could have developed. Before 1600 Sir Walter Raleigh concluded that dogs had turned into wolves and that the different races of men were related. Several philosophers also declared that new conditions caused plants to change into new varieties or species.

Comte de Buffon (1707–1788) went still further. In his 36-volume 'Natural History', he declared that modern animals had evolved, or "degenerated," from others and so on back to the beginning. Some changes, he thought, were produced when different forms interbred; others were caused by food, climate, pressure, and so on. According to Buffon's theory, the hippopotamus and elephant are large because their ancestors ate a great deal of food; the hair of

This drawing of the famous biologist was made about 15 years before he published his famous book on the origin of species.

lions is tawny because it has been bleached by the brilliant sunlight of the tropical plains.

Chevalier de Lamarck (1744–1829) maintained that plants and animals evolved because of an inborn tendency to progress from simple to complex forms. Environment, however, modified this progression and so did use or disuse of parts. Giraffes, for example, developed long necks by straining to reach the leaves of trees; snakes lost their legs by crawling. Birds, said Lamarck, came from hairy ancestors. Their attempts to fly forced air into the hairs and so turned them into feathers.

Darwin knew about these attempts to explain evolution. His grandfather, Erasmus Darwin, had published several books containing ideas much like Lamarck's theory of use and disuse. He felt, however, that early writers on the subject had speculated too much and had collected too few facts. As a result, they failed to convince the scientific world that evolution had actually taken place. They also failed to give a reasonable explanation of how changes might have produced the different organisms found upon the earth today.

Darwin Attacks the Great Problem

Darwin determined to avoid these mistakes and to collect and test facts scientifically before explaining them. After his return to England he followed this course for 15 months, meanwhile also writing up the 'Journal' of his scientific work on the *Beagle*.

Then he happened to read 'An Essay on the Principle of Population', by a British economist, Thomas Malthus. Malthus undertook to prove that human populations tend to increase more rapidly than food and other necessities. The result is a struggle in which some people succeed and become wealthy while others fail or even starve.

Darwin applied this theory to the world of nature. Plants and animals, he knew, reproduce so rapidly that the earth could not hold them if all their young survived. This meant that there was a constant struggle for space, food, and shelter, as well as against enemies and unfavorable conditions. Young trees, for example, struggle for space. Those that grow most rapidly survive while those that grow slowly become stunted and die. Certain hawks struggle, or compete, with each other for the mice they eat, and the poorest hunters go hungry. Mice, in turn, struggle to keep from being caught by hawks. In frigid winters all living things struggle against cold. Some endure it and others keep themselves warm, but many die because they can do neither.

Struggling and living or dying could not lead to evolution if all members of each living kind or species were exactly alike. Darwin found that members of a single species vary greatly in shape, size, color, strength, and so on. He also believed that most of these variations could be *inherited*.

Under the constant struggle to exist, organisms with harmful variations were almost sure to die before they could have young ones. Living things with useful variations, however, survived and reproduced. When their descendants varied still more, the process was repeated. In other words, the struggle for existence selected organisms with helpful variations but made others die out. This was the critical point in Darwin's reasoning.

This *natural selection* had two further effects that were important. Many newly developed organisms remained in their old habitats, where they struggled successfully against older forms, crowding them out of existence. Other new organisms made their way into different surroundings, where they prospered and kept on changing. Over the ages, these two factors produced a steady succession of new plants, animals, and other organisms. They enabled living things to go into all sorts of environments and become fitted, or adapted, to many different types of life. Thus mammals, which started out on dry land, also spread into swamps, lakes, and seas. Some climbed trees, some burrowed, and some even learned to fly.

Darwin wrote a short sketch of his theory in 1842 and a longer one in 1844. Instead of publishing the second statement, however, he continued to collect information. He also took time to write books on coral reefs, volcanic islands, barnacles, and the geology of South America. Not until 1856 did he begin what would have been a three- or four-volume book on the subject of evolution.

In 1858 he received a manuscript from a young naturalist, Alfred Russel Wallace, who also had developed a theory of natural selection. Although Darwin was willing to withdraw in favor of Wallace, associates insisted that he publish his own discoveries without further delay. With Wallace's approval, short statements by both men were published late in 1858. Darwin went on to write his famous book 'On the Origin of Species by Means of Natural Selection', which appeared in 1859.

After completing the 'Origin of Species', Darwin began 'The Variation of Animals and Plants under Domestication', which showed how rapidly some organisms had evolved under artificial, instead of natural, selection. 'The Descent of Man', published in 1871, elaborated the theory of sexual selection and applied Lamarck's unsound theory of use and disuse (*see* Lamarck). Later books dealt with earthworms, orchids, climbing plants, and plants that eat insects. 'The Power of Movement in Plants' was written with the help of Darwin's son Francis, who became a botanist. Another son, George, was an astronomer and Horace was a noted engineer.

Darwin, who was a semi-invalid for much of his life, became very weak in 1881 and complained that he no longer could work. He died on April 19, 1882, and was buried among England's greatest men in Westminster Abbey.

Darwin himself never claimed to provide proof of evolution or of the origin of species. His claim was that if evolution had occurred, a number of otherwise mysterious facts about plants and animals could be easily explained. Recently, however, direct evidence of evolution has been observed, and evolution is now supported by a wealth of evidence from a variety of scientific fields.

In spite of this evidence, evolution has been rejected by the members of certain religious groups who prefer what they term the theory of creationism. This attempts to explain some features of plant and animal life through a literal interpretation of the Bible. In the scientific community, however, there is little doubt that the general outline of Darwin's theory of evolution is correct.

A recently proposed modification of evolutionary theory suggests that from time to time evolution may proceed relatively rapidly. These bursts of activity are then followed by long periods of little change. This modification, called punctuated equilibrium, goes a long way toward explaining what has been called the incompleteness of the fossil record; that is, the scarcity of fossils intermediate between earlier and later members of the same plant or animal family.

DARWIN, Australia. A fast-growing and cosmopolitan city, Darwin is the capital and chief port of Australia's Northern Territory. It is located on the Timor Sea at the northern edge of the central Australian continent. Almost totally destroyed by a cyclone in 1974, the city has been rebuilt and is one of the most modern in Australia.

With major shipping and international air facilities, Darwin is the port-of-entry to northern Australia. Its location makes it a distribution and communication center. While business generated by government activity is a major part of the city's economy, tile and brickmaking, fruit canning, meat-packing, sawmilling, and the export of cattle, rice, uranium ore, and pearl shell are also important.

The harbor at Darwin was sighted in 1839 by a surveyor on board the *HMS Beagle* and named for the British scientist and naturalist Charles Darwin. Surveys for a town at the harbor site were not made until 1869, and the original settlement was known as Palmerston. In 1911, when control of the Northern Territory passed from South Australia to the Commonwealth government, Palmerston was renamed Darwin. The town's early growth was accelerated by the discovery of gold at nearby Pine Creek in 1872 and the completion in that same year of the Overland Telegraph Line. Discovery of pearl shell in 1884 and the completion of railroad service to Pine Creek in 1889 also spurred development. Uranium was discovered in the Darwin vicinity in 1949.

Japanese air raids damaged Darwin during World War II, and a Dec. 25, 1974, cyclone nearly destroyed the city. Thirty thousand residents were evacuated, and approximately 9,000 homes had to be built or rebuilt. Growth has continued, however, and the population is now greater than it was before the cyclone. During the 1970s Darwin was a haven for refugees fleeing from troubled southeast Asian areas.

Darwin became a city in 1959 and has a mayor and a municipal council. Population (1981 census), 56,482.

DAUDET, Alphonse (1840–97). As novelist, dramatist, and short story writer, Alphonse Daudet was a leading figure in the 19th-century school of French Naturalism. This movement, according to author Émile Zola, intended to study the "human temperament and the profound modifications of the human organism under the pressures of environment and events."

Daudet was born on May 13, 1840, at Nîmes, France, and grew up there at Lyon. His first significant work, 'The Little Good-for-Nothing', was published in 1868, the year he moved to Paris. There he formed a long and troubled relationship with a model, Marie Rieu, to whom he dedicated his only book of poems, 'The Lovers' (1858). His relationship with her also formed the basis for a later novel, 'Sapho' (1884).

Not all of Daudet's works were well received during his lifetime. His first play, 'The Last Idol', made a great impact in 1862; but 'Woman of Arles' (1872) did not. His novel 'The New Don Quixote' (1872) was disliked, but 'Young Fromont and Old Risler' (1874) received an award.

Throughout most of his adult life, Daudet was poor and his health was very bad. He died in Paris suddenly on Dec. 16, 1897.

DAUMIER, Honoré (1808–79). The caricaturist, painter, and sculptor Honoré Daumier is best known for his cartoons and drawings satirizing 19th-century French politics and society. Also important were his paintings that helped introduce techniques of impressionism into modern art. The paintings were hardly known, however, during his lifetime.

Daumier was born in Marseilles, France, on Feb. 20 or 26, 1808. His parents were artists but were not successful. Daumier received a typical lower middle-class education, but his studies did not interest him. He wanted to draw. His family therefore arranged for him to study with Alexandre Lenoir, a fairly well-known artist who had studied with Jacques-Louis David, a leading classicist painter.

At age 13 Daumier became a bailiff's messenger in the law courts. He then worked as a bookstore clerk at the Palais-Royal, one of the busiest spots in Paris. There Daumier saw picturesque personalities— men and women of fashion, intellectuals, artists, and swindlers—who lent themselves to caricature.

At age 18 or 20, Daumier decided to embark on the artistic career he longed for. He soon found he could not make a living from painting or sculpting what he pleased and therefore accepted commissions for portraits and cartoons of morals and manners. From 1830 to 1847, Daumier was a lithographer, cartoonist, and sculptor.

In his cartoons Daumier created unforgettable characters as he attacked a regime, form of society, or concept of life that he scorned. His types were universal: businessmen, lawyers, physicians, professors, and petits bourgeois. After two uncomplimentary caricatures of King Louis-Philippe in 1832, Daumier was thrown into prison for six months.

'Past, Present, and Future', a three-faced cartoon by Daumier, was sketched in 1834.

In 1848 Daumier discovered impressionism, a form of art in which faces and bodies tend to be devoured by the surrounding light and become one with the atmosphere. From lack of demand, Daumier's impressionist lithographs are not very numerous, but these and his paintings, also few in number, show that he had been converted to impressionism.

As a cartoonist, Daumier enjoyed a wide reputation, though as a painter he remained unknown. He died in Valmondois on Feb. 11, 1879, having produced 4,000 lithographs and an equal number of drawings.

DAVID. One of the greatest heroes of ancient history was David, a poor shepherd boy who killed the giant Goliath. According to the Biblical story of his life, which is told in detail in the Old Testament, David was born about 3,000 years ago.

David was the youngest son of Jesse, a man of Bethlehem. While a shepherd, he learned to play the harp and to hurl stones from a sling with deadly accuracy to protect the flocks.

Saul, at that time king of Israel, called for music to soothe his troubled spirit. David was so handsome and his music on the harp so pleasing that Saul made him his armor bearer and musician.

Then David met Goliath. This Philistine had challenged Saul for 40 days to send out a man to fight him. No one had responded, for Goliath stood more than nine feet tall. He brandished a spear that had a 20-pound head of iron and a shaft "like a weaver's beam." David wore no armor and carried only a sling hidden in his hand and five smooth stones in a shepherd's bag at his side.

As Goliath came into range, David reached into his bag, put a stone in his sling, and let go with all his might. The stone pierced Goliath's forehead, and he fell dead. David then cut off the giant's head as a present to Saul. The Philistines fled in terror. David's heroic deed aroused Saul's jealousy.

An engraving entitled 'David Forgiving Absalom' shows the compassionate side of the king toward his rebellious son.

Brown Brothers

At that time, David became a very good friend of the king's son Jonathan. Jonathan gave the humble shepherd boy his royal garments, his sword, and his bow. David, now a full-fledged warrior, fought so bravely against the Philistines that according to the Bible the women of Israel said, "Saul hath slain his thousands, and David his ten thousands."

Fearing that the people would make David king, Saul tried to kill him. He even tried to kill his own son Jonathan for shielding David. Jonathan, however, helped David to escape. Saul's army followed and David had to hide. Twice David could have killed Saul, but he would not seize the throne by murder.

In the battle of Gilboa both Saul and Jonathan were killed. With Saul gone, David ruled at Hebron as king of Judah for almost eight years. When the king of Israel was murdered, the Israelites made David their king in about 1000 BC.

David ruled Judah and Israel as a united nation until he died 33 years later. He moved from Hebron to Jerusalem, which his nephew Joab had captured for him. Joab also conquered Israel's neighbors until the nation's power reached into Syria.

Years of bloodshed and famine marked David's reign. The treason and death of his favorite son, Absalom, filled the king with grief. David's worst crime was his betrayal of his faithful captain Uriah, so that he might marry Uriah's wife, Bathsheba.

DAVID, Jacques-Louis (1748–1825). Often considered the leader of the neoclassical school of painting, David actually combined neoclassicism with the seeds of the later romanticism, realism, and academicism. He was the leading painter during the years of the French Revolution, but he also became the court painter of the Napoleonic empire.

Jacques-Louis David was born in Paris on Aug. 30, 1748. He entered the Royal Academy of Painting and Sculpture when he was 18 and, after failing four times, won in 1774 the Prix de Rome, the much sought-after prize awarded by the government for study in Italy. In Italy David absorbed many influences, including the neoclassical ideas being developed in Rome.

David returned to Paris in 1780 and was elected to the Académie Royale in 1784 for his 'Andromache Mourning Hector'. His 'Oath of the Horatii' created a sensation at the official Paris Salon of 1785 and immediately became the model for all future noble historical art. By 1789, when his 'Brutus and His Dead Sons' was exhibited, the French Revolution was underway. The patriotic Roman condemning his traitorous sons to death had unexpected political significance, and the Roman dress and furnishings shown in the picture influenced French fashion.

A member of the extremist Jacobin group led by Robespierre, David was elected in 1792 to the National Convention. He became virtually the art dictator of France, known as "the Robespierre of the brush." In that role he abolished the Académie. It was during this period that he painted perhaps his greatest work, the realistic 'The Death of Marat'.

After the fall of Robespierre, David was imprisoned, but he was allowed to paint, and he began what he considered his masterpiece, the giant 'Sabines'. When it was exhibited in 1799, it attracted much attention, including that of Napoleon. He again became a government painter, the most important work produced being the huge 'Coronation', begun in 1805 and finished in 1807. After Napoleon's fall, David was exiled to Brussels, where he died on Dec. 29, 1825.

'The Death of Marat' was one of Jacques-Louis David's most realistic paintings.

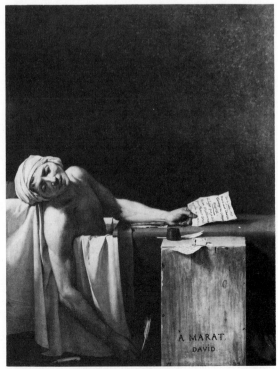

Musees Royaux des Beaux-Arts de Belgique, Brussels

DAVIS, Jefferson (1808–1889). During the Civil War, Jefferson Davis was president of the Confederate States and Abraham Lincoln led the United States. Both were born in Kentucky, several months apart, Davis on June 3, 1808. The Lincolns moved to Indiana soon after, then to Illinois, while the Davises moved to a small plantation in Mississippi.

Jefferson was the tenth child of Samuel Davis, a planter. Jefferson's father was not wealthy, but the oldest son, Joseph, became well-to-do and helped the boy. Jefferson attended academies in Kentucky and Mississippi, and in 1821 he entered Transylvania University in Kentucky. Three years later he was appointed to West Point and was graduated in 1828, becoming an officer in the United States Army.

He served in frontier posts in Illinois and Wisconsin and in the Black Hawk War in 1832. Next year he fell in love with Sarah Taylor, the daughter of his commandant, Col. Zachary Taylor. The colonel did not approve of the match; so Davis resigned his commission in June 1835. Sarah went to an aunt in Kentucky, and there the two were married. Joseph helped him establish a plantation (Brierfield) on land in Mississippi. Within three months, tragedy struck. The young couple fell ill with malaria and Sarah died.

Davis spent the next few years living quietly at Brierfield. In 1845 he married Varina Howell (*see* Davis, Varina). By this time he was a successful planter. He developed a deep devotion to Southern plantation life and his own attitude toward his slaves led him to deny fiercely all Northern claims that slavery was cruel.

Elected to Public Office

He was elected a representative to Congress in 1845, but he resigned the next year when the Mexican War broke out. He became a colonel of Mississippi volunteers and served under his former father-in-law, now General Taylor. At the battle of Buena Vista, Davis and his regiment probably saved the American army from defeat. Davis was severely wounded. This action made him widely known as "the hero of Buena Vista." It also convinced him that he was a military genius. This belief later handicapped him in his relations with Confederate commanders.

In 1847 Mississippi sent him to the United States Senate. His ability as a speaker soon made him a Democratic leader, championing the South and slavery. In 1851 he resigned to run for governor of Mississippi. He was defeated; but he re-entered public life when Franklin Pierce became president in 1853. Davis became secretary of war, serving until the end of Pierce's term in 1857.

Mississippi again sent him to the Senate. By this time the tension between the North and the South over slavery was at fever heat. Davis took an unyielding attitude in favor of slavery. In 1860 he helped nominate a proslavery Democrat, John C.

Jefferson Davis and his second wife, Varina Howell Davis, were a devoted pair. Despite the 18 years' difference in their ages, Mrs. Davis was her husband's valued adviser in political affairs.

Breckinridge, to run against both Abraham Lincoln, the Republican nominee, and Stephen A. Douglas, the northern Democratic nominee. This party split caused Lincoln to be elected.

Southern bitterness made secession inevitable. On Jan. 21, 1861, Davis made an impassioned speech to the Senate and resigned. When the Southern states formed the Confederacy he hoped to be named commander of the Confederate forces. Instead he was named president. He was inaugurated Feb. 18, 1861. (*See also* Confederate States of America.)

In spite of poor health, Davis assumed his new duties. At first his administration was highly popular. Time brought military reverses, and criticism began. He took more power into his hands, until even his own officials at Richmond complained.

Davis was not indifferent to the personal liberty of his people, but he was dictatorial in manner. His experience had developed in him self-confidence and habits of command. On the whole he made few blunders.

As the blockade of the Southern coasts became more effective, the uneven struggle appeared hopeless. Still confident, Davis declared in his last message of March 13, 1865, that success might yet be secured. Less than 30 days later Lee surrendered. Soon after, Davis was captured by United States troops near Irwinsville, Ga. (*See* Civil War, American.)

Davis was confined at Fortress Monroe. His sufferings there aroused the sympathy of the Southern people. Even those who had found fault with his policies now regarded him as a martyr. After two years he was released on bail.

As soon as he was free he journeyed to Canada and Europe to try to regain his health. Upon his return to the United States he tried to retrieve his broken fortunes. His business ventures proved failures, and in 1878 he retired. The rest of his life was spent writing his book 'The Rise and Fall of the Confederate Government'. He died in New Orleans on Dec. 6, 1889. A monument now stands in Richmond to the memory of "Jefferson Davis, the first and only President of the Confederate States of America."

DAVIS, Miles (born 1926). The most important jazz bandleader after World War II was Miles Davis. Outstanding among trumpet soloists, he led many small ensembles, including three that were the original sources of major jazz idioms: cool jazz, modal jazz, and fusion music.

Born in Alton, Ill., on May 25, 1926, Miles Dewey Davis III grew up in East Saint Louis, Ill. His father, a prominent dentist and landowner, gave him a trumpet for his 13th birthday, and soon he was playing in local jazz bands. His father, delighted with young Miles's talent and determination, sent him to study at the Juilliard School in New York City. Instead of attending classes, Miles joined Charlie Parker's quintet, developed a simplified bebop trumpet style, and performed on many of Parker's greatest recordings. In 1948 Davis formed a nine-piece band to play a new kind of jazz that featured low, muted tone colors. This band, although never commercially successful, was the beginning of cool jazz, which became widespread during the 1950s.

By that time, however, Davis had abandoned cool jazz and was playing a more blues-influenced music, as in his 'Bags Groove' and 'Walkin' ' solos. He performed with his quintet, which often included tenor saxophonist John Coltrane, and with Gil Evans' big band. Davis began to create music based on modes, the scales used by ancient Greek musicians, instead of traditional keys and harmonic patterns. 'Kind of Blue' by his sextet in 1959 was the first major modal jazz recording, beginning a trend that remained popular among jazz musicians for the next ten years.

Miles Davis in 1969

Votavafoto from London Daily Express—Pictorial Parade/EB Inc.

His modal jazz quintets of the 1960s, which usually included drummer Tony Williams and tenor saxophonist Wayne Shorter, progressed steadily toward greater harmonic and rhythmic freedom. In 1969 Davis adopted a new approach that combined elements of rock music with jazz, resulting in fusion music. This featured several rhythms played at the same time. His fusion music recordings brought him to the height of his popularity, but in 1975, following a series of severe leg and hip injuries, he retired from performing. He began playing concerts again in 1980, resuming an active touring schedule amid wide public acclaim.

DAVIS, Varina (1826–1906). The first lady of the Southern states during the time of the United States Civil War was Varina Davis. As the wife of Jefferson Davis, she shared in the rise and fall of his political fortunes. For a time after the war, she shared his imprisonment. She was a bride of 19 when Davis entered Congress. When Davis left for service in the Mexican War, she proved herself a capable manager of their Mississippi plantation, Brierfield.

Varina Howell was born on May 7, 1826, near Natchez, Miss. She was tutored at home and later attended a girls' school in Philadelphia. She married Davis in 1845. She followed her husband's career closely, advised him, and often served as his personal secretary. After his death she wrote a two-volume biography of him. She died on Oct. 16, 1906, surviving all but one of her six children.

DAVY, Humphry (1778–1829). The English scientist who invented the miner's safety lamp was Humphry Davy. He was also known for his researches in electrochemistry that led to the isolation of sodium and potassium. He proved that these substances were elements and not compounds.

Humphry Davy was born on Dec. 17, 1778, in Penzance, England. He was the eldest of five children and showed an early interest in reading. His father died when the boy was 16 years old. Humphry was sent to work for and learn the trade of a surgeon-apothecary and developed a keen interest in chemistry. Before he was 20 he was appointed laboratory head of the Pneumatic Institute at Bristol.

In his new work Davy directed experiments on the effect of breathing certain gases. On one occasion, he nearly killed himself by inhaling a mixture of toxic gases. He recorded the properties of nitrous oxide, or laughing gas. In 1801 he was appointed assistant lecturer in chemistry and director of the laboratory at the new Royal Institution.

Davy completed many studies in tanning and agricultural chemistry. He married Jane Apreece, a wealthy widow, in 1812, and during the same year he was knighted. In 1820 Sir Humphry was elected president of the Royal Society of England. For several years Michael Faraday, another scientist who was later to achieve great fame, served as Davy's laboratory assistant (*see* Faraday).

Davy, W.R. Clanny, and George Stephenson made discoveries that led to the design of a successful safety lamp for miners. Davy's main contribution was a wire gauze to surround the lamp's flame. This cooled or quenched the flame and prevented it from passing through the gauze to the gaseous surroundings. Before the introduction of Davy's lamp, frequent explosions occurred in mines from the methane in the air. The safety lamp was first used in British mines in 1816. It reduced the number of explosions, and Davy was made a baronet for his invention. He died on May 29, 1829.

Gamma/Liaison

Moshe Dayan

DAYAN, Moshe (1915–81). As a soldier and statesman, Moshe Dayan was the architect of Israel's military policy in three wars. These were the 1956; 1967, or Six-Day; and 1973, or Yom Kippur, wars with neighboring Arab countries.

Dayan was born on May 20, 1915, at Deganya, Palestine (now Israel). As a young man, he learned guerrilla warfare tactics from British Captain Orde Wingate, the leader of special night patrols organized to fight Arab rebel bands. These patrols formed the nucleus of the later Israeli army. His organizing of the Haganah, an illegal military force in British-occupied Palestine, caused his arrest and imprisonment from 1939 to 1941. After his release he served with British forces during World War II. While in combat against pro-German French soldiers in Syria, he lost his left eye. The black patch he wore thereafter became a distinguishing trademark.

Dayan remained with the Haganah until 1948, the year Israel became a nation. During the war for independence in 1948, he was in command of the Jerusalem area, and in 1949 he participated in armistice negotiations with Jordan. While serving as chief of staff of the armed forces from 1953 to 1958, he planned and led the invasion of the Sinai Peninsula during a conflict with Egypt.

In 1958 Dayan retired from the military and joined Israel's labor party, Mapai. The following year he was elected to the Knesset (parliament) and was appointed minister of agriculture under Prime Minister David Ben-Gurion. He resigned in 1964 but joined Ben-Gurion in forming the new Rafi party (Alliance of Israel's Workers) in 1965 and was reelected to the Knesset.

Dayan served as minister of defense during the 1967 war and remained in the cabinet until the 1973 war. He resigned over criticism of Israel's lack of preparedness. Four years later, as Menachem Begin's foreign minister, he was instrumental in drawing up the Camp David Accords, a peace agreement with Egypt. He later resigned over Begin's policy of settlements by Israel in formerly Arab-occupied territories. In 1981 he formed a new party, Telem, to counter Begin, but he died shortly thereafter, on Oct. 16, 1981, at Tel Aviv.

DAY CARE. Organized care for the children of working parents has been known since 1770, when a pastor in eastern France instructed a serving girl to feed and care for the village children while their parents worked full-time at woodworking. This developed into an institution known as crèche, which is French for "crib." Other terms to describe similar services are nursery, nursery school, and day-care center.

As the world became industrialized, mothers increasingly worked outside the home, requiring assistance in child care. By the 1980s large numbers of women in many countries were working, nearly 90 percent in the Soviet Union, more than 60 percent in East Asia, more than half in Europe and North America, 42 percent in Africa, 40 percent in South Asia, and 28 percent in Latin America.

In European countries day-care facilities are either state operated or licensed and subsidized by the state. The United States is one of the few industrial nations that does not have a day-care policy except for tax

The children's day-care center at Chicago's Hull House combines schooling with custodial care.

David Walberg

incentives that allow tax deduction of some or all such expenses for the parents or employers who pay them. Japan's traditional emphasis on the family as the center of child care has worked against the development of day care. Hungary, on the other hand, has more than 3,000 state-operated day-care facilities, and in Sweden almost 60 percent of all preschool children are enrolled in state-run day-care centers.

Some day-care centers are entirely custodial, offering only care; others also offer schooling. Because licensing is loosely enforced by the separate states in the United States, it is possible for almost anyone to open a day-care center. There are also chains of commercial facilities, such as Kinder-Care and Children's World, that operate well-equipped centers across the country. In many communities day-care institutions are run by civic groups and churches.

Many business firms find it beneficial to offer day-care facilities to their employees. By the mid-1980s in the United States, there were about 1,500 firms that assisted their workers with day care in some way, many having facilities in company quarters. Costs are usually shared between employer and employee. Some governments require employers to provide such services.

DAYTON, Ohio.

A group of Revolutionary War veterans founded the city of Dayton in 1796. Their energetic pioneer spirit has marked its history. It has been a city of bold and successful experiments.

Dayton straddles the Great Miami River, in southwestern Ohio, at the point where it is joined by the Mad and the Stillwater rivers. In 1913 the three rivers, swollen by heavy rains, flooded the city, causing great losses of life and property.

In Dayton Wilbur and Orville Wright built the planes they used for their first flights, and Orville's home has been preserved by the city (*see* Wright Brothers). Their experimental field is now part of Wright-Patterson Air Force Base, headquarters of the Air Force Logistics Command and site of the Air Force Museum. The Defense Department's Institute of Security Assistance Management is here. In Dayton are an art institute, the University of Dayton, Wright State University, United Theological Seminary, and the home of the poet Paul Laurence Dunbar.

Dayton is an industrial, trade, and transportation center. The manufacture of machinery and electrical equipment is a leading industry. Printing, the making of transportation equipment and cash registers, and the processing of foods are also important.

The city was named for Jonathan Dayton, one of its early promoters. It became the Montgomery County seat in 1803 and was chartered as a city in 1841. In 1913 it adopted the city-manager form of government. Population (1980 census), 203,588.

DAYTONA BEACH, Fla.

A year-round resort, Daytona Beach is famous throughout the world for its beach that is a natural automobile speedway of hard, white sand. The city is on the Atlantic Ocean and Halifax River, which is part of the Atlantic Intracoastal Waterway. The resort area and a residential section are on the beach and peninsula between the river and the ocean. A business and residential section are on the mainland west of the river.

Twenty-three miles (37 kilometers) long and up to 500 feet (150 meters) wide, the beach has been used for automobile speed trials since 1903. In 1935 Sir Malcolm Campbell drove his *Bluebird* over the course at 276.82 miles per hour (445.49 kilometers per hour). The city is also known for the Daytona International Speedway and greyhound racing.

There is some light industry in the area. Educational facilities include Bethune–Cookman College, Daytona Beach Community College, and Embry Riddle Aeronautical University. The Halifax Historical Museum has mementos of early families, period clothing, portraits, and Civil War memorabilia. The collections of the Museum of Arts and Sciences include paintings, prints, and photos by major Florida artists.

Mathias Day of Mansfield, Ohio, founded the original city, Daytona, in 1870. In 1926 the cities of Seabreeze, Daytona, and Daytona Beach were consolidated, or united, under the latter's name. Population (1980 census), 54,176.

DEAD SEA.

Between Israel and Jordan lies the Dead Sea. It is actually a rather small lake that is about 45 miles (72 kilometers) long and 10 miles (16 kilometers) wide. Its surface level is 1,292 feet (394 meters) below that of the Mediterranean, making it the lowest body of water in the world.

The Dead Sea extends from north to south in a great depression between rocky cliffs. The depression is a rift valley, caused by the slipping down of the Earth's crust between two parallel fractures. The valley is a part of the Great Rift Valley, which continues north through the Jordan River valley and Sea of Galilee and south through the Gulf of Aqaba and the Red Sea and across East Africa.

The Jordan River flows into the Dead Sea from the north. Evaporation carries off most of its waters, for the climate is very hot and rainfall seldom exceeds 5 inches (12.7 centimeters) a year. No river flows out of the lake. As a result, the Dead Sea is about 25 percent salt, or about seven times as salty as the ocean. A swimmer cannot sink deeper than the armpits. No fishes live in its waters. Those brought down by the Jordan die on the northern shore and provide food for flocks of seabirds.

Jutting out from the southeastern shore is a peninsula called El Lisan (Arabic for "the tongue"). South of the peninsula the lake becomes very shallow, varying from 3 to 30 feet. North of the peninsula is the point of greatest depth (1,310 feet).

The lake shores yield salt, potash, and bromides. Bitumen, or native asphalt, is also found. The cities Sodom and Gomorrah were on the shores of the Dead Sea. The Biblical manuscripts known as the Dead Sea Scrolls were found on the northwest shore, near the ruins known as Khirbet Qumran (*see* Dead Sea Scrolls).

DEAD SEA SCROLLS. The Biblical manuscripts known as the Dead Sea Scrolls have been called by scholars "the greatest manuscript discovery of modern times." They include Old Testament books and non-Biblical texts dating from 100 B.C. to A.D. 68. They are not original manuscripts but copies made by scribes. They are a thousand years older than the oldest known Masoretic (traditional Hebrew) text of the Old Testament, which is the basis of the English translation (*see* Bible).

The first scrolls were found in 1947 in a cave at the northwest corner of the Dead Sea, in Jordan. They were found by a Bedouin shepherd. His account of details varied in later years. One version was that a runaway goat jumped into the cave. The shepherd threw in a stone and heard the sound of breaking pottery. He called another boy, and the two crawled into the cave. They saw several large pottery jars, most of them broken. Protruding from the necks of the jars were scrolls of leather wrapped in linen cloth. Although they were badly decomposed, it was possible to see that they were inscribed in a strange writing. There were seven scrolls.

Dr. G. Lankester Harding, former director of the Department of Antiquities for Jordan, sorts fragments of the Dead Sea Scrolls in the Palestine Archaeological Museum, Jerusalem.

Either the boys themselves or older members of their tribe sold the seven scrolls to two Bethlehem dealers in antiquities. Three scrolls were bought for the Hebrew University in Jerusalem by Dr. Eleazar L. Sukenik, professor of archaeology. The other four were sold to the head (metropolitan) of the Syrian Orthodox Christian church, at the Monastery of St. Mark in the Arab quarter of Jerusalem.

The metropolitan took his scrolls to the American School of Oriental Research in Jerusalem for examination. Satisfied that they were genuine, the American School photographed them and announced the discovery to the world in April 1948.

The metropolitan then took his scrolls to the United States. In 1954 Professor Yigael Yadin, son of Sukenik, was lecturing in the United States on the three scrolls acquired by his father for the Hebrew University. By chance he learned that the metropolitan was advertising the other four scrolls for sale in a New York newspaper. He purchased them for $250,000 for the government of Israel.

Meanwhile Bedouins were looting every cave near the first one and selling thousands of fragments to dealers. In 1949 G. Lankester Harding, British-born director of the Department of Antiquities for Jordan, and Father Roland de Vaux, head of the French Dominican School of Archaeology in Jerusalem, took charge of the exploration of the caves. Eventually hundreds of manuscripts were found, including almost all the books of the Old Testament.

The seven scrolls found in the first cave were the most important. There were two scrolls of the *Book of Isaiah*, one complete, the other incomplete. The *Manual of Discipline*, also called the *Rule of the Community*, gives detailed information on all matters concerning a Jewish sect which lived an ascetic communal life on the shores of the Dead Sea. This sect is believed by most scholars to have been the Essenes. They were one of three parties within Judaism, the other two being the Sadducees and the Pharisees. The members of the sect referred to themselves only as the Sons of Light.

The *War of the Sons of Light with the Sons of Darkness* discusses the coming victory over the Sons of Darkness, how it will happen, and the military preparations necessary for it. It includes beautiful prayers. The *Commentary on the Book of Habakkuk* tells of the defiling of the sanctuary of God and the persecution of the Teacher of Righteousness, who was driven into exile by the Wicked Priest. Enemies called the Kittim are described as plundering and slaying. The scroll of the *Thanksgiving Hymns* is a collection of songs similar to the Psalms. It was written by a sect leader, possibly the Teacher of Righteousness.

The *Book of Lamech* was so fragile that seven years went by before it could be unrolled. It was assumed to be the lost Apocryphal Book of Lamech, but it proved to be a document in Aramaic relating to the Book of Genesis. It is now called the *Scroll of the Apocryphal Genesis*. It describes the journeys of

Abraham. One passage describes the beauty of Sarah, his wife. Another gives a legend of Noah's birth.

Of the later discoveries, one of the most interesting was a copper scroll found in 1952. It was broken in two pieces and was too brittle to unroll. The Jordan government sent it to the Manchester (England) College of Technology. Professor H.W. Wright-Baker devised a way of mounting the pieces on a spindle and cutting them into paper-thin strips through which the letters could be read. The scroll contains a long list of hiding places of treasures of enormous value. Some 200 tons of silver and gold are itemized. They were hidden in wells, in tombs, and near certain trees and springs. Some scholars believe the list to be imaginary or symbolic. Some think it may be a catalog of the treasures of King Solomon's Temple, others that it lists the treasures of the Essenes.

An eighth scroll, the longest and most complete of the Dead Sea Scrolls, was acquired by the Israeli government during the Six-Day War in 1967. Called the *Temple Scroll,* it was probably found in the late 1950s. Yadin, who published a translation of the 27-foot scroll in 1977, dated it between the second century BC and AD 70. The document establishes clear links between early Christian doctrines and the religious teachings of the Essenes.

Near the caves is a ruined building long known to the Arabs as Khirbet Qumran. It had been assumed to be the ruins of a Roman fort of the first few centuries AD. Archaeologists began excavating the ruins in 1951 in the hope of finding some link between the building and the scrolls. They discovered that this was the community center of the Essenes who made the scrolls. They also found the scribes' writing tables of plastered clay, benches, and inkwells.

From the evidence of silver coins, pottery shards, and other materials, the archaeologists believe that the building was erected no later than the reign of Alexander Jannaeus (103–76 BC). It was destroyed by an earthquake in 31 BC. It was probably restored in the time of Herod's son Archelaus (4 BC–AD 6) by the same community that occupied it before.

In the war that followed the Jewish revolt against the Romans, the people who lived in the community center at Khirbet Qumran were driven away or exterminated in AD 68. Before the Romans arrived, however, the Essenes hid their library in jars in the surrounding caves. All historical, archaeological, and paleographical (the science of ancient writing) evidence indicates that the scrolls were copied during the first or second century BC and the first century AD.

The Dead Sea Scrolls were written during one of the most decisive periods in the history of the Jewish people, on the eve of the birth of Christianity. When the tens of thousands of scroll fragments have been pieced together and translated, scholars will have a great amount of new material for the study of Biblical texts and the people who wrote them as well as of Jewish history after the 4th century BC. The scrolls shed new light on the foundations of Christianity and the influence of Judaism on the Christian faith.

DEAFNESS.

Ears are the most noticeable portion of anyone's hearing apparatus, but the most important hearing parts—mechanical and neural components—are within the skull (*see* Ear). Damage to either set of components, or to both, results in a loss of hearing that may be partial or complete. The word deafness is used to describe any degree of hearing loss, though it is most commonly used where there is a total inability to hear.

Two major categories of hearing impairment are recognized: conductive and sensorineural. Conductive, or transmission, hearing loss is caused by any obstruction to the sound-conducting mechanism of the outer or middle ear that prevents sound waves from reaching the inner ear. Sensorineural, or perception, hearing loss results from a loss of function of the sensory apparatus of the inner ear or its connecting nerve pathways to the cortex of the brain (*see* Brain, "The Cerebral Cortex").

Age Groups

Infants may suffer hearing loss from heredity or infection. In loss by heredity, normally the child inherits a failure in the development in the nerve components of the ear. There are, however, cases of inherited deformities that result in the partial or complete closure of the external canal or the middle ear.

Many babies are born with hearing defects that were brought on by infection of the mother during

The Manual Alphabet is used as part of sign language to communicate with deaf persons.

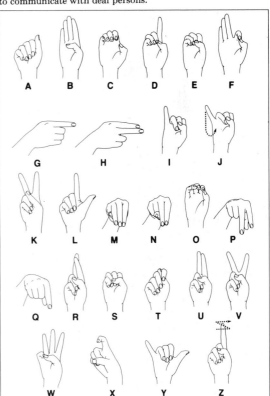

pregnancy. German measles, chicken pox, and other diseases, when contracted by a pregnant woman, can cause damage to the developing inner ears of the fetus. Infants who get virus infections during the first year may also develop hearing loss.

The most frequent causes of deafness in persons between the ages of 20 and 50 are long exposure to loud noise and a condition called otosclerosis, in which new bone growth in the middle ear blocks off the passage of sound waves. Exposure to noise levels above 90 decibels (about as loud as a truck passing 16 feet away) for extended periods of time can damage the delicate structures and nerves of the inner ear. A typical rock music concert creates 100 or more decibels. Sudden loud noises, such as explosions, can very quickly damage the ears.

Old people tend to lose their hearing gradually. This is the natural result of problems such as failing blood circulation, which deprives nerve tissues of oxygen.

Deaf-mutism

When children can hear, they learn to speak, saying what they have heard others say. If a young child is deaf, he or she is unable to hear voices and does not, therefore, develop speech. Such an inability to speak is normally not related to a condition in the vocal cords, nor is it an indication of low intellect.

Restoration of Hearing

Depending on the cause of deafness, there are two options available that may restore hearing: surgery and hearing aids. The objectives of surgery are to open the outer ear canal if it is blocked; to repair or replace damaged eardrum membranes; to eliminate chronic infection; or to reestablish the connection between the inner ear fluids and a chain of tiny bones needed to carry sound vibrations from the eardrum to the cochlea, which transforms the vibrations to electrical signals for the brain.

Hearing aids are types of electromechanical, battery-operated devices that are attached to the outer ear or inserted into the ear canal. Their purpose is to collect sound waves, make them stronger, and introduce them into the ear canal; or they may introduce sound vibrations directly into the skull. Hearing aids are quite helpful to persons with conductive hearing loss, and, to a lesser degree, to individuals with damaged inner ears.

In the early 1980s a new procedure combining surgery with a mechanical device gained increased acceptance as an aid for the profoundly deaf. Called a cochlear implant, it consists of a synthetic cochlea made of tiny wires implanted in the inner ear. This cochlea is connected to a plug inserted under the skin behind the ear. The plug, in turn, is connected to an external microphone attached to a small microprocessor that can be worn on a belt or carried. The synthetic cochlea transmits sounds in the form of electrical signals through the auditory nerves to the cerebral cortex where the signals are perceived by the individual as sound.

Courtesy of the U.S. Army

The military cemetery, with its rows of identical tombstones, is a particularly strong and vivid reminder of death.

DEATH. The last words of the author Rabelais were quite brief: "I go to seek a great perhaps." This little sentence expresses the mystery, if not the fear and anxiety, with which humans have traditionally viewed death. Dying, the halting of all life functions, is the great unknown that neither science nor religion has ever been able to penetrate. Philosophers have only been able to speculate about it. Because it is both unknown and inevitable, death has always been an object of fascination and fear. Whether it is good or bad depends on an individual's perspective. For many, as for Socrates, it is an open question. His farewell remarks to his friends were: "The hour of departure has arrived, and we go our ways—I to die, and you to live. Which is better only God knows." In whatever light it is regarded, death has always played a significant role in the culture of human societies, and it has strongly influenced the way people live their lives.

Biomedical and Legal Aspects

Contrary to appearances, nothing dies all at once—not a plant, an animal, or a human being. Major vital organs, such as heart, lungs, or brain, may fail very rapidly in the case of a human or of an animal. But lesser noticed signs of life can continue for some time after an individual has been pronounced dead. Hair and fingernails can continue to grow, and individual cells continue to function (*see* Cell).

Because the heart has long been considered the central organ of the body, its failure once indicated with certainty an impending death. Failure of the breathing mechanism was known to bring about cessation of heartbeat, thereby inducing death. But now there are techniques of resuscitation, or revival, for both the heart and lungs, including life-sustaining machines. The operation of the heart and lungs may be stopped and their functions taken over by a heart–lung machine—during heart transplants and other major surgery, for instance.

The use of these new medical techniques has raised the question: When is a person really dead? If only a machine is keeping a person's vital functions going, is that individual really alive? Such machines can support an undamaged brain, but once the brain fails no machine can yet revive and support it. Such complexities have confronted modern medical scientists with the need to define exactly when the moment of death occurs. This need is complicated by legal, moral, and religious issues as well.

If the heart and lungs cease to operate, the brain will die for lack of oxygen. Conversely, if the brain dies, the heart and lungs will soon fail to function unless they are regulated by a respirator. It only takes about six or eight minutes for the brain to expire for lack of oxygen.

Failure of heart and lungs is fairly easy to determine, but determining brain death is more difficult. It is done by examining a combination of life signs. Is there a total lack of response to any kind of stimulation? Can the person breathe without artificial aid? Is there any eye movement, swallowing, or coughing? Does an electroencephalogram, or tracing of brain waves, show any evidence of electrical activity coming from the brain? Is there any blood flow through the brain? A negative answer to all of these questions would indicate brain death, but no single sign is enough to warrant such an assumption.

Even if the brain has been determined to be dead, it is possible to keep the heart and lungs operating by machine. Other bodily functions will continue. Yet a physician would say that the person is dead. Who has the right to "pull the plug"? In the absence of the ability of a person to respond, only family members can authorize turning off the machine. Sometimes a patient may stipulate that no special measures be taken to prolong life.

Some states have passed statutes recognizing the legality of living wills. An individual signing such a document asks that life not be prolonged under specified circumstances. When a person has been declared dead by a physician, this fact must normally be reported to a governmental agency charged with keeping records of births and deaths. Specific laws relating to the presumption of death and the disposition of property vary widely.

Stages of Dying

Dying is something everyone endures essentially alone. Nothing, therefore, so engages the mind and the emotions as does the ending of one's life. Except in the case of sudden death, an individual who is ill centers hope on medical treatment and possible cure.

People often go through a series of stages in accepting the reality of their own mortality. Diagnosis of a terminal illness brings shock, which soon gives way to denial. This denial may take the form of searching for any possible cure for the disease. From denial the patient may go on to anger—at himself, at everyone around him, and even at a God who seems not to hear his pleas for recovery.

Anger eventually gives way either to hope for a temporary respite or to deep depression over the impending loss of everyone and everything. This grief over oneself then turns to resignation and acceptance in the face of the inevitable.

How an individual responds depends, of course, on the quality of one's personal life. For most people it is probably true, as Sir Thomas Browne said, that "The long habit of living indisposes us for dying." For those to whom life has been an ordeal, death may come, in Hamlet's words, as "a consummation devoutly to be wished." In the face of such an unknown quantity, however, death often becomes a matter of fear: Aristotle asserted that it "is the most terrible of all things, for it is the end."

On the other hand, people of great religious faith are often able to face dying with composure: They know it as the final ill of life, but they also view it as a transition, not a termination.

Papier-mâché cattle conceal bodies of the dead from evil spirits at a Hindu cremation in Indonesia.

Ewing Krainin—Stockpile

Funeral Rites and Customs

The bodies of the dead have traditionally been disposed of in two ways: burial or cremation, or burning of the body. Burial has been customary in most societies dating as far back as prehistoric mankind. The ritual burial of the dead probably stems from an instinctive refusal on the part of people to accept death as the complete end of an individual's existence. This notion was unknown until it first appeared in Buddhist thought in India during the 6th century BC.

The belief that humans somehow survive death in some form occurs in nearly all religions. Funeral rituals and customs reflect this belief. Prehistoric and ancient burial customs testify to the conviction that the person somehow survives; hence burial with supplies of food, ornaments, and tools. This was true for Paleolithic mankind as it was for the Egyptians who at a much later date built elaborate tombs and pyramids. Proper preparation of the body and burial were regarded as necessary if the dead individual was to depart to the place where he belonged.

Some religions have held that the dead must cross some barrier that separated their new existence from the land of the living. Ancient Greeks and Romans believed that the dead were ferried across a river, the Acheron or the Styx, by a demonic boatman called Charon. To pay his fee, a coin was placed in the mouth of the body before burial.

Preparation of the body for burial has traditionally included washing the body and dressing it in special garments. The most elaborate preparation took place in Egypt. The body was embalmed, a procedure of using preservatives either externally or internally to keep the body intact for as long as possible. The body was then carefully wrapped in cloth and buried beyond the reach of the Nile River to preserve the corpse. Other ancient societies also used embalming, among them prehistoric Indian tribes of Peru and Ecuador and the aborigines of the Canary Islands. In Tibet bodies are still often embalmed according to ancient formulas.

The modern embalming practice of injecting fluids into the arteries to preserve the body began in the 18th century in England, following techniques developed by William Harvey to study the circulation of blood. Embalming came into wide acceptance in the United States as a result of the Civil War, when casualties were very high and some means had to be used to preserve the bodies to be sent home for burial.

In modern embalming procedures, the blood is drained from the body and replaced by a solution of formaldehyde in water, called Formalin. Cavity fluid is removed and replaced with a preservative of Formalin mixed with alcohols, emulsifiers, and other substances. Such embalming does not permanently preserve the body; its use is to give the corpse a lifelike appearance during the time it is viewed by mourners. To enhance the effect, cosmetics and other substances are customarily used on visible portions of the body.

Cremation has been practiced in Western societies since about 1000 BC, when it was first used by the Greeks. It is also an ancient practice among the Hindus of India. Such cremations were always performed in the open, as they are in India today. The waterfront of Benares, India, is lined with concrete and marble slabs on which funeral pyres, structures on which the dead are burned, are erected. After burning, the remains are cast into the Ganges River.

In modern Western cremations the body is placed into what amounts to an oven, where intense heat transforms it into a few pounds of powdery ash. The ash may be kept in an urn, buried, or scattered in some favored place. Cremation has been looked upon with disfavor by members of many religious groups, but the growing shortage of burial space in urban centers makes it a practical way of disposing of the dead.

Bodies have been buried under the earth, on top of the ground under a mound of earth or rocks, in caves, in large above-ground burial sites called mausoleums, and in water. Communal burial places, called cemeteries, mark some of the oldest locations of human settlement.

Water burial was a custom in many ancient cultures. Often the bodies of heroes were cast adrift in boats. In the South Pacific it was customary to place the body in a canoe and to launch it on the water. In Western society water burial is commonly used when a person dies at sea.

DEATH VALLEY, Calif. Long known for its scientific and human interest value, Death Valley is also famous as a scene of suffering in the gold rush of 1849. Here many gold seekers nearly lost their lives in searing heat. They gave the valley its grim name.

The valley is a deep trough between the Panamint Range on the west and the steep slopes of the Amargosa Range on the east. It is about 140 miles (225 kilometers) long and 4 to 16 miles (6.4 to 25.7 kilometers) wide. Nearly 550 square miles (1,425 square kilometers) of its area lie below sea level, and it contains the lowest dry land in the country, 282 feet (86 meters) below sea level. Less than 100 miles (160 kilometers) away towers Mount Whitney, 14,495 feet (4,418 meters) above sea level.

The scorching heat has reached a record of 134° F (60° C) in the shade. Despite this heat, more than 600 kinds of plants thrive here as well as rattlesnakes, lizards, and other animals. The average annual rainfall is a little over 2 inches (5 centimeters). Most of the year the bed of the Amargosa River is only a series of dry channels. White salts, mostly borax, crust great areas of the soil. These once provided nearly all the country's domestic borax. Death Valley National Monument was created in 1933. It consists of about two thirds of the valley and a small area in Nevada.

DEBATE.

DEBATE. Since 1960, when United States presidential candidates John F. Kennedy and Richard M. Nixon met in a series of televised debates, political debates have become commonplace in campaigns even between candidates for state and local offices. But these are not really debates in the formal sense. They are more like news conferences or panel discussions. Only on occasion do the candidates respond to each other's remarks, and such response is a key element of true debating.

Such true debate is an encounter between speakers or teams of speakers and follows formal rules. It is an exercise in argumentation, also called forensics. There are procedures that the speakers must follow, and the competition is normally on two levels. The first level is the specific competition between two teams to decide which presents its arguments more effectively. Second is the general competition among teams, with the same issue being debated by all.

Format

The subject to be argued is stated as a positive resolution; for example, "Resolved: That the Federal Government Should Guarantee Comprehensive Medical Care for All Citizens in the United States." The speakers are divided into two teams of two or three members each. The affirmative side upholds the resolution; the negative opposes it. Each has equal time to present its views.

The presentation of a debate falls into two parts: the constructive speeches and the rebuttals. In a typical debate, with two speakers on each side, the following order is generally observed: constructive speeches—affirmative, negative, affirmative, negative; and rebuttal speeches—negative, affirmative, negative, affirmative. The length of the speeches varies. A chairman who is neutral reads the resolution and introduces the speakers in turn.

When a subject has been decided upon, the teams plan the case. Each side analyzes the resolution carefully. Often more than one interpretation can be given a resolution. The affirmative decides which interpretation to use. The negative must prepare its side of the case to argue any interpretation the affirmative presents.

From the evidence each side chooses three or four major contentions to support its case. A contention is a statement of belief that can be proved with evidence and sound reasoning. Minor contentions support major contentions. The choice of evidence and the way of presenting it depend upon the audience before which the debaters speak. The debater must never forget that the main purpose of a debate is to win the audience to a desired point of view. A debate brief, setting forth all probable contentions for both sides, is a valuable aid in planning a case.

There is no set rule that governs how many contentions each debater presents. The first speaker, however, covers as many points as possible. This gives the second speaker a chance to refute the opposition's opening arguments.

The importance of the rebuttal in a debate cannot be overemphasized. A debate is often won by an effective rebuttal. In rebuttal speeches the debaters must limit themselves to answering the attacks of their opponents. No new contentions may be introduced. A speaker, however, may introduce new evidence to refute or support an argument that has been put forward by the opposition.

History

College debating has a long history in both Great Britain and the United States. Harvard and other colleges had debate clubs early in the 18th century. Intercollegiate and interscholastic high school debating competitions did not start, however, until the late 19th century. Today there are thousands of high schools and hundreds of colleges that enter teams in local and national competitions.

Some of the best-known and most prestigious college tournaments are those held at Harvard, Dartmouth, Wake Forest, the University of Wyoming, the University of Southern California, Georgetown University, Northwestern University, and the University of California at Los Angeles. There is also a national debate tournament held at West Point, N.Y., every April. These debates are sponsored by the American Forensic Association, which is affiliated with the Speech Communication Association.

There are, in addition, regional high school debate tournaments. In Sioux Falls, S.D., for example, Augustana College hosts an annual midwestern tournament that brings together between 500 and 600 speakers from high schools in Minnesota, North and South Dakota, Wisconsin, Iowa, Nebraska, Wyoming, Michigan, and Illinois.

DEBS, Eugene V. (1855–1926). The only candidate to run for the presidency of the United States from a prison cell, the labor organizer Eugene V. Debs had been sentenced to prison for criticizing the government's prosecution of persons charged with violating the 1917 Espionage Act. It was the fifth time he had run for the presidency on the Socialist ticket.

Eugene Victor Debs was born in Terre Haute, Ind., on Nov. 5, 1855. He left home at 14 to work on the railroad and soon became interested in union activity. In 1875 he helped organize the Brotherhood of Locomotive Firemen. As president of the American Railway Union, he led a successful strike against the Great Northern Railroad in 1894. Two months later he was jailed for his role in a strike against the Chicago Pullman Palace Car Company.

Within a few years he had become a socialist and a founder of the Socialist Party of America. He was a presidential candidate in 1900, 1904, 1908, 1912, and 1920, when he received his highest popular vote—about 915,000. He was released from prison in 1921. In 1905 Debs helped found the Industrial Workers of the World (*see* Labor Movements), but he soon quit the organization over its radicalism. He died at Elmhurst, Ill., on Oct. 20, 1926.

DEBUSSY, Claude (1862–1918). As a child the French composer Debussy was already a rebel. Instead of practicing his scales and technical exercises, the boy would sit at the piano and experiment with different chord combinations. In later years Debussy's unusual chords, based on the whole-tone scale, laid the groundwork for an unconventional style of music called impressionism.

Achille Claude Debussy was born in Saint-Germain-en-Laye, near Paris, on Aug. 22, 1862. He did not come from a musical family. His father was a shopkeeper. When he was 7 years old, young Debussy began taking piano lessons. When he was 9, his playing attracted Madame Mauté de Fleurville, a former pupil of Frédéric Chopin. Under her tutoring he was able to enter the Paris Conservatory two years later.

Debussy was 22 years old when he won the Grand Prix de Rome. Debussy's entry was a cantata, 'L'Enfant prodigue'. Part of the award was three years of study at the French Academy in Rome. After two years in Rome he returned to Paris. About this time he began signing his name Claude.

Among Debussy's friends were many artists and writers. They too had broken with tradition. They were known as impressionists and symbolists (*see* Painting). Debussy was particularly friendly with the poet Stéphane Mallarmé. It was Mallarmé's poem that inspired Debussy's composition 'L'Après-midi d'un faune' (The Afternoon of a Faun).

In 1892 Debussy began his most notable work, the opera 'Pelléas et Mélisande'. It was based on a play by Maurice Maeterlinck. Debussy also composed a number of other works in the 1890s. Best known of these was his cycle of 'Nocturnes' for orchestra. They are 'Nuages', 'Fêtes', and 'Sirènes'. 'Clair de lune' is one of his most popular compositions. His famous 'La Mer' (The Sea) was first heard in 1905.

Debussy was married twice. For his daughter Chou-Chou he wrote the piano work 'The Children's Corner'. In it is the amusing 'Golliwog's Cakewalk'. In his last years Debussy was a semi-invalid. Many of his best piano pieces, however, were composed during this period. He died in Paris on March 25, 1918.

Stephen Decatur

Courtesy of the U.S. Navy

DECATUR, Stephen (1779–1820). "The most daring act of the age," said Lord Nelson, the famous British admiral. He was speaking of Stephen Decatur's exploit in Tripoli Harbor on the night of Feb. 16, 1804. Pirates from the Barbary States had captured the United States frigate *Philadelphia* and taken it into the harbor. Stephen Decatur, with a little ship and a small crew, slipped into the harbor, burned the *Philadelphia,* and escaped without the loss of a man. For this deed Decatur was made a captain in the United States Navy.

Pirates from the shores of Morocco, Algeria, Tunis, and Tripoli had for centuries been the terror of the Mediterranean. They had preyed on the commerce of many nations and captured many sailors as slaves. Decatur gave them their first great setback, and in 1815 he returned with an American fleet. He forced them to stop attacking United States ships and to surrender all the people they held captive.

Stephen Decatur was born on Jan. 5, 1779, at Sinepuxent, Md. As a boy he was close to the sea, for his father was a sailor. Stephen became a midshipman when he was 19 years old, a lieutenant at 20, and a captain at 25.

In the War of 1812 his frigate, the *United States,* captured the British *Macedonian* after a desperate fight near Madeira Island. On Jan. 14, 1815, before news of the war's end reached the United States, four British frigates surrounded his ship, the *President,* off Long Island. After being wounded twice and losing one fifth of his men, Decatur was forced to surrender his ship.

Decatur became a commodore in 1813 and in 1815 a navy commissioner. At the peak of his fame he was killed by Commodore James Barron in a duel on March 22, 1820. The duel came about after Barron had been court-martialed, and Decatur had refused to reinstate him.

Decatur has been called the most conspicuous figure in United States naval history for the hundred years between John Paul Jones and David Farragut. His most quoted saying is a toast he made in 1816: "Our country . . . may she always be in the right; but our country, right or wrong!"

DECEMBER *see* FESTIVALS AND HOLIDAYS.

Claude Debussy in an 1884 painting by Marcel-André Baschet

Giraudon—Art Resource/ EB Inc.

DECLARATION OF INDEPENDENCE

DECLARATION OF INDEPENDENCE. July 4, 1776, the members of the Continental Congress assembled at the State House in Philadelphia to take up a matter of vital importance. Two days earlier the Congress had voted to declare the colonies to be "free and independent states." Now they were considering how to announce that fact to the world. By the end of the day, the final wording had been determined and the Congress voted unanimously to adopt one of history's greatest documents—the Declaration of Independence.

The stirring phrases of the Declaration inspired the patriots to defeat the British, thus guaranteeing independence (*see* Revolution, American). Since that time the Declaration has been a source of pride and strength for every generation of Americans.

The Movement Toward Independence

When the Revolutionary War broke out at Lexington and Concord, April 19, 1775, few colonists desired independence. Most of them wanted only a larger measure of self-government within the British Empire. In June 1775 General Washington promised to work for "peace and harmony between the mother country and the colonies." As late as September, Thomas Jefferson "looked with fondness towards a reconciliation."

Although they wanted to remain in the British Empire, most of the colonies insisted that they have the right of self-government. As the year 1775 wore on, however, it became clear that both of these goals could not be achieved. Parliament would not repeal the "five intolerable acts" or admit that only the local assemblies could tax the colonists. In August the king called the patriots "rebels," and summoned all British subjects to aid in bringing them to terms. In December he removed the colonies from his protection and blockaded their ports. In effect, then, the king had begun war almost a year before the Declaration was adopted.

The ravages of war were making the people more and more bitter. In October 1775 the British burned the town of Portland, Me., destroying the homes of a thousand people just at the approach of winter. The siege of Boston inflicted severe hardships on its people. Then came the news that 20,000 Hessian troops had been hired to put down the revolt. "The king," wrote Jefferson, "has plundered our seas, ravaged our coasts, burnt our towns, and destroyed our people." The German mercenaries were intended "to complete his works of death, desolation, and tyranny." On the frontiers he had aroused "the merciless Indian savages, whose known rule of warfare" was the destruction of women and children. If the colonists had to preserve their rights by fighting, then they had to have the means of making war and trading with other nations. They could not, however, secure aid abroad so long as they were British subjects, nor could they make a treaty of commerce with a foreign state.

The Declaration Is Framed

The time was ripe. In January 1776, Thomas Paine wrote a vigorous pamphlet 'Common Sense'. How, he asked, could the people at once fight against the king and profess their loyalty to him? The day of compromise had passed. "The blood of the slain, the weeping voice of Nature cries, 'Tis time to part'.

Thomas Jefferson is discussing his draft of the Declaration of Independence with Benjamin Franklin, who is reading the document, while John Adams listens. This picture, painted by J. L. G. Ferris, hangs in Independence Hall, Philadelphia.

Here is the vast continent of North America, suited to become the home of a race of free men; let it no longer lie at the feet of an unworthy king." Thousands of men read this challenge and accepted the idea of complete separation from Great Britain.

In the spring of 1776 North Carolina was the first of several states to direct its delegates in Congress to declare for independence. Virginia voted to have its delegates make the necessary motion. As a result, on June 7, 1776, Richard Henry Lee introduced the dramatic resolution. It declared that "these United Colonies are, and of a right ought to be, free and independent states, that they are absolved from all allegiance to the British Crown, and that all political connection between them and Great Britain is and ought to be totally dissolved."

The Declaration Adopted

The resolution could not be adopted immediately because not all the states had yet told their delegates to vote for independence. Therefore a committee was appointed to prepare a statement of the American case. It was made up of John Adams, Thomas Jefferson, Benjamin Franklin, Roger Sherman, and Robert Livingston. Jefferson was chosen to draw up the necessary declaration. It was brought to the floor of Congress on June 28.

On July 2 the Lee resolution was adopted and debate on Jefferson's declaration began. In a list of charges against King George III, Jefferson had attacked slavery and the slave trade. Representatives from southern slaveholding colonies refused to accept this clause, and after heated debate it was dropped.

The Declaration of Independence was adopted on July 4. A copy was ordered engrossed on parchment. This formal document was signed on August 2 by members of Congress present on that date. Those who were absent signed later.

The Declaration did not establish the independence of the American Colonies. It only stated an intention and the cause for action. Complete separation would have to be accomplished by force. Once the Declaration had been adopted, however, there was no turning back.

Origin of the Declaration

Jefferson put little that was new into the famous document. Its ideas had already been much discussed in America. They had previously been popular in England; John Locke had used them in his book 'On Civil Government', a defense of the English Revolution of 1688 (see Locke, John).

The Declaration is a statement of the American theory of government. Three basic ideas were involved: (1) God had made all men equal and had given them the rights of life, liberty, and the pursuit of happiness; (2) the main business of government was to protect these rights; (3) if a government tried to withhold these rights, the people were free to revolt and to set up a new government. These three ideas formed the groundwork for the state governments that were established after the Declaration was adopted.

Charges Against the King

The colonists had good reasons for taking their stand of protest against the king. If the Declaration had attacked the British Parliament, the American people would be attacking the representatives of the British people, particularly in the elected House of Commons. The Americans, therefore, leveled their charges against the person of the king. It was George III, they said, who had no real power over the American Colonies. Thus they sought to gain the sympathy of the British people.

The king had powerful enemies at home who might help the colonists if they believed that the Americans were fighting solely against the monarch. To foreigners the Revolution would not seem to be a revolt against the authority of the British Parliament, but a revolt against the tyranny of the British king. It would seem to be only a defense of rights long enjoyed and impossible to give up.

Boston Historical Society

The excited crowd is listening to the Declaration of Independence being read from the porch of the Old State House in Boston. Messengers carried copies of the document to all parts of the country. The news aroused great enthusiasm.

Liberty Bell and the Declaration

When the Declaration was adopted, racing horsemen and the noise of cannon fire carried the news far and wide. General Washington had the document read to the army, and its ringing sentences strengthened the morale of his troops.

On July 8, 1776, the people of Philadelphia gathered at the old State House to hear a reading of the Declaration. They were called together by the ringing of the Liberty Bell in the belfry of the building. It has been said that the bell cracked on that joyful occasion. This is not true, however. The Liberty Bell cracked for the first time in 1752, after it had been brought from London. It was recast the following year by Charles Stow and John Pass. After its use in 1776 the bell was rung each year on the anniversary of the Declaration. In 1835 a crack developed while it was tolling for the death of John Marshall, famous chief justice of the Supreme Court. When the bell was rung on Washington's birthday in 1846, it cracked beyond repair. It was struck lightly by officials of Philadelphia on April 6, 1917, when the United States entered World War I.

The historic old bell hung in the hallway of the State House (renamed Independence Hall) until the bicentennial year of 1976, when it was moved to a new pavilion nearby. The original document of the Declaration is preserved in a helium-filled glass case in the National Archives in Washington, D.C.

Text of the Declaration of Independence *
IN CONGRESS, JULY 4, 1776.

THE UNANIMOUS DECLARATION OF THE THIRTEEN UNITED STATES OF AMERICA,

WHEN in the Course of human events, it becomes necessary for one people to dissolve the political bands which have connected them with another, and to assume among the powers of the earth, the separate and equal station to which the Laws of Nature and of Nature's God entitle them, a decent respect to the opinions of mankind requires that they should declare the causes which impel them to the separation.——We hold these truths to be self-evident, that all men are created equal, that they are endowed by their Creator with certain unalienable Rights, that among these are Life, Liberty and the pursuit of Happiness.——That to secure these rights, Governments are instituted among Men, deriving their just powers from the consent of the governed, ——That whenever any Form of Government becomes destructive of these ends, it is the Right of the People to alter or to abolish it, and to institute new Government, laying its foundation on such principles and organizing its powers in such form, as to them shall seem most likely to effect their Safety and Happiness. Prudence, indeed, will dictate that Governments long established should not be changed for light and transient causes; and accordingly all experience hath shewn, that mankind are more disposed to suffer, while evils are sufferable, than to right themselves by abolishing the forms to which they are accustomed. But when a long train of abuses and usurpations, pursuing invariably the same Object evinces a design to reduce them under absolute Despotism, it is their right, it is their duty, to throw off such Government, and to provide new Guards for their future security.——Such has been the patient sufferance of these Colonies; and such is now the necessity which constrains them to alter their former Systems of Government. The history of the present King of Great Britain is a history of repeated injuries and usurpations, all having in direct object the establishment of an absolute Tyranny over these States. To prove this, let Facts be submitted to a candid world.——He has refused his Assent to Laws, the most wholesome and necessary for the public good.——He has forbidden his Governors to pass Laws of immediate and pressing importance, unless suspended in their operation till his Assent should be obtained; and when so suspended, he has utterly neglected to attend to them.——He has refused to pass other Laws for the accommodation of large districts of people, unless these people would relinquish the right of Representation in the Legislature, a right inestimable to them and formidable to tyrants only.—— He has called together legislative bodies at places unusual, uncomfortable, and distant from the depository of their public Records, for the sole purpose of fatiguing them into compliance with his measures.——He has dissolved Representative Houses repeatedly, for opposing with manly firmness his invasions on the rights of the people.——He has refused for a long time, after such dissolutions, to cause others to be elected; whereby the Legislative powers, incapable of Annihilation, have returned to the People at large for their exercise; the State remaining in the mean time exposed to all the dangers of invasion from without, and convulsions within.——He has endeavoured to prevent the population of these States; for that purpose obstructing the Laws for Naturalization of Foreigners; refusing to pass others to encourage their migrations hither, and raising the conditions of new Appropriations of Lands.——He has obstructed the Administration of Justice, by refusing his Assent to Laws for establishing Judiciary powers.——He has made Judges dependent on his Will alone, for the tenure of their offices, and the amount and payment of their salaries.——He has erected a multitude of New Offices, and sent hither swarms of Officers to harass our people, and eat out their substance.——He

*This text follows exactly the spelling and punctuation of the original document.

SOME SIGNERS OF THE DECLARATION

Some prominent persons are not included below because they are covered in the main text of this article or in other articles in Compton's Encyclopedia (see Fact-Index).

Bartlett, Josiah (1729–95). Born in Amesbury, Mass. Became a physician and settled at Kingston, N.H. Member of the colony's Provincial Assembly from 1765 to 1775. Elected to the Continental Congress. Member of New Hampshire's Committee of Correspondence. Cast the first vote for the proposed Articles of Confederation. Chief justice of New Hampshire court of common pleas (1779–82). Associate and later chief justice of the state's supreme court (1782–90). First governor of the state (1790–94). First president of the New Hampshire Medical Society.

Carroll, Charles (1737–1832). Born in Annapolis, Md. Outlived all other signers of the Declaration. Cousin of John Carroll, first Roman Catholic bishop in the United States. Educated in France and studied law at the Inner Temple in London. Member of the Second Continental Congress. Served in the Maryland Senate from 1777 to 1800. Elected United States senator 1789 and served until 1792. Returned to the state Senate until 1801. A founder of the Baltimore and Ohio Railroad.

Gerry, Elbridge (1744–1814). Born in Marblehead, Mass. Educated at Harvard. Member of the Continental Congress from 1776 to 1781 and 1783 to 1785. Delegate to the Constitutional Convention of 1787. Served in Congress (1789–93). Member of the commission to France during the "XYZ affair" that caused an undeclared war with France. Governor of Massachusetts (1810–12), when his name gave rise to the term gerrymander. Served as James Madison's vice president (1813–14).

Gwinnett, Button (1735?–77). Born in Gloucestershire, England. Immigrated to Georgia by 1765. Member of the Continental Congress 1776. Member of the Georgia Assembly. Became president (equivalent to governor) of Georgia 1777. Died from wounds received in a duel with the state's military commander.

Hooper, William (1742–90). Born in Boston. Studied law under James Otis. Settled in North Carolina 1764. Elected to the colonial assembly 1773. Member of the Continental Congress from 1774 to 1777. Returned to North Carolina 1777. Much of his property was destroyed during the Revolution. Did not again hold public office.

Hopkins, Stephen (1707–85). Born in Providence, R.I. A merchant and businessman, served several terms in the colonial assembly and as colonial governor. Chief justice of the superior court. Member of the Continental Congress from 1774 to 1776. A founder, in 1762, of the *Providence Gazette*. First chancellor of Rhode Island College (now Brown University), founded 1764.

Hopkinson, Francis (1737–91). Born in Philadelphia. Lawyer, composer, poet, and businessman. Settled in New Jersey 1773. Elected to the Continental Congress 1776. One of the great anti-British pamphleteers of the Revolution. Author of the popular poem, "The Battle of the Kegs," published in 1778. Helped design the first American flag 1777. Judge of the Pennsylvania admiralty court from 1779 to 1789. District judge (1789–91).

Lee, Francis Lightfoot (1734–97). Born in Westmoreland County, Va. A member of the Lee family of Virginia from which Robert E. Lee was descended. Served in the colonial House of Burgesses from 1758 to 1768 and 1769 to 1776. Member of the Continental Congress (1775–79).

Livingston, Philip (1716–78). Born in Albany, N.Y. Wealthy land owner and merchant. Settled in New York City as an importer and privateer. Donated to many philanthropic causes. A founder of King's College (now Columbia University), of the New York Society Library, and of the New York Chamber of Commerce. Elected to the colonial assembly 1758, the first of several terms. Member of the Stamp Act Congress. Member of the Continental Congress from 1774 to 1778.

Morris, Lewis (1726–98). Born in Westchester County, N.Y. A member of the landed aristocracy, owner of the manor of Morrisania. Elected to the Continental Congress 1775. Became brigadier general in charge of the Westchester County militia 1776 and served until the end of the war. County judge from 1777 to 1778. Member of the state Senate intermittently (1777–90). Member of the first board of regents for the University of the State of New York.

Paca, William (1740–99). Born in Harford County, Md. Studied law at the Inner Temple in London. Member of the Maryland Committee of Correspondence. Elected to the Continental Congress 1774. Appointed chief judge of the state's General Court. Served as governor from 1782 to 1785. A founder of Washington College. Member of the Society of the Cincinnati. Appointed a federal district judge by President George Washington 1789.

Paine, Robert Treat (1731–1814). Born in Boston. Attended Harvard. Served briefly as a clergyman. Became a lawyer 1757. Served as associate prosecuting attorney for the "Boston Massacre" trial. Served five terms in the Provincial Assembly. Elected to the Continental Congress 1774. Elected first attorney general of Massachusetts 1777. Helped draft state constitution from 1779 to 1780. Judge of the state supreme court (1790–1804). A founder of the American Academy of Arts and Sciences 1780.

Rodney, Caesar (1728–84). Born near Dover, Del. Sheriff of Kent County from 1755 to 1757. Elected to the colonial legislature 1758 and served until 1776 (except for 1771). Member of the Stamp Act Congress. Elected to the Continental Congress 1774. Became brigadier general of Kent County militia 1775. Elected president (equivalent of governor) of Delaware 1778. Spent most of the term furnishing the state's quota of men and money for the Revolution. Elected to the state Senate 1783.

Rush, Benjamin (1745–1813). Born near Philadelphia. Studied at the College of New Jersey (now Princeton University) and at Edinburgh, Scotland. Became one of the best-known physicians in early American history. Professor of chemistry at College of Philadelphia (now University of Pennsylvania). Elected to the Continental Congress 1776. Appointed surgeon general of the Continental Army 1777. An organizer of the medical school at the University of Pennsylvania 1791. Treasurer of the Mint of the United States from 1797 to 1813. Author of 'Medical Inquiries and Observations Upon the Diseases of the Mind', published 1812.

Rutledge, Edward (1749–1800). Born in Charleston, S.C. Admitted to the English bar 1772. Returned home to practice law 1773. Elected to the Continental Congress 1774. Became captain of artillery 1776. Captured by the British at the fall of Charleston 1779. Returned to South Carolina 1782. Member of the state legislature from 1782 to 1796. State senator (1796–98); elected governor 1798.

Sherman, Roger (1721–93). Born in Newton, Mass. Settled in New Milford, Conn., 1743. Held a number of local offices and served in the legislature intermittently from 1755 to 1766. A judge of the superior court (1766–89). Elected to the Continental Congress 1774. Helped draft Articles of Confederation. Delegate to the Constitutional Convention of 1787. The only man who signed the Declaration, the Articles of Association, the Articles of Confederation, and the Constitution. Served in the House of Representatives (1789–91) and in the Senate (1791–93).

Thornton, Matthew (1714–1803). Born in Ireland. Went with his family to America 1718. Studied medicine and settled in Londonderry, N.H. Colonel in the colonial militia. Active in colonial and state politics from 1758 to 1786. Associate justice of the superior court (1776–82). Elected to the Continental Congress 1776.

Wilson, James (1742–98). Born in Carskerdy, Scotland. Studied at Scottish universities before immigrating to America in 1765. Settled in Philadelphia, where he was admitted to the bar. Moved to Carlisle 1770 and established an outstanding reputation as a lawyer. Elected to the Continental Congress 1774. Author of 'Considerations on the Nature and Extent of the Legislative Authority of the British Parliament' published 1774. Played pivotal role at the Constitutional Convention of 1787. Appointed associate justice of the United States Supreme Court 1789.

Wolcott, Oliver (1726–97). Born at Windsor, Conn. Graduated from Yale College 1747. Sheriff of Litchfield County from 1751 to 1771. Held other public offices and became a colonel in the militia 1774. Elected to the Continental Congress 1775. Appointed commissioner of northern Indian affairs from 1775 to 1785. Served as a soldier in several campaigns until the end of the Revolution. Governor of Connecticut (1796–97).

Wythe, George (1726–1806). Born in Elizabeth City County (Hampton), Virginia. Admitted to the bar 1746. Served in the House of Burgesses from 1754 to 1755 and 1758 to 1768. Elected to the Continental Congress 1775. Judge on the high court of chancery (1778–1806). One of the first American justices to enunciate the doctrine of judicial review. Professor of law at College of William and Mary (1779–90). Delegate to the Constitutional Convention of 1787.

At the top are the first lines and the final phrase of the Declaration of Independence as it was written. At the bottom are the actual signatures (see following page for names by states).

has kept among us, in times of peace, Standing Armies without the Consent of our legislatures.——He has affected to render the Military independent of and superior to the Civil power.——He has combined with others to subject us to a jurisdiction foreign to our constitution, and unacknowledged by our laws; giving his Assent to their Acts of pretended Legislation: —For quartering large bodies of armed troops among us:—For protecting them, by a mock Trial, from punishment for any Murders which they should commit on the Inhabitants of these States:—For cutting off our Trade with all parts of the world:—For imposing Taxes on us without our Consent:—For depriving us in many cases, of the benefits of Trial by Jury:—For transporting us beyond Seas to be tried for pretended offences:—For abolishing the free System of English Laws in a neighbouring Province, establishing therein an Arbitrary government, and enlarging its Boundaries so as to render it at once an example and fit instrument for introducing the same absolute rule into these Colonies:——For taking away our Charters, abolishing our most valuable Laws, and altering fundamentally the Forms of our Governments:—For suspending our own Legislatures and declaring themselves invested with power to legislate for us in all cases whatsoever.—He has abdicated Government here, by declaring us out of his Protection and waging War against us.——He has plundered our seas, ravaged our Coasts, burnt our towns, and destroyed the lives of our people.——He is at this time transporting large Armies of foreign Mercenaries to compleat the works of death, desolation and tyranny, already begun with circumstances of Cruelty & perfidy scarcely paralleled in the most barbarous ages, and totally unworthy the Head of a civilized nation.—— He has constrained our fellow Citizens taken Captive on the high Seas to bear Arms against their Country, to become the executioners of their friends and Brethren, or to fall themselves by their Hands.—— He has excited domestic insurrections amongst us, and has endeavoured to bring on the inhabitants of our frontiers, the merciless Indian Savages, whose known rule of warfare, is an undistinguished destruction of all ages, sexes and conditions. In every stage of these Oppressions We have Petitioned for Redress in the most humble terms: Our repeated Petitions have been answered only by repeated injury. A Prince, whose character is thus marked by every act which may define a Tyrant, is unfit to be the ruler of a free people. Nor have We been wanting in attentions to our Brittish brethren. We have warned them from time to time of attempts by their legislature to extend an unwarrantable jurisdiction over us. We have reminded them of the circumstances of our emigration and settlement here. We have appealed to their native justice and magnanimity, and we have conjured them by the ties of our common kindred to disavow these usurpations, which, would inevitably interrupt our connections and correspondence They too have been deaf to the voice of justice and of consanguinity. We must, therefore, acquiesce in the necessity, which denounces our Separation, and hold them, as we hold the rest of mankind, Enemies in War, in Peace Friends.——

WE, THEREFORE, the Representatives of the united States of America, in General Congress, Assembled, appealing to the Supreme Judge of the world for the rectitude of our intentions, do, in the Name, and by Authority of the good People of these Colonies, solemnly publish and declare, That these United Colonies are, and of Right ought to be FREE AND INDEPENDENT STATES; that they are Absolved from all Allegiance to the British Crown, and that all political connection between them and the State of Great Britain, is and ought to be totally dissolved; and that as Free and Independent States, they have full Power to levy War, conclude Peace, contract Alliances, establish Commerce, and to do all other Acts and Things which Independent States may of right do.——And for the support of this Declaration, with a firm reliance on the protection of divine Providence, we mutually pledge to each other our Lives, our Fortunes and our sacred Honor.

(GEORGIA)	(NORTH CAROLINA)	(MASSACHUSETTS)	(PENNSYLVANIA)	(NEW YORK)	(NEW HAMPSHIRE)
Button Gwinnett	William Hooper	John Hancock	Robert Morris	William Floyd	Josiah Bartlett
Lyman Hall	Joseph Hewes		Benjamin Rush	Philip Livingston	William Whipple
George Walton	John Penn		Benjamin Franklin	Francis Lewis	
		(MARYLAND)	John Morton	Lewis Morris	(MASSACHUSETTS)
	(SOUTH CAROLINA)	Samuel Chase	George Clymer		Samuel Adams
	Edward Rutledge	William Paca	James Smith		John Adams
	Thomas Heyward,Jr.	Thomas Stone	George Taylor		Robert Treat Paine
	Thomas Lynch, Jr.	Charles Carroll	James Wilson		Elbridge Gerry
	Arthur Middleton	of Carrollton	George Ross	(NEW JERSEY)	(RHODE ISLAND)
				Richard Stockton	Stephen Hopkins
		(VIRGINIA)	(DELAWARE)	John Witherspoon	William Ellery
		George Wythe	Caesar Rodney	Francis Hopkinson	(CONNECTICUT)
		Richard Henry Lee	George Read	John Hart	Roger Sherman
		Thomas Jefferson	Thomas McKean	Abraham Clark	Samuel Huntington
		Benjamin Harrison			William Williams
		Thomas Nelson, Jr.			Oliver Wolcott
		Francis Lightfoot Lee			(NEW HAMPSHIRE)
		Carter Braxton			Matthew Thornton

The names of the 56 men who signed the Declaration of Independence are listed under the names of the states they represented. John Hancock, then president of the Congress, signed on July 4. Most of the others signed on August 2.

DECORATIVE ARTS. Art forms that have a primarily decorative rather than expressive or emotional purpose are often called decorative arts, a term that first appeared in 1791. Related to the visual arts, decorative arts are associated with the major crafts that are considered practical or useful as opposed to such fine arts as painting and sculpture, though these, too, may be used decoratively in architecture as decorative arts.

The decorative arts began to be thought of as a separate category of art during the beginnings of the Industrial Revolution in the mid-19th century. It soon extended from such productions as Josiah Wedgwood's stoneware to the whole field of mechanically produced minor arts. Decoration gradually came to be thought of as an artistic varnish that could be transferred to a surface, therefore also referred to as an applied art. It then became associated with the economical production of readily salable products, and, so, also became industrial art (*see* Industrial Design). This caused a reaction in what is known as the Arts and Crafts Movement centered in Great Britain and led by William Morris (*see* Morris).

Between World Wars I and II, an individual decorative arts style that the public particularly liked helped make thousands of products commercial successes. It was called Art Deco—a term coined from the name of the Exposition Internationale des Arts Décoratifs et Industriels Modernes, held in Paris in 1925. The term moderne also came from that title, and the two styles were applied to a variety of products and a style of architecture. The decorative arts as a whole began to be considered "design," but during shortages caused by World War II the word came to mean adaptation of objects to mass production.

All these terms still cause confusion. In recent years, however, the words decorative arts have been increasingly applied to those objects of a relatively practical and useful nature that exhibit a high degree of fine craftsmanship and artistic integrity.

Representative Articles

The decorative arts include such things as body adornment (*see* Dress; Dress Design; Bead and Beadwork; Button; Glove; Hat and Cap; Shoe; Jewelry and Gems; Fabergé; Cosmetics; Perfume; Tattoo), household and commercial interiors (*see* Interior Design; Furniture; Aalto; Adam; Chippendale; Le Corbusier; Wallcovering), crafts associated with the printed word (*see* Book and Bookmaking; Calligraphy; Type and Typography), metalwares (*see* Metalworking; Cellini; Knife, Fork, and Spoon; Revere), glassware and ceramics (*see* Glass; Pottery and Porcelain), embossing and enameling (*see* Embossing; Enamel), and such miscellaneous items as basketry, candles, and fans (*see* Basketry; Candle; Fan). Decorative arts also include certain aspects of textiles as in the areas of rugs and carpets; the making of lace, fine linens, and quilts; and such nationalistic designs as batik (*see* Rug and Carpet; Lace; Linen; Quilt; Batik). (*See also* Arts, The; Fashion; Advertising.)

DEEP-SEA LIFE. Far below the limit of light penetration in the ocean is the abyssal zone, which lies below about 6,560 feet (2,000 meters). The major environmental features of such depths are pressures greater than 200 atmospheres, or 2,940 pounds per square inch (207 kilograms per square centimeter); temperatures ranging from 30° to 41° F (−1° to 5° C); total darkness; calm, relatively motionless water; and soft sediments on the ocean floor. Green plants cannot grow in the absence of light—that is, below about 1,970 feet (600 meters)—so the primary food base and energy source of deep-sea life is organic matter that falls from waters much closer to the surface. (*See also* Ocean.)

Most animal species living in the abyssal zone belong to groups that also live in shallower marine environments. Deep-sea species of squids, octopi, worms, and mollusks, for example, have been discovered living in the abyssal zone. A wide variety of fish families also live in the deep sea. Fish living under such pressures and in perpetual cold and darkness must be biologically specialized to survive. Most deep-sea fishes, for example, are small, usually only a few inches in length, with soft bodies and minimal bone structure, which are adaptations to the tremendous pressures.

Bioluminescence, or the generation of light by living organisms, is common among deep-sea fishes. Such light is produced by special cells or by bacteria

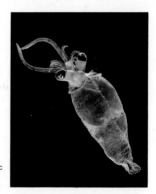

Two examples of deep-sea life are a small squid (right) and an angler fish (below).

(Right) Peter Parks—Oxford Scientific Films; (below) Peter David—Seaphot Limited: Planet Earth Pictures

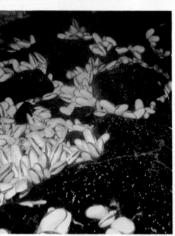

ties at the Galapagos Rift, at a depth of 8,200 feet (2,500 meters). The area is a major rift, or fissure, between two of the plates making up the Earth's crust. The gradual separation of the plates and the exposure of the underlying volcanic activity result in a mixing of cold seawater with hot minerals on the ocean bottom. The environmental conditions have created habitats that support deep-sea communities that were formerly unknown.

When magma, molten rock in the Earth's crust, breaks through the surface of the ocean floor in the abyssal zone, lava slowly enters the zone and cools rapidly because of the high pressure and low temperatures. Seawater circulates downward into fissures and exits the fissures laden with dissolved minerals. These hydrothermal, or hot-water, vents, called smokers, contain high concentrations of iron, manganese, zinc, copper, nickel, and other metals. Much sulfur is also present in the form of hydrogen sulfide, which is believed to be the primary energy base of the vent communities. Organisms known as chemosynthetic bacteria thrive on the hydrogen sulfide and form the bottom of the food chain.

The life forms huddled around these vents are characterized by large body size and high numbers of individuals, presumably because of the abundance of nutrients and the warmer temperatures. Among the remarkable finds were colonies of large red worms encased upright in white tubes anchored to the ocean floor. These worms measure up to 5 feet (1.5 meters) in length. Their red color results from hemoglobin, which performs the usual function of binding with oxygen. The hemoglobin also reacts with sulfur compounds, which may be used as an energy source. Previously unknown species of clams, mussels, crabs, jellyfish, and other animals have been discovered in the rift communities. Newly discovered clams with white shells and tissues rich in hemoglobin are among the largest clams known, some reaching lengths of more than 10 inches (25 centimeters).

Deep-sea fishes, also common around the thermal vents, live in the warm-water areas amid the clams and tube worms. A species of blind crab is a common scavenger in some areas. Colonial jellyfish were also discovered attached to the bottom by stalks and bearing yellow spheres looking much like dandelions. Although the members of rift communities have close relatives that inhabit the warmer, sunlit seas, many are species new to science.

Rift communities have been discovered on other parts of the ocean floor and presumably could occur wherever fissures are formed by the separation of the Earth's crustal plates. Some species are common to rift communities separated by thousands of miles of cold, dark ocean. Each community discovered so far, however, has a unique assemblage and diversity of species. The discovery of rift communities created much excitement in deep-sea biology. Knowledge of the behavior and ecology of most deep-sea species is scarce because of the difficulty of observing and studying animals at great depths in the ocean.

(Top left) John M. Edmond, Massachusetts Institute of Technology; (top right) Robert R. Hessler—Scripps Institution of Oceanography, University of California at San Diego; (above left) Richard A. Lutz; (above right) Dudley B. Foster, Woods Hole Oceanographic Institution

A "smoker" (top left) at a mid-ocean rift vent spews hot minerals. Life forms at the site include crabs (top right); a colony of large white clams (above left); and a cluster of tube worms (above right).

that live within the fish. Some fishes have lights of different colors and on various parts of the body that flash on and off constantly. Although the exact purposes of the light displays are unknown, they presumably function as a form of communication.

Some predatory species use bioluminescence to lure prey. Deep-sea angler fish, for example, have long filaments with a light on the end dangling over the top of the head. These anglers feed on other fishes that mistake the light for small prey and swim into the angler's enormous mouth (*see* Fish).

Mid-Ocean Ridge Vent Life

A discovery in 1977 revealed how some organisms cope with some of the harsh conditions of the ocean depths. Scientists discovered ocean-floor communi-

Two male elk follow their instincts to fight for the right to mate with a female of their species.

John Running—Stock, Boston

DEER. Members of the deer family are found throughout the Western Hemisphere, Europe, and Asia. They are not native to Australia nor to most of Africa. Included among the approximately three dozen species in the deer family are wapiti, moose, and reindeer. Solid horns, called antlers, distinguish most species in the deer family from the other hoofed mammals. Except for female caribou, only male deer grow antlers, which they shed each year. In contrast, both sexes of many other hoofed mammals have permanent, hollow horns. Among deer, the antlers serve as weapons during the mating season, when the males fight to win the right to breed with females.

Members of the deer family live in a wide variety of places, including forests, swamps, deserts, and tundra. They feed exclusively on such plant materials as grass, young shoots, twigs, and bark. Some deer travel in herds and go on seasonal migrations. Deer are extremely cautious animals with keen senses of smell and hearing. Most deer reach maturity in one to three years, and the female gives birth to one or two young or, occasionally, to triplets. The offspring nurse for several months.

Deer are mammals belonging to the family Cervidae in the order Artiodactyla (the even-toed, hoofed mammals). The order Artiodactyla also includes pigs, cattle, goats, sheep, camels, antelope, giraffes, and hippopotamuses.

North American Deer

The most common deer in the eastern United States is the white-tailed deer, whose scientific name is *Odocoileus virginianus*. These deer range throughout eastern North America from southern Canada through Central America. In colonial times they were one of the most important wild game animals. Their meat, called venison, was a major food source for early settlers. Deer hides were used to make buckskin jackets, moccasins, and other leather articles. Even today the white-tailed deer is the most popular large game animal in the eastern United States.

White-tailed deer are larger in the northern part of their range where bucks, or males, often weigh more than 470 pounds (213 kilograms). As in most deer species, the does, or females, are somewhat smaller. Both sexes are reddish brown in summer and gray in winter. When they run, they lift their tails straight up like white flags. The young, called fawns, have reddish coats with white spots.

A buck develops a pair of spiked antlers by the fall of its second year. Between January and April, after mating, the buck sheds his antlers and grows a larger set. The autumn mating season transforms timid bucks into fierce fighters, though, in contrast to many European and Asian species, the North American deer do not utter sounds. The winner in a contest of clashing antlers inherits mating privileges with the does in the vicinity.

A closely related species, the mule deer (*O. hemionus*) lives in western North America from the southern Yukon to northern Mexico. It has large ears, and the tail is tipped with black. Both white-tailed and mule deer can run as fast as 40 miles (64 kilometers) per hour and are good swimmers.

South American and European Species

Several species of deer are found in Central and South America. The brockets (genus *Mazama*) are small deer, 1.1 to 2.5 feet (.35 to .75 meter) tall and weighing less than 55 pounds (25 kilograms). Brockets inhabit thick forest areas from sea level to as high as 16,400 feet (5,000 meters) from eastern Mexico to northern Argentina. Two species of pudu (genus *Pudu*), found in forests of the lower Andes,

Leonard Lee Rue III—Animals Animals

A fawn born to a white-tailed doe less than 20 minutes previously struggles valiantly to stand.

are the smallest deer. The Chilean pudu (*P. pudu*), which is in danger of extinction, stands about 1 foot (.3 meter) high and weighs less than 20 pounds (9 kilograms). The nocturnal marsh deer (*Blastocerus dichotomus*), resembling the mule deer in size and antler shape, lives in wet lowlands of eastern South America. The pampas deer (*Ozotoceros bezoarticus*) is a small, reddish-brown species that lives in the plains of Argentina and Brazil. Hunters can smell pampas deer some distance away because of a strong scent that is released from sacs in the hind feet.

Roe deer (*Capreolus capreolus*) are small and reddish with no visible tail. They are found from the British Isles to China. Fallow deer (*Dama dama*) are a woodland species now mostly in Europe that are more restricted in their range than red or roe deer.

Asian Deer

Included among the Asian deer are the five species of muntjacs, also known as barking deer (genus *Muntiacus*), which are found from India and Sri Lanka to China and parts of Malaysia and Indonesia. These are small deer of the forests. They are noted for barking like dogs when alarmed and during the breeding season, and for having tiny antlers and tusklike canine teeth. The Chinese water deer (*Hydropotes inermis*) of China and Korea have tusks but no antlers. They live in marshy areas among tall reeds and grasses. The axis deer, or chital (*Axis axis*), of India and Sri Lanka are medium-sized deer of forested areas. They have reddish coats and, for part of the year, keep their white spots as adults. Other species found in Asian forests are sika deer and sambar, which are closely related to wapiti and tufted deer.

Moose

The largest member of the deer family is the moose (*Alces alces*), called elk in Europe. The bull, or male, stands as high as 7.7 feet (2.35 meters) at the shoulder and may weigh more than 1,800 pounds (816 kilograms). The cow, or female, is about three fourths the

size of the bull. The color of moose ranges from black to brown. Moose occur across Canada from New England to Alaska and extend down into Wyoming. They also are found from northern Europe to Mongolia.

The bull moose has a large head with a broad muzzle that curves downward. Beneath his neck hangs a hairy fold of skin called a bell. The antlers of a moose are flattened and may spread 6.6 feet (2 meters) across. The antlers are shed in winter, sprout again in spring, and reach full size by early summer. In late spring the cow gives birth to one or two calves that stay with her until the following spring.

Moose occur in forested areas, particularly near water. They feed on willow tips, saplings, and bark. They wade along the shores and thrust their heads under water for mouthfuls of tender plants that grow on the bottom. Moose swim very well.

Wapiti

The North American wapiti (*Cervus elaphus*), or elk as it is often called in North America, is the second largest member of the deer family. Wapiti bulls grow to nearly 5 feet (1.5 meters) in height at the shoulders and may weigh more than 750 pounds (340 kilograms). The cows are smaller. Wapiti are dark brown in the head and chest region and light brown on the rest of the body with a large white patch on the rump. They have huge antlers that may spread 5 feet across. Wapiti were once found throughout most of the United States but are now restricted to the western states and southern Canada. Their range includes Europe (where they are called red deer), central Asia, Siberia, and northern and western China.

Wapiti roam in herds, moving from the mountains to the valleys in winter. During the mating season in the fall, fights between males are common. They challenge one another with a loud bellow. Two animals face each other from a distance of about 20 feet (6 meters), paw the ground, and then charge and crash their antlers together. Bellowing as they fight, they continue the struggle until one goes down. The loser usually survives but leaves the area. Occasionally the antlers of the fighters lock together so that neither can eat, and both animals die from starvation. (This also sometimes happens with other fighting species of deer.) In March the bulls lose their antlers, but they can still ward off predators with their sharp front hooves. In early summer each cow gives birth to one or two white-spotted calves.

Caribou

Caribou (*Rangifer tarandus*), or reindeer as they are sometimes called, inhabit the far northern regions of North America, Europe, and Asia. An almost pure-white subspecies lives in northern Greenland. In North America the woodland caribou is found in Canada and Alaska in swampy forest habitats. Farther north, the northern, or barren ground, caribou roam the desolate Arctic tundra. Their original range included northern Maine and Minnesota as well as the Rocky Mountain region of Idaho and Wyoming.

Moose
(Alces alces)

Height: 1.4–2.35 m (4.6–7.7 ft)

Axis Deer
(Axis axis)

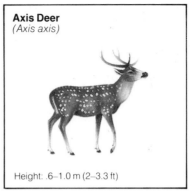

Height: .6–1.0 m (2–3.3 ft)

Roe Deer
(Capreolus capreolus)

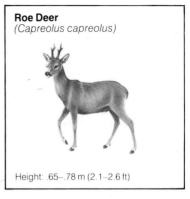

Height: .65–.78 m (2.1–2.6 ft)

North American Wapiti
(Cervus elaphus)

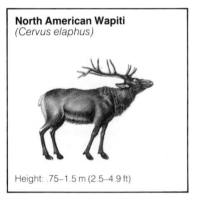

Height: .75–1.5 m (2.5–4.9 ft)

Fallow Deer
(Dama dama)

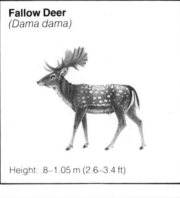

Height: .8–1.05 m (2.6–3.4 ft)

Chinese Water Deer
(Hydropotes inermis)

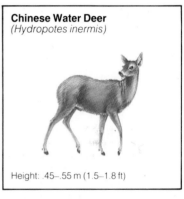

Height: .45–.55 m (1.5–1.8 ft)

Brocket Deer
(Mazama americana)

Height: .35–.75 m (1.1–2.5 ft)

Muntjac
(Muntiacus muntjak)

Height: .45–.58 m (1.5–1.9 ft)

Mule Deer
(Odocoileus hemionus)

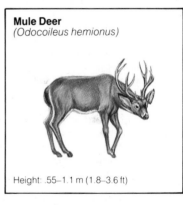

Height: .55–1.1 m (1.8–3.6 ft)

White-tailed Deer
(Odocoileus virginianus)

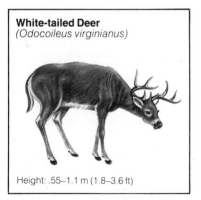

Height: .55–1.1 m (1.8–3.6 ft)

Pudu
(Pudu pudu)

Height: .32–.42 m (1–1.4 ft)

Woodland Caribou
(Rangifer tarandus)

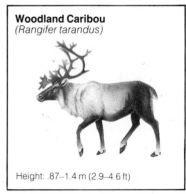

Height: .87–1.4 m (2.9–4.6 ft)

In the table above, the heights of the animals are measured from the shoulder. This table represents a selection of some species of deer and is not intended to be inclusive.

63

The reindeer of the Lapps in northern Norway are used to pull sleds and are valued for their meat, milk, and hides.

The last natural band south of Canada disappeared from Isle Royale, Michigan, in the 1920s.

Caribou move continually, migrating in herds that travel south for winter and north in summer. In the warmer months they can be found in the farthest northern reaches of the Arctic tundra.

Caribou have thicker bodies and shorter legs than do most deer. Their hooves are broad. Their coats are brown. They have white tails, necks, and sides. The colors vary with the seasons, as do those of many other deer, becoming lighter in color during winter. Those in the northernmost parts of their range may be almost white.

Both sexes of caribou have large, irregularly branching antlers, though those of the female are somewhat smaller and more slender. The males also reach larger sizes, with some reaching weights of more than 700 pounds (318 kilograms) and shoulder heights of up to 4.6 feet (1.4 meters). Caribou eat grasses and browse on low-lying vegetation. They are noted for consuming large quantities of a lichen called reindeer moss that grows in the tundra regions. When alarmed, caribou break into a clumsy gallop, changing to a steady trot that carries them across the tundra. Their large, spreading hooves, with sharp cup-shaped edges, give them a firm footing on the soft, mucky surface of their summer homes and on winter ice and snow.

Caribou are the most domesticated of the deer. In the region of Lapland in northern Europe, they are kept for milk and meat and for pulling sleds over the snow. Their hides furnish clothing, blankets, and harnesses.

DEFOE, Daniel

DEFOE, Daniel (1660?–1731). The author of 'Robinson Crusoe' was Daniel Defoe. A man of many talents, he was also a businessman, secret agent, and journalist.

He was born in London in about 1660. His father, James Foe, was a butcher. The Foes were Dissenters, or Nonconformists, who did not believe in certain practices of the Church of England. Young Daniel was brought up in the strict yet independent beliefs of the Dissenters.

At 14 he was sent to a Dissenters' academy. In addition to the traditional Latin and Greek, he studied French, Italian, Spanish, and history and became especially well educated in geography. He studied for the ministry, but in 1685 he went into business. Engaged in foreign trade, he visited France and lived in Spain for a time. Meanwhile he was writing and speculating financially. He began to use the name Defoe, which may have been the original Flemish family name.

Defoe was more interested in writing than in business. His lively mind was taken up with problems of the day. In pamphlets, verse, and periodicals, he called for reforms and advances in religious practices, economics, social welfare, and politics. In his 'Essay on Projects', written in 1698, he suggested a national bank, reformed bankruptcy laws, asylums, and academies of learning. He stressed the need for tolerance, often using satire for emphasis.

In 1702 he wrote a pamphlet titled 'The Shortest Way with Dissenters', satirizing the Tories' persecution of Dissenters. The government arrested him. For three days in 1703 he stood locked in the pillory while people brought him flowers. They admired his spirit. Defoe wrote of his experience in verses called 'Hymn to the Pillory'.

After some months in prison he was released in 1704 through the influence of Robert Harley, a statesman who became his patron. Defoe then wrote political pamphlets for Harley and served as his secret agent in working for the union of Scotland and England.

In 1704 Defoe started *The Review,* a periodical. It was the first of many such periodicals with which Defoe was connected—forerunners of the modern newspaper (*see* English Literature, section "The 18th Century"). As people of that era did not care for fiction, Defoe wrote "true histories" of pirates and thieves, spicing facts with imagination. In 1719 he published 'Robinson Crusoe', which was drawn from the experiences and memoirs of a British sailor, Alexander Selkirk.

Defoe's other major works include a satirical poem, 'The True-born Englishman' (1701); 'Moll Flanders' (1722); 'A Journal of the Plague Year' (1722); and 'Roxana' (1724). He died in London on April 24, 1731.

DE FOREST, Lee

DE FOREST, Lee (1873–1961). The broadcasting of sound, or radio broadcasting, began when Lee De Forest invented the Audion tube. His invention changed the living habits of millions; yet he made almost nothing from it.

Lee De Forest was born in Council Bluffs, Iowa, on Aug. 26, 1873. His father, a Congregationalist minister, became head of Talladega College for Negroes in Alabama in 1881. The white community was unfriendly to the family, and young Lee made few friends. To fill his lonely hours, he turned to science.

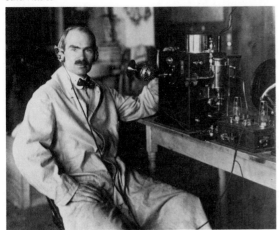

Lee De Forest

By the age of 13 he had invented several mechanical gadgets.

A scholarship enabled him to attend the Sheffield Scientific School at Yale University. Some classmates called him the "homeliest and nerviest student in school." He worked hard and earned his doctor of philosophy degree in 1899.

While he earned his living at various jobs, he steadily experimented after hours. One problem especially challenged him. Marconi had already sent the "dot-dash" of the telegraph code through the air by radio waves, but no one had found a way to broadcast music or speech. Experimenting with Fleming's vacuum tube, De Forest introduced a third part—a grid between the filament and the plate (see Radio). He patented this Audion tube in 1907 and broadcast a live Metropolitan Opera performance of Enrico Caruso in 1910.

Radio broadcasting was born, but the public was not interested. Discouraged, De Forest sold the rights to the tube to a telephone company. In the following years he took out more than 300 patents on radio and other electronic devices. One invention was phonofilm, a forerunner of sound-track motion-picture film. In 1923 he showed the first public "talking" movie.

Wider recognition came to him in his later years, but he was bitter about the financial gains made by others on his inventions. He died on June 30, 1961, in Hollywood, Calif.

DEGAS, Edgar (1834–1917). Famed as the "painter of dancers," Edgar Degas put ballet performers on canvas with great skill. Through his choice of indoor multifigure groups in movement as subjects, he found new and brilliant solutions to the problems of form, composition, and color.

Hilaire-Germain-Edgar Degas was born in Paris on July 19, 1834. His father was a wealthy banker. His mother, of Creole descent, was from New Orleans. Degas went to school at the Lycée Louis-le-Grand, then studied law. He went to the Louvre

art museum often. When he was 20 he persuaded his father to let him become a painter. He studied at the École des Beaux-Arts and with private teachers.

During his 20s Degas visited Italy frequently. He copied old masters and made imitative historical paintings. By 1862, however, he was already beginning to paint the world around him. He met other French painters who would one day become famous—Manet, Monet, Pissarro, Renoir, and Cézanne.

In 1870 Degas served in the Franco-Prussian War. Two years later he spent several months in New Orleans. Back in Paris, he and his artist friends formed a group called the impressionists.

Degas was a sculptor as well as a painter. Only one of his pieces was exhibited during his lifetime. By 1885 his eyes were beginning to cause him serious trouble. He continued to paint and to model in wax, but his sight kept failing. He was forced to spend more and more time working with wax, where eyesight was less important than in painting. After his death bronze casts were made of the 70 works in wax he left behind.

For the last 20 years of his life, Degas lived in seclusion. He died in Paris on Sept. 27, 1917. (See also Painting.)

The pastel study 'Dancer with a Fan' was painted by Edgar Degas in 1879.

DE GAULLE, Charles (1890–1970).

Twice in 20 years France looked to Charles de Gaulle for leadership in a time of trouble. General de Gaulle led the Free French government in the dark days of World War II. In 1958 he returned to power in an attempt to save France from civil war. Throughout his career as military leader and statesman De Gaulle was guided by a belief in the greatness of France.

Education and Early Military Career

Charles de Gaulle was born Nov. 22, 1890, at Lille, in northern France. His father was a philosophy professor. His mother was a descendant of Scottish and Irish refugees who had fled to France with the Stuarts. In 1911 De Gaulle was graduated near the head of his class from the military school at Saint-Cyr, the "West Point" of France.

He was wounded three times in World War I. At the battle of Verdun in 1916 he was captured by the Germans. De Gaulle made five unsuccessful attempts to escape. He was released after the 1918 armistice.

Teaching and Writing Between Wars

In 1921 De Gaulle married Yvonne Vendroux, the daughter of a biscuit manufacturer from Calais. They had three children. Their only son, Philippe, was named after De Gaulle's old commander, Marshal Henri Philippe Pétain.

Between World Wars I and II De Gaulle taught military history at Saint-Cyr. He served on a military mission to Poland and later became aide to Pétain. He wrote several books on military subjects. Perhaps the most important was 'The Army of the Future', in which he was one of the first to suggest the use of mechanized infantry.

Leader of Fighting French in World War II

When Germany invaded France in 1940 De Gaulle was made a general and was given command of an armored division. France failed to check the German advance, and Pétain signed a truce with Hitler.

De Gaulle flew to London for a series of conferences with Winston Churchill. With Churchill's approval he took command of the Free French resistance movement and broadcast to the world: "France has lost a battle, but she has not lost the war."

De Gaulle kept in constant touch with the French underground. After the American invasion of North Africa he joined Gen. Henri Giraud in Algiers to serve as copresident of the French Committee of National Liberation. De Gaulle later became sole president of the committee and chief of the armed forces. He returned to Paris in 1944 on the heels of the retreating Germans.

Provisional President

Appointed president of the newly established French provisional government, De Gaulle tried to unite France's many political parties into a strong national administration. He fought the extremist measures of both the Communists and the reaction-

An official photograph of French President Charles de Gaulle in state dress was taken in 1959. At 6 feet 4 inches tall, he was an imposing figure.

aries, urged cooperation among the political groupings, and tried to establish a moderately liberal regime.

De Gaulle had always been opposed to France's historic system of an all-powerful legislature. He advocated a strong presidency as a check on the National Assembly. De Gaulle's proposed constitutional reforms met with increasing hostility from the Assembly, and early in 1946 he resigned as president.

In 1947, still working for a strong central government, he organized a new political party—the Rally of the French People. His influence declined, however, and he dissolved the party in 1953. In the years that followed, De Gaulle's warnings against unstable government were justified. No French government was able to stay in power for more than a few months. One of the chief causes of the political uproar was the civil war raging in Algeria (see Algeria).

Return to Power in 1958 Crisis

De Gaulle was popular with the French army, whose leaders distrusted the country's politicians. In 1958 a group of officers in Algeria appealed to him to restore order to the French government. De Gaulle then went to Paris for an interview with President René Coty. Coty asked him to try to form a new government. De Gaulle agreed but only if the National Assembly would vote him the executive powers that he had long sought. France's Fifth Republic

At the history-making meeting pictured here Charles de Gaulle addressed the French Assembly. The date was June 3, 1958. He demanded full emergency powers to establish political stability. The Assembly granted his request.

was formed in December, and De Gaulle took office as its first president on Jan. 8, 1959.

De Gaulle sought to end the civil war in Algeria but was blocked by repeated armed uprisings of French settlers who opposed his actions. In a nation-wide referendum, however, the voters of France overwhelmingly supported a cease-fire agreement announced by him in March 1962. De Gaulle attrib-uted the attainment of peace to his broad presidential powers. He declared Algeria's independence on July 3.

In a move to consolidate the powers he had added to the French presidency, De Gaulle proposed that future presidents be chosen by popular election. His plan was approved in a national referendum.

In the November 1962 parliamentary elections De Gaulle's party was the first in the history of France to win a majority in the National Assembly. After the elections De Gaulle increased his efforts to make France a leading world power. At his urging the French developed a nuclear force and a space pro-gram. In international affairs De Gaulle pursued an independent course. He rejected the nuclear test ban treaty; opposed the establishment of a multilateral Polaris-armed submarine force; blocked Great Brit-ain's entry into the European Economic Community, or Common Market; and granted formal recognition to Communist China.

After a runoff election, De Gaulle was inaugurated president for a second seven-year term in January 1966. Later in the year he ended French participa-tion in the military activities of the North Atlantic Treaty Organization (NATO). In 1967, at De Gaulle's insistence, all NATO military personnel were evacuated from France.

In the 1967 parliamentary elections De Gaulle's control of the National Assembly was weakened. His power was threatened further by a national strike wave in 1968. On June 23 he dissolved the National Assembly and called new elections. His party won an overwhelming majority in the National Assembly.

Nevertheless, dissatisfaction continued to grow. In 1969 De Gaulle again demanded a vote of confi-dence when he submitted a number of constitutional changes to a national referendum. On April 27 the people of France voted down his proposals. The fol-lowing day France's 78-year-old president submitted his resignation and retired to his home at Colombey-les-Deux-Églises, 120 miles southeast of Paris. De Gaulle died there on Nov. 9, 1970. A memorial Cross of Lorraine was erected near his grave in 1972.

DE KALB, Johann (1721–1780). When only 16 years old, ambitious Johann Kalb left his peasant home in Bavaria to find adventure. Six years later, he turned up in the French army as "Jean de Kalb," with the assumed title of "baron." Young "Baron de Kalb" rose swiftly to the rank of brigadier general.

In 1767 the French government sent him to Amer-ica to investigate secretly the possibilities of a revolt by the American Colonies against England. They were not yet ready. When they did rebel, he offered his services. With his protégé, the young Marquis de Lafayette, he sailed from France and joined Wash-ington's army in 1777. He was made a major general.

In 1780 he was sent south with some 2,000 men to relieve besieged Charleston, S. C. At the battle of Camden, S. C., August 16, he was second in com-mand to Gen. Horatio Gates. When Gates fled the field, De Kalb and his men fought off the British force until De Kalb fell, with 11 wounds. Three days later he died, a British prisoner. A monument to him was erected in Camden in 1825. His former companion-in-arms, Lafayette, laid the cornerstone.

DE KOONING, Willem (born 1904).

A major abstract expressionist painter, Willem De Kooning is best known for his controversial paintings of women. He was considered by some to be the foremost American artist of the 1950s.

De Kooning was born on April 24, 1904, in Rotterdam, The Netherlands. He attended evening classes for eight years at the Academie voor Beeldende Kunsten en Technische Wetenschapen and graduated in 1924. He went to New York City in 1926 and worked as a free-lance commercial artist. In 1935 he worked for the Works Progress Administration (WPA) Federal Art Project and in 1939 designed a mural for the Hall of Pharmacy at the New York World's Fair. He taught art at Black Mountain College in North Carolina in 1948 and at Yale University from 1950 to 1951.

He started painting in an abstract style around 1934 and was considered a major avant-garde painter by the mid-1940s. His paintings of the 1930s and 1940s centered around men, women, and abstractions, though he finished only a small number of them. In 1946, too poor to buy artists' pigments, he turned to black and white household enamels to paint a series of large abstractions. His works became progressively more violent, and in 1950 De Kooning began to explore the subject of women to the exclusion of others. His paintings caused a sensation and controversy at their gallery showing in 1953 because of De Kooning's blatant figurative technique and imagery used to create harsh, grossly sexual women. By the late 1950s he painted in a more symbolic style, absorbing female figures into landscape backgrounds.

The painter Willem De Kooning poses with his wife, Elaine, before one of his works.

Hans Namuth

'Liberty Guiding the People' is one of Eugene Delacroix's more famous examples of realism.

DELACROIX, Eugène (1798–1863).

Eugène Delacroix is numbered among the greatest and most influential of French painters. He is most often classified as an artist of the romantic school. His remarkable use of color was later to influence impressionist painters and even modern artists such as Pablo Picasso.

He was born Ferdinand-Victor-Eugène Delacroix on April 26, 1798, at Charenton-Saint-Maurice, France. In 1815 he became the pupil of the French painter Pierre-Narcisse Guérin and began a career that would produce more than 850 paintings and great numbers of drawings, murals, and other works. In 1822 Delacroix submitted his first picture to the important Paris Salon exhibition: 'Dante and Virgil in Hell'. A technique used in this work—many unblended colors forming what at a distance looks like a unified whole—would later be used by the impressionists. His next Salon entry was in 1824: "Massacre at Chios'. With great vividness of color and strong emotion it pictured an incident in which 20,000 Greeks were killed by Turks on the island of Chios. The French government purchased it for 6,000 francs.

Impressed by the techniques of English painters such as John Constable, Delacroix visited England in 1825. His tours of the galleries, visits to the theater, and observations of English culture in general made a lasting impression upon him.

Between 1827 and 1832 Delacroix seemed to produce one masterpiece after another. He again used historical themes in 'The Battle of Nancy' and 'The Battle of Poitiers'. The poetry of Lord Byron inspired a painting for the 1827 Salon, 'Death of Sardanapalus'. Delacroix also created a set of 17 lithographs to illustrate a French edition of Goethe's 'Faust'.

The French revolution of 1830 inspired the famous 'Liberty Leading the People', which was the last of Delacroix's paintings that truly embodied the romantic ideal. He found new inspiration on a trip to Morocco in 1832. The ancient, proud, and exotic culture moved him to write "I am quite overwhelmed by what I have seen."

In 1833 Delacroix received his first commission to paint for a government building: a group of murals for the king's chamber at the Palais Bourbon. He continued in this type of painting, including panels for the Louvre and for the Museum of History at Versailles, until 1861. Much of the architectural painting involved long hours on uncomfortable scaffolding in drafty buildings, and his health suffered. He died on Aug. 13, 1863, in Paris. His apartment there was made into a museum in his memory.

DE LA MARE, Walter (1873–1956).
The verses that Walter de la Mare wrote for his four children became favorites of children everywhere. His 'Songs of Childhood' and 'Peacock Pie' sparkle with the fancy and humor of a child's world of discovery and dreams.

Walter John de la Mare was born on April 25, 1873, in the village of Charlton in Kent, England, of Huguenot and Scottish descent. He was educated at St. Paul's Cathedral School in London. When he was 16 years old, he founded *The Choristers' Journal*, the school magazine.

In 1890 he went to work for the Anglo-American Oil Company as a bookkeeper. He held the monotonous job for 18 years, later saying, "I think that one can find interest in any task which has got to be done." Meanwhile he continued to write, often working on a story or poem during his lunch hour.

Writing under the name Walter Ramal, he sold his first story, 'Kismet', in 1895. At that time he dressed "like a poet"—long hair, flowing tie, and broad hat. Every night when he went upstairs to say good night to his two sons and two daughters, he "took them a poem as naturally as other parents took a drink of water."

In 1908 his writings earned him a government pension. He retired to the country life he loved and devoted himself exclusively to writing. About half his work was prose, some of it about the supernatural. In 1922 he won the James Tait Black prize for his 'Memoirs of a Midget'—a fictional account of a tiny gentlewoman. His works for children include fairy books, short stories, and 'The Three Mulla-Mulgars'— a story of three royal monkeys.

His poems for adults include 'The Listeners' and 'Winged Chariot'—the latter written when he was nearly 80. At that time a middle-aged friend said, "I always come away from a visit with him feeling refreshed and happily stretched in mind." De la Mare died on June 22, 1956, in Twienenham, Middlesex.

DELAUNAY, Robert (1885–1941).
One of the earliest painters of abstract art, Robert Delaunay transformed the style called cubism with the use of vibrant colors into a variety called orphism by the poet Guillaume Apollinaire. The essential element of orphism, named after the Greek poet and musician Orpheus, was that "color is both form and subject."

Deposited by Emanuel Hoffman-Foundation in Kunstmuseum Basel, Switz.; photo, Hans Hinz

'Eiffel Tower' was one of Robert Delaunay's contributions to the style called cubism.

Delaunay was born in Paris on April 12, 1885. He became an apprentice to a stage designer in 1902. Influenced by the post-impressionists, he began to paint during vacations in Brittany, and by 1909 he was associated with the cubists. His first major paintings were the series of 'Cathedrals' and 'Cities' in the cubist style. His 'St-Severin' and the three large paintings of 'Eiffel Tower' are also cubist but show an expanded use of color. Delaunay's dynamic perceptions of the world of light produced his first purely abstract paintings in 1912, in two series that were known as 'Windows' and 'Disks'. He was admired by the Blue Rider group in Munich, Germany, and exhibited in their shows of 1911 and 1912 and at Berlin's Der Sturm Gallery in 1913.

Delaunay married the Ukrainian painter Sonia Terk in 1910, and from 1915 to 1920 they lived in Spain and Portugal. Among other things they designed sets for Serge Diaghilev's ballet 'Cléopâtre' in 1918. When they returned to Paris in 1921, their home became a meeting place for the Dadaists, but they were little influenced by the group. They collaborated on a major decorative project for the 1937 Exposition Internationale in Paris.

Delaunay's love of rhythmic motion inspired still another subject for his painting—sporting events. 'Cardiff Team' dates from 1913, 'Hommage to Blériot' (1914), and the series 'Sprinters' from 1924 to 1926. These led to pure rhythmic patterns, or total abstraction, in the nonobjective series 'Rhythms' and 'Eternal Rhythms'. Delaunay died in Montpellier, France, on Oct. 25, 1941.

Delaware River Port Authority

At Delaware's Port of Wilmington, ships to and from all over
the world load and unload at quay-type docks. Beyond the
dock area stretches the modern industrial city of Wilmington.

DELAWARE

DELAWARE. Although it is small in size and population, Delaware is of great importance historically.
It was the first of the 13 original colonies to ratify
the federal Constitution in 1787. Delaware thus
became the First State of the Union, a nickname by
which it has been known ever since.

Thomas Jefferson called Delaware "a *jewel* among
the states," and a later writer specified the jewel
as a diamond. Delaware has always lived up to the
nickname Diamond State. From its research laboratories have come synthetic fibers and fabrics that
have made living easier. Its productive farms supply
the Eastern seaboard with poultry, fruits, and vegetables. A third nickname, the Blue Hen State, came
from the game chickens carried by a Delaware
regiment during the Revolutionary War.

The state is named after Lord De la Warr, governor
of Virginia in the early 1600's. In 1610 Capt. Samuel
Argall of the Virginia colony saw the bay and named
it for the governor. Later the river and the land
along the western shore were also called Delaware.

Population (1980): 595,225—rank, 47th state. Urban, 70.7%;
rural, 29.3%. Persons per square mile, 289.4 (persons per
square kilometer, 111.7)—rank, 7th state.

Extent: Area, 2,057 square miles (5,328 square kilometers),
including 112 square miles (290 square kilometers) of
water surface (49th state in size).

Elevation: Highest, Ebright Road, New Castle County, 442 feet
(134 meters); lowest, sea level; average, 60 feet (19 meters).

Geographic Center: 11 miles (17.7 kilometers) south of Dover.

Temperature: Extremes—lowest, $-17°$ F $(-27.2°$ C), Millsboro, Jan. 17, 1893; highest, 110° F (43.3° C), Millsboro,
July 21, 1930. Averages at Wilmington—January, 33.6° F
(0.89° C); July, 76.3° F (24.6° C); annual, 54.2° F (12.3° C).

Precipitation: At Wilmington—annual average, 43.05 inches
(1,093 millimeters).

Land Use: Crops, 42%; pasture, 1%; forest, 31%; other, 26%.

**For statistical information about Agriculture, Education,
Employment, Finance, Government, Manufacturing, Mining,
Population Trends, and Vital Statistics, see DELAWARE
FACT SUMMARY.**

Location, Size, and Boundaries

Delaware is on the East coast, about midway between Maine and Florida. It is one of the Middle Atlantic states. The state is 2,057 square miles in area, including 112 square miles of water surface. Its greatest length, north to south, is 96 miles. Its greatest width, east to west, is 35 miles. Delaware is the 49th state in size. Only Rhode Island is smaller.

The state is bounded on the east by the Atlantic Ocean and by the Delaware River and Delaware Bay, which separate it from New Jersey. To the south and west is Maryland. Delaware's northern boundary curves into Pennsylvania. This boundary was set in a land grant made to William Penn by the duke of York in 1682. It was to be within a circle with a 12-mile radius from "the end of the horse dyke" at New Castle.

Most of Delaware lies on the Delmarva Peninsula, which also includes part of Maryland and Virginia. The state has only three counties: New Castle, Kent, and Sussex. For taxing and other purposes the counties are divided into "hundreds" rather than townships. Delaware is the only state to use this old English method of political division.

Natural Regions

Delaware is divided into two natural regions—the Piedmont Plateau and the Coastal Plain.

The Piedmont Plateau lies in the extreme northern part of the state. It begins at the Christina River and runs northward into the foothills of southeastern Pennsylvania. Erosion is a great problem in the Piedmont region. East of Centerville is Ebright Road (442 feet), the highest point in the state.

The Coastal Plain covers most of Delaware. It is a region of sandy soil that makes good farmland. Altitudes are low, ranging from sea level to 60 feet. Poor drainage is the big problem in this region.

The watershed in Delaware begins in the north as a low ridge along the western boundary and turns southeast below the center of the state. The Appoquinimink, Smyrna, Saint Jones, and Mispillion rivers empty into the Delaware River or Delaware Bay. The Nanticoke River empties westward into Chesapeake Bay. In the southeast are Rehoboth and Indian River bays, shallow lagoons behind narrow sandy coastal barriers.

Climate and Weather

Delaware's winters are mild; its summers, hot and humid. The average annual temperature for the state is about 55°F. Winter temperatures average about 34° in the north and about 37° in the south-central part of the state. Summer temperatures vary less, from just under 74° in the north to a little more than 74° in the south. The record low is −17°; the record high, 110°. Both records were established at Millsboro in the southeast. The growing season lasts about 185 days. The average annual precipitation (rain and melted snow) is about 44 inches, evenly distributed through the seasons.

Natural Resources and Conservation

Delaware is rich in natural resources. Its sandy soil is fertile and well watered. The state is divided into three soil conservation districts, all managed by working farmers. There are no sizable dams or reservoirs in Delaware.

Pine, gum, oak, hickory, sycamore, walnut, tulip, beech, maple, ash, plum, and cedar trees are abundant. The State Forestry Department, created with the help of Coleman du Pont in 1927, supervises Redden, Ellendale, Blackbird, and other state forests. All state forests are game sanctuaries. Many game refuges have been created on unused farms. Foxes, otters, minks, muskrats, chipmunks, moles, beavers, and deer are found in Delaware.

A variety of fish and shellfish live in the state's river, bay, and ocean waters. The State Game and Fish Commission, created in 1911, supervises conservation areas at Assawoman Bay and Petersburg. Delaware lies along the Atlantic wild bird migration flyway. Many birds are seen in the state throughout the year. The United States Fish and Wildlife Service maintains the 14,000-acre Bombay Hook National Wildlife Refuge as well as the smaller Killcohook refuge, about 600 acres of which lie in Delaware.

Some minerals are found in the state, mainly sand and gravel, stone, and kaolin (a pottery clay). Delaware rivers provide waterpower and transportation. The state lies close to busy East coast cities, which offer ready markets for Delaware products.

Rodney Square, with its statue of Caesar Rodney, Revolutionary War statesman and signer of the Declaration of Independence, lies in midtown Wilmington.

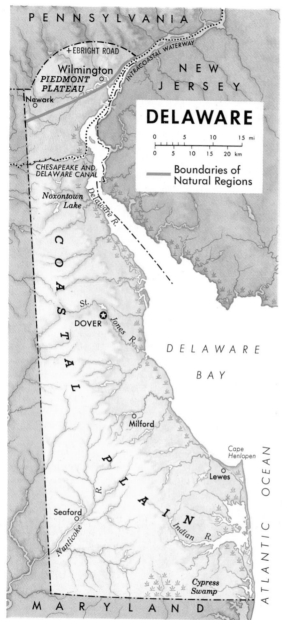

This map shows the two natural regions and the surface features of Delaware. The use that can be made of the land is related to the physical features of each region.

Delaware People

The first people in the state were the Delaware Indians. They called themselves Lenni-Lenape, meaning "original people." About 8,000 Delaware lived in Pennsylvania, New Jersey, and Delaware. They belonged to the Eastern Woodland group and spoke an Algonquian language. A branch of the Delaware, the Nanticoke, lived in southern Delaware and on the Eastern Shore of Maryland. The Minqua, from Pennsylvania and Maryland, made frequent raids on the Delaware. (See also Indians, American.)

The first white settlers in Delaware were Swedes, Dutch, and English. A colony of Mennonites, a Dutch religious group, lives in Dover. Modern immigrants have come from the British Isles, Italy, Germany, Poland, and Canada. Delaware has a small foreign-born population. Blacks make up 16 percent of the total. With only 595,225 people, Delaware is the seventh most densely populated state.

Farms, Forests, and Fisheries

Almost 80 percent of Delaware's farms are commercial operations. About a fifth of the state's farms are operated on a part-time basis by semiretired people or by people who are employed in neighboring industrial plants.

In New Castle County much of the land is silt loam. Here are most of the large dairy and grain farms. In Kent and Sussex counties, with their sandy soil, are the big poultry, fruit, and truck farms.

Poultry, corn, soybeans, milk, truck crops, and potatoes are the chief farm products. Broilers are by far the most important in value. Delaware is one of the leading states in raising broilers. A variety of truck crops are grown: lima and snap beans, sweet corn, tomatoes, asparagus, peppers, peas, cucumbers, pumpkins, squash, spinach, and cantaloupe. Canneries operate from midsummer until frost time. The state also produces fruits (mainly apples and peaches), wheat, oats, hay, eggs, barley, rye, turkeys, hogs, and beef cattle.

Commercial forests in the state yield loblolly, shortleaf, and Virginia pine for piling, red gum for veneer, and holly, pine, and other forest greenery for Christmas decorations. The state has about 400,000 acres of forest land.

For its size Delaware ranks high in fisheries. Menhaden make up the largest catch by far. Also caught are flounder, shad, and sea trout. Valuable seafood catches include crabs, clams, and oysters, which are shipped fresh throughout the East and frozen for the markets of the Midwest.

Cities and Industries

Wilmington is the only large city in Delaware. All the other cities have fewer than 26,000 people. Wilmington has been a mill town since colonial days. First flour mills, then paper mills brought wealth to the city. Today it is called the "world's chemical capital" because of its production of plastic materials, synthetic fibers, dyes, paints, and varnishes. Several powder companies have their main offices in Wilmington, but no explosives are manufactured in the state. The Port of Wilmington, at the mouth of the Christina River, ships Delaware products all over the world. Because of favorable corporation laws, many nationally known businesses are incorporated in Delaware and have offices in Wilmington. (See also Wilmington.)

Newark is the home of the University of Delaware. Dover, the third city in size, is the state capital (see Dover, Del.). Seaford is called the "nylon capital of the world." Rehoboth Beach has earned the title of

Nylon yarn is produced by the Du Pont company at Seaford (left). Nylon, Orlon, and Dacron were developed in Delaware.

A chicken range on this farm (right) houses young broilers. Delaware is one of the leading states in raising broilers.

the "nation's summer capital" because many Washington, D. C., government officials spend summer vacations here.

Chemical products and canned foods rank high on the list of Delaware's manufactures. Also important are apparel and leather goods, especially glazed kid for women's shoes. Textile mills produce many natural and synthetic fabrics. Iron and steel products; nonelectrical machinery; and stone, clay, and glass products are made in several Delaware cities.

Transportation in Delaware

The Chesapeake and Delaware Canal crosses the state 15 miles south of Wilmington. It unites Delaware Bay with Chesapeake Bay. It is part of the In-

tracoastal Waterway that runs down the Atlantic and Gulf coasts. The canal, begun in 1801 and completed in 1829, was 19 miles long and 90 feet wide. The channel was widened to 250 feet in 1935-39.

The Delaware Memorial Bridge spans the Delaware River from a point near New Castle to Deepwater, N. J. Nearly 11,000 feet long, it was opened in 1951. It is on the main highway route from Maine to Florida. A parallel, twin suspension bridge was opened in 1968. The new bridge handles southbound traffic; the older span, northbound.

Delaware has thousands of miles of primary and secondary state highways. Du Pont Highway, a principal thoroughfare, runs from the southern boundary to Wilmington. Governor Printz Boulevard, named for

At the Du Pont Experimental Stations near Wilmington, fundamental and applied research in chemistry goes on. Scientists seek new facts about chemistry and new uses for chemical substances. Many aids to modern living were developed here.

73

an early governor of New Sweden, continues from Wilmington to the northern boundary.

The state's first railroad was the New Castle-Frenchtown Railroad, opened in 1831. It replaced a turnpike of the same name and ran 16½ miles between the Delaware and Elk rivers. Delaware is now served by a number of railroads, bus lines, and airlines.

Recreation and Places of Interest

Delaware's mild climate invites its people to enjoy the outdoors. Rehoboth Beach, Bethany Beach, and Woodland Beach are popular saltwater beach resorts. Many inland lakes offer fishing and swimming.

The State Park Commission supervises the following state parks: Fort Delaware, on Pea Patch Island opposite Delaware City; Delaware Seashore, on the Atlantic Ocean; Trap Pond, near Laurel; Cape Henlopen, near Lewes; Killen Pond, near Felton; Brandywine Creek and Brandywine Springs, both near Wilmington; Lums Pond, near Kirkwood; and Holts Landing, on Indian River Bay. The Public Archives Commission administers Fort Christina Monument in Wilmington.

The Zwaanendael Museum in Lewes was built in 1931 to celebrate the 300th anniversary of the first Dutch settlement in Delaware. It is modeled after an old Dutch town hall. The Henry Francis du Pont Winterthur Museum, at Winterthur, has more than 100 rooms furnished in the styles of 1640 to 1840.

New Castle is rich in historic interest. Its Green was laid out under the direction of Peter Stuyvesant during the period of Dutch rule. Around the Green stand the Immanuel Church, the New Castle Academy, the Old Court House, and several other 18th-century buildings. The Amstel House, built about 1730, houses the New Castle Historical Society. There are many fine private homes, some of which are open to the public once a year on Old New Castle Day.

Dover also has many fine old homes. Some of them circle the Green, which was the site of early fairs and slave markets. The Green was laid out in 1717. In Wilmington regular services are still held at the Holy Trinity (Old Swedes) Church, begun in 1698 and consecrated a year later. Fort Christina Monument is another major Wilmington attraction. The first permanent European settlement in Delaware was established here by Peter Minuit in 1638.

Delaware Schools

The first teachers in the Dutch and Swedish colonies of the 1600's were mainly clergymen. The first school buildings were churches. The state constitution of 1792 provided for the establishment of public schools.

Today Delaware has a six-member State Board of Education. It chooses a superintendent of public instruction and four assistant superintendents. The major school administrative units are the City of Wilmington, the Special Districts, and the State Board Units. Public school costs are paid primarily out of the state general fund, but a small percentage comes from taxes collected by the school districts.

The schools supported by the state include the University of Delaware, at Newark, and Delaware State College, at Dover. The university was opened in 1834 as Newark College. In 1843 the name was changed to Delaware College. From 1859 to 1870 it was closed. The Women's College opened in 1914. In 1921 the two schools were combined for administrative purposes as the University of Delaware. In 1944 the two were completely merged.

State Government

Dover has been Delaware's state capital since 1777 (see Dover, Del.). Before that the capital was New Castle. The historic State House, still used for state offices, was built between 1787 and 1792. The seat of government was transferred to the new capitol building, Legislative Hall, in 1933.

The General Assembly is the lawmaking body. It consists of the Senate, with 21 members, and the House of Representatives, with 41 members. The governor is elected for a four-year term. He may serve only two terms. He has the "item veto" power on appropriation bills. The secretary of state is appointed by the governor.

Delaware has had four constitutions, adopted in 1776, 1792, 1831, and 1897. The present constitution's bill of rights guarantees freedom of religion, the right of free elections, freedom from improper arrest, and the right of fair trial. Delaware is the

A wave-borne ship carved by Carl Milles was given to Delaware by the Swedish people in 1938 to mark the 300th anniversary of Swedish settlement on this site, in what is now Wilmington. It stands in Fort Christina State Park.

The Henry Francis du Pont Winterthur Museum, at Winterthur, exhibits rooms decorated in the styles of 1640 to 1840.

HISTORY OF DELAWARE

Although small in size and population, Delaware has had a rich history. In colonial days it was ruled successively by the Dutch, Swedes, and English. It was the first of the 13 original states to ratify the federal Constitution. Throughout its history it has had many "firsts" in invention and industrial development. Today these firsts are giving the world a continuing stream of new synthetics. The following sketch traces the history of Delaware from its beginning to the present.

Colonial Days

The history of Delaware began in 1609 when Henry Hudson sailed the *Half Moon* into Delaware Bay and River. For the next few years Dutch captains explored the Delaware waters. In 1621 the Dutch West India Company was formed. The company allowed its patroons (owners of lands) to rule like great lords. The first land in the area was bought in 1630. The next year 28 Dutchmen settled on Blommaert's Kill (now Lewes) and started the Zwaanendael colony. It was soon wiped out by the Indians.

Several Dutchmen withdrew their support of the Dutch West India Company and offered it to Sweden. With their help a Swedish colony was set up in 1638 at what is now Wilmington. This first permanent white settlement in Delaware was called Fort Christina, and the area was called New Sweden. Although they had many setbacks, the Swedes built well and generally prospered. For example, they built the

only state in which constitutional amendments do not have to be ratified by the voters. They become law after they pass both houses of the General Assembly by a two-thirds vote of the elected members at two successive sessions.

The state's judicial system is headed by the Supreme Court. There are also chancery, superior, and common pleas courts. New Castle County is governed by a county executive and a six-member county council. Kent County is governed by a levy court, and Sussex County is governed by a county council.

Delaware sends only one congressman to the national House of Representatives. In presidential elections the state has voted for the Democratic and Republican candidates about an equal number of times.

At Wilmington is Holy Trinity (Old Swedes) Church (left). Built in 1698, it is the oldest Protestant church in America.

Zwaanendael Museum (right), at Lewes, was built in 1931 to celebrate the settlement made by the Dutch in 1631.

first log cabins in America. These were trim, tight, snug, and warm.

In 1655 the Dutch captured Fort Christina, and the Swedes were forced to give up New Sweden. The Dutch did not stay in power long. In 1664 the English seized all the Dutch colonies in America.

Delaware became part of the province granted to the duke of York by his brother, Charles II. Marcus Jacobsen led the Swedes in a revolt, but it was put down. The Dutch regained control for a year, but the colony reverted to English hands in 1674.

In 1682, the duke of York gave Delaware, then called the Three Lower Counties, to William Penn. The counties became part of Pennsylvania Province. In 1704 the Delaware counties left the Pennsylvania assembly and formed their own. However, they remained under the rule of the Pennsylvania governor.

New State in a New Nation

Delaware shared in the colonial tension by refusing to obey the Stamp Act in 1765. When in 1776 the Continental Congress met to vote on the Declaration of Independence, the Delaware delegates were tied. Caesar Rodney rode from Dover to Philadelphia, Pa., on July 1 to break the tie and vote for independence.

Delaware adopted its first constitution on Sept. 21, 1776. On Dec. 7, 1787, it became the first state to ratify the federal Constitution.

In 1802 a Frenchman named Éleuthère Irénée du Pont settled on the Brandywine and started making gunpowder. His business grew into one of the richest and most diversified manufacturing companies in the world. Early Delaware inventors included Oliver Evans, who devised many machines.

United States Navy forces at Delaware fought in the War of 1812, and for a time the Delaware River was blockaded by a British fleet. Although it was a border state, Delaware stayed in the Union when the Civil War came. After the war, industry expanded. It has continued to do so, spurred by such inventions as nylon, which was developed in the 1930s under the direction of Wallace H. Carothers.

Today Delaware is prosperous and productive. Its industries seek countryside locations that give workers the chance for part-time farming and country living. Its schools rank among the nation's best. Its welfare agencies care for the aged and the poor. (*See also* United States, section "Middle Atlantic Region"; individual entries in Fact-Index on Delaware persons, places, products, and events.)

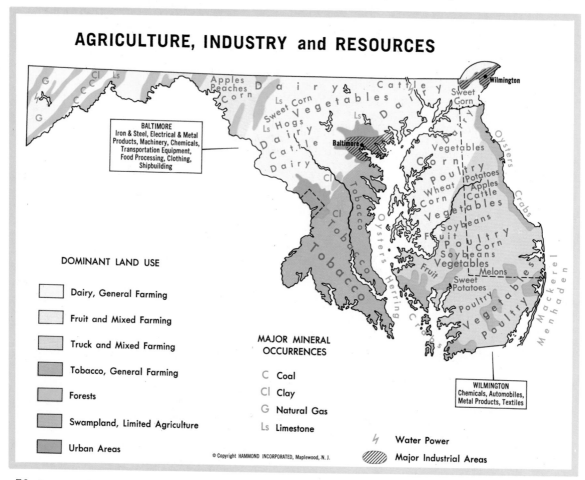

AGRICULTURE, INDUSTRY and RESOURCES

BALTIMORE
Iron & Steel, Electrical & Metal Products, Machinery, Chemicals, Transportation Equipment, Food Processing, Clothing, Shipbuilding

WILMINGTON
Chemicals, Automobiles, Metal Products, Textiles

DOMINANT LAND USE

- Dairy, General Farming
- Fruit and Mixed Farming
- Truck and Mixed Farming
- Tobacco, General Farming
- Forests
- Swampland, Limited Agriculture
- Urban Areas

MAJOR MINERAL OCCURRENCES

- C Coal
- Cl Clay
- G Natural Gas
- Ls Limestone
- ⚡ Water Power
- ▨ Major Industrial Areas

© Copyright HAMMOND INCORPORATED, Maplewood, N.J.

Notable Events in Delaware History

1609—Henry Hudson discovers Delaware Bay and River.

1631—Dutch plant colony of Zwaanendael near present Lewes. Indians massacre settlers.

1638—Swedish colonists settle in present Wilmington, first permanent settlement in Delaware; build Fort Christina; name area New Sweden.

1651—Peter Stuyvesant, governor of Dutch New Amsterdam (now New York), builds Fort Casimir on site of New Castle. Swedish settlers capture fort in 1654; call it Fort Trinity. Stuyvesant recaptures fort in 1655; takes Fort Christina; Swedish claims surrendered to Dutch.

1664—England conquers Dutch American colonies; Delaware area becomes part of Duke of York's Province.

1672—Dutch and English at war; Dutch capture New York and recover colonies in 1673; English regain control by Treaty of Westminster in 1674.

1682—**Duke of York grants Three Lower Counties (present Delaware) to William Penn as part of Pennsylvania Province. Penn lands at New Castle.** Lord Baltimore of Maryland begins dispute over Penn's Delaware grant.

1704—Lower Counties form own assembly at New Castle; continue under rule of Pennsylvania governor.

1761—James Adams sets up printing press at Wilmington.

1763–68—Mason and Dixon survey Delaware boundaries.

1776—**Caesar Rodney, born 1728 in Dover, rides from Dover to Continental Congress at Philadelphia, Pa., to cast Delaware's vote for independence.** State constitution framed at New Castle.

1777—Capital moved from New Castle to Dover. Only battle of Revolution in state fought at Cooch's Bridge near Newark; British occupy Wilmington.

1779—Assembly ratifies Articles of Confederation.

1781—Delaware's delegate Thomas McKean elected president of Continental Congress.

1787—Delaware is first state to ratify U. S. Constitution, December 7. State House, built in 1787–92 at Dover, is State Capitol until Legislative Hall is completed in 1933.

1790—John Fitch's steamboat goes into service on Delaware River at Philadelphia.

1802—E. I. du Pont builds first powder mill near Wilmington.

1812—*Wasp*, under Capt. Jacob Jones of Delaware, captures British ship *Frolic* in War of 1812; British blockade Delaware River.

1814—Capt. Thomas Macdonough of Delaware defeats British in battle on Lake Champlain.

1829—**Chesapeake and Delaware Canal opened.**

1833—University of Delaware founded at Newark.

1844—First iron, propeller-driven seagoing ship built in U. S., the *Bangor*, launched at Wilmington.

1861—Delaware refuses to secede from Union.

1897—Present state constitution adopted.

1905—State abolishes pillory.

1911–24—State-long Du Pont Boulevard built.

1937—**Wallace H. Carothers of Du Pont Company invents nylon, a synthetic fiber, at Wilmington.**

1951—Delaware Memorial Bridge opens; twin span opened in 1968.

1961—Congress approves first federal-interstate compact to develop Delaware River basin resources.

1966—State acquires its first executive mansion—Woodburn, historic 1790 house, in Dover.

1971—Legislature passes Coastal Zone Act to forestall heavy industry along state's shore.

1682

1776

1829

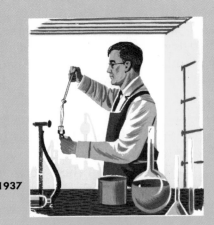

1937

STATE FLOWER:
Peach Blossom

STATE TREE:
American Holly

STATE BIRD:
Blue Hen Chicken

STATE SEAL: Wheat, corn, and ox on shield signify agriculture; above, a ship; at either side, farmer and soldier.

Delaware Profile

FLAG: *See* **Flags of the United States.**
MOTTO: Liberty and Independence.
SONG: 'Our Delaware'—words,
George B. Hynson; music,
William M. S. Brown.

Delaware, the first state to ratify the federal Constitution in 1787, combines elements that enter into the character of all the United States. The First State's economy is firmly based upon both agriculture and industry. Delaware cherishes and preserves the beautiful things of the past, while creating in its laboratories the products that have revolutionized modern living. Settled originally by Dutch, Swedes, and British, it has successfully absorbed the many other peoples who followed them.

Closeness to the large markets of the Eastern United States, good transportation facilities, good climate, and the well-watered, sandy soil of the broad Coastal Plain that comprises most of Delaware make it an important agricultural state. The extreme northern part of Delaware is in the Piedmont Plateau, from which short, swift streams tumble to lower levels. Abundant waterpower and easy access to the Delaware River and Delaware Bay helped make Wilmington a manufacturing center and seaport. Flour mills were built on the Brandywine and other streams when the state was first settled. Paper mills were built as early as 1787; the first cotton mill, in 1795. Leathermaking has been a leading industry since 1732, when the Quakers began preparing buckskin and chamois in Wilmington. Here in 1802 Éleuthère Irénée du Pont de Nemours founded the great company which in the 20th century made Wilmington the "world's chemical capital."

Delaware has taken pains to preserve its stately old houses and public buildings. Old Dover Days and A Day in Old New Castle are celebrated with 18th-century music and dances. Many private homes are open to the public on these occasions, and collections of antiques, paintings, and old documents are also on display. Far from living in the past, however, the First State continues to grow in population and in economic productivity.

Delaware picture profile

Legislative Hall, Delaware's seat of government in Dover, was opened in 1933. It replaced the State House, in use since 1792. Like the State House, the new Capitol was built of handmade red bricks in Georgian style.

Christ Church in Dover was built in 1734. Since then many major structural changes have been made in the building. The tower was added in 1876.

Wilmington, Delaware's largest city, has been an important seaport since colonial times. The Wilmington Marine Terminal on the Christina River serves oceangoing ships, though the Atlantic is 70 miles away.

The University of Delaware, chartered as Newark College in 1833, bisects the city of Newark. Its open-stack Hugh M. Morris Library opened in 1963. The library contains about 750,000 volumes and provides a variety of research facilities.

Delaware picture profile

Schoolchildren celebrate Old Dover Days by dancing on the green in front of the State House. The structure, originally erected in 1722, was rebuilt in 1792. It served as Delaware's seat of government until 1933.

The Birkenhead Mills, on Brandywine Creek, were built by E. I. du Pont de Nemours and Company in 1822–24. Gunpowder was manufactured here until 1921. The mills are now part of the Hagley Museum.

Fenwick Island Lighthouse is on the Maryland state line in southeastern Delaware. The 80-foot-high white tower was built in 1857. Fenwick Island is actually a narrow sandy peninsula 12 miles long.

Thoroughbred horse racing is an attraction at Delaware Park, a racetrack near Stanton. Delaware offers a great variety of vacation activities, including hunting, fishing, bathing in the ocean, and boating on rivers and bays.

Facing New Castle's Green is the Immanuel Church, begun in 1703 and completed about 1710. The tower and spire were added in 1820–22. Next to the church is the New Castle Academy, begun in 1798.

This is the spinning area in the Du Pont nylon plant at Seaford. Here the nylon filaments are gathered into yarn and spun onto bobbins.

This colonial kitchen is in Amstel House, New Castle. The kitchen wing, which was built in 1706 or earlier, probably served as the original residence.

The Port Royal Parlor is one of the most beautiful of the many period rooms in the Henry Francis du Pont Winterthur Museum. The woodwork—mantelpiece, chimney breast, and paneling—came from the Port Royal House near Philadelphia, built in 1762. The Chippendale furniture dates from the same time. On the mantel are Chinese porcelains.

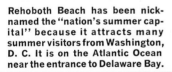

Rehoboth Beach has been nicknamed the "nation's summer capital" because it attracts many summer visitors from Washington, D. C. It is on the Atlantic Ocean near the entrance to Delaware Bay.

Fort Delaware, a state park on Pea Patch Island, overlooks the Delaware River below Wilmington. Work began on the present fort in 1848. Earlier forts on the site had been destroyed, one by fire, another by a tidal wave.

DELAWARE FACT SUMMARY

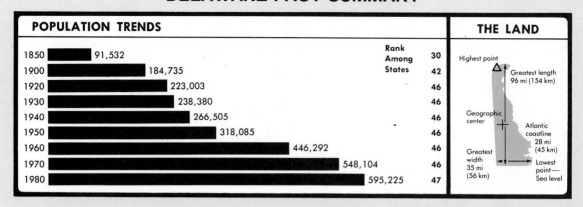

POPULATION TRENDS

Year	Population	Rank Among States
1850	91,532	30
1900	184,735	42
1920	223,003	46
1930	238,380	46
1940	266,505	46
1950	318,085	46
1960	446,292	46
1970	548,104	46
1980	595,225	47

THE LAND

Highest point

Greatest length 96 mi (154 km)

Geographic center

Atlantic coastline 28 mi (45 km)

Greatest width 35 mi (56 km)

Lowest point— Sea level

LARGEST CITIES AND TOWNS (1980 census)

Wilmington (70,195): industrial city; numerous corporate headquarters; port on Delaware River; banking center; Winterthur Museum (*see* Wilmington).

Newark (25,247): University of Delaware; chemical research area; auto manufacturing.

Dover (23,512): state capital; large Amish community nearby; U.S. Air Force base; food processing (*see* Dover, Del.).

Brookside (15,255): residential suburb of Newark.

Claymont (10,022): residential suburb of Wilmington.

Wilmington Manor (9,233): city between Wilmington and New Castle.

Edgemoor (7,397): west of Wilmington; on Christiana Pike; Delaware Race Track nearby.

Talleyville (6,880): town on north side of Wilmington; on Concord Pike.

Elsmere (6,493): residential town near Wilmington; rail center; auto manufacturing.

Stanton (5,495): residential area, north of Wilmington.

Milford (5,366): farming community; fertilizer; food processing; weakfish tournament.

Seaford (5,256): nylon production.

New Castle (4,814): original state capital; George Reading House.

Smyrna (4,750): garment manufacturing; industrial manufacturing.

VITAL STATISTICS 1980 (per 1,000 population)

Birthrate:	16.06
Death Rate:	7.81
Marriage Rate:	7.5
Divorce Rate:	3.9

GOVERNMENT

Capital: Dover (since 1777).

Statehood: First state to ratify the U.S. Constitution, on Dec. 7, 1787.

Constitution: Adopted 1897; amendment may be passed by two-thirds vote of two consecutive legislatures.

Representation in U.S. Congress: Senate—2. House of Representatives—1. Electoral votes—3.

Legislature: Senators—21; term, 4 years. Representatives—41; term, 2 years.

Executive Officers: Governor—term, 4 years; may succeed self once. Other officials—lieutenant governor, attorney general, treasurer, auditor; all elected; terms, 4 years. Secretary of state, appointed by the governor.

Judiciary: Supreme Court—5 justices; term, 12 years. Court of Chancery—4 judges; term, 12 years. Superior Court—11 judges; term, 12 years.

County: 3 counties. New Castle County and Sussex County, governed by County Council. Kent County, governed by Levy Court. All officials elected for 4-year terms.

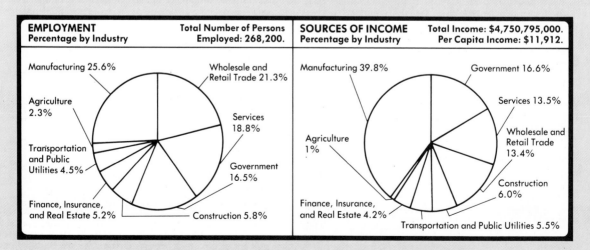

EMPLOYMENT Percentage by Industry — Total Number of Persons Employed: 268,200.

- Manufacturing 25.6%
- Wholesale and Retail Trade 21.3%
- Agriculture 2.3%
- Services 18.8%
- Transportation and Public Utilities 4.5%
- Government 16.5%
- Finance, Insurance, and Real Estate 5.2%
- Construction 5.8%

SOURCES OF INCOME Percentage by Industry — Total Income: $4,750,795,000. Per Capita Income: $11,912.

- Manufacturing 39.8%
- Government 16.6%
- Services 13.5%
- Agriculture 1%
- Wholesale and Retail Trade 13.4%
- Construction 6.0%
- Finance, Insurance, and Real Estate 4.2%
- Transportation and Public Utilities 5.5%

MAJOR PRODUCTS

Agricultural: Broiler chickens, corn, soybeans, potatoes, fruits, vegetables, fish.

Manufactured: Automobiles, food processing, chemicals, textiles, nylon, petroleum products.

EDUCATION AND CULTURE

Universities and Colleges: Delaware State College, Dover; Delaware Technical and Community College, campuses in Georgetown, Wilmington, and Dover; Goldey Beacom College, Wilmington; University of Delaware, Newark; Wesley College, Dover; Brandywine College of Widener University, Wilmington; Wilmington College, New Castle.

Libraries: Henry Francis du Pont Winterthur Library, near Wilmington; Historical Society of Delaware, Wilmington; Kent and Sussex Community Public Libraries; New Castle County Public Libraries; Wilmington Institute Libraries.

Notable Museums: Delaware Agricultural Museum, Dover; Delaware Art Museum, Hagley Museum, Nemours Mansion and Garden, Henry Francis du Pont Winterthur Museum, Rockwood Museum, all in or near Wilmington; Delaware Museum of Natural History, Greenville; Island Field Museum, near South Bowers Beach; John Dickinson House, near Dover; George Read II House, New Castle; Zwaanendael Museum, Lewes.

PLACES OF INTEREST

Barratt's Chapel: near Frederica; called "cradle of Methodism"; first service in 1784.

Belmont Hall: near Smyrna; old mansion, begun about 1684; family heirlooms on display.

Bethany Beach: resort on Atlantic Ocean.

Bombay Hook National Wildlife Refuge: near Smyrna; waterfowl sanctuary on Atlantic Flyway.

Brandywine Springs State Park: west of Wilmington; woodland paths; picnic areas and fireplaces for cooking.

Cape Henlopen State Park: near Lewes; site marks entrance to Delaware Bay; rare plants thrive in area; nature tours.

Chesapeake and Delaware Canal: connects Chesapeake Bay and Delaware River; wildlife area.

Christ Episcopal Church, Broad Creek Hundred: near Laurel; Georgian Colonial style (1771).

Cooch's Bridge: near Newark; site of only battle of Revolutionary War fought in Delaware (1777).

Delaware Memorial Bridge: great suspension bridge over Delaware River near New Castle.

Delaware Seashore State Park: along Atlantic coast, Dewey Beach to Fenwick Island Lighthouse; picnicking, fishing.

Dover Air Force Base: near Dover; large military air cargo terminal.

Eleutherian Mills-Hagley Foundation: on Brandywine Creek near Wilmington; Du Pont Company began in 1802; Hagley Museum.

Fort Christina State Park: in Wilmington; commemorates landing of Swedish colonists at The Rocks in 1638—first permanent white settlement in Delaware; in 1938 people of Sweden donated monument depicting one of the ships, the *Kalmar Nyckel* (Key of Kalmar).

Fort Delaware State Park: on Pea Patch Island in Delaware River opposite Delaware City; great pentagon-shaped fortress built in 1848–60; Civil War prison.

Grand Opera House: Wilmington; built in 1871 as part of Masonic Temple.

Henry Francis du Pont Winterthur Museum: in Winterthur; many period rooms of 1640–1840.

Indian River Inlet State Park: south of Rehoboth Beach along Atlantic Ocean; swimming, fishing.

John Dickinson Mansion: near Dover; home of the "penman of the Revolution," built in 1740.

Lewes: resort town at mouth of Delaware Bay; fishing and crabbing; Zwaanendael Museum, modeled after ancient Town Hall at Hoorn, The Netherlands.

Lums Pond State Park: near Kirkwood; fishing, swimming, picnicking.

Odessa: Corbit-Sharp House and Wilson-Warner House, 18th-century homes.

Old Drawyers' Presbyterian Church: near Odessa; fine old brick church dating from 1773.

Old State House: Dover; second oldest state house in U.S.

Old Swedes Church: Wilmington; oldest church in U.S. standing as originally built.

Prince George's Chapel: near Dagsboro; old country frame church erected in 1757.

Rehoboth Beach: resort on Atlantic Ocean; nation's "summer capital"; beach; boardwalk.

St. Anne's Episcopal Church: near Middletown; built 1768; altar cloth embroidered by Queen Anne.

Sussex County Court House on the Square: in Georgetown; built in 1839; handsome clock tower.

Trap Pond State Park: near Laurel; wooded recreation area; beautiful lake and stream; beaches; camping, boating, picnicking.

Valley Garden: near Greenville; landscaped gardens.

Welsh Tract Baptist Church: near Newark; built in 1746; Welsh bought land from William Penn in 1703.

BIBLIOGRAPHY FOR DELAWARE

Bleeker, Sonia. The Delaware Indians: Eastern Fishermen and Farmers (Morrow, 1953).

Bodine, A.A. Chesapeake Bay and Tidewater (Bodine, 1969).

Carpenter, Allan. Delaware (Children's, 1979).

Fagan, Michael. Beautiful Delaware (Beautiful America, 1980).

Federal Writers' Project. Delaware: a Guide to the First State (Somerset, 1938).

Fradin, D.B. Delaware in Word and Pictures (Children's, 1980).

Hoffecker, C.E. Delaware: a Bicentennial History (Norton, 1977).

Munroe, J.A. Colonial Delaware: a History (Kraus International, 1978).

Swindler, W.F. and Frech, Mary, eds. Chronology and Documentary Handbook of the State of Delaware (Oceana, 1973).

Weslager, C.A. Delaware's Buried Past: a Story of Archaeological Adventure (Rutgers Univ. Press, 1968).

All Fact Summary data are based on current government reports.

Delaware River Port Authority

The two giant spans of the Delaware Memorial Bridge tower over the Delaware River to connect Delaware with New Jersey at a point about three miles south of Wilmington. Each span is more than two miles long.

DELAWARE

COUNTIES

Kent, 98,219 .... C 4
New Castle, 398,115 .... C 2
Sussex, 98,004 .... D 6

CITIES AND TOWNS

Arden, 516 .... C 1
Ashland, 100 .... C 1
Ashley, 500 .... C 2
Bear, 200 .... C 2
Bellefonte, 1,279 .... D 1
Bellemoor, 275 .... C 2
Belltown, 500 .... E 6
Belvidere, 750 .... C 2
Bethany Beach, 330 .... E 6
Bethel, 197 .... C 6
Blades, 664 .... C 6
Bowers Beach, 198 .... D 4
Bridgeville, 1,238 .... C 6
Brookside, 15,255 .... C 2
Camden, 1,757 .... C 4
Cannon, 150 .... C 6
Canterbury, 150 .... C 4
Centerville, 800 .... C 1
Cheswold, 269 .... C 4
Christiana, 500 .... C 2
Clarksville, 350 .... E 6
Claymont, 10,022 .... D 1
Clayton, 1,216 .... C 3
Concord, 200 .... C 6

Dagsboro, 344 .... D 6
Delaware City, 1,858 .... C 2
Delmar, 948 .... C 7
Dover (cap.), 23,512 .... C 4
Dupont Manor, 1,059 .... C 4
Edgemoor, 7,397 .... C 1
Ellendale, 361 .... D 5
Elmhurst, 300 .... C 2
Elsmere, 6,493 .... C 2
Farmington, 141 .... C 5
Farnhurst, 1,110 .... C 2
Felton, 547 .... C 4
Fenwick I., 114 .... E 7
Frankford, 828 .... E 6
Frederica, 864 .... D 4
Georgetown, 1,710 .... D 6
Glasgow, 350 .... B 2
Greenwood, 578 .... C 5
Harbeson, 300 .... D 6
Harrington, 2,405 .... C 5
Hartly, 106 .... C 4
Highland Acres, 2,994 .... C 4
Hockessin, 950 .... C 1
Holloway Terrace, 1,466 .... C 2
Holly Oak, 1,140 .... D 1
Houston, 357 .... C 5
Kent Acres, 1,590 .... C 4
Kenton, 243 .... C 4
Kirkwood, 350 .... C 2
Laurel, 3,052 .... C 6
Leipsic, 228 .... C 4
Lewes, 2,197 .... E 5

Lincoln, 757 .... D 5
Little Creek, 230 .... D 4
Magnolia, 197 .... D 4
Marshallton, 1,240 .... C 2
Middletown, 2,946 .... C 3
Midway, 250 .... E 6
Milford, 5,366 .... D 5
Millsboro, 1,233 .... D 6
Millville, 178 .... E 6
Milton, 1,359 .... D 5
Minquadale, 1,774 .... C 2
Montchanin, 500 .... C 1
Mt. Pleasant, 149 .... C 2
Nassau, 150 .... E 5
New Castle, 4,814 .... C 2
Newark, 25,247 .... C 2
Newport, 1,167 .... C 2
Oak Grove, 109 .... C 6
Oak Orchard, 350 .... E 6
Ocean View, 495 .... E 6
Odessa, 384 .... C 3
Overbrook, 100 .... D 5
Port Penn, 300 .... C 2
Red Lion, 150 .... C 2
Rehoboth Beach, 1,730 .... E 6
Richardson Park, 2,600 .... C 2
Rising Sun, 2,176 .... C 4
Rodney Village, 1,753 .... C 4
Roxana, 250 .... E 7
Saint Georges, 450 .... C 2
Seaford, 5,256 .... C 6
Selbyville, 1,251 .... E 7

Slaughter Beach, 121 .... D 5
Smyrna, 4,750 .... C 3
Summit Bridge, 100 .... C 2
Thompsonville, 60 .... D 5
Townsend, 386 .... C 3
Viola, 167 .... C 4
Westover Hills, 1,250 .... C 1
Willow Grove, 200 .... C 4
Wilmington, 70,195 .... D 2
Wilmington (met. area), 523,221 ... D 2
Wilmington Manor, 9,233 .... C 2
Winterthur, 100 .... C 1
Woodside, 248 .... C 4
Wyoming, 960 .... C 4
Yorklyn, 600 .... C 1

OTHER FEATURES

Bombay Hook (isl.) .... D 3
Broadkill (riv.) .... D 5
Chesapeake and Delaware (can.) .... C 2
Christina (riv.) .... B 2
Delaware (bay) .... E 4
Delaware (riv.) .... C 2
Dover A.F.B. .... D 4
Henlopen (cape) .... E 5
Mispillion (riv.) .... D 5
Murderkill (riv.) .... C 5
Nanticoke (riv.) .... C 6
Rehoboth (bay) .... E 6
St. Jones (riv.) .... D 4
Smyrna (riv.) .... C 3

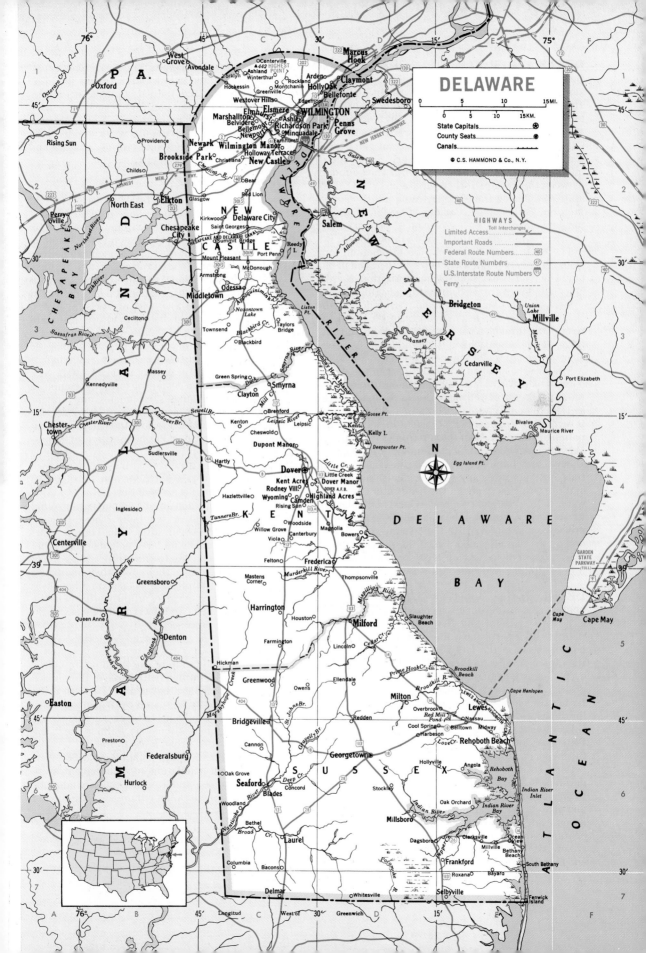

DELAWARE RIVER. The famous river that George Washington and his troops crossed on a stormy Christmas night in 1776 was the Delaware. The river flows through the rich and densely populated Middle Atlantic region of the United States. It rises in two branches on the westward slopes of the Catskill Mountains. These join to become one river at the New York-Pennsylvania boundary. For about 70 miles (110 kilometers) the river forms the boundary between these states. It then turns southward to separate New Jersey from Pennsylvania and Delaware. Trenton, Philadelphia, Camden, Chester, Wilmington, and other cities have grown on its banks. Finally the river empties into the broad Delaware Bay.

The Delaware is 280 miles (450 kilometers) long from the junction of its branches to the head of the bay. The river is navigable as far as Trenton, N.J. Its chief tributaries are the Schuylkill and Lehigh rivers.

Most spectacular of its scenic stretches is the Delaware Water Gap near Stroudsburg, Pa. There the river pours through a narrow gorge in the Kittatinny ridge of the Appalachian Highlands. The gorge is about three miles (4.8 kilometers) long.

The river has had an important part in the development of its basin since colonial times. Its navigable lower reaches first welcomed the ships that brought settlers to Pennsylvania, Delaware, and New Jersey. It carried the commerce that made Philadelphia the nation's first port. Waterpower from the Delaware aided the early development of industry in the area. Today this rich industrial region brings in raw materials and ships out many of its products on the river and the bay. Reservoirs on the headwaters impound water for the cities of the area. In 1961 the Delaware River Basin Compact—the first such federal-state project—was approved by the federal government and by the four states bordering the river. Its major objectives were to develop electric power, prevent water pollution, and control floods.

DELHI, India. A metropolitan area made up of the cities of Old Delhi and New Delhi, Delhi is particularly important because the latter is the capital of India. Delhi also occupies a strategic crossroads position in South Asia. From Delhi various Hindu and Muslim dynasties, and finally the British, ruled the Indian subcontinent. The city served as the capital of the British Indian Empire from 1912 until India became independent in 1947.

Between 1920 and 1930 the city of New Delhi was developed to the southwest of the old city according to the design of Sir Edwin Lutyens, a British architect and planner. Although physically the two cities have become integrated, they maintain certain distinctive characteristics.

New Delhi is a city of parks, tree-shaded boulevards, and mansions. Two main landmarks—the Secretariat and the Presidential Palace, known as Rashtrapati Bhavan—are located in New Delhi. The dividing line between New and Old Delhi is quite sharp and is marked by a transformation from spacious avenues and arcades of shopping centers in New Delhi to a complex arrangement of small streets studded with mosques, temples, monuments, crowded bazaars, and residential areas in the old city.

Physical Description

Situated 700 feet (210 meters) above sea level, Delhi lies between the Delhi Ridge and the west bank of the River Yamuna. The railway from Calcutta enters the city via a magnificent bridge across the Yamuna. Extensive growth following India's independence has led to the expansion of the city on and across the ridge.

Old Delhi is a traditional Indian city, crowded with people and bustling with commercial and industrial activity. Chandni Chowk—with its twisting lanes, narrow streets, and crowded bazaars—is the main commercial center of Old Delhi.

New Delhi, south of the old city, is a majestic colonial city that emerged as a new city when it became the capital of British India in 1912. New Delhi was planned in a geometric form that combines hexagons, circles, triangles, rectangles, and straight lines. Spacious roads, a magnificent residence for British viceroys (now the Presidential Palace), a circular council chamber (now Parliament House), imposing Secretariat buildings, a Western-style shopping center called Connaught Place with a large open space in the middle, officers' residences, and a garden-like environment are major parts of New Delhi.

Large-scale public housing developments surround the initial settlement of New Delhi. These developments, which were begun after India became independent in 1947, make up large neighborhoods that are segregated according to the rank of the government employees living in them. Wealthy Indians and diplomats, for example, are housed in Chanakyapuri, the diplomatic enclave; military officers in the Dhaulakaun complex; and lower middle-class workers in the Vinay Nagar section.

People

In 1981 the population of the Delhi metropolitan area was about 5.5 million, with three million males and 2.5 million females. Between 1971 and 1981 the population of the city increased by 57 percent. With an average density of about 11,000 persons per square mile (4,200 per square kilometer), Delhi is one of the most densely settled urban areas in India.

In 1941 the area's Hindu population, at 53.2 percent, and Muslim population, at 40.5 percent, were reasonably balanced. India's independence and partition in 1947 brought a large number of Hindu and

This article was contributed by Pradyumna P. Karan, Professor of Geography, University of Kentucky; author of numerous articles and books on South Asia.

Sikh refugees from Pakistan. These refugees filled a vacuum left by Muslims migrating from India to Pakistan. The Hindu proportion of the population rose to 82 percent by 1951. Sixty-two percent of Delhi's population in 1951 was classified as refugee. The change in the religious composition was followed by an enormous increase in the overall population: 106 percent in the period 1941 to 1951, 64 percent in the next decade, and 53.9 percent between 1961 and 1971.

Interestingly, while the suburbs of Delhi were expanding in response to the population growth, the highly constricted old core of the city became even more overcrowded. Today more than 1,000 persons per acre (400 per hectare) live in some Old Delhi neighborhoods, called mohallas.

More than 84 percent of Delhi's population in 1984 was estimated to be Hindu; Muslims comprised about 7 percent, and Sikhs made up 8 percent. Other religious groups in Delhi are Christian, Jain, and Buddhist. More than 62 percent of Delhi's population was classified as literate in the 1981 Indian census. The government has given priority to power development, water supply, sewage disposal, and housing to meet the needs of the growing population.

Culture, Education, and Recreation

Delhi is a major cultural and educational center. Many historic monuments depict various periods in India's history. The most important of these historic sites, dating to the early 16th century, are: Qutab Minar, Asoka Pillar, Purana Qila, Nizam-ud-din's shrine, the Lodi Tombs, Hauz Khas, and Safdarjang's Tomb. Cultural and historic sites belonging to the Mughal period, from 1526 to 1857, include Humayun's Tomb, Red Fort, and Jama Masjid, or Mosque. Among the historic monuments of the contemporary period are the India Gate, Parliament House, the Presidential Palace, the Lakshmi Narayan Hindu Temple, Rajghat, and Connaught Place.

In the National Museum one can see a wide variety of India's and Central Asia's artistic treasures, including the 5,000-year-old relics of the Indus Valley civilization. Also housed there are Hindu, Jain, and Buddhist sculptures in stone, bronze, and terra cotta from the early and medieval periods of Indian history. The museum also contains a fine collection of paintings of the Mughal, Rajput, Deccani, and Pahari schools; ancient jewelry; and painted pottery. The National Art Gallery, known as Jaipur House, exhibits the works of modern Indian artists.

Other cultural facilities include the Hall of Nation Builders, a kind of national portrait gallery, located on the spot where Mahatma Gandhi was assassinated, the Nehru Memorial Museum, Red Fort Museum, Tibet House (for Tibetan antiquities and religious objects), and the Museum of Natural History.

The goals of India's developmental plans are an adequate supply of food, health conditions equal to the best that modern medicine can provide, and high technological and industrial production. Accomplishing these goals requires advanced professional

Barbara Klutinis—CLICK/Chicago

The Central Secretariat Building complex in New Delhi houses many of India's government offices.

and technical education, particularly in the fields of agriculture, medicine, and technology. With more than 62 arts and sciences colleges and 17 colleges of engineering and technology, Delhi has emerged as an important center of professional and technical education in India. Among the major institutions are the Indian Agricultural Research Institute, the University of Delhi, Jawaharlal Nehru University, the All India Institute of Medical Sciences, and the Indian Institute of Technology.

Economy

Many people in Delhi work for the government. Many are also employed in wholesale and retail trade as well as in a variety of industries. Since the 1950s industry has grown in Delhi. Approximately 450,000 persons worked in industry in the early 1980s.

Delhi's industrialization started toward the end of the 19th century, but World War II, and later India's independence, accelerated industrial development. There were neither zoning regulations nor a comprehensive plan for urban development, so most industries located wherever space could be found. This led to overcrowding, traffic bottlenecks, and unhealthy living conditions.

Newer industries, though, are located on the Najafgarh Road and the Kalkaji Road, west of the Delhi–Mathura railroad. Some older industrial plants such as the Delhi cloth mills, Birla cotton and weaving mills, and the Ganesh flour mills are also in this area. Electronic goods, electrical appliances and accessories, lathes and drilling machines, small tools, paints and varnishes, rubber goods, plastic goods, auto parts and batteries, precision instruments, television sets, radios, and transistors are now manufactured in Delhi.

Different areas of Delhi specialize in different trades. The area around Chandni Chowk, for instance, is the center for textiles and general merchandise. The market in which copper and brass utensils are sold is in the Chawri Bazaar, which also houses a market for hardware. The Khari Bhawli area and adjoining streets specialize in dry fruits, pickles, spices, and other condiments. Lal Kuan Bazaar is noted for building materials, while Sadar Bazaar deals in wholesale hosiery, glass and china, and general merchandise. Silverware is marketed in Dariba Kalan, while the bullion market is localized in Chandni Chowk. Major Indian and foreign banks have branches in Connaught Place, which is New Delhi's chief shopping area.

Tourism has grown into a major activity. Foreign as well as Indian airlines have offices in New Delhi. Delhi is easily reached through the network of national railways, highways, and air transport systems. The main railroad station is located in Old Delhi, from which railway lines radiate to Punjab, Uttar Pradesh, Bombay, Calcutta, and Madras. The Delhi airport is at Palam, to the southwest of the city.

Government

Under India's constitution, Delhi is a union territory. It is administered by the president of India through an appointed administrator designated as lieutenant governor. Delhi has a metropolitan council, which can make recommendations, and an executive council. The entire metropolitan area is covered by three local governments—the Delhi Municipal Corporation, the New Delhi Municipal Committee, and the Delhi Cantonment Board.

The Delhi Development Authority is responsible for planning and implementing a 20-year Delhi master plan. More than 21,555 acres (8,723 hectares) have been developed for residential, industrial, and commercial uses.

History

The Delhi area, where the northernmost spur of the Aravalli Hills, known as the Delhi Ridge, meets the Yamuna River, has been the site of one great city after another. The earliest of these was the city of Indraprastha, founded in prehistoric times on the right bank of the Yamuna as the capital during the Mahabharat period. About 100 BC Raja Dilli of the Mauryan Dynasty rebuilt the town, and later Delhi would be named after him. In AD 1052, Anangpal, a Rajput chief, built Delhi. In the wake of the changing regimes of different dynasties of the Delhi sultanate and the later various Mughal emperors, as many as ten new cities were built between 1288 and 1648.

Mughal Emperor Shah Jahan rebuilt the city Shahjhanbad on the present site of Old Delhi, surrounding it with fortifications. He also built the Jama Masjid, or Mosque. Soon afterward he was deposed and imprisoned by his son Aurangzeb, who brought Delhi to its period of greatest glory. Delhi's decline began with Aurangzeb's death in 1707.

In 1739 the city was attacked by Nadir Shah, a Persian, who made off with the fabulous Peacock Throne. Alamgir II, the last real emperor, was murdered in 1759. Shah Alam, who assumed the title of emperor, was unable to establish his authority. Delhi became the alternate prey of Afghans and Marathas

until 1771, when the Marathas helped to maintain an emperor. In 1788 a Maratha garrison occupied the palace permanently. Shah Alam remained a prisoner in the hands of the Marathas until the British conquest of Delhi.

On March 14, 1803, Lord Lake, having defeated the Marathas, entered Delhi and took Shah Alam under his protection. Delhi was administered by the British in the name of the emperor, but only the palace remained under the emperor's rule. The last of the Delhi emperors was Bahadur Shah II. He was emperor during the first struggle for India's independence, the mutiny of 1857. Delhi was restored to British civil administration on Jan. 11, 1858.

In 1912 Delhi became the capital of India once more, replacing Calcutta. Delhi is now the nerve center of independent India. Population (1981 census), Old Delhi, 4,865,077; New Delhi, 271,990; metropolitan area, 5,350,928.

SCALA/Art Resource

'The Resurrection', a glazed terra cotta lunette, was created by Luca della Robbia for Florence's cathedral.

DELLA ROBBIA FAMILY.
Members of the Della Robbia family were artists and craftsmen who lived in Florence, Italy, during the 15th and 16th centuries. They were especially skilled at creating sculptured figures of glazed terra cotta, enameled in various colors. Their shop in Florence supplied ceramic works to cathedrals, palaces, and guildhalls all over Italy.

Luca della Robbia

Luca della Robbia (1400?–82) was the first and finest artist of this talented family. He may have started his training as a goldsmith, but he early turned to marble as his material. In 1431 he created a marble "singing gallery"—a group of singing boys carved in low relief—for the cathedral in Florence.

His first terra-cotta work was at the church of Saint Mary in Peretola. Here he used a glazed terra cotta in three ways—as a background for marble reliefs; as reliefs against a marble background; and as a mosaic in combination with marble. His glaze was a mixture of tin, litharge, antimony, and other minerals. This was applied to the modeled clay figure that was then fired in a kiln. The glaze was milky white, varied with a glowing blue. Other colors were occasionally added. Generally regarded as the best of Luca della Robbia's terra cottas are the glazed reliefs of the 'Resurrection' and the 'Ascension' in Florence. He also created bronze doors, medallions, and altarpieces.

Andrea and His Sons

Andrea della Robbia (1435?–1525?) was Luca's nephew and pupil. He entered his uncle's shop as a boy and soon mastered the craft.

Andrea experimented with the use of colors and with rich ornamentation, especially garlands of fruit and flowers to frame his low reliefs. His best-known work is the decoration of the Loggia dei Innocenti in Florence. Under Andrea's management the Della Robbia shop became a kind of factory where workers and apprentices turned out large quantities of terra-cotta work of various kinds, now called Della Robbia ware.

Andrea's two sons, Giovanni (1469–1529) and Girolamo (1488–1566), carried on the family tradition. On the death of his father in 1525, Giovanni assumed control of the family workshop. His early works were executed in collaboration with or under the strong influence of his father. Giovanni's most ambitious work was a frieze with representations of the works of mercy on the hospital Ospedale del Ceppo at Pistoia, done between 1525 and 1529. He evolved a coarser, more pictorial style in which color became more important than composition.

The younger brother, Girolamo, was trained in Andrea's studio and collaborated with his father and brother until about 1527. But he also developed a separate career as an accomplished architect. It was this and his reputation for terra-cotta work that led to his being invited to France to work on the terra-cotta decoration of the Chateau de Madrid. After the death of King Francis I in 1547, Girolamo returned to Florence for 12 years. In 1559 he went back to France to resume work on the Chateau de Madrid. He also was employed on the chateau at Fontainebleau not far from Paris. The superintendent of royal buildings later asked him to work on the monuments of Francis II and Catherine de' Medici at Saint Denis, where many of the royalty of France are buried. Girolamo died in France in August 1566. (*See also* Pottery and Porcelain; Sculpture.)

DELMONICO, Lorenzo (1813–81). For nearly 50 years Lorenzo Delmonico operated the foremost and largest restaurant in the United States. No one in the 19th century contributed more than he did to make the concept of fine restaurant dining a reality in America.

Delmonico was born in Marengo, Switzerland, on March 13, 1813. He went to New York City at the age of 19 and worked with relatives in a catering firm. He soon opened a restaurant that offered an unusually large menu, including a great variety of European dishes never before served in the United States. He also served American wild game and fish as well as a selection of wines.

The success of the restaurant inspired him to open branch restaurants, including the internationally renowned Delmonico's on the corner of Broadway and 26th Street in New York City. His organization also operated its own farm in nearby Brooklyn and temporarily ran a hotel. His fame as a restaurateur brought many imitators, and between them they helped make New York City one of the primary culinary centers in the world. He was largely responsible for making the restaurant an accepted and popular institution. He died at Sharon Springs, N.Y., on Sept. 3, 1881.

DELPHI. In ancient Greece, the people turned to their gods for answers to questions and problems that worried them. Both the god's answer and the shrine where worshipers sought his advice were called an oracle. The most celebrated oracle was at Delphi on the south slope of lofty Mount Parnassus. Here a sacred stone supposedly marked the exact center of the Earth. Nearby flowed the sacred fountain of Castalia. Over the centuries, several temples were built at Delphi to Apollo, the god of light, of poetry and music, and of prophecy. Inquirers came from every part of Greece to learn the future through the wisdom of Apollo. (*See also* Apollo.)

In ancient days there was a crack in the earth here. From it came volcanic vapors with strange powers. A priestess, called the Pythia, sat on a tripod placed over this cleft. After first bathing in a sacred stream and eating the leaves of the sacred laurel, she breathed the intoxicating vapors and went into a trance. The weird sounds she spoke were taken down by priests and put into verse form. They were given to the

The theater and temple of Apollo are among the ruins that can be seen today at Delphi, Greece.

Toni Schneiders

inquirer as the revelations of Apollo. These oracles were worded to suggest two or more meanings.

Everyone who asked advice at Delphi brought gifts. Great treasuries were built to hold the offerings presented by kings, states, and individuals. Many were of pure gold or silver. Enemies who conquered Greece looted these treasuries. Nero, the Roman emperor, is said to have stolen 500 statues; still 3,000 remained. Modern excavations have uncovered temple ruins, pieces of sculpture, and historic inscriptions.

The oracle at Delphi was consulted before any important step was taken in affairs of state. Thus it exerted a powerful influence on the history of the Greeks. The common reverence for its words, together with the Pythian festivals and games held near the shrine every four years, made for unity in the political and religious life of the Greek world.

The Delphic oracle, the most famous, was only one of several Greek oracles. The oldest was that of Zeus at Dodona, in Epirus. Here Zeus was believed to speak through the rustling of the leaves of the sacred oak tree. There were also oracles in Rome and in Egypt, Babylonia, and other countries.

DELTA. The Greek equivalent to the English letter "D" is Delta: In print it appears as an equilateral triangle (**Δ**). The ancient Greek historian Herodotus gave the letter's name to the similarly shaped low-lying plains composed of sediment deposited at the mouths of rivers.

Rivers often carry large amounts of soil, sand, and other suspended matter in their waters. When a stream runs swiftly, its strong current erodes the earth from the banks and carries it along with the current. As the river slows, some of this sediment settles. When a river flows into the sea, its current is abruptly slowed, and the sediment tends to drop faster than when the river is flowing freely between its banks. Over the centuries this sediment builds up into generally fan-shaped plains.

As the delta grows, the course of the river becomes impeded by the buildup of sediment. The river then splits into a network of smaller branches called distributaries before it empties into the sea.

Herodotus was observing the Nile Delta in Egypt when he gave this landform its name. Not all deltas,

National Air Survey Center, Corp.

The intense cultivation of the Nile Delta makes it stand out from the surrounding desert in a photograph from space.

however, are triangular in shape. There are three main types, each determined by waves, currents, flood conditions, geological formations, and other factors. An arcuate delta is essentially triangular—the Nile Delta is the best-known example. A bird-foot delta consists of projections built out along river branches as they flow toward the sea; the Mississippi Delta at New Orleans is representative of this type. A cuspate delta, such as that of the Tiber River in Italy, is made up of two cusps, or horns, similar to breakwaters extending the river channel.

Deltas form most readily where a river carries a heavy load of suspended matter and where the sea is calm. Seas with strong tides and shore currents tend to wash away the sediment as fast as it is deposited. The Amazon River has a large underwater delta, but tides and waves keep the deposit from reaching sea level. Deltas are not present in regions such as the Atlantic Coast of North America where the land has sunk or subsided in recent geologic times. The Saint Lawrence and Hudson rivers have bays called estuaries instead of deltas at their mouths.

The total land area comprising a delta may be enormous, sometimes tens of thousands of square miles. The Ganges–Brahmaputra river system of Bangladesh has the largest delta in the world, followed by the Mekong Delta in Vietnam.

Deltas have been of great significance to mankind since prehistoric times. The silts, sands, and clays deposited by floodwaters have proved extremely fertile. As human agricultural ingenuity increased, large civilizations emerged and flourished in the deltaic plains of the Nile, Tigris-Euphrates, Indus,

MAJOR DELTAS OF THE WORLD

River system	Country	Area (sq mi)	Area (sq km)
Ganges–Brahmaputra	Bangladesh	23,000	59,600
Mekong	Vietnam	19,300	50,000
Niger	Nigeria	14,000	36,300
Mississippi–Missouri	United States	10,100	26,200
Lena	Soviet Union	10,000	25,900
Orinoco	Venezuela	9,500	24,600
Nile	Egypt	7,800	20,200
Irrawaddy	Burma	7,700	19,900
Río de la Plata–Paraná	Argentina	5,500	14,200

and Huang rivers (*see* Ancient Civilization; Indus Valley Civilization). The huge Ganges–Brahmaputra delta region has supported large farming populations for centuries. A large part of the fertile farm land of The Netherlands, as well as the country's cities, lies on the delta of the Rhine River.

Mazes of interconnecting waterways common in a delta provide natural avenues for both communication and trade. River mouths give seagoing vessels access to interior ports, and many of the world's great port cities are located in delta plains. Alexandria in Egypt and New Orleans in Louisiana are both flourishing examples.

The majority of the world's delta areas have not been exploited to their full economic potential. The Mekong Delta is the rice bowl of Southeast Asia, but present agricultural practices, combined with political upheaval, do not allow maximum utilization of this fertile region. Other large tropical deltas, such as the Orinoco and the Niger, are virtually untouched.

DE MILLE, Agnes (born 1909).

Ballerinas often seem fragile and dainty, but dancer-choreographer Agnes George de Mille had her first hit playing a cowgirl. She went on to choreograph not only ballets but musicals like 'Oklahoma!' and 'Carousel', and her use of folk themes formed the basis for a distinctly American dance style.

De Mille was born in New York City and then moved with her family to Hollywood. She received a degree in English from the University of California at Los Angeles in 1926 and spent the years 1929 to 1938 touring the United States and Europe staging her own humorous mime–dance concerts. In 1940 she became a choreographer for what is now the American Ballet Theatre. She composed many works for that company, including a dance about Lizzie Borden, 'Fall River Legend', first performed in 1948.

In 1942 de Mille choreographed 'Rodeo' for the Ballet Russe de Monte Carlo. This very American ballet includes tap dance as well as bronco-riding and steer-roping movements. On opening night it received 22 curtain calls, and de Mille was truly on her way. Rogers and Hammerstein asked her to choreograph

Agnes de Mille and her partner Yurek Lazowski appeared in 'Three Virgins and a Devil' in 1955.

Fred Fehl

their Broadway musical 'Oklahoma!', opening in 1943, in which she made dance an essential part of the story line for the first time in the American theater.

De Mille went on to choreograph many musicals, including 'Carousel' (1945) and 'Brigadoon' (1947). She worked in television and film and formed the Agnes de Mille Dance Theater in 1953 and the Heritage Dance Theater in 1973. Her 11 books include 'Dance to the Piper', an autobiography published in 1952; 'To a Young Dancer' (1962), a handbook; and 'Reprieve' (1982), an account of her recovery from a severe stroke.

DEMOCRACY.

The word democracy comes from two Greek words—*demos,* meaning "the people," and *kratos,* meaning "authority" or "rule." A democracy means literally "rule by the people." Any government, therefore, in which the people have supreme power is a democracy.

Throughout the history of civilization people have struggled to get the power to govern themselves. Some won it, only to lose it again. Some fought and kept it. There has been slow but steady progress toward democratic government for more and more people.

The history of civilization began in Western Asia and Egypt about 5,000 years ago. At that time democracy was almost unknown. Government was by autocracy—the unrestricted rule of one person.

In the great Asian nations, such as Babylonia, an absolute monarch ruled. He made laws by his own decrees and had the power of life or death over his subjects. The only curbs on him were custom, the fear of arousing rebellion, and the power of the great nobles. Some rulers, such as Sennacherib of Assyria, were cruel. Others, such as Cyrus of Persia, were generous and wise. (*See also* Babylonia and Assyria; Government; Persian History.)

In some parts of the world the heads of families governed some clans or tribes. Usually, however, people were ruled by a chief or king, sometimes aided by a council of elders. Throughout this period the people as a whole seldom had a voice in their rule.

Democracy Appears in Ancient Greece

The first major development of democracy took place in the city–states of ancient Greece (*see* City-State). Each was small, usually with a population of less than 10,000. Thus all the freemen could meet in a general assembly to speak and vote. This was direct democracy, the simplest form of democracy. There was no need for the more complicated representative democracy, in which one person is elected to speak for many others.

At first the city–states were ruled by kings. The king had to consider the opinion of an assembly and a council. Later, rule by a king gave way to rule by the principal families (*see* Greece, Ancient). This type of government was called an oligarchy. The name comes from two Greek words—*oligos,* meaning "few," and *archein,* meaning "rule." It thus means "rule by a few."

The Bettman Archive

Democracy began in the city-states of ancient Greece. Here members of the Council of aristocrats meet to discuss government affairs. They will send their decision to the king.

As more and more people demanded a greater share in the government, democracy gained strength. By about 500 B.C. the Athenians were virtually self-governing. They made their own laws and elected the magistrates.

In Athens all final authority was placed in the *ecclesia*. This was an assembly of the freemen. In peacetime the assembly took measures to keep any man from becoming supreme. Terms of office seldom ran longer than one year. Military power was usually divided among a number of generals, all equal in rank. Some of the major civil officers were chosen by lot, so that the weakest citizens had the same opportunity as the strongest. Political parties, in the modern sense, played no part in the government.

When the leaders were able and honest, this democratic government of the Greek city-states worked well. At other times the assembly acted like a fickle mob. Sometimes it yielded to evil or dangerous men. Demagogues could get control too easily under the system. Moreover, it lacked the power of healthy continuity. When a great monarchy arose in Macedonia, the Greek democracies crumbled before its onslaught (*see* Alexander the Great; Macedonia).

Roman Struggle for Freedom

Originally settled by a people called Latins, Rome was conquered around 600 B.C. by the Etruscans (*see* Roman History; Etruscans). In 509 B.C., the Romans expelled the Etruscan kings and later established what has become known as the Roman Republic.

Thereafter two consuls were chosen each year by the *comitia curiata*. This was an assembly of all the fighting men. The consuls administered the laws. Even then, however, the government was not a true democracy, for most members of the comitia curiata were *patricians*—members of the wealthy class. The comitia curiata divided its power with the Senate. This was also made up of patricians.

The common people of Rome, the *plebeians*, gained some victories in self-government. Rome, however, never achieved as much democracy as Greece. The Senate became the most powerful body in the nation.

As Rome extended its conquests powerful military commanders arose. At last, in 48 B.C., the greatest of them, Julius Caesar, overthrew the power of the Senate (*see* Caesar). His triumph led to the establishment of the Roman Empire. Except among the Germanic tribes of northern Europe, whose kings were guided somewhat in their policies by the assent or disapproval of their warriors, democracy appeared dead. (*See also* Government.)

Free Cities of the Middle Ages

Centuries passed before democracy revived. In the early Middle Ages democracy as we know it was practically unknown. Early medieval government rested on feudalism, which was a system of aristocracy (*see* Feudalism; Middle Ages).

Gradually democracy began to rise in the cities of Western Europe—in France, Germany, and England. At first cities were usually governed by a feudal lord or a great churchman. Gradually many towns attracted large numbers of artisans and merchants. They wanted peaceful trade, not feudal wars. They demanded charters to guarantee their business rights.

The kings held out, but by 1250 many towns all over Europe were partly or wholly free of their feudal lords. These towns were well on the road to true democracy. Their qualified citizens—the burghers or burgesses—elected aldermen who made the laws and mayors who enforced them.

There was an important difference, however, between most of these medieval cities and modern cities. In the medieval city the individual merchant, weaver, or ironworker counted for little. It was his trade or calling that was important. In the typical free city of this period the government was based on the different trades or industries, such as the merchant guilds and various craft guilds (*see* Guilds).

Democracy developed most fully in England. The English people had inherited democratic institutions from the Teutonic invaders who colonized Britain. The villages of the Teutonic tribes governed themselves by meetings of all the freemen. In England, such self-governing communities in early times combined into "hundreds." These were governed by a "hundred moot." This was a meeting made up of the priest, the reeve (steward), and four men from each township in the hundred. Above this was a "folkmoot," a tribal or national council. All England became a single Saxon kingdom. The king was aided by a national council of the chief men, called the Witenagemot.

After the Norman Conquest the towns rapidly became important. They revived the old Teutonic spirit of democracy. Henry I, who ruled 1100–35, granted London a charter. Other towns demanded and got similar charters. Then Richard I, to get the money he needed for his Crusade, sold charters to towns.

Citizens ponder a problem at a town meeting in the village of Njoornlole Ujamaa in the United Republic of Tanzania.

The spirit of democracy in these places was alert. In London, for example, special bodies of citizens frequently gathered in borough meetings to elect aldermen. They were also active in guild meetings. When the bell of old St. Paul's clanged, they all met in a single great town meeting, with their aldermen presiding. Every townsman could claim the right to be tried by his equals in the town court or "hustings." When danger threatened the city, the townsmen mustered their own army. In time town governments had as much power as nobles (barons) who ruled great domains or churchmen who controlled many parishes.

Magna Carta and Its Effect

Meanwhile, the English nation as a whole tended toward democracy. By force of custom, law, or local charters, both the people and the barons gradually won many rights. When King John tried to override them, the barons forced him in 1215 to sign the Great Charter (Magna Carta). This document restored the feudal privileges of the nobles. It included several clauses protecting townsmen and a few reforms of peasant conditions (see Magna Carta).

Democracy made another great advance in 1265. Until then the parliament was made up only of the barons, bishops, and knights of the shires. The knights had been summoned only occasionally since they were first called by King John in 1213. In 1265 Simon de Montfort called together a parliament in which the towns and boroughs were represented (see Montfort). The representation of the towns was made permanent and regular in the "model parliament" of 1295.

By the mid-1300's, Parliament had two bodies—the hereditary House of Lords (with the bishops) and the House of Commons (town members and knights of the shires). The Commons was democracy's great new arm. (See also Parliament, British; Parliament, Australian; Parliament, Canadian; Parliament.)

Parliaments Abroad and Britain's Power

Parliaments sprang up similarly in other European nations. Each of the early kingdoms in Spain had a Cortes, and members chosen by the towns sat in León as early as 1188. France had a States-General, in which burgesses of the towns also had representatives. Sweden had the Riksdag, to which even the peasant farmers sent their own members.

In none of these countries, however, did the parliament become so important as in England. By the time of Cromwell, in the 17th century, the House of Commons was so strong it overthrew the king and governed the whole country (see Cromwell). A little later Britain established ministerial government; that is, government by men controlled by Parliament and not by the king.

In the 18th century the House of Commons lost ground for a time. Under the influence of the king, it became more an aristocratic body than a democratic institution. This changed in the 19th century. Reform acts gave more people the right to vote for members of Commons. The climax was the woman's suffrage act of 1928. The House of Commons became one of the world's most democratic legislatures.

The Spread of Democracy

In the 19th century most of the civilized world seemed to be swept by democracy, or "government of the people, by the people, for the people." Even before the American Revolution the English colonies in North America had highly democratic forms of government. Rhode Island and Connecticut governed themselves almost entirely.

After the Revolution the United States was considered a leading democracy, although at first the government was somewhat of an aristocracy. Most state governments required voters to own property. By the mid-1800's, however, every male citizen supposedly had a vote and the right to hold office. This did not apply to most black men until the 15th Amendment (1870) to the Constitution guaranteed universal male suffrage. The 19th Amendment (1920) granted women the right to vote.

In France the revolution of 1789 overthrew the royal rulers and led to the establishment of a democracy. Both the French and American democracies took the form of a *republic*. A republic, in the modern sense, is a representative government based on free, popular election. There is no hereditary ruler or ruling class. Following the example of France and the United States, most Latin American countries became republics early in the 19th century. They had no training in self-rule, however, and so democracy was slow to develop (see Latin America; South America).

This is the annual opening of Norway's parliament (Storting). The king sits at the left. The Storting can override his veto.

Democracy spread too in another form—the constitutional monarchy. In Denmark, Norway, and Sweden—as in Britain—the rulers strictly abided by constitutional restrictions on their power. The freedom-loving peoples of those nations developed excellent democratic institutions.

Democracy Gains over Autocracy

The spread of democracy in Europe left only central and eastern Europe under *autocracy,* or rule by an absolute sovereign. The two great European autocracies were Germany and Austria–Hungary.

The overthrow of autocracy in Germany and Austria, following their defeat in World War I, made these countries republics. From the shattered Russian Empire arose the republics of Finland, Estonia, Latvia, Lithuania, and Poland. The republic of Czechoslovakia was carved out of Austria. A spirit of democracy appeared in the Balkans and in Turkey. Greater self-rule spread throughout the British Empire. Democratic ideas arose also in Asia.

Modern Dictators Crush Some Democracies

But rival systems arose. In Russia the overthrow of the imperial government brought an attempt to set up a democracy. A Bolshevik revolution in 1917, however, established a "dictatorship of the proletariat." The Bolsheviks became Communists in 1918, and the country became the Union of Soviet Socialist Republics, or Soviet Union (*see* Communism; Russian History). In Italy the constitutional monarchy gave way in 1922 to the Fascist dictatorship of Mussolini (*see* Fascism; Mussolini). Other countries—for example, Spain and Portugal—fell into the hands of "strong men," who ruled as despots.

These one-party regimes were called "totalitarian." The one that most menaced democracy was the Nazi government of Germany under the dictatorship of Adolf Hitler in 1933 (*see* Hitler). Hitler built Germany into a mighty military machine and forced concessions from the democracies, which sought to keep peace.

World War II

The extension of German aggression into Poland in 1939 plunged the democracies into World War II (*see* World War II).

Later Hitler attacked the Soviet Union. The Communist-dictated Soviets then fought on the same side as the democracies. The Fascist nations—Germany, Italy, and Japan—were defeated. The democracies, however, feared the rise of new dictators in lands that had known very little of freedom. To guard against new dictatorships, the democracies launched programs in Japan and Western Germany to teach the people democratic ways.

Communism Challenges Democracy

The Soviet Union came out of the war as a world power second only to the United States. Immediately it began to force Communism on neighboring nations. Its army formed a solid wall across eastern Europe from the Baltic Sea to the Adriatic. East of this "iron curtain" only Greece and occupied Austria remained democracies.

Communists took over the governments of Yugoslavia, Czechoslovakia, Poland, Hungary, Bulgaria, Romania, Albania, and East Germany and gained strength in Finland. The Baltic countries became "republics" of the Soviet Union—the Estonian, Latvian, and Lithuanian Soviet Socialist Republics (*see* articles on these republics).

Even in some of the democracies, especially in Italy and France, the Communist party increased in strength. In some democratic nations Communists worked secretly in efforts to undermine national strength and the democratic way of life. The United States, for example, took security measures against "un-American" activities.

Supported by the Soviets, Communism continued to make gains, especially in Asia. By 1950 Chinese Reds had seized control of vast China. In 1954 the

94

Communist Vietminh party conquered much of Vietnam. In 1959 Fidel Castro made Cuba a Communist state. (*See also* China; Cuba; Indochina; Vietnam.)

Russia claims that its system is the "only true democracy." This is not so. Like Fascists, Communists consider the state more important than the individual. Russia has a rigid dictatorship. It does not permit freedom of speech or freedom of the press. It discourages freedom of worship and indeed of religion itself. It permits only one political party, the Communist party. It virtually forces the people to vote, but usually the ballots carry only a single list of candidates. The government runs all business and industry and crushes any possible opposition to its policies. (For details, *see* Russia, sections on education and on government.)

Kinds of Democratic Government

The processes of democratic government have developed slowly. They are continually being changed to meet new conditions. For example, self-government may take the form of *direct democracy*. This is government by all the citizens meeting together. The growth of population now makes this impossible except for small units of local government. It exists in town meetings in parts of the United States and in the assemblies of the Swiss cantons.

Today the usual form of self-government is the *representative democracy*. In this the people elect persons to represent them in government matters. There are several types of representative democracies. One is the *parliamentary* system of Britain, Canada, and other sovereign states that are members of the Commonwealth of Nations.

Another type is the *presidential* system, used by the United States and most Latin American nations. A third type is the *executive council* system. Only Switzerland, which began it, uses the system today. Each system has advantages and disadvantages.

This man and woman are being shown how to use a voting machine. Voting is an important democratic right. Exercising that right is a major responsibility of a democracy's citizens.

Structure of the Democratic Systems

The parliamentary system began in England. It consists of an upper and a lower house. The cabinet is appointed, but the majority in parliament can replace it. When the cabinet and prime minister (or premier) lose the support of the parliament, a new popular election may be called. In this system the will of the people usually finds immediate expression. (For details, *see* Cabinet.)

The parliamentary system is unstable when there are three or more strong political parties. It is hard for a cabinet to get and hold a majority in parliament. France before the Fifth Republic is an example.

In the presidential system the government is carried on by a legislature and a president. They are largely independent of each other. Both hold office for a fixed term of years. This plan gives greater stability and safety than the parliamentary system, because the president and the legislature tend to check each other. Such a government, however, is often slow to act. Moreover, critics say that second-rate men, controlled by professional politicians, have a good chance of becoming president.

In the Swiss plan the people elect the legislature. This body chooses a small administrative council to execute the laws. The council has a fixed term of office, and its members do not have seats in the legislature. The president of the nation is chosen from members of the council (*see* Switzerland).

This plan works well for the Swiss. Success comes partly from the fact that Switzerland is a small country, and the people are highly literate. The little nation has, moreover, no extremes of wealth or poverty and few great problems. In 1952 Uruguay adopted a similar plan, but in 1966 it voted to return to the presidential system. Students of government are not certain that the Swiss council plan would do well in large and complex nations.

Responsibilities in Democracy

In all types of democracy some perils and difficulties have arisen. In all democracies government has to be carried on by the aid of political parties, and party bias can rise dangerously (*see* Political Parties). It causes unwise legislation, and sometimes even civil wars, as in Spain in 1936–39 (*see* Spain).

Another peril is the wrong use of money in popular government. Where the political parties must reach great masses of voters, as in all large democracies, the rival parties must spend huge sums. Sometimes it is used for bribery or other improper purposes. Another defect in large democracies is the difficulty of judging public opinion. During elections there are often so many confusing issues that it is hard to say just what the people have really decided.

The greatest danger, perhaps, is that in a democracy of many millions of people the government may lose touch with the masses. The men elected to office may try to please the political bosses and machines instead of the people.

An ancient marble statue of Demosthenes stands today in a Copenhagen museum.

Courtesy of the Ny Carlsberg Glyptotek, Copenhagen

DEMOSTHENES (about 383–22 BC). When Demosthenes was a youth in ancient Athens, no one would have believed that he would become the greatest orator of all time. He had a speech impediment, and when he addressed his first large public assembly, people laughed and jeered at his poor delivery.

Demosthenes was born into a wealthy family. He was orphaned when he was only 7 years old. His guardians so misused his estate that little was left when Demosthenes came of age. Seeking justice, he boldly pleaded his own case and won some damages.

He was not yet an outstanding speaker, however. To learn to speak distinctly, he talked with pebbles in his mouth. To strengthen his voice, he spoke on the seashore over the roar of the waves.

Demosthenes' rigid work was successful. By the time he was about 25 he had entered public life. He had won popularity and power when King Philip of Macedon was beginning the conquest of Greece. Demosthenes realized the peril. In eloquent appeals he urged his countrymen to unite and preserve their freedom. These powerful orations against Philip were known as philippics, a term still in use to describe any impassioned denunciation or criticism.

The Athenians were too late in heeding Demosthenes' warnings. Then he was falsely accused of taking a bribe. He was fined and imprisoned but escaped into exile. After his final effort to obtain freedom for Greece failed, he poisoned himself.

Demosthenes' greatest oration is entitled 'On the Crown'. He delivered it in 330 BC. It was a review and justification of his public life.

DEMPSEY, Jack (1895–1983). Regarded by many as the perfect boxer, Jack Dempsey, known also as the Manassa Mauler, held the world heavyweight boxing title from 1919 to 1926. The most popular fighter of his time, Dempsey attracted the first five million-dollar "gates," or attendance receipts, in boxing history.

William Harrison Dempsey was born on June 24, 1895, in Manassa, Colo. He began boxing in 1914 under the name of Kid Blackie. He had fought more than 80 professional fights by the time he was 24 and had compiled enough knockouts by 1919 to earn a fight with Jess Willard, the 37-year-old title holder. Dempsey attacked ferociously from the starting bell and knocked Willard to the floor seven times in the first round. Dempsey captured the title in the third round after Willard's side threw in the towel.

In 1923 Dempsey defended his title in New York City against the Argentine heavyweight Luis Angel Firpo. It was a wildly intense fight from the start and, after being knocked out of the ring in the first round, Dempsey won the fight in the second, thus successfully defending his title for the fifth time. For the next three years he fought only exhibition matches. In 1926 Dempsey lost the title to Gene Tunney in a ten-round decision fight. The two boxers met again one year later in Chicago in the famous "Battle of the Long Count." Dempsey missed his chance for a seventh-round knockout by standing over the fallen Tunney rather than going to a neutral corner of the ring, and Tunney recovered and won another ten-round decision. During the 1930s Dempsey competed in many exhibition fights but was never again a serious contender for the championship. He later became a successful restaurant owner in New York City and died there on May 31, 1983.

DENG XIAOPING (born 1904). Although he was twice a victim of political purges, Deng Xiaoping emerged as the most powerful leader of China in the years after the death of Mao Zedong (also spelled Mao Tse-tung). By the 1980s he had downgraded Mao's legacy and turned his country in the direction of economic development, unhindered by rigid Communist ideology.

Deng was born in 1904 to a wealthy family in Sichuan Province. At age 16 he went to Paris to study. While there he was befriended by Zhou Enlai (also spelled Chou En-lai), who was to become premier of China in 1949. In 1924 Deng returned home, where he joined the Chinese Communist Party, and then he was sent to the Soviet Union for further study from 1925 to 1926. Returning in 1926, he became active in the Communist movement led by Mao. He participated in the Long March of 1934 and 1935, when the Communists were forced to retreat to northwestern China by the Nationalist armies.

With the establishment of the People's Republic in 1949, Deng became a vice premier and general secretary of the Communist Party. During the Cultural Revolution of the 1960s, he was driven from office, allegedly for calling for "capitalist methods of production." He returned to power in 1973 as the chosen successor to Zhou Enlai, but, after Zhou's death in 1976, he was again dismissed from all government posts. In 1977 he returned to power and stifled opposition led by Mao's associates, the notorious "gang of four." By June 1981 Deng had arranged for a party resolution condemning Mao's policies as "tragic errors." In the Communist Party congress of 1982 he restructured the party and began to put China on the road to economic renewal.

Courtesy of the Danish Information Office

Christiansborg Palace in Copenhagen is the home of
Denmark's one-house parliament, the Folketing.

DENMARK

DENMARK. One of
the most prosperous na-
tions of Europe, Den-
mark is a small country
with few natural riches.
Its location on the North
Sea, however, makes it
easily reached by the in-
dustrial states of West-
ern Europe, and it is a

physical, cultural, and commercial bridge between
Scandinavia and Central Europe. Although it is dependent on foreign trade, Denmark has one of the
highest standards of living in the world.

Denmark proper is made up of a long peninsula
called Jylland, or Jutland; two large islands—Fyn,
or Fünen, and Själland, or Zealand; and 483 smaller
islands that dot the entrance to the Baltic Sea. People
live on 97 of those islands. A strip of land about
30 miles (48 kilometers) wide joins Jylland to the
German Plain at the south. The long peninsula at
its northern tip is 70 miles (113 kilometers) from
Norway across the Skagerrak, a rectangular arm of
the North Sea. The North Sea itself lies to the west.
To the east, between Denmark and Sweden, stretch
the strait called Kattegat, meaning "cat's throat,"
and the narrow strait called Öresund.

The Lowland and Its Climate

Denmark has an area of 16,633 square miles (43,-
081 square kilometers) without counting Greenland,
the world's largest island, and the Faeroe Islands,

located in the North Atlantic between Iceland and
the Shetland Islands. Both are self-governing parts
of Denmark. (*See also* Greenland.)

The surrounding sea makes Denmark's climate
quite mild for its location between 54° and 58° N.
latitude. The temperature averages 61° F (16° C) in
summer and 32° F (0° C) in winter. Periods of frost seldom last long. Rainfall is plentiful, with the greatest
monthly amounts occurring in August and October.

The Jylland peninsula makes up two thirds of
the area of the country proper. The western side is
a broad plain of moor, heath, and sand. Swept by
winds, it is rimmed at the coast by dunes and low
cliffs. This part of the peninsula was all wasteland
at one time. As a result of the efforts of the Danish
Heath Society, a large part of it is now producing
grains, sugar beets, pasturage, and pine trees. The
middle of the peninsula is a wide strip of irregular
hills. The eastern shore is fertile and wooded with a
coast indented by shallow fiords, each with a small
town or fishing village at its head.

The harbor of Frederikshavn, at the northern end
of Jylland, is the sailing point for Sweden. Aarhus,
halfway down the east coast, is an important seaport
and Denmark's second largest city. The only city of
any importance on the west coast is Esbjerg, from
which food exports go to Great Britain.

The islands are fertile spots, alike in formation,
with low hills, tiny lakes, and sandy beaches. Even
the smallest ones are richly green and wooded by the
typical beech trees. The soil is of glacial origin, constantly moistened by the damp sea winds and fogs.

97

Just to the east of Jylland, across the Little Belt, by ferry or over the half-mile bridge, is the garden island of Fyn. Its largest city, Odense, is famous as the birthplace of the beloved writer of charming fairy stories, Hans Christian Andersen.

East from Fyn, 10 to 15 miles across the Great Belt, lies Zjälland, the largest of the islands and the seat of the capital city of Copenhagen. The city is the country's largest port, its only important industrial center, and the metropolitan area for more than a quarter of the population (*see* Copenhagen).

The two-mile Storstrom Bridge links Själland to the southern island of Falster. West of Falster is Lolland Island; east is Möen. Some 100 miles farther east is Bornholm Island, site of Denmark's deposits of brown coal and the kaolin used in making porcelain. These deposits were long thought to be Denmark's only minerals, but great salt beds were found elsewhere in the years 1946 to 1948.

Efficient Farming

The Danes were once primarily a farming people, but only about 8 percent of the workers now are farmers. Many are dairy or stock farmers. About three fourths of the land can be cultivated. Much of it is difficult to work. The soil is kept fertile by the use of fertilizers. The combination of mild climate, usable soil, skillful scientific farming, and government aid has made Denmark one of Europe's richest farming countries. Most farmers are small landowners. Laws forbid the merging of small farms into larger units.

Denmark has the most successful system of rural cooperatives in the world. They include nearly nine tenths of the farmers in the country. The cooperative societies pool capital and buy farm machinery. They handle the marketing of milk, butter, cheese, eggs, and bacon. They also help to keep members informed about the best agricultural methods.

Much of the farmers' prosperity depends upon pigs, cows, and chickens. These provide the bacon, eggs,

and dairy products for their export business. The crops of grain and vegetables are now raised almost exclusively for home use or to feed the livestock. Until the mid-19th century, grains and cereals were Denmark's largest exports. Then American competition made it impossible for the farmers to market these products profitably. Many of the farmers were ruined. They changed to stock and dairy farming.

Fishing and Industry

Fishing is a profitable occupation for many Danes. Some of the fishing villages are shining and modern; others are old and weathered. All along the coast fishermen are hard at work with boats and nets to bring in the plaice, or flatfish, herring, cod, eels, and other fishes that, with fish products, make up a large part of the country's food and exports.

Industry now provides more of the national income than does agriculture. Each year more people are employed in manufacturing and handicrafts. Artistic designers and skilled craftsmen turn out elegant modern silver goods, china and ceramics, textiles, and furnishings that are admired and widely bought abroad. The leading industries are iron and other metal manufacturing and the processing of foodstuffs. Also important are the paper and graphics industries, transport, footwear and clothing, wood and furniture, and mineral extraction industries.

People

The cities, even around the port districts, are so clean that they look as if they are carefully scrubbed every night. The buildings and streets are modern and well constructed. The most popular method of transportation is the bicycle. Here and there rise old castles, many built in the 16th century.

The Danes seem to have discovered a fine philosophy of living well and vigorously. They are happy, friendly, and helpful. The farmer and his family do most of the work on the land. Their home is equipped

Cows graze on a dairy farm near Aarhus, seaport and commercial center. Denmark's dairy exports are highly regarded.

Modern multistory apartment buildings provide housing for many residents living in a suburb of Copenhagen.

J. Allen Cash—Rapho Guillumette

Fritz Henle—Photo Researchers

The bronze statue of the 'Little Mermaid' by the Danish sculptor Edvard Eriksen perches on a rock in Copenhagen Harbor.

with central heating, telephone, and refrigeration. Most farms have low, white-plastered buildings built around small courts. They have either thatched or red-tile roofs. In front of the house, a neatly fenced flower garden grows in gay colors. A little summerhouse offers an outdoor dining room for use in the brief summer months, as the sun-loving Danes never stay inside when the weather is good.

Education and Social Welfare

The Danes have no racial problems. They are almost all of the same northern stock—tall and blond. Neither have they any racial prejudices. There are no extremes of wealth and poverty; there is almost no illiteracy, as education is compulsory.

An outstanding feature of Danish education is the system of folk high schools. Though called high schools, they are institutions of advanced education and part of the adult education movement. Their founding was inspired by the writer and teacher Bishop Nikolai Grundtvig (1783–1872). He believed that understanding and love of country would arouse his people to an active interest in their government. The schools specialize in Danish history, literature, folklore, and methods of democracy.

Denmark has kept in advance of many other countries in social legislation. Its government, a constitu-

tional monarchy with legislative powers delegated to the Folketing, or Parliament, was founded in 1849. Before the end of the 19th century, Denmark's laws had provided for old-age pensions, health and hospital insurance, and trade unions. The government also maintains the National Health Service. Its members give instruction in hygiene, nutrition, and related subjects. Living standards are so nearly uniform that it has been possible to organize these measures along similar lines for all the people. There is uniformity of religion also, as a large majority of the people belong to the established Lutheran church.

The principal universities in Denmark are the Copenhagen University, founded in 1479, and the University of Aarhus, opened in 1933. Since the days of the famous 16th-century astronomer Tycho Brahe, Denmark has produced many distinguished scientists. Perhaps the best known is Niels Bohr, world authority on atomic theory (*see* Bohr).

History

The ancient history of the Danes previous to the Viking period is founded on tradition and sagas. The Norse heroes were savage and warlike and loved fighting for its own sake. The Vikings were pirates whose galleys sailed to the shores of all the countries of the known world. They were a scourge to all the lands within their reach.

Although the "wild Danes" were mentioned in a document written in the 6th century, the first authentic historical record of these people dates from AD 800. From 800 to 1042 they constantly raided the British shores. They conquered and sent colonists to southern England (*see* Canute).

In 826 the missionary monk Ansgar brought the first Christian teachings to the wild northland. True Christianization of Denmark was not accomplished until the Viking period ended in the reign of Harold Bluetooth (960).

Under King Canute, Norway was conquered. After Canute's death the kingdom was in a state of chaos, with bitter jealousy and fighting among the nobles. The free Danes were forced to accept a feudal system under which they became serfs. Poverty and dissatisfaction were widespread.

With the reign of Valdemar I (1157–82) Denmark

The setting of Shakespeare's 'Hamlet', Kronborg Castle (left) was built about 1580 near the port of Helsingör (English, Elsinore) on the narrow Sound. There the play 'Hamlet' is produced each summer. At the right, adult students learn about their country's history, literature, government, and economics in one of the famous folk high schools of Denmark. The schools are institutions of higher learning designed to educate adults.

regained its power. The Danes conquered northern German territory as far as Hamburg. The Baltic became Denmark's sea. After the reign of Valdemar II (1202–41) the whole political structure of the nation again fell apart through internal strife and religious differences. It was not until the reign of Valdemar IV (1340–75) that the country became reunited. This monarch again made Denmark a great Baltic power. His work for the welfare of his people was carried on by his daughter, Margrethe I.

Union of Kalmar

In 1397, during Queen Margrethe's reign, the Union of Kalmar was formed. This agreement gave each of the Scandinavian countries—Norway, Sweden, and Denmark— the right to manage its own affairs, but it united them against aggression. Sweden was never satisfied with the Union, as Denmark was the powerful member. After many quarrels it withdrew in 1523. Norway and Denmark kept the Union until 1814, when the Peace of Kiel ceded Norway to Sweden.

There were then 50 years

DENMARK

0   10   20   30   40 mi
0   10 20 30 40 50 60 km

CAPITAL ⊛   HIGH POINT △

INT'L BOUNDARY ------

Jutland peninsula and the islands are flat to rolling lowlands. The highest point is 568 feet. Bornholm Island, in the square at right, lies eastward in the Baltic Sea.

of peace. But in 1864 Denmark was attacked by Austria and Prussia and lost the provinces of Schleswig and Holstein. After that war the Danes were at peace until the German invasion in 1940. In the intervening period they built their present strong democratic structure. In World War I the country remained neutral, though its sympathies were with the Allies. After Germany's defeat, a plebiscite gave back to Denmark the northern third of the province of Schleswig.

Resistance to German Occupation

In April 1940, disregarding its nonaggression pact with Denmark, Germany sent in its troops. King Christian X asked his people not to resist. He remained in Copenhagen, regarding himself a prisoner. He refused to appoint a new cabinet, as the Germans wished him to do. Later, all semblance of authority was taken from the Danish government. The people's trade, homes, and lives were controlled by the invaders. Sabotage against the Germans increased. Trains were

wrecked, manufacturing plants were blown up, and general strikes were called.

The Danes saw few battles and little bombing, and Denmark fared better than other occupied nations. In 1947 Frederick IX succeeded his father, Christian X, as king. Denmark joined the European Recovery Plan in 1948 and ratified the North Atlantic Treaty in 1949. In 1953 it amended the constitution and changed the parliament to one body, the Folketing. Greenland was made part of Denmark and given representation in the Folketing, with full home rule granted in 1979. Denmark was one of the seven charter members of the European Free Trade Association formed in 1959. In 1967, faced with severe economic difficulties, Denmark applied for membership in the European Economic Community (EEC), based on Britain's acceptance into the organization. Membership became effective on Jan. 1, 1973. Frederick IX died in 1972, and his eldest daughter succeeded to the throne as Margrethe II.

Denmark Fact Summary

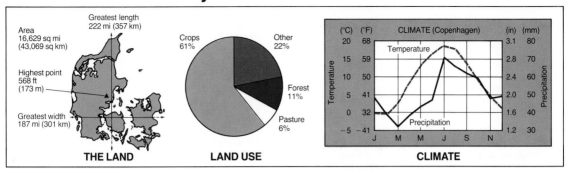

THE LAND

Area 16,629 sq mi (43,069 sq km)

Greatest length 222 mi (357 km)

Highest point 568 ft (173 m)

Greatest width 187 mi (301 km)

LAND USE

Crops 61%

Other 22%

Forest 11%

Pasture 6%

CLIMATE

CLIMATE (Copenhagen)

Temperature

Precipitation

Official Name: Kingdom of Denmark.
Capital: Copenhagen.

NATURAL FEATURES

Highest Peak: Yding Skovhöj.
Major Rivers: Gudenaa, Stor, Varde, Skjern.

PEOPLE

Population (1983 estimate): 5,013,412; 301 persons per square mile (119 persons per square kilometer); 83.9 percent urban, 16.1 percent rural.
Major Cities: Copenhagen (1,377,064, including metropolitan area); Aarhus (181,518), Odense (137,427), Aalborg (114,159).
Major Religion: Evangelical Lutheran.
Major Language: Danish.
Literacy: Virtually 100 percent.
Leading Universities and Colleges: Aarhus University, Copenhagen University, Odense University, Technological Institute (Taastrup).

GOVERNMENT

Form of Government: Limited constitutional monarchy.
Chief of State: Monarch.
Head of Government: Prime minister.
Legislature: Crown and Folketing (Diet) of 179 members elected for four-year terms.

Voting Qualification: Age 18.
Political Divisions: 14 counties: Aarhus, Bornholm, Copenhagen, Frederiksborg, Fyn, Nordjylland, Ribe, Ringköbing, Roskilde, Sönderjylland, Storström, Vejle, Vestsjaelland, Viborg; and one borough, Frederiksberg.
Flag: Red background with a white cross, the upright of the cross being left of center (*see* Flags of the World).

ECONOMY

Chief Agricultural Products: *Crops*—sugar beets, barley, potatoes, wheat. *Livestock*—chickens, pigs, cattle, ducks.
Chief Mined Products: Natural gas, limestone flux and calcareous stone, crude petroleum, unrefined salt.
Chief Manufactured Products: Metal products, food products, machinery, printed products, footwear and clothing, transportation equipment, electrical machinery, chemical products.
Chief Exports: General industrial machinery, equipment, and parts; dairy products and eggs; fish and shellfish; meat and meat products; specialized industrial machinery; textile yarns and products.
Chief Imports: Petroleum and petroleum products, motor vehicles, industrial machinery and equipment, textile yarns and fabrics, paper and paper products, electrical machinery and parts.
Monetary Unit: 1 krone = 100 ore.

After 1973 rising petroleum prices and the international depression hurt the economy and increased unemployment to about 10 to 14 percent. A tax bill controversy in 1973 led to the dissolution of the Folketing. Two new parties were elected, and Poul Hartling became prime minister. His Venstre party, under pressure to prevent further increases in unemployment, was defeated in 1975 elections. A Social Democratic government was in control until 1982, when economic problems forced Prime Minister Anker Jörgensen to resign. He was replaced by conservative Poul Schlüter. Population (1984 estimate), 5,112,100.

BIBLIOGRAPHY FOR DENMARK

Eriksen, Peter and others. Fünen—the Heart of Denmark (Nordic, 1980).
Linker, Robert, trans. Misfortunes of Ogier the Dane (Blair, 1964).
MacHaffie, I.S. and Nielsen, M.A. Of Danish Ways (Harper, 1984).
Wohlrabe, R.A. and Krusch, W.E. The Land & People of Denmark, rev. ed. (Harper, 1972).

DENTISTRY. As part of the medical profession, dentistry began in Egypt about 3700 BC. Modern dentistry emerged in the 19th century; and today it includes the study, treatment, and prevention of the diseases of the mouth, teeth, gums, and jaw bones.

Dental disease can affect a person's general health, and conversely, illness can cause dental problems. The most common dental problem is caries—that is, tooth decay or cavities. Tooth decay is caused by acids secreted by bacteria that adhere to the tooth surface in a film called dental plaque. The acids cause minerals in the tooth enamel to soften, allowing bacteria and food particles to enter. If left untreated, decay causes substantial loss of the tooth structure and can eventually lead to loss of the entire tooth.

Periodontal diseases involve the gingiva, or gums, and underlying structures, and they usually affect adults rather than children. Improper dental hygiene and lack of professional care promote periodontal disease. Gingivitis, or inflammation of the gums, is caused by bacteria. One type of gingivitis called trench mouth is a bacterial infection that occurs in people who have nutritional deficiencies or other infections.

Periodontitis is a bacterial inflammation at the base of the teeth including the ligament that holds the teeth to the bone and the bone itself. The main cause is the buildup of tartar, which irritates the gums and permits bacteria to become established. If untreated, the gums recede, the bone leeches away, and the teeth loosen and fall out. Periodontitis is the major cause of tooth loss in adults.

Most tooth decay and periodontal disease are preventable. Sodium fluoride has aided greatly in preventing tooth decay. The fluoridation of water with sodium fluoride began on a small scale in 1944 in the United States, and by the mid-1980s approximately 50 percent of the population drank fluoridated water. Community water fluoridation has reduced decay as much as 70 percent. Fluoride is also readily available in mouthwashes, in toothpastes, and in solutions that dentists apply directly to the teeth. Devices are sometimes inserted in the mouth by the dentist that release fluoride slowly over a period of months. Researchers are working actively on a vaccine to prevent tooth decay.

Prophylaxis, or prevention of tooth decay, involves thorough cleaning of the teeth by a dental hygienist. Abrasives and scraping tools are used to remove tartar and other material from the teeth. Tartar is formed from mineral salts that react with dental plaque and saliva to form crusty areas that cannot be removed by daily brushing. This buildup of tartar encourages tooth decay and irritates the gums. Prophylaxis should be repeated every six months.

Proper brushing, daily flossing between the teeth to remove food particles, and professional cleaning every six months are important for preventing both tooth decay and periodontal disease. Since sugar seems to promote tooth decay, a diet that is low in sugar is also recommended by most dentists.

The Dental Visit

The dental examination usually begins with X rays of the teeth to detect decay or other problems, such as an impacted tooth. An impacted tooth is one that is unable to erupt normally through the gum. The condition of the gums and other soft tissue is inspected, and previous dental work such as fillings, inlays, and bridges are examined for irregularities that need correcting.

When a tooth is found to have a cavity, the decay is removed with a high-speed drill before the cavity can be filled. Usually the area where the work is to be done is numbed first with a local anesthetic such as novocaine or procaine, and sometimes the anesthetic gas nitrous oxide is used. The material used to fill the cavity may be an inert, nontoxic mixture of silver and mercury, or it may be gold, porcelain, or plastic. This is packed tightly into the cavity and the outer surface is smoothed.

When decay reaches the pulp of a tooth and inflames the nerve, causing pain and infection, root canal, or endodontic, treatment is necessary. The pulp is removed from the tooth and replaced with metal, cement, or some other material. A crown, gold inlay, or filling material is used to close the cavity. Crowns, or caps, cover the entire tooth. These are used when the enamel of a tooth has been removed. Crowns are made of porcelain, plastic, or gold.

Pulling a tooth, or tooth extraction, is usually considered a last resort. Dentistry today strives to preserve the teeth and avoid dentures, if at all possible.

Some exceptions to this rule improve the health of the mouth. For example, an impacted wisdom tooth, or third molar, can crowd the teeth and cause discomfort. Such impacted teeth are removed by an incision in the gum. Teeth may also be removed when the jaw bone is too small to have room for all the teeth.

Dentures, either partial or complete, must be carefully fitted to the patient. Partial dentures can be used when some of the natural teeth remain in the mouth. When removable, they are held in place by clasps that attach to nearby teeth. A fixed bridge is permanently attached to natural teeth. Complete dentures are removable and are held in place, if properly fitted, without adhesive pastes and powders, which are irritating if used over long periods. Treatment of periodontal disease consists of scraping and scaling the gums and teeth, applying chemicals to retard further loss of tissue, and surgery.

Misaligned teeth can be slowly realigned by the use of removable plates, fixed metal bands, and wires, popularly known as braces. The best results are obtained when this treatment, called orthodontia, begins in childhood or adolescence, though adults are often helped by orthodontia as well.

Temperomandibular joint (TMJ) syndrome is a disorder of the hingelike joint between the upper and lower jaw. The cause can be malocclusion, or misaligned bite; injury; arthritis; or abnormal clenching or grinding the teeth. Symptoms of TMJ syndrome are varied and can include headache, popping of the jaw, sore teeth, ear problems, or neck ache. The treatment depends on the cause, but often a bite appliance worn at night will correct TMJ syndrome. When the cause is serious malocclusion, orthodontic treatment or jaw surgery is needed.

Specialization and Training

Dentistry includes so many techniques that most dentists specialize. Oral surgery is concerned with tooth extraction, jaw fractures, correcting malformation of the bones, and plastic surgery of the mouth. Orthodontics treats maloccluded teeth using wires and appliances. Prosthodontics builds dentures and bridges. Periodontics is the treatment of gums and underlying bones. Endodontics is concerned with protection or removal of the tooth's pulp in root canal therapy. Pedodontics is dental practice limited to treating children.

At least two years of college training is required before one can be admitted to a dental school in the United States. The basic 4-year dental school course includes both basic science and clinical study. Most of the 52 accredited dental schools in the United States are associated with medical schools. Graduates earn a degree of Doctor of Dental Surgery (DDS) or Doctor of Dental Medicine (DDM). Before a dentist can go into practice, he or she must pass a state licensing examination. The American Dental Association is a national professional organization that promotes research, publishes several periodicals, and evaluates drugs and materials. (*See also* Teeth and Gums.)

DENVER, Colo. Between the Missouri River and the Pacific coastal states, the largest city is Denver, a transportation, industrial, and commercial center and the capital of Colorado. Rich in gold rush history, it has developed from a mining town into a modern city that is recognized as both a business and a cultural area.

The state capitol, with its 272-foot (83-meter) gold-leafed dome, stands in downtown Denver. It was completed in 1895 in the Corinthian architectural style. Nearby is the Denver branch of the United States mint, which was opened in 1906. It produces about 75 percent of United States coins and is the country's second largest gold depository. Larimer Square is a turn-of-the-century neighborhood of landmark row houses. The Denver Center for the Performing Arts is a complex of theaters that includes performance halls for the Denver Symphony, plays, and touring Broadway productions.

There are many museums in the area, including the Denver Art Museum with a collection of art from around the world, the Museum of Western Art, and the Denver Museum of Natural History. The University of Denver is a private university founded in 1864. Other educational facilities include Regis College, founded in 1888, Colorado Women's College (1909), Iliff School of Theology (1892), Loretto Heights College (1918), Metropolitan State College (1963), and medical and extension centers of the University of Colorado. The Colorado School of Mines is in nearby Golden.

In addition to more than 200 parks in the city, about 50 parks extend into the foothills of the Rocky Mountains and are scattered over a wide scenic area. The city's nickname, "The Mile-High City," comes from its altitude, which is one mile (1.6 kilometers) above sea level. Winter Park is one of many ski areas in the vicinity. Denver has a crisp, dry climate and stands at the western edge of the Great Plains, just east of the Rocky Mountains' Front Range.

Denver has many industries and manufactured products. As the gateway to a major tourist area and the largest city in an extensive region, Denver's top industry is in services. These include retail and wholesale trade, eating establishments, transportation, and financial services. Major industries also include the manufacture of electronic and aerospace equipment. In addition there are several petroleum companies. With army bases in the vicinity, government is a big industry. Military and related installations in the area include Fitzsimmons Army Medical Center, Lowry Air Force Base, Rocky Mountain Arsenal, the Air Force Accounting and Finance Center, and the United States Air Force Academy. The Denver Union Stockyards is one of the largest livestock markets in the United States.

Denver was settled during the gold rush of 1859. It was a stopping point for trappers, traders, and Indi-

ans. Denver and the town of Auraria formed a single municipality called Denver, in 1860, and seven years later Denver was designated the capital of Colorado Territory. A fire destroyed the city in 1863, and a year later a flash flood swept away many buildings, including the city hall. Indian wars on the plains during the 1860s also held back the town's growth. Denver's citizens organized their own railroad company to build a line to connect with the Union Pacific at Cheyenne, Wyo. Denver citizens bought stock in the company, and the railroad line was completed in 1870. The Kansas Pacific Railroad reached Denver a short time later. An economic boom resulted, and the population increased from 4,759 in 1870 to 106,713 within 20 years. When Colorado was admitted to the Union in 1876, Denver became its capital.

Silver surpassed gold in economic importance during the 1870s and 1880s. A period of wealth began, and many people got rich almost overnight. The collapse of the silver markets in 1893, however, brought an end to much of the wealth. Banks failed, smelters shut down, and silver kings were suddenly poor. New gold discoveries helped prevent a major decline, and farming, cattle and sheep ranching, and commerce began to provide a more stable economy. Denver has a mayor-council form of government. Population (1980 census), city, 491,395; metropolitan area, 1,620,902.

DEPRESSION *see* BUSINESS CYCLE.

DE QUINCEY, Thomas (1785–1859). Although the collected writings of English essayist and critic Thomas De Quincey consist of more than 14 volumes, he published very little during his lifetime. He is remembered basically for one book, 'The Confessions of an English Opium-Eater', that brought him immediate fame when it was published.

De Quincey was born in Manchester, England, on Aug. 15, 1785. Feeling alienated from his family, he ran away from home at 17, first to Wales, then to London. He returned home in 1803, and his family sent him to Worcester College at Oxford, where he decided to become a writer. While in school he began taking opium to relieve the pain of neuralgia. By 1813 he confessed that he had become a "regular and confirmed opium-eater."

In 1817 he married Margaret Simpson, with whom he had already had a son. He continued to write a great deal, but his financial situation became desperate because he published almost nothing. At the invitation of the editors of *London Magazine*, he wrote two articles that later appeared as a book, 'The Confessions of an English Opium-Eater'. This account of his addiction was expanded into a fuller story of his life in an 1856 edition. He continued to take opium for the rest of his life, but his interest in the drug in the 1856 edition centered on its medical value and on its power "over the grander and more shadowy world of dreams."

De Quincey wrote on many other subjects in the years after the 'Confessions' was first published, including history, economics, and biography. His most important works were his autobiographical writings, literary criticism, and an unfinished book, 'Suspiria de Profundis' (Sighs from the Depths), a work explaining his philosophy of life as a result of his sufferings. His critical efforts focused on the poets John Milton and Alexander Pope as well as William Wordsworth and Samuel Taylor Coleridge, with whom he had been closely associated early in life. De Quincey died at Edinburgh on Dec. 8, 1859.

DESCARTES, René (1596–1650). Both modern philosophy and modern mathematics began with the work of René Descartes. His analytic method of thinking focused attention on the problem of how we know, which has occupied philosophers ever since. His invention of coordinate geometry prepared the way for advances in mathematics. Descartes offered one of the first modern theories to account for the origin of the solar system of the Earth.

René Descartes was born on March 31, 1596, at La Haye in the Touraine region of France. At the renowned Jesuit school of La Flèche, René was taught philosophy, the humanities, science, and mathematics. After getting a law degree at the University of Poitiers in 1616, he served as a volunteer in Dutch and Bavarian armies to broaden his experience. He resumed his study of mathematics and science when his duties permitted. Dissatisfied with the haphazard methods of science then in use, he began to doubt all but mathematical knowledge.

In 1619 Descartes arrived at the conclusion that the universe has a mathematically logical structure and that a single method of reasoning could apply to all natural sciences, providing a unified body of

A painting of René Descartes was done by Frans Hals, the noted Dutch artist, in 1649.

Cliché Musées Nationaux, Paris

knowledge. He believed he had discovered such a method by breaking a problem down into parts, accepting as true only clear, distinct ideas that could not be doubted, and systematically deducing one conclusion from another.

Descartes soon gave up army life. Living on private means, he spent several years traveling and applying his analytical system to mathematics and science. Finding, however, that the sciences rested on disputed philosophical ideas, he determined to discover a first principle, which could not be doubted, on which to build knowledge. Retiring to seclusion in Holland in 1629, he methodically doubted all accepted traditions and evidence about the universe and mankind. He could not doubt the statement "I think, therefore I am," and thus his first principle was established.

Descartes's major writings on methodology and philosophy were his 'Discourse on Method' (published in 1637) and 'Meditations' (1641). His application of algebra to geometry appeared in his 'Geometry' (1637). He also published works on his studies in natural science.

Descartes's work brought him both fame and controversy. In 1649 he was invited to teach philosophy to the queen of Sweden. Unused to the climate, he became ill and died in Stockholm on Feb. 11, 1650.

DESERT. Any barren region that supports very little life may be called a desert. The cold expanses of Antarctica, extreme northern Asia, and Greenland are therefore true, but cold, deserts. Most commonly, however, the term desert is used for regions that are barren because they are arid, or dry. Arid deserts receive little precipitation and are characterized by specialized plants that tolerate drought conditions and salty soils, and by distinctive land features.

Most desert areas get less than 5 inches (13 centimeters) of rain in a year. The rainfall is not only scanty but also uncertain. Records at Iquique in northern Chile showed no rain for a period of four years. The fifth year brought 0.6 inches (1.5 centimeters), making a five-year average of 0.12 inches (0.3 centimeter). At another time 2.5 inches (6.4 centimeters) fell in a single shower.

Desert Climates

Temperatures range widely in deserts. The greatest daily fluctuations occur in deserts near the equator. Temperatures above 100° F (38° C) occur regularly in summer. Azizia, 25 miles (40 kilometers) southwest of Tripoli, in Libya, holds the record with 136.4° F (58° C), while Death Valley, Calif., comes close with 134° F (56.7° C).

Winters are cold in middle-latitude deserts, located far from the equator. At Luktchin in central Asia the average temperature in July is 90° F (32° C), while the January average is 13° F (−10.6° C)—a range of 77 Fahrenheit degrees (42.6 Celsius degrees).

The temperature drops sharply in the desert night. Dry air, cloudless skies, and bare, dry earth furnish ideal conditions for the cooling of air after sunset.

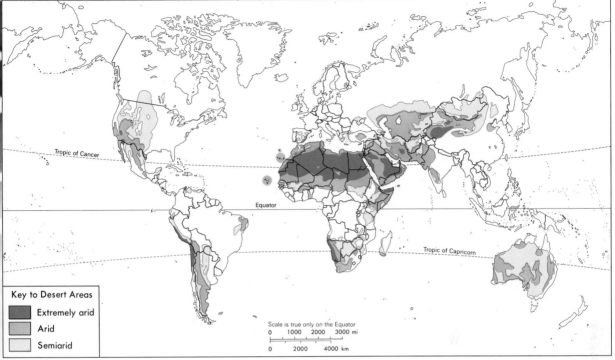

Adapted from FAO/UNESCO 'Desertification Map of the World', 1977

Key to Desert Areas
- Extremely arid
- Arid
- Semiarid

Scale is true only on the Equator
0   1000   2000   3000 mi
0   2000   4000 km

Most of the world's hot, dry deserts are between the Tropic of Cancer and the Tropic of Capricorn.

A 24-hour range of 25 to 45 Fahrenheit degrees (14 to 25 Celsius degrees) is common, and it may be as great as 60 to 70 Fahrenheit degrees (33 to 39 Celsius degrees).

In coastal fog deserts, such as the Namib of Southwest Africa/Namibia, relative humidity may be high, ranging from 60 to 100 percent. In interior deserts, however, relative humidity tends to be low, ranging from 5 to 15 percent. Such deserts are windy places. Travelers constantly struggle against wind and sand. The air is often dark with a fine dust that fills the eyes, nose, and throat. Cloudiness is rare, and the sunlight reflected from the bare earth is blinding. The hot, dry air evaporates moisture rapidly. In the Sonoran Desert a year's possible evaporation amounts to 100 inches (254 centimeters). This is about 20 times the rainfall. Additional moisture evaporates as it rises from under the ground.

Land Forms of Desert Regions

Desert areas differ greatly in the appearance and nature of their surface features, which range from mountains to plateaus to plains. These diverse arid landscapes occupy about 11,500,000 square miles (29,785,000 square kilometers) of the continental masses of the Earth—about 20 percent of the surface area—and occur on all continents except Europe. Although sand dunes are spectacular features of deserts, they are not as common or widespread as generally believed. In the deserts of the southwestern United States, dunes occupy less than 1 percent of the surface. In the most sandy of all deserts, the Arabian, dunes occupy only about 30 percent of the total area. If sand accumulations on plains are extensive and appear as a "sand sea," they are called ergs.

The more common type of desert consists of rugged mountains separated by basins called bolsons. The mountains receive most of the rains in downpours. As the water rushes down the steep slopes it cuts deep gullies and carries rock fragments, gravel, and sand to the bolson. These materials are freed from the water when it slows, and they are deposited as alluvial fans or cones. The rugged forms produced in this way, such as the terrain in Death Valley, Calif., are termed badlands. Sometimes the flood waters make a temporary shallow lake in the basin. The temporary lakes that form in basins with no outlet are called playa lakes. There are two general playa types: clay pan or clay flat playas in valleys where the water table, or underground water, is relatively deep, and salt pan or saline playas where the water table is within 10 feet (3 meters) of the surface. Those portions of playas that contain water throughout the year or that are kept moist are called salinas. In narrow basins, alluvial fans and badlands may extend to the edge of the playa. In broad valleys there is a surface of low relief and gentle downward slope that occurs between the playa and other alluvial fans of the mountain front. Such a surface is called a desert flat, or llano.

Other deserts consist of rocky plateaus, called hammadas, separated by sand-filled basins, or ergs. Here differences in altitude are usually slight. Many hammadas are broad, flattish, dome-shaped areas.

Where streams or wind wear away the weaker rocks, strong rock formations stand out boldly as mesas or cuestas. Pinnacles, needles, and arches carved in colored rocks lend fantastic beauty to the deserts of the American Southwest. Gullies are cut deep into the hammadas by the wearing force of the torrents. Gullies are known as wadis in Arabia and arroyos in the Southwest.

Water and Drainage in the Desert

People can live and grow crops in the desert only at places where they can get water, called oases. In some spots ordinary shallow wells reach the water table, but usually ground water lies at greater depths in deserts than in humid lands. In alluvial fans the water sinks deep into the porous material, but it may be reached by a well at the tip of the fan. In the wadis, ordinary wells can usually tap a supply of good water. Oasis settlements therefore are most often found where wadis are numerous. Ergs into which many wadis drain may have a water supply. Desert shrubs in the hollows between the dunes signal its presence. Deep artesian wells may be bored where the rock structure holds water under pressure (*see* Water). In some oases an artesian spring flows through a crack in the rock.

Streams that rise in rainy regions outside deserts bring the most generous supply of water for irrigation. All the large deserts except those of Australia are crossed by these so-called exotic rivers. The largest and best known of them are the Nile in Egypt, the Tigris and Euphrates in Iraq, the Indus in Pakistan, and the Colorado in the United States. (*See also* articles on these countries and rivers.)

Desert soils are usually productive when given water. They are coarse textured and highly mineralized. Most widely cultivated are the water-transported soils of flood plains and alluvial fans (*see* Soil).

Plants and Animals of Arid Lands

Few parts of the desert are entirely barren. Where water seeps toward the surface, a great variety of plants spring up. After a rain low shrubs and grasses come to life. At blooming time, the plants are fragrant and bright with color. They grow quite far apart, instead of providing complete ground cover.

Desert plants differ in the ways they adapt themselves to arid places. Those that depend on the rain sprout when it falls, bloom quickly, ripen their seed in a few days, then wither and die. Others depend upon underground water and have long root systems. Various adaptations of the leaves prevent loss of moisture through transpiration. Cactus leaves, for example, are reduced to spines. (*See also* Plants; Cactus; Sagebrush.)

Animals live in all but the most barren stretches. The camel is the most useful domestic desert animal. Its physical structure permits it to travel far without water (*see* Camel). Various wild mammals, birds, and reptiles of arid regions must get all their moisture from their food.

World Distribution of Deserts

Most of the Earth's deserts are strung along the Tropic of Cancer and the Tropic of Capricorn between 20° and 35° in both north and south latitudes. These low-latitude deserts lie mainly on the west coasts of continents, though deserts extend across North Africa and far into Asia. Deserts inside continents extend poleward. These are sometimes called middle-latitude deserts. Usually interior deserts are dry. This is because mountain ranges have taken the moisture from ocean winds.

The low-latitude deserts lie mainly in the path of the northeast and southeast trade winds or in the adjacent horse latitudes (*see* Wind). The air is descending (subsiding), and the weather tends to be warm and dry. There are few clouds and variable winds. When winds blow from the cold ocean to these warm lands, the air is heated. It drops little rain because moist air must be cooled to bring rainfall.

Ice cap and tundra regions around the poles are sometimes called cold deserts. They have little precipitation—usually less than ten inches—but the dearth of vegetation is caused chiefly by the cold.

Land Use and Livelihood

The total human population of all desert regions is estimated at some 85 million, or less than eight to the square mile. The only densely settled spots are irrigated places such as the lower Nile River.

Land is precious in oases, so it is intensively cultivated. In North Africa and Asia oasis farmers have commonly raised crops for their own use. The chief food crops are dates, figs, wheat, barley, rice, and beans. Today they also raise such commercial crops as cotton and sugarcane. In the United States irrigated lands are mainly used for commercial crops—citrus fruits, dates, winter vegetables, and cotton.

Proper development of critical water resources has recently focused on improving surface-water management techniques, improving control and storage of surface runoff, reducing loss from shallow aquifers, and desalting brackish waters. The buildup of salts in the soil has become a serious problem that is being studied in several nations. The introduction of cultivated plant species with greater salt tolerance, as has been done in Israel, seems to be a promising alternative to abandoning arid land. In the arid lands of Africa and Asia, nomads make a livelihood by grazing stock, moving often to find grass.

Desert life is changing. Irrigated lands are being extended by giant river-control systems (*see* Irrigation; Dam). Oases once reached only by slow camel caravan now have airports and service stations for motor vehicles. Settlements have sprung up in deserts to obtain valuable minerals. These include the petroleum of Saudi Arabia, Iraq, and Iran and the copper and other metals of arid North and South America. Typical desert minerals are soluble salts deposited by the high evaporation. Sodium nitrate, the most valuable, comes from the north Chile desert (*see* Chile).

DESIGN. The field of design goes beyond painting and drawing, sculpture, architecture, and handicrafts. It includes thousands of mass-produced objects that were designed for everyday use. Many industrial designers' products—from chairs to stereo equipment—are exhibited in art museums.

Throughout the ages man has designed things to meet his needs. The armor worn by knights was designed to protect them in medieval warfare. Birchbark canoes were designed to meet the needs of the American Indians. Skyscrapers were designed to provide the best use of valuable ground space in crowded cities.

As new materials and new methods are found, new designs are created to make use of them. As man's needs change, new designs are made to meet those needs. The telephone in use today could not have been designed 100 years ago. Some of its materials did not exist. The methods of making it were unknown.

The modern telephone, with its swift automatic dialing, is designed to make the dial convenient to use and difficult to break. It blends with office or home furnishings. The design of the modern telephone housed in strong plastic makes it simple, usable, and compact. Its surfaces are smooth and easy to clean and come in a variety of colors to match room decoration.

Functional Design

The first step in design is to consider the use of the object. This determines its shape, material, color, and size. Its parts need to be large enough to do their work but no larger. It has no needless ornaments. This is design for use—or *functional design.*

The eye is attracted by a sharp contrast of lights and darks. Artist Charles Howard has achieved this effect in the painting 'California' done for the Container Corporation of America.

Container Corp. of America

Modern functional design appears in many homes today. This is especially true in the kitchen, because clean, simple lines save work. Manufacturers of refrigerators, stoves, and washing machines combine the talents of fine engineers and designers to produce machines that are beautiful as well as useful.

People are slower to accept improved design in some home furnishings. The common dining-room chair, for example, is often still made of straight slabs of wood. It is heavy to lift. Its shape has little in common with the shape of the human body. After a time it becomes uncomfortable.

Designers have been developing lightweight chairs. These conform to the natural curves of the body and support it with ease and comfort. The molded plywood chair designed by Charles Eames and Eero Saarinen in 1940 is a classic of contemporary design.

This quality of good design extends to the styling of clothes, the sleek lines of automobiles, the patterns of superhighways, and the planning of growing cities. In these and in other areas man uses his creative ability to design things for better living.

Who Makes Designs?

Most professional designers specialize in a particular field such as dresses, furniture, automobiles, or books. These people usually have special training and experience. Yet, to some degree, each of us is a designer. The choices we make in our clothing, the way we set a table, arrange flowers and furniture, and decorate the walls of our homes—all these involve planning and organizing to meet our needs. These may be functional needs of the body or they may be nonfunctional needs of the spirit, but each is creative.

Types of Design

There are two important types of designs made by man. First are designs which are made for flat, two-dimensional surfaces. Second are designs made for three-dimensional objects.

Two-dimensional designing includes such activities as drawing, painting, and producing surface patterns on fabrics, rugs, and wallpaper and in advertising layouts. Three-dimensional designing includes sculpture; architecture; handicrafts such as jewelry, pottery, and leatherwork; clothing; and machine-made objects such as automobiles, stoves, chairs, and pencil sharpeners.

Design is also found in nature. The pebble, washed by the rains of the ages, wears to a beautiful free-flowing form. There is design in the swelling, spiraling form of seashells and the upward soar of a pine. There is design in the arrangement of petals on a flower, the spacing of leaves on a stem. Man has studied the basic rhythms in natural forms so that he might also design pleasing relationships.

ELEMENTS AND PRINCIPLES OF DESIGN

To make anything, whether it is a painting, a chair, or a house, materials suitable for the purpose must first be chosen. These might be wood, stone, metal,

The fan-shaped interior of the Mount Angel Abbey Library (left) at St. Benedict, Ore., exemplifies the use of space as a design element. Tony Smith's plywood sculpture 'Smoke' (right) was made for the "Scale as Content" exhibit.

glass, or paint. The materials must then be organized within an area or volume. To do this we use the *elements of design*. These are line, color, value, space, mass, and texture. The arrangement of these elements is determined by the *principles of design*—proportion, rhythm, and balance.

Elements of Design

Line. Line defines the shapes we use in design. Lines may be straight or curved, delicate or bold. They may be vertical, horizontal, or diagonal. Their directions can suggest movement, mood, or emotion.

Color. Color has three basic properties. They are hue, value, and saturation. *Hue* refers to a particular color such as red, blue, or yellow. The hue of an apple is red. *Value* refers to the lightness or darkness of a color. Some colors, such as yellow or orange, are light in value. Some colors, such as purple or brown, are dark in value. We can lighten the value of a color by adding white or darken it by adding black. *Saturation*, also called *chroma*, refers to the purity of a color. If we wish to decrease the saturation of a color, we dull it by adding a mixture of other colors. (*See also* Color.)

Colors also have other important qualities. Those which contain yellow or red are *warm* colors. They seem to be solid, advance toward us, and expand in their size. *Cool* colors are those which contain blue. They seem to be spacious, withdraw from us, and contract in size. Colors can affect our emotions. Some colors make us feel happy and excited. Other colors make us feel sad. We surround ourselves in our homes with the colors we like.

Value. Value is the amount of light reflected by a surface. If there is little contrast in the amount of light reflected from surfaces near each other, the eye has difficulty in distinguishing them. A sharp contrast of light and dark values is necessary to attract attention.

Even with brilliant color contrasts, a painter must carefully balance the distribution of lights and darks throughout his picture. A drawing or any type of design in one color requires careful consideration of light and dark values.

Space. There is a real space in which we move about. The architect is concerned with dividing this space by walls, ceilings, and floors. There is also the illusion of space which can be created on a two-dimensional surface by drawing or painting.

Mass. Mass is the three-dimensional volume which occupies space. It may be the *actual* mass of a sculpture or a building or the *suggested* mass on a two-dimensional surface in a drawing or painting.

Texture. Texture is the nature of a material's surface. We usually notice texture by our sense of touch. However, we also "feel" texture through our eyes after we are familiar with its touch. A texture may be smooth like satin or rough like burlap. It may be hard like stone or soft like butter. The architect is interested in varying the texture of walls on a building. He may contrast the texture of rough brick with polished marble and smooth painted wood. The painter may emphasize texture in

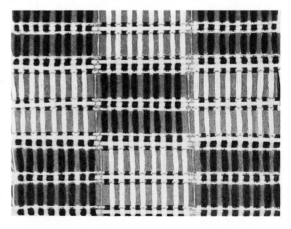

This hand-woven fabric by Robert D. Sailors uses leather strips, matchstick wood, and metallic yarn in a cotton warp.

This is a pleasing display in which the proportion follows a rhythmic progression of numbers in a 3 by 5 space.

his painting by applying his paint more thickly. The weaver uses contrasts of yarn; heavy and light, coarse and smooth.

Principles of Design

If the elements of design are thrown together without plan, the result is confusion. The elements must be carefully organized into a unified design. This is done by following the *principles* known as proportion, rhythm, and balance.

Proportion. The principle of proportion is concerned with relative measure or amount. The effectiveness of a design depends upon the good proportion of its elements. There may be different sizes, shapes, and lengths of line. The relationship between these differences is proportion.

In design proportions are sometimes determined by structural needs and sometimes by visual appearances. Occasionally it is a combination of both. For example, the architect must determine the size and shape of windows for his building. He decides after considering how much light is needed inside the building as well as the appearance from outside. In a portrait painting, the artist must decide how large to make the figure and where to place it on his canvas. The potter decides how large to make the mouth of a bowl or of a vase. These are all problems in proportion.

Artists have learned much about good proportions by studying nature. Many centuries ago the Greeks discovered the formula of nature's proportions as it occurs in such living things as plant forms, shells, and the arrangement of seeds in a pod. This plan of proportion is based upon a curious relationship of numbers known as the *summation series*. The series is built by always adding the last two numbers in the series to get the next. Let us start with the numeral 1. By adding 1 and 1 we get 2. By adding 2 and 1 we get 3. By adding 3 and 2 we get 5. Continuing in this manner we get the series 1-2-3-5-8-13-21-34-55 and so on. This series of numbers has what is called a *rhythmic progression*, because the relationship between each succeeding pair of numbers is about the same. The proportion of 3 to 5 is almost the same as 5 to 8.

The plan of proportion appears frequently in nature. In a pineapple, for example, the scales are arranged to form two sets of spiraling curves running up the fruit. One of these curves is quite steep and its spiral is counterclockwise. The other, a more gradual spiral, runs clockwise. By counting the scales on the two sets of spirals we find that their numbers are in the same proportion as the summation series.

The general proportion of 3 to 5 is often used. There are many proportions which are pleasing to the eye. It is the artist's job to develop interesting proportions whether the object be a clock, a dinner fork, or a sewing machine.

Rhythm. Rhythm is movement which we feel in looking at a design. It often results from a repetition of forms which flow in a given direction like the upward thrusts of a picket fence.

Rhythm may be seen in a polka dot design or in a checkerboard design. The simple shapes and spaces between them are always the same. We call this a *static* rhythm. It has no variety and is therefore somewhat monotonous. Other types of rhythm have more variety and interest. Instead of a single shape there may be a group of *related* shapes whose height, width, or depth may change as well as the space between them. Ocean waves are an example.

Balance. You may have seen two children on a seesaw. If they are the same weight, they balance each other when they sit the same distance from the center. This is *equal*, or symmetrical, balance. If a heavier child wants to seesaw with a small child, the larger must move closer to the center to be balanced by the weight of the small child. This is *unequal* balance.

Nature provides us with many examples of equal and unequal balance. The formal symmetry of a pine tree is an equal balance; but the irregular, unequal jutting limbs of an oak are also in balance.

In designs made by artists we also find examples of equal and unequal balance. If two shapes are about the same size and color, they will balance each other if placed about equal distance from the center of the design. However, if two shapes are unequal in size, the smaller will need to be placed farther from the center to make them appear balanced.

The artist learns to deal with many problems of balance. He learns how to balance each of the elements of design: line, color, value, space, mass, and texture. He finds that horizontal lines can be used to balance vertical ones. A small area of complex shape will balance a large area of simple shape. Small areas of bright color balance larger areas of dull color. There is no mathematical formula for determining balance in design. Through experience and practice the artist develops an ability to *feel* when all the parts of his design are in balance.

A design achieves *unity* when (1) it has pleasing proportions; (2) its parts are so organized that we enjoy following the rhythms of the patterns; and (3) we feel it is in balance. We enjoy looking at designs that have unity.

DESIGN IN PAINTING AND DRAWING

Painting is perhaps the most popular of the visual arts. More children and adults draw and paint today than ever before in the history of the world.

Whether a painter works in oil or in water color, he has only a flat, two-dimensional surface on which to express his idea. The idea may be one which lends itself to a decorative pattern as in Picasso's painting 'The Studio'. Or it may suggest deep space as in Ben Shahn's 'Handball'. The painting may be based upon the visual world as the artist sees and understands it. His painting will then achieve some degree of realism as in Christian Bérard's 'Portrait of Jean Cocteau'.

On the other hand, the composition may be formed by lines, shapes, colors, and textures which have no relation to nature or man-made objects. One type of picture composition is not necessarily better than another. Each is an individual and original expression by the artist. Its merit rests on his skill in handling the elements and principles of design.

Beginnings of Design in Painting

The beginnings of painting go back thousands of years to the prehistoric cave men. Realistic drawings and paintings of animals believed to be more than 20,000 years old were discovered in the caves of Lascaux in southern France (see Drawing). In spite of their fine craftsmanship and remarkable realism, there is little if any planned design in the total effect.

The earliest known paintings which had planned design were Egyptian. The forms used in Egyptian paintings were not what the eye sees. Their paintings of a human figure were distorted and used only the simplest proportions, but they were carefully composed (see Egypt, Ancient).

Simple arrangement and exaggerated outlines, leaving out all details, give force and strength to the composition. This emphasis upon making paintings flat with a two-dimensional linear pattern appears in many periods. Even in the 20th century, many painters feel that they should limit the depth to which the eye can be led. This is true whether the painting is realistic or abstract.

Three-Dimensional Painting

Painters first began to achieve a feeling for visual reality early in the Renaissance. Giotto, born in the city of Florence about 1266, was the first great artist to make his figures look human and to give them an emotional quality. He organized them into compositions in such a way that each figure became an active part of the design (for picture, see Painting).

In the 15th century the great Florentine architect Brunelleschi (Brunellesco) discovered the laws of scientific linear perspective. The discovery enabled painters to create the illusion of depth.

This was an important milestone in painting but it created new problems in design. Now artists had to develop new ways of leading the eye into space and yet provide a return to the picture surface. They

THREE USES OF DESIGN

Artist Christian Bérard achieves realism in his 'Portrait of Jean Cocteau' by painting the subject as he sees him.

Ben Shahn's painting 'Handball' has a movement of forms and shapes which leads the eye into the distance and back again.

In his painting 'The Studio' Picasso expresses a decorative pattern which stretches itself upward, down, and across.

The Art Institute of Chicago

The 'Toreador from Knossos' illustrates the two-dimensional linear pattern used in ancient Crete and early Greece.

solved this by the arrangement of lines, planes, textures, colors, and values.

Painting Today

With the invention of the camera, which more accurately reproduces nature, interest in realism declined. New efforts were made to achieve other qualities in pictures that emphasized imagination. Artists began to think of painting as a more personal expression of the artist rather than a picture of what was seen. Cubism, for example, was an attempt to create a new way of seeing things. It reduced objects into planes and rearranged their parts so they might be seen from several positions at the same time.

Twentieth-century painting in America and Europe has become increasingly abstract. However,

Metropolitan Museum of Art

Botticelli's 'The Last Communion of St. Jerome' shows how lines can be used expertly to create the illusion of depth.

whether a painting is realistic, abstract, or completely nonobjective, the same principles of design are used. If the painting is two-dimensional, its design is a controlled movement of surface patterns. If the painting is three-dimensional, the design is so organized that the eye is carried rhythmically into space and back again. (*See also* Painting.)

DESIGN IN SCULPTURE

Sculpture is a three-dimensional art. It deals with the arrangement of solid mass and space. The choice of material affects the design in sculpture. If a sculptor works in a hard brittle material such as stone, the sculpture must have a compact design on a firm base. Because this material tends to chip, the design must be simple, without great detail. 'Child with a Cat', by William Zorach, is an example of sculpture carved directly in stone (for picture, *see* Arts, The).

Wood permits more complex carving. With planning, the carver can make grain an effective part of the design and add to the surface beauty of the work. (*See also* Woodworking and Wood Carving.)

Clay is soft and lends itself to more delicate designs. Metal can be melted and cast in molds to reproduce sculptures designed in clay. Metal can also be worked directly with cutting tools and welding torch. In this new type of sculpture, formed of bars and rods, open space is as important an element as solids in the total design.

Ancient Sculpture

Throughout the ages human beings have felt a need to surround themselves with carved images. Prehistoric humans carved bone and ivory into sculptural forms. They used both animal and human shapes, often with amazing craftsmanship.

Designs in primitive sculpture reappear in modern sculpture. It is interesting to compare the two sculptures of heads on the following page. The ivory head was made by an artist of Zaire. The second sculpture was done by an English sculptress, Barbara Hepworth. Each reduces the head to a simple egg shape. Facial features are primarily accents on an otherwise abstract shape.

Ancient Egyptians produced a great amount of sculpture carved of hard stone such as basalt. Only portrait heads were accurately reproduced. The figure was always rigid and stiffly erect. The Greeks developed a highly realistic type of stone sculpture. Their figures twisted and turned, forming compositions that were pleasingly curved.

DESIGN IN ARCHITECTURE

The purpose of architecture has always been to provide some type of shelter. It might be a tomb, a tem-

111

Museum of Modern Art

Arts Council of Great Britain

Sculptor Peter Grippe's 'The City' (left) is a terra-cotta work in which clay is arranged in an interesting manner. 'The Fisheater' (right), by Lynn Chadwick, is a mobile sculpture made of copper and brass. It moves in a constantly changing pattern.

ple, a factory, or a dwelling. The plan, the method of construction, and even the final appearance of a structure should be determined by its purpose.

The oldest known examples of architecture are in Egypt. Some of the most important structures were built as tombs. They were made of great stone blocks and are now called pyramids (*see* Pyramids). Egyptian temples were thick walled, with heavy pillars.

The Greeks developed a much lighter, smaller type of architecture in their temples. Out in front a portico was supported by columns. In some of the more important temples, such as the Parthenon, the columns circled the entire building (for pictures of the Parthenon, *see* Architecture). Greek architects designed the columns and their parts very carefully. Certain excellent designs became famous and were known as orders. These were called Doric, Ionic, and Corinthian (for pictures, *see* Architecture).

The Romans needed huge public buildings such as market places, public baths, and arenas. To provide large open spaces, they built curving masonry walls. These turned inward until they met in a rounded arch.

The Romans were the first to build with concrete. They used it for huge domed buildings such as the Pantheon and vast amusement centers such as the Colosseum. Roman architecture achieved a feeling of strength and dignity through its massiveness (for pictures, *see* Rome).

In the Middle Ages religion was the center of life. There was need of cathedrals that could house throngs of people. This led architects in northern France to design a new method of construction. It used pointed stone arches held up by slim pillars and narrow ribs. This permitted large open areas on the sides of buildings. These were filled with stained glass windows. It was called the Gothic style of architecture.

During the early Renaissance, architects returned to Greek and Roman methods of building. The walls, however, were more open with windows and doors, and they became more elaborate with surface decorations.

By the early 19th century there were so many styles based on the past that the art of this period was known as eclectic—composed of elements drawn from various sources.

New Materials and Techniques

As early as 1848 cast iron was used for a building constructed in New York City. By about 1855 architects had developed a type of construction that used a skeleton of metal—cast iron. Cast iron made possible floor spans of greater width than ever before. A second important material was concrete, which the Romans had used. By 1900 concrete had taken the place of a great deal of masonry and wood.

The development of structural steel and plate glass revolutionized the walls of shops and department stores. They afforded far more height and light. The invention of the elevator in 1852 made the

Harry N. Abrams, Inc.

City Museum and Art Gallery (Birmingham, England)

The ivory head (left) was carved by an African artist. 'Cosden Head' (right) was done by Barbara Hepworth, an English sculptress.

'Beau Dieu' (left) is a simplified statue of Christ in the Amiens cathedral in France. It is typical of medieval sculpture. Ancient

Egyptians built temples of simple design and great mass to suggest permanence. This is the Temple of Horus at Edfu (right).

dream of the skyscraper a possibility (*see* Building Construction). An American architect, Louis Sullivan, pioneered in modern methods and design.

Frank Lloyd Wright's Architecture

Another great American architect was Frank Lloyd Wright. He was chiefly interested in designing houses. (For pictures, *see* Wright, Frank Lloyd.)

Wright's earliest style was called "prairie architecture." His homes had low-lying roofs which seemed

The Cologne cathedral, built in Germany during the Middle Ages, shows stained-glass windows within the stone framework.

to hover over the house and give it added protection. Windows no longer were mere glass holes in walls. They formed bands which extended the full length of the wall.

His floor plans were informal, based upon the needs of the individual family. Rooms extended out from a central area. This design let light into each room from three different directions.

The International Style

Examples of Wright's work in architectural publications interested young architects in Europe. Four of them were to make important contributions to the new architecture. They were Walter Gropius, Mies van der Rohe, J. J. P. Oud, and Le Corbusier. Their experiments during and immediately after World War I created the International Style in architecture.

These young men agreed that most of the architecture around them was not designed for its purpose either structurally or decoratively. Because these buildings were based upon ancient styles, they were not meeting the needs of people living in the 20th century.

As they experimented with new designs, they discovered a basic principle of all true architecture. This was that architecture must *function* according to the needs of people who would use it. As Louis Sullivan had said earlier in America, "Form follows function."

Being engineers as well as architects, these men sought suitable building materials. They used steel and glass and reinforced concrete for the structural elements. For surfacing, they used stucco, tile, marble, and brick. These materials did away with the need for massive bases and top-heavy cornices. The new steel and concrete skeleton made heavy masonry walls unnecessary (*see* Building Construction).

Now the surfaces of their buildings could have many openings without weakening the structure of the building. At last it was possible to flood the whole

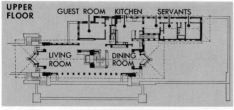

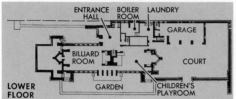

At the left are floor plans of Frank Lloyd Wright's Robie House in Chicago. The informal arrangement resembles early American houses. The bedrooms are on the top floor (not shown).

Outside, the house seems part of its natural setting. Vertical and horizontal surfaces flow into each other. The building now houses the Adlai E. Stevenson Institute of International Affairs.

structure with the natural light of day. They tried to eliminate all ornaments and let the buildings be frankly machines for living. This new type of design strongly influenced American architects.

The Contemporary House

The plan for a home of contemporary design is based upon the needs of the family. Its interior space is divided freely into sleeping, living, recreation, and service areas. It does not try to be quaint or pretty. The building itself should be so well designed that it does not need decoration. The choice of materials depends upon climate, cost, and serviceability.

Mass-produced homes can follow this principle. By standardizing such units as floors and walls architects have been able to design low-cost buildings with some individuality. This is also true of prefabricated houses (see Housing).

DESIGN IN HANDICRAFTS

Handicrafts are items used in daily living that have been made by man with his hands. These include tools, weapons, vessels, jewelry, and fabrics. The finest of these blend the useful and the beautiful. Man has always desired objects which function well and are pleasing to the eye at the same time.

The earliest stone implements of prehistoric cave men were made only as useful objects. Gradually there appeared a feeling for proportion and balance. Such a refinement took place in the shape of the hand ax and other items.

The pottery of prehistoric man

was simple and rugged. Some was decorated with lines, spirals, zigzags, and dots. These often served to strengthen the structural lines and surfaces. Later, primitive artists developed quite elaborate designs based upon animal and human forms.

Egyptian artists developed great skill in handicrafts. They learned to cast, hammer, and solder gold. They made elegant vases of alabaster. Small toilet articles such as cosmetic boxes were carved from wood. The perfecting of ceramic glazing made possible handsome beads, pendants, scarabs, figu-

Technological advances characterize Louis Sullivan's Carson Pirie Scott & Co. building (left) and the Lake Point Tower apartments (right), both in Chicago, Ill.
By courtesy of (left) Carson Pirie Scott & Co., (right) American Institute of Architecture

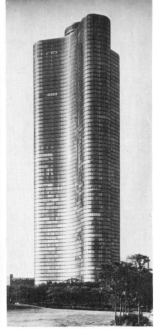

Architect Mies van der Rohe (right) studies his model for a housing and shopping center in New York City's Battery Park.

rines, and even architectural decorations. (*See also* Jewelry and Gems.)

In Crete the potter was of special importance since his wares were articles of commerce. Greece also developed pottery to a fine art. The Greeks used only a few basic shapes but gave special attention to refining proportions, contours, handles, and decorations. Probably no other people have used the human figure in pottery decoration as much as the Greeks. (*See also* Pottery and Porcelain.)

Handicrafts flourished during the Middle Ages. Luxurious fabrics were required for church vestments and castle tapestries (*see* Tapestry). Vessels for church services and jeweled ornaments were also much in demand. Enameling on metal, an art that has been revived in the 20th century, was highly developed (*see* Enamel).

During the Renaissance handicrafts alternated between the decorative arts and the useful arts. Among the decorative arts were enameling, tapestry work, and goldwork. Outstanding among useful handicrafts were ironwork, furniture, and glassware. One of the high points of the 16th century was the perfection of glass blowing in the city of Venice (*see* Glassware).

In the 17th and 18th centuries furniture making developed as a handicraft. After the massively carved and gilded furniture of the period of Louis XIV came a period of transition. It introduced lighter, more graceful forms. Cabinetmakers began to use more curved designs. Later, craftsmen copied both Greek and Roman styles. These included the use of lyres, urns, festoons, and decorative animal forms. Among the famed English cabinetmakers were Thomas Chippendale, the Adam Brothers, Thomas Sheraton, and George Hepplewhite. (*See also* Furniture; Chippendale; Adam; for pictures, *see* Interior Design.)

Development of American Handicrafts

In America the work of the early craftsmen was about the equal in quality of European wares. Cabinetmakers, silversmiths, and workers in pewter and iron continued the forms introduced in Europe. They also developed some that were truly American.

The first makers of furniture in America were called "joyners" (joiners). Their furniture was built entirely of straight pieces of wood, "joined" at right angles. By the 18th century furniture makers put emphasis upon new types of construction, including the curve and some decorative elements. Perhaps the most famous cabinetmaker of the early republic was Duncan Phyfe.

The favorite pottery of early America was stoneware. Its strength and low cost made it practical for many uses, such as crocks, jars, and bottles. It

The octopus vase (left) shows curving, naturalistic lines. It was created in Crete about 1500 B.C. The jeweled pendant (center) in the form of a mermaid is an example of designs in metal created in Italy during the Renaissance. The silver creamer (right) is beautiful in its simple design and decoration. It was made by Paul Revere, silversmith and Revolutionary War hero.

Stoneware pottery dates from early America. A modern example is the vase, 40 inches tall, created by Peter Voulkos of California.

was usually made of tan or gray clay with a transparent glaze. Ornamentation was in cobalt blue and consisted of flowers and animals. Toward the middle of the 1700s the designs became elaborate with domestic and patriotic scenes. (*See also* Pottery and Porcelain.)

American craftsmen also developed glasswork of high quality. Henry William Stiegel was perhaps the most famous of the early glassmakers. He made window glass and bottles as well as many household utensils. His colors included a rich blue, amethyst, green, amber, opaque, and clear white. For decoration he modeled, engraved, and enameled the surface and combined different colors of glass. (*See also* Glass.)

By the close of the 17th century, America had many fine silversmiths. The colonists measured their wealth largely in silverware. The most popular items were drinking vessels, such as the tankard. One of the greatest silversmiths was Paul Revere, famous hero of the midnight ride (*see* Revere).

The weaving of textiles has been an important activity of every pioneer society. Colonial weaving was necessarily a useful art. The woven coverlet was truly an American expression. No one knows the source of most of their designs. Some had simple, realistic names such as Sunrise, Cat Tracks, and Dog Tracks. Others were nationalistic in design and were given such names as E. Pluribus Unum and the Declaration of Independence.

Today the machine has eliminated much of the need for handicrafts. Even so, people are willing to pay extra money for unique hand-blown goblets or hand-woven and hand-printed fabrics.

DESIGN IN INDUSTRY

The Industrial Revolution brought the use of power machinery in many fields (*see* Industrial Revolution). These machines began turning out objects cheaply and in large quantities. The ease of production led to many abuses. Manufacturers, lacking in art experience and training, often produced unattractive objects. Because the machine could reproduce ornaments easily, decoration was used to excess. It was applied to everything, often hiding defects in structure.

Mechanized ugliness led to the Arts and Crafts Movement in Britain and America. The movement was founded by William Morris of England (*see* Morris). He insisted that only handmade objects were really beautiful, and he encouraged a return to the simple handicrafts of the past. The movement failed to achieve its goal, but it did succeed in calling attention to the need for good design in industry.

Competition in the mass sales of identical objects was probably the chief cause of the final union between art and industry. During the 1920s manufacturers first felt the need for expert advice on designing highly competitive articles such as home appliances. The new industrial designers created better products by following three basic design principles.

First, materials should be honestly used. For example, metal should never be painted to look like wood. Second, all forms should be kept simple in their shape. One of the best arguments in favor of this principle was the ease of cleaning simple surfaces. Third, products should be designed in such a way that their appearance expressed their function. A bed should not be disguised to look like a bookcase.

Some of the influential figures in the development of American industrial design were Norman Bel Geddes, Walter Dorwin Teague, Henry Dreyfuss, Harold Van Doren, and Raymond Loewy. They made America "streamline" conscious. Streamlining originally implied a bullet or tear-drop shape. Now everything from a pencil sharpener to a radio has been designed for this effect, though it may bear no relationship to its usefulness.

The idea of simplifying exterior surface on all types of machine-made objects has gained favor. Surface interest is provided by the contrast of dull and bright, and by the simple beauty of such materials as porcelain, enamel, glass, copper, aluminum, brass, and steel. Any added ornament is closely related to the structure and seems to be an actual part of the object itself. (*See also* Industrial Design.)

BIBLIOGRAPHY FOR DESIGN

Bevlin, M.E. Design Through Discovery, 4th ed. (Holt, 1984).
De Sausmarez, Maurice. Basic Design, rev. ed. (Van Nostrand Reinhold, 1983).
Graves, M.E. The Art of Color and Design, 2nd ed. (McGraw, 1951).
Maier, Manfred. Basic Principles of Design (Van Nostrand Reinhold, 1981).
Papanek, Victor. Design for the Real World, 2nd ed. (Van Nostrand Reinhold, 1984).
Wolchonok, Louis. The Art of Three-Dimensional Design (Dover, 1969).

DES MOINES, Iowa.

The capital and largest city of Iowa, Des Moines is located on the Des Moines River. Its name may come from the mound-building Indians who once lived in the area and called the

river *Moingola,* meaning River of the Mounds. It is also possible that the name is a French word for "middle," as the Des Moines River is the principal river midway between the Mississippi River to the east and the Missouri River to the west.

Although it is located in the heart of a fertile agricultural area, Des Moines is heavily industrialized. There are tire and rubber factories, farm machinery manufacturers, tool and implements manufacturers, and publishing companies. These firms account for the largest share of Des Moines's manufacturing jobs, but the city's real economic strength lies in the trade, financial services, and government parts of its economy. Dozens of insurance companies are headquartered there, and the state government is a major employer.

The capital complex is a large park on a hill overlooking the rest of the city with the golden domed Capitol at its center. Nearby is the Iowa State Historical Museum and Archives and several state office buildings. The new Civic Center, constructed in the late 1970s, has both convention and theater facilities. In a plaza outside the center is a sculpture by Claes Oldenburg. Near the Civic Center is the old post office, which has been restored and now houses the Polk County Heritage Gallery. Greenwood Park, in a residential area west of downtown, has two museums—the Art Center and the Center of Science and Industry. The Art Center is a building designed by Finnish architect Eliel Saarinen.

The city's best-known educational institution is Drake University, which was founded in 1881 by the Disciples of Christ. The most important professional school is the College of Osteopathic Medicine and Surgery (1898). Des Moines has several theaters and a symphony orchestra and hosts the Iowa State Fair.

Sauk and Fox Indians inhabited the area before the coming of white settlers. The site was explored in 1835, and Fort Des Moines was established in 1843 near the junction of the Raccoon River and the Des Moines, which empties into the Mississippi. In 1845 the area was opened for settlement, and in 1857 a city charter was adopted. That same year Des Moines became the state capital.

Growth was spurred in the early 20th century by the development of coal deposits near the city. In 1903 the United States Army established a military base, also known as Fort Des Moines, that was active until the 1960s. Part of the old fort grounds are now the Des Moines Children's Zoo and the College of Osteopathic Medicine and Surgery. The city has a council-manager form of government. Population (1982 estimate), city, 191,506; metropolitan area, 371,700.

Hernando De Soto, from an engraving by Antonio de Herrera y Tordesillas (1559-1625)

Library of Congress

DE SOTO, HERNANDO (1500?–42).

One of the most famous gold seekers in history was Hernando De Soto. He was born about 1500 in Barcarroto, Spain. When he was 19 he sailed to the New World with Pedrarias Dávila, governor of Darien (now Panama). He became a ruthless soldier whose men feared his temper but admired his horsemanship.

In 1524 and 1526 he took part in expeditions to Central America. In 1532 he joined Pizarro in the conquest of Peru (*see* Pizarro). De Soto's share of the Peruvian treasures made him rich. He returned to Spain and married Dávila's daughter Isabel.

The Spaniards did not know the country north of Florida. Captive Indians told stories of lands there richer than Mexico or Peru. De Soto decided to win another fortune from this region. He persuaded the king of Spain to appoint him governor of Cuba and Florida. He recruited a thousand men and helped pay for their equipment. This great army set sail from Spain in April 1538. At Havana they set up an advance base and made final preparations.

On May 30, 1539, De Soto and his men went ashore at Tampa Bay in Florida. They marched northward to Georgia, then turned westward and followed the Alabama River to Mobile Bay. When their supplies and spirits ran low, De Soto rallied his men with the prospect of riches ahead.

Along the way they met many Indian tribes. De Soto forced the Indians to furnish supplies and tortured their chiefs in a useless effort to make them tell where gold was hidden. This brutality led to many battles. The bloodiest was fought near Mobile Bay. About 70 Spaniards were killed, and many more were hurt. De Soto himself was severely wounded.

De Soto first saw the Mississippi near the present site of Memphis in the spring of 1541. The men built boats and crossed the river. By the next autumn they reached the Neosho River in northeastern Oklahoma before they turned eastward again.

Everywhere De Soto searched, the Indians reported gold "just ahead" in order to escape his torture, but after three years he still had found no gold. In the spring of 1542 De Soto led his worn and tattered men southward. Near the junction of the Red and the Mississippi rivers, De Soto fell ill and died.

DETECTIVE STORY. Whodunit? (never "Who did it?") is both a question and the name of a type of fiction—the detective story. The answer to the question is found by the clever detective as he wends his way through a maze of clues that leads to the identity of the murderer. The detective story is one of the most popular kinds of fiction in the 20th century. Each year hundreds of novels and short stories of this type are turned out by countless authors. Many of these stories have been presented on radio, television, and as movies.

First there had to be detectives. The profession was invented in France by François-Eugène Vidocq, who started his own private detective agency in 1817. His memoirs, published about 1830, inspired the American author Edgar Allan Poe to write the first detective story. Published in 1841, it was called 'The Murders in the Rue Morgue' and featured, as its detective, C. Auguste Dupin. Poe followed this tale with two more stories, but a lukewarm public response led him to turn his talents to other kinds of writing (*see* American Literature, "Poe and Hawthorne"; Poe). However, in France, about 25 years later, Émile Gaboriau had great success with his 'Affaire Lerouge'. Public response was so great that Gaboriau wrote several more, similar detective novels.

Detective fiction was introduced into England by Wilkie Collins, a close friend of Charles Dickens, in 1868 with the publication of 'The Moonstone' and its memorable detective, Sergeant Cuff. It is still, after more than a century, one of the best mystery stories ever written. Dickens himself was so taken with this type of fiction that he tried his hand at it in 'The Mystery of Edwin Drood', but he died before finishing it. The popularity of detective fiction continued to grow, and it was permanently established by the enormous commercial success of 'The Mystery of a Hansom Cab' (1886) by the Australian Fergus Hume.

Had Hume not published his book, the detective story would have been assured a permanent place in the annals of fiction by a British physician named Sir Arthur Conan Doyle. It was he who in 1887 introduced the reading public to Sherlock Holmes, the world's most famous and memorable detective (*see* Doyle). The last of the Holmes stories was published by Doyle in 1927. These 60 tales were for decades models of what the detective story should be.

The first generation of Holmes imitators firmly established the detective story in England and the United States. Among the best-known English authors were R. Austin Freeman, whose detective, Dr. John Thorndyke, first appeared in 'The Red Thumb Mark' in 1907; and G.K. Chesterton, creator of the Father Brown series of stories. The first of these, 'The Innocence of Father Brown', was published in 1911. The publication of 'Trent's Last Case' by E.C. Bentley in 1913 was hailed by critics as one of the masterpieces of detective writing.

In the United States one of the best storytellers was Mary Roberts Rinehart, author of 'The Circular Staircase' (1908) and other novels. Carolyn Wells, beginning with 'The Clue' in 1909, wrote more than 70 detective novels. America's most oustanding contribution to detective fiction in this period was Melville Davisson Post, author of the stories collectively titled 'Uncle Abner, Master of Mysteries'. He had begun writing his stories in 1896, but they were not published until 1918.

The era of modern detective story writing began in England in 1920 with the publication of Freeman Wills Crofts's 'The Cask', with its detective, Inspector Joseph French. Between 1920 and 1940 some of the best-known fictional detectives made their appearance. Agatha Christie brought Hercule Poirot to life in 1920 in 'The Mysterious Affair at Styles' (*see* Christie). Christie's now-famous Miss Jane Marple did not appear until 1942. Lord Peter Wimsey, a creation of Dorothy Sayers, first appeared in 'Whose Body?' (1923).

In the United States, Chinese detective Charlie Chan was introduced to the public in 1925 by Earl Derr Biggers in 'The House Without a Key'. Philo Vance,

In the 1939 film 'The Adventures of Sherlock Holmes' (left), Holmes, seated (played by Basil Rathbone), and Dr. Watson (Nigel Bruce) get information from Ann Brandon (Ida Lupino). Swedish actor Warner Oland played Charlie Chan, in white suit (right), in 'Charlie Chan at the Race Track'.

SOME POPULAR DETECTIVE-STORY WRITERS

Some prominent persons are not included below because they are covered in the main text of this article or in other articles in Compton's Encyclopedia (see Fact-Index). Many detective fiction writers use pen names. The article notes, for instance, that Ellery Queen was really Manfred B. Lee and Frederic Dannay. The real names of others mentioned are: Willard H. Wright (S.S. Van Dine), C. Day-Lewis (Nicholas Blake), John I. M. Stewart (Michael Innes), Alfred A. G. Clark (Cyril Hare), and Evan Hunter (Ed McBain). The following list presents the pen names of some authors with the real name, if it is different, and birth and death dates in parentheses. The author's detective creation and at least one popular title and its publication date follow this information.

Bell, Josephine (Doris Bell Ball, born 1897). Inspector Steven Mitchell, among others. 'The Port of London Murders' (1938) and 'Wolf! Wolf!' (1979).

Brown, Carter (Alan Geoffrey Yates, born 1923). Larry Baker and others. 'Venus Unarmed' (1953), 'A Bullet for My Baby' (1955), and 'Night Wheeler' (1975).

Chandler, Raymond (1888–1959). Philip Marlowe. 'The Big Sleep' (1939), 'Farewell, My Lovely' (1940), 'The Long Goodbye' (1953), and 'Playback' (1958).

Charteris, Leslie (Leslie Charles Bowyer Yin, born 1907). Simon Templar, the Saint. 'Meet the Tiger' (1928), 'The Saint in New York' (1935), 'Vendetta for the Saint' (1965), and 'Send for the Saint' (1977).

Cleary, Jon (born 1917). Scobie Malone. 'The High Commissioner' (1966) and 'The Beaufort Sisters' (1979).

Davis, Dorothy Salisbury (born 1916). Mrs. Norris and Jasper Tully. 'The Judas Cat' (1949), 'Death of an Old Sinner' (1957), and 'A Death in the Life' (1976).

Francis, Dick (Richard Stanley Francis, born 1920). Sid Halley. 'Odds Against' (1965), 'Rat Race' (1970), 'Trial Run' (1978), 'Whip Hand' (1979), 'Twice Shy' (1981), 'Banker' (1982), and 'The Danger' (1984).

Freeling, Nicholas (born 1927). Inspector Van der Valk and others. 'Love in Amsterdam' (1962), 'Double Barrel' (1964), 'Over the High Side' (1971), and 'Wolfnight' (1982).

Gardner, Erle Stanley (1889–1970). Perry Mason. 'The Case of the Velvet Claws' (1933), 'The Case of the Lame Canary' (1937), 'The Case of the Postponed Murder' (1973). Gardner also published a number of crime stories under the pen name A.A. Fair.

Hughes, Dorothy (born 1904). Inspector Tobin. 'The So Blue Marble' (1940), 'The Candy Kid' (1950), and 'The Expendable Man' (1963).

Innes, Hammond (born 1913). 'The Doppelganger' (1937) and 'The Big Footprints' (1977).

Innes, Michael (John Innes Mackintosh Stewart, born 1906). John Appleby. 'Death at the President's Lodging' (1936), 'Hamlet, Revenge!' (1937), and 'The Ampersand Papers' (1979).

James, Phyllis Dorothy (born 1920). Adam Dalgliesh. 'Cover Her Face' (1966), 'Shroud for a Nightingale' (1971), 'An Unsuitable Job for a Woman' (1972), and 'The Skull Beneath the Skin' (1982).

Lathen, Emma (Mary J. Latis and Martha Hennissart, no dates available). John Putnam Thatcher. 'Banking on Death' (1961), 'A Stitch in Time' (1968), 'Ashes to Ashes' (1971), 'Double, Double, Oil and Trouble' (1978), and 'Going for the Gold' (1981).

McBain, Ed (Evan Hunter, born 1926). Officers of the 87th Precinct. 'Cop Hater' (1956), 'He Who Hesitates' (1965), 'Calypso' (1979), 'Beauty and the Beast' (1982), and 'Lightning' (1984).

MacDonald, John D. (born 1916). Travis McGee. 'The Brass Cupcake' (1950), 'A Deadly Shade of Gold' (1965), 'The Girl in the Plain Brown Wrapper' (1968), 'The Dreadful Lemon Sky' (1975), and 'The Green Ripper' (1979).

Macdonald, Ross (Kenneth Millar, 1915–83). Lew Archer. 'The Moving Target' (1949), 'The Way Some People Die' (1951), and 'The Blue Hammer' (1976).

Marquand, John P. (1893–1960). Mr. Moto. 'Ming Yellow' (1935) and 'Stopover: Tokyo' (1957).

Mason, F. Van Wyck (1901–78). Hugh North. 'Seeds of Murder' (1930) and 'The Deadly Orbit Mission' (1968).

Pentecost, Hugh (Judson P. Philips, born 1903). Luke Bradley and others. 'Cancelled in Red' (1939), 'The Cannibal Who Overate' (1962), and 'The Homicidal Horse' (1979).

Simenon, Georges (born 1903). Jules Maigret. 'The Strange Case of Peter the Lett' (1933), 'My Friend Maigret' (1956), 'Maigret and the Wine Merchant' (1971), and 'Maigret and the Apparition' (1975).

Spillane, Mickey (Frank Morrison Spillane, born 1918). Mike Hammer. 'My Gun is Quick' (1950), 'Kiss Me, Deadly' (1952), and 'The Body Lovers' (1967).

Stout, Rex (1886–1975). Nero Wolfe and Archie Goodwin. 'Fer-de-Lance' (1934), 'Please Pass the Guilt' (1973), and 'A Family Affair' (1976).

Tey, Josephine (Elizabeth Mackintosh, 1897–1952). Alan Grant. 'The Man in the Queue' (1929) and 'The Singing Sands' (1952).

Van Gulik, Robert (1910–67). Judge Dee. 'The Chinese Maze Murders' (1957), 'The Emperor's Pearl' (1963), and 'The Phantom of the Temple' (1966).

Wahlöö, Per (1926–75) and **Sjöwall, Maj** (born 1935). Martin Beck. 'Roseanna' (1967), 'The Laughing Policeman' (1970), 'The Locked Room' (1973), 'Cop Killer' (1975), and 'The Terrorist' (1977).

Chan's immediate successor, was introduced by S.S. Van Dine in 'The Benson Murder Case' (1926). And Ellery Queen, considered by many critics to be the premier American detective, made his debut in 'The Roman Hat Mystery' in 1929. The books were also written by Ellery Queen, a pen name of two men, Manfred B. Lee and Frederic Dannay. The last, and perhaps most significant, writer of this period was Dashiell Hammett. His narratives established new standards of realism in the detective story. He invented what has been called the "hard-boiled school" of detective fiction, a distinctly American style divorced from its English counterparts. The first of his books was 'Red Harvest' (1929), but the best known was 'The Maltese Falcon' (1930), with its detective hero, Sam Spade. Hammett also created the 'Thin Man' in 1934. Hammett's style of fiction was carried on by Raymond Chandler, Ross Macdonald, and Mickey Spillane.

Other popular American writers of the period were Erle Stanley Gardner, author of the Perry Mason novels; Rex Stout, creator of Nero Wolfe and his sidekick, Archie Goodwin; and John Dickson Carr, who also wrote under the name Carter Dickson. In England the popular writers were Nicholas Blake, Michael Innes, Ngaio Marsh, and Cyril Hare.

Elsewhere in Europe the modern detective story took hold slowly after 1930 and then primarily in the stories of Georges Simenon, with his masterful Inspector Maigret. These stories of police procedure found a popular following, and the style was taken up by Ed McBain in the United States, J.J. Marric in England, and by Maj Sjöwall and Per Wahlöö in Sweden. In The Netherlands, Robert van Gulik wrote the Judge Dee mysteries, set in medieval China.

DETERGENT see SOAP AND DETERGENT.

The Detroit skyline is framed by the Ambassador Bridge, which connects Detroit with Windsor, Ont.

DETROIT, Mich.

Detroit has been a city of industrial excitement ever since Henry Ford rolled his first rickety contraption out of his shed and onto the streets of the city back in 1896. Detroiters were fascinated by cars back then, and they still are. Anybody driving the freeways of the city sees electric signs on big billboards ticking off annual automobile production. When it comes to cars, Detroiters like to keep score.

Most people will forgive them this. Detroit, the nation's sixth largest city, is a land of immense industrial power, and it owes almost all of it to the automobile. The industrial output of Detroit dwarfs that of a good many countries in the world. Steel, cars, robots, and computers are all produced there, but cars are king. In a real sense they make Detroit "America's muscle."

Cars even affect the feel of the city. Detroit is not as sophisticated as New York City or San Francisco, but it is a no-nonsense town. It is a town where a good many believe that people get ahead by hard work, not by inherited wealth, connections, or boasting. Many of the city's top leaders today—politicians, professors, engineers, business executives—are the offspring of factory workers who punched a time clock and carried lunch pails. Their belief in hard work has stuck with them. And Detroiters seem to be rewarded for this work. Wages are higher than the national average, and the cost of living is lower than in many other large American cities.

Physical Description

Detroit has some unattractive concentrations of heavy industry and of poverty. But much of the Detroit area is a pleasant place to live. Because of the prevailing westerly winds, Detroit has low pollution

This article was contributed by Gary Hoffman, Senior Editor, *Monthly Detroit*.

for a large city. For a northern city, the climate is surprisingly mild, largely because of the Great Lakes. The lakes are relatively warm in winter and cool in summer, moderating the temperatures on land. The warmest month is July with an average high of 80° F (26.6° C); the coldest is January with an average high of 33° F (0.6° C). The average annual precipitation is about 32 inches (81 centimeters).

Detroit has some unusual features. On the map it seems to lean against the Detroit River and southwestern Ontario so that some of Canada actually lies to the south of most of Detroit. The Canadian city of Windsor can be seen from Detroit's downtown riverfront. Another surprise is that the river is not actually a river but a strait. It connects Lake Saint Clair to the north and Lake Erie to the south. On it are lake freighters and oceangoing vessels carrying goods between the Midwest and the rest of the world. It is a part of the Saint Lawrence Seaway, providing passage to the Atlantic Ocean.

The city of Detroit sits mostly on a flat plain. The highest natural elevation is just 110 feet (33.5 meters) above the level of the river. On this plain downtown are tall buildings dating back mostly to the 1920s. The magnificent 28-story Fisher building and the 36-story Penobscot building are among the most notable examples. The Detroit neighborhoods begin nearby. The ones closest to downtown are deteriorating badly, but the neighborhoods farther out become progressively more prosperous.

Detroit is a city that grew out, not up. The great majority of the homes and businesses are one-story structures. Detroiters have always found it easiest to build rambling ranch-style homes and bungalows that took advantage of the plentiful land. One sign of Detroit's historic sprawl is that the city actually grew around the cities of Highland Park and Hamtramck. Both are separate cities, yet they exist entirely within the Detroit city limits.

The automobile not only dominates the city's economy but its transportation system as well. An extensive network of expressways was completed by the early 1970s that provides relatively easy access to most areas. The city is served by three airports.

People

Detroiters come from a variety of backgrounds. Although 89 percent of Michigan's population is white, some 63 percent of Detroit's 1.2 million people are black. The city and suburbs also have large numbers of Americans of Polish, Italian, Arab, German, and Irish extraction. The Arab population of Detroit, for instance, has been put at between 200 thousand and 250 thousand. This makes the Detroit area the largest concentration of people of Arab descent in the Western Hemisphere. Their families and the families of most ethnic Detroiters came to the city during the first three decades of the 20th century to work in the automobile factories.

The area retains a strong ethnic flavor, reminiscent of earlier decades. In the early 1980s it had about 135 thousand foreign-born persons. Of these, some 20 thousand were born in Poland, and a somewhat larger number were from Italy.

Detroit is also populated by former farmers from the South and Midwest who came to Detroit for many of the same reasons that the foreign immigrants did, especially jobs. Many Southern whites and blacks came north when hard times hit agriculture in their home states after 1910. The arrival of blacks was especially dramatic. Their numbers jumped from 6,000 in 1910 to 41,000 in 1920. Many were recruited by manufacturers when World War I closed the supply of immigrant labor.

Since World War II many Detroiters have displayed a preference for life in the suburbs over life in the city. Between 1970 and 1980 alone about 21 percent of the city's population moved out of Detroit. Although some black families left, those who departed were mostly whites. In 1980 there were about 415,000 whites in Detroit. In 1970 the figure was about double that. Detroit is not alone, of course, in having "white flight" from the city to the suburbs.

These changes have brought problems. As people left the city, there were fewer people remaining to support the police and other municipal services with their taxes. And, since the people who stayed tended to make less money than those who left, Detroiters in general could not easily afford to have their taxes raised to cover the difference. The median household income in the early 1980s in the city was just about $17,000. In many of the suburbs the figure was twice that. To help support the city, Detroit has turned to the state of Michigan and the federal government for financial aid. The state helps with extra support for the city's cultural institutions, and the federal government has provided hundreds of millions of dollars for the redevelopment of Detroit's inner city.

Government

The responsibility for solving most of these problems falls to the mayor of Detroit. Under the 1974 city charter, he is the official that holds most of the power. Like most major United States cities, Detroit has a "strong mayor" type of government. Under it the mayor initiates most legislation and makes 150 political appointments. (Under the pre-1974 charter, he could make just 26 appointments.) This arrangement gives considerable authority to the heads of city departments. The Detroit City Council, which must approve ordinances, is composed of nine members elected at large.

Since 1974 the mayor of Detroit has been Coleman A. Young, who was raised in Detroit's "black bottom" on the east side. The first black bombardier in the Army Air Corps and an early labor organizer, he enjoys considerable popularity among the city's residents and is the longest-serving mayor in the city's history. He is especially well-known for bringing the $327 million Renaissance Center and other projects along Detroit's riverfront into being.

Industry

Although it is racked by recession from time to time, Detroit's automobile industry is still an awesome economic force. About one third of the nation's new cars each year are produced in southeastern Michigan, and the Big Three automakers all make their home in metropolitan Detroit—the Ford Motor Company in Dearborn, the Chrysler Corporation in Highland Park, and General Motors in Detroit itself. These are huge multinational corporations whose decisions affect business life in countries across the globe—from South America to Africa to Japan. Their combined sales regularly top $100 billion a year. Two smaller automakers—American Motors Corporation and Volkswagen of America—also make their home in the Detroit area as do the Burroughs Corporation, a computer manufacturer, Stroh's Brewery, and Bendix, a high-tech company. And, largely because Detroit is an automotive center, about 226 foreign companies have established branches that employ some 25,000 workers. (See also Automobile Industry.)

Although about 425,000 workers in Detroit are employed in the car industry, it would be a mistake to consider Detroit strictly a blue-collar town. Before 1958 most people did work in manufacturing, but afterward the majority worked in offices, stores, restaurants, and other non-factory settings. More recently the introduction of robot devices in car factories has further reduced the number of blue-collar workers.

But whatever their occupation, the people of Detroit depend indirectly on the automobile industry. No other major American city depends so much on a single industry for its livelihood. When the automobile industry suffers, the entire population suffers. And since people tend to postpone car purchases during recessions, the whole industry can go into a tailspin during hard times. This is why Detroit had an unemployment rate of more than 15 percent during the recession of the early 1980s. But when times are good, the workers in the car industry command salaries about four dollars an hour higher than wages in manufacturing in the rest of the country.

One of the reasons wages are higher is that Detroit has long been a center of organized labor, and the unions have fought hard to keep wages high. Detroit is the home of the United Auto Workers union, and all the legendary leaders—Walter Reuther, Douglas Fraser, and Owen Bieber—have occupied the executive offices of the union headquarters along the river on Detroit's east side. Some critics say that high labor costs have hurt United States car companies in their competition with those of Japan.

Culture and Recreation

Industry, industrialists, and taxpayers of Detroit have given a considerable amount of support to the arts and education. The city has seven colleges and universities, two of which stand out for their excellence. The University of Detroit, founded in 1877 by Jesuit fathers, has an enrollment of more than 6,000, and Wayne State University, founded in 1858, is state-supported with an enrollment of about 20,000. Both have well-respected schools of liberal arts, business, medicine, and law.

In addition, Henry Ford was instrumental in founding the Henry Ford Museum and Greenfield Village, two sister museums in suburban Dearborn that trace the history of the United States through the homes, vehicles, and everyday objects of its people. Detroit also has a world-class symphony and an excellent art museum that contains a surprising number of well-known masterpieces: paintings by Vincent Van Gogh, Pieter Bruegel, and other great masters draw visitors from around the world.

Still another Detroit area cultural institution had a part in shaping the art and design history of the United States. It is the Cranbrook Academy in suburban Bloomfield Hills. It was founded during the 1920s by George G. Booth, son-in-law of James E. Scripps, founder of the *Detroit News.* An art and design school, Cranbrook Academy was dedicated to teaching freedom of expression in these disciplines and was long directed by the Finnish architect Eliel Saarinen. The school has affected trends in sculpture, furniture, and architecture. A commonly seen contribution of Cranbrook is the famous Charles Eames chair of molded wood so often seen in business conference rooms across the country.

The Renaissance Center stands behind the Ford Auditorium, home of the Detroit Symphony.

Dick Pietrzyk—CLICK/Chicago

Cultural institutions are not the only things that occupy Detroiters' time. Detroit is the scene of a lively recreational life. Situated as it is on the Detroit River and near two large lakes—Lake St. Clair and Lake Erie—water-related activities are a major attraction. Smelt and coho salmon can be caught along the banks of the Detroit River. Many residents of the metropolitan area also like to hunt, fish, camp, and swim in northern Michigan, just a few hours away. It has been said that Michigan's north—with its lakes, streams, and forests—is one big backyard for Detroiters.

History

Indians were the first people to lay eyes on the region after glaciers withdrew northward about 15,000 years ago—after the last Ice Age. The first Indians hunted caribou and deer, and later immigrants from the south brought agriculture. The first Indians to be seen by white men were of the Chippewa, Wyandot, and Huron tribes. Those white men were hardy French explorers and trappers from Quebec, known as voyageurs, who passed the present site of the city dozens of times without taking notice of it. The first recorded sighting of the area was by Father Louis Hennepin, a French priest aboard the *Griffon,* a ship built above Niagara Falls to explore the Great Lakes in the 17th century. He described the area as teeming with deer, goats, and other game and full of meadows and wooded groves.

It was one of his countrymen, Antoine Laumet de la Mothe Cadillac, who actually founded Detroit. A swashbuckling figure resembling someone out of the Three Musketeers, Cadillac was an expert dueler and social climber. Originally named simply Antoine Laumet, he changed his name when he arrived in the New World, presumably to make it sound more noble. An army officer from the south of France, he had already been stationed in the north of present-day Michigan when he persuaded Louis XIV of France to allow him to establish a fort on the strait between Lake St. Clair and Lake Erie. His argument was that the fort would protect the French fur trade. Thus it has been said that Detroit was born to keep Louis XIV in fur hats.

Originally the settlement at Detroit was simply a rough fort on the banks of the Detroit River in what is now downtown. French trappers, many married to Indian women, settled and farmed nearby on long, narrow plots later known as ribbon farms. These early farms produced wheat and oats; Indian slaves—mostly Pawnees from far to the west—helped the settlers work the land.

The name Detroit comes from the French word *détroit,* meaning "strait"; the early French were more precise in their geographic terms than were the later English inhabitants. The name, however, survived. In 1760 Detroit was conquered by the British in the French and Indian War and remained in British possession until 1896—well after the American Revolution. Under the British, the character of the community hardly changed at all. The settlers were still predominantly French, though a large group of them became very unhappy with their new rulers and fled to an area about 30 miles (50 kilometers) south, where they established their own community. The Indians, too, disliked the British. Chief Pontiac of the Ottawa tribe nearly took Detroit from the British in a military action that historians would later call the Pontiac Conspiracy.

During the Revolutionary War Detroit had little military action. The British used it mostly as a launching point for attacks on American settlers and forces in New York, Pennsylvania, and Kentucky. After the war Detroit remained a sleepy little outpost with hundreds of French farmers and a handful of English and American traders. One of the few exciting things that happened during this time was the fire in 1805 that started in the stable of a baker named John Harvey and burned the entire town. But Detroit came of age in 1825, when the Erie Canal was completed. Suddenly the time it took to travel from the East coast to Detroit was reduced from a month to a mere five and a half days.

The small town boomed. Yankees from New England brought their families to Michigan, cleared the virgin woods, and began farming. Fortunes were made and lost in land speculation. Merchants grew rich through the sale of farming implements, and lumber barons began carving up the state's forests. The population of Detroit grew from 2,000 in 1830 to more than 30,000 in 1855. One of the immigrants was an Irishman named John Ford. His grandson, Henry, would later become famous for putting Detroit and the world on wheels. After the discovery of copper and iron in northern Michigan, Detroit started to prosper as a manufacturing center. Long before the first car rolled on its streets, the city was known as the potbelly stove capital of the nation. In addition it produced railway equipment, boats, and marine engines. So there was no shortage of the skilled labor needed to build the first American cars.

In 1910, 38 companies were making automobiles in the Detroit area. In 1917 the total annual production reached one million. As the competition intensified, Henry Ford and other pioneers turned to innovations in mass production to cut the costs of the new vehicles. Ford's mass production techniques reached a high point in 1919, when he established the first automotive assembly line in his massive new plant in Highland Park. (*See also* Automobile, section "History"; Ford, Henry.)

It was this industry and the high-paying jobs with it that attracted so many American and immigrant workers to Detroit. By 1920 Detroit's population reached 993,000. Detroit boomed during the 1920s but fell to desperate straits during the depression of the 1930s, when all but the biggest automakers went bankrupt and disappeared. During the summer of 1931 about one third of the city's workers were without jobs, and landlords were evicting families at the rate of 150 a day. Battles frequently erupted between police and labor demonstrators who protested

Dick Pietrzyk—CLICK/Chicago

A replica of Rodin's 'The Thinker' sits before the main entrance to Detroit's Institute of Arts.

wage cuts and long hours in the factories. One of the most famous Detroiters during this period was probably Father Charles Coughlin, who preached against Communism but fostered his form of right-wing extremism from the pulpit and on his national radio show from suburban Royal Oak.

It was only at the onset of World War II that the growing need for tanks, trucks, planes, and jeeps brought Detroit out of the Great Depression. During this time Detroit became the nation's arsenal of democracy. In a single plant, for instance, 8,000 B-24 bombers were produced during the war.

After the war, returning GIs chose the suburbs over the city, and the urban sprawl began. Tract homes extended to the north, east, and west of the city. The car industry boomed until the 1970s. Henry Ford II, a grandson of Henry Ford, became a folk hero for saving the failing Ford Motor Company with the introduction of the popular 1949 Ford.

In the 1950s Detroit produced cars with great fins and large amounts of chrome, and Americans bought them by the millions. But all metropolitan Detroiters did not share in the prosperity. The city itself began a slow decline as the suburbs prospered. The poverty of many sections of Detroit has been blamed for the race riots of August 1967, which started with a police raid on an after-hours drinking establishment. Similar disturbances have not recurred, and reforms in the police department, designed to ease racial tensions, and improvements in the economic conditions of some blacks are believed to have made the difference in recent years. Population (1980 census), city, 1,203,339; metropolitan area, 4,227,762.

BIBLIOGRAPHY FOR DETROIT

Babson, Steve. Working Detroit: the Making of a Union Town (Watts, 1984).
Fischhoff, Martin, ed. Detroit Guide (Detroit Guide, 1983).
Kornhauser, Arthur. Detroit As the People See It: a Survey of Attitudes in an Industrial City (Greenwood, 1977).
Levine, D.A. Internal Combustion: the Races in Detroit 1915–1926 (Greenwood, 1976).
Vexler, R.I. Detroit: a Chronological and Documentary History 1701–1976 (Oceana, 1977).

DE VALERA, Eamon (1882–1975). An American-born schoolteacher, Eamon De Valera became one of Ireland's greatest leaders in its struggle for independence. After the country was freed from British rule in 1922, he led it from 1932 to 1948, first as president of the executive council and later as prime minister. After the Republic of Ireland was proclaimed, he served two terms as its prime minister before he was elected president in 1959 and in 1966.

Edward De Valera was born in New York City on Oct. 14, 1882. His father was Spanish, and his mother Irish. When the boy was 2 years old his father died, and Edward went to live with his grandmother in County Limerick, Ireland. In school he was a brilliant student and a good athlete, especially in track. At 16 he won a scholarship to Blackrock College. In 1904 he got a degree in mathematics at Royal University, now the National University of Ireland.

For years De Valera gave little thought to politics. He taught languages and mathematics at several schools. He also joined the Gaelic League, which aimed to revive Irish culture and the ancient Gaelic language. In 1910 he married Jane O'Flanagan, a teacher of Gaelic. They later adopted the Gaelic versions of their names—Eamon and Sinead. The couple had five sons and two daughters.

In 1913 he joined the Volunteers, an underground army pledged to fight British rule. During the Easter Week rebellion in 1916 he led a group of 50. All the leaders were executed except De Valera. His life was spared because of his American birth, but he was sentenced to life imprisonment. In jail he studied mathematics and read widely. In 1917 the British released all political prisoners. De Valera was at once elected to the Irish Parliament and rose to leadership in the Sinn Fein, the Irish revolutionary party.

Again jailed for revolutionary activity, he escaped to America in 1919 and raised millions of dollars for the Irish cause. The Anglo-Irish Treaty of 1921 was far short of De Valera's ideal of an independent Ireland. He refused to accept it. His republican group fought the Free State government, and in 1923 De Valera was again sent to prison.

The Sinn Fein returned him to Parliament in 1924, but the party split on taking the oath of allegiance to the king. In 1926 he formed a new party, Fianna Fail (Soldiers of Destiny). It won control in 1932. He became president of the executive council.

In 1933 and 1938 to 1939 De Valera was president of the League of Nations Assembly. In 1938 he became prime minister of Ireland. Defeated for office in 1948, he was prime minister again from 1951 to 1954 and from 1957 to 1959, when he resigned to seek election as president. He won and was reelected in 1966. De Valera retired in 1973. He died in Dublin on Aug. 29, 1975.

DEWEY, George (1837–1917). On the night of April 30, 1898, six United States war vessels commanded by Commodore George Dewey moved boldly into Manila Bay in the Spanish-held Philippine Islands. Dewey had been ordered to "capture or destroy" the Spanish fleet. On the following day he won a battle that made naval history.

George Dewey was born in Montpelier, Vt., on Dec. 26, 1837. He was graduated from the Naval Academy at Annapolis in 1858. During the Civil War he served under Admiral David G. Farragut in the battle of New Orleans. After the war he rose through the ranks of lieutenant commander, commander, and captain. Finally as commodore he was placed in command of the Asian naval squadron.

When war between the United States and Spain was declared in 1898, the squadron was docked off Hong Kong. Ordered to attack the Spanish at Manila, Dewey pushed his vessels there at full speed. In the early dawn of May 1, the American warships, steaming in column formation, bore down on the Spanish ships. They were drawn up in front of Cavite Point. Within a few hours Dewey destroyed the enemy ships, silenced the Spanish land batteries, and captured the Philippines' chief port. The victory was achieved without the loss of a ship or a man.

As soon as the news reached America, President William McKinley appointed Dewey a rear admiral. Before the hero's return to the United States in 1899, he had been made admiral. This rank had been given only to Farragut and David D. Porter. Congress voted that Dewey should never be placed on the retired list of the Navy. He was still considered in active service when he died on Jan. 16, 1917, though he was 79 years old at the time.

DEWEY, John (1859–1952). One of the most notable American philosophers of the 20th century, John Dewey was also a pioneer in educational theory and method. Out of his ideas developed the progressive education movement that was very influential in schools until about 1950. In philosophy he shares with William James and Charles Sanders Peirce the distinction of founding the movement called pragmatism. (*See also* Education.)

Dewey was born in Burlington, Vt., on Oct. 20, 1859. He attended the University of Vermont and Johns Hopkins University. In 1884 he went to the University of Michigan as an instructor in philosophy and psychology. From 1894 to 1904 he headed a department of philosophy, psychology, and education at the University of Chicago. In 1904 Dewey moved to Columbia University in New York City as professor of philosophy. He remained there for the rest of his teaching career.

Dewey and his wife, the former Alice Chipman, started the Laboratory School at the University of Chicago to test his educational theories. Learning by doing was the heart of his method. The children were given freedom to learn in accordance with their needs and experiences. The faculty was able to study child behavior, a new area of study at the time.

Dewey regarded the school as a community—a part of society. He looked upon education as a process of living, not as preparation for later living. His ideas were incorporated in a number of books, including the influential 'The School and Society' published in 1899 and 'Experience and Education' (1938). In philosophy, Dewey's pragmatic theories insisted that the way to test ideas was to check them against their consequences rather than to claim their agreement with supposedly self-evident truth. His philosophy was suited to American life, characterized by its respect for science and technology, diversity, and practicality. When faced with a problem, said Dewey, a person must logically examine the options open to him to find the best solution supported by the facts. This method of inquiry and testing should be applied to moral and social questions, as well as to technological and scientific ones. His theories were set forth in a number of books, including 'Reconstruction in Philosophy', published in 1920, 'Experience and Nature' (1925), 'Art as Experience' (1934), and 'Freedom and Culture' (1939). Dewey retired from teaching in 1930. He died in New York City on June 1, 1952.

DHAKA, or DACCA, Bangladesh.

The capital city of Bangladesh, Dhaka is also the largest of the cities in the country. The city's name is said to refer either to the *dhak* tree that once flourished in the area or to Dhakeswari, "The Hidden Goddess," whose shrine is located in the western part of the city.

Together with its river port of Narayanganj, 10 miles (16 kilometers) to the south, Dhaka is the largest industrial area in the country. Its products include embroidery, silk, jewelry, and fine-quality muslin. The city is also an educational center and houses the University of Dhaka, which was founded in 1921. There is also a university of engineering and technology, an agricultural university, a nuclear-science training and research center, and a library. Museums include the Balda Museum and the Dhaka Museum, both of which have collections of art and archaeology. Recreational facilities include a stadium and Ramna Park, which is a mile (1.6 kilometers) from the city center.

Dhaka is located in the center of the country and occupies about 100 square miles (260 square kilometers). The city is served by three rivers, which help to make the area fertile. To the south is the old city, where there are many historic buildings. There are more than 700 mosques, the oldest dating back to 1456. Buildings of the Muslim period include Lal Bagh fort, dating back to 1678, with hidden passageways and the tomb of Bibi Pari, who was the wife of a governor of Bengal; the Bara Katra, the great caravansary, or inn, (1664); the Chhota Katra (small caravansary, 1663); and Husayni Dalan, a religious monument of the Shi'ite sect (1642). Other 17th-century buildings include the Hindu Dhakeswari temple and Tejgaon church, which was built by the Portuguese. The National Capitol, designed by American architect Louis

Kahn and completed in 1983, was built with large geometric holes and shafts to admit light while preventing glare.

Dhaka became prominent in the 17th century, when it flourished as a provincial capital of the Mughal empire. It was the center of an active sea trade, attracting English, French, and Dutch merchants. When the provincial capital was moved to Murshidabad in 1704 and the muslin industry slowed, Dhaka entered a period of decline. It passed to British control in 1765 and became a municipality in 1864, but decay continued until Dhaka was designated the capital of Eastern Bengal and Assam province in 1905. During the early 20th century, Dhaka served as a commercial center and seat of learning. It became the capital of East Bengal province in 1947 and of East Pakistan in 1956. Dhaka was the scene of heavy fighting in 1971 during the war of independence, when East Pakistan separated to become Bangladesh. Population (1981 census), 3,160,200.

DIABETES. The word diabetes, meaning "a siphon," was first used by the Greek physician Aretaeus in AD 2 to describe patients with great thirst and excessive urination. In the 17th century it was noticed that the urine of diabetic patients was sweet, so the word mellitus, meaning "like honey," was added to the name of the disease. Another disease called diabetes is diabetes insipidus. It is rare.

Diabetes mellitus is characterized by abnormally high levels of sugar in the form of glucose in both the blood and the urine. The disease occurs when the body does not produce enough of the hormone insulin or when the body's cells cannot use the insulin that is available even if there is a sufficient amount. Insulin is produced in the pancreas and regulates the body's use of glucose. When the amount of insulin is inadequate, glucose in the blood cannot be taken up by the body's cells. Glucose, therefore, remains in the blood stream and then is passed out of the body in the urine (*see* Disease, "Metabolic and Deficiency Diseases"; Hormones).

There are two main types of diabetes mellitus: Type I, or insulin-dependent, and Type II, or non-insulin-dependent. Type I, sometimes called juvenile-onset diabetes, often develops during childhood but may occur at any age. People with Type I diabetes have low or absent levels of insulin and must inject insulin into their bodies each day.

Type II diabetes mostly affects adults, usually over the age of 40, and tends to run in families. People with this form of the disease may have normal, high, or low insulin levels, but the insulin is blocked from getting to receptor sites on the body's cells and, therefore, cannot be used by them. Type II diabetes is more common in women than men, and 60 to 90 percent of these diabetics are overweight.

Symptoms and Complications

If Type I diabetes goes untreated the life-threatening condition called ketoacidosis develops rapidly.

The symptoms include excessive urination, thirst, appetite loss, and vomiting. If not treated quickly, coma and death can follow. Type II diabetes symptoms include excessive urination and thirst, hunger, some weight loss, and fatigue. These symptoms usually appear gradually and may even go unnoticed at first.

Prolonged, high levels of blood sugar can cause the walls of small blood vessels to thicken. This condition, called arteriosclerosis, can lead to heart disease and stroke. Impaired circulation in the legs can cause gangrene, requiring the amputation of toes or even legs. A condition called diabetic retinopathy causes hemorrhages, or bleeding, in the tiny capillaries of the retina in the eye, leading to blindness. Kidney failure can also occur from inadequate circulation. Neuropathy is a complication in which the nerves are damaged, usually in the arms and legs, causing either pain or loss of feeling.

Diagnosis and Treatment

Although high glucose levels are present in the urine in diabetes, a urine test alone cannot confirm that the disease is present since other things can cause sugar to appear in the urine. Diabetes is diagnosed with a glucose-tolerance test, which measures the rate at which sugar is removed from the blood. Glucose is usually given in a beverage, and blood samples are drawn at intervals. Because the pancreas normally responds to a rise in blood sugar by producing more insulin, a high glucose level after several hours indicates insufficient insulin.

The correct diet is essential for all people with diabetes, and in many people with Type II diabetes, the disease can be controlled by diet alone. Intake of calories should be consistent. Carbohydrates, fats, and proteins should be evenly distributed into three main meals and between-meal snacks. Exercise and weight control are also important. Researchers have found that overweight people with Type II diabetes often begin to manufacture insulin again after losing weight and getting regular exercise.

For approximately 50 percent of the people with diabetes, diet alone cannot control the disease and insulin is necessary. In some mild cases drugs called sulfonylureas can be taken orally to lower blood sugar. People with Type I and some with Type II diabetes require insulin injections. Insulin dosages are specific to the individual and must be monitored closely, since diet, activity, or illness can affect a person's insulin needs. Glucose levels in the urine or blood must be checked daily so that the insulin dosage can be adjusted when necessary. Special paper or tablets that change color on contact with sugar are used to monitor glucose levels in the urine. Measuring the sugar level in a drop of blood from a finger prick is more accurate and is often done daily by the diabetic at home.

Diabetes insipidus is characterized by excessive thirst and a large production of urine. It is caused by a lack of the hormone vasopressin, which is produced in the hypothalamus gland in the brain.

Sergei Diaghilev

Courtesy of the Dance Collection, the New York Public Library at Lincoln Center, Aster, Lenox and Tilden Foundations

DIAGHILEV, Sergei (1872–1929). The man who revolutionized ballet in the early 20th century was not a dancer. He was Sergei Pavlovich Diaghilev, who combined great music, painting, and drama with new types of choreography in the dance company he founded and directed, the Ballets Russes.

Diaghilev was born in the Novgorod province (now in the Russian S.F.S.R.). He was trained in music and law. He began organizing art exhibitions and publications while in his 20s. His career took off when he moved to Paris, where in 1909 he started the Ballets Russes to combine many art forms into one. Diaghilev used the best artists available. He employed the talents of dancers Pavlova and Nijinsky; choreographers Fokine, Massine, and Balanchine; painters Bakst and Picasso; composers Stravinsky and Ravel; and poet Cocteau, among others.

What the Ballets Russes presented was unusual to audiences. The choreography was more expressive and the music more forceful than ever before, with sometimes unsettling consequences. Stravinsky's masterpieces 'The Firebird', performed in 1910, and 'Petrushka' (1911) were appreciated, but the music of his 'The Rite of Spring' (1913) caused such booing from the audience that the dancers could not even hear the orchestra.

Diaghilev toured his company extensively, permanently rekindling enthusiasm for the dance. He died in Venice on Aug. 19, 1929. (*See also* Ballet, section on European History.)

DIAGNOSIS. The examination of a person to determine the cause of an illness results in a diagnosis, or the determination of what disease is present. The correct diagnosis is necessary if the illness is to be treated properly. Sometimes a diagnosis can be made quickly when the symptoms of an illness are specific for a disease, such as the distinctive rash of chicken pox. But often a physician must play detective by matching clues to the disease in order to arrive at a diagnosis. (*See also* Disease; Medicine.)

The process of diagnosing a disease begins with the person's health history. This includes questions on both present and past illnesses, family history of disease, and habits. The general physical examination that follows includes measuring height, weight, and taking blood pressure; listening to the heart and lungs with a stethoscope; and examining eyes, ears, and mouth. Tests of hearing and vision are sometimes performed in routine physical examinations. Reflex tests are simple tests of nerve conduction that involve, among several other tests, tapping with a rubber hammer in areas such as the knee. The remainder of the examination will usually depend on the person's symptoms.

Diagnostic Procedures

The body's fluids often reveal important information about disease. Blood tests can determine whether the person has anemia—that is, insufficient amount of healthy red blood cells—infection, or a blood disease such as leukemia. Blood analysis can also uncover nutritional deficiencies and other disorders. The functioning of the thyroid gland, which regulates the body's rate of metabolism, and the immune system can be evaluated from blood samples. The glucose tolerance test, which is used to diagnose diabetes, measures insulin activity by monitoring the level of glucose, or sugar, in the blood (see Diabetes).

Urine is also tested for glucose as well as for bacteria, protein, and other materials. Glucose in the urine is sometimes caused by diabetes. Bacteria in the urine can indicate a kidney or bladder infection, and the presence of protein may result from a kidney disorder. A stool sample is tested for disease-causing microorganisms and for blood, which is often a symptom of intestinal disease.

Spinal fluid is examined for microorganisms and other unusual contents when a nervous system disorder is suspected. Mucus from the nose and throat can be tested to identify the organisms responsible for respiratory infections.

A sample of tissue can be taken from an organ or any other part of the body by a process called biopsy. The tissue is then sliced into very thin sections, stained with special dyes, and studied under the microscope to discover abnormalities in the cells. Breast lumps, for example, are biopsied to find out if they are cancerous. Bone marrow is usually biopsied when a blood disease, such as leukemia, is suspected.

Radiographs, or X-ray photographs, are used to examine various parts of the body. A chest X ray, for example, can help diagnose tumors, pneumonia, and tuberculosis. X rays can also show bone fractures and other conditions of the musculoskeletal system.

Radiopaque liquids are injected into the urinary tract, spinal column, circulatory system, and other areas. These materials do not allow X rays to pass through them. Thus they allow X-ray examination of soft tissues that would otherwise be invisible by X ray. Spinal cord disorders, for example, often show up in myelograms after a radiopaque liquid has been injected into the spinal canal. Various kinds of angiograms show heart and circulatory disease. In these procedures a radiopaque dye is injected into a vein or artery. X-ray photographs will then show if there is a blockage or an aneurism—an outpocketing.

X-ray examination of the esophagus and stomach is carried out by having the patient swallow a radiopaque solution to highlight details in the upper gastrointestinal tract. For X raying the lower intestinal tract, the solution is given in an enema.

CAT, or CT, scanners (computerized axial tomography scanners) are specialized X-ray cameras that take highly detailed images of hard and soft tissues. By picturing one layer of the body's tissues at a time, CAT scanners can detect very small tumors and other disorders.

In the procedure termed scintigraphy, a small amount of a radioactive isotope is introduced into the body. A scintiscan camera, or scintillascope, measures the uptake and concentration of the isotope in certain tissues, such as the brain, kidney, or thyroid gland. Metabolic diseases and other disorders can be uncovered by this technique.

Ultrasonography is useful in locating tumors of the lung and abdominal cavity. It employs ultra high frequency sound waves to form television images of internal organs. Because it produces no x-radiation, ultrasound is sometimes used during pregnancy to determine the size and position of the fetus.

Both the heart muscle and the nervous system produce electrical impulses that can be measured with special machines. The electrocardiograph (ECG) is useful for diagnosing certain heart conditions. With electrodes taped to a person's chest, the electrical activity of the heart can be recorded while the patient is either resting or performing some activity, such as walking on a treadmill. The electroencephalogram (EEG) measures the electrical activity of the brain through electrodes attached to the head. This test detects whether there is an area of irritability in the brain, such as occurs in epilepsy. The electromyogram (EMG) records the activity of nerves in muscles. The EMG is helpful in diagnosing degenerative nerve disorders such as multiple sclerosis.

Tests of pulmonary function measure the breathing capacity of the lungs and airways. By exhaling into a tube connected to a machine called a spirometer, information is obtained on respiratory functions.

Fiber optic technology has allowed physicians to see parts of the body that previously could be seen only by performing surgery. Fiber optic tools are essentially hair-thin glass fibers that can enter small areas and can be moved deep into the body cavities. Fiber optic light sources and lenses are used to examine the colon, and the fiberbronchoscope can be used to view the bronchial tubes in the lung.

A pelvic examination is performed to assess the general reproductive health of a woman. The Pap smear (Papanicolaou's test) is a test for cancer of the cervix. A breast examination can detect lumps that may indicate cancer.

Skin tests are used to diagnose hypersensitivity conditions, or allergies. Psychological tests are used to diagnose learning and mental disorders. With the aid of these and other tests, the physician can arrive at a diagnosis and institute the appropriate treatment.

DIAMOND

The rough diamond, center, gives little hint of its potential beauty—surrounded as it is with its matrix, the natural material in which it was found in South Africa.

Courtesy of the Field Museum of Natural History

DIAMOND. The fiery brilliance of the diamond has made it the world's favorite jewel. The word comes from the Greek term *adamas*, which means "unconquerable." The diamond is the hardest natural substance found on Earth. Diamond-tipped industrial tools can cut through granite as easily as a steel saw cuts through wood.

Diamonds are crystals of pure carbon that have been subjected to tremendous pressure and heat. This process is believed to have taken place deep in the Earth. Synthetic, or man-made, diamonds became possible in 1955, when the General Electric Company used laboratory equipment to subject graphite to great pressure and heat.

The weights of both gem and industrial diamonds are expressed in metric carats. One carat equals one fifth of a gram. (*See also* Carbon.)

Sources

Diamonds were probably formed millions of years ago in molten lava. As the lava flowed to the Earth's surface through vents known as pipes, it cooled and solidified into kimberlite, a blue rock. Kimberlite contains the diamonds and is known to diamond miners as blue ground.

Diamonds have been found on all continents. India was once a chief source. About AD 600 diamonds were found in Borneo and are still mined there. The rich fields of Brazil were discovered in the 1700s. In the 19th century even richer diamond fields were found in South Africa. Most of the world's diamonds are mined in African countries. Zaire produces mostly industrial diamonds. South Africa is the major source of gem-quality diamonds. Congo, Ghana, Namibia (South West Africa), and Angola are other major suppliers. The Soviet Union has diamond-mining operations in northeastern Siberia. Since the late 1970s many diamond finds have been made in Australia.

About 20 percent of the world's output is used for industrial purposes, with the United States importing some 60 percent of the industrial diamonds mined. A few diamonds are found in Pike County, Ark., near Murfreesboro, and diamonds have also been found in the Upper Peninsula of Michigan.

How Diamonds Are Mined

In mining kimberlite, shafts are sunk some distance from the blue-ground pipe. Tunnels are then driven from the mine shaft to the pipe. Elevators take the kimberlite aboveground, where it is processed. The shaft of the Kimberley mine in South Africa is more than 3,500 feet (1,000 meters) deep. Pipe mines are found in South Africa and Tanzania. Arkansas diamonds are also taken from a pipe.

In other parts of Africa and in the rest of the world, diamonds are found in alluvial soils, or soils of sediment that have been deposited by running water. In 1962, however, diamonds were for the first time taken from the ocean floor, near Namibia. In this process a rubber hose 12 inches (30 centimeters) in diameter is extended from a barge to the bottom of the sea. Like a huge vacuum cleaner, it sucks up gravel. The diamonds are then removed, and the gravel is dumped. On the average a ton of gravel contains one diamond, whereas it requires some 20 tons of kimberlite to yield a diamond.

Qualities of a Gem Diamond

The brilliance and fire of a gem diamond result from its properties of refraction, reflection, and dispersion. Upon passing through a diamond facet (one of many small planes cut onto the gem surface), a light ray is refracted, or bent. The bent ray is reflected from a bottom facet upward through a top facet. In refraction each color of the ray is bent at a slightly different angle. This spreading of colors is called dispersion. Since refraction occurs both as the ray enters and as it leaves the diamond, dispersion also occurs twice. Thus the ray is emitted as a glittering rainbow. Of all gems the diamond has the highest property, or index, of refraction: 2.419. (*See also* Light.)

Most diamonds are tinged with color. If a diamond's color is sufficiently intense, it is prized as a gem and called a "fancy." Blue and pink diamonds are

PIGOTT   POLAR STAR   HOPE BLUE   SANCY   STEWART

TIFFANY YELLOW   KOH-I-NOOR (RECUT)   JUBILEE   KOH-I-NOOR (1ST CUT)   AKBAR SHAH

DRESDEN GREEN   STAR OF SOUTH AFRICA   ORLOFF   EMPRESS EUGÉNIE   ENGLISH DRESDEN

BLUE TAVERNIER   STAR OF THE SOUTH   CULLINAN I   JONKER   WHITE TAVERNIER

PASHA OF EGYPT   NASSAK   GREAT MOGUL   FLORENTINE   STAR OF ESTE

MATAN   SHAH OF PERSIA   NIZAM   DARYAINOOR   REGENT, OR PITT

These are replicas of famous diamonds. Tales of slaves, royalty, theft, and murder are told about the real gems. Some, such as the Great Mogul, have disappeared. The Pigott was reported smashed by order of its dying owner, Ali Pasha, vizier of Albania. The Matan, a Borneo stone, has never been examined by an expert. It may be a crystal and not a diamond at all.

CULLINAN ROUGH   CULLINAN I   CULLINAN IV   CULLINAN III   CULLINAN II

These are glass replicas of the Cullinan rough, largest diamond ever found, and the nine largest gems cut from it. The originals are among the English crown jewels. The four largest are: I, a pendeloque cut, set in the scepter; IV, a square; III, a pendeloque; and II, a square brilliant. The bottom row cuts are: emerald, marquise, heart shape, marquise, and pendeloque.

129

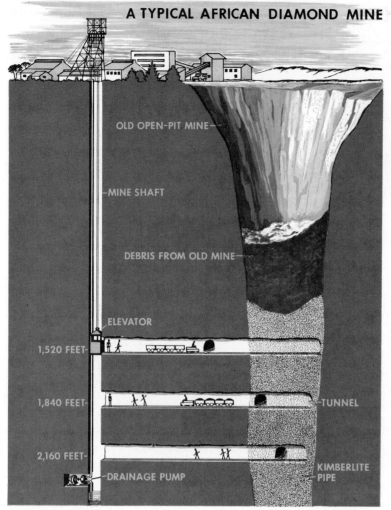

A TYPICAL AFRICAN DIAMOND MINE

OLD OPEN-PIT MINE

MINE SHAFT

DEBRIS FROM OLD MINE

ELEVATOR

1,520 FEET

1,840 FEET — TUNNEL

2,160 FEET

DRAINAGE PUMP

KIMBERLITE PIPE

Diamond-bearing kimberlite is often found in the vents, or pipes, of old volcanoes. After it has been blasted loose by dyna-mite it is carried to the elevator in ore cars. Then it is taken to the surface and processed to eliminate waste materials.

cut is the most popular. This has 58 facets, 33 above the girdle (circle at greatest diameter) and 25 below. (For diagrams of the cuts, see Jewelry and Gems.)

The diamond cutter's trade is highly skilled. His task is to place the facets so that the most light rays will reflect through the top facets. Antwerp and Amsterdam are the traditional centers of the diamond-cutting industry. New York City also is an important cutting center.

How Industry Uses Diamonds

In even the best gem-producing areas only about 25 per cent of the diamonds mined are of gem quality. The rest, of poor gem quality because of color or faults, are used in industry. An old saying, "it takes a diamond to cut a diamond," is true. Diamonds are employed by the lapidary (gem cutter) to shape and polish diamonds and other gems.

The stones also are used to true the surfaces of precision grinding wheels. In machine shops tools tipped with diamonds cut grooves around automobile pistons and perform other precision-cutting tasks. Needles tipped with diamond dust drill holes through some diamonds. A new process does this electrically. Diamonds with holes are used as feeder nozzles for oil furnaces and as wire-drawing dies. Some 400 tons of copper can be drawn through a diamond die into a wire fine enough to circle the world 20 times before the die shows signs of wear (see Wire). Geologists and engineers use diamond-tipped hollow steel bits for drilling into the earth to secure samples of deep-lying rock formations (see Mines and Mining).

Famous Old Diamonds

The Koh-i-noor is probably the best known of all diamond gems. There is a tradition that it was taken in 1304 from a rajah at Malwa, whose family had held it for centuries. It is believed to have been guarded with other treasures at Delhi until 1739, when it was carried off by Nadir Shah of Persia. After further adventures the diamond was surrendered to the East India Company, whose directors presented it to Queen Victoria of England. It weighed 186 carats. Queen Victoria had it recut in 1852, and the gem now weighs 106 carats. It is among the English crown jewels.

The Great Mogul was the largest Indian diamond

the most valuable. Red diamonds are very rare. Clear white diamonds are called diamonds of the first water.

Cutting and Polishing the Gem Diamond

When found or mined diamonds look like fragments of glass. Two or more gems are usually cut from a rough stone. Diamonds are first split or sawed along the grain of the stone. The pieces are then mounted in a lathe. The fast-turning gem is shaped roughly by a diamond-tipped tool. The stone is then placed in solder in a *dop* (holder), and a facet is ground on the surface by a spinning iron disk bearing a paste made of diamond dust and olive oil. The cutting of each facet requires changing the position of the stone in the dop. In order to grasp the larger diamonds, dops are equipped with mechanical holding fingers.

Diamond gems have been cut in many different shapes. Some of these are shown on the preceding page of pictures of famous diamonds. The *brilliant*

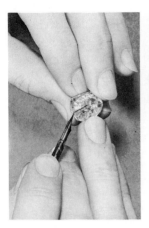

known. The rough stone weighed 817 carats, but inexpert cutting later reduced it to $287\frac{1}{2}$ carats. The Orloff, now part of the Soviet diamond treasury, was one of the Russian crown jewels. Legend says that it was one of the eyes of an idol in a Brahman temple. It was eventually sold to Count Orloff, once a favorite of Catherine the Great. He gave the gem to Catherine, hoping the gift would restore him to favor, but it did not. As cut, the stone weighs 199.6 carats.

The Blue Tavernier, a $112\frac{1}{2}$-carat Indian diamond, was taken to France in the 17th century. King Louis XIV bought it and had it recut to about 68 carats. In 1792 it was stolen, along with the Regent and the Sancy. The Regent was recovered quickly, and the Sancy in about 1828, but the Blue Tavernier was never found. In 1830, however, the $44\frac{1}{2}$-carat blue diamond now called the Hope appeared on the market. Some gem experts believe that the Hope diamond is a recut version of the lost Blue Tavernier.

The Regent, or Pitt, diamond, which weighed 410 carats in the rough, was found in India in 1701. Sir Thomas Pitt, governor of Madras, India, bought it and had it cut down to 143.2 carats. In 1717 Pitt sold it to the regent of France. Later Napoleon had it set in the hilt of his sword. After his fall it was placed in the Louvre. The Excelsior, discovered in South Africa in 1893, weighed $969\frac{1}{2}$ carats. From this stone were cut ten fine stones, ranging in weight from 13 to 68 carats.

Famous Diamonds Found Since 1900

The largest diamond ever found was the Cullinan. It was taken in 1905 from the Premier mine in Transvaal, South Africa. It was as large as a man's fist and weighed 3,106 carats ($1\frac{1}{3}$ pounds). In 1907 the Transvaal government presented it to King Edward VII. The next year it was cut into 9 large and more than 90 small stones. Edward desired the larger stones to be called Stars of Africa, but they are also known as Cullinan I, II, III, and so on. Cullinan I (530 carats) is set in the British scepter; Cullinan II (309 carats) is in the British state crown.

The Jacobus Jonker (726 carats) was named for the prospector who found it in Transvaal in 1934. In 1935

A rough diamond is marked for splitting (left). A light tap of a mallet (center) cleaves the stone in two. Shaping, or girdling (top right) is done by rotating it on a lathe. Facets are cut on the diamond by pressing it against an iron wheel coated with olive oil and diamond dust (right).

(Top right) Courtesy De Beers Consolidated Mines, Ltd.; (others) N.W. Ayer & Sons, Inc.

it sold for more than $750,000. Twelve gems were cut from it by a New York City cutter. It was the first large diamond cut in the United States. The Vargas diamond (726.6 carats), discovered in 1938 in Brazil, was cut into 29 gems. In 1945 a 770-carat diamond, the fourth largest ever found and the largest ever taken from alluvial deposits, was dug up alongside the Woyie River in Sierra Leone.

DIAPHRAGM. After the heart, the diaphragm is perhaps the most important muscle in the body. It is a dome-shaped membrane, extending across the body below the chest cavity and separating the lungs and heart from the abdomen. Its edge follows the general outlines of the lower ribs, being fastened to the breastbone in front. When the diaphragm straightens out and compresses downward, it sucks air into the lungs. It is thus the chief muscle of breathing. The muscles between the ribs are also used in breathing (see Respiration).

Diaphragm breathing means using the diaphragm almost entirely, leaving the upper ribs extended in a stationary position. Singers and speakers use diaphragm breathing to obtain great volume and control of the voice. For ordinary purposes it is better to use both the ribs and the diaphragm in breathing. Anything that restricts breathing, such as tight clothing, should be avoided.

DIARY. A diary is a daily personal record. In it the writer is free to record anything at all. This may include events, comments, ideas, reading notes, or any subject on one's mind as the entry that covers the day is written. People on vacation journeys often keep diaries, noting new sights, new friends, and new experiences. Reading one's own travel diary in later years helps recall the pleasures that may have slipped from memory.

In past centuries people in public life often kept diaries. These have become valuable sources of fact and interpretation for later historians. The private, candid observations set down in these personal journals often provide truer pictures of an age than do official records or books published—and often censored—during that time. For the most part, these diaries were never intended to be read by others. The entries were made simply as aids to memory or as a form of relaxation.

In modern times, however, statesmen and other important people realize that their diaries will very likely be read by historians or, in published form, by the public. Thus they make entries with these readers in mind, and many of their diaries lose the confidential, intimate nature of older ones. On the other hand, they tend to make their entries more complete and self-explanatory.

The most famous diary ever written in English was that kept by Samuel Pepys. A civilian official of the British navy, Pepys made regular entries between 1660 and 1669. His diary starts at the beginning of the Restoration period in English history and describes many of the court intrigues and scandals of his day. The diary reveals Pepys as a man with many human weaknesses but honest with himself. He wrote his entries in a combined code and shorthand that was not solved until more than 100 years after his death. (*See also* Pepys.)

The most famous diary of the 20th century was published in English in 1953 with the simple title 'Diary of a Young Girl'. It is more commonly known as 'The Diary of Anne Frank'. Anne was a young Jewish girl whose diary records the two years her family spent in hiding, mostly in The Netherlands, trying to escape the Nazi persecutors of the Jews. She was finally caught by the Gestapo in August 1944, and she died at the Bergen–Belsen concentration camp near Hanover in March 1945.

DIATOM. Tiny one-celled plants called diatoms are found by the billions in all the waters on the face of the Earth. The largest of them are barely visible to the unaided eye, and the smallest are less than a thousandth of an inch long. Biologists classify diatoms as golden or golden-brown forms of algae (*see* Algae). Like other algae, diatoms have no leaves, stems, roots, or flowers, but the cell of every diatom contains chlorophyll, the substance that is responsible for the green color of leafy plants.

Just as it does in other plants, chlorophyll absorbs sunlight to help diatoms make sugars from carbon

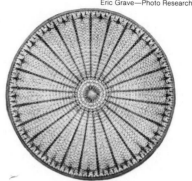
Magnification of a diatom reveals its beautiful symmetry.

dioxide and water (*see* Plants, Physiology of). Unlike diatoms, most plants next change these sugars to cellulose to make their cell walls strong. Diatoms, on the other hand, take up dissolved silica from the water and form it into a pair of glassy shells adorned with intricate patterns. There are thousands of species of diatoms, each with its own shape. The two shells of a diatom fit together like the top and bottom of a box and are held together along the edges by a softer band called a girdle.

Most diatoms float helplessly in the water or fasten themselves with a sort of jelly to stones or other water plants. Diatoms reproduce themselves by various methods. Sometimes the cell divides, the shells separate, and each half grows a new shell on its exposed surface. Two diatoms may combine after shedding their old shells. The united cells then separate into two new individuals, each of which grows a new pair of shells. Some species reproduce by means of spores.

In cold waters, where diatoms are most plentiful, the dead and the discarded shells may form thick deposits on the bottom. After long ages, the shell deposits turn into a porous mineral mass called diatomite (also called diatomaceous earth, tripolite, and kieselguhr). Diatomite deposits are found on the sites of many ancient oceans and lakes. (*See also* Oceanography.) Diatomite is used as a chemical filter, particularly in the sugar industry, and in the preparation of heat-insulating materials and polishing compounds and for mixing with concrete.

DIAZ, Bartholomew (1450?–1500). The first European to see the stormy Cape of Good Hope at the southern tip of Africa was Bartholomew Diaz (or Dias), a courageous Portuguese sea captain and explorer. Diaz was one of the great Portuguese seamen who helped find the southeastern water route between western Europe and Asia.

As a youth Diaz entered the hazardous gold and ivory trade along the African Gold Coast and rose to the rank of captain. At this time the Italian cities were growing rich on their trade with India and the Far East. Portugal and other European nations were eager for a share of this trade. However, the Italians controlled the Mediterranean, which was the chief trade route to the East. The Portuguese dreamed of

Courtesy of the Department of Anthropology,
Smithsonian Institution, Washington, D.C.

DICE

finding an all-water route around Africa. The groundwork was laid by Prince Henry, who had sent ships on voyages down the African coast (*see* Henry the Navigator). Exploration continued under his nephew, King John II. When Diogo Cam (or Cão) returned to Portugal with word that he had sailed past the mouth of the Congo River, John planned to send another expedition to sail even closer to the southern end of the continent. He chose Diaz to lead the venture.

With two caravels and a storeship Diaz left Lisbon in August 1487. He sailed straight from Cape Palmas to the mouth of the Congo, then kept close to the coast until he reached Cabo da Volta (present-day Lüderitz). About New Year's Day 1488 a gale hit his ships and blew them southward, past the southernmost tip of land. After 13 days he managed to turn east, but found no sheltering shore. Turning north, he sighted Mossel Bay, beyond the Cape of Good Hope. Unknowingly and out of sight of land, he had rounded the cape.

Almost at the entrance to the Indian Ocean, Diaz' crew, weary and afraid, virtually forced him to turn back. On the return voyage he charted the southern waters, and in May 1488 he saw the Cape of Good Hope for the first time (*see* Cape of Good Hope). Diaz called it Cabo Tormentoso—"stormy cape."

Diaz was welcomed home in December 1488. The task that he began was completed ten years later by Vasco da Gama, who sailed around the Cape of Good Hope and on to India (*see* Gama). Diaz supervised the building of Da Gama's ships.

In 1500 Diaz sailed as one of the captains in a large fleet headed by Pedro Álvares Cabral (*see* Cabral). Their destination was India, but they made a wide sweep into the South Atlantic and touched on the shores of Brazil. Then they headed southeastward and encountered fierce storms. Four ships went down, and all on board, including Diaz, were drowned.

DÍAZ, Porfirio (1830–1915). The soldier–statesman Porfirio Díaz built Mexico from a weak nation into a country of great promise. His dictatorial rule earned him the title of "Iron Man of Mexico."

Díaz was born on Sept. 15, 1830, in Oaxaca. His parents were poor. Determined to better himself, Díaz studied for the church and later read law. At 17 he interrupted his studies to serve in the war against the United States. After passing his law tests in 1853, he entered politics.

At that time Mexico was torn by civil wars, with numerous armed forces struggling for power. Díaz seized the advantage afforded by the national unrest. With ruthless daring he led revolts against the government until, in 1877, he won the presidency. He was reelected in 1884 and, by special law, served continuously until 1911. His regime was devoted to the economic development of his country. However, his disregard of the social needs of Mexico aroused public resentment, and in 1911 a revolt forced him into exile in Europe. He died on July 2, 1915, in Paris. (*See also* Mexico.)

An Egyptian die, top, probably from the tomb of Osiris, is from Abydos, Egypt. Etruscan dice, bottom, both from Chiusi, Italy, date from about the 7th to the 6th century BC.

DICE. The oldest game-playing equipment known to mankind consists of small cubes today usually made of cellulose or some other plastic. They are called dice: one is called a die. Each cube is marked with a number of dots, ranging from one to six. Dice were first used so long ago that no one knows what they were then used for. Dice very similar to modern ones have been found in Egyptian tombs built earlier than 2000 BC. Before the invention of plastics, dice were made from wood, ivory, jade, stone, glass, amber, nutshells, and other materials. Probably the earliest dicelike objects were made from sheep anklebones.

There are basically three kinds of dice games. The simplest uses only the dice during the play. Another uses dice on a marked table layout. The third uses them as part of the play in board games.

In dice-only games, the dice are thrown, by hand or from a dice cup, and tumble to rest on a flat surface. The combination of what is on the topmost surfaces determines whether one wins or loses. One such game is poker dice. It is played with five dice. Each player rolls to try to get the equivalent of a poker hand. Each roll is allotted a specific score. The player who finishes with the highest score wins. (For the ranking of poker hands *see* Card Games.)

The most popular and complicated dice games are craps, chuck-a-luck, and hazard. Any number of people may play craps. Each person in turn casts two dice in an attempt to roll a winning combination. Before rolling, the shooter, or thrower, bets, and the other players place bets against him. The players may also bet among themselves as to whether the shooter will win or lose. Bank craps, the most popular of casino gambling games, is played on a table about the size of a billiard table.

In many board games dice are thrown to determine how many moves a player makes on the board. Among the best-known board games using dice are Monopoly®, backgammon, and Trivial Pursuit®. (*See also* Board Games.)

Charles Dickens in 1859

DICKENS, Charles (1812–70). On a pier in New York Harbor in 1841 a crowd watched a tall sailing ship from England being towed to the pierhead. There was no ocean communication cable as yet and the ship brought the latest news. A question was yelled from the pier to the ship: "Is Little Nell dead?" Little Nell was the heroine in a serial called 'Old Curiosity Shop'. The latest installment was on the ship, and the people were anxious to learn how the story came out.

The author who could stir people to such excitement was Charles Dickens, then a young man of 29. The next year, on his visit to America, he received a reception second only to that of Lafayette in 1824. Six years before, with his 'Pickwick Papers', he had become the world's most celebrated writer.

Charles Dickens was born on Feb. 7, 1812, in Portsmouth. His father, John Dickens, was a minor clerk in the navy offices, a friendly man with a large family (Charles was the second of eight children) and only a moderate income. The family drifted from one poor home in London to another, each shabbier than the last. Presently John Dickens ended up in the Marshalsea Prison for debt and took his wife and younger children with him.

Meanwhile young Charles worked in a ramshackle warehouse, lived in a garret, visited his family in prison on Sundays, and felt that his life was shattered before it had begun. For a fictionalized account of his early life, read 'David Copperfield'. Then a timely inheritance restored the family to something like comfortable means, and Charles had a few quiet years at a private school.

Later he immortalized his father, for whom he always had a great love, as Mr. Micawber. When his own rising fortune and fame gave him control of a great newspaper, he put his father on the staff to preside over the dispatches and bought him a small country house. Dickens' mother, unsympathetic and

unconscious of his genius, meant less to him; she begrudged his leaving work to go to school. He made her immortal as Mrs. Nickleby.

Dickens made his own career. A few years of secondary school was his basic education. He never attended college. His real education came from his reading and observation and daily experience. Except for the English novels of the 18th century, he knew little of great literature. Of history and foreign politics, he knew practically nothing. His novels all deal with his own day and his own environment, except for his two historical novels—'A Tale of Two Cities' and 'Barnaby Rudge'—and these were set in the recent past of the French Revolution and the Gordon Riots.

The qualities that made up Dickens' genius did not depend on formal education for development. Dickens had a reporter's eye for the details of daily life and a mimic's ear for the subtleties of common speech. Further, he had the artist's ability to select what he needed from these raw materials of observation and to shape them into works of enduring merit.

Preparation for a Career

By teaching himself shorthand, Dickens secured the position of court reporter in the old Doctors' Commons, a survival from Elizabethan days that handled marriage, divorce, wills, and other "ghostly" causes. This experience gave Dickens a peculiar dislike of law that never left him; forever after it seemed either comic as in "Bardell vs. Pickwick" or terrible with tragedy as in 'Bleak House'. Dickens moved up in 1831 to the Reporters' Gallery of the "old—the unburned and unreformed—House of Commons." He also went

Mister Pickwick, the humorous hero of the 'Pickwick Papers', addresses fellow members of his club. The drawing was done by artist Robert Seymour.

to other cities and towns to report election speeches, transcribing his notes on the palm of his hand "by the light of a dark lantern in a post-chaise and four." This experience gave him a detailed and sometimes cynical view of government. To him the voters were often represented by the Eatanswill Election in 'Pickwick', parliamentary government by Doodle and Foodle and Coodle ('Our Mutual Friend'), and civil service by the Circumlocution Office ('Little Dorrit').

Thus equipped, Charles Dickens set out to conquer the world. The stage was his first dream. Night after night for two or three years he sat entranced with the melodrama of the London theaters—lurid with love, battle, treachery, and blue fire, in which a heroic young man would knock over 16 smugglers like ninepins. Melodrama put a stamp on Dickens for life. His characters, if they get excited, drop into the ranting language of the old Adelphi Theatre. On the other hand, Dickens' intense concentration on acting helped to give him that weird, almost hypnotic, power that he showed in the public reading of his works.

However, fate led him to a different career. He had a passion for creative writing, and he has told of his great joy, of his eyes dimmed with tears when a manuscript sent anonymously to an editor appeared in print. So he began writing sketches under the name of "Boz," the family nickname of a younger brother. To "Boz" came sudden and great success. The publishers, Chapman and Hall, had a plan for some serial pictures of cockney sportsmen, a Nimrod club, having all sorts of misadventures. The humor of the period turned very much on such horseplay. An artist named Seymour had drawn one or two pictures. They asked young "Boz" to write a set of stories to go with the pictures. Knowing nothing of sport, Dickens suggested changing the activities of the Nimrod club from sport to travel. When the publishers agreed, then, says Dickens, "I thought of Mr. Pickwick," which is all that has ever been known of the origin and genesis of one of the greatest characters in humorous literature. The young author was to receive 14 guineas (about $70) for each monthly installment.

The very week that the 'Pickwick Papers' began their monthly appearance, in April 1836, Dickens married Catherine Hogarth, one of the three pretty daughters of a newspaper associate. The young couple moved into rooms in Furnival's Inn. They did not realize that one day they would separate with bitter words because they believed they had made a love match. Dickens looked on Catherine, beautiful and silent, and saw nothing but the reflection of himself. Catherine looked at Charles and did not realize that genius and egotism often lie close together. Dickens indeed was not so much in love with Catherine as in love with love.

At first the 'Pickwick Papers' failed to sell more than a few hundred copies a month. Then the serial introduced the character of Mr. Sam Weller, polishing boots at the White Hart Inn. The narrative took off on the wings of imagination, down English lanes, past

Mario Scacheri

The Old Curiosity Shop on Portugal Street in London is still a landmark visited by tourists.

gabled inns, and along the highways as varied and as cheery as a flying coach at a gallop, and the world was at the author's feet. The phenomenal 'Pickwick Papers' and the books that followed steadily lifted young "Boz" to the height of success, from poverty to wealth, from obscurity to fame, all in a few brief years. The great novels of this period were 'Oliver Twist' (published in 1838), 'Nicholas Nickleby' (1839), 'Old Curiosity Shop' (1841), and 'Barnaby Rudge' (1841).

Dickens in America

Dickens now looked around for other worlds to conquer. America had welcomed his books from the start, in part because the lack of international copyright permitted American publishers to print them without paying him. Dickens, in his youth a radical who hated Toryism and aristocracy, longed to study America and its freedom at first hand. Leaving their four children at home, he landed with his wife in Boston in January 1842. The town blazed with excitement; society was thrilled; there were dinners, receptions, adulation. Young Dickens, dressed in a bright velvet waistcoat, reveled in his new and adoring audience and wrote home of the freedom of America and the comforts of the workers. H.W. Longfellow, William Ellery Channing, and others of the New England elite joined in the welcome. Young Dr. Oliver Wendell Holmes was one of those who helped to organize it.

Dickens found in Boston friendships that he never lost, even when bitterness and disillusion altered his

135

view of America. From Boston he went to New York and a "Boz" ball of 3,000 people; to Philadelphia and a huge public reception; then to Baltimore and to Washington, where he met President John Tyler and the Congress; then to Richmond, which offered him a taste of Southern culture. Such was the triumphant progress of the young author, only a few years before a member of the shabby-genteel class of London.

Always ready to raise his voice in defense of a cause he believed in, Dickens spoke everywhere of the need for an international copyright agreement that would protect the rights of both American and British writers. He felt that it was unfair and unjust that American publishers should print and sell his books without permission from him and without paying him any royalties. Dickens did not speak of himself as the sole victim of this practice. He pointed out that all British authors were equally victimized; he also acknowledged that American authors, such as Edgar Allan Poe, suffered from the pirating of their works in England.

The newspapers in America attacked these forthright statements and accused Dickens of bad taste and of abusing American hospitality. In time Dickens' rosy view of America faded. The proof of his disillusion and disgust is revealed in his 'American Notes' (published in 1842), his letters to friends, and 'Martin Chuzzlewit' (1844). From Dickens' viewpoint, Americans all seemed to chew tobacco. They kept slaves, whom he never stopped to compare with the factory slaves of England. American government seemed all plunder and roguery. Then he went West, traveling as far as Cairo, Ill. His vision of the West contained nothing but foul and reeking canal boats, swamps, bullfrogs, and tobacco juice.

Dickens lacked the eye to see the pageant of America, the great epic of the settlements of the West; the eye to compare the canal boat with the raft and the scow of earlier settlers. He became peevish, impatient of small discomforts, resenting the fact that hotel-keepers dared to talk to him. He spent two weeks in Canada, consoled there by the presence of friends at the English garrison in Montreal. Then he returned home to discredit America with his pen.

Fame and Fortune

The years that followed Dickens' return from America—the middle period of his life—were filled with more activity, fame, and success. In 1851 he took a fine residence at Tavistock Square and lived in great style. His friends were the leading authors, artists, and actors of the day. Later on, his purchase of a country house at Gad's Hill fulfilled an ambition of his childhood. His books, appearing in monthly serial

Secondary characters in Dickens' novels are numerous and often as interesting as the main characters of the story. Captain Cuttle (left) is a kindly sea captain in 'Dombey and Son'. The villainous Uriah Heep (right) is the bookkeeper in 'David Copperfield'.

parts, enjoyed a popularity that slackened only to rise again. It is generally thought that 'David Copperfield', written as a serial in 1848 and 1849, when he was at the height of his powers, is the greatest of his novels. Contrasted with the 'Pickwick Papers', it shows the transition of Dickens' genius from the exuberance of youth to the somber acceptance of middle age.

One of his books, 'Dombey and Son', is a sort of epic of great sorrow. Dickens' books indeed appealed to his generation of readers as much for their tears as for their laughter.

Reformer-Journalist

Book writing did not entirely satisfy Dickens' ego. The onetime reporter wanted to be a newspaper editor. Dickens felt the need to reform all England. The way to do it, he felt, was to control and edit a great daily newspaper, where he should preside like Jupiter handing out lightning. Enthusiastic friends subscribed £100,000 and founded the *Daily News*. In January 1846 Dickens threw himself eagerly into the editorial chair of the fledgling publication and threw himself out again in 19 days. He found that in the newspaper business the lightning hits in two directions. So in 1850 he founded instead a weekly journal, *Household Words*, and carried on with it and a later magazine, *All the Year Round* (1859), until his death. Several of his own stories, 'Christmas Stories', 'A Tale of Two Cities', 'Great Expectations', and others ran in his magazine.

Dickens as Actor and Lecturer

Another activity, and this a special delight to him, was amateur theatricals that carried on Dickens' love of the stage. He himself had incomparable dramatic power. With it he had a great talent for management and an energy and enthusiasm that carried all before it. On May 16, 1851, at a performance that was given at the duke of Devonshire's London house for a charity, the young Queen Victoria and her Prince Consort and the duke of Wellington were in the audience. The queen came to a later performance in 1857 and graciously "commanded Mr. Dickens' presence"—an invitation of great honor—after the show. Mr. Dickens being in "farce" dress asked to be excused from appearing, thus defying all royal precedents.

To theatricals he soon added public lectures and readings from his works. This activity began after he had read one of his famous Christmas stories to a group of friends who received it enthusiastically. He made a number of successful tours in England, Scotland, and Ireland—from 1858 to 1859, 1861 to 1863, 1866 to 1867, and 1869 to 1870.

Relief in Work

Dickens separated from his wife in 1858. Georgina Hogarth, his wife's younger sister, had lived with the couple since 1842. She remained with Dickens until his death. His will provided for both women.

Dickens sought relief from a public curious about his personal life in the excitement of work. He made

Bettmann Archive

Bill Sykes, in 'Oliver Twist', is a brutal burglar and a henchman of the evil Fagin. Dickens was skilled at depicting society's outcasts and criminals.

a second American tour in 1867 to 1868. It was an overwhelming success but extremely fatiguing. At home again, he resumed lecturing. His last appearance was in March 1870.

In retirement he struggled with his last task, 'The Mystery of Edwin Drood', a tale of night and storm and murder. The book was still unfinished on June 9, 1870, when Dickens died.

In the opinion of many, Dickens is England's greatest creative writer. The names and natures of his characters are unforgettable. His humor is unsurpassable, not only in the laughter that lies on the surface, but in the warmth of human kindliness below. His books are still being read all over the world. 'A Christmas Carol', conceived and written in a few weeks in 1843, is the ultimate, enduring Christmas myth of modern literature.

BIBLIOGRAPHY FOR CHARLES DICKENS

Barlow, George. The Genius of Dickens (Folcroft, 1977).
Chesterton, G. K. and Kitton, F. G. Charles Dickens (Folcroft, 1973).
Clark, Cumberland. Dickens' London (Haskell, 1973).
Crotch, W. W. The Soul of Dickens (Haskell, 1974).
Ford, G. H. Dickens and His Readers (Gordian, 1974).
Gissing, George. Charles Dickens (Haskell, 1974).
Johnson, Edgar. Charles Dickens: His Tragedy and Triumph (Viking Press, 1977).
Johnson, Spencer. The Value of Imagination: the Story of Charles Dickens (Value Communications, 1977).
Miller, J. H., Jr. Charles Dickens: the World of His Novels (Harvard Univ. Press, 1959).
Quiller-Couch, A. T. Charles Dickens and Other Victorians (Kraus Reprint, 1968).
Wagenknecht, E. C. The Man Charles Dickens: a Victorian Portrait, rev. ed. (Telegraph Books, 1983).

Courtesy of the Harvard College Library

Emily Dickinson

DICKINSON, Emily

DICKINSON, Emily (1830–86). A New England spinster whose work was unknown in her lifetime was one of America's finest poets. Emily Dickinson's life was uneventful, but she enjoyed a full and exciting existence in her imagination.

Emily Elizabeth Dickinson was born on Dec. 10, 1830, at Amherst, Mass. Her father, Edward Dickinson, was a lawyer and leading citizen of Amherst. Her mother was Emily Norcross Dickinson. Emily had an older brother, William Austin, and a younger sister, Lavinia.

Emily Dickinson had more formal education than most women of her time. She attended public schools, the Amherst Academy (of which her father was treasurer), and spent one year at Mount Holyoke Female Seminary in South Hadley.

In the spring of 1854 Emily, her mother, and Lavinia went to Washington, D.C., where her father was in Congress. On their return they stopped in Philadelphia. There she met the Reverend Charles Wadsworth. Most scholars agree that he was the subject of her love poems, the "atom I prefer to all the lists of clay." He was a famous preacher and married.

Dickinson returned to Amherst and spent the rest of her life quietly at home. She seldom left her room, appearing only occasionally and briefly, in a white dress, when guests visited downstairs.

She probably saw Wadsworth only three additional times, when he visited her at Amherst. In 1861 he was transferred to San Francisco. It was then that Dickinson began to write her poems in earnest, scribbling hundreds of them on scraps of paper. Only six were published in her lifetime.

After Emily Dickinson died on May 15, 1886, Lavinia found her poems. They were published, extensively edited, in various collections from 1890 to 1925. Not until 1955, however, were all her poems actually published. They appeared, unedited, in a three-volume 'Poems of Emily Dickinson'. The poems are brief and condensed, characterized by unusual rhyming and swift flashes of insight. The collection 'Letters of Emily Dickinson' was published in 1958.

DICKINSON, John (1732–1808). One of the foremost statesmen and patriots during the period of the American Revolution, John Dickinson served as a member of the Stamp Act Congress of 1765, the first and second Continental Congresses of 1774 and 1775 to 1776, and the Constitutional Convention of 1787.

Dickinson was born on Nov. 8, 1732, in Talbot County, Md. After studying law in London, he conducted his own practice in Philadelphia from 1757 to 1760. From 1765 to 1775 he was one of the most productive writers against British colonial tax policies. His 'Letters from a Farmer in Pennsylvania, to the Inhabitants of the British Colonies' made him famous. Published in 1767 and 1768, they opposed the Townshend Acts that imposed import duties on the colonies. In the Second Continental Congress, he was a principal author of the 'Declaration . . . Setting Forth the Causes and Necessity of Their Taking up Arms' (1775). He at first opposed the Declaration of Independence but fought against the British during the Revolution. He helped draft the Articles of Confederation in 1776 and 1777.

After helping draft the United States Constitution in 1787, he supported the document in a series of letters signed "Fabius." Dickinson College at Carlisle, Pa., chartered in 1783, was named in his honor. He died in Wilmington, Del., on Feb. 14, 1808.

DIDEROT, Denis (1713–84). The essayist and philosopher Denis Diderot was one of the originators and interpreters of the Age of Enlightenment. This 18th-century movement was based on the belief that right reason, or rationalism, could find true knowledge and lead mankind to progress and happiness. He was the chief editor of its leading testament, the 'Encyclopédie'.

Diderot was born at Langres, France, on Oct. 5, 1713. He studied in Paris from 1729 to 1732, showing an interest in a wide variety of subjects, including languages, theater, law, literature, philosophy, and mathematics. In his early adult life he turned away from Christianity and embraced rationalism.

In 1745 Diderot was hired by publisher André Le Breton to translate an English encyclopedia. When he and his co-editor, mathematician Jean d'Alembert, undertook the task, they created a virtually new work, the 'Encyclopédie'. Published in 28 volumes from 1751 to 1772, it was a literary and philosophic work that was to have profound social and intellectual effects. Its publication was troubled by strong reactions against it by both church and state. The atheism and materialism apparent in some articles enraged many readers. Some of Diderot's writings foreshadowed the evolutionary theories of Charles Darwin. He also formulated the first modern notion of the cellular structure of matter.

Besides his work on the 'Encyclopédie', Diderot also wrote novels, short stories, and plays in which he frequently criticized society and argued for political revolution. He died in Paris on July 30, 1784, only five years before the outbreak of the French Revolution.

DIE AND DIEMAKING. A tool or other device for imparting a desired shape, form, or finish to a material is called a die. Examples of dies include a metal block with specially shaped holes through which metal or plastic is drawn or extruded, the hardened steel forms for producing the patterns on coins and medals by pressure, and the hollow molds into which metal or plastic is forced. Many dies are made by a process called diesinking in which a cavity is machined in a steel block to be used for molding plastics or metals or in conjunction with presses of various types for hot and cold forging and coining. Diecasting forms plastic or metal objects by injecting molten metal into dies, or hollow molds.

In the diemaking process of diesinking, the die block is mounted on a table while a milling machine is used to shape the die. In simple machines the movement of the milling machine may be controlled by moving it manually by means of transverse, horizontal, and vertical feeds. Patterns of sheet metal or plastic may be used as guides.

Diesinking is done chiefly by automatic machines. The movement of the milling machine's cutting head against the die block is controlled by a gauge that automatically traces around a model made of soft metal, plaster of paris, or wood. The template, or model, is attached to the bed beside the die block. The movement of the gauge over the template is transmitted to the cutter by hydraulic or electrical controls. The surface of the sunken die is finished to the desired size and surface quality by hand scrapers, files, small grinding wheels, and polishing cloths. In addition to diesinking, dies are made by any of a number of machine tools, including turning machines, shapers and planers, drilling machines, grinding machines, power saws, and presses (see Tool).

Presses are nearly always used in conjunction with dies for forming metal and plastic parts through the application of a variety of processes, including shearing, or cutting; blanking, or punching; extrusion; open and closed forging; coining; and bending, among others. All of the processes require presses that are provided with a movable ram that is pressed against an anvil, or base. Power to the movable ram may be furnished through gravity, mechanical linkages, or through hydraulic or pneumatic systems.

Appropriate die sets, with one part mounted on the movable ram and the matching part mounted on the fixed bed or platen, are an integral part of the machine. Punch presses punch out metal parts from sheet metal and form the parts to the desired shape. Dies with cavities having a variety of shapes are used on forging presses that form white-hot metal blanks to the desired shape. Power presses are also used for shearing, bending, flanging, and shaping sheet metal parts of all sizes. Power presses are made in various sizes, ranging from small presses mounted on a workbench to machines weighing more than 1 million pounds (450,000 kilograms).

An early and important use of the die-casting technique was in the Mergenthaler Linotype machine, invented in 1884, to cast whole lines of type for use on printing presses. The development of mass-production techniques in the automobile industry, however, sparked the widespread use of die-casting. Great precision is possible, and products range from tiny parts for sewing machines and automobile carburetors to aluminum engine-block castings.

The two major die-casting techniques differ only in how the molten metal is introduced. In the cold-chamber process, the metal is ladled into a chamber; a plunger forces the metal into the cold die cavity, in which it quickly hardens.

In the piston, or gooseneck, process the plunger and its cylinder are submerged in the molten metal, the metal being admitted through a hole in the top of the cylinder when the plunger is retracted; the advance of the plunger forces the metal into the die cavity as before. In both techniques when the metal hardens, the die is opened and the finished casting is ejected. In modern die-casting, the sequence is governed electronically.

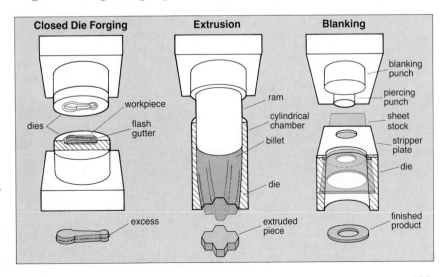

Closed Die Forging **Extrusion** **Blanking**

workpiece
dies
flash gutter
excess

ram
cylindrical chamber
billet
die
extruded piece

blanking punch
piercing punch
sheet stock
stripper plate
die
finished product

Closed die forging, extrusion, and blanking are among the more common industrial processes used to form materials into desired shapes. Other important processes include bending, drawing, heading, and open die forging.

139

John Diefenbaker

National Film Board of Canada

DIEFENBAKER, John (1895–1979). For 22 years Canada's Liberal party had controlled the government under two successive prime ministers. Then in June 1957 John Diefenbaker led the Progressive Conservatives to victory, but by a very close margin. Nine months later, as prime minister, he called for another election. This time his party won by the greatest landslide in Canada's history.

John George Diefenbaker was born on Sept. 18, 1895, in Newstadt, Ont. His father was a schoolteacher. When the boy was 8, the family moved to a homestead in Saskatchewan. His father tutored him until he was ready for high school. Then the family sold their wheat farm and moved to Saskatoon.

In 1916 John Diefenbaker received his M.A. in political science from the University of Saskatchewan in Saskatoon. After serving in World War I, he returned to the university and got a law degree in 1919. He made his home in Prince Albert, Sask., after 1922 and became an outstanding criminal lawyer. In 1929 he married Edna May Brower. She died in 1951. In 1953 he married Olive Freeman Palmer.

The "prairie lawyer" lost five elections until at last, in 1940, he won a seat in the House of Commons. In 1956 he became leader of the opposition. In the 1957 elections, charging that the Liberals had become too powerful, he replaced Louis St. Laurent as prime minister (*see* St. Laurent).

In March 1958 Diefenbaker campaigned against the new Liberal leader, Lester B. Pearson, former minister for external affairs and winner of a Nobel peace prize (*see* Pearson). A new spirit of nationalism had developed in Canada. Diefenbaker sensed this and gave the people a "vision of a new and greater Canada," less dependent economically upon the United States. He won 10 of the 12 provinces and territories.

In 1962 he was reelected by a small margin and formed a coalition government. It fell in 1963 on the issue of his refusal to accept nuclear weapons from the United States. Pearson became prime minister after the April elections. Diefenbaker remained the opposition leader until 1967, when he was succeeded by Robert L. Stanfield of Nova Scotia. He was elected for a record 13th term in the House of Commons in May 1979. He died on Aug. 16, 1979, in Ottawa. (*See also* Canada, section on History.)

DIENBIENPHU, Battle of. A major turning point in the history of Vietnam, the battle of Dienbienphu ended any hope of French control in Indochina and paved the way for the heavy American involvement in the area from 1965 to 1975. It ended the First Indochina War, which had begun in 1946, when France attempted to regain control of its former Southeast Asian colony. France was opposed by a coalition of groups, the strongest of which was the Viet Minh, headed by Ho Chi Minh.

From 1946 to 1951 the Viet Minh waged a relentless guerrilla war against the French forces. Despite large amounts of American aid, the French were losing badly by 1952. By the end of 1953 the Viet Minh controlled most of the countryside in northern Vietnam and neighboring Laos. Late in 1953 the French occupied a small mountain outpost named Dienbienphu, located in the northern part of Vietnam near the Laotian border. The French hoped to cut Viet Minh supply lines into Laos and to set up a base from which to attack.

The Vietnamese, in control of the countryside, quickly cut off all roads to Dienbienphu, so the French could only be supplied from the air. The French remained quite confident of their position, and they were thus completely taken by surprise when General Vo Nguyen Giap of North Vietnam surrounded their base with 40,000 troops and used heavy artillery to batter the French lines. In spite of massive infusions of American aid, the outpost was overrun on May 7, 1954.

By this time support in France for the war had virtually evaporated, and the American Congress refused any more aid to support a lost cause. The French government sought an end to the fighting, and an agreement was signed in Geneva on July 21, 1954. The agreement also divided Vietnam in half along the 17th parallel. The Viet Minh controlled the north, and the stage was set for their eventually successful attempt to conquer the south. French dismay at the defeat, which was soon to be followed by a similar turn of events in Algeria, led to the end of the French Fourth Republic in 1958.

DIESEL, Rudolf (1858–1913). When people travel by ship or railroad train, it is often thanks to an invention by the German engineer Rudolf Diesel. Modern diesel engines, which commonly power such vehicles, have changed little since Diesel devised the first ones in the 1890s.

Diesel was born to German parents in Paris on March 18, 1858. The family went to England in 1870, and soon Rudolf was sent to school in Germany. After his graduation from the technical college in Munich, he moved to Paris and worked for a refrigeration company. He also devoted much of his time to developing an engine that would use fuel more efficiently than did gasoline engines.

About 1890 Diesel came up with the idea for the diesel engine, which uses highly compressed, high-temperature air to ignite its fuel. He obtained a German development patent for this invention in 1892 and published a description of it in 1893. By 1897 his refinements of the machine resulted in an engine that was a commercial success, bringing him honors and wealth.

Diesel apparently drowned on Sept. 29, 1913. He mysteriously disappeared from the mail steamer *Dresden* while crossing the English Channel.

DIESEL ENGINE.

DIESEL ENGINE. Of all internal-combustion engines, the diesel engine is the most efficient—that is, it can extract the greatest amount of mechanical energy from a given amount of fuel. It achieves this high level of performance by compressing air to high pressures before injecting very small droplets of fuel into the combustion chamber. The high temperatures created when air is highly compressed in a diesel engine cause the fuel to burn without the spark plug required in a gasoline engine. Very large diesel engines, which are used for stationary power production and to power boats and ships, can be twice as efficient as a conventional automobile gasoline engine. However, the high pressures created inside diesel engines make heavy engines with thick cylinder walls necessary. High weight and the need for careful maintenance of the fuel-injection system have made the diesel engine most useful for trucks, buses, small and medium-size ships and tugs, movable industrial-power systems, and diesel-electric railroad locomotives. Its weight makes the diesel engine unsuitable for use in aircraft, and it has found only limited acceptance in passenger automobiles.

How the Diesel Engine Works

Diesel engines use a conventional cylinder and piston arrangement. The cylinders may be arranged vertically in line, in two banks forming a V, or with the cylinders radiating from the center like spokes in a wheel (*see* Internal-Combustion Engine; Automobile, "Power Plant").

In the widely used four-stroke engine, the piston draws air into the cylinder during the first stroke. During the second stroke the air is compressed in the cylinder to about one fifteenth of its original volume. Engineers call this a 15:1, or 15 to 1, compression ratio. At the end of compression the air pressure is more than 40 times atmospheric pressure, and the air temperature exceeds 1,000° F (540° C). At this point a predetermined amount of finely atomized fuel, or fuel in the form of very small droplets, is injected into the cylinder through the fuel pump. The very high air temperature in the cylinder causes the fuel to burn very rapidly without the use of a spark plug. The high-temperature, combusted gas pushes the piston to the bottom of the cylinder, delivering power to the crankshaft during the third stroke. During the fourth stroke, the low-pressure, combusted gases are pushed through the exhaust port. Thus only one stroke in four delivers power.

In two-stroke engines, which are generally smaller than four-stroke diesel engines, air is admitted just before compression begins, and the burned gases are exhausted near the end of the power stroke. The two-stroke engine therefore delivers power once every second stroke. A two-stroke engine is generally less efficient than a four-stroke engine but can develop greater power for a given engine size and speed. Two-stroke engines are used where small one- or two-cylinder engines are needed and where the intermittent action of a four-stroke engine would require too large a flywheel to keep the engine running at nearly constant speed.

The heart of the diesel engine is its fuel-injection system. Each cylinder has a separate fuel pump that

Unlike a gasoline engine the diesel engine does not draw into its cylinders a fuel-air mixture; fuel is not injected into the cylinder until the air has been compressed to its maximum and thereby heated to about 1,000° F (540° C).

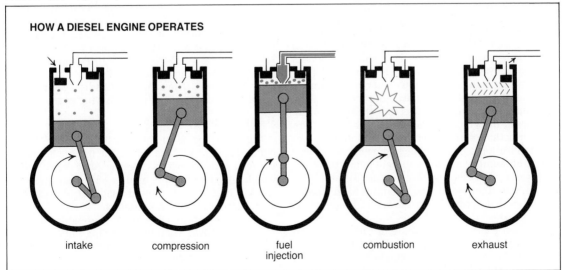

HOW A DIESEL ENGINE OPERATES

intake   compression   fuel injection   combustion   exhaust

can develop pressures in excess of a thousand pounds per square inch (70 kilograms per square centimeter) to force a measured amount of oil through very small nozzle holes into the cylinder. The high pressures coupled with the small holes cause the atomization of the fuel. The amount of fuel injected at every stroke must be varied to meet the power requirements imposed on the engine. Various types of oils can be used for diesel engines. The most commonly used oil, usually called diesel fuel, is similar to that used in home heating systems.

The high pressures developed during compression demand large starting motors for automotive diesels. Large, nonautomotive diesel engines are usually started with a supply of compressed air from an auxiliary compressor and air storage tank. For a cold small diesel engine, an in-cylinder heat source called a glow plug is required during start-up to assist the initial combustion. During very cold weather longer warm-up periods are needed, and care must also be taken that the fuel is able to flow readily from the tank to the engine. Diesel engines are therefore not recommended for automotive use in very cold climates unless the fuel can be preheated. The performance of large diesel engines can be improved by the addition of a supercharger, which precompresses the air before it is admitted to the cylinder, thereby increasing the amount of air and fuel available for combustion during each power stroke.

History and Applications

The diesel engine was first developed by the German engineer Rudolf Diesel, who tried to improve on the efficiency of the steam engine and of the gasoline engine, which was invented shortly before (see Diesel). The modern diesel engine is still very similar to the one described by Diesel in his initial 1892 patent and his 1893 description. The first diesel engine for commercial service was built in the United States and installed in Saint Louis, Mo., by a brewing company in 1898. The design of the engine was based on an engine exhibited in Germany. Within a few years thousands of diesel engines were in service.

Diesel engines typically range in size from 10 to 1,500 horsepower. They are used widely in buses and trucks where fuel efficiency is important. They drive tractors, power shovels, air compressors, pumps, hoists and winches, air-conditioning and refrigeration equipment, and many other industrial machines. Slow-speed diesel engines are very reliable and are used for both electric power production and for marine applications. Until the development of nuclear power, all submarines were diesel-engine powered. Nearly all railroad locomotives now use a diesel-electric drive in which the engine is coupled to an electric generator that feeds electric power to motors that drive the wheels.

In recent years the agriculture of China has been revolutionized by replacing farm draft animals with locally built, 12-horsepower, single-cylinder diesel tractors on a wheelbarrow-like support.

THE STORY OF A FOOD MOLECULE

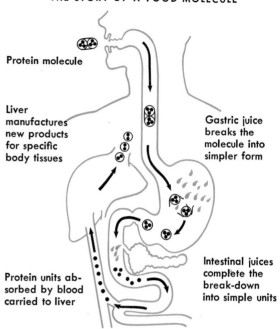

Protein molecule

Liver manufactures new products for specific body tissues

Gastric juice breaks the molecule into simpler form

Intestinal juices complete the break-down into simple units

Protein units absorbed by blood carried to liver

A protein molecule is changed by the digestive juices in the stomach and small intestine before being passed on to the liver. All foods must be processed by digestion before being used by the body.

DIGESTIVE SYSTEM. What happens to food after it is eaten? The human body uses various kinds of food for energy and growth. To be used, however, food must be changed into a form that can be carried through the bloodstream. The body's process of extracting useful nutrients from food is called digestion.

The digestive system is the group of organs that changes food—carbohydrates, fats, and proteins—into soluble products that can be used by the body. The illustration above shows how protein is taken apart and rebuilt into a simpler form. Both mechanical action and chemical action are necessary to do this.

Human digestion, or the change that food undergoes in the digestive system, takes place in a long tubelike canal called the *alimentary canal*, or the *digestive tract*. The whole canal is lined with a *mucous membrane*. The structure of the digestive tract is shown in drawings on the following pages.

Where Digestion Begins

Digestion begins in the mouth. Here the food is cut and chopped by the teeth. The tongue helps mix the food particles with a digestive juice called *saliva*, which is secreted in the mouth. Saliva moistens the food so it can be swallowed easily. It also changes some starches into simple sugars.

It is important to chew food thoroughly to mix it well with saliva. Thorough chewing cuts food into small pieces that are more easily attacked by digestive juices. Food should not be washed down with quantities of liquid to avoid chewing.

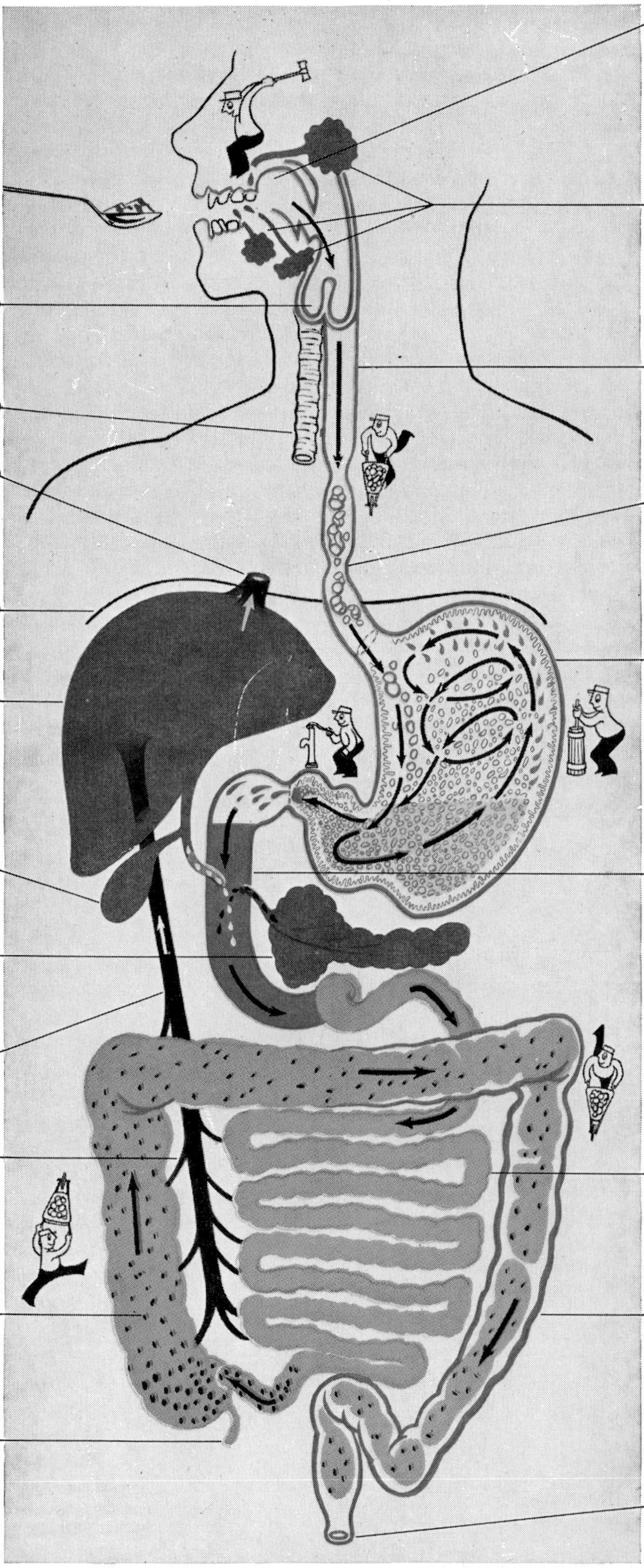

MOUTH: Grinds food and mixes it with saliva; digestion begins.

SALIVARY GLANDS: Make saliva, starting digestion of starch.

EPIGLOTTIS: Flap which closes windpipe during swallowing.

TRACHEA: Windpipe

HEPATIC VEIN: Vein which carries blood away from liver.

ESOPHAGUS: Passes food from mouth to stomach.

PERISTALSIS: Contractions by walls of digestive tract which move food forward.

DIAPHRAGM: Wall between chest and abdomen.

LIVER: Stores food and makes chemical changes in it.

STOMACH: Holds and mixes food; glands in lining of upper two thirds produce digestive juice which acts on protein; lower third serves as pump.

GALL BLADDER: Stores bile.

PANCREAS: Makes enzymes which break down all types of food.

DUODENUM: First part of small intestine; bile from liver breaks up fat, and juice from pancreas digests all food types.

PORTAL VEIN: Carries blood from entire digestive tract to liver.

VEINS: Drain intestinal tract, carrying digested food into portal vein.

SMALL INTESTINE: Fluid from intestinal glands dilutes food; food absorbed into blood stream.

BACTERIA (represented by dots): Live in intestines; make vitamins used by human body.

APPENDIX

LARGE INTESTINE: Fluid absorbed from indigestible foodstuffs; wastes become solid; last part of intestine a container for waste.

ANUS: End of digestive tract, where the food wastes leave body.

Primary digestive organs in red; secondary digestive organs in gray.

143

From the mouth the food is swallowed into a transport tube, named the *esophagus*, or *gullet*. A flap called the *epiglottis* closes the windpipe while food is being swallowed. *Peristalsis*, a wavelike muscular movement of the esophagus walls, forces food down the tube to the stomach. Peristalsis takes place throughout the digestive tract. It is an *automatic*, or *involuntary*, action, carried out in response to nerve impulses set up by the contents of the tube. When digestion is working normally, a person is unaware of the movements of the gullet, stomach, and most of the intestine. Swallowing is a *voluntary* muscular action.

Work of the Stomach

At the end of the esophagus there is a muscular valve, or *sphincter*, through which food enters the stomach. This sphincter muscle keeps food in the stomach from being forced back into the esophagus. Peristalsis in the stomach churns the food and mixes it with mucus and with *gastric juices*, which contain *enzymes* and hydrochloric acid (*see* Enzymes). These gastric juices are secreted from millions of small glands in the lining of the upper stomach walls. Drawings of them are shown below on this page. These glands pour about three quarts of fluid into the stomach daily. Similar glands in the small intestine also secrete enzymes and fluid. Hydrochloric acid secreted by the stomach sets up the sour or acid condition necessary for digestion. Certain remedies for indigestion are advertised as correcting this acid condition. If these remedies actually do get rid of

the stomach acids it is not wise to take them. Acid is required for digestion in the stomach.

The stomach churns the food into a thick liquid, called *chyme*, before it is passed on by peristalsis into the small intestine (*see* Stomach). Another strong sphincter muscle further mashes the chyme and has some control over the rate at which it is passed out of the stomach into the *duodenum*, or upper small intestine. The sphincter also prevents the chyme from passing back into the stomach.

Little by little, as the digestive process in the stomach is completed, all the chyme is passed through the sphincter into the duodenum. This peristalsis is regulated by the autonomic nervous system (*see* Nerves). This process does not take place all at once. It continues over a period of time.

It takes from 30 to 40 hours for food to travel the length of the alimentary canal. Different kinds of food are held in the stomach for varying lengths of time. Starch and sugar are held in the stomach for a short time only, usually no more than one to two hours. Protein foods are there from three to five hours. Fat foods may remain in the stomach even longer than proteins. This is why eating a heavy dinner of meat, potatoes, and gravy satisfies our hunger longer than one made up of sweets or greens. Food made up of easily digested carbohydrates passes quickly from the stomach and into the small intestine.

The stomach is an extremely important organ, but it is not essential to life. People who have had their stomachs removed are frequently able to live

STRUCTURE OF THE LINING OF THE DIGESTIVE TUBE

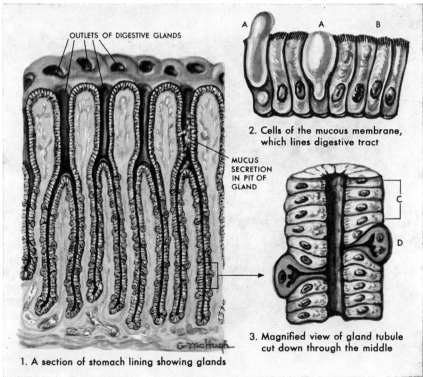

OUTLETS OF DIGESTIVE GLANDS

MUCUS SECRETION IN PIT OF GLAND

1. A section of stomach lining showing glands

2. Cells of the mucous membrane, which lines digestive tract

3. Magnified view of gland tubule cut down through the middle

1. The mucous membrane of the stomach is honeycombed with millions of glands that secrete mucus, enzymes, and acid. These secretions do the chemical work of digestion.

2. Cells (A) are mucus-secreting cells. These are called "goblet cells" because of their shape and because they hold the mucus. Cells (B) that secrete enzymes and fluid are called columnar epithelial cells.

3. Cells lining the tubules in the stomach glands are of two kinds. Chief cells (C) that are modified epithelial cells which secrete enzymes, and acid-secreting cells (D) that are only found in the stomach.

STRUCTURE OF THE DIGESTIVE TUBE

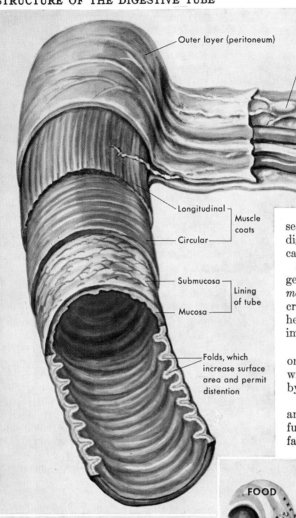

Outer layer (peritoneum)

Lymph node and vessels

Vein
Nerve
Artery

Longitudinal
Circular
} Muscle coats

Submucosa
Mucosa
} Lining of tube

Folds, which increase surface area and permit distention

Muscle
Submucosa
Intestinal glands
Villi

The large picture at the top shows the layers that make up the walls of the small intestine. The inside layer is in the form of folds. These increase the surface area and help in food absorption. They also permit the tube to enlarge, or distend, itself. The small picture above shows a part of the intestinal lining greatly enlarged. Fingerlike villi further increase the surface area. At right is a magnified section of the villi and of a digestive gland acting upon food. Shown here are: (A) an artery, (B) a digestive gland, (C) cross section of a villus, (D) a lymph vessel which transports fats, (E) a vein. White symbols indicate fat (in lymph). Black symbols indicate proteins and carbohydrates.

by taking special foods in small quantities many times a day. The small intestine is then able to perform all necessary digestion.

Work of the Small Intestine

Food remains in the small intestine for several hours. Two large glands, the liver and the pancreas, connect with the small intestine by *ducts*, or tubes. Through these ducts the liver and pancreas pour secretions which further aid digestion. Fluid from the pancreas is called *pancreatic juice*. Fluid from the liver is called *bile*. The pancreas is one of the most important glands in the body. It secretes up to a pint of pancreatic juice a day. This digestive fluid contains enzymes which help digest carbohydrates, proteins, and fats.

One of these enzymes is *trypsin*, which helps digest protein foods. Other enzymes are *amylase* and *maltase*, which help digest carbohydrates. The pancreatic enzyme *lipase*, along with bile from the liver, helps digest fat. Bile, however, does not contain important enzymes.

Bile is stored in the *gall bladder*, a small hollow organ located just under the liver. We could not live without the liver but the gall bladder can be removed by surgery without serious effect.

The liver stores *glycogen* for later use by the body and furnishes clotting material for the blood. When fully digested, proteins are changed into *amino acids;* fat foods are changed into *fatty acids;* and carbohy-

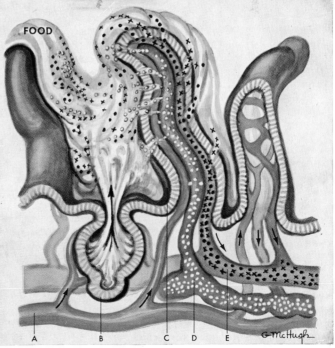

FOOD

A   B   C   D   E   G. McHugh

drates are changed into sugars. These soluble food products are dissolved and then absorbed into the bloodstream through the walls of the small intestine.

While food is in the small intestine it is further diluted by fluid secreted by the intestinal glands. In an adult the small intestine is about 21 feet (6.4 meters) long. By the time the diluted food products have traveled its length, most of their nutrients have been absorbed into the bloodstream.

How Food Is Absorbed

The lining of the small intestine contains many folds. These folds increase the surface area that can be in contact with the food products. The lining surface of the intestinal folds is further increased by many microscopic fingerlike projections called *villi*. The digested food is passed through the cell membranes of the villi into the blood and lymph, which carry it to the cells. The body can then use the food for energy and growth (*see* Blood).

Peristalsis moves material from the small intestine into the large intestine. Peristalsis continues in the large intestine but at a much slower rate. Although the large intestine is only five or six feet long, waste material takes 10 to 20 hours to pass through it. Here most of the water that was mixed with the food is removed through the walls of the large intestine. The waste is turned into solids that are passed from the body by excretion. A semivoluntary sphincter at the anus controls elimination.

In addition to the rectum, anus, and other parts, the large intestine is made up of the ascending colon, the transverse colon, and the descending colon (*see* Physiology; Anatomy, Human). The contents of the small intestine enter the ascending colon through a sphincter muscle, which prevents their return.

In the ascending colon, fluids and salts are absorbed. Water taken with meals is absorbed here. Water drunk between meals is mostly absorbed in the small intestine. In the transverse colon more water is removed from the waste materials until they are in solid form. The descending colon is a container for waste.

In the colon there are large numbers of bacteria. These bacteria aid in digesting the remaining food products. They also produce *folic acid,* which prevents anemia, and several vitamins.

Enzymes help plants and animals digest their food just as enzymes help humans digest theirs. An enzyme, *diastase,* helps break down starch into sugar. Another enzyme, *maltase,* acts upon malt sugar. Some plants produce fatty foods. *Lipase* changes these fats to usable forms for the plant.

Carnivorous, or meat-eating, animals have digestive systems that are shorter and simpler than those of herbivorous, or plant-eating, animals. The latter frequently have longer small and large intestines having several additional sections. The cow, for example, has four sections to its stomach (*see* Ruminants; Stomach). Bacteria in the intestines of herbivorous animals do much of the digestive work.

DIKE AND LEVEE.
Embankments of stone and earth that hold back water from dry land are called dikes or levees. Dikes usually protect land that would otherwise be under water most of the time. Levees protect land that is normally above water but that may be flooded when rain or melting snow raises the water level in a river.

River Valley Levees

By far the most famous of the levees that have been built along the course of streams in the United States are those that run along the Mississippi from the mouth of the Ohio River to the Gulf of Mexico. The first of these was built at New Orleans when the city was founded in the 18th century (*see* New Orleans). Shortly afterward the landowners along the river began to build small levees in front of their own plantations. Later the states along the Mississippi formed commissions for organized levee construction. In 1879 the Mississippi River Commission was formed by the United States government to assist the states. Working under the authority of the Army Corps of Engineers, the commission has built about 1,900 miles (3,000 kilometers) of levees.

The Mississippi levees are made of hard-packed earth, more than 100 feet (30 meters) wide at the base and about 15 to 30 feet (4.5 to 9 meters) high, tapering to a narrower top. The top and sides are planted with Bermuda grass to bind the earth together. The underwater foundations are protected by mattresses of woven willow or by concrete slabs. A careful watch is always kept to assure that no breaks in the levees are made by outside elements, such as burrowing animals. During floods a patrol is always ready to fill in gaps with bags of sand.

A disastrous flood in 1927 showed the need for additional water-control measures. One of these measures provides for diverting the Mississippi water into other rivers during times of danger. Another plan calls for blasting the levee at certain points to allow flooding of selected areas.

The Loire River in France is another site where levees have been built to protect agriculture and populated areas. At one time, a large section of the river called the Val de Loire flooded easily. Its once marshy floodplain is now protected from flooding by levees built progressively from the 12th to the 19th century.

Some rivers, as their flow slows, may deposit sediment in their beds between the two levees. This will eventually build up their channels higher than the surrounding floodplains. The rivers can, during high water, spill over the levees and cause devastating floods. The lower portions of the Chinese river Hwang Ho (or Huang He), which means Yellow River, are noted for this type of behavior.

The Dikes of The Netherlands

The name of The Netherlands means "lowlands": most of the country's territory ranges from below sea level to only about 66 feet (20 meters) above sea level.

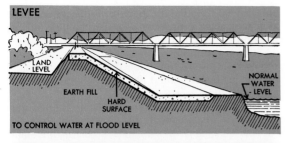

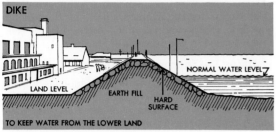

A great portion of the land of this country was once under lakes or the North Sea. In the greatest feat of hydraulic engineering ever executed, the water has been eliminated and the land made useful.

As early as 500 BC a growth in population resulted in people moving into the low-lying areas in the northwest near the sea. To protect themselves from flooding, they built mounds, or hills, of sod and debris on which they built their villages. These mounds, called terps, proved to be the easiest way to keep small areas unflooded. The terps were only a defensive measure against the sea, however. There was no guarantee that the land around them would remain dry.

Beginning in the 13th century, land reclamation on a large scale was begun with the construction of dikes. The earliest of these dikes were merely embankments connecting the terps. Eventually much larger areas came to be enclosed by dikes. These tracts of lowland reclaimed by the building of dikes are called polders. In the 13th century about 135 square miles (350 square kilometers) of land was reclaimed. By the end of the 20th century about 2,540 square miles (6,575 square kilometers) may have been added to that amount.

The most massive polder-creating project began in the 1920s in the Zuiderzee (now Lake IJssel). The scheme was developed by an engineer named Cornelius Lely. From 1927 to 1932 a barrier dam 19 miles (30 kilometers) long was built across the Zuiderzee, separating it from the Waddenzee. A great part of Lake IJssel was to be reclaimed into five polders. The first of the polders, the Wieringermeer, was finished by 1930. Three more have since been added, and one has still to be completed. The total area of the reclamation project is about 506,500 acres (205,000 hectares). (For map, *see* Netherlands.)

Although The Netherlands has the best-known dikes, there are other areas where cultivation is made possible by use of them. In Denmark and Germany there are low-lying districts that are protected against flood by dikes. There are also large dike-controlled areas at the mouths of the Vistula River in Poland, the Po in Italy, and the Danube in Germany.

DINOSAUR *see* ANIMALS, PREHISTORIC.

DIOGENES (412–323 BC). Many stories are told about the eccentric Greek philosopher Diogenes. According to one legend, he was seen carrying a lantern through the streets of Athens in the daytime. When he was asked why he was doing this, he answered, "I am seeking an honest man."

Diogenes came to Athens from the Greek colony of Sinope, on the Black Sea. He adopted the philosophy of the Cynics, who taught that to attain wisdom and virtue one must give up all the pleasures of life, which stand in the way of self-mastery. Thus he discarded all his possessions except a cloak and purse and a wooden bowl. He even threw away the bowl as unnecessary when he saw a boy drinking from his hand. He lived in a cask or tub.

At one time he made a voyage and was captured by pirates. They sold him as a slave in Crete. When asked his trade, he replied that he knew no trade but that of governing men and that he should be sold to a man who needed a master. He was sold to a wealthy man who took him to Corinth to tutor his children. There he became famous. Diogenes died at Corinth, and a pillar was erected to his memory.

DIONYSUS. One of the most widely worshiped gods of Greek mythology was Dionysus. At first, he was only the god of wine. Later he became the god of vegetation and warm moisture. Still later he was the god of pleasures and of civilization.

Dionysus was the son of Zeus and Semele, who was daughter of the king of Thebes. Legend says that Semele was consumed by flames when she glimpsed Zeus, without disguise, in his godlike splendor. Zeus put her unborn infant in his thigh. When the time came for the child's birth, Zeus drew him forth again. Thus Dionysus had a double birth.

In his early years the young god was cared for by an old satyr called Silenus. Dionysus learned to make wine and journeyed across the world to give it to mortals. The god enjoyed many adventures on his travels. He finally went into the infernal regions to find his mother and bring her back. He renamed her Thyone and brought her with him to Mount Olympus, the home of the gods.

Dionysus was represented in works of art as a beautiful youth, crowned with vine leaves or ivy and wearing a faun (a mythological animal) skin over his shoulders. His festivals were celebrated with processions, dances, and choruses, out of which grew the Greek drama and the Greek theater (*see* Drama). The Romans called this god Bacchus and celebrated the Bacchanalia, or festival of Bacchus, every third year. It became so immoral, however, that in 186 BC the Roman Senate forbade it.

A diorama in the American Museum of Natural History, New York City, shows a pair of mountain lions in a setting carefully designed to re-create their natural habitat.

DIORAMA. A popular type of exhibit found in many natural history museums is the diorama. It is a reproduction of a natural scene that is made by posing mounted specimens of animals among preserved or sculpted trees, grass, flowers, and rocks in front of a realistically painted background. The foreground is then skillfully made to merge with the painting, increasing the illusion of distance and space.

Collecting the Habitat Group

The groups of animals and plant life displayed in a diorama are often referred to as habitat groups. The idea for a display of a habitat group often begins with a curator in a department of a natural history museum. The museum's mammalogist, for example, may decide to display a particular mammal in its natural habitat and attempt to show as much as possible about the animal and its environment. In doing this the curator will often decide to include other species that are usually associated with the animal. In showing a bison group, for example, tick birds and prairie dogs would also be displayed.

Large museums with extensive resources are able to send teams to collect materials for a diorama of a habitat group. The team may consist of an artist, a taxidermist, a botanist, the curator, and other naturalists. Ideally the team goes to the actual spot from which the animals are taken. The artist makes sketches of the land forms and other physical features as well as the plant and animal life. The artist also takes many photographs of the area. The taxidermist or another member of the team is responsible for collecting—that is, killing—the animals.

Team members collect a wide variety of materials needing more or less preservation, depending on the perishability of the materials. Any woody branches and bushes collected need little preservation. If whole trees are to be part of the diorama, the bark of trees is carefully peeled off and sent back to the museum to be used as the outer portion of an artificial tree. Fragile, perishable specimens such as leaves may be preserved in a formaldehyde and glycerin solution and taken back to the museum for additional processing. Alternatively, impressions of the leaves, flowers, and other fragile plant materials may be made in the field. Boxes of soil and rocks are also collected.

When an animal is collected, it is skinned and the hide is treated in the field separately from the carcass. Casts and intricate measurements are made of the carcass, which is then treated to remove all the flesh except for the ligaments holding the skeleton together. The skeleton is then sun-dried in the field and returned to the museum.

Building the Diorama

Back at the museum, before the diorama is built, at least one small-scale model is made by the artists for the scientists, who then can comment on it and make suggestions. After the model has been approved, it gets translated into the large permanent exhibit.

In preparing the diorama, the artist does the background painting. The floor of the diorama is built up with wooden forms over wire mesh and plaster to get the contours desired. On top of this the soil is placed, usually about an inch deep. The color and texture of the rock specimens serve as guides for making reproductions of much larger rocks and boulders.

Although the plant life in a diorama appears to be real, in fact most of the foreground materials are replicas. Real leaves, for example, cannot be used because as they die they usually shrivel out of shape, lose their colors, and become brittle. The artificial leaves are made by a process called vacuum forming. In this method a plaster impression is taken of the real leaf. A sheet of cellulose acetate is placed over it, and the sheet is heated until it becomes plastic. It is then drawn onto the plastic mold by a vacuum. The resultant cast is a perfect replica of the original leaf. It is trimmed, the center vein or stem is attached with cement, and the color is sprayed on with a device called an airbrush. These artificial leaves are then attached to real tree branches, which need no preservative treatment. The bark that was shipped back is placed on a light cylindrical form to make a tree trunk. The petals and leaves of flowers are reproduced in the same way that the leaves are. Grasses are preserved in a formaldehyde and glycerin solution, dried, and sprayed with color.

The skeletons of the animals are set up in armatures to hold them in the positions in which the animals are to be displayed. Clay is then used to build up the animals based on the casts and measurements of the carcasses. Meanwhile the hides have been tanned and made soft and supple. When the clay models are finished, molds are made and hollow castings produced out of fiberglass or a similarly light, strong material. The hides are then brought together with the castings and glued on. Artificial eyes are inserted, and the original horns, if any, are then put back. The finished products are extremely lifelike.

UPI/Bettmann

Secretary of State Henry Kissinger and Egyptian President Anwar el-Sadat share a light moment during one of Kissinger's many exercises in shuttle diplomacy.

DIPLOMACY. The conduct of negotiations between nations is called diplomacy. As President Lyndon Johnson once said of politics, it is the art of the possible. Those who carry out diplomacy are, naturally, called diplomats. Their duty is to pursue, gain, and maintain as much peace and harmony for the countries they serve as a given situation will permit.

Agencies and Diplomats

Every independent nation has some government agency that handles foreign affairs. In the United States it is called the Department of State, and its chief officer is the Secretary of State (*see* United States Government). In Great Britain it is the Foreign Office, whose chief officer is the Foreign Secretary. These agencies act under the direction of the head of government to carry out foreign policies. In the United States, for example, it is the president who makes foreign policy in consultation with advisors. In Britain it is the prime minister.

Every foreign service agency sends out field agents who are stationed in foreign countries to protect and promote the interests of the nations from which they come. Before the days of rapid communication by radio, cable, and telegraph, four ranks of diplomats were established according to their authority to speak for their countries. The chief officer was given the title of ambassador. His word in negotiations was considered decisive and binding upon his country. Now that communication between an ambassador and his home country can be on a daily—or hourly—basis, he has far less authority to make foreign policy decisions on his own.

Second in rank was the minister plenipotentiary, who was sent on special missions with an authority equal to that of an ambassador. (Plenipotentiary means "having full authority.") The third grade was a minister resident, who handled routine affairs but lacked the full authority of an ambassador. The lowest rank was that of chargé d'affaires, who had temporary authority in absence of a diplomat of superior rank.

Today these ranks still exist, but the differences in their authority have largely disappeared. Diplomats of every grade can refer significant matters instantly to their home governments for a decision. Nevertheless, the highest ranking officer in any embassy is still the ambassador. It is a title that carries a good deal of dignity and prestige, and nations feel somewhat slighted if not sent persons of ambassadorial rank from other countries. On formal occasions, such as state dinners, ambassadors take precedence over everyone except heads of state and of government.

Certain others in the foreign service have different titles. The Vatican City calls its representatives nuncios, but they rank as ambassadors. Representatives of a country's army, navy, or air force are called military attachés. They act only as observers for their services, however, and do not conduct diplomatic negotiations.

The Foreign Service

In the 19th century, steps were taken in most countries to establish a professional corps of foreign service officers. The jobs were open to men and women on the basis of competitive examinations; advancement was by merit; and retirement was required by law at specific ages. A person hired is generally commissioned as a foreign service officer and classified into an established grade that determines salary. Promotion to the level of ambassador, however, is usually by appointment of the head of government. In the United States an ambassador must be appointed by the president and receive the approval of the Senate. Ambassadors need not be trained in the foreign service. This is especially true in the United States, where many ambassadors are appointed because of political loyalty and support; they may have no diplomatic training whatsoever.

The modern foreign service officer is usually a university graduate with an education in languages, history, law, and economics along with studies in foreign affairs. Officers often find it useful to specialize in certain areas of the world, making necessary in-depth study of the economics, politics, and culture of a region or country.

Great Britain. The modern British Diplomatic Service was formed in 1965 through the joining of other agencies. It staffs the Foreign and Commonwealth Office in London and British diplomatic missions abroad. It consists of administrative, executive, clerical, communications, secretarial, and guard branches.

United States. Foreign service officers of the United States below the rank of ambassador were put under civil service regulation. In 1924 the foreign service was established on a professional career basis by an act of Congress. It was further developed by the Foreign Service Act of 1946 and subsequent amendments and executive orders. Apart from regular foreign service officers, there is a Foreign Service Reserve composed of specialists serving for limited time, a Foreign Service staff to provide technical and cleri-

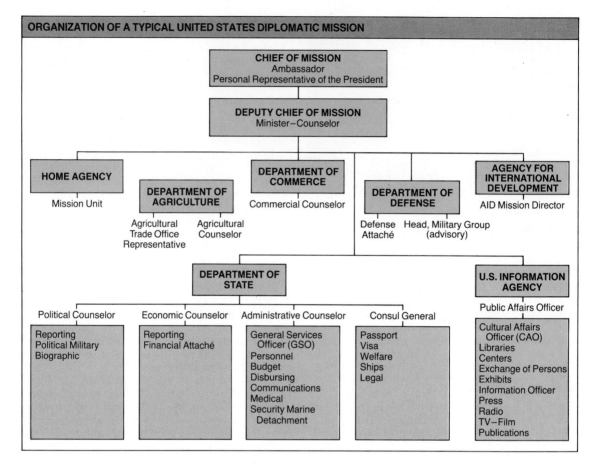

ORGANIZATION OF A TYPICAL UNITED STATES DIPLOMATIC MISSION

CHIEF OF MISSION
Ambassador
Personal Representative of the President

DEPUTY CHIEF OF MISSION
Minister–Counselor

HOME AGENCY
Mission Unit

DEPARTMENT OF AGRICULTURE
Agricultural Trade Office Representative — Agricultural Counselor

DEPARTMENT OF COMMERCE
Commercial Counselor

DEPARTMENT OF DEFENSE
Defense Attaché — Head, Military Group (advisory)

AGENCY FOR INTERNATIONAL DEVELOPMENT
AID Mission Director

DEPARTMENT OF STATE

Political Counselor
- Reporting
- Political Military
- Biographic

Economic Counselor
- Reporting
- Financial Attaché

Administrative Counselor
- General Services Officer (GSO)
- Personnel
- Budget
- Disbursing
- Communications
- Medical
- Security Marine Detachment

Consul General
- Passport
- Visa
- Welfare
- Ships
- Legal

U.S. INFORMATION AGENCY
Public Affairs Officer
- Cultural Affairs Officer (CAO)
- Libraries
- Centers
- Exchange of Persons
- Exhibits
- Information Officer
- Press
- Radio
- TV–Film
- Publications

cal services, and a Foreign Service Institute to train personnel progressively throughout their careers.

Embassies and Consulates

The headquarters of a permanent mission established in a foreign capital is called an embassy. It consists of one or more buildings where the foreign service staff does its work and where the ambassador has his office. Permanent missions may also be set up in the vicinity of an intergovernmental agency: there are many of them, for example, in New York City near the United Nations headquarters (*see* United Nations).

A consul is not a diplomat but a public officer authorized by a government to establish an office in another country to protect the interests of fellow nationals who may be in that country. This includes fellow citizens engaged in business there. While there can only be one embassy of a given nation in another capital city, there may be several consulates distributed in major cities throughout a country. Consulates handle routine tasks such as renewing passports. They also issue visas to citizens of the country in which they are located who may want to travel to the nation represented by the consulate. Americans wishing to travel to Japan, for example, get visas permitting them to do so from the nearest Japanese consulate.

Diplomatic Immunity

According to the Vienna Convention on Diplomatic Relations of 1961, diplomats are immune from the jurisdiction of the nation in which they are living. This means that they and their families are not subject to the criminal laws of the host state, nor—with some exceptions—to the civil law. When traveling from place to place, their luggage may not be searched. Should they be guilty of flagrant violation of the law or other unseemly behavior, however, they may be expelled from the host country.

Foreign embassies are similarly protected. Under a principle called extraterritoriality, an embassy and its grounds are considered not to be within the territory of the host state but within the territory of the state represented by the embassy. The embassy may not be entered by anyone without the permission of the head of the mission. If, for instance, a Soviet citizen who wishes to leave his country takes refuge in the American embassy in Moscow, no officials of the Soviet Union are permitted to follow and apprehend him. Because diplomatic immunity is an arrangement between nations, most nations respect it. Some few countries, however, have openly violated this principle in recent years. American embassies in Iran, Pakistan, Kuwait, and other places have been sacked.

How fragile the concept of diplomatic immunity has become was demonstrated early in 1984. On April 17, while exiled Libyans were demonstrating outside the Libyan embassy in London, shots were fired from the building, killing an English policewoman and wounding 11 demonstrators. British authorities cordoned off the building but did not enter it. Great Britain broke diplomatic relations with Libya over the incident but allowed the embassy staff to leave the country. Those who fired the shots escaped because the British government insisted on complying with international law concerning diplomatic immunity. This incident, along with others, has led some governments to consider revising the whole concept.

The World of Modern Diplomacy

Nations negotiate with one another on a wide array of issues, ranging from serious problems of war, peace, and disarmament to the more ordinary matters of boundary disputes, fishing rights, foreign aid, immigration quotas, and international trade. The issues themselves have remained fairly constant over the centuries, but the environment of diplomacy is quite different from what it was before World War II. Since 1945 six conditions have emerged that bear heavily on the conduct of diplomacy.

1. The great improvements in communication and transportation have, in effect, shrunk the size of the world. What happens almost anywhere is known almost everywhere else virtually immediately, and reaction time is therefore much shorter than it was formerly. An ambassador can convey news to a home government instantly and receive a policy directive without delay.

2. The Cold War has necessarily polarized the whole international community between the United States and the Soviet Union. Diplomacy everywhere is executed under the shadow of this bipolarization: diplomats must constantly have in mind "What will Moscow and Washington think about this issue?"

3. There are many more nations in the world now than there were in 1945. The colonial empires have disappeared, and dozens of new nation–states have emerged in Asia and Africa. Each of these wishes to make its voice heard in the international forum. These nations are in competition with one another and with the great powers, and they frequently succeed in playing the great powers against each other to gain favor from one or another. Many of these new countries are poor and underdeveloped, constituting what has been called the "Third World." Their problems pose a heavy burden on the diplomacy of the industrialized nations; many of these countries have rich supplies of natural resources, but so many also have unstable governments.

4. The possession of vast arsenals of nuclear weapons by the United States and the Soviet Union has created a "balance of terror," a situation in which world war is supposedly unthinkable. Theoretically, then, every nation in the world has a vital stake in striving for peace.

5. If nuclear war is unthinkable, conventional war is not. There have been more than 40 conventional wars since 1945. The world of the 1980s is saturated with "hot spots," such as Central America, the Middle East, the Far East, portions of South America, South Africa, Central Asia, and sub-Saharan Africa. In addition to trouble spots, there is a tendency of many nations to interfere in the affairs of other countries in order to destabilize their governments for economic or political advantage.

6. The sixth factor affecting diplomacy is the existence of the United Nations and other international organizations. These have not replaced bilateral diplomacy, but they have created larger forums for the airing of national points of view.

The effect of these six factors is to limit the independence of each nation as it pursues its foreign policy goals. The growing number of independent nations has led to increased interdependence in the world as a whole. Especially significant is economic interdependence. Economic well-being or disaster knows no national boundaries. A singular example was the impact that huge increases in the price of petroleum had on the economies of all nations in the 1970s.

Extraordinary Diplomacy

The ordinary matters of foreign policy are carried out in the day-to-day business at embassies around the world. But the critical issues of disarmament, economics, and conventional war trouble spots have called forth some bolder and more imaginative ways of carrying out international negotiation.

Summit meetings. In August 1941, a few months before the United States entered World War II, President Franklin D. Roosevelt and British Prime Minister Winston Churchill met on board ship in the North Atlantic. This was the first modern summit meeting between heads of government (*see* Atlantic Charter). This summit was followed by others during the war, the most famous of which was at Yalta in the Soviet Union between Roosevelt, Churchill, and Joseph Stalin. Shortly before the war ended, another summit was held at Potsdam, near Berlin, between President Harry S. Truman, Churchill, and Stalin.

Since then every American president has been involved in at least one summit meeting with other heads of state. Presidents Eisenhower, Kennedy, Johnson, Nixon, Ford, and Carter all had meetings with leaders of the Soviet Union. Presidents Nixon, Ford, Carter, and Reagan have all visited China to meet its leaders.

One of the most notable and successful summit meetings of the postwar era took place in 1977 when Egyptian President Anwar el-Sadat traveled to Israel to obtain a peace settlement with Israeli Prime Minister Menachem Begin. Out of this trip came the Camp David talks, arranged and hosted by United States President Jimmy Carter in 1978, from which came the Camp David accords outlining the principles for peace in the Middle East.

Not all summit meetings arise out of emergency

situations. Since 1975 there has been an annual economic summit between the heads of government of the United States, Japan, West Germany, Great Britain, Italy, and Canada to settle areas of disagreement among the various nations and to forge policies that will lead to greater international prosperity.

Shuttle diplomacy. John Foster Dulles, who served under President Dwight D. Eisenhower, was a widely traveled secretary of state, but it was Henry Kissinger who made such shuttle diplomacy a basic tool in the conduct of foreign relations. He traveled hundreds of thousands of miles on diplomatic missions to all parts of the globe during the administrations of Richard M. Nixon and Gerald R. Ford (*see* Kissinger).

Sometimes special envoys are used for shuttle diplomacy. In 1982 President Reagan sent Philip Habib and other negotiators to the Middle East to try to settle the crisis over Lebanon that had arisen from Israel's invasion of that country in June 1982. He traveled between Damascus, Jerusalem, and Cairo in what proved to be a futile attempt to reach a settlement of the discord (*see* Lebanon, section "History").

Diplomacy in the late 20th century has become a challenging, exasperating, and often frustrating attempt to reconcile seemingly irreconcilable differences between independent nation–states and between cultures that often have little understanding of each other. (For more information on the problems of foreign policy, *see also* Foreign Aid; International Monetary Fund; International Relations; and International Trade.)

DIRAC, P.A.M. (1902–1984).

One of the foremost theoretical physicists of the 20th century was Nobel prize winning English scientist P.A.M. Dirac. He was known for his work in quantum mechanics, for his theory of the spinning electron, and for having predicted the existence of antimatter.

Paul Adrien Maurice Dirac was born in Bristol, England, on Aug. 8, 1902. His mathematical ability showed itself at an early age and was encouraged by his father, a Swiss-born French teacher. Dirac studied electrical engineering at the University of Bristol. After receiving his degree he entered the University of Cambridge. In 1926, while still a graduate student, he devised a form of quantum mechanics, the laws of motion that govern particles smaller than atoms. Dirac's theoretical investigations led him to agree with other physicists that the electron, one such particle, must rotate on its axis. He also concluded that there must be states of negative energy. This idea was confirmed in 1932 when the positron—the anti-electron—was discovered.

In 1933 he was awarded the Nobel prize for physics. Dirac taught at Cambridge after receiving his doctorate there, and in 1932 he was named professor of mathematics. He served in that capacity until 1968, when he moved to the United States. In 1971 he was made professor emeritus at Florida State University, Tallahassee, Fla. He died in Tallahassee on Oct. 20, 1984. (*See also* Atomic Particles; Matter; Physics.)

DIRECTING.

A play's opening night or a movie premiere is the culmination of work by many people. Directing is the management of that technical and creative joint effort.

The director of a live performance has the primary responsibility for interpreting the play script, deciding on its meanings and method of presentation, and bringing that interpretation to life through the processes of rehearsal and staging. Motion pictures and television are forms of indirect communication using recording media such as film or videotape, both of which will be called "film" in this article. Here creating a production is a technical process usually employing a team of specialists. The director is a prime partner in this group. On an American feature film the production team may include a producer, director, writer, editor, and cinematographer, who is responsible for lighting and camerawork.

Various media, differing goals (such as promotion, instruction, or entertainment), and methods (animation, finding and joining existing film footage, or shooting live-action sequences) produce different kinds and levels of directing. Moreover, practices vary, depending on whether an individual is working within what has become a highly-structured industry or independently and according to how much creative control the production circumstances allow.

The duties of a stage director are relatively well-defined. Known as a *régisseur* in France and other European countries, the director was called a producer in England until 1956, when the American title was adopted. Though the stage director must have a thorough understanding of how a play is constructed and of lighting, set, and costume design, the ability to communicate successfully with actors is fundamental. Not surprisingly, many of the leading theatrical directors have been actors.

Both in terms of working on particular projects and as a profession film directing demands a more flexible definition. The director of a 10-second commercial "spot" for television may function as producer, set designer, cameraman, and editor—and may write and perform a musical score as well. Many skills are also required of the amateur filmmaker.

Despite the complexity of feature filmmaking, the professional director, through working with talented collaborators on several projects, may achieve considerable creative control. From D.W. Griffith to Francis Ford Coppola, there have been a number of directors who have earned reputations equal to or greater than those of the actor superstars of their day. Such a director's "name above the title" on a theater marquee has been a recognition of a personal vision expressed through a vast collaborative enterprise.

Increasing numbers of directors for both stage and the media now are trained in colleges, universities, or

---

This article was contributed by Christopher Lyon, Editorial Director, St. James Press; Art Critic, Chicago *Sun-Times*; and Editor, 'International Dictionary of Films and Filmmakers'.

Alfred Hitchcock (center, pointing), the most noted director of horror and thriller films, gives instructions in 1943 to the camera crew on the set of 'Shadow of a Doubt'.

professional schools. But there remains no substitute for experience, and the aspiring director seeks every opportunity to become involved with stage and film production in any capacity.

The Production Process

Plays may be developed through improvisation, based on a plot outline, for example. If a written play is to be used, an interpretation—an overall concept of the play's meaning—must evolve and be translated into terms understood by the actors, designers, and technical staff.

A play script is more than written dialogue and stage directions. It implies a world—modern, historic, fantastic, or absurd—in which the play is set and which sets the play in motion. The director must construct a version of that world that is both faithful to the playwright's vision and meaningful to the audience. The personal histories of the play's characters and their psychological relationships are at the center of this imagined world.

A stage director does not ordinarily work closely with a playwright except in the case of a new play, while a film director is frequently involved in the extensive rewriting typically required of film scripts. Before a script is given final form, the director and producer will have made many decisions. Money and time are the two most important factors to be considered. Whether to shoot on location or in a studio, to work in black and white or color—these are examples of such decisions.

Once a script is revised according to such considerations, and to suit the director's vision of the final film, a process of pre-visualization may be undertaken. For example, the director and production designer may "storyboard" the film in a series of hand-drawn sketches.

Casting for a live-action feature or a play is one of the director's most crucial jobs. The financial risks of filmmaking often dictate that actors be chosen to play types of roles that they have already done successfully. This may be less of a rule in theater, where casting "against type" is one means of realizing a new interpretation of a familiar play. In film small roles are often filled by a casting director.

Substantial rehearsal is rare in commercial film production, but it is the essential task of the stage director. Stage actors in rehearsal are finding out who their characters are and what they want in the world of the play. Traditionally actors were simply given directions for stage movement and line delivery, but now directors are more likely to participate with the actors in their discovery process, allowing movement and line reading to develop instinctively as the actors' understanding of character and motivation progresses. The director cannot teach acting in a rehearsal but may use a variety of techniques to remove tension or other obstacles to spontaneous performance. In addition the director may have to be something of a psychologist, devising exercises that allow an actor to experience an emotion needed for the role. The only necessary elements for a performance are actors and audience. In a rehearsal one of these is missing. The director's most important function may be to become, in the words of director Sir Tyrone Guthrie, "an audience of one."

153

© Martha Swope

Director James Lapine, right, works out a scene in the Broadway musical 'Sunday in the Park with George'.

Once a unified performance is achieved, the stage director's job is largely done. The film director, however, must keep a unified conception in mind while shooting hundreds of separate pieces of film usually not in the order in which they will appear. For the film actor this means that the sense of emotional continuity that is natural in a stage play is not present. For example, an actor may do a scene requiring joy, then a scene from much later in the film requiring anger, then go back to a joyous scene that will immediately follow the original one. Often in such cases, actors must rely more heavily on the director for instruction. But the film director also enjoys certain advantages. The stage actor has only one chance in each performance to realize his and the director's intentions, but the film director may order many "takes" of a particular shot or scene.

During the shooting of a film, the director's partner is the director of photography. Film is often discussed as if it were a kind of language. The raw vocabulary is ordinarily composed of many kinds of shots, ranging from a master shot containing all the elements in a scene to a powerful close-up emphasizing the significance of an object or facial expression. Angle of shot, placement of a subject within the frame, camera movement, depth of focus, and many other devices, as well as the modern array of special effects, all may modify a shot or sequence.

Working with the film editor, the director "writes" the film, selecting the most expressive "takes" and putting them together in sequences that can have very different meanings—depending on the order and duration of the individual shots that compose them. Other aspects of film production in which the director may become involved are sound effects and musical scoring—and even promotion of the film.

History

Stage. In ancient and Renaissance theater, and in such Eastern forms as the Japanese *No* drama, the poet or playwright commonly instructed the actors in their parts. During the Middle Ages plays based on episodes from the Bible were directed by the medieval *maître de jeu,* who supervised amateur actors in productions sponsored by the cities.

Rehearsal began to assume greater importance under 19th-century managers such as Madame Vestris, who took over London's Olympic Theatre in 1830. Playwright and manager Dion Boucicault worked under her and introduced her methods to the United States, where his work influenced David Belasco, often considered America's first modern director.

The attempt to create a total stage picture—using all the resources of set design, lighting, and ensemble acting in which the actors emphasize the coordination of their roles—has its roots in the Renaissance. It grew to maturity in the productions of an artistic nobleman, the Duke of Saxe-Meiningen. The appearance of his troupe in Berlin in 1874 may be considered the birth of modern stage direction.

Stage directing thereafter must be considered according to its two principal functions: conducting rehearsals and the actual mounting of a production on stage. The introduction of naturalistic drama—looking to everyday life for models of behavior—made necessary a psychologically realistic approach to acting that was pioneered by Konstantin Stanislavsky in Russia at the turn of the century. The development of rehearsal technique since Stanislavsky parallels the development of acting methods in the 20th century (*see* Acting).

Innovative methods of staging were pioneered by such director–designers as the Swiss Adolphe Appia and British Gordon Craig. Jacques Copeau in France and Max Reinhardt in Germany attempted to integrate stagecraft and ensemble acting techniques.

After World War II various attempts were made to create forms of theater that would address working-class concerns. Notable efforts in this direction were by Bertolt Brecht, who founded the famed Berliner Ensemble in East Berlin in 1948, and by Roger Planchon in France and Joan Littlewood in England in the 1950s.

Most theater was increasingly coming to resemble opera or ballet in that it appealed to a limited and specialized audience. In the 1960s, however, a brief flowering of radical experimentation was led in the United States by Judith Malina and Julian Beck, whose Living Theater company developed original works through improvisational methods. Joseph Chaikin, a member of that company, led the Open Theater through the mid-1970s, producing convincing examples of collaborative theatrical creation. The most influential director internationally during this period was Poland's Jerzy Grotowski, whose "theater laboratory" emphasized a total mental and physical approach to performance.

Film. While the conditions of stage production have changed very little since the early 20th century, the history of film directing must be considered in relation to a rapidly-developing technology and the explosive growth of the film industry. Directors in a position to exploit new techniques and equipment, or more sophisticated forms of industrial organization, have frequently been the first in the film industry to create elements of film "language" that are now part of its basic vocabulary.

Georges Méliès, for example, a magician and master illusionist of the Parisian theater, was the first to appreciate the illusionistic potential of film. He made use of multiple exposure and other in-camera manipulations, as well as primitive but convincing special effects, in some 500 short films produced between 1896 and 1914. The American Edwin S. Porter, having worked on camera design for Thomas Edison, understood Méliès's camera tricks. Porter introduced the technique of intercutting—paralleling shots of a racing fire engine with shots of a mother and child in a burning building—in his 1903 'The Life of an American Fireman'.

The best of early American filmmaking is the work of D.W. Griffith. Assisted by cameraman G.W. "Billy" Bitzer, he not only established many of the standard story-telling devices of film but also exploited the ability of the new industry to organize and finance movies of unprecedented scale. Among them are 'The Birth of a Nation' and 'Intolerance', which remain among the greatest films ever made.

Griffith's work had a profound effect on the first Soviet filmmakers. Lacking blank film because of a ban on trade to the Soviet Union, these directors concentrated at first on editing and re-editing foreign features or documentary footage. In the work of Sergei Eisenstein editing technique was raised to the level of a "theory of montage," in which the contrast of contradictory shots was used to shock and agitate the audience. The great French innovator of the 1920s, Abel Gance, pioneered wide-screen and multi-screen effects in his epic 'Napoleon'.

Such visionary directors often found themselves at odds with a highly-structured industry organized to produce a standardized product. It is within this studio system that most directors worked between the world wars. With the decline of movie attendance after World War II, the studio system began to disintegrate, and by the 1960s independent production was once again very important. A renewed appreciation of the director's contribution was given impetus by a group of young French film critics in the 1950s, who considered the film director to be the *auteur,* or author, of the motion picture.

BIBLIOGRAPHY FOR DIRECTING

Allensworth, Carl and others. The Complete Play Production Handbook (Harper, 1982).

Bronfeld, Stewart. How to Produce a Film (Prentice, 1984).

Clurman, Harold. On Directing (Macmillan, 1972).

Cole, Toby and Chinoy, H.K., eds. Directors on Directing (Bobbs, 1963).

Geduld, Harry, ed. Film Makers on Film Making (Univ. of Ind. Press, 1967).

Kantor, B.R. and others, eds. Directors at Work: Interviews with American Film-makers (Funk & Wagnalls, 1970).

Lipton, Lenny. Independent Filmmaking (Simon & Schuster, 1983).

Macgowan, Kenneth. Behind the Screen: the History and Techniques of the Motion Picture (Delacorte, 1965).

Marowitz, Charles and Trussler, Simon, eds. Theatre at Work: Playwrights and Productions in the Modern British Theatre (London, Methuen, 1967).

Sarris, Andrew. The American Cinema: Directors and Directions, 1929–1968 (Octagon, 1982).

SOME MAJOR FILM AND STAGE DIRECTORS

Some prominent persons are not included below because they are covered in the main text of this article or in other articles in Compton's Encyclopedia (see Fact-index). The following list gives the names of directors with their birth and death dates and place of birth. At least two titles that the subject directed are given with the year of release in parentheses. If a film won an Academy Award for best director, it is indicated in the parentheses.

Film Directors

Buñuel, Luis (1900–83; Calanda, Spain). 'Land Without Bread' (1932), 'Viridiana' (1961).

Coppola, Francis Ford (born 1939; Detroit). 'The Godfather' (1972), 'The Godfather, Part II' (1974, Academy Award), 'Apocalypse Now' (1979).

DeMille, Cecil B. (1881–1959; Ashfield, Mass.). 'The Cheat' (1915), 'The Sign of The Cross' (1932; re-released with added footage, 1944).

Flaherty, Robert (1884–1951; Iron Mountain, Mich.). 'Nanook of the North' (1922), 'Man of Aran' (1934), 'Louisiana Story' (1948).

Ford, John (1895–1973; Cape Elizabeth, Me.). 'The Informer' (1935, Academy Award), 'The Searchers' (1956), 'The Man Who Shot Liberty Valance' (1962).

Hawks, Howard (1896–1977; Goshen, Ind.). 'Scarface: The Shame of a Nation' (1932), 'Red River' (1947), 'Gentlemen Prefer Blondes' (1953).

Hitchcock, Alfred (1899–1980; London). 'Rear Window' (1954), 'Vertigo' (1957), 'Psycho' (1960).

Kurosawa, Akira (born 1910; Tokyo). 'Rashomon' (1951), 'Kagemusha' (1980).

Lang, Fritz (1890–1976; Vienna). 'Hangmen Also Die!' (1943), 'While the City Sleeps' (1956).

Ray, Satyajit (born 1921; Calcutta). 'Charulata' (1964), 'Jana Aranya' (1975), 'Pikoo' (1981).

Renoir, Jean (1894–1979; Paris). 'Madame Bovary' (1934), 'The Rules of the Game' (1939).

Scorsese, Martin (born 1942; Queens, N.Y.). 'Taxi Driver' (1976), 'New York, New York' (1977), 'Raging Bull' (1980).

Truffaut, François (born 1932; Paris). 'The 400 Blows' (1959), 'Day for Night' (1973).

Welles, Orson (born 1916; Kenosha, Wis.). 'Citizen Kane' (1941), 'The Lady from Shanghai' (1947).

Stage and Stage-and-Film Directors

Brook, Peter (born 1925; London). 'The Marat/Sade' (1965), 'Antony and Cleopatra' (1978), 'The Cherry Orchard' (1981).

Kazan, Elia (born 1909; Constantinople). 'J.B.' (1958), 'Gentlemen's Agreement' (film, 1947, Academy Award), 'On the Waterfront' (film, 1954, Academy Award).

Littlewood, Joan (born 1914?; London). 'Oh, What a Lovely War!' (1963), 'Sparrers Can't Sing' (film, 1962).

Nichols, Mike (born 1931; Berlin). 'The Odd Couple' (1965), 'Plaza Suite' (1968), 'The Graduate' (film, 1967, Academy Award), 'Silkwood' (film, 1983).

A group of hikers stops to check their location and in what direction to travel. They are using a topographical map of the area.

Boy Scouts of America

DIRECTIONS. Animals have a wonderful sense of direction. Cats and dogs do not have to be taught how to find their way home. Birds travel thousands of miles from their winter to their summer homes and do not get lost. Some even return to the same meadow or tree where they nested the year before. The Pacific salmon swims across the ocean to lay its eggs in the very stream in which it was born. Even an ant knows its way about.If you pick it up and move it, it will turn around and find its way back. Scientists are still unable to explain this remarkable direction sense. (*See also* Animal Migration.)

People are the greatest travelers of all, but they get lost easily. When blindfolded, a child cannot even walk across a room in a straight line to pin a tail on the donkey. That is why many people become lost in dense woods and in blinding snowstorms. Tests have shown that when people cannot see, they wander around in circles. The reason seems to be that the two sides of the body are not equal in weight or in muscle strength.

When a person is described as having a good sense of direction, this means that he notices and remembers objects that he passes and is conscious of the various turns in a road or the corridors in a building. This helps him if he returns by the same route. If he takes another route, he will need directions to help him find his way.

THE LANGUAGE OF DIRECTIONS

Fortunately people have maps and compasses to guide them; and when the sky is clear they have the sun and stars. To learn how to use these aids, they need to know the exact meanings of words used in the language of directions.

Some of these direction words pertain to the body. Such words are "forward," "back," "right," and "left." Others are related to the earth. These are "up," "down," "north," "south," "east," and "west."

Right and Left

Right and *left* are names for the two sides of the body. People tell them apart by the different way they feel. If someone is right-handed, the right hand is stronger and is used for most skilled work. Someone who is left-handed prefers to use the other hand. A few people seem to do things as well with one hand as with the other. They are called ambidextrous. Even these people usually choose to train one hand for writing or for throwing a ball.

When right and left are used as location words, they are usually qualified as *right hand* and *left hand*. These terms mean the two sides of something as it appears to the viewer. This sentence is on the left-hand page of the book and in the right-hand column of that page.

RIGHT HAND AND LEFT HAND
The cat has its own right and left sides. The desk does not.
Right-hand drawer means on the right of a person using the desk.

RIGHT BANK AND LEFT BANK
The right bank of a river will be on your right hand only if you
are facing downstream—the direction in which the river flows.

Animals, like people, have their own right and left
sides. Cars, ships, trains, and airplanes also have
their own right and left because we think of them as
facing in the direction in which they usually move.
On ships and airplanes the left side is called the *port*
side. The right side is called *starboard*.

All rivers flow downstream—from higher to lower
ground. We think of them as "facing" downstream
and call the rising ground that borders them the *right
bank* and the *left bank*. When you read that a city is
on the left bank of a river, think of yourself as facing
downstream. The city will be on your left.

Up and Down

If you drop a ball it falls to the ground or floor.
If you drop a stone into the ocean it sinks to the ocean
bottom. We say that the ball and the stone "fall."
Actually they are pulled toward the center of the
earth by the force called gravity. *Down* therefore

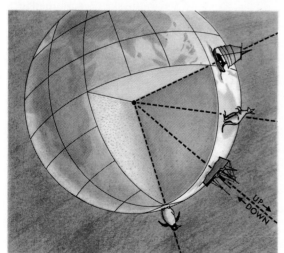

UP AND DOWN
Down means in a direct line toward the center of the earth.
Up is the direction away from the center.

means toward the earth's center. *Up* means away
from the earth's center. (*See also* Gravitation.)

"Up" and "down" are direction words. So are "upstream" and "downstream," "uphill" and "downhill."
We also use these words to locate things, as when we
say upper story, downstairs, top drawer, bottom shelf.
"Upstage" means toward the rear of the stage because
in early theaters the rear was higher than the front.

North and South

The round world we live on spins in space like a
curve ball thrown by a baseball pitcher. We say that
the earth spins, or rotates, around a straight line
through its center. We call this imaginary line the
earth's axis; and we call the two ends of the axis
poles—the North Pole and the South Pole.

A globe is a small model of the earth. On it you
will see lines drawn from the North Pole to the South
Pole, as in the diagram on the next page. Follow any
one of of these lines and you will be going straight
north or straight *south*. From the North Pole you can
move in only one direction—south. From the South
Pole you can move only north. Map makers invented
these lines and gave them numbers to help locate
places on the earth. They are called meridians of
longitude.

The earth, like a ball, has no top or bottom. We
think of the North Pole as the top only because all
globes and most maps are made that way. We sometimes say "up north" or "down south" when we mean
simply north and south. The long mountainous
peninsula in Mexico that extends south from California was named Lower California because on maps it
is below the state of California.

East and West

The earth's rotation gives us two more directions
—*east* and *west*. East is simply the direction toward
which the earth is turning. West is the direction from
which it turns. The earth makes one complete turn,
or rotation, every 24 hours.

DIRECTIONS

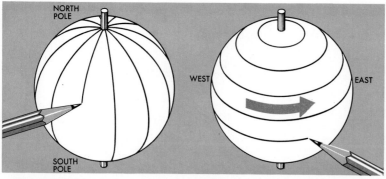

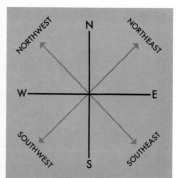

NORTH AND SOUTH
North is the direction toward the North Pole. South is the direction toward the South Pole.

EAST AND WEST
East is the direction toward which the earth is turning. West is the direction from which it turns.

IN-BETWEEN DIRECTIONS
Halfway between the "true" directions are northeast, southeast, southwest, and northwest.

East and west are not directions to particular points such as the North and South Poles. An airplane could circle round and round the Earth and go always straight west or always straight east.

The east-west lines get smaller and smaller toward the poles. The longest is the line halfway between the poles. It is called the equator because it divides the world into two equal parts. These parts are called hemispheres (half spheres). The Northern Hemisphere is north of the equator. The Southern Hemisphere is south of the equator.

There is no natural dividing line, such as the equator, separating east from west. Map makers needed such a line as a starting point for measuring both time and space. Almost all countries adopted as the prime meridian the line passing through Greenwich, England, because this was the site of a famous observatory. This line, like the equator, is numbered zero. Unlike the equator, it is a half circle. It runs only from one pole to the other. (*See also* Latitude and Longitude; Time; International Date Line.)

In-Between Directions

North, south, east, and west are the only true directions. On a compass they are called the cardinal points. The directions halfway between the cardinal points are called northeast, southeast, southwest, and northwest. The forms "eastnorth" or "westsouth" are not used because the entire system of directions is pinned to the North and South Poles.

Globes and maps show only north-south and east-west lines. If one tried to draw on a globe a line going straight northeastward, it would curve more and more as it got nearer the North Pole.

FINDING DIRECTIONS BY THE SUN

The sun lights only one side of the Earth. It is the turning of the Earth that causes day and night. Because it turns toward the east, the sun seems to rise in the east. Throughout the day the sun appears to move westward across the sky because the Earth itself is moving eastward. It disappears, or sets, in the west when the turning Earth blots it from view.

It might seem that the sun would be most useful for giving east-west directions, but it is not very reliable for this use. In winter (north of the equator) it rises and sets far to the south of true east and west; and in summer, far to the north. On only two days in the year does the sun rise exactly in the east and set exactly in the west. These days are about March 21 and September 23. This is true anywhere in the world except near the poles. One can check by looking down an east-west street at sunset or at sunrise. (*See also* Earth, section "The Moving Earth"; Season.)

One thing is certain at any season. For those who live in the United States or Canada, the sun will always be in

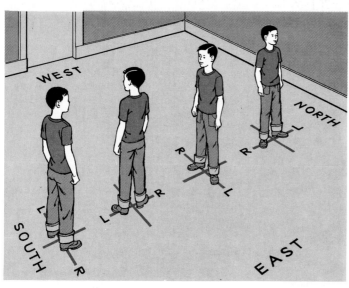

If you are sure of one direction, you can easily figure out the other three. The boy at the left is facing north. East is to his right and west is to his left. What directions are to your right and left when you face west? When you face south? When you face east?

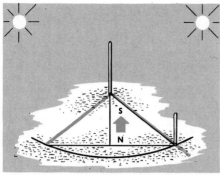

GETTING DIRECTIONS WITH A SHADOW STICK OR A WATCH

the south at noon. On any sunny day you can find south with a shadow stick or with a watch.

How to Find South with a Shadow Stick

In the morning drive a long stick straight into the ground. Where the shadow of this stick ends, drive in a short stick. Tie a loop at the end of a cord and slip it over the shadow stick. Stretch the cord tight and tie another loop around the short stick. Then use the short stick, still in the loop, to scratch a circle around the shadow stick.

The shadow will grow shorter up to noon. Then it will grow longer. As soon as it touches the circle again, mark this point. Draw a straight line connecting this mark with the hole you made in the morning with the short stick. Exactly halfway along this line, draw a straight line to the shadow stick. This line will run north-south. South will be toward the stick.

How to Find South with a Watch

Put your watch down flat on the ground in the sun. Hold a match upright at the edge of the watch so that it casts a shadow across the watch dial. Then turn the watch so that the shadow lies exactly along the hour hand. If you do this at exactly noon, the shadow line will, of course, point south, with south the direction toward the sun. Your watch, of course, must be set for standard (not daylight-saving) time.

In the morning and afternoon, south will lie halfway between the shadow line and 12:00. In the morning use the left-hand side of the watch to locate the halfway line. In the afternoon use the right-hand side of the watch, reading the numbers backward.

FINDING DIRECTIONS BY THE STARS

If you stood at the North Pole and looked up, you would see a star directly over your head. You can see this same star from any place in the Northern Hemisphere. When you point to it, you are pointing very nearly true north. The star was named Polaris, after the pole, but it is usually called the North Star, or the polestar. Before the compass was invented the North Star was the best guide for travelers on land and sea. It is not a very bright star, but it is easy to find.

Since very early times, people have imagined that

certain groups of stars form pictures. The groups are called constellations. The best known of all the constellations is the group of seven bright stars that form the Big Dipper. The two stars in the bowl that are farthest away from the handle are called the Pointers. The star charts on this page show you how to use the Pointers to find the North Star.

When you have found the North Star, look for the Little Dipper. The North Star is the last star in the handle of this smaller constellation. Then find Cassiopeia's Chair.

The North Star never sets; and it is the only star that is always in the same place in the sky. The stars close to it—called circumpolar (around-the-pole) stars—appear to circle around the North Star. Sometimes the Big Dipper seems to be standing on its handle and sometimes hanging by it.

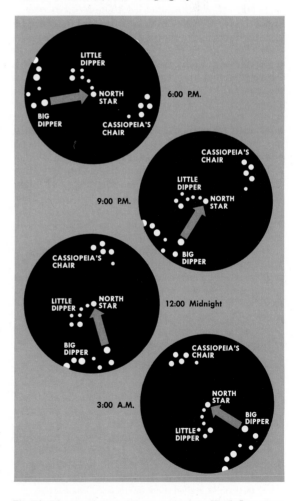

The Big Dipper swings completely around the North Star every 24 hours; but wherever it is the two Pointers in its bowl point to the North Star. These charts show four positions of the circumpolar stars during the night of September 21.

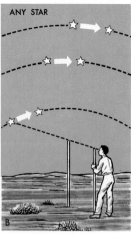

SIGHTING STARS FOR DIRECTIONS

HOW TO SIGHT A STAR

After locating the North Star, you need to "bring it down to the earth." Picture A above shows how to sight the North Star. Picture B shows how to find a general direction by sighting any other bright star.

A. Drive a long stake into the ground. Then take a shorter stick and get down on the ground with it. Move it around until you can sight across the tops of the two sticks as if you were aiming a gun at the North Star. When the three points—the two sticks and the star—are in an exact line, drive the short stick into the ground. Then scratch a line joining the two sticks. The line will run north-south, with the tall stick marking north.

B. If the North Star is behind a cloud, any other bright star will give you a general direction. Sight the star across two sticks in the same way. Then watch for a while to see which way the star is moving. Remember that stars, like the sun, rise in the east, circle across the sky, and set in the west.

If the star you are watching is low in the sky, it will appear to move either up or down. If it is rising, you are facing east. If it is setting, you are facing west. If you are watching a star high in the sky, it will appear to move sideways instead of up or down. The direction toward which it moves is west. If it moves to your right, you are facing south. If it moves to your left, you are facing north.

UNDERSTANDING THE COMPASS

Everyone who likes to sail, hunt, camp, hike, or climb mountains should carry a small pocket compass. If you use it correctly, you can always find your way back to the place you started from.

Lay a compass down flat and leave it until the swinging needle comes to rest. In what direction does the arrow point? Most people think it points to true north—the North Pole. It does not. The earth has two other poles, called *magnetic poles*. The north magnetic pole is in northern Canada. The south magnetic pole is on the opposite side of the earth in the Antarctic. The compass needle points to magnetic north.

How to Make a Floating Compass

If you have a toy horseshoe magnet or a bar magnet, try this experiment. You will also need two bowls (not metal), two sewing needles, and a piece of cork.

Your toy magnet pulls to itself small iron and steel objects, such as paper clips. This pull is called magnetic force. It is very much stronger at the two ends of the magnet than in the middle. The ends are called poles. (*See also* Magnets and Magnetism.)

The poles look alike and they have equal magnetic force. Your floating compass will show, however, that each pole behaves differently.

Mark one pole of your magnet with a pencil. Rub the *point* of one sewing needle on this marked pole and the *eye* on the unmarked pole. To prepare the second needle, rub its *eye* on the marked pole and its *point* on the unmarked pole. Both needles are now magnetized, like the needle in a compass.

Run each needle through a small piece of cork so it will float. Drop one needle in each bowl. When the needles come to rest, each will lie in the same direction as a compass needle. One needle, however, will lie with its eye end toward magnetic north; the other, with its point end toward magnetic north.

Put both needles into the same bowl and they will join eye to eye or point to point. The reason is that we made the eye of one needle a north-seeking pole and the eye of the other a south-seeking pole. Unlike poles attract each other. Like poles repel each other.

We give the name north pole, or north-seeking pole, to the end of a magnet or to a magnetized needle that is attracted to the earth's north magnetic pole. We call the other end the south pole. This is convenient but not really correct. Since unlike poles attract each other, the end of the needle that points to magnetic north is really the south pole of the needle.

Errors of the Compass—
Deviation and Declination

Hold a steel knife close to the needle of your floating compass and watch the needle swing toward the blade. It no longer points to magnetic north and

This simple experiment shows how the compass works. All you need to perform it are a toy horseshoe magnet or a bar magnet, sewing needles, bits of cork, and bowls of water.

is quite useless as a direction finder. If you are depending upon a compass to find your way, be sure that there is no iron or steel near it. This compass error, caused by iron or by any other magnetic substance, is called *deviation*.

The other compass error is called *declination*, or *variation*. It is the difference between true north and magnetic north. You need to know how much the variation is for the place where you are and allow for it. Your compass will point straight north only if you happen to be on a line that runs roughly from Savannah, Ga., through Lake Superior. East of this line a compass points west of true north. West of this line it points east of true north. (For map, *see* Compass, Magnetic.)

HOW TO READ A ROAD MAP

A globe is a small, round model of our round earth. Maps are flat. Only a globe can show distances, directions, and shapes as they really are. For most purposes, however, maps are more useful than globes. They can be larger and show more. They can be printed in books, such as in this encyclopedia. They can also be carried about easily, folded or rolled.

There are many kinds of maps and each kind tells a different story. For finding directions there are sea charts and aeronautical charts, railroad maps, road maps, and contour maps. Most common of all are the road maps used by automobile drivers.

When you unfold a road map, you will naturally hold it so that you can read the words on it. Then you can be pretty sure that north will be at the top of the sheet, but you had better check by looking for a direction arrow or a compass rose. If there is none, north will be at the top.

If north is at the top, the right-hand edge is east, the left-hand edge is west, and south is at the bottom. When you spread a map on a table, turn it so that the map north is toward the north. Then the directions east and west on your map will be east and west on the earth. If you hang the map on a wall, try to hang it so that east is to the east as you face the map.

Map Symbols—Spacesaving Signs

Everything on a road map is a word, a number, or a symbol. The usual symbol for a city is a circle. If there is a star inside the circle, the city is a capital. Some symbols are small pictures. An airplane, for example, may stand for an airport. Even the lines are symbols. Some line symbols show the kind of road surface. Others represent canals, railways, or boundaries. Colors also have a meaning.

All maps do not use exactly the same symbols. On every road map you will find a *key* that explains what each symbol means.

Index, Grid, and Frame of Reference

When you are planning a trip, you first look on the map for the place where you are and then for the

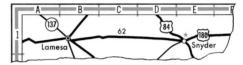

place where you are going. Somewhere on the road map you will find the *index*. This is an alphabetical list of all towns and cities shown on the map. Suppose you are looking for Snyder. You find it in the index, followed by E-1. Remember E-1 and turn to the map.

Thin lines divide the map into a network of squares, called the *grid*. (Sometimes only the ends of the lines are shown.) Inside the *frame of reference* (the border) you will see letters on two opposite sides and numbers on the other two sides. Locate the square E-1. Inside this square you will find Snyder.

A Large-Scale Map May Be Very Small

The map maker, like the architect, draws *to scale*. If he decides to make an inch represent 20 miles, this must be true on every part of the map.

Many state road maps have separate maps of important cities. These maps are very small compared to the state map; but because they are drawn to a much larger scale, they can show streets, parks, and main buildings. The larger the scale, the more details a

Map makers today use special air photos, checking them with ground surveys. The camera is pointed straight down. That is why the photograph does not show the heights of hills and build-

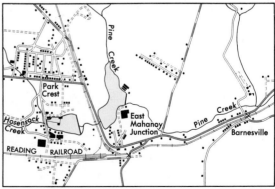

ings. Maps also are made as if you were looking straight down on the land. The map is simpler than the picture because the map maker uses symbols for roads, railways, and other features.

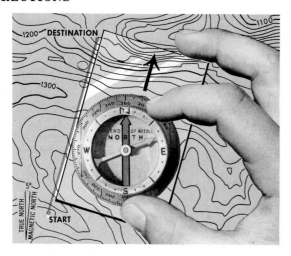

Set your compass so that the Direction of Travel arrow will point along your route when the compass needle is pointing

north. Use the direction arrow to sight a landmark, then walk to it. Do not watch the compass while walking.

map maker can show. If one inch represents 20 miles, one can easily figure the distance from point to point "as the crow flies." Roads, however, twist and turn. To figure the actual driving distance, one must total the mileage figures shown on the map along the main highways.

ORIENTATION WITH MAP AND COMPASS

There are still many large areas in the United States and Canada where one might wander for days without meeting another person or crossing a road. In such places the fisherman, the hunter, the camper, the hiker, and the mountain climber need both map and compass to help them find their way.

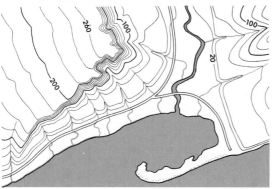

A topographic map is clearer than a picture. Contour lines connect places that are the same height above sea level. Numbers on the lines give the height in feet. (Sea level is zero.) Lines close together show that the slope is steep.

The best kind of map for this purpose is a topographic sheet in the scale of 1 inch to 2,000 feet. Topographic maps use line symbols, called contours, to show ups and downs. They also show every creek, pond, and woodland, as well as man-made features. Such maps may be obtained from a map store or from the United States Geological Survey.

The best compass for hikers is the kind used by Boy Scouts. It is mounted on a transparent plastic plate. The magnetic needle swings inside a metal housing. The housing can be turned easily on the plate. The circular edge of the housing is marked into 360 parts, called degrees. The degrees are numbered in clockwise order from zero through 360. North is zero, or 360. East is 90, south is 180, and west is 270. Each degree indicates a possible direction of travel, called a bearing.

If a starting place and destination are marked on a map, the best route—which may not be the shortest one—may be determined by using a compass. The following steps will provide a bearing, ignoring the swinging needle.

On the plastic plate at the top is an arrow marked Direction of Travel. The compass should be placed on the map so that this arrow (or either long edge of the plate) lies along the chosen route. Then the compass housing is turned until the N–S line that runs through it is aligned with north–south on the map. The degree reading below the Direction of Travel line should then be noted.

The direction arrow on the topographic map may show a considerable difference between magnetic north and true north. If, for example, the declination is 10 degrees west, 10 degrees are added. If the declination is to the east, the degrees are subtracted.

When one starts out, the bearing must be transferred from the map to the land. The entire compass—held level—is turned until the magnetic needle points to N. The line indicated by the arrow on the plate can then be followed. (*See also* Maps and Globes.)

DISABILITY. In medicine, the inability to perform an activity because of some physical or mental disorder is called disability. Disabilities can range from relatively minor to crippling. They may also be temporary, such as a broken leg, or permanent, correctable or not, congenital, meaning present at birth, or acquired. A disabled person is not necessarily handicapped, however. A handicap is a limitation that a disability may impose on a disabled person.

Types

A relatively minor disability might be caused by the loss of a finger in an accident. Some learning would be necessary to perform certain actions, but over time the average person learns to adapt. The same injury to a concert pianist, however, would constitute a major disability, so the degree of disability depends to some extent on the individual.

A person who loses a leg or arm generally has more adapting to do, much of it depending on how much of the limb is lost. Usually a prosthesis, or false limb, can be fitted if a stump remains, and with rehabilitation the person is often able to resume most activities.

Injuries to the spinal cord can result in profound disability. The extent to which a person is disabled depends on the portion of the spine injured. Paraplegia, or paralysis of the legs, results when the injury occurs around the thoracic or lumbar vertebrae of the spine. These extend from about shoulder level to below the waist. Neck injuries can cause quadriplegia, or paralysis from the neck down. People with these disabilities are often confined to wheelchairs. Loss of bowel and bladder control occurs with quadriplegia and with paraplegia when paralysis is from the waist down.

Many diseases can cause disability. A person who has a stroke, for example, may lose the use of a limb, speech, or comprehension. Chronic diseases, such as heart disorders, can limit a person to walking short distances. Arthritis is a common cause of disability. Though it is often considered a disease of older people, rheumatoid arthritis, which is sometimes called "crippling arthritis," can affect young people and even infants (*see* Arthritis).

Congenital disabilities include spina bifida (open spinal cord), absent arms or legs, cystic fibrosis, muscular dystrophy, and mental retardation. Some congenital abnormalities that once caused disability, such as cleft palate and club foot, can now be corrected surgically in infancy.

The degree of disability that arises from mental retardation varies. Many mentally retarded people can be taught to care for themselves, to become productive citizens, and to earn a living. The profoundly retarded, however, require total care.

Rehabilitation

Learning to adapt to a disability usually takes time and the assistance of professionals who work with disabled people. Physicians, physical and occupational therapists, social workers, psychologists, and others can assist in this process, which is called rehabilitation. Disabled people can learn to compensate, and many develop careers in areas that might otherwise have been unexplored.

Loss of hearing or sight requires special education as part of rehabilitation. Lip reading and sign language are important skills for the deaf person to learn. Braille, seeing eye dogs, canes, and tape recorders can help blind persons maintain their independence (*see* Blindness; Deafness).

Rehabilitation and exercise are especially important for people with musculoskeletal disabilities. The affected limbs are exercised passively by having another person move the arm or leg through the normal range of motions. The portions of the body not affected can be actively exercised; for example, a paraplegic can pull up on a bar suspended over a bed or chair. Bladder and bowel training is effective for many people who have lost sensation in these areas.

Rehabilitation often includes occupational training. People who have developed disabilities because of an injury or disease may not be able to resume their former occupations, but often they can lead productive lives after job training. Counseling is an important facet of rehabilitation because the loss of function often leads to depression and other psychological problems.

Aids

The physical environment poses many barriers for people with disabilities. Although architects and city planners are increasingly aware of the needs of disabled people, there are still areas where a person confined to a wheelchair cannot enter. Wheelchair access at doorways, curbs, ramps, and public restrooms are designs that accommodate the disabled. Braille signs in public areas, such as in elevators, are a great help to blind people.

Other important accommodations both for public areas and in the home are toilet bars for aid in transferring between toilet seat and wheelchair. Tub grab bars and shower grab bars permit independence in hygiene. Kitchens can be modified by lowering cabinets, countertops, sink, refrigerator, and stove so that a person in a wheelchair can easily reach everything for food preparation. Numerous household aids are available to assist the disabled person. Special eating utensils allow a person with hand disabilities to eat with a minimum amount of discomfort.

DISARMAMENT. The single most vital issue to confront the nations of the world since World War II has been the prevention of nuclear warfare. This task has been the focus of diplomatic discussions between the United States and the Soviet Union and a leading item on the agenda of the United Nations. Despite all the effort that has been put into disarmament talks, however, there have been few positive results. Both the United States and the Soviet Union have enormous and growing stockpiles of nuclear weapons. Great Britain, France, China, India, and other countries also possess them. In addition, annual sales of more conventional weapons to nearly every nation total hundreds of billions of dollars.

Modern History

Modern attempts at international disarmament began with the Hague Peace Conferences of 1899 and 1907 (*see* Hague Peace Conferences). The failure of these conferences became evident with the outbreak of World War I in 1914. Between this war and World War II there were several attempts at arms limitation and at total disarmament. The two most notable were the London Naval Conference of 1930 and the Permanent Disarmament Commission of the League of Nations of 1932. The London Naval Conference had some success, but it was very temporary. Great Britain, the United States, France, Italy, and Japan agreed to a five-year moratorium on the construction of battleships and to a limitation of submarines and aircraft carriers. Within a couple of years, however, Japan was building a large navy, and Germany was doing the same. The League commission produced little in the way of results, and what it did accomplish was soon undone as Germany began to rearm.

The invention in World War II and spread of nuclear weapons—atomic and hydrogen bombs—lent greater urgency to the need for disarmament. Immediately after the founding of the United Nations in 1945, an international Atomic Energy Commission was set up to make plans for controlling all major weapons of mass destruction. What prevented any accord from being reached was the Cold War between the United States and the Soviet Union (*see* Cold War). Under the auspices of the United Nations, only two significant agreements were reached. The first was the Moscow Agreement of 1963, in which the two superpowers and Britain pledged not to conduct atomic tests in the atmosphere, under water, or in outer space. The second agreement was the Nuclear Nonproliferation Treaty of 1970, signed by 47 nations. This attempt to keep other countries from joining the "atomic club" has been generally successful.

Tensions between the United States and the Soviet Union have made it clear that unless agreement is reached between these two superpowers, nuclear disarmament is impossible. A start toward that goal was made during the presidency of Richard Nixon. In November 1969 the first series of Strategic Arms Limitation Talks (SALT) began at Helsinki, Finland. After about 130 meetings, the first SALT treaty was signed in Moscow by Nixon and Soviet leaders. This agreement outlawed construction of comprehensive antiballistic (ABM) systems and limited construction of intercontinental ballistic missiles. SALT II began in Geneva in 1972 and resulted in an agreement signed by leaders of the two countries in June 1979. The treaty was not ratified by the United States Senate, however, and the arms race continued at a heightened pace into the 1980s. A major obstacle to slowing the race remains the need for a means of checking each nation's compliance to any agreement.

DISCIPLES OF CHRIST.

Frontier life in early 19th-century America was informal and straightforward. Many Christians attempted to blend the independence and practicality of wilderness life with an equally uncomplicated biblical faith. They looked only to the New Testament to discover what Christians should believe and how they should worship and live.

One of the first to sound this call was Thomas Campbell, a Presbyterian who had immigrated to the United States in 1807. In 1809 he published a 'Declaration and Address' with, as he said, "the sole purpose of promoting simple evangelical Christianity, free from all mixture of human opinions and inventions of men." Campbell's son, Alexander, took up his father's work and became a leader in religious reform and a champion of popular democracy. In the 1820s he began an association with a like-minded reformer named Barton Stone. In 1832 the two men and their followers founded what they called simply the Christian Church.

Divisions

Today the denomination is most commonly called the Disciples of Christ. Since its founding the denomination has undergone divisions through doctrinal differences. In the 20th century there are three major bodies that stem from the original church: the Christian Church (Disciples of Christ), the Churches of Christ, and the Undenominational Fellowship of Christian Churches and Churches of Christ.

Divisions within the denomination began late in the 19th century over the view of New Testament authority. Conservatives believed that only what the New Testament specifically authorized was permissible. Others felt that what was not prohibited was allowed. Another leading issue was organization. Campbell and his followers advocated a general church organization. They eventually became the present Christian Church (Disciples of Christ). Their opponents believed that general religious institutions other than the congregation are not permitted. This is the view of the Churches of Christ and of the Fellowship of Christian Churches and Churches of Christ. By 1906 the divisions resulting in the present three bodies had taken place.

The Christian Church (Disciples of Christ) accepts its status as a denomination. It has a full-time clergy, a national headquarters, and regional organizations. The congregations are fully independent, but corporate unity is expressed by representatives from congregations to national and international conventions. Its membership in the early 1980s was about 1,156,-000. The Churches of Christ are strictly congregational and have no national organization. Membership in the 1980s was about 1,240,000. The congregations loosely related in the Undenominational Fellowship of Christian Churches and Churches of Christ with a membership of about 1,000,000 were formerly identified with the Disciples, but they refused to follow them into the Christian Church (Disciples of Christ) when the denomination was reorganized in 1968.

HUMAN DISEASE

DISEASE, HUMAN. A disease is a condition that impairs the proper function of the body or of one of its parts. Every living thing, both plants and animals, can succumb to disease. People, for example, are often infected by tiny bacteria, but bacteria, in turn, can be infected by even more minute viruses.

Hundreds of different diseases exist. Each has its own particular set of *symptoms* and *signs*, clues that enable a physician to diagnose the problem. A symptom is something a patient can detect, such as fever, bleeding, or pain. A sign is something a doctor can detect, such as a swollen blood vessel or an enlarged internal body organ (*see* Diagnosis).

Every disease has a cause, though the causes of some remain to be discovered. Every disease also displays a cycle of *onset*, or beginning, *course*, or time span of affliction, and *end*, when it disappears or it partially disables or kills its victim.

An *epidemic* disease is one that strikes many persons in a community. When it strikes the same region year after year, it is an *endemic* disease.

An *acute* disease has a quick onset and runs a short course. An acute heart attack, for example, often hits without warning and can be quickly fatal. A *chronic* disease has a slow onset and runs a dragged out, sometimes years-long, course. The gradual onset and long course of rheumatic fever, for example, makes it a chronic ailment.

How Germs Invade the Body

Humans live in a world where many other living things compete for food and places to breed. The pathogenic organisms, or pathogens, often broadly called "germs," that cause many diseases are able to invade the human body and use its cells and fluids for their own needs. Ordinarily, the body's defense system can ward off these invaders.

Pathogenic organisms can enter the body in various ways. Some—such as those that cause the common cold, pneumonia, and tuberculosis—are breathed in. Others—such as those that cause venereal diseases—enter through sexual contact of human bodies. Still others—such as those that cause bacillary dysentery, cholera, and typhoid fever—get in the body through contaminated food, water, or utensils.

This article was contributed by Theodore R. Van Dellen, M.D., syndicated medical columnist and Associate Professor of Medicine, Northwestern University; Thomas Killip, M.D., Professor of Cardiovascular Medicine, Cornell University; Albert M. Kligman, M.D., Professor of Dermatology, University of Pennsylvania; William C. Thomas, Jr., M.D., Professor of Medicine, University of Florida; Bernard S. Leibel, M.D., Associate Professor of Medicine, University of Toronto; and Daniel J. Feldman, M.D., Professor of Rehabilitative Medicine, University of California at Irvine.

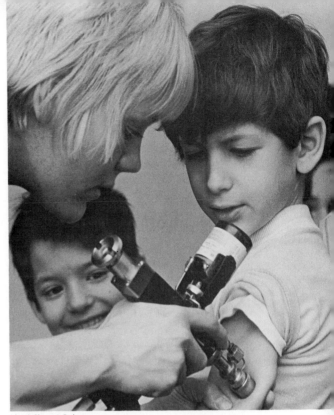

Merck Sharp & Dohme

Rubella (German measles) vaccine, painlessly given by a special air gun, gives immunity against the disease. Effective vaccines against other diseases are available, too.

FACT FINDER FOR HUMAN DISEASE

Human Disease is a vast subject. Additional information appears in the articles listed here. (*See also* related references in the Fact-Index.)

Acne	Eye
Acupuncture	Folk Medicine
Aging	Health
Alcoholism	Health Agencies
Allergy	Health Education
Analgesic	Immune System
Anatomy, Human	Industrial Medicine
Anesthesia	Kidneys
Anorexia Nervosa	Leprosy
Antibiotic	Liver
Antihistamine	Lungs
Antiseptic	Medicine
Antitoxin	Mental Health
Arthritis	Muscles
Autopsy	Nursing
Bioengineering	Pharmacy
Bioethics	Physiology
Blood	Psychology
Cancer	Serum
Chiropractic	Stomach
Diabetes	Surgery
Diagnosis	Vaccines
Drugs	Venereal Disease
Ear	Virus

Charles C. Randall, M.D., University of
Mississippi Medical Center, Jackson, Miss.

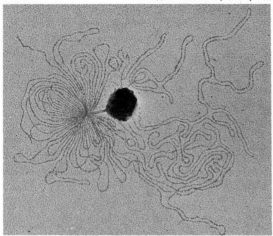

The diagram, right, shows how viruses can capture a cell by infecting it with their nucleic acids, DNA or RNA. The electron micrograph, above, shows a virus releasing its DNA.

Insects can spread disease by acting as *vectors,* or carriers. Flies can carry germs from human waste or other tainted materials to food and beverages. Germs may also enter the body through the bite of a mosquito, louse, or other insect vector.

Kinds of Disease

Infectious, or communicable, diseases are those that can be passed between persons such as by means of airborne droplets from a cough or sneeze. Tiny organisms such as bacteria and fungi can produce infectious diseases. So can viruses. So can tiny worms. Whatever the causative agent might be, it survives in the person it infects and is passed on to another. Or, its eggs are passed on. Sometimes, a disease-producing organism gets into a person who shows no symptoms of the disease. The *asymptomatic carrier* can then pass the disease on to someone else without even knowing he has it.

Noninfectious, or noncommunicable, diseases are caused by malfunctions of the body. These include organ or tissue degeneration, erratic cell growth, and faulty blood formation and flow. Also included are disturbances of the stomach and intestine, the endocrine system, and the urinary and reproductive systems. Some diseases can be caused by diet deficiencies, lapses in the body's defense system, or a poorly operating nervous system.

Disability and illnesses can also be provoked by psychological and social factors. These ailments include drug addiction, obesity, malnutrition, and pollution-caused health problems.

Furthermore, a thousand or more inheritable birth defects result from alternations in gene patterns (*see* Genetics). Since tiny genes are responsible for producing the many chemicals needed by the body, missing or improperly operating genes can seriously impair health. Genetic disorders that affect body chemistry are called inborn errors of metabolism. Some forms of mental retardation are hereditary.

A WAY VIRUSES INFECT A CELL

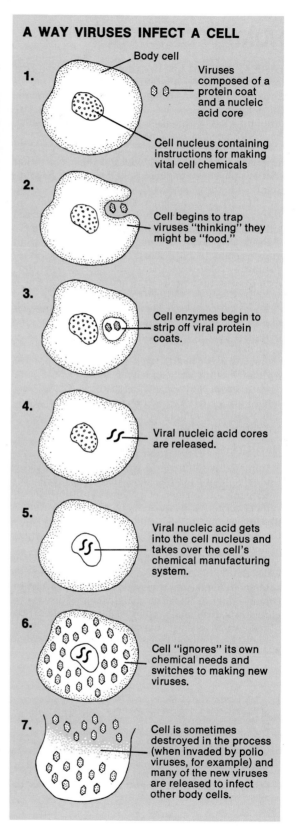

Body cell

1. Viruses composed of a protein coat and a nucleic acid core

Cell nucleus containing instructions for making vital cell chemicals

2. Cell begins to trap viruses "thinking" they might be "food."

3. Cell enzymes begin to strip off viral protein coats.

4. Viral nucleic acid cores are released.

5. Viral nucleic acid gets into the cell nucleus and takes over the cell's chemical manufacturing system.

6. Cell "ignores" its own chemical needs and switches to making new viruses.

7. Cell is sometimes destroyed in the process (when invaded by polio viruses, for example) and many of the new viruses are released to infect other body cells.

How the Body Fights Disease

As a first line of defense, a healthy body has a number of physical barriers against infection. The skin and mucous membranes covering the body or lining its openings offer considerable resistance to invasion by bacteria and other infectious organisms. If these physical barriers are injured or burned, infection resistance drops. In minor cases, only boils or pimples may develop. In major cases, however, large areas of the body might become infected.

Breathing passages are especially vulnerable to infection, but they have a unique defense. The airways are lined with mucus-secreting cells that trap tiny organisms and dust particles. Also, minute hairs called *cilia* line the breathing passages, wave like a field of wheat, and gently sweep matter out of the respiratory tract. In addition, foreign matter in the breathing passages can often be ejected by nose blowing, coughing, sneezing, and throat clearing. Unfortunately, repeated infection or strong chemicals can damage the respiratory passageways and make them more susceptible to infection.

Scavenger cells are present too in the walls of the *bronchi*, the branched air tubes to the lungs. Foreign matter reaching the bronchi after evading the other defenses can be "eaten" by the scavengers and disposed of in the lymph glands of the lungs.

Many potential invaders cannot stand body temperature (98.6° F or 37° C). Even those that thrive at that temperature may be destroyed when the body assumes higher, fever temperatures.

Wax in the outer ear canals and tears from eye ducts can slow the growth of some bacteria. And stomach acid can destroy certain swallowed germs.

The body's second line of defense is in the bloodstream and the lymphatic passageways. Certain white blood cells flock to infected areas and try to localize the infection by forming pus-filled abscesses. Unless the abscess breaks and allows the pus to drain, the infection is likely to spread. When this happens, the infection is first blocked by local lymph glands. For example, an infection in the hand travels up the arm, producing red streaks and swollen, tender lymph glands in the armpit. Unless the infection is brought under control, it will result in blood poisoning (*see* Blood).

Scavenger cells, or *phagocytes*, are located at various sites to minimize infection. One type in the spleen and liver keeps the blood clean. Others in such high-risk areas as the walls of the bronchi and the intestines remove certain bacteria and shattered cells.

How We Become Immune to Disease

The body has a special way of handling infection. It has a system that fends off the first traces of an infectious substance and then, through a "memory," gives the body a long-lasting immunity against future attacks by the same kind of invader.

Many substances in the outside world could harm the body if they ever entered it. These substances, or *antigens*, range from bacteria and pollen to a transplanted organ (viewed by the body as an invader). To fight them the body makes special chemicals known as *antibodies*.

Antibodies are a class of proteins called *immunoglobulins*. Each antibody is made of a heavy chain of chemical subunits, or *amino acids*, and a light chain of them. The light chain has special sites where the amino acids can link with their complements on the antigen molecule (*see* Biochemistry). When an antibody hooks up with an antigen, if often puts the antigen out of action by inactivating or covering a key portion of the harmful substance. In some cases, through the process of *opsonization*, antibodies "butter" the surface of some antigens and make them "tastier" to phagocytes, which engulf the antigens. Sometimes an antibody hooks to a bacterial antigen but needs an intermediate, or *complement*, to actually destroy the bacterium. As the antibody-antigen complex circulates in the blood, the complex "fixes" complement to it. In turn, the complement causes powerful enzymes to eat through the bacterial cell wall and make the organism burst.

There are several kinds of immunoglobulins—IgM, the largest; IgG, the most plentiful and versatile; and IgA, the next most plentiful and specially adapted to work in areas where body secretions could damage other antibodies. Other immunoglobulins are tied in with allergic reactions (*see* Allergy). IgM is made at the first signs of an antigen. It is later supplanted by the more effective IgG.

When infection first strikes, the immunity system does not seem to be working. During the first day or so, antibodies against the infection cannot be found in the blood. But this is only because the basic cells involved in antibody production have been triggered by the presence of antigen to multiply and form many more of their kind. The antibody level starts to rise on about the second day of infection and then zooms upward. By the fifth day the antibody level has risen a thousandfold. The first antibodies, the large IgM type, are not the best qualified to fight a wide range of antigens, but they are particularly effective against bacteria. The more versatile IgG is circulating in the blood on about the fourth day of infection. Its production is stimulated by the rising level of IgM in the blood. At this time, IgM production drops off and the immunity system concentrates on making IgG. The IgG type of antibody sticks well to antigens and eventually covers them so that the antigens can no longer stimulate the immune response and IgG production is switched off. This is an example of negative feedback control (*see* Bioengineering).

Antibody Production

Antibodies are made by two kinds of cells—*plasma cells* and a class of white blood cells, *lymphocytes*. Plasma cells actually originate from lymphocytes and

HOW THE BODY FIGHTS GERMS

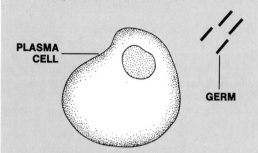

PLASMA CELL

GERM

When an antigen—a germ or foreign chemical substance—enters the body, certain defense cells found throughout the body called plasma cells are triggered into action.

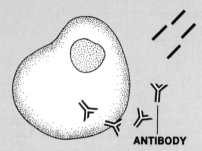

ANTIBODY

The plasma cell begins to produce special proteins called antibodies. Antibodies are also produced by blood cells called lymphocytes. Each antibody has a shape that enables it to "recognize" and inactivate a specific type of antigen.

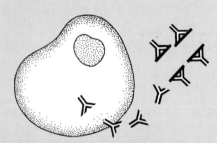

One way an antibody destroys a germ is by attaching to it and puncturing its protective cell wall with enzymes. Or antibodies may inactivate key structures on bacteria or viruses, thus depriving these germs of vital parts. Or a group of antibodies may surround an antigen and make it "appetizing" to other body cells that "eat" germs.

are found throughout the lymphatic tissue. Lymphocytes stem from cells in the blood-forming sections of bone marrow (*see* Blood). When the bone-marrow cells circulate to the *thymus*, a lymphatic structure in the chest, they receive "orders" to become lymphocytes and make antibodies. Most lymphocytes last for only a few hours, but a few wander through the blood and body tissues for years. These lymphocytes are responsible for "remembering" old antigens and for inducing the immunity system to produce antibodies against those or similar antigens if they ever again enter the body.

When people develop antibodies against a disease by the action of their own immunity system, they have *active immunity*. When they are given someone else's antibodies, however, they just have *passive immunity* to a disease. Passive immunity is only temporary. Some people may also get temporary relief from a disease through injections of serum containing gamma globulin, a portion of the blood rich in antibodies.

Without protective antibodies, we could die of the first disease that struck us. This would be true, too, of newborn babies, except that they receive passive immunity from their mothers. During her lifetime, a mother accumulates a wide variety of antibodies against a host of diseases. Enough of them are passed to the developing baby in her womb to give it a temporary immunity to many diseases during the early months of its life, until it can develop its own set of antibodies.

What Happens When Immunity Backfires

Paradoxically, a person's immunity system can backfire and develop *autoantibodies* against his own body tissue. In many diseases of unknown cause, doctors have found many unusual antibodies in the blood serum of patients. They think the patients become sensitive to something made by their own bodies. Only a slight change in certain proteins in normal body tissue is necessary for them to become antigens. Most diseases marked by the production of autoantibodies cannot be traced to infection or drug allergy. In rheumatoid arthritis, for example, the rheumatoid factor is the presence of autoantibodies in the victim's blood. These autoantibodies may stick to the membranes lining the bone joints and cause a reaction that destroys tissue in the joints. In other disorders associated with reversed immunity, autoantibodies strike red blood cells, tissues surrounding small blood vessels, or other target areas. Ulcerative colitis, a disorder marked by an inflamed portion of the intestine, often with ulcers, is also believed to be an autoimmune disease.

In some cases, lymphocyte defects or discrepancies in antibody production lead to an immune deficiency. When this happens, the victim is helpless against recurring infections. A simple head cold can soon become pneumonia. Antibiotics or serums with antibody-rich gamma globulin offer temporary relief in such cases.

How Drugs Fight Disease

With the advent of drug therapy in the 20th century, doctors began to use lifesaving drugs to fight disease. The clinical use of sulfanilamide, the predecessor of sulfa drugs, in the 1930's and the mass production of penicillin, the first antibiotic, in the 1940's gave physicians extremely powerful tools with which to fight infection. A disease-fighting drug never acts by itself. It always works in conjunction with the body's immunity system. Vaccines have also become available for the prevention of certain diseases.

How Certain Drugs Quell Infection

Such antibiotics as penicillin, streptomycin, and tetracycline are very effective against bacterial infections. The name "antibiotic" comes from *antibiosis*, or the use of substances made by one living thing to kill another (*see* Antibiotics). Antibiotics are made by bacteria and molds that are specially cultured in commercial drug laboratories.

Antibiotics kill bacteria and other disease organisms in various ways. Some destroy the cell walls of bacteria. Others interfere with bacterial multiplication or fatally alter the way bacteria make vital proteins. Still others mix up the genetic blueprints of the bacteria.

Ordinarily, an antibiotic tricks bacteria into using the antibiotic's chemicals instead of closely related ones that the organisms really need for making the key enzymes required for their growth and reproduction. With the antibiotic assimilated into their systems instead of the vital chemicals, an essential activity or structure of the pathogens is lacking and they die.

Sulfa drugs act in a somewhat similar but less effective way. Weakened but not killed by the sulfa drugs, the pathogens fall easy prey to the body's scavenger cells. Drugs are also available against parasitic worms, infectious amoeba, and other pathogenic organisms.

Antibiotics are not very effective against viruses because the drugs cannot get into the body cells where viruses hide and multiply. However, the body produces a protein called *interferon* that inhibits viral reproduction.

A drug is sometimes recognized by the body's immunity system as an antigen. It then triggers a severe reaction. In some cases, a person can suffer *anaphylaxis*, or extreme sensitivity, to penicillin after repeated injections. Without quick medical aid, severe cases of anaphylactic shock can be fatal.

How Bacteria Become Drug Resistant

Once in every several hundred million cell divisions a mutation makes a bacterium immune to an antibiotic drug. The mutation alters the bacterium's genetic code and thus its ability to use certain chemicals for its life activities. Mutations can be caused by the radiations from outer space that stream into the earth's atmosphere, as well as by some atmospheric chemicals. As a result of the mutation, all bacteria that stem from the immune germ will be resistant to the drug unless any of them undergoes a mutation that makes the strain susceptible again. Hence, whenever a new antibiotic is developed, there will be a chance that bacteria will develop an immunity against it. But because mutations are fairly rare, doctors have a good chance of fighting a bacterial disease with the new drug before future strains become resistant. (*See also* Genetics.)

Some members of a bacterial strain are resistant to certain drugs naturally. In the course of time they can eventually become selected through evolutionary forces to become the dominant drug-resistant forms of a pathogenic strain. (*See also* Evolution.)

More importantly, some bacteria can pass on their drug resistance to bacteria of another strain by "infection." Since the passing of resistance factors does not depend upon the lengthy process of mutation, it poses a much greater problem of drug immunity. As a consequence, doctors often must prescribe more than one antibiotic to fight certain diseases in the hope that this will slow bacterial resistance.

Use of Vaccines and Hormones

A person can become artificially immune to some diseases by means of a vaccine. Vaccines contain antigens that stimulate the production of protective antibodies.

Immunity to smallpox, polio, measles, rabies, and certain other diseases, is induced by injecting a person with vaccines containing living but *attenuated*, or weakened, disease organisms. A vaccine containing only dead organisms protects against typhoid fever and whooping cough, as well as against measles and polio. Vaccines containing *toxins*, or poisons, are used to prevent diphtheria and tetanus. When injected into a person, they trigger the production of special antibodies called *antitoxins* (*see* Antitoxins; Vaccines).

Some body disorders are caused by too much or too little hormone production. Hormones are body chemicals that influence many vital biochemical reactions. When someone suffers a hormone deficiency, a doctor usually can treat the deficiency with hormone shots (*see* Hormones).

Antibiotics kill bacteria. A culture of *Staphylococcus aureus*, a species of disease-causing bacteria, is shown, left. Growth of such germs is inhibited by a disc of *penicillin*, right.

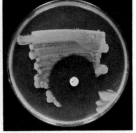

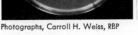
Photographs, Carroll H. Weiss, RBP

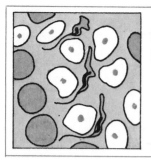

INFECTIOUS DISEASES

will become the victim of a disease after being infected. The number of invading germs—the dose of the infection—influences the outbreak of disease. So does the virulence of the pathogens; that is, their power to do harm. In addition, the condition of the body's immunological defenses also affects the probability of catching a disease.

Contagious Disease

A great many infectious diseases are contagious; that is, they can easily be passed between people. To acquire certain contagious diseases someone need only be in the presence of someone with it, or come in contact with an infected part of the body, or eat or drink from contaminated utensils.

Someone can be a carrier of a contagious disease in several ways. He can be an asymptomatic carrier, or have a disease without ever developing its symptoms. He can be an incubationary carrier and pass on the pathogens at any time during the "silent" incubation period. He can be a convalescent carrier and transmit some of the infectious organisms remaining in the body even after recovery. Of course, anyone suffering the frank symptoms of a contagious disease can pass it on to others while the disease is running its course.

The tables on the next two pages contain information about many of the now or once common infectious diseases found in the world. As in the case of all diseases, certain symptoms may or may not be present. Furthermore, the tables are for general information purposes only and are not for self-diagnosis of any disease. A physician should always be consulted for diagnosis and treatment of all but the most minor ailments.

Infectious diseases can be transmitted in many ways. They can be spread in droplets through the air when infected persons sneeze or cough. Whoever inhales the droplets can then become infected. Some diseases can be passed through contaminated eating or drinking utensils. Some can be spread through sexual activity. Others can even be spread in the course of medical or surgical treatment, or through the use of dirty injection equipment, especially by drug abusers.

Once an infectious organism gains a foothold in the body, it begins to thrive and multiply. Its success is slow or fast, depending upon the nature of the pathogen. The symptoms of the common cold, for example, appear within a few days of infection. However, the symptoms of kuru, an uncommon disease of the nervous system, often appear three years or longer after infection. Every infectious disease has an *incubation period*, which is the length of time between the pathogen's gaining a foothold in the body and the appearance of the first symptoms of the disease.

Several factors also determine whether a person

Infectious organisms, greatly magnified below, have many forms. *Entamoeba histolytica* (1) causes amebic dysentery. *Trichinella* worms (2) in uncooked pork cause trichinosis in man. *Klebsiella pneumoniae* (3) is responsible for pneumonia.

Center for Disease Control, Atlanta, Georgia

Corynebacterium diphtheriae (4) causes diphtheria and also makes a toxin capable of damaging the heart. *Staphylococcus* (5), a cluster-forming group of bacteria, causes a variety of diseases, as does *Streptococcus* (6), a chain-forming group.

Upjohn International   Dr. Leon Le Beau, University of Illinois

1
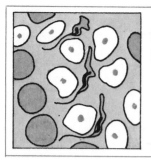

3
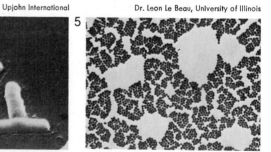

5
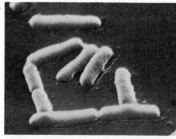

2
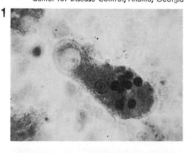

4

6
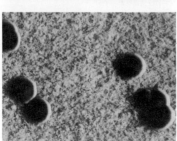

Center for Disease Control, Atlanta, Georgia

Center for Disease Control, Atlanta, Georgia

Center for Disease Control, Atlanta, Georgia

SOME NOTABLE INFECTIOUS DISEASES

Name	Cause	Typical Sources	Incubation Period	Some Common Symptoms	Usual Treatment	Preventive Measures
AIDS (Acquired Immune-Deficiency Syndrome)	HTLV-III virus (human T-lymphotropic virus, type III)	sexual contact with carrier, contaminated blood and hypodermic equipment	6 months to several years	severe viral, fungal, protozoal, and bacterial infections; Kaposi's sarcoma	antimicrobial agents, radiotherapy for Kaposi's sarcoma	avoid sexual contact with carriers, avoid contaminated blood and hypodermic equipment
Amebiasis	Entamoeba hystolytica (a parasitic ameba)	contaminated water or raw vegetables, flies	variable; commonly 2–4 weeks	stomach pain, fever, chills, bloody diarrhea	tinidazole, metronidazole, dehydroemetine	improved sanitation and food handling, health education, fly control
Bacillary Dysentery (Shigellosis)	Shigella bacteria	contaminated food and water	1–7 days	diarrhea, fever, stomach pain, vomiting	fluids, antibiotics	food protection, improved sanitation
Chicken Pox (Varicella)	Varicella-zoster (a herpesvirus)	airborne droplets	2–3 weeks	slight fever, small red bumps on skin	lotion to relieve itching	isolation of high risk individuals
Cholera	Vibrio cholerae (a bacterium)	contaminated food and water	a few hours to 5 days	profuse watery diarrhea, vomiting, dehydration	tetracycline, oral and intravenous fluids	improved sanitation and food handling, water purification
Common Cold (Coryza)	more than 100 rhinoviruses cold	airborne droplets	1–3 days	sneezing, sore throat, runny coughing	rest, pain relievers,	none effective
Diphtheria	Corynebacterium diptheriae (a bacterium)	contact with carrier	2–5 days	sore throat, fever, swollen neck glands	diphtheria antitoxin, antibiotics	immunization
German Measles (Rubella)	Rubella virus	airborne droplets	14–21 days	headache, stiff joints, rash	lotion to relieve itching	immunization
Gonorrhea	Neisseria gonorrhoeae (a bacterium)	sexual contact with carrier	2–7 days	pus discharge from sex organs	penicillin and other antibiotics	prostitution control, condom use, sex education
Hepatitis (Types A; B; Non-A, Non-B)	hepatitis virus and other pathogens	contaminated food, water, blood, syringes, sexual contact	2–39 weeks	fever, drowsiness, loss of appetite, jaundice	special diets, rest	sterilized injection equipment, screening for infected blood, vaccine for type B
Herpes Simplex (Fever Blister, Cold Sore)	Herpes simplex virus (HSV) types 1 and 2	contact with saliva of carrier	2–12 days	small blisters about mouth, lips, or genitals	keep lesions clean and dry	personal hygiene, health education
Influenza ("Flu")	Influenza viruses A, B, C	airborne droplets	2–3 days	chills, fever, muscle pain, sore throat	fluids, bed rest, pain relievers	vaccines for some virus strains
Legionnaire's Disease (Legionellosis)	Legionella bacteria	airborne transmission	2–10 days	appetite loss, muscle pain, headache, high fever, cough	erythromycin	disinfecting cooling-tower water of air conditioners
Leprosy (Hansen's Disease)	Mycobacterium leprae (a bacterium)	long exposure to carrier	7 months–6 years	bumpy skin nodules, sores, muscle weakness, numbness	dapsone, acedapsone, rifampicin	acedapsone, BCG vaccine
Malaria	one-celled Plasmodium parasites	Anopheles mosquito bite	12 days–10 months	chills, fever, headache, sweating	quinine-based drugs	drugs for treatment are also used for prevention
Measles (Rubeola)	Morbillivirus	airborne droplets, contact with carrier	7–14 days	fever, cough, spots on gums, skin rash	lotion to relieve itching, bed rest	immunization
Mononucleosis ("Mono")	Epstein-Barr (EB) virus	contact with carrier's saliva	4–6 weeks	fever, sore throat, fatigue, swollen lymph nodes	fluids, bed rest, pain relievers	none known

SOME NOTABLE INFECTIOUS DISEASES (continued)

Name	Cause	Typical Sources	Incubation Period	Some Common Symptoms	Usual Treatment	Preventive Measures
Mumps (Infectious Parotitis)	*Paramyxovirus*	airborne droplets, contact with carrier	2–3 weeks	painfully swollen salivary glands, fever	soft diet, bed rest, pain relievers	immunization
Polio (Poliomyelitis)	poliovirus types 1, 2, 3	contact with carrier	3–35 days	headache, stiff neck and back, fever, paralysis	mechanical respirators for some patients	immunization
Rabbit Fever (Tularemia)	*Francisella tularensis* (a bacterium)	contact with infected animals	2–10 days	ulcer at entry site, swollen and burst lymph glands	antibiotics	rubber gloves when handling animals, immunization
Rabies (human) (Hydrophobia)	rabies virus	bite by infected animal	10 days–more than a year	headache, fever, painful throat spasms	antirabies serum followed by rabies vaccine series	vaccination of all dogs and cats
Rheumatic Fever	*Streptococcus pyrogens* (a bacterium)	contact with "strep" throat or scarlet fever carrier	7–21 days after first "strep" infection	painful joints, inflamed heart, bumps near joints, rash	aspirin, steroid drugs, rest	antibiotic treatment to kill "strep" germs
Salmonella Infection (Salmonellosis)	numerous strains of *Salmonella* bacteria	contaminated food, egg, and dairy products	6–72 hours	stomach pain, diarrhea, nausea, fever, vomiting	fluids	thorough cooking of animal-derived foodstuffs, refrigerate foods, avoid raw eggs
Scarlet Fever (Scarlatina)	*Streptococcus pyrogens* (a bacterium)	contact with "strep" throat carriers	1–5 days	sore throat, red bumps on tongue, skin rash	antibiotics, pain relievers	antibiotic treatment to kill "strep" bacteria
Smallpox[1] (Variola)	Variola virus	contact with carrier	7–17 days	fever, headache, skin lesions	antibiotics to hinder other infections	immunization no longer necessary
Syphilis	*Treponema pallidum* (a spirochete)	sexual contact with carrier	10 days–10 weeks	painless chancre, rash, lethargy, gummy tumors	penicillin and other antibiotics	health and sex education, condoms, prostitution control
Tetanus	*Clostridium tetani* (a bacterium)	wounds containing contaminated soil or other matter	4–21 days	stiff, painful jaw and neck muscles	cleaning wound, antibiotics, tetanus immune globulin	immunization
Toxic Shock Syndrome	a strain of *Staphylococcus aureus* (a bacterium)	associated with use of vaginal tampons	1–2 days	high fever, vomiting, rash, diarrhea, shock	hospitalization, fluid replacement, antibiotics	avoid vaginal tampons, or use intermittently during each menstrual period
Tuberculosis, Pulmonary	*Mycobacterium tuberculosis* (a bacterium)	airborne droplets	4–12 weeks	cough, bloody sputum, chest pain, weight loss	isoniazid, antibiotics, surgery (rarely)	Improvement of social conditions, tuberculin tests, chest X rays
Typhoid fever	*Salmonella typhi* (a bacterium)	contaminated food or water	1–3 weeks	fever, headache, appetite loss, red skin spots	chloramphenicol, antibiotics	improved sanitation, immunization
Undulant Fever (Brucellosis)	*Brucella* organisms (a group of bacteria)	infected milk, contact with infected farm animals	5 days–several months	high fever, aches, headache, sweating, weakness	tetracycline, streptomycin, bed rest	pasteurized milk, careful handling of farm animals
Whooping Cough (Pertussis)	*Bordetella pertussis* (a bacterium)	airborne droplets	7–21 days	spasmodic cough, ending "whoop" breath, vomiting	hospitalization of infants; small, frequent meals; fluids	erythromycin, immunization (vaccine has some associated risk)

[1]The last naturally acquired case of smallpox in the world occurred in 1977. In 1979 the World Health Organization certified that the disease had been eradicated.

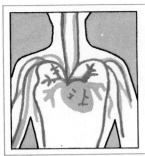

HEART AND BLOOD SYSTEM DISEASES

Disease of the heart or of the blood vessels, called *cardiovascular disease*, is the leading cause of death in the United States and Canada. It claims more than a million lives each year in the United States; more than 70,000 each year in Canada.

The heart is a muscular pump. When its own tissue or blood vessels become diseased, serious and sometimes fatal harm can follow. (For diagrams showing the heart's structure and function, *see* Heart.)

Coronary Artery Disease

Disease of the coronary arteries that supply oxygen and nutrients to the heart is the most common heart ailment. Coronary artery disease accounts for more than a third of all deaths among males in the United States between the ages of 35 and 55. It also strikes many women past the age of 50. Hypertension (high blood pressure), overweight, cigarette smoking, diabetes mellitus, excess cholesterol, triglycerides and other fats in the blood, and probably lack of regular exercise contribute to the chance of getting coronary artery disease.

Coronary artery disease is characterized by an *atheroma*, a fatty deposit of cholesterol beneath the inner lining of the artery. The atheroma obstructs the passage of blood, thereby reducing the flow of nourishing blood to the heart muscle. It also sets up conditions for a blood clot in the coronary artery (*see* Blood). Atheroma formation seems to run in families. Eating foods rich in saturated animal fat and cholesterol is also thought to contribute to atheroma formation.

Many persons with coronary artery disease do not experience symptoms. If the obstruction is bad enough, however, it may cause angina pectoris, myocardial infarction, or heart enlargement and failure.

Angina pectoris is a chest pain that feels like something is squeezing or pressing the chest during periods of physical exertion. It takes place when the heart's oxygen needs cannot be met because of a blocked coronary artery. Rest will relieve the pain. Some persons have angina pectoris for years and still live active lives.

Myocardial infarction is commonly called *heart attack*. Tissue death that results from a lack of blood is called infarction. When the coronary artery becomes so obstructed that the *myocardium*, or heart muscle, does not receive oxygen, it dies. Once, it was believed that a blood clot occluded the coronary artery and caused the infarction. This is why a heart attack is sometimes called a *coronary occlusion*. However, it now appears that most clots form in the artery after the infarction.

The first few hours after a heart attack are the most critical because abnormal heart rhythms may develop. *Ventricular fibrillation* is the most dangerous. The ventricles of the heart contract so fast that the pumping action is balked. Death follows in three or four minutes. Heart attack patients are usually treated in the coronary care unit of a hospital for a few days to enable electronic monitoring of the heart rate and rhythm (*see* Hospitals).

Heart failure can occur when repeated heart attacks put too much strain on the remaining healthy heart muscle. As attacks destroy more and more heart muscle, the remaining muscle *hypertrophies*, or enlarges, to maintain effective pumping. Pressure builds up in a weakened heart, however, and causes fluid backup in the lungs. As a result, the heart output cannot keep pace with the body's oxygen demands.

Heart Rhythm and Pacemakers

A node of special cells in the heart controls its rhythm by regularly producing energizing electrical signals. Sometimes, abnormal signals cause extra heart beats, or *tachycardia*. At other times, especially in older persons, the signals might not be conducted too well through the heart, thus slowing it. When a person's heart rate drops below 40 beats a minute, he usually feels faint and cannot function well. In that case, he often can be fitted with an artificially powered heart pacemaker.

Diagnosis and Treatment of Heart Trouble

A doctor carefully questions and examines anyone suspected of heart trouble for evidence of pain, fatigue, abnormal heartbeat, and so on. He listens to the heart and lungs with a stethoscope. Sometimes, a heart *murmur*, a rushing noise heard through the stethoscope, provides a clue to a heart problem. A faint murmur can be normal, but a loud one usually indicates a diseased heart valve or other trouble. A chest X ray is usually taken to get a picture of the heart and lungs. An electrocardiogram reveals the electrical activity of a patient's heart.

A doctor can also rely on cardiac catheterization and angiography to diagnose heart disease. Cardiac catheterization involves slipping a catheter, a long tube, through veins into the heart to learn such things as how much blood the heart is pumping, whether its valves are damaged, and whether it is contracting as it should. Angiography involves injecting dye through a catheter into the heart so that subsequent X rays will reveal the internal anatomy of the heart and the blood flow through it.

Rheumatic Heart Disease

Rheumatic heart disease has both an acute form and a chronic form. The acute form, *rheumatic fever*,

173

Photographs, American Heart Association

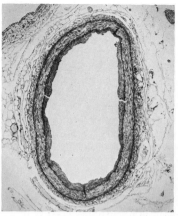 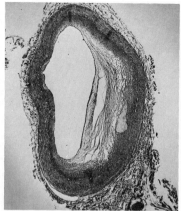 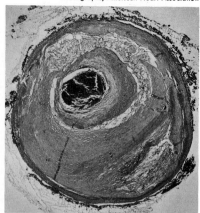

Atherosclerosis is a disease process in which substances thicken and harden the walls of arteries. The micrograph at the left shows a cross section of a normal artery. The middle one shows deposits forming under the inner lining of the artery. At the right the artery is so thickened by an atheroma and cholesterol deposits that blood has a difficult time passing through.

inflames joints and heart muscle. The joints always recover, but if the condition becomes chronic the heart valves may eventually become scarred. Rheumatic fever most often affects the mitral, or bicuspid, valve of the heart and produces a blockage called *mitral stenosis.*

Rheumatic fever is a health problem in many of the world's developing nations. It is caused by an unusual body response to an infectious sore throat sparked by the bacterium *beta hemolytic streptococcus.* Uniquely, the bacterial cell wall and the human heart muscle have a protein in common. A person with a "strep" throat develops antibodies against the bacterial protein. However, the antibodies may also attack that person's own heart muscle, damaging it over the years. Penicillin and other antibiotics treat strep throat and can prevent heart damage. In severe cases after many years, however, surgery might be needed to repair or even replace a damaged heart valve.

Hypertensive Heart Disease

Hypertension, or high blood pressure, is a fairly common disorder. Ordinarily, the heart creates sufficient pressure to send blood throughout the body. However, sometimes resistance to blood flow from the arteries is high and the blood pressure rises above normal. Because the heart must then work harder to maintain the higher pressure, it enlarges.

Blood pressure is maintained by means of a complex interaction between the heart, the nervous system, and a kidney hormone called *renin.* Some persons with hypertension have too much renin in their blood. High blood pressure increases the wear and tear on blood vessels. It also can cause heart failure, strokes, and kidney disorders. When discovered soon enough, it can be treated with drugs.

Other Kinds of Heart Disease

Sometimes the heart does not develop properly and a child can be born with a serious congenital heart disease. Heart valves might be too narrow or missing altogether, or the *septum,* a wall separating the heart chambers, might be incomplete. As a result, a hole exists between the heart chambers. Such congenital heart diseases can be discovered by means of cardiac catheterization and angiography and often can be corrected by a heart surgeon.

Some substances are dangerous to the heart. For example, diphtheria bacteria produce a toxin that damages the heart. Excessive alcohol drinking weakens and enlarges the heart. Persons with heart murmurs caused by faulty valves or congenital heart disease are susceptible to *endocarditis,* a bacterial infection of the inner lining of the heart. Also, certain viruses can cause *myocarditis,* inflammation of the heart muscle, and *pericarditis,* inflammation of the outer lining of the heart.

Blood Vessel Disorders

Atherosclerosis, the thickening and hardening of arterial walls, may occur in many arteries. Cholesterol and other fats that form in the process obstruct the affected arteries and, at times, produce a *thrombus,* or clot, in them. Sometimes, these clots break away, especially from the heart, and *embolize,* or travel to some other part of the circulatory system. There, they can block a blood vessel and keep oxygen away from a vital body part. Embolism in the brain, for example, can cause a stroke.

Aneurysm occurs when the walls of a large artery, especially the aorta, become weak and balloon out. Atherosclerosis can cause an aneurysm. So can syphilis. The venereal disease can also make the aortic valve leak.

Varicose veins, bulging veins in the leg, develop when the walls of the veins weaken. The condition may be inherited or may stem from *phlebitis,* an inflammation of the veins. Phlebitis may trigger clots in the veins, which sometimes break away, travel to the lungs, and form a *pulmonary embolus.* Drugs used to prolong clotting time often correct clotting disorder. (For a discussion of some blood disorders, *see* Blood.)

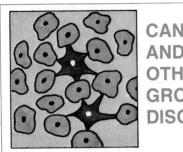

CANCER AND OTHER GROWTH DISORDERS

Cancer—the collective name for any of the dangerous *tumors*, or growths, that can arise in the body—is the second ranking cause of death in the United States and Canada. It claims more than 460,000 lives each year in the United States; some 87,000 each year in Canada (*see* Cancer).

Cancer is characterized by rampant, abnormal cell growth. It can arise in muscle, bone, connective tissue, blood vessels, and fatty tissue. This kind is called *sarcoma*. Cancer can also arise in skin cells and in cells that line the body's cavities and organs. This kind is called *carcinoma*. Abnormal proliferation of white blood cells is called *leukemia*. An aberrant tumor in the body's lymphatic tissue is a *lymphoma*.

Cancer can strike many parts of the body. Some cancerous tumors are fast growing; they may double their size within a month or so. Others are slow growing and may not spread for many months or even years.

The Cancer Process

Tumors, or *neoplasms,* are purposeless bulges of excessive cell growth in tissue. If they are local and harmless, they are *benign*. If they can spread to other tissues and cause the body harm, they are *malignant.* Malignant tumors are cancerous.

Cell multiplication goes on normally in the body for replacement of dead cells, but in cancer the multiplication goes awry. Local malignant tumors often can be removed by surgery, thus ending the problem. However, if the cancer cells are not destroyed by surgery or other means, they may *metastasize,* or leave the local site and spread to other parts of the body. When they do, the entire body can succumb to the disease.

Cancer is believed to begin with one wildly multiplying cell in a given tissue. The process so resembles the action of cells in an embryo as they divide and shape the body that scientists think that cancer is tied in with the basic chemistry of the cell. After the embryonic cells have performed their tasks, certain chemical repressors lock up portions of DNA in genes in the cell nucleus. These repressed pieces of DNA no longer trigger the biochemical reactions associated with rapid embryonic cell division. Thus, the seeds of cancer might be in everyone's body. Then, at some time in the future, an event such as virus infection, radiation intake, inhalation of a

This computer printout of the absorption of fluorine-18 in the bones of a patient shows areas (encircled) where abnormal uptake of the radioisotope indicates spreading bone cancer.

National Cancer Institute, Washington, D.C.

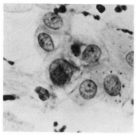 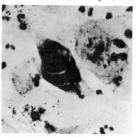

Medical scientists can readily notice cancer cells under the microscope. Each of the cluster of normal cells, left, has a relatively large amount of cytoplasm surrounding a darker but clear nucleus. Also, each nucleus has a fairly round border. By contrast, the cancer cell, right, has an irregular nuclear border, and a nucleus that engrosses most of the cell.

CANCER SIGNS

There are seven warning signs of cancer. If you notice any of these symptoms be sure to call them to the attention of a physician:

1. A sore that does not heal.
2. A lump or thickening anywhere in the body.
3. Nagging hoarseness or cough.
4. Unusual bleeding or discharge.
5. Persistent indigestion or difficulty in swallowing.
6. A change in bowel or bladder habits.
7. A change in a wart or a mole.

carcinogen, or cancer-causing chemical, or an imbalance of hormones might free the genes and permit a mature body cell to revert back to an embryoniclike cell. One theory even holds that the gene-bearing chromosomes of normal cells have certain sections capable of making viruslike particles. These particles could then infect neighboring cells and make them produce more particles, until many cells were proliferating wildly.

Cancer cells produce antigens against which the body reacts with antibodies. Small pockets of cancer cells, called silent cancers, might constantly be springing up in a person's body, only to be destroyed by the body's immunity system before they could do any harm. If the antibodies are ineffective, however, the cell mass grows to the size of a pinhead. Unless it gets enough blood, the pinhead mass will not get bigger. However, such tumors can give off a substance called *tumor angiogenesis factor,* which "fertilizes" rapid growth of tiny blood vessels into the tumor. Then, it starts growing again because it has an ample supply of food from the blood. When it grows large enough to interfere with a vital body activity, the sufferer dies.

Treatment of Cancer

Cutting out the cancerous tissue through surgery is probably the most effective way of fighting cancer, as long as it has not had a chance to spread. Radiation treatment using radioactive cobalt or radium salts is another method of inhibiting the spread of cancer. Certain anticancer drugs hinder the growth of cancer cells and prevent their spread.

Early detection of cancer through annual physical examinations has been effective in reducing cancer death rates. In its early stages, cancer can often be stopped before it spreads. Surgery performed early enough can remedy most women suffering from cancer of the uterus or cancer of the ovaries. A simple test, the Pap smear, given by a physician at regular intervals can indicate the presence of these cancers before they become dangerous.

Lung cancer, which is often linked with cigarette smoking, affects males more than any other type of cancer. The next most frequent type among males is prostate cancer. Cancer of the breast is the leading type of cancer among females. Cancer of the colon/rectum ranks second. A woman can frequently discover breast cancer herself before it becomes serious by regular examination of her breasts for lumps. (*See also* Cancer.)

Other Growth Changes

Some alterations in tissue growth are not cancerous. *Atrophy,* for example, is a lessening in size. It is the shrinking of cells or tissues for various reasons. Starvation, for instance, causes atrophy of the *adipose,* or fatty, tissues. Disuse of a body part may also lead to atrophy. When a fractured arm is placed in a cast, the arm's muscles decrease in size from lack of use.

Hypertrophy is an increase in size of individual cells or fibers. It results in an enlargement of the body part containing these muscles or fibers. Hypertrophy of the heart has already been discussed. *Compensatory hypertrophy* is best seen in paired organs. When a diseased kidney is removed from the body, the remaining kidney grows larger because it now must do the work of two kidneys.

A patient is shown undergoing radiation therapy against cancer. The radiation given off by the radioactive decay of cobalt-60 is used in the treatment of certain kinds of cancer.

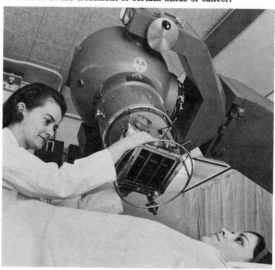

University of Wisconsin Center for Health Sciences

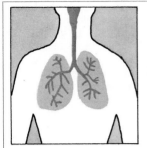

RESPIRA-
TORY
SYSTEM
DISEASES

The lungs are spongy organs through which vital oxygen enters the body and needless carbon dioxide exits. Oxygen and carbon dioxide are exchanged in and out of capillaries in the many tiny air sacs, or *alveoli*, in the lungs. Although the breathing passages have defenses against invading germs and irritants, the lungs can be stricken by a number of serious diseases.

Chronic bronchitis is a disease that results from infection of the air passages by bacteria or viruses. It is marked by cough and increased production of *sputum*, an accumulation of saliva, mucus, and pus. Air pollution and cigarette smoking both can aggravate the malady.

Tuberculosis is a complicated disease that most often strikes the lungs. The bacilli that cause it grow from place to place in the lung, leaving cavities in the unoccupied sites. Symptoms of tuberculosis may include weight loss, fever, chest pain, cough, and sputum. After the active infection is arrested, a period follows when the disease may break out again. Tuberculosis is treated with isoniazid and other drugs.

Pneumonia, or acute infection of the lungs, may occur suddenly in a seemingly healthy person. It is usually marked by fever, cough, and chest pain. Lung X rays show patches of inflammation. Though once quite fatal, the threat of pneumonia has been reduced as a result of antibiotic treatment.

Pleurisy is severe chest pain accompanying each deep breath in a person with an inflamed *pleura*, the twin membrane around each lung and lining the chest cavity. Pleurisy can attend pneumonia or result from direct infection of the pleura.

Emphysema is a serious lung disease that follows destruction of the elastic and connective tissue fibers supporting the lung. It is linked with advancing age. Certain forms of emphysema are inherited. Heavy cigarette smoking and long exposure to air pollutants seem to encourage the disease. A person with emphysema wheezes and has trouble breathing. Without sufficient lung elasticity, he must work hard to breathe properly. Furthermore, air movement in the lungs is reduced and the patient is easily fatigued because he fails to get enough oxygen or get rid of enough carbon dioxide.

Asthma is the wheezing or whistling sound that accompanies each breath when the air passages contain too much mucus. It may follow lung infection or result from an allergic reaction that causes muscle spasms and swelling in the air passages.

Acute pulmonary edema results when fluid quickly accumulates in the lungs and fills the alveoli. The fluid buildup is caused by heart trouble that, in turn, produces back pressure in the pulmonary veins and the left atrium of the heart to which they carry oxygen-rich blood from the lungs. A person suffering acute pulmonary edema is suddenly breathless and turns blue because of oxygen-poor blood. The condition is treated with oxygen, digitalis to strengthen heart action, and diuretics to speed fluid removal by the kidneys.

Pneumothorax occurs when air gets into the chest between the pleural lining. The lung then collapses. A collapsed lung may occur when the chest is pierced in some way or when an abnormal *bleb*, or blister, on the lung surface bursts.

Lung abscess is an accumulation of a mass of pus inside the lung. A lung abscess can increase the seriousness of pneumonia and other lung infections, especially in chronically ill persons.

Hyaline membrane disease is a disorder of some prematurely born infants. The alveoli of afflicted babies are lined with a protein material, limiting the amount of oxygen their blood can receive. The disease is often fatal.

Histoplasmosis is a fungus infection of the lungs. Fungi lodge in the lungs and multiply until body defenses wall them off. In some areas it was once called "summer flu" because its symptoms resemble those of influenza. Serious cases involve weight loss and a long convalescent period.

Pneumoconiosis means "dust disease." It can strike miners and industrial workers who inhale damaging amounts of dust. One of the most serious is *silicosis*, which results from inhaling quartz dust. Another, *anthracosilicosis*, arises from inhalation of coal and quartz dust. (*See also* Lungs.)

When a person breathes into a spirograph, the instrument registers the vital oxygen capacity of his lungs. It is useful in determining the extent of chronic lung disease.

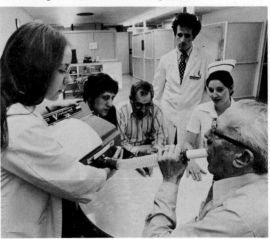

Arthur Shay from *Medical World News*

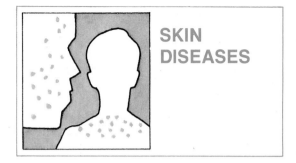

SKIN DISEASES

Because of its location the skin is perhaps more susceptible to disease than any other body organ. Even so, it is marvelously designed for its particular jobs of protecting the inner body against harm from the outside surroundings, receiving clues about what is happening externally, and keeping the body cool by means of the evaporation of sweat produced by its sweat glands. The skin is thick, leathery, and tough enough to prevent mechanical injury to the body. It is also covered with a barrier of dead cells that block harmful chemicals from getting into the body.

The skin is richly supplied with nerves that enable the perception of pain, touch, heat, and cold. Blood vessels in the skin can either contract or expand on response to nerve signals. A person's emotional state can often be observed through changes in skin color. Shame or rage reddens the skin; fear blanches it. The skin may react to disease in a great many ways—including formation of blisters, pimples, ulcers, tumors, and by hemorrhage.

Blackheads are an accumulation of a horny material in special follicles of the face. The characteristic black dots in blackheads are not dirt but *melanin*, the pigment responsible for skin color (*see* Skin).

Acne is an outcropping of blackheads or pimples on the face of an adolescent. It is brought on by hormonal changes that accompany sexual maturity. It is not caused by food, emotions, or uncleanliness. Antibiotics are available for the treatment of severe acne, but most cases respond well to local application of a peeling agent.

Warts are horny growths caused by virus infection. They are spread from person to person. Although warts cannot be prevented, they can be burned away with an electric needle or a caustic chemical such as nitric acid.

Hives, or *urticaria*, are itchy, whitish elevations of the skin. They appear and disappear rapidly. Hives are often the result of an allergic reaction to certain foods or medicines. Persons who suffer severe cases of hives can receive a series of desensitizing shots (*see* Allergy). Antihistamine drugs sometimes can relieve a bout of hives.

Birthmarks are the result of an overgrowth of blood vessels. They usually show up after birth as port-wine-colored stains or strawberry-colored marks. The strawberry marks may eventually disappear but at times can be destroyed quickly by the application of extreme cold. Port-wine stains and other long-lasting skin blemishes can be concealed by special cosmetics.

Eczema, or *dermatitis*, is a superficial inflammation of the skin. It can be an allergic reaction to poison ivy, dyes, or drugs. It can be provoked by such irritants as acids, solvents, or excessive use of soap or detergents. Sunburn can also cause eczema. Some forms of it, such as infantile eczema and seborrheic dermatitis, stem from an unknown cause. Nonetheless, nearly all types of eczema can be relieved by the application of corticosteroid creams.

Athlete's foot is a fungus infection of the skin between the toes. The infected area is scaly, moist, and itchy. It usually has a disagreeable smell. Athlete's foot can be relieved when antifungal drugs are applied to the infected skin each day. Fungus infections that cause a loss of hair or nails must be treated with griseofulvin, an antibiotic.

Bacterial infections such as the psoriasis caused by "staph" germs are rare because of modern standards of hygiene and sanitation. However, the bacterial disease gonorrhea, which passes between the skin of the sex organs, has risen to epidemic proportions among teenagers in recent years (*see* Venereal Disease). This and other bacterial infections of the skin are remedied with antibiotics.

This child, left, suffered from eczema, or dermatitis, of the face. Eczema is marked by inflamed, thickened, and itchy skin. The cause of infantile eczema is unknown. However, irritants such as solvents and detergents can cause a similar skin affliction called contact dermatitis. Treatment, which may include use of corticosteroid ointments, can clear the skin, right.

Carroll H. Weiss, RBP

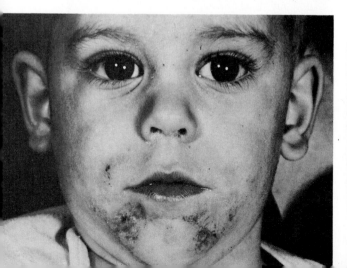

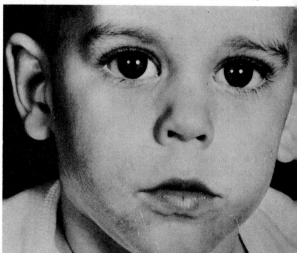

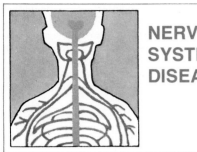

NERVOUS
SYSTEM
DISEASES

The nervous system is the quick communication system of the body. Information from the outside world enters the body through the sense organs and is sent to the spinal cord for instant response or is relayed to the brain for further processing. (See Nerves; Brain and Spinal Cord.)

Nerves and the membranes that protect portions of the nervous system are susceptible to breakdown or infection. Sometimes, the organisms that cause such diseases as mumps or infectious hepatitis can infect the nervous system, too.

Nervous System Infections

Meningitis is an inflammation of the *meninges*, or membranes around the brain and spinal cord. It can occur through viruses, bacteria, fungi, or yeasts that get into the nervous system. Meningitis is a serious disease and can be fatal.

Shingles, or *herpes zoster*, is a virus-caused inflammation of certain nerve tissue. Painful skin bumps occur over the line of the inflamed nerve or its branches. Shingles and chicken pox are both caused by the same virus.

Noninfectious Nerve Disorders

Neuritis is the degeneration of one or more nerves. It is often marked by a pins-and-needles feeling, a burning sensation, or a stabbing pain. Neuritis can result from infection, especially of the facial nerve, hard body blows, or bone fracture causing nerve injury. Everyday hard grasping of tools and activities requiring cramped body positions can also trigger neuritis.

Neuralgia is often confused with neuritis but is a distinct problem. Neuralgia is characterized by sudden, sharp bursts of pain along any of the sensory nerves near the body surface.

Sciatica is severe leg pain resulting from an inflamed sciatic nerve or its branches. A ruptured, or "slipped," disk—one of the pads between the vertebra of the spine—often causes sciatica.

Tics are usually habitual muscle twitches in the face or neck that seem to serve no purpose. A tic is generally intensified by an emotional situation or by fatigue.

Vertigo is a dizziness or disorientation that occurs when something is wrong with the body's balancing system, part of which is located in the inner ear (see Ear). The sufferer feels as though he is falling through space.

Parkinsonism, or *Parkinson's disease*, is thought to stem from changes in brain chemistry. Victims of the disorder walk with a slow, shuffling gait, have a wide-eyed, unblinking facial look, and experience muscle tremors, or shakes. They also have trouble speaking and swallowing. Parkinsonism can be treated with a drug called levodopa, or L-dopa.

Multiple sclerosis is a slow-developing disease that eventually involves the entire brain and spinal cord. Its cause is not yet known, but the disease eats away the fatty myelin sheath around many nerves. As a result, it interferes with proper nerve-signal transmission to muscles and organs (see Nerves). Muscle control, vision, mental abilities, and many other body functions are eventually impaired. Physical therapy is often required because the limbs of victims become weak and they are easily tired doing ordinary tasks.

Stroke

A *stroke*, or *cardiovascular accident*, occurs when blood can no longer nourish brain tissue and key nerve cells are thereby destroyed. A blood clot in one of the brain's blood vessels, hemorrhage from a broken blood vessel there, or hardening of a brain artery can cause a stroke.

Depending upon the brain area affected, a stroke can culminate in loss of limb use—particularly the arms—speech difficulties, and partial blindness. In time, victims of relatively unsevere strokes often regain most or all of the impaired body functions. In more severe cases, extensive physical or speech therapy is needed for partial rehabilitation of the stroke victim.

Epilepsy

Epilepsy is a brain disorder in which nerve signals "fire" abnormally and cause convulsive seizures, or alternating muscle contractions and relaxations. Scar tissue in the brain can provoke some seizures. In many cases, however, doctors cannot pinpoint the reason for an epileptic attack. Someone might have a seizure once and never again. If someone has more than one seizure, the second and any that may follow are officially called epileptic attacks.

Doctors generally recognize several types of epilepsy, including grand mal, petit mal, and infantile spasms. A *grand mal* attack is usually marked by rigidly contracted muscles, loss of consciousness, and collapse. The attack may last from two to five minutes, followed by deep sleep. A *petit mal* attack usually comes as a lapse of awareness for less than a minute. The victim then resumes whatever activity he was engaged in before the attack without realizing anything out of the ordinary took place. Infants under the age of three sometimes have *infantile spasms* during which sharp muscle contractions force the body to jackknife for a few seconds. Anticonvulsive drugs are used to treat and prevent all such attacks.

METABOLIC AND DEFICIENCY DISEASES

Disease can sometimes follow from alterations in normal body metabolism caused by deficiencies in diet, hormones, and vitamins. It can also stem from malfunctions in the body's immunity system.

Malnutrition and Vitamin Deficiencies

Malnutrition can be either overnutrition or undernutrition. Obesity resulting from overeating can lead to high blood pressure, heart disease, and diabetes. Undereating can stifle the development of body and mind.

Marasmus is the condition that results when a child's diet lacks both total calories and protein. A child with marasmus is always hungry and wastes away. *Kwashiorkor* is a protein deficiency that saps a child's strength even though his diet contains enough calories. A child with kwashiorkor lacks an appetite and is sullen. Both conditions occur in underdeveloped nations (*see* Food and Nutrition).

Vitamin deficiencies are uncommon among people in the world's richer nations, except in the cases of pregnant women and those who breast-feed their babies. Since ample vitamins are in the general diet in those lands, there is no medical justification for daily doses of multivitamins to stimulate vigor or prevent colds or infections. (For a discussion of the vitamin-deficiency diseases, *see* Vitamins.)

Mineral deficiencies can also produce body disorders. Iron is indispensable for the prevention of anemia. Magnesium is a cofactor in many enzymes. Deficiency of it causes dizziness, weakness, and convulsions. Iodine is a major part of the thyroid hormones. Without it a person can develop a goiter. Fluorine is not considered essential, but it plays a great part in minimizing dental *caries*, or cavities. Trace elements, such as chromium, cobalt, and manganese are also needed for a healthy body.

Hormone Deficiencies

The body's endocrine system produces a variety of hormones. When the endocrine glands are not working properly, certain disease processes can begin.

Abnormal output of growth hormone from the pituitary gland early in life can result in one of two disorders—dwarfism if there is too little or gigantism if there is too much. Abnormal output of certain hormones from the adrenal glands causes misregulation of the body's water balance and disturbs the normal retention and excretion of salts. Malfunction in sex hormone production can stem sexual activity, as well as produce excessive hair growth and distribution. Malfunction of the thyroid gland affects the rate at which food is burned for energy, causing the metabolic rate to run too fast or too slow for everyday needs. When part of the pancreas breaks down, diabetes develops (*see* Hormones).

Diabetes Mellitus

Diabetes mellitus, a fairly common disease, is caused by lack of biologically active *insulin,* a hormone secreted by the pancreas. Without insulin the body cannot use sugars and starches in the food. It must then rely upon its stored fat for energy. This storehouse is soon exhausted, however, because without insulin the body can no longer make and store fat. In addition, protein is no longer manufactured and the muscle mass of the body dwindles. The effect of growth hormone is reduced too. All this adds up to a rise in the level of blood sugar and increased urination, which, in turn, dehydrates the body and makes the diabetic thirsty. The sufferer loses weight, experiences muscle cramps, and has an itchy skin. If diabetes is not treated, sodium and potassium are lost in the urine and the products of fat breakdown, called *ketones,* build up in dangerous proportions in the blood. The blood also becomes increasingly acid and body dehydration reaches a dangerous level. Finally, the untreated diabetic goes into a potentially fatal coma.

Diabetes is treated by limiting the patient's diet and injecting him with insulin derived from cattle or hog pancreases. This treatment was pioneered by the Canadian physicians Frederick G. Banting and Charles H. Best in the 1920's (*see* Banting). Recently, an oral medication has proved capable of lowering the blood sugar of diabetics who develop a mild form of the disease after they reach adulthood. These tablets do not contain insulin but are helpful as long as the pancreas of the diabetic still produces some insulin.

Long-term diabetes is often associated with blood vessel degeneration. When this complication occurs, the diabetic can suffer heart disease, stroke, eye hemorrhage and blindness, kidney failure, gangrene of the feet, and serious neuritis.

The normal blood-sugar level ranges between 60 and 100 milligrams per 100 cubic centimeters of blood. It rises slightly higher after a meal. When the level falls below normal, a person has *hypoglycemia* and may develop headache, irritability, sweatiness, and other symptoms. Later, the patient has trouble keeping balance, speaks incoherently, and may even become violent or act listless and withdrawn. Finally, the hypoglycemic person falls into a coma and may have convulsions.

A diabetic may experience hypoglycemia when he gets an excessive dose of insulin or oral medication. Hypoglycemia can also result from diseases of the adrenal, pituitary, and pancreas glands, as well as from starvation, liver damage, and alcohol intake.

Moreover, some otherwise healthy persons, especially those with a nervous disposition, can suffer mild hypoglycemia. The immediate treatment for hypoglycemia is sugar dosage, either orally or by intravenous injection. *Glucagon*, a pancreatic hormone that raises the blood-sugar level, can also be injected. Long-range treatment involves correcting the disorder engendering the low blood sugar.

Other Metabolic Diseases

Gout is faulty metabolism of *purine*, an amino acid, resulting in the accumulation of uric acid in the blood and urate salts in the tissues, especially the joints where they cause painful arthritis. It may stem from an inborn error of metabolism or from other diseases. It usually strikes middle-aged men. The joint at the base of the big toe is the typical site of a sudden acute attack of gout. The affected joint becomes red, hot, swollen, and painful. Fever accompanies the attack. Joints of other limbs might become similarly affected. Attacks of gout recur, but the sufferer enjoys complete relief in between them. Some patients develop chronic arthritis from gout. Gout is treated with low-purine foods and such drugs as allopurinol that lower the uric acid level of the blood.

Cystic fibrosis is a genetic disorder involving the pancreas and the lungs. It appears during the first 10 years of life, although sometimes it is not discovered until later. Certain glands of the pancreas become plugged by thick mucus, which bottles important digestive enzymes. Intestinal troubles result. Furthermore, the lungs suffer scarring, infection, and eventual emphysema. Cystic fibrosis is treated with substitute pancreatic enzymes, vitamins, and a high-calorie diet. Antibiotics are given to fight the lung troubles.

Other metabolic disorders include *phenylketonuria* (PKU) and *galactosemia*. PKU is an inherited inability to metabolize *phenylalanine*, an amino acid. Galactosemia is an inherited inability to change *galactose*, one type of sugar, into *sucrose*, another, because a necessary enzyme is missing. Both diseases can result in mental retardation of children if not corrected in time.

Arthritis and Lupus

When the body fails to recognize itself, it makes antibodies against its own tissues. Rheumatoid arthritis and systemic lupus erythematosus are two among a rising number of such autoimmune diseases.

Rheumatoid arthritis is a chronic crippling disease that deforms bone joints and their adjacent tissues. It can strike nearly anyone. Although arthritis is not especially prevalent in damp climates, its symptoms are more bothersome there. It is marked by inflammation of an entire joint, including its *synovial* lining. Tendon coverings and *bursas*, or fluid-filled cushions, can become inflamed too. Cartilage in the joint and adjacent bone are destroyed, causing painful stiffness and eventual *ankylosis*, or "freezing," of the joint. Skin over the joint is taut, shiny, and clammy. Arthritics often suffer aches and pains. The rheumatoid factor, a large protein molecule, is present in the blood of so many adult patients that it aids in the diagnosis of the disease. Rheumatoid arthritis is usually treated with rest, physical therapy, and aspirin and other salicylates.

Systemic lupus erythematosus (SLE), or lupus, is a serious degenerative disease that can strike one or many body systems over a period of years. The blood serum of afflicted persons contains a number of peculiar proteins, including the so-called L. E. factor, the antibody characteristic of the disease. Symptoms of SLE resemble other diseases, including cancer and tuberculosis, but lesions around the nail beds and fingertips that destroy the skin in those areas earmark lupus. In addition, the spleen and lymph glands of the neck and armpits may enlarge. The pericardium and heart valves are affected too. The kidneys and portions of the central nervous system may also become damaged. Females between the ages of 20 and 40 years most often develop this incurable disease.

Osteoarthritis is a painfully disabling disease of the spine and other weight-bearing joints. Cartilage in the joint is destroyed, followed by overgrowth of nearby bone. The incurable but nondeforming disease develops with advancing age.

Ankylosing spondylitis is a disabling and deforming disease of the spine, sacroiliac joints, and sometimes the shoulders, hips, and knees. The synovial lining of the affected joint becomes inflamed, the bone is weakened by loss of calcium, and the spine is bent forward. Eventually, the spinal vertebrae fuse and the spine becomes locked in the deformed position.

Gout sufferers long ago believed that sweating would relieve the disorder and therefore took "treatment" in "sweathouses."

The Bettmann Archive

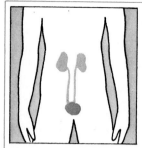

KIDNEY AND GENITAL DISEASES

Disease can affect any of the parts of the closely related urinary and genital systems. Both can be infected or malfunction because of a shortcoming in development.

Kidney Inflammations

Glomerulonephritis is a serious inflammatory disease of the kidneys (*see* Kidneys). It usually is triggered by a prior infection, often by streptococcal bacteria, which inflames the *glomeruli*, the tiny tufts through which blood is filtered. The inflammation may go away after a few weeks or may slowly destroy all the glomeruli. In the early stages, the inflammation may reduce filtration enough to cause blood to retain some excess fluid, salts, and wastes. Blood pressure might also rise. If the inflammation persists, the glomeruli are destroyed, blood pressure soars, and urine formation may stop. Mechanical means must be taken to cleanse the blood.

Pyelonephritis is a bacterial infection of the inner portions of the kidneys and the urine. If quickly treated, the infection can be cured. If untreated, however, the infection may scar and eventually destroy kidney tubules, resulting in a need for mechanical cleansing of the blood. Once damaged by a bout of pyelonephritis, the kidneys are easily reinfected.

Toxemia of pregnancy is a disorder stemming from other kidney problems experienced by some women in the last half of pregnancy. During a pregnancy, the kidneys must work more than usual. However, a woman entering pregnancy with a kidney disease such as glomerulonephritis may not be able to step up kidney function enough to meet the new demands. In severe cases of toxemia, the fetus may die or have to be aborted to save the mother's life. In lesser cases, however, medical treatment poses little risk to either life. Once a woman develops toxemia, she is likely to develop it again in later pregnancies.

Calculi and Other Urinary Disorders

Calculus disease occurs when certain substances in urine crystallize into compact stones called *calculi*. A stone may be formed within a kidney and become swept by urine into the ureters and the bladder. It may cause pain, obstruct urine flow, or grow large enough to damage the kidney or bladder. Small calculi may be passed in urine, and large ones can be pulverized without surgery by means of energetic sound waves.

Most calculi contain calcium, but some may consist mostly of urates, cystine, or other crystals. The tendency to form kidney stones, especially of the cystine type, sometimes runs in families.

Polycystic disease, an inherited failure of normal kidney development, strikes infants as well as adults. Many fluid-filled cysts spring up throughout the kidneys and cause them to malfunction. Polycystic disease sufferers eventually become uremic.

Uremia means "urine in blood." It describes the condition in which the kidneys almost totally fail to operate. The blood then retains the nitrogenous products of protein metabolism instead of having them removed by the kidneys. Also, the concentration of many of the *electrolytes,* or salts, in the blood rises too high. The breath or perspiration of affected persons smells of urine. Each of the previously mentioned kidney ailments could cause uremia. Artificial kidneys have been developed to cleanse the blood of uremic patients (*see* Bioengineering). In some cases, patients with destroyed kidneys can receive a human kidney transplant.

Genital Disorders

Sometimes portions of the genital system fail to develop normally. In some rare cases, the *gonads*—male testes and female ovaries—or other sex structures fail to develop at all. Without gonads, a person neither achieves puberty nor develops secondary sexual characteristics, such as breasts and uterus growth in females and penis growth and muscle development in males.

Infections such as gonorrhea can cause sterility by blocking the *oviducts,* or egg passages, of females or the *vas deferens,* or sperm passages, of males. In males, gonorrhea may also interfere with urination.

The prostate gland at the neck of the bladder in males enlarges slowly with age. It eventually may hamper urination and need surgical correction. (*See also* Reproduction and Reproductive Organs.)

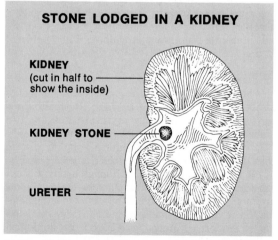

STONE LODGED IN A KIDNEY

KIDNEY
(cut in half to show the inside)

KIDNEY STONE

URETER

A kidney stone, or *renal calculus,* can grow in the organ, lodge in the ureter, and block the flow of urine to the bladder. If small, such stones can be passed from the body in the urine.

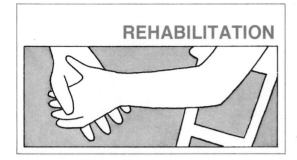

REHABILITATION

Rehabilitation Institute of Chicago

Rehabilitation can strengthen the limbs of a disabled person. Here, the patient builds up his arm by sanding a piece of wood. In the process, he may also acquire a new skill.

Rehabilitation is a fairly new medical specialty, although the notion of helping someone cope with a disabling disease or disorder is an old one. As an increasing number of people become disabled by stroke, paraplegia (paralysis of the lower body), limb losses, and many chronic nervous system and other physical disorders, it has been shown that medical rehabilitation can help many of them live a reasonably normal life. This is true even when the handicapping problem is not medically correctable.

Rehabilitation means getting utmost use from the limbs, senses, or other body systems that remain in operation after a chronic disability. Its goal is to help the patient become as independently active as possible. The disabling condition might result from a disease, birth defect, or severe accident. Sometimes rehabilitation involves fitting an amputee with an artificial limb, fitting a lame person with a brace, or teaching a paraplegic how to maneuver a wheelchair. Sometimes it only involves counseling and other psychological techniques for persons who are mentally disabled.

In its early days medical rehabilitation concentrated on helping people who had walking and other movement problems. The advances made in rehabilitating them sparked efforts to aid people who were stricken by stroke, chronic arthritis, and spinal cord disease and other chronic nervous system disorders. Afterward, it was learned that rehabilitation could also help patients with heart disease, chronic lung disease, and a variety of conditions that slowed recovery from surgery. Bioengineers have been successful in devising artificial limbs and other life-support structures that function so much like natural ones that recipients no longer suffer a disabling handicap (*see* Bioengineering).

Rehabilitation is a team effort. It requires the work and dedication of physicians, physical therapists, occupational therapists, psychologists, social workers, and vocational counselors. The doctor and the physical and occupational therapists work to restore those body functions impaired by the disability. The psychologist, social workers, and vocational counselor help the patient get a mental grip on himself to better deal with the emotional and social problems brought on by the disability. Members of a coordinated rehabilitative team can do wonders in restoring a handicapped person to a functional life.

In addition, the rehabilitative team works with a disabled person to prevent the physical deterioration that takes place when muscles are not used. Furthermore, the team aims at getting the maximum output from the patient's remaining body functions. Exercises and other means are used to develop fully the remaining physical reserves because disabled persons expend more energy and need more stamina to do ordinary things than do nondisabled persons.

Teaching new tasks to the disabled is an integral part of physical rehabilitation. For example, a crippled person may be trained to use a wheelchair or other motive device well enough to manage into the driver's seat of an automobile and thus achieve a measure of independence, the important goal of the entire rehabilitative process.

A chronically disabled person often suffers mental depression. The rehabilitation team tries to restore that person's confidence so that he can take an optimistic view on resuming daily activities. Positive attitudes of patient, friends, and family toward any disability are important factors in the success of rehabilitation. During rehabilitation the patient is encouraged to find meaning in life, overcome feelings of being a "permanent patient," and resume his place as an active member of society. Counseling is also important in rehabilitating alcoholics and the mentally ill.

Treatment for the disabled is given at special rehabilitation centers or in the rehabilitation departments of some hospitals (*see* Hospitals). Rehabilitation units are designed so that patients can do many things by themselves; the quarters are built to simulate conditions the patients will encounter when discharged. As a consequence, patients get practice in dealing with such problems as opening and closing doors, going up and down stairs, and a host of other environmental situations that they will face when the rehabilitation program is over.

183

RESEARCH AGAINST DISEASE

Stanford Research Institute

A computer electrically stimulates a monkey's brain to generate arm-moving nerve signals. Through this kind of research, scientists hope someday to restore impaired human brain activity.

Although medical science has made great strides to eradicate disease, a number of ailments remain to be conquered. Medical scientists have not yet discovered what causes muscular dystrophy, an inherited disorder that strikes nerve tissue and cripples its victim. Nor do they know what causes sudden death syndrome, or crib death, a disease that fatally strikes infants less than a year old. Nevertheless, research is under way against these and other baffling diseases in the hope that someday they will be wiped out or at least made manageable.

Medical scientists perform many kinds of experiments when they are on a research adventure. They may grow tiny cells in test tubes, infect them with the germs or chemicals they think might cause the disease, and watch the aftereffects. Or they might infect a laboratory animal with a disease and observe how its body fights off or succumbs to the ailment. At other times medical scientists test the effects of a drug, a pathological environment, or a possible disease organism on human volunteers. However, before human experimentation ethically can be permitted, the volunteers must give their informed consent to any unconventional treatment. That is, they must be fully aware of the harmful as well as helpful consequences possible before taking part in the research. Also, prior experiments should have been made on laboratory animals to establish some idea of the project's safety.

Medical research is an ongoing endeavor at many laboratories and scientific institutions throughout the world. Medical schools and major hospitals maintain research programs for the benefit of their patients with unchecked or rare diseases. Research programs are also undertaken at many universities where scientists divide their time between teaching and laboratory study. Government agencies such as the National Institutes of Health also engage in research against disease (see Health Agencies).

Research programs are delving into the problems of aging. As more and more is learned about the biochemical changes that go on in the body as it grows older, scientists may someday be able to modify those changes to ensure better health for the aged. The biochemical basis of certain forms of mental illness are being explored, too, as are the causes and possible remedies of drug abuse (see Mental Health; Drugs, section "Drug Abuse").

Some physical disorders still require surgery for correction. As a result, there has been research into improving surgical techniques and into devising artificial parts for the body. Surgeons, for example, have been trying to improve their ability to rejoin severed limbs. Bioengineers have designed heart pacemakers, sensory aids for the blind, and many other spare parts for the body.

The very foundations of life are being explored in *genetic engineering*. This recent endeavor is an attempt to alter the genetic makeup of developing embryos in the hope that inborn errors of metabolism can be corrected.

Although some scientists doubt that genetic engineering will ever be practical, if it became so, the ability to alter mistaken genes in unborn children would open a remarkable medical frontier. In the meantime, doctors have encouraged *genetic counseling*, in which couples planning marriage can learn of the possible consequences of childbearing when they are the carriers of certain inherited disorders, such as Down's syndrome, also called mongolism, or sickle-cell anemia. (*See also* Medicine; Surgery; Nursing; Hospitals; Physiology; Health.)

BIBLIOGRAPHY FOR DISEASE

Asimov, Isaac. How Did We Find Out About Germs? (Avon, 1981).
Astor, Gerald. The Disease Detectives (New American, 1984).
Baldry, Peter. The Battle Against Bacteria (Cambridge Univ. Press, 1976).
Blanzaco, André. VD: Facts You Should Know (Lothrop, 1970).
Brooks, S.M. and others. Handbook of Infectious Diseases (Little, 1980).
De Kruif, Paul. Microbe Hunters (Harcourt, 1966).
Donahue, Parnell and Capellaro, Helen. Germs Make Me Sick: a Health Handbook for Kids (Knopf, 1975).
McNeill, W.H. Plagues and People (Doubleday, 1977).
Wolfe, Louis. Disease Detectives (Watts, 1979).

DISNEY, Walt (1901–66). An American cartoonist, Walt Disney made the world love an ugly duckling and dozens of other animal characters. At the same time he raised the making of animated cartoon motion pictures to an art.

Walter Elias Disney was born on Dec. 5, 1901, in Chicago, Ill., the fourth of five children. In 1906 the family moved to a farm near Marceline, Mo. The boy's first drawings were of the farm animals. In 1910 the family moved to Kansas City, Mo., where young Disney got his first job as an artist. He did weekly sketches for a barber, for which he received either 25 cents or a haircut. The family returned to Chicago in 1917. Disney attended McKinley High School, but his real interest was in the evening courses he took at the Chicago Academy of Fine Arts. He left high school without graduating.

Disney enlisted as a Red Cross ambulance driver in World War I. He returned to Kansas City after the war and worked as an artist with an advertising firm. At this time he made his first animated cartoons, 'Laugh-O-Grams'. By 1923 Disney had decided his future lay in Hollywood with the film industry. He formed a partnership with his brother Roy and produced the 'Alice Comedies' series. In 1925 Disney married an employee, Lillian Marie Bounds. They had two daughters, Diane Marie and Sharon Mae.

The first cartoon to use synchronized sound, 'Steamboat Willie', appeared in 1928. It starred a new personality, Mickey Mouse. In a decade Mickey, Minnie Mouse, Pluto the dog, and Donald Duck became world famous. Disney's films have been made with sound tracks in 14 languages to be shown around the world. (*See also* Cartoons.)

Disney's first full-length film, 'Snow White and the Seven Dwarfs', was released in 1937. 'Seal Island', produced in 1948, was the first of Disney's True-Life Adventures, featuring real wildlife. He also made films with real actors, such as 'Mary Poppins'. Disney won more than 100 prizes for his films, including many Academy awards. In 1964 he was awarded the Presidential Medal of Freedom. His films,

Walt Disney

© Walt Disney Productions

which include 'Fantasia' and 'Bambi', are rereleased periodically.

In 1955 Disney opened a large themed amusement park, Disneyland, at Anaheim, Calif. Several million people a year visit the 180-acre (75-hectare) park. Disney died on Dec. 15, 1966, in Burbank, Calif. Five years after his death, Walt Disney World, a 28,000-acre (11,300-hectare) amusement park and vacation area, opened near Orlando, Fla. Epcot Center opened nearby in 1982. (*See also* Amusement Park.)

DISRAELI, Benjamin (1804–81). A clever novelist and a brilliant statesman, Disraeli led the Tory (now Conservative) political party in Great Britain. Twice he held the post of prime minister.

Benjamin Disraeli was born on Dec. 21, 1804, in London. Although his parents were Jews, he became a Christian in 1817. This affected his political career since, before 1858, Jews were excluded from Parliament. He was educated by tutors. He studied law but gave it up in order to write. In 1837 he won a seat in Parliament.

As a young man Disraeli needlessly handicapped himself by dressing like a dandy and by affecting dramatic manners. The first time he tried to make a speech in the House of Commons, the other members ridiculed him. He shouted, "I shall sit down now, but the time is coming when you will hear me."

Disraeli's prophecy came true. The debates between him and William E. Gladstone, who was the leader of the Whig (Liberal) party, were some of the keenest ever held in the House of Commons.

In 1848 Disraeli became the leader of the Conservative party in the House of Commons. Under his leadership the party no longer opposed all progressive measures. In 1867 he persuaded the Conservatives to carry through a Parliamentary Reform Bill that extended the right to vote even further than the Whigs had suggested.

In 1868 Disraeli became prime minister. His ministry fell within a year, but in 1874 he was again made prime minister. This time he remained in office for six years.

Disraeli is known as the founder of British imperialism. He personally purchased for Britain shares in the Suez Canal from the khedive of Egypt and so safeguarded England's route to India.

In 1876 he had Queen Victoria proclaimed empress of India. He played a clever part against Russia in the Congress of Berlin in 1878, blocking its progress in the Balkans and saving Turkey from its domination. The queen rewarded him with the title earl of Beaconsfield and a seat in the House of Lords. In 1880 the Conservatives were defeated and he retired. He died the next year.

Disraeli's success as a writer resulted largely from his political experience. He was the first successful author of political novels. Some of his best-known writings are 'Vivian Grey', published in 1826; 'Henrietta Temple' (1837); 'Coningsby' (1844); 'Sybil' (1845); 'Tancred' (1847); and 'Lothair' (1870).

Whether from a tuck position (left), pike position (center), or straight position (right), a diver tries to enter the water straight for a minimum of splash.

DIVING. Whether from the side of a pool or from a springboard, diving is a sport performed by plunging into water. When done by trained athletes, it is one of the most graceful of exhibitions.

Diving as a sport demands a spirit of daring from its participants. It also demands coordination, muscular control, and exact timing. Diving requires body conditioning through daily exercise and constant practice. It is gymnastics performed over water.

Dives may be performed from either a springboard or a platform. The springboard is a flexible, light, and springy aluminum-alloy board with a non-slip surface. The diver can spring upward to obtain extra height in the dive, giving more time in the air to do somersaults and twists. Springboards are either 1 or 3 meters high; the distance is measured from the surface of the water to the bottom of the board. In Olympic, regional, national, and international competitions, the 3-meter springboard is used.

The platform is a rigid fixture covered with a nonslip surface 5, 7.5, or 10 meters high. Competition is generally held only at the 10-meter height, with divers plummeting headfirst at more than 30 miles per hour.

In competitive diving the water is the landing medium as a mat is for the gymnast. It is the flight through the air that is the dive and that provides the challenge. Competitive diving is really diving gymnastics. It enables one to do something that can be achieved in few other sports: flying through the air without any means of support and landing safely without discomfort.

There are approximately 70 different dives listed for competition. Each dive has a designated number and may be performed in one of four positions. In the

This article was contributed by Albert Schoenfield, Vice Chairman, United States Swimming Olympic International Committee, 1972–88; Secretary, Technical Swimming Committee, Fédération Internationale de Natation Amateur, 1980–84. He has been inducted into the International Swimming Hall of Fame.

straight position the body is not bent either at the knees or at the hips, the feet are together, and the toes pointed. In the pike position the body is bent at the hips, but the legs must be kept straight at the knees, the feet together, and the toes pointed. In the tuck position the body is compact, bent at the knees, feet together, hands on the lower legs, and toes pointed. In free position the body position is optional, but the legs are together and the toes pointed.

All dives are divided into six categories. They are: forward dives—the diver both faces and dives forward; backward dives—the diver faces backward and dives so that the body rotates away from the board; reverse dives—the diver faces forward but dives so that the body rotates toward the board; inward dives—the diver faces backward but dives so that the body rotates toward the board; twisting dives—the diver, from either of the starting positions, twists the body in the air before reaching the water; handstand dives—the diver begins the dive from a motionless handstand at the edge of a platform only.

Professionals have dived from temporary towers, often more than 60 feet (18 meters) high, into tanks of water for exhibitions at fairgrounds, marine lands, and carnivals. A big tourist attraction at Acapulco, Mexico, is divers going headfirst off the high cliffs into the sea. At many competitions comic diving has been added as a crowd-pleasing event. The divers are clad in funny costumes, performing dives that are unorthodox and amusing.

Like gymnastics and figure skating, diving is judged by experts. For Olympic games and world championships, seven judges make up a panel; for all other competitions, five are sufficient. Each judge rates every dive on the approach, takeoff, elevation, execution, and entry into the water. A score from zero to ten is given. In major competitions the highest and lowest are cancelled. The remaining scores are added and multiplied by the degree of difficulty to give the final score. The difficulty ratings are from 1.0 for simple dives to 3.4 for very difficult. A complicated rating table has been devised by the Fédération Internationale de Natation Amateur (FINA), the world governing body that controls the sport.

Diving did not become a formal competition until about 1880. In 1883 the Amateur Swimming Association of Great Britain began a distance competition—plunging. This was a standing dive made headfirst from a firm base. The body was kept motionless face downward.

The plunge terminated when the competitor raised his face from the surface of the water or when 60 seconds had elapsed. The distance traveled from takeoff to the farthest point reached by any part of the body determined the winner. The event was discontinued with a record of 86 feet 8 inches.

In the 1800s divers from Sweden came to England and demonstrated fancy high diving. In 1895 the English Royal Life Saving Society staged the first National Graceful Diving Competition. It was for men only and consisted of running plain dives from heights of 15 and 33 feet (5 and 10 meters). In Europe divers graduated from plain diving to fancy diving, from platforms to springboards. Fancy diving began the era of somersaults and twists.

Springboard diving was included in the 1904 Olympic games in Saint Louis. Platform diving was added to the supplementary Olympic games at Athens in 1906. In 1928 plain and fancy high diving events were combined into one competition and renamed highboard diving, and fancy was dropped from the diving vocabulary.

In the 1912 Olympic games at Stockholm, women were allowed to compete in plain diving for the first time. This remained in effect until 1920, when the events were divided into springboard and platform diving. Prior to 1918 Sweden dominated the fancy high diving events and Germany the men's springboard diving. When the Olympic games resumed after World War I, United States men and women dominated, sweeping all six springboard medals in 1920. American domination continued with only occasional losses. In the 1984 Olympics, held in Los Angeles, the Peoples' Republic of China emerged as a serious competitor, winning the women's platform and placing second in the men's springboard and third in the men's platform.

Diving competitions take place in high schools and colleges but are confined to springboard. In open competition, Olympic, World, and international events the 3-meter springboard and 10-meter platforms are the events. Diving is now part of amateur aquatic programs in more than 35 countries and on all continents.

Somersault and twisting dives that once were considered impossible for experienced adults are now performed by school children. Training for Olympic class divers now starts when a child reaches 10 years of age and in the United States sometimes even younger.

Recommended reading includes the 'FINA Handbook', published every four years, and Charles Batterman's 'The Techniques of Springboard Diving', published in 1968. (*See also* Swimming.)

DIVING, UNDERWATER. With the oceans comprising more than 70 percent of the Earth's surface, it is no wonder that human beings have been curious about the undersea realm since the beginnings of history. Plato and Aristotle wondered about deep-sea life and speculated about going underwater. Roger Bacon, a 13th-century English friar, wrote about the possibility of submarine operations. Leonardo da Vinci designed a diving helmet of leather. It had spikes to protect the diver from monsters, and a breathing tube stretched from the helmet to the surface with a cork float. (*See also* Deep-Sea Life.)

In 1716 the English astronomer and mathematician Edmund Halley, who discovered Halley's Comet, invented two types of diving bells. One was made of wood and looked like an upside-down wastebasket with eyes. The two "eyes" were not to see out of but to let light in. Air was provided by two 36-gallon (136-liter) barrels that alternated from surface to bottom with cargoes of fresh air, and a flexible tube transferred the air from the barrel to the bell and the diver inside.

Halley's second diving bell was made of lead. It was 8 feet (2.5 meters) in height, 3 feet (1 meter) in diameter at the top, and 5 feet (1.5 meters) at the bottom. There was a seat inside for several divers, and the air-supply system was essentially the same as for the first bell. Halley and four other daring divers reportedly stayed at 10 fathoms (60 feet, or 18 meters) for an hour and a half in the lead bell. Their only problem, he reported, was a pain in the ears "as if a quill had been thrust into them." In those days they did not understand the problems of increased pressure and depth.

Development of Scuba

Modern exploration of the undersea world had its beginnings in June 1943, when Jacques Cousteau made his first dive with a revolutionary breathing device he had developed with Émile Gagnan, a French engineer. Captain Cousteau, then a French Navy gunnery officer, had not been satisfied with the superficial probing of the ocean surface. It was not enough that humans could stay underwater and look only as long as they could hold their breath.

Gagnan had designed a gas-flow demand regulator for use on automobiles and in hospital operating rooms during World War II. Cousteau thought that the invention could be modified for use underwater. The two tried several concepts and finally came up with a successful model of an open-circuit, compressed air scuba (Self-Contained Underwater Breathing Apparatus). (*See also* Cousteau.)

Not only did Cousteau realize his own dream of "flying" underwater like a fish, but he also enabled many others to peer into the ocean and study its

This article was contributed by Hillary Hauser, a frequent author of articles that appear in *Skin Diver Magazine, Oceans,* and other periodicals.

Dave Woodward—CLICK/Chicago

A scuba diver explores a shallow portion of the ocean floor while being investigated by curious fishes.

innermost secrets. Today thousands of scuba divers explore reefs in every ocean of the world, studying marine life and exploring shipwrecks. Divers have explored the frigid waters of the North Pole, and they have cruised the steep drop-offs of tropical subsea canyons in the Caribbean.

Learning Process

For most people, learning how to dive is not difficult. The first step is often snorkeling, or so-called free diving. The only equipment required for snorkeling is a face mask and a snorkel. The snorkeler swims along the surface of the water, looking at the underwater scenery through the face mask while breathing through the snorkel. Most snorkelers also wear rubber or plastic fins on their feet to make swimming as effortless as possible. For a closer look at the reef below, the diver holds his breath and dives down. Breathhold diving, as this is called, is a safe, enjoyable pastime as long as the diver guards against excessive hyperventilation, or rapid breathing, on the surface before a dive. This can result in an excessive buildup of carbon dioxide and cause what is called shallow-water blackout.

When a diver decides to explore deeper ocean areas, it is necessary to enroll in a certified scuba training course. Here the diver first learns how to handle the equipment: Along with the mask, fins, and snorkel used in free diving, the scuba diver uses a scuba tank, regulator, pressure and depth gauges, weightbelt, and buoyancy compensator (BC)—essentially an inflatable lifejacket that serves as a safety device and helps a diver to regulate buoyancy underwater.

A diver's early training also includes how to deal with the two major physiological problems associated with diving: air embolism and bends. Both problems are caused by the increase in pressure that occurs as a diver goes deeper. The pressure of the atmosphere at sea level is 14.7 pounds per square inch (1.03 kilograms per square centimeter). This pressure is termed 1 atmosphere. Every foot of sea water contributes 0.445 pounds per square inch (0.3 kilogram per square centimeter) of pressure on the diver. The result is that at 33 feet (10 meters) the pressure doubles. At 66 feet (20 meters) it is again increased by 1 atmosphere.

A diver equalizes for these pressure changes: on the way down, most notably by clearing the ears; on the way up, breathing must be normal—never holding one's breath—because the air in the lungs will expand. Pressure decreases on the way up in the same ratio as the increase on the way down. If a diver takes a deep breath at 33 feet (10 meters), holds it, and rises to the surface, the air in the lungs will expand to twice its original volume and the diver will suffer what is called an air embolism.

Air embolism occurs when the lungs overexpand to the point that air bubbles are forced through the lungs into the circulatory system. The bubbles can become lodged in the heart, the arteries, or the brain. The symptoms of air embolism appear within minutes—even seconds—after surfacing. There can be dizziness, confusion, weakness, blurred vision, convulsions, and even death.

Bends, also known as decompression sickness and caisson disease, also results from differences in underwater pressure. Because of the increased pressure under water, the nitrogen in the compressed air that is breathed is absorbed by the fluids and tissues of the diver's body. If a diver who has been in deep water comes up properly, as pressure is reduced, the nitrogen is released from the fluids and tissues, passes through the veins, is freed in the lungs and is breathed out.

The key to coming up properly is time. The United States Navy developed dive, or decompression, tables to indicate the amount of time it takes for nitrogen to dissolve from the diver's bloodstream. Divers overextending their stay in deep water must make stops on their way back to the surface to allow these nitrogen bubbles to dissolve. If a diver comes up too rapidly, it causes bends: The bubbles can go into the bloodstream and lodge in the brain, lungs, or spinal cord. In minor cases the bubbles can cause itchy skin and stiff joints; in more extreme cases there can be pain, partial or total paralysis, and death.

Most divers learn the time and depths to which they can go without requiring decompression—called no-decompression diving—and stay within those limits. A diver can stay at 30 feet (9 meters) indefinitely, but can stay at 130 feet (40 meters) for only 10 minutes without decompressing on the way up.

Depths greater than 130 feet are not recommended for recreational diving. At about 100 feet (30 meters), and sometimes shallower, nitrogen affects the diver's nervous system with results similar to intoxication. This is called nitrogen narcosis. It does not happen suddenly but increases by degrees with increasing depth. It is not a permanent or traumatic condition, but it is known to impair judgment seriously. At 130 feet it can be very noticeable, another reason 130 feet has been established as a maximum depth for sport diving.

Commercial Diving

Commercial diving technology has made significant strides in ushering in the age of undersea exploration. Commercial operations have extended into deeper and deeper waters because of the needs of the offshore petroleum industry. After an oil platform is placed offshore, the subsea support structure must be maintained, serviced, and inspected by divers.

Until the 1960s divers went only to depths above 300 feet (90 meters). In these depths diving practices have remained the same. Divers descend from the surface breathing mixed gas, rather than compressed air, to prevent the nitrogen narcosis problem. They wear either hard hats—brass and copper helmets with glass portholes—or band masks—plasticized helmets with built-in faceplates. Both systems are tied to the surface by hoses that supply both breathing gases and communication lines that allow the

A navy diver is readied to be lowered into the water on a platform in a procedure for testing diving equipment.

Courtesy US Navy

diver to talk with the surface support team. The gas mixture is generally a helium-oxygen mixture called heliox, the helium replacing nitrogen. Helium, however, produces a high, squeaky "Donald Duck" voice in the diver, and sometimes communication can be nearly impossible because of it.

Heliox also is often used in submersible chambers, in which divers rest between dives during their underwater work periods. The chambers also serve for decompressing, or being brought back to surface pressure, at the end of a job. The problem with this type of procedure is the length of decompression. A diver working at 900 feet (275 meters) for six hours, for example, must decompress for nine days.

In 1974 a United States diving company, Oceaneering International, introduced a revolutionary armored diving suit called Jim. It had been developed over many years by a British company and named after Jim Jarratt, who had explored the wreck of the *Lusitania* in the 1930s in a preliminary model of the suit. Jim is a one-person submersible device that is essentially a pressurized suit of armor that lets a diver work at depths of up to 2,000 feet (600 meters) while remaining at surface pressure. Because the diver is never subjected to the pressure of the depths, there is never a need to undergo decompression. The first Jim dives were to 905 feet (275 meters) in the Canadian Arctic, and the diver was able to surface in minutes instead of decompressing for the usual nine days.

This introduced a sort of technological wizardry into the ocean arena, and today the bottom of the sea in busy petroleum locations looks like a subsea Cape Canaveral. Included in this inner-space fleet are the Mantis and Wasp that look like the insects they are named for and take divers to 2,000 feet (600 meters). Wasp, with its yellow body and acrylic dome head, allows a diver to hover mid-water because it has thrusters in the place of feet. In 1982 marine scientists from the University of California at Santa Barbara used the Wasp to explore deep areas off Santa Barbara. Other 1-atmosphere diving systems, including one called Deep Rover, have been developed that allow a diver to go to 3,000 feet (900 meters). Eventually 7,000 feet (2,100 meters) will be a common depth in which divers and scientists can work and study.

How much deeper will human beings want to go? The average depth of the Pacific Ocean is 13,739 feet (4,188 meters), and the average depth of the Atlantic, 12,257 feet (3,736 meters). There is much unexplored territory, and with advanced submersibles humans may eventually see large portions of it.

There is more down there than petroleum. There are manganese nodules loaded with valuable copper, cobalt, and nickel, and many believe there is twice as much gold in the sea as on land. There are long-lost wrecks, as well as uncharted ridges, to be mapped by future explorers. But the ultimate lure for deep diving is the quest for knowledge.

DIVORCE *see* MARRIAGE.

Dorothea Dix
Courtesy of Saint Elizabeth's
Hospital, Washington, D.C.

DIX, Dorothea (1802–87). A social reformer and humanitarian, Dorothea Dix devoted her life to the welfare of the mentally ill and the handicapped. Through her efforts, special hospitals for mental patients were built in more than 15 states, and in Canada, Europe, and Japan.

Dorothea Lynde Dix was born on April 4, 1802, in Hampden, Me. When she was a young teenager, she opened a school in Worcester, Mass. She later operated a school in Boston until ill health forced its closing in 1835. In 1841 she began to teach a Sunday school class in the East Cambridge (Mass.) jail. There the thoughtless confinement of mentally ill persons with criminals disturbed her deeply. After touring similar jails throughout Massachusetts, she revealed in a public report the shocking conditions she found. In addition to bringing about prison reforms, she worked in behalf of blind and deaf mutes. Dorothea Dix died on July 17, 1887, in Trenton, N.J.

DJIBOUTI. A small nation on the eastern coast of Africa, Djibouti faces the Strait of Bab el Mandeb between the Red Sea and the Gulf of Aden. Formerly known as Afars and Issas, it has been called officially the Republic of Djibouti since 1977.

Djibouti is bordered almost entirely by Ethiopia; Somalia borders on the southeast, and the Gulf of Aden is on the east. It covers an area of 8,900 square miles (23,200 square kilometers). Its coastline, deeply indented by the Golfe de Tadjoura, runs some 500 miles (800 kilometers) from north to south. The capital is the port city of Djibouti.

Djibouti is both a desert land of nomads, or wandering peoples, and traders and a busy commercial trade center at the western end of the Gulf of Aden. The nation has few natural resources. Its location, however, gives it strategic value. Djibouti city, a deep-water port located on the southern shore of the Golfe de Tadjoura, is the only seaport to which neighboring Ethiopia is connected by rail.

The climate is extremely hot most of the year: Temperatures average 86° F (30° C) at Djibouti city. There is a less warm season from November to April. Precipitation is scarce and irregular, and plants are mostly scrub bush. Animal life includes hyenas, jackals, antelopes, and gazelles.

The two major ethnic groups of the country are the Afars, who are of Ethiopian ancestry, and the Issas, who are of Somalian ancestry. The Afars are concentrated in the north and west and the Issas in the south and east. Both groups share a language, are largely nomadic, and adhere to the religion of Islam.

Agriculture is limited to small-scale production of dates, other fruits, and vegetables. Livestock, raised largely by pastoral nomads, includes camels, sheep, goats, and cattle. There is limited fishing along the coastline but more is being developed at Obock. Salt mining, cement manufacturing, and a bottling plant are in early stages of development.

Djibouti's economy relies almost entirely on services and external trade. Imports are mainly textiles, coal, and cement. Exports include local products such as hides and skins. Djibouti city has several piers, warehouses, water reservoirs, and fuel-storage tanks. The closing of the Suez Canal from 1967 to 1975 severely affected trade in Djibouti. Destruction of parts of the Djibouti-Addis Ababa railway during the Ethiopian civil war of 1977 led to further disruption of Djibouti's economy.

From the Djibouti airport there are international flights to and from France, parts of the Middle East, and East African countries. There is one radio and one television station. They broadcast programs in French, Afar, Issa, and Arabic. The country's cultural life is centered in Djibouti city. A weekly newspaper is issued by the government.

The port of Djibouti was created in 1888 by Léonce Lagarde, the first governor of French Somaliland, as the area was then called. Shortly after it became the capital in 1892, work began on the railway that finally linked the port city to Addis Ababa in 1917. The area was a French colony until 1967, when it became an overseas territory of France. It remained so until it became a republic in 1977.

Djibouti is governed by a president elected by the National Assembly. A prime minister heads the Council of Ministers. Population (1981 estimate, excluding refugees), 323,000.

DNEPR, or DNIEPER, RIVER. The fourth longest river in Europe (after the Volga, the Danube, and the Ural) is the Dnepr, in the southwestern Soviet Union. With its many tributaries, the river drains much of the Belorussian and Ukrainian S.S.R.s. It originates in the low Valday Hills west of Moscow and flows about 1,400 miles (2,250 kilometers) to the Black Sea through one of the most industrialized regions of the Soviet Union.

The Dnepr flows in great curves across the vast Russian plain. Before reaching Kiev, it is joined by the Pripyat', or Pripet, River. At Kiev it meets another tributary, the Desna. Leaving Kiev, it spreads to a mile in width. The center of the river's basin consists of broad lowlands. Its mouth is a swampy delta on a long inlet called Dnepr Liman.

Bending to the southeast, the river breaks through a rocky plateau from Dnepropetrovsk to Zaporozh'ye. A series of rapids here made possible a giant hydroelectric development, the Dnepr Dam (Russian Dneproges) at Zaporozh'ye. This raised the river level by 121 feet (37 meters) and made possible the construction of a bypass canal with locks for navigation. It is one of the largest dams in the Soviet Union. More than 300 hydroelectric plants operate in the Dnepr Basin. The Dnepr Bend district is now one of the largest centers of heavy industry in the Ukraine.

The canal made the Dnepr navigable throughout most of its length. High water follows the spring thaw, and the river flows well until early autumn. Timber is floated from the upper course to the treeless steppe region of the lower course, which carries the bulk of the river's commerce. The principal cargoes are coal, ore, mineral building materials, lumber, and grain. The chief ports on the river are Dorogobuzh, Smolensk, Osha, Kiev, and Kherson. Canals connect the upper course with the Bug, Niemen, and Western Dvina rivers. More than 60 species of fishes live in the Dnepr. Commercially important species are pike, roach, carp, goldfish, perch, and catfish.

DNESTR, or **DNIESTER, RIVER.** The Dnestr River is the second longest river in the Ukrainian Soviet Socialist Republic and the main water artery of the Moldavian S.S.R. It originates in the Carpathian Mountains and flows in a southeasterly direction, emptying into the Black Sea through an estuary, or sea arm. The middle course winds a great deal. Its mouth is near Odessa. The river's entire length of 839 miles (1,350 kilometers) is within the Soviet Union.

The climate of the river's basin is humid with warm summers. The river freezes from December to March and frequently floods when the ice melts, causing extensive damage to settled areas. Annual precipitation varies within a range of from about 40 to 50 inches (1,000 to 1,250 millimeters) in the Carpathians to 20 inches (500 millimeters) near the Black Sea. A large proportion of the land of the basin is under cultivation.

The Dnestr has three parts: the upper river as far as the village Nizhny, about 170 miles (270 kilometers); the middle river from Nizhny to Dubossary, about 450 miles (720 kilometers); and the lower river from Dubossary to the mouth, about 210 miles (340 kilometers). For the first 30 miles (50 kilometers) of its course, the Dnestr is a rushing mountain stream flowing through a deep gorge. At Dubossary there is a hydroelectric station and reservoir. Below Dubossary the valley gradually widens, with slopes several hundred feet high on which there are orchards, vineyards, and forests.

About 750 miles (1,210 kilometers) of the river are navigable. Regular passenger and freight lines run from Soroki to Dubossary and from the latter to the Black Sea. The river is used extensively for carrying logs. Fishing is of little importance except near the coast. In the lower reaches and in the Dubossary Reservoir, there are fish hatcheries for sturgeon, whitefish, pike, perch, and carp. The Dnestr's chief tributaries are the Seret and Stry.

Although the basin of the Dnestr is densely populated, there are no large towns on the river itself. L'vov, Ternopol', Ivano-Frankovsk, Kishinev, and other urban centers lie above the main valley on the river's tributaries. The Dnestr's main ports are Mogilev-Podol'skiy, Soroki, Bendery, and Tiraspol'.

DOBZHANSKY, Theodosius (1900–75). A Russian-American scientist, Theodosius Dobzhansky had a major influence on 20th-century thought and research in genetics and the study of evolution. From 1918 he published more than 400 research papers that provide an important part of the factual evidence for modern evolutionary theory.

Theodosius Dobzhansky was born on Jan. 25, 1900, in Nemirov, Ukraine. He began school at age 10 and was graduated from the University of Kiev in 1921. In 1927 he went to Columbia University in New York City, where he spent most of his teaching career. He became a United States citizen in 1937.

Dobzhansky's work was involved with that of other theorists who were trying to link Darwin's theory of evolution with Mendel's theory of genetics. His book 'Genetics and the Origin of Species', published in 1937, was the first substantial synthesis of these related subjects.

Dobzhansky's most important experiments showed that genes could vary far more than geneticists had believed. After retiring, he moved in 1971 to the University of California at Davis, where he died on Dec. 18, 1975.

DOG

DOG. The dog is one of the most popular pets in the world. It ordinarily remains loyal to a considerate master, and because of this the dog has been called man's best friend. Class distinctions between people have no part in a dog's life. It can be a faithful companion to either rich or poor.

Dogs have endeared themselves to many over the years. Stories have been told about brave dogs that served admirably in war or that risked their lives to save persons in danger. When Pompeii—the Roman community destroyed by Mount Vesuvius in A.D. 79—was finally excavated, searchers found evidence of a dog lying across a child, apparently trying to protect the youngster. Perhaps few of the millions of dogs in the world may be so heroic, but they are still a source of genuine delight to their owners.

A dog fits easily into family life. It thrives on praise and affection. When a master tells a dog that it is good, the animal happily wags its tail. But when a master scolds a dog, it skulks away with a sheepish look and with its tail tucked between its legs.

People in the city as well as those in other areas can enjoy a dog. Medium-size or small dogs are best

This article was contributed by Arthur F. Jones, internationally known authority on dogs and author of numerous books and articles about them. Illustrations of the breeds in this article were prepared by Harry Michaels, expert illustrator of canine features in newspapers and periodicals.

Scientific Classification

Phylum: Chordata **Family:** Canidae
Subphylum: Vertebrata **Genus:** *Canis*
Class: Mammalia **Species:** *C. familiaris*
Order: Carnivora

Dogs are in the order of carnivorous animals, Carnivora, and belong to the family Canidae. All domestic dogs are genus *Canis*, species *C. familiaris*. For information on other members of the dog family, *see* Jackal; Wolf.

---

suited for the confines of the city. Large dogs need considerable exercise over a large area.

Dogs are not always well thought of, however. In recent years dogs in the city have been in the center of controversy. Some people have criticized dog owners for allowing their pets to soil sidewalks and lawns, although in some cities laws oblige owners to walk their dogs along street curbs. In turn, dog owners have argued that the animals serve as protection against vandals and burglars and thus protect their detractors as well as their owners.

When a person decides to own a dog, he should be prepared to care for it properly. For a dog to stay healthy it must be correctly fed and adequately groomed, and its medical needs must be met. For a dog to be well-mannered it must be properly trained. It should never be ill-treated or mishandled. Otherwise, it will bite in its own defense.

The wild ancestors of all dogs were hunters. Wolves and other wild relatives of the dog still hunt in packs for their food. Dogs have retained the urge to be with the pack. This is why they do not like to be left alone for long. Some breeds of dogs still retain the hunting instinct.

Dogs exist in a wide range of sizes, colors, and temperaments. Some, such as the Doberman pinscher and the German shepherd, serve as alert and aggressive watchdogs. Others, such as the beagle and the cocker spaniel, are playful family pets, even though they were bred for hunting. Still others, such as the collie and the Welsh corgi, can herd farm or range animals. Each of the dogs just mentioned is a purebred. A mongrel dog, however—one with many breeds in its background—can just as easily fit into family life. Only proper training and affection are needed to raise any happy dog.

Dogs have been with man since prehistoric times. Over the years they have performed various services for man. They have pulled his sleds over snowy tracts. They have delivered messages, herded sheep and cattle, and even rescued persons trapped in the snow. Dogs have served as a source of food, too. The ancient Romans are said to have prized certain kinds of dog stew. The Aztecs of ancient Mexico raised tiny dogs, thought to be the forebears of the chihuahua, to feed the large carnivores in the private zoos of the Aztec rulers. In the past dogs have even been worshiped as gods. Recently, they have been used in drug research, medical experimentation, and space science. Russian scientists launched dogs into space to test the ability of mammals to survive the rigors of space travel before men were sent up.

Dogs are trained as guard dogs in peacetime by the United States Army and other military services. Because of their keen sense of smell, dogs are used by police at times to track down escaped prisoners. Law enforcement agencies also rely on the dog's acute sense of smell to uncover illegal drugs. And specially trained dogs serve as the "eyes" of the blind, guiding the steps of their sightless masters around obstacles and hazards.

SOME NOTEWORTHY DOGS IN HISTORY

Soter—one of 50 watchdogs of ancient Greece that alone survived attack by invaders and ran to the gates of Corinth to warn the citizens.

Saur, or Suening—a dog that was "king" of Norway for three years during the 11th century A.D. The Norwegian king, angry that his subjects once deposed him, put Saur on the throne and demanded it be regally treated.

Le Diable—a notorious French dog that smuggled lace and other costly items across the French border under a false skin dyed various colors by its owners to baffle the customs guards.

Rin Tin Tin—a German shepherd who ranked as one of the all-time famous canine movie stars. "Rinty" was in 19 movies before its death in 1932.

Laika—the first dog in space. Laika was aboard the Russian satellite Sputnik 2 in 1957.

Lassie—any of a line of popular collies in movies and in a television series. The first Lassie starred in the 1942 movie 'Lassie Come Home'.

SOME FACTS ABOUT DOGS

A dog is more apt to chase and perhaps bite a stranger who runs away from it than a person who remains still.

Smell is a dog's sharpest sense.

When a dog is hot, it pants with its tongue hanging out so that perspiration from the tongue will evaporate and cool the animal.

A dog has 42 teeth, 20 in the upper jaw and 22 in the lower jaw.

Each of the dog's body cells contains 39 pairs of chromosomes (heredity-carrying structures), the most of any mammal.

A dog experiences emotion. For example, it appears to become upset during a family dispute, and it apparently suffers anxiety when lost.

A GLOSSARY OF DOG TERMS

Bitch—a female dog.

Breed—a variety of dog with consistent traits.

Crop—to clip off the top of a puppy's ears to make them stand erect; illegal in some countries.

Dock—to shorten a puppy's tail by cutting off a portion.

Dog—strictly speaking, a male canine.

Feathering—long fringes of hair on the ears, legs, and tail of some dogs.

Kennel—a place where dogs are bred and boarded.

License—permission by a government agency enabling anyone to keep a dog; usually requires a fee.

Mongrel—a dog whose parents were not of the same breed.

Mutt—another name for a mongrel.

Pedigree—a listing of the names of a dog's recent ancestors.

Purebred—a dog whose parents and other ancestors were all of the same breed.

Registration Papers—proof that the names of a purebred and its parents are on record at a dog registry, such as the American Kennel Club (AKC).

Stud—a male used for breeding.

The Body of a Dog

Dogs grow to various sizes. The Irish wolfhound, for example, stands about 32 inches high at the withers, or top of the shoulders. The chihuahua, however, stands about five inches.

The color of a dog's coat, or hair cover, also ranges widely, even within a breed. Some dogs are all black. Others are all white. Some have light markings on portions of their bodies and darker coloration elsewhere. Or, they may have a solid color other than black. All dogs have some hair cover, even the so-called hairless ones.

The shape of a dog is determined by three major structures—the head, the body, and the legs. The size and form of these structures vary greatly as do, for example, coloration and hair characteristics.

The Head

There are two basic head shapes—a narrow skull with a long face and a wide skull with a short face—plus several intermediate head shapes. Long-faced dogs, such as the German shepherd and the cocker spaniel, may have jaws eight inches long. By contrast, the nose of small-faced dogs, such as the Pekingese and the pug, may be less than an inch from the eyes.

Dogs have 42 teeth. Six pairs of sharp incisor teeth are in front of the mouth, flanked by two pairs of large canine ("dog") teeth. The other teeth are premolars and molars. The incisors and the canines are very important because the dog bites and tears at its food with these teeth.

Air breathed in through the dog's nose passes on its way to the lungs through the two nasal cavities behind the nose. These cavities are lined by a mucous membrane containing many nerve endings stimulated by odors. Smell is the dog's most acute sense. A dog continually sniffs the air, the ground, and nearby objects to learn what is happening around it. The indentation in the dog's forehead just above eye level is called the stop. The stop in some dogs is deeper than that in others.

The fairly thin tongue of the dog is used mainly for guiding food to the throat, for licking the coat clean, and for perspiration. When a dog is overheated, it cools off by hanging its tongue out and panting. As it pants, the evaporation of perspiration from its tongue cools the animal. The dog also sweats through the pads on its paws and—slightly—through its skin.

A dog's ears either stick up or hang down. The earliest dogs probably had erect ears, but the ears began to droop in smaller, later breeds because of excessive ear skin. Dogs have a fine sense of hearing. They can hear sounds at frequencies too high for man to hear. This is why dogs can respond to "silent" whistles.

Each eye of a dog has three eyelids, the main upper and lower lids and a third lid hidden between them in the inner corner of the eye. The third eyelid can sweep across the transparent cornea of the eye and clean it like a windshield wiper.

The head and body of a dog are connected by its neck. The neck may be long or short, depending on the size of the seven bones that support it. The length of the vocal cords in the neck is a factor influencing the pitch and loudness of a dog's voice—its barks, grunts, and howls.

The Body

The body of a dog contains most of its vital organs. The heart, lungs, stomach, and intestines are located there. So too are its sex organs, kidneys, and bladder. The 13 ribs of the dog's chest wrap around the heart and lungs. Since these organs influence the animal's speed and stamina, chest size can be an indication of these traits.

All dogs have 27 bones from the skull to the point where the tail begins. The number of tailbones, however, and therefore the length of the tail, varies from breed to breed.

The body may be covered with straight or with wavy hair. Hair shafts emerge from tiny follicles in the skin. The shafts are connected to tiny muscles that cause the dog's hair to stand up, or bristle, when they contract. During times of stress, a dog raises its hackles—the hair along the neck and spine. Special sensory hairs called whiskers are near the nose, but their usefulness is doubtful because a dog rarely relies on the sense of touch.

The Legs

The front legs and back legs of a dog are also called the forelimbs and hind limbs. A dog uses its legs for movement, for scratching, and, in some breeds, for digging.

Each of the forelimbs is connected to the body by a long, narrow scapula, or shoulder blade. Its lower part, in turn, forms a shoulder joint with the humerus, the upper forelimb bone. The lower forelimb bones, the radius and the ulna, are fused at two points and act as a single bone.

The foot, or paw, has five toes. One of them—the dewclaw—is too high to be of any use. It is a vestigial part and is often surgically removed from puppies. The toes of the foot are composed of a number of bones. A toenail, or claw, emerges from the end of each toe. The foot also has cushiony pads for each toe and two larger pads farther up the paw. Dogs perspire through their pads.

Each of the two hind limbs is connected to the body at the pelvic bone. The upper portion of the femur, or thighbone, fits into a socket in the pelvic bone to form the hip joint. The tibia and the fibula are beneath. They make up the lower thigh. The joint where their upper portions link with the femur is called the stifle. The joint where their lower portions link with the foot bones of the hind limbs is called the hock. Like the forefeet, the hind feet have pads and four functional toes, although a dewclaw is sometimes present.

THE DOG'S BODY

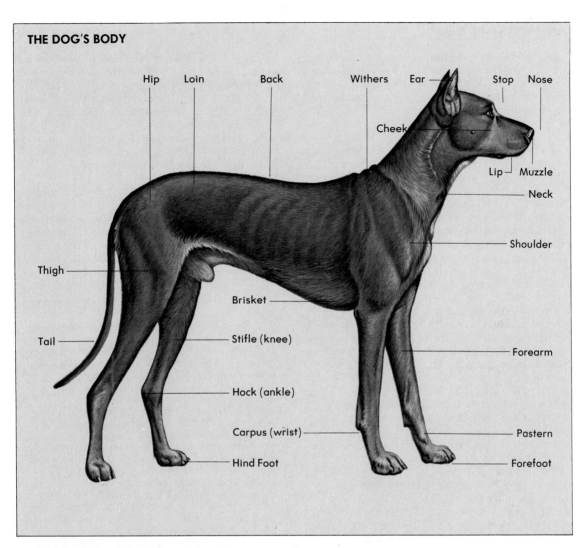

Hip — Loin — Back — Withers — Ear — Stop — Nose

Cheek

Lip — Muzzle

Neck

Shoulder

Thigh

Brisket

Stifle (knee)

Forearm

Tail

Hock (ankle)

Carpus (wrist) — Pastern

Hind Foot — Forefoot

THE DOG'S FEET

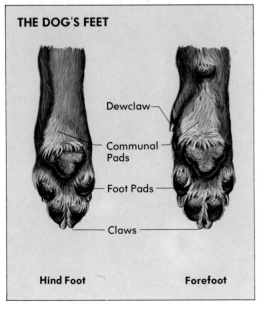

Dewclaw

Communal Pads

Foot Pads

Claws

Hind Foot **Forefoot**

THE DOG'S SKELETON

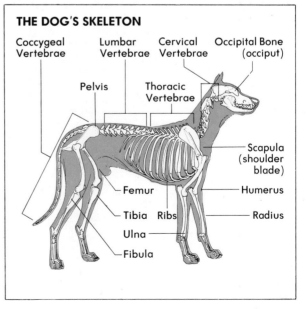

Coccygeal Vertebrae — Lumbar Vertebrae — Cervical Vertebrae — Occipital Bone (occiput)

Pelvis — Thoracic Vertebrae

Scapula (shoulder blade)

Femur — Humerus

Tibia — Ribs — Radius

Ulna

Fibula

Life History of a Dog

The normal life span of a small or medium-size dog is about 15 years. A large dog lives only about ten years, however. On the average, a ten-month-old dog is sexually mature. Smaller bitches go into their first heat (become responsive to their first mating) at an earlier age than larger ones.

Fetal puppies grow and develop in their mother's womb before they are whelped, or born. Whelping is usually a painless task for the bitch. After each of her litter is whelped, she licks the pup as dry as she can. The newborn, hungry puppies snuggle by the teats on the bitch's underside, where she nurses them. The puppies draw nourishing milk from their mother until they are weaned, or given food more solid than milk to eat. The time of weaning depends on the size of the litter and the amount of milk in the bitch. Sometimes, it occurs as early as three weeks. Puppies should not be weaned, however, any later than their seventh week.

After its birth the puppy grows, becomes stronger, and gains in alertness. Its eyes, which are closed at birth, open when it is between one and two weeks old. It then begins to see. Its first teeth, the puppy or milk teeth, erupt through the gums during the third to sixth week of its life. Puppy teeth are mostly incisors and canines. By the third month, the first of the permanent teeth work through, and by the seventh month they all do. By the time it reaches its first birthday a puppy is considered a dog.

Although sexually mature beforehand, a dog ordinarily does not attain full growth until its first birthday or even later. By this time, however, it is capable of a wide range of responses to its environment. When it meets another dog, its ear position indicates how interested it is in the newcomer. If its ears are erect, it is concentrating on the other. If its ears are pointing forward, it is on the alert. If the dog holds its tail high and wags it, the animal is happy and confident.

If it drops its tail and remains still, the dog is apprehensive. If it pulls its tail between its legs, the dog is afraid. If on meeting a person or another dog it pulls back its lips and growls, it is making a threat. If it bares its teeth without growling, the dog is ready to attack and bite. A male dog establishes a territory by marking the boundaries with urine, scent from the anal glands, or even feces. The dog will then defend that territory against intruders. Every six or seven months a female dog goes into heat and will mate with nearly any available male within the three-week length of her heat.

When a dog reaches old age, its eyes begin to weaken. Cataracts may also form in the lenses of its eyes. The hair on its muzzle turns gray. The old dog begins to feel numerous aches and pains and might become easily irritated and snap at members of the family. Its body systems are breaking down, and it can no longer behave as it did when younger.

BARRY TO THE RESCUE

The monks of the Hospice of St. Bernard, high in the Great St. Bernard Pass between Switzerland and Italy, for several hundred years have raised a hardy breed of dogs able to move through snow and rescue trapped persons. About 150 years ago lived a St. Bernard named Barry. The dog was so brave and determined that it saved some 40 persons at different times. Barry's keen sense of smell guided it to the snow-trapped victim. Like all St. Bernards on rescue missions, Barry would clear away snow from the victim if it was not too deep, lie on top of the person to warm him, and bark to summon the monks. Once, Barry even pulled a boy off an icy ledge. In honor of the exploits of this brave dog the monks have given the name Barry to the best of each new litter of St. Bernards whelped at the hospice. St. Bernards have never carried small casks of brandy around their necks on rescues, as popularly believed. Sometimes, however, they are posed with casks to please tourists.

The mother dog nurses her puppies until they are weaned —usually between three and seven weeks.

Walter Chandoha

Breeds of Dogs

Several hundred dog breeds exist throughout the world. For a puppy to be a purebred dog, its sire and dam (father and mother) both must be of the same breed, as must its ancestors dating back to the establishment of the breed. Kennel clubs in many countries set their own standards. In the United States the American Kennel Club (AKC) determines the standards for breeds it recognizes.

The AKC recognizes six groups of breeds—sporting dogs, hounds, working dogs, terriers, toys, and non-sporting dogs. *Sporting dogs* hunt, locate (point), and retrieve game birds. *Hounds* hunt all game except birds. *Working dogs* can do such jobs as herding farm animals, pulling sleds and carts, and guarding life and property. *Terriers* were once bred to ferret out rodents but are now bred as house pets. *Toys* are tiny dogs bred mainly as pets. *Non-sporting dogs* are those purebreds not included in the other categories. AKC-recognized breeds are illustrated here and on the following pages.

Country of Breed Origin
Each breed is accompanied by the flag of its country of origin, as best determined by authorities.

🇲🇽 Mexico

Type of Dog
△ Sporting Dog   ☐ Terrier
✚ Hound   ◯ Toy
◇ Working Dog   ▽ Non-Sporting

Shoulder Height and Weight
Many height and weight ranges of the breeds are derived from American Kennel Club sources.

Relative Size of Each Breed
Each illustration contains a scale arrow that indicates the size of a dog of the illustrated breed in relation to the height of a page of Compton's Encyclopedia.

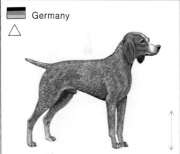
United Kingdom
△

Pointer
Height: 23–28 in.
Weight: 45–75 lbs.

Germany
△

German Shorthaired Pointer
Height: 21–25 in.
Weight: 45–70 lbs.

Germany
△

German Wirehaired Pointer
Height: 22–26 in.
Weight: 45–70 lbs.

United States
△

Chesapeake Bay Retriever
Height: 21–26 in.
Weight: 55–75 lbs.

United Kingdom
△

Curly-Coated Retriever
Height: 22–24 in.
Weight: 55–70 lbs.

United Kingdom
△

Flat-Coated Retriever
Height: 21½–24 in.
Weight: 60–70 lbs.

United Kingdom
△

Golden Retriever
Height: 21½–24 in.
Weight: 60–75 lbs.

Canada
△

Labrador Retriever
Height: 21½–24½ in.
Weight: 55–75 lbs.

197

 United Kingdom

English Setter
Height: 23–25 in.
Weight: 50–70 lbs.

 United Kingdom

Gordon Setter
Height: 23–27 in.
Weight: 45–80 lbs.

 Ireland

Irish Setter
Height: 25–27 in.
Weight: 60–70 lbs.

 United States

American Water Spaniel
Height: 15–18 in.
Weight: 25–45 lbs.

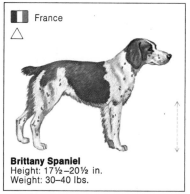 France

Brittany Spaniel
Height: 17½–20½ in.
Weight: 30–40 lbs.

 United Kingdom

Clumber Spaniel
Height: 14–18 in.
Weight: 35–65 lbs.

 United States

Cocker Spaniel
Height: 14–15½ in.
Weight: 22–28 lbs.

 United Kingdom

English Cocker Spaniel
Height: 15–17 in.
Weight: 26–34 lbs.

 United Kingdom

English Springer Spaniel
Height: 17–20 in.
Weight: 35–55 lbs.

 United Kingdom

Field Spaniel
Height: 17–18 in.
Weight: 35–50 lbs.

 Ireland

Irish Water Spaniel
Height: 21–24 in.
Weight: 45–65 lbs.

 United Kingdom

Sussex Spaniel
Height: 14–16 in.
Weight: 35–45 lbs.

United Kingdom

Welsh Springer Spaniel
Height: 15½–17 in.
Weight: 35–45 lbs.

Hungary

Vizsla
Height: 21–24 in.
Weight: 40–60 lbs.

Germany

Weimaraner
Height: 23–27 in.
Weight: 55–85 lbs.

France

Wirehaired Pointing Griffon
Height: 19½–23½ in.
Weight: 45–60 lbs.

Afghanistan

Afghan Hound
Height: 24–28 in.
Weight: 50–60 lbs.

Egypt

Basenji
Height: 16–17 in.
Weight: 22–24 lbs.

France

Basset Hound
Height: 10–15 in.
Weight: 25–40 lbs.

United Kingdom

Beagle*
Height: 13 in. and under; 13–15 in.
Weight: 18 lbs.; 30 lbs.

United States

Black and Tan Coonhound
Height: 23–27 in.
Weight: 70–85 lbs.

United Kingdom

Bloodhound
Height: 23–27 in.
Weight: 80–110 lbs.

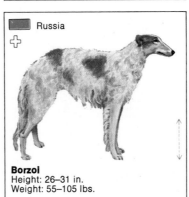

Russia

Borzoi
Height: 26–31 in.
Weight: 55–105 lbs.

Germany

Dachshund
Height: 5–9 in.
Weight: 5–20 lbs.

*Two categories of the beagle breed are recognized by the American Kennel Club.

 United States

American Foxhound
Height: 21–25 in.
Weight: 60–70 lbs.

 United Kingdom

English Foxhound
Height: 21–25 in.
Weight: 60–70 lbs.

 Egypt

Greyhound
Height: 25–27 in.
Weight: 60–70 lbs.

 United Kingdom

Harrier
Height: 19–21 in.
Weight: 40–50 lbs.

 Ireland

Irish Wolfhound
Height: 30–33 in.
Weight: 105–140 lbs.

 Norway

Norwegian Elkhound
Height: 19¼–20½ in.
Weight: 40–50 lbs.

 United Kingdom

Otter Hound
Height: 24–26 in.
Weight: 55–65 lbs.

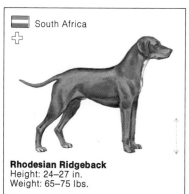 South Africa

Rhodesian Ridgeback
Height: 24–27 in.
Weight: 65–75 lbs.

 Egypt

Saluki
Height: 18–28 in.
Weight: 45–60 lbs.

 United Kingdom

Scottish Deerhound
Height: 28–32 in.
Weight: 75–110 lbs.

 United Kingdom

Whippet
Height: 18–22 in.
Weight: 12–28 lbs.

 United States

Alaskan Malamute
Height: 20–25 in.
Weight: 50–85 lbs.

Belgium

Belgian Malinois
Height: 22–26 in.
Weight: 50–60 lbs.

Belgium

Belgian Sheepdog
Height: 22–26 in.
Weight: 50–60 lbs.

Belgium

Belgian Tervuren
Height: 22–26 in.
Weight: 50–60 lbs.

Switzerland

Bernese Mountain Dog
Height: 21–27½ in.
Weight: 50–70 lbs.

Belgium

Bouvier des Flandres
Height: 22¾–27½ in.
Weight: 60–70 lbs.

Germany

Boxer
Height: 21–25 in.
Weight: 60–75 lbs.

France

Briard
Height: 22–27 in.
Weight: 70–80 lbs.

United Kingdom

Bullmastiff
Height: 24–27 in.
Weight: 100–130 lbs.

United Kingdom

Collie
Height: 22–26 in.
Weight: 50–75 lbs.

Germany

Doberman Pinscher
Height: 24–28 in.
Weight: 60–75 lbs.

Germany

German Shepherd Dog
Height: 22–26 in.
Weight: 60–85 lbs.

Germany

Giant Schnauzer
Height: 23½–27½ in.
Weight: 65–78 lbs.

 Germany

Great Dane
Height: 28–34 in.
Weight: 120–150 lbs.

 France

Great Pyrenees
Height: 25–32 in.
Weight: 90–125 lbs.

 Hungary

Komondor
Height: 23½–31½ in.
Weight: 75–90 lbs.

 Tibet

Kuvasz
Height: 24–26 in.
Weight: 60–70 lbs.

 United Kingdom

Mastiff
Height: 27½–33 in.
Weight: 165–185 lbs.

 Canada

Newfoundland
Height: 25–28 in.
Weight: 110–150 lbs.

 United Kingdom

Old English Sheepdog
Height: 21–25 in.
Weight: 55–65 lbs.

 Hungary

Puli
Height: 16–19 in.
Weight: 25–35 lbs.

 Germany

Rottweiler
Height: 21¾–27 in.
Weight: 75–90 lbs.

 Switzerland

St. Bernard
Height: 25½–29 in.
Weight: 140–170 lbs.

 Russia

Samoyed
Height: 19–23½ in.
Weight: 35–65 lbs.

 United Kingdom

Shetland Sheepdog
Height: 13–16 in.
Weight: 14–16 lbs.

Russia

Siberian Husky
Height: 20–23½ in.
Weight: 35–60 lbs.

Germany

Standard Schnauzer
Height: 17½–19½ in.
Weight: 27–37 lbs.

United Kingdom

Welsh Corgi (Cardigan)
Height: 11–12 in.
Weight: 15–25 lbs.

United Kingdom

Welsh Corgi (Pembroke)
Height: 10–12 in.
Weight: 18–24 lbs.

United Kingdom

Airedale Terrier
Height: 22–23 in.
Weight: 40–50 lbs.

Australia

Australian Terrier
Height: 9–10 in.
Weight: 12–14 lbs.

United Kingdom

Bedlington Terrier
Height: 15–17½ in.
Weight: 17–23 lbs.

United Kingdom

Border Terrier
Height: 11–13 in.
Weight: 11½–15½ lbs.

United Kingdom

Bull Terrier
Height: 19–22 in.
Weight: 30–60 lbs.

United Kingdom

Cairn Terrier
Height: 9½–10 in.
Weight: 13–14 lbs.

United Kingdom

Dandie Dinmont Terrier
Height: 8–11 in.
Weight: 18–24 lbs.

United Kingdom

Fox Terrier
Height: 14½–15½ in.
Weight: 15–19 lbs.

 Ireland

Irish Terrier
Height: 16½–18 in.
Weight: 25–27 lbs.

 Ireland

Kerry Blue Terrier
Height: 17½–19½ in.
Weight: 29–40 lbs.

 United Kingdom

Lakeland Terrier
Height: 13–15 in.
Weight: 15–17 lbs.

 United Kingdom

Manchester Terrier †
Height: 14–16 in.; 6–7 in.
Weight: 12–22 lbs.; 5–12 lbs.

 Germany

Miniature Schnauzer
Height: 12–14 in.
Weight: 13–15 lbs.

 United Kingdom

Norwich Terrier
Height: 9–11 in.
Weight: 10–14 lbs.

 United Kingdom

Scottish Terrier
Height: 9–10 in.
Weight: 18–22 lbs.

 United Kingdom

Sealyham Terrier
Height: 10–10½ in.
Weight: 20–21 lbs.

 United Kingdom

Skye Terrier
Height: 7½–10 in.
Weight: 23–25 lbs.

 United States

Staffordshire Terrier
Height: 17–19 in.
Weight: 35–50 lbs.

 United Kingdom

Welsh Terrier
Height: 14–15 in.
Weight: 18–20 lbs.

 United Kingdom

West Highland White Terrier
Height: 10–11 in.
Weight: 13–19 lbs.

†Standard and toy varieties of the Manchester terrier breed are recognized by the American Kennel Club. The larger figures are for the standard; the smaller for the toy.

Germany

Affenpinscher
Height: 8–10¼ in.
Weight: 7–8 lbs.

Belgium

Brussels Griffon
Height: 7–8 in.
Weight: 5–12 lbs.

Mexico

Chihuahua
Height: 5 in.
Weight: 1–6 lbs.

United Kingdom

English Toy Spaniel
Height: 9–10 in.
Weight: 9–12 lbs.

Italy

Italian Greyhound
Height: 13–15 in.
Weight: 7–10 lbs.

Japan

Japanese Spaniel
Height: 8–9 in.
Weight: 6–7 lbs.

Malta

Maltese
Height: 5 in.
Weight: 4–6 lbs.

Germany

Miniature Pinscher
Height: 10–11½ in.
Weight: 8–10 lbs.

Italy

Papillon
Height: 8–11 in.
Weight: 5–11 lbs.

China

Pekingese
Height: 6–9 in.
Weight: 6–14 lbs.

Germany

Pomeranian
Height: 5½–7 in.
Weight: 3–7 lbs.

China

Pug
Height: 10–11 in.
Weight: 14–18 lbs.

Tibet

Shih Tzu (pronounced "shid zoo")
Height: 8–11 in.
Weight: 9–18 lbs.

Australia

Silky Terrier
Height: 9–10 in.
Weight: 8–10 lbs.

United Kingdom

Yorkshire Terrier
Height: 8–9 in.
Weight: 4–7 lbs.

United States

Boston Terrier
Height: 14–17 in.
Weight: 13–25 lbs.

United Kingdom

Bulldog
Height: 13½–15 in.
Weight: 40–50 lbs.

China

Chow Chow
Height: 18–20 in.
Weight: 50–60 lbs.

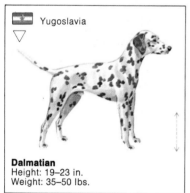

Yugoslavia

Dalmatian
Height: 19–23 in.
Weight: 35–50 lbs.

France

French Bulldog
Height: 11–12 in.
Weight: 19–28 lbs.

Netherlands

Keeshond
Height: 17–18 in.
Weight: 32–40 lbs.

Tibet

Lhasa Apso
Height: 10–11 in.
Weight: 13–15 lbs.

France

Poodle‡
Height: over 15 in.; 10 in. or under
Weight: 40–55 lbs.; 5–7 lbs.

Belgium

Schipperke
Height: 12–13 in.
Weight: 14–18 lbs.

206

‡Standard and toy varieties of the poodle breed are recognized by the American Kennel Club.
The larger figures are for the standard; the smaller for the toy.

Over the years dogs have entertained man, joined him on the hunt, herded his other domestic animals, and pulled his loads. Greyhound racing (top), related to the ancient sport of coursing, has avid fans throughout the world today. The swift greyhounds streak around the track in pursuit of a mechanical rabbit at speeds of almost 40 miles an hour. Duck hunters rely on the retrieving skills of their sporting dogs, such as the Labrador retriever (left), to snag their game. The "soft mouth" of retrievers and spaniels permits them to return game in an undamaged condition. This trait is due to the underdevelopment of the cheek muscles of these dogs. Some working dogs, such as the border collie (above), do an amazing job of herding animals. The border collie can dominate a flock of sheep with its strong stare and keep the flock in a tight group. Dogsleds pulled by rugged teams of huskies, malamutes, or samoyeds were for years an important form of transportation in the frozen North. Dogsled races featuring teams of these breeds or mixtures of them are still held in the colder parts of the United States and Canada (below).

207

Walter Chandoha

Whether the puppy you choose is male or female, large or small, purebred or mongrel, it should be a healthy dog whose personality and needs fit into your way of life.

A balanced diet that is nourishing and that your dog enjoys is necessary for his scheduled feedings. A puppy must also have a bowl of fresh water available at all times.

Walter Chandoha

Choosing a Dog

An important thing to consider when buying a dog is whether it will fit comfortably into your quarters when it reaches adult size. The presence of young children in the family should also be a factor in selection. A dog for a growing family must be able to stand rough treatment. A toy dog would be a poor choice for such a family because its tiny bones are fragile enough to break when children handle it roughly. In general larger dogs are better adapted both physically and temperamentally for a young family.

A dog can be acquired from a number of sources. It can be bought from a reputable pet shop or from a kennel. Newspaper advertisements describe pups for sale from private parties. Local humane societies have dogs available, too. From whatever source you get a dog, however, make certain it is healthy. Ask for proof, if possible, that it has received all the necessary immunizing shots. Also, get a written reminder of whatever shots and other care the pup will need after you take it home. Even if a puppy has had shots against distemper and hepatitis, it will need booster shots. Later, it will need a rabies shot. A reputable pet shop or kennel ordinarily will have taken care of these details but get a signed verification from a veterinarian anyway.

Should you acquire a male or a female dog? Males are usually larger, stronger, and more aggressive, and they make excellent watchdogs. On the other hand, females are usually more affectionate and gentle, and if they are purebred dogs and are mated with males of their breed, their pups can be sold for profit. The female has a strong maternal instinct and will guard children as well as she does her own pups. Dogs of either sex, however, can be neutered. Castration, the removal of the testes, makes a male dog infertile and more docile. Spaying, or removal of the ovaries, makes a female dog infertile.

Should you buy a purebred or a mongrel? This question is hard to answer because a purebred dog sometimes turns out to be less desirable than expected, while a mongrel often makes an alert, intelligent, and delightful family pet. As a rule, a purebred pup inherits the traits of its breed. As a result, few surprises in body form and temperament arise when the pup reaches adulthood. If you want to buy a purebred but are unfamiliar with the breed, first look at a full-grown dog of the breed. The puppy will grow to resemble it. If you want to buy a mongrel, try to see its sire and dam. They will display any unwanted trait that may lie hidden in the puppy.

Ideally, children and puppies should grow up together. Caution should be taken, however, when dog owners bring a newborn baby home. Pampered dogs sometimes resent the newcomer because the baby receives most of the parents' attention. They should make an effort to pay attention to the dog, too.

A puppy should be at least eight or nine weeks old before it is taken from its home kennel. By this time it will have been weaned and eating regular food. At first, the puppy must be fed four times a day. By the time it is mature, feedings should be down to twice a day or even once a day in the case of a dog that gets little exercise. Diet and feeding instructions should accompany the puppy. If it was eating a prepared dog food at the kennel, the same diet should be maintained until the puppy shows its dislike of it by "going off its feed," or refusing to eat. Several types of dog food may have to be tried before the dog settles on a favorite. If it refuses all the choices offered, however, consult the breeder—or, even better, your veterinarian —for help.

Caring for a Dog

Dog owners are responsible for feeding, housebreaking, and cleaning their pets. They should also oversee the health of their dogs. It's best to consult a veterinarian at the first sign of a dog ailment.

A dog can be fed either the dry meal, biscuit, semimoist and cellophane-wrapped, or canned type of dog food. Whichever type is selected must contain the carbohydrates, fats, proteins, minerals, and vitamins essential for the animal's well-being. As a rule, the cost of feeding a large dog can be kept low by giving it the inexpensive dry meal type.

A puppy should be housebroken as soon as possible. When the puppy takes its first water or food, note how long it takes for the puppy to urinate or defecate. When you discover the schedule, take the pup outside when the prescribed time has elapsed after feeding or drinking. Soon, the puppy will associate the outdoors with toilet function and will no longer soil the house or the newspapers that have been spread around its living area.

Young puppies should not be excessively groomed. A daily brushing with a soft brush is sufficient to remove surface dust and dirt. Authorities disagree as to whether a puppy should be bathed or not. Some believe that to conserve its natural skin oils a pup should not be completely bathed until its first birthday. Mud and deep dirt in its coat, however, can be removed with a damp, warm washrag. Afterward, the puppy should be completely dried with a rough towel. A dog can then have a complete bath when it is old enough, but it must be kept in the house until thoroughly dry, especially during winter.

Dog nails should be trimmed periodically. Cut only the transparent part of the nail past the foot pads. Close clipping can cut into the "quick,"—the portion of nail that has nerves and blood vessels—and hurt the animal. Special clippers can be purchased for trimming dog nails.

Canine Pests and Diseases

The flea is the dog's most common pest. Washing the dog with special soap can remove fleas. Flea-preventive collars are also available to protect dogs with thin coats. Flea collars, however, should not be used on short-haired, single-coated dogs—such as greyhounds, whippets, and pointers—because of skin irritation.

The tick poses a greater danger to the dog. This pest attaches itself to the dog's skin and sucks its blood. It also carries certain canine and human diseases. An owner can remove ticks from his dog by first dabbing alcohol on the infested area and then picking the parasites off with tweezers, making sure that the entire tick is removed.

Worms and other intestinal parasites often infest puppies. A puppy's fecal stools should be checked periodically for them. If worms are detected, take a sample of the infested stool to a veterinarian so that the type of parasite can be determined and the proper

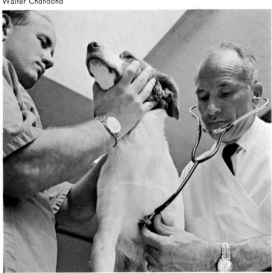

It is always best to consult a trusted veterinarian at the first sign of a dog ailment. He will also make certain that all shots and grooming needs are taken care of.

treatment rendered. Commercial deworming medicines should be avoided unless prescribed by a veterinarian.

A dog is obviously sick when it becomes listless and eats without enthusiasm. Its bowel movements may be irregular. It might also have pale, whitish gums and tongue, dull eyes, and a dry coat. A sick dog often runs a fever. A dog's temperature is best taken with a rectal thermometer. Normal body temperature of a dog is 101.5° F. A dog's pulse can be taken by pressing your finger against the blood vessel in the V formed where the undersides of the hind legs attach to the body. Normal pulse rate of a dog is between 75 and 100 beats per minute.

A dog can be infected by several viruses, including those that cause distemper, canine hepatitis, and rabies. A spirochete-caused ailment called leptospirosis is also common among dogs. Puppies should be vaccinated against each of these diseases. If any of them should arise, however, the suffering dog must be taken to a veterinarian for treatment.

Distemper affects the mucous membranes of the dog's respiratory tract. The symptoms resemble those of human influenza. Distemper causes the dog's temperature to rise two to three degrees above normal. *Canine hepatitis* affects the dog's liver and abdominal organs. It is marked by a fever as high as 105° F, thirst, diarrhea, and vomiting. A dog with hepatitis may hump its back and try to rub its belly against the floor to relieve the pain.

Rabies is a disease that can pass to humans who have been bitten by infected dogs. Rabies is almost always fatal when the virus gets to the brain. Brain inflammation causes the erratic behavior that is sometimes seen in a rabid dog. *Leptospirosis* is sometimes confused with hepatitis. However, leptospirosis is characterized by discolored and abnormal-smelling urine. At the onset of the disease, the dog's body temperature might soar as high as 105° F.

Training a Dog

Any young dog can be trained to understand commands and to do simple tricks. When correctly trained, it is conditioned to respond to your commands, noises, or gestures. Once an owner decides to train his puppy, however, he must be willing to stick with the job until the puppy learns the task. First, the owner should select a simple "call" name for the animal. The call name should be used frequently so the puppy can learn to recognize the sound of it.

A training session is best begun when the puppy is hungry because it is more alert at that time. Also, the owner can reinforce the dog's correct responses to commands with a dog biscuit or meat tidbit, as well as with enthusiastic petting and praise. The hungry dog is more apt to associate the correct performance of a task with a food reward.

To get the puppy into a collar at first, entice it to you by extending your open hands, pet it and say "good dog" (and include its name) when it comes, and finally slip the collar around its neck. Then attach a leash to the collar. If the puppy has confidence in you, it will walk along with you even though it is wearing the leash. A metal chain leash is usually

After being effectively trained, purebred pedigreed dogs may be entered in shows sponsored by kennel clubs under the auspices of the AKC. Field trials (above) judge hunting abilities and such skills as tracking, pointing, flushing, and retrieving. Bench shows and obedience trials (below) judge appearance and performance.

(Above) Ronny Jaques—Photo Researchers, (below) Walter Chandoha

best because the puppy will not be able to chew and play with it.

Wait until a puppy is at least six months old before trying to teach it tricks, but do teach it the meaning of "no" at an earlier age. The young dog must be corrected vocally each time it does something that you disapprove of. If you are consistent, it soon learns by your tone of voice what pleases you and what displeases you. Formal training sessions should entail no more than ten minutes of work at a time, and they should never tire the dog.

To teach the command "sit," keep the dog on your left side and pull up on its leash with your right hand while gently but firmly pushing its hindquarters to the floor. While doing this, say the command "sit" with authority. Reinforce its correct actions with a tidbit.

To teach the command "stay," work with the puppy after it has learned to sit. While it is sitting, raise your palm to the dog and order it to "stay." It will probably try to get up, so tell it "no." Whenever it remains in the sitting position after you have given the "stay" command, reward the dog with a tidbit.

More effort might be needed to teach the command "come." When the dog has learned to stay, command it to "come" and call it by name. When it comes to you, lavish the dog with praise and give it a snack. A very stubborn dog might have to be pulled with a cord tied around its collar while the command is given. If this is necessary, be firm but accompany the command with a friendly hand gesture. Many tugs may be necessary until the reluctant dog learns the meaning of "come."

Do not be impatient with a puppy when teaching it simple tricks, and never get angry. If the training sessions are not going well, break them off and resume them later in the day or even on another day. In addition, give praise and tidbits to the dog only when they are earned.

Dog Shows

When their dogs are effectively trained, owners of purebred, pedigreed dogs may enter them in shows sponsored by local kennel clubs, under the auspices of the American Kennel Club (AKC). Winners are awarded points based on how well they conform to breed standards. Five points is the top mark a dog can win in any single show. To gain the coveted title "Champion," a dog must have accumulated 15 points in a series of shows, with at least two major wins (three points or more). Dog shows are usually called *bench shows* because the dogs wait in raised stalls or benches before being judged in the show ring. *Obedience trials* may be held separately or as part of a larger show. These trials test how well dogs can perform various tasks. The top mark in obedience trials is 200 points. *Field trials* judge the hunting abilities of sporting dogs and hounds in realistic outdoor settings. Such skills as tracking, pointing, flushing, and retrieving are tested in these trials.

The unique partnership of dog and man has long been depicted in various art forms. The Flemish painter Pieter Brueghel painted dogs in 'Hunters in the Snow' (above) and also in his 'Massacre of the Innocents', 'Netherlandish Proverbs', and 'Bridle Procession'.

The Egyptian god Anubis was always depicted with a doglike head.

Evolution of the Dog

The dog traces its ancestry back to a five-toed, weasellike animal called *Miacis*, which lived in the Eocene epoch about 40 million years ago. This animal was the forebear of the cat, raccoon, bear, hyena, and civet, as well as of the wolf, fox, jackal, and dog. Miacis, undoubtedly a tree climber, probably also lived in a den. Like all den dwellers, it no doubt left its quarters for toilet functions so that the den would remain clean. The ease of housebreaking a modern dog probably harks back to this instinct. Next in evolutionary line from Miacis was an Oligocene animal called *Cynodictis*, which somewhat resembled the modern dog. Cynodictis lived about 20 million years ago. Its fifth toe, which would eventually become the dewclaw, showed signs of shortening. Cynodictis had 42 teeth and probably the anal glands that a dog still has. Cynodictis was also developing feet and toes suited for running. The modern civet—a "living fossil"—resembles that ancient animal (*see* Civet Cat). After a few more intermediate stages the evolution of the dog moved on to the extremely doglike animal called *Tomarctus*, which lived about 10 million years ago during the late Miocene epoch. Tomarctus probably developed the strong social instincts that still prevail in the dog and most of its close relatives, excluding the fox. The Canidae, the family that includes the true dog and its close relatives, stemmed directly from Tomarctus. Members of the genus *Canis*—which includes the dog, wolf, and jackal—developed into their present form about a million years ago during the Pleistocene epoch.

The Partnership of Dog and Man

Authorities agree that the dog was the first of man's domesticated animals. How and when this domestication took place, however, remains unknown. A 50,000-year-old cave painting in Europe seems to show a doglike animal hunting with man. But most experts believe the dog was domesticated only within the last 15,000 years. Moreover, fossil remains that would substantiate the presence of dogs with humans have not yet been unearthed for periods earlier than about 10,000 B.C. One theory holds that humans took wolf pups back to their camp or cave, reared them, allowed the tame wolves to hunt with them, and later accepted pups of the tame wolves into the family circle. Another theory suggests that dogs were attracted to food scraps dumped as waste near human living sites. As they scavenged and kept the site clean, the dogs rendered a service to the humans. In turn, the humans would accept the presence of the scavengers and would not drive them away. Still other theories maintain that the dog was domesticated to pull sleds and other conveyances bearing the heavy game killed by man, to provide a ready source of food, or to act as a sacrificial animal for magical or religious purposes.

Studies of primitive human societies still in existence tend to substantiate some of these theories. Whatever the ultimate reason for the domestication of the dog, however, the final submission must have been the consequence of thousands of years of caution and "deliberation" by the dog before it would cast its lot with man. Also, the dog, itself a hunter, had

Polished, iridescent green-glazed pottery dog of the Han Dynasty, China (206 B.C.-A.D. 220)

'The Cup of Coffee', Pierre Bonnard, France (about 1914)

Pre-Columbian ceramic spout vessel of a dog gnawing a bone, Tiahuanaco Culture, South America (A.D. 700–1000)

to suppress its desire to kill the other animals domesticated by man. Instead, it had to learn to protect them.

Some *feral* dogs live today; that is, they have returned to the wild state. The dingo of Australia, for example, spends only a portion of its time with man. When the mating urge seizes it, the dog runs off to the wild. Another, the dhole of India, is reputed to be a fierce, untamable dog.

The partnership between dog and master has long been shown in paintings and other art forms and in writings. Prehistoric paintings done about 15,000 years ago on the walls of Spanish caves show doglike animals accompanying humans on a hunt. Dogs are amply illustrated in the sculptures and pottery of ancient Assyria, Egypt, and Greece. The ancient Egyptians worshiped Anubis as the god of death. Anubis was portrayed with the head of a jackal or a dog. The Egyptians were great lovers of dogs and were responsible for developing many breeds by crossing dogs with jackals, wolves, and foxes.

Homer, the Greek author of the 'Odyssey' in the 9th century B.C., is believed to be one of the first to write about dogs. They were mentioned often in his classic epic. The ancient Greeks believed that the gates of the underworld were guarded by a savage three-headed dog named Cerberus. The belief might have been derived from the widespread practice in Greece of using watchdogs. The ancient Romans relied on watchdogs, too. So many dogs were kept in the larger Roman cities that any house with a watchdog was required to have a sign warning "Cave Canem" (Beware the Dog). The Romans also used

dogs for military purposes, some as attack dogs and some as messengers.

During the 400 years of the Han Dynasty of China, which began in the 3rd century B.C., dogs were portrayed in many pieces of pottery. These were effigy pieces that symbolized the burial of favored dogs with their masters. Toy dogs were also popular among the ancient Chinese to provide warmth in the wide sleeves of their gowns.

Many of the European hound breeds were developed in the Middle Ages, when coursing was popular with the nobility. In coursing, the prey is pursued until exhausted. Then it is killed. Coursing was eventually replaced by fox hunting, which was considered less cruel.

Throughout the years dogs have been bred for many reasons, such as for hunting, for herding, and for guarding. Breed histories and pedigrees, however, were not methodically compiled until the 19th century with the establishment of the first kennel clubs. The world's first dog show took place in Great Britain in 1859. The first all-breeds show in the United States was held in Detroit, Mich., in 1875, although Chicago, Ill. was the site a year earlier of a show exclusively for sporting dogs. In 1884 the AKC was organized in New York City.

Today's breeds are a standardization of the desirable traits of the older breeds. Dog breeders try to perpetuate those traits while maintaining a friendly disposition in a dog, a trait so important for a family pet.

Man has been amply repaid for this long partnership and rapport with the dog. Care and love have been exchanged for loyalty, companionship, and fun.

From Sheila Burnford (© 1961), 'The Incredible Journey' (reprinted by permission of Atlantic, Little, Brown and Co.), illustration by Carl Burger

From 'R. Caldecott's Picture Book, No. 1': Dr. Goldsmith, "An Elegy on the Death of a Mad Dog" (reprinted by permission of Frederick Warne & Co., Inc.), illustration by Randolph Caldecott

From Eric Knight, 'Lassie Come-Home' (© 1968 by Jere Knight; reprinted by permission of Holt, Rinehart and Winston, Inc.), illustration (© 1971) by Don Bolognese

The Dog in Literature

FICTION

Armstrong, W. H. Sounder (Harper, 1969). A Newbery Medal story of a black sharecropper and his coon dog.

Ball, Zachary. Bristle Face (Holiday, 1962). Tale of a tramp dog with a face full of whiskers and an orphan boy. Also by the author is 'Sputters' (Holiday, 1963).

Burnford, Sheila. The Incredible Journey (Little, 1961). A 250-mile trek home by a Labrador retriever, a bull terrier, and a Siamese cat. Carl Burger illustrates.

Carroll, Ruth and Latrobe. Tough Enough (Walck, 1954). The adventures of the Tatum family and their mischievous dog, realistically set in the Smokies.

Cleary, Beverly. Ribsy (Morrow, 1964). One of the genuinely funny Henry Huggins stories. Illustrated by Louise Darling. Others are 'Henry Huggins' (Morrow, 1950) and 'Henry and Ribsy' (Morrow, 1954).

Cole, William, ed. Man's Funniest Friend (Collins, 1967). A collection of famous and not-so-famous stories, poems, cartoons, and anecdotes to delight dog lovers.

Gipson, F. B. Old Yeller (Harper, 1956). A dog saves a boy from a mad animal. Illustrated by Carl Burger.

Goldsmith, Oliver. An Elegy on the Death of a Mad Dog (Warne, 1879). A familiar ditty made especially enjoyable by the drawings of Randolph Caldecott.

Kjelgaard, J. A. Big Red, rev. ed. (Holiday, 1956). A story of a champion Irish setter. Others by the author are 'Snow Dog' (Holiday, 1948) and 'Fire-Hunter' (Holiday, 1951). His dog stories are true to the breed.

Knight, E. M. Lassie Come-Home, rev. ed. (Holt, 1971). A welcome new edition of an appealing dog story. Illustrated by Don Bolognese.

Lippincott, J. W. Wilderness Champion (Lippincott, 1944). A red setter pup is lost in the mountains and raised by a wolf. Illustrated by Paul Bransom.

London, Jack. The Call of the Wild (Macmillan, 1963). A tame dog escapes from his captors and must survive in the wilderness. Enjoyed by young and old.

O'Brien, Jack. Silver Chief: Dog of the North (J. C. Winston, 1933). A classic story of a police dog that is part husky, part wolf. Illustrated by Kurt Wiese.

Terhune, A. P. Lad: a Dog (Dutton, 1959). A favorite.

White, A. H. Junket (Pocket Books, 1976). A wise Airedale shows a family how to run a farm. Robert McCloskey illustrates. See also 'A Dog Called Scholar' (Viking Press, 1963).

Will and Nicolas. Finders Keepers (Harcourt, 1951). Two dogs fight over one bone. A Caldecott Medal winner.

NONFICTION

American Kennel Club. The Complete Dog Book, 15th ed. (Howell Book, 1975). Officially recognized breeds of dogs.

Broderick, D. M. Training a Companion Dog (Prentice, 1965). Dog behavior for young dog trainers.

Carter, R. G. Dogs and People (Abelard, 1969). The relationship of dogs and their masters through the ages.

Dangerfield, Stanley and Howell, Elsworth, eds. The International Encyclopedia of Dogs (Howell Book, 1971). Alphabetically arranged entries on all subjects.

Fiennes, Richard and Alice. The Natural History of Dogs (Natural History, 1970). For the layman, a scientific treatment of the domestic dog.

Henry, Marguerite. Album of Dogs, rev. ed. (Rand, 1970). Anecdotes that describe the personalities of major breeds for the young person. Illustrated by Wesley Dennis.

Levin, J. W. Bringing Up Puppies: a Child's Book of Dog Breeding and Care (Harcourt, 1958). Practical advice.

National Geographic Society. Man's Best Friend, rev. ed. (National Geographic, 1974). A beautifully illustrated guide to the characteristics of the various breeds.

Sabin, Francene and Louis. Dogs of America (Putnam, 1967). Purebreds of the United States; illustrated.

Smythe, R. H. The Dog: Structure and Movement (Arco, 1970). The anatomy of the dog.

Whitney, L. F. Dog Psychology: the Basis of Dog Training (Howell Book, 1971). The behavior, instincts, and learning abilities of the domestic dog.

Whitney, L. F. How to Select, Train, and Breed Your Dog (McKay, 1969). A complete guide for dog owners.

National Greyhound Racing Club Ltd.

Greyhounds race on a track in the British Isles. In Britain and Ireland the dogs run on grass tracks instead of sand tracks.

DOG RACING. Specifically, dog racing is the racing of greyhounds, the fastest of dogs. As a sport, dog racing has its origin in a kind of race called coursing, in which hounds chased game by sight, not by scent. The popularity of coursing dates back many centuries. It was fully described by the Greek writer Arrian about AD 150. It is still practiced to a limited extent in Great Britain, Australia, and the United States.

In its present form dog racing takes place on a track that is usually round or oval. In the United States most tracks are composed of finely sifted loam and sand, while in Britain and Ireland the tracks normally have a grass surface. The size of the standard track in the United States is one quarter mile (400 meters). In Britain and Ireland the length of the race must be from 230 yards (210 meters) to 1,200 yards (1,097 meters). The greyhounds pursue an electrically propelled model of a rabbit around the track. People bet on the outcome of each race.

Modern dog racing was first tested in 1909 by a promoter named Oliver P. Smith at a track in Tucson, Ariz. By 1919 Smith had perfected the mechanical rabbit, and he successfully demonstrated it at Emeryville, Cal. In the next few years tracks were opened in many places around the country, including Tulsa, Okla.; Chicago; and Hialeah, Fla. Many of the early tracks eventually went out of existence, but the one that opened on Jan. 3, 1925, in Saint Petersburg, Fla., has remained open to become the longest in continuous operation. It is internationally known as Derby Lane. In 1926 modern dog racing was introduced into Britain, where it gained a greater following than in the United States. It later spread through Europe and to China, Mexico, and Australia.

Because of its association with gambling, racing fell into disrepute, and many courses were raided. Florida was the first state to legalize dog racing, doing so in 1931. Because the state derived considerable income from the taxes on the betting and on licensing and admission fees, other states followed suit. Today in the United States the sport is popular primarily in Florida, Massachusetts, and the western states.

British dog racing is governed by the rules of the National Greyhound Racing Club formed in 1928. On most days not more than eight races are allowed at any one track. No more than six greyhounds run in a race, and the owner of the winning dog is awarded the prize money. This money can amount to several thousand dollars at such classic races as the Greyhound Derby at White City, London. Each greyhound wears a distinctive coat and begins the race from a trap, or starting box. As the mechanical rabbit passes the starting point, the dogs are automatically released from the trap. The finish of the race is photographed in order to confirm the judges' decision.

In the United States racing greyhounds are registered with the National Coursing Association and the American Kennel Club. The method of racing is similar to that in Britain, but the number of dogs in a race is usually eight and the number of races on a program 10 or 11.

Ireland has long been noted as the breeding place for racing greyhounds and is the main supply source for other countries. Britain and the United States, however, have also developed some breeding lines.

DOLE, Sanford Ballard (1844–1926). A Supreme Court judge of the former Kingdom of Hawaii, Sanford Ballard Dole helped establish the Republic of Hawaii and was its only president. He was instrumental in the annexation of the islands by the United States and became the first governor of the Territory of Hawaii.

Sanford Ballard Dole was born near Honolulu, Hawaii, on April 23, 1844. He was the son of Emily Ballard and the Reverend Daniel Dole, Protestant missionaries from Maine. From 1866 to 1868 he studied at Williams College in Williamstown, Mass., and studied law in Boston. He became a lawyer in Honolulu in 1869.

In 1884 and 1886 Dole was elected to the Hawaiian national legislature. Dole and other legislators of New England descent resented King Kalakaua's opposition to the domination of the islands' economy by United States business interests. In 1887 they forced him to accept a new constitution. It gave the vote only to property holders, most of whom were American and European. This assured foreign control of the government. That year Dole was appointed an associate justice of the Hawaiian Supreme Court.

Dole desired the annexation of Hawaii by the United States so that Hawaiian sugar planters could favorably compete in United States markets. He was angered when Queen Liliuokalani, who succeeded her brother Kalakaua in 1891, tried to restore royal power (see Liliuokalani). In 1893 Dole joined a group of businessmen who, aided by United States Marines, overthrew the monarchy. The next year he became president of the new Republic of Hawaii.

Dole pressed for annexation, but it was delayed until 1898, when Hawaii became a strategic naval base during the Spanish-American War. In 1900 Dole was appointed governor of the new territory. In 1903 he became presiding judge of the Federal District Court.

Dole married Anna Prentice Cate, who died in 1918. They had no children. Dole died in Honolulu on June 9, 1926. He was a cousin of James Drummond Dole, who organized Hawaii's canned pineapple industry in 1901.

DOLL

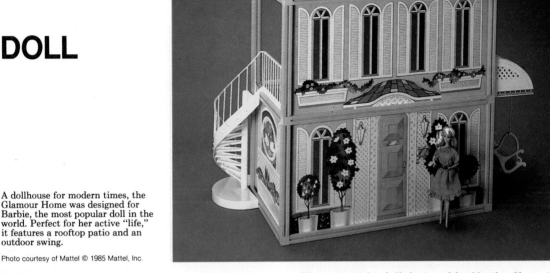

A dollhouse for modern times, the Glamour Home was designed for Barbie, the most popular doll in the world. Perfect for her active "life," it features a rooftop patio and an outdoor swing.

Photo courtesy of Mattel © 1985 Mattel, Inc.

DOLL. Although dolls have been around ever since there were children to play with them, dolls have always been more than toys. Prehistoric people made miniature human figures of stone or clay that were apparently used as magic charms in religious ceremonies. The doll-like pieces found in ancient Egyptian tombs probably were substitutes for the real servants who were formerly buried alive with their dead masters. During the Middle Ages bread dolls were designed to represent various saints and were eaten on their feast days. In about 1400 the first fashion dolls were used to show off the latest Paris styles in hats and gowns.

One of the oldest American dolls was the kachina, which was made primarily by the Hopi Indians of Arizona. Kachinas were carved from cottonwood or cactus root, painted in symbolic colors, and dressed traditionally. The dolls were not toys, but sacred objects for the children to study. At annual kachina ceremonies they were passed out by masked adults representing the legendary gods concerned with the people's prayers and needs.

In addition to the fashion dolls, so-called "working" dolls included the peddler, or pedlar, and the Chase Hospital doll. In a basket tray held by a ribbon around the English pedlar's neck were displayed miniature samples of household goods—kitchen tools, pots and pans, pincushions and other sewing notions—that were for sale in full-size versions. Some German and French peddlers were surrounded by baskets filled with seaweed and shells or garden produce and baked goods. The fortune-telling doll was a type of peddler with a skirt made of folded paper fortunes that were to be purchased.

The watertight doll designed by Martha Chase in 1910 was used in hospitals to help train student nurses in handling babies, feeding them, giving them enemas, and other treatments. Chase Hospital dolls were made in five life sizes. For instruction in newborn care offered by some hospitals, baby dolls are used for practice by the parents-to-be.

The ivory dolls kept by Chinese physicians made it possible for female patients to pinpoint the areas of their ailments without having to undress. In cases of child abuse, anatomically correct dolls are used to help victims describe what happened to them.

A doll is not just a plaything even for the child who owns one. Babies find comfort by snuggling with soft stuffed dolls in their cribs. For preschoolers, dolls are almost-real companions who can share gossip on make-believe visits or confidences on long trips. Often children identify with their favorite dolls and, in imitation of their own parents, scold or praise, spank or cuddle them. Older youngsters, who can dress their dolls themselves to suit their fantasies, may play school or stage battles or give parties.

No one is ever too old for dolls. Many parents enjoy helping their children act out life situations with a new generation of dolls. Some men and women—including Montezuma II, the last chief of the Aztecs, and Britain's Queen Victoria—become doll collectors. Members of the Doll Collectors of America, founded in 1935, study a different kind of doll, dollmaker, or dollmaking process each month.

Schools and museums also collect dolls for their educational value. By examining the costumes of dolls from other countries and other times, students learn something about other people's lives and cultures.

215

An Egyptian paddle doll (left) has hair of clay beads. Raggedy Andy® and Raggedy Ann® (center) were originally homemade dolls. The 19th-century doll is made from corn husks.

Dolls from Guatemala, for example, are usually garbed in cotton or wool. Those wearing cotton represent the Indians who live in the steaming coastal lowlands. The wool-clad dolls show the dress of the Indians in the cool highlands, where most of the people live. When Guatemalan dolls carry huge head baskets or *cacastes* (wooden back packs), students can visualize that transportation in Guatemala is largely primitive.

Ceremonial Dolls in Asia and Africa

In Japan dolls are often part of traditional rites and festivals. A Japanese bride takes her doll collection to her new home. At the girls' festival dolls representing the emperor, the empress, and their court are displayed; girls from 7 to 17 visit each other's collections and offer real food, first to the dolls, then to the guests. This ritual, nearly 1,000 years old, may reflect an early rite in which a scapegoat doll, treated as if alive, was given to Japanese mothers to ward off evil from their children. Japanese boys have an annual doll festival, from the first May after they are born until they are about 15 years old. Warrior dolls, weapons, banners, and legendary figure groups are displayed to encourage chivalrous virtues. Some modern dolls are even attired as athletes. In Korea, for the children's festival, a paper image of a woman is made with a clay base to stand erect. In Japan the corresponding toy, identified as the Buddhist Daruma, is bought by boys at a temple. The face is painted and in place of eyes are white paper disks, upon which black dots are inked if the god answers a prayer.

In India elaborately dressed dolls were given to child brides by both Hindus and Muslims. In Iraq dolls are considered unlucky; little girls must improvise their own dolls of pillows and blocks of wood. In Syria girls of marriageable age hang dolls in their windows.

In South Africa, among the Mfengu people of the Orange Free State, every grown girl is given a doll to keep for her first child. After its birth, the mother receives a second doll to keep for the second child. Voodoo dolls and fertility dolls still play a role in many tribal cultures.

What Dolls Are Made of

Dolls can be made out of almost anything. Some of the earliest dolls were fashioned from perishable materials such as wood and fur or cloth, as well as clay and stone. The dolls found in ancient Egyptian graves were carved out of flat pieces of wood and decorated with paint and hair made of strings of clay or wooden beads. Clay horses and knights and small figures of tin and glass were made in the Middle Ages.

For centuries people made dolls out of whatever raw materials were available. Primitive Japanese dolls were made of shaved willow sticks with paper clothes and wood shavings or string for hair. Korean children had similar dolls made of bamboo sticks with grass hair stuffed into the top of the head. In colonial America homemade dolls were fashioned from corn husks, corncobs, fruits, nuts, and gourds. The Eskimos and northern Indians used whalebone, walrus tusk, and mammoth teeth.

In commercial dollmaking the use of molded plastic was the major development in the 20th century. Yet the most enduring dolls of the century have been rag dolls—Raggedy Ann and Raggedy Andy, which were originally homemade. Stocking dolls, felt dolls, and paper dolls are also easily made at home.

Before the introduction of all-plastic and all-rubber dolls, a doll's body and its head were usually manufactured from different materials. The body was generally made of kid-covered wood or of leather stuffed with sawdust. Eventually composition bodies, which were cheaper to make, became popular. The head was made of wood, terra-cotta, alabaster, wax, or waxed papier-mâché. After 1820 glazed, or shiny, porcelain doll heads and then unglazed, or matte, bisque heads were introduced.

The Antique China Doll

The glazed porcelain dolls made in 19th-century Germany had heads of Dresden china. Generally lady dolls, with pink or white cloth bodies, they were sometimes used for fashion dolls. Almost all of them

This rare Peddler doll, or Vendor doll, stands 14½ inches high. Her head and hair are china. She was made about 1860.

She came from Holland in 1805. Her wood body is jointed; her hair is real. She wears clothes made for her about 1844.

The wax doll smiles demurely. She has real blonde hair. Her bootees are crocheted. She dates from about 1840.

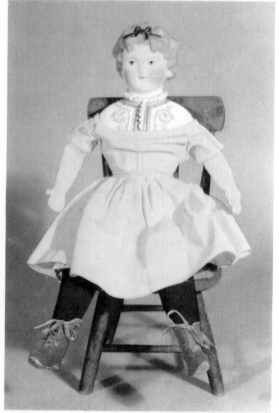

The stuffed rag doll rests in his toy wicker chair. He stands 16 inches high. He first delighted some child about 1880.

Her head and hair are bisque. When her bisque hands broke, she got cotton ones. Made about 1840, she is 15 inches high.

NORWAY

SCOTLAND

SWITZERLAND

WALES

BRITTANY

ITALY

SPAIN

The lovely costume dolls shown on these two pages are imported. Their historic dress is representative of their native countries or regions. Even today, where people have adopted less colorful dress for work, many persons still appear in costumes like these on fete days. The detailed and careful handwork on these beautiful dolls reflects the skilled handicraft that is still practiced in many parts of the Old World and of the Far East. These dolls were provided by Marshall Field and Company, Chicago, Ill. They were especially photographed in their original colors by the Compton art staff.

GREECE

SLAVIC

BRITTANY

BALI

ALBANIA

INDIA

JAPAN

CHINA

The imported dolls shown on these two pages vary in actual size. The Japanese male actor doll stands only 7 inches high. The Spanish dancer, on the opposite page, is nearly 18 inches high. The Bali dancer figurine, which was made by an American after much study, is only 5 inches tall. The beauty and significance of these dolls make them "collectors' items." Their prices range from a few dollars to hundreds. The Brittany dolls are unique. They recall an old Breton legend. Ages ago an evil witch snatched newborn babies. When a brave mother released them, she dressed them all in festive finery.

The rich hues and lavish embroideries of old China brighten the dress of the mandarin doll couple, right, and their attendants.

The dainty ladies above are shown in actual size in tiny glass domes. They are done in the style of the old-time fashion dolls.

The doll replica of Jane Seymour, third wife of Henry VIII, wears a bell-like canvas underskirt—forerunner of the hoop.

This Henry VIII doll shows the splendor of the nobles' dress in 16th-century England. The waistcoat is richly embroidered.

The young Queen Victoria doll is resplendent in an exact reproduction of the coronation regalia worn June 28, 1838.

These paper dolls were more than playthings. They were exhibited to display high fashion in the United States about 1866. In the center stands a fashion magazine, *The American Lady and Her Children*. Americans followed European styles.

had dark hair, for contrast to the fair skin, and blue eyes. China heads were also sold separately to people who wanted to make their own dolls or for pincushions. There were two-faced porcelains, with one side depicting youth and the other old age.

Perhaps the first celebrity doll portrayed the Austrian dancer Fanny Elssler, posed in a ballet position in the 1840s. Jenny Lind, named after the "Swedish Nightingale," had molded hair scooped into a bun.

The littlest china dolls, called Frozen Charlottes, came in sizes from 2 to 12 or 15 inches (5 to 30 or 38 centimeters). The bigger ones were called Frozen Charlies because they looked like boys. The jointless Charlottes and Charlies had extended forearms as if frozen stiff. Their origin is a ballad, 'Fair Charlotte', about the death of a Vermont country girl who rode in a sleigh, without a blanket, to a New Year's party.

The Bisque Doll

The china doll was the forerunner of the bisque doll. Bisque comes from the word biscuit, which refers to a piece of porcelain when it comes out of the kiln, or oven, before the glaze is applied. One day a German dollmaker was taking unglazed heads out of the kiln when he noticed that the matte finish looked more like a young woman's cheek than the glossy porcelain did.

The French soon started making bisque dolls in their own factories. Some of the so-called "French bisque," used for the famous dolls made by the Jumeau family, was actually made in Germany. Said to be extremely fine, the Jumeau bisque was faintly flesh colored in the clay before it was fired to give it a permanent tint. Later some brown bisque faces were introduced.

The head of a bisque doll was sculptured by an artist. Then a mold of the head was made and hundreds of copies produced. Next porcelain clay was rolled, like piecrust, and pressed into the mold. When it was dry, it was taken from the mold and fired in a kiln for many hours. After being fired and cooled, the bisque heads were washed and smoothed and sent into the various painting rooms for coloring of the features by artists.

Endless hours were required to turn out perfectly tinted cheeks and perfect lips with deeper rose shading. Sometimes a one-stroke eyebrow was used. More often the best dolls were designed with full brows made with many single, clean strokes, one over the other, until the right thickness was achieved. Eyelashes too were the work of a steady, practiced hand that could paint endless even strokes. Some bisque dolls, like the Jumeau, had particularly beautiful glass eyes. After the bodies were assembled and attached to the heads, wigs were added. Finally, the dolls were dressed.

The Jumeau bisque dolls had their own professional dress designers and hatmakers, with separate departments for shoes and accessories—all set up in the family factory. Hand needlework on the costumes was done by women who worked at home. The dolls wore pearl necklaces to hide the joining of neck and body. Some had pierced ears.

The Parian doll was named for the Greek island of Paros, which was noted for its pure white marble. However, the doll was made of pure white bisque. Only the cheeks, lips, hair, and eyes were colored. Its hair was usually blond and elaborately styled. Eyes were usually painted on, but sometimes were glass.

Most bisque doll companies also made small all-bisque dolls with movable arms and legs. They were from 3 to 7 inches (8 to 18 centimeters) high. They came to be called Candy Store dolls because they were sold in candy stores.

Other Famous Dolls and Dollmakers

As early as 1862 E.R. Morrison of New York patented a walking doll, and within a few years there were several other models. In the 1890s Thomas Edison developed a "phonograph doll" that "said" nursery rhymes. Other inventors soon produced dolls that sang or said their prayers. Mechanical dolls, fitted with tiny music boxes, appeared very early in the 19th century in European countries. Today there are baby dolls, teenage dolls, bride dolls, character dolls, storybook dolls, costume dolls, collectors' dolls, celebrity dolls, and just plain dolls in every stage from diapers to fancy dress.

Hilda Baby, made by J.D. Kestner of Germany, often was sold with a bent-leg baby body, but the same head was sometimes attached to a toddler body.

Topsy Turvey was a so-called two-way doll made of fabric. One end was a black-faced doll in a bandanna; turned upside-down she revealed a white face under a bonnet. Their skirts overlapped.

Kewpie doll had an impish smile, side-turned eyes, topknot, and blue wings. Based on a drawing by Rose O'Neill, the Kewpie was so loved from its debut in 1912 that Kewpie clubs still flourish. They were made in bisque, composition, and celluloid.

Gibson Girl, also by Kestner, was modeled on Charles Dana Gibson's drawing of a fashionable young lady of 1910. She had a haughty look and a Gay Nineties hairdo under a wide-brimmed hat. A Gibson Girl with a sweeter expression was made by Simon Halbig, another German dollmaker.

Boudoir dolls, later called sofa dolls and Vamps or Flappers, were made by many companies. They were long-legged dolls, often with silk- or cotton-covered faces, that could be tossed about for decoration.

Campbell Kids, copied from the soup characters, were the most popular of the advertising dolls created by E. I. Horsman & Company. Another was the Fairy, which was made to publicize Fairy soap.

Bye-Lo Baby, introduced in 1924, was called the "million dollar baby" because of its instant popularity. Grace Storey Putnam, an art teacher, created it in the image of a 3-day-old infant.

Patsy, another 1920s doll, was a little-girl doll, and the first American doll with a wardrobe.

Dy-Dee Baby, the first doll to drink from a bottle and wet its diapers, came out in 1932.

DOLL

The Shirley Temple celebrity doll (left) was introduced in the 1930s. GI Joe® (center) was popular in the 1950s. The Cabbage Patch Kids were the doll craze of the 1980s.

Shirley Temple, modeled after the curly-topped child actress of the same name in 1934, became the best-selling celebrity doll ever. Originally a composition doll, she was reissued in vinyl in 1967.

Magic Skin Baby was introduced in 1946 as the first doll with texture resembling human skin.

Madame Alexander dolls were the creation of Beatrice Behrman, whose parents had a dolls' hospital. For decades these portrait dolls have been collected for their authentic costumes as well as their perfect faces. Among the most popular have been Alice in Wonderland, the four Little Women, and Charles Dickens characters. The company's miniature dolls are costumed in the traditional dress of many lands. A 1962 doll came with a wardrobe of interchangeable wigs attached by Velcro.

Patti Play Pal, a lifelike 1950s doll, was the same size as a 3-year-old child and often wore clothes her owner had outgrown.

Barbie, a shapely young woman, has been the all-time best-selling doll since she was introduced 150 million dolls ago in 1959. She soon had a boyfriend doll, Ken, and a little sister, Skipper, as well as a girlfriend, Midge.

Betsy McCall was a magazine's paper-doll feature who became a miniature plastic doll. (In the 19th century many popular bisque dolls had been adapted as paper dolls.)

G.I. Joe was an outstanding action doll of the 1960s, when it became more acceptable for boys to have dolls. His accessories included a rifle, hand grenades, and a cartridge belt. He was later replaced by Action Joe, an explorer–adventurer equipped with a space capsule and underwater diving gear.

Strawberry Shortcake, the first doll success of the 1980s, is one of a collection of miniatures who smell like their names and have scented pets. Others in the group are Blueberry Muffin, Orange Blossom, Huckleberry Pie, Mint Tulip, and the twins Lem and Ada.

Cabbage Patch Kids were called Little People before 1983. Beginning in 1977, the original dolls were handmade of cloth for display as pieces of soft

sculpture. Babyland General Hospital was set up in 1978 in Cleveland, Ga., with a staff of salespeople and dollmakers dressed as doctors and nurses. There was even an incubator unit for smaller "preemie" baby dolls in the converted medical clinic. All the kids are sold with birth certificates and adoption papers for "fees" that range from 25 to a thousand dollars. Each kid, whether handmade in Georgia or manufactured with computer technology in Hong Kong, has one-of-a-kind features and individualized names. The Flower Kid imitations, which were marketed to cash in on the Cabbage Patch craze, have no belly buttons.

Doll Accessories

Most dolls today have more clothes and personal play equipment than their young owners. And, through licensing agreements, a doll's name or face can create a demand for still more related items. For example, the Cabbage Patch Kids have umbrella strollers, convertible car beds, chairs that hook on the family kitchen table, dishes, playpens, sleeping bags, and Snuggle Close carriers, as well as complete outfits. And there are Cabbage Patch sheets, bedspreads, lunch boxes, tote bags, pajamas, T-shirts, shoes, children's cosmetics, jewelry, games, and bikes.

About 20 million clothing items for Barbie and her friends are sold annually. Every year 50 new outfits are designed, from bathing suits to ballgowns, each with appropriate accessories to be added from head to toe, or to carry or use.

The Barbie of the 1980s could live in her own special van, or townhouse, or Dream House with a pool. She could get around in a sportscar or on a motor bike or horse. Dressed in a leotard and leg warmers, she could keep her slim shape in her own workout center, with an exercise machine, weights and pulleys, and locker. On her 25th birthday, in 1984, she became a truly modern woman with her own dress-for-success suit, credit and business cards, attaché case, and computer terminal. In a flashback to Barbie's frivolous 1960s image, the skirt of her business suit was reversible for an evening on the town.

Common Dolphin
(Delphinus delphis)

Bottle-nosed Dolphin
(Tursiops truncatus)

Harbor Porpoise
(Phocoena phocoena)

Dall's Porpoise
(Phocoenoides dalli)

DOLPHIN AND PORPOISE. Dolphins are small members of the whale order, Cetacea. Although the terms dolphin and porpoise are sometimes used interchangeably to refer to any member of the group, biologists recognize three distinct families: the true porpoises, with six marine species; the river dolphins, with five freshwater species; and the true dolphins, with more than 30 marine species. The killer whales and pilot whales are closely related to the true dolphins and are included in the same family.

Although they are similar in appearance, a dolphin is distinguished from a porpoise by its long, sharp snout that is flattened like a beak; a porpoise has a short, blunt snout. The teeth of dolphins are cone-shaped while those of porpoises are flatter.

Dolphins and porpoises, often called simply "small whales," are mammals, not fishes, and are thus warm-blooded, keeping their body temperature nearly constant even when they are exposed to different environmental temperatures. The mothers provide milk for the young and nurse them for a year or more. Like other whales, dolphins have lungs and breathe through a single nostril called the blowhole located on top of the head. The blowhole is opened during their frequent trips to the surface to expel and inhale air. In contrast to some of the large whales, dolphins and porpoises have teeth, which they use to seize their food, consisting primarily of marine fishes and larger invertebrates, such as squid.

Dolphins and porpoises have two flippers, fins that serve as forelimbs, and an upright triangular fin on the back. The tail is horizontal—to propel the animal in its lunges and dives—not perpendicular like the tails of fishes. Dolphins and porpoises are noted for being graceful swimmers, arcing through long, slow curves that bring the blowhole to the surface of the water and then expose the back fin as the animal dips downward. At first glance, the high dorsal fin somewhat resembles that of a shark and has sometimes caused false alarms at beaches. Dolphins and porpoises have been clocked at sea traveling at speeds of more than 25 miles (40 kilometers) per hour.

The largest dolphins reach a length of about 15 feet (4.6 meters), but most species are 7 to 10 feet (2.1 to 3 meters) long. Porpoises are somewhat smaller. Dolphins and porpoises have smooth skin with a rubbery texture. Most species have color patterns that are some combination of black, white, and gray. Like other whales, they have an insulating layer of blubber beneath the skin.

Most dolphins and porpoises have declined in numbers during this century. Some species are hunted commercially, particularly in Asian marine waters. Many individuals of several species are accidentally drowned each year when they become entangled in fishing nets.

True dolphins belong to the family Delphinidae; true porpoises to the Phocoenidae; and river dolphins to the Platanistidae. All are in the toothed-whale suborder Odontoceti.

Dolphins and porpoises are noted for their intelligence and learning abilities. They have proved to be superb acrobats under certain conditions and can be trained to perform impressive tricks in oceanariums. Their social behavior and organization are among the most complex and advanced in the animal kingdom. Dolphins and porpoises exhibit an intricate communication and detection system in the form of underwater sonar that consists of high-pitched whistles and squeaks, some of which may be of ultrasonic frequency—that is, above range of human hearing. They are able to detect objects underwater by using "echolocation" in which the sounds are reflected off solid surfaces back to their sensitive ears. By means of echolocation they can recognize schools of fish or even smaller organisms such as shrimp. The time it takes for a reflected sound to return indicates how far away an object is from the animal.

Dolphins and porpoises also use sounds for communication among themselves as members of a school (also called herd or pod), which may consist of more than 1,000 individuals in some open-ocean species. Often an entire school will function as a unit to accomplish some objective, such as trapping fish.

Dolphins

Certain species of marine dolphins are the best known biologically because they survive well in captivity, allowing them to be more carefully observed. The bottle-nosed dolphin, whose scientific name is *Tursiops truncatus,* has been the most intensively studied because of its adaptability to salt-water holding tanks. It is a major participant in the acrobatic shows at oceanariums and is noted for its curiosity toward humans. Bottle-nosed dolphins, so called because of their long beaks, are found in all oceans of the world from the tropics to the temperate regions. They grow up to 12 feet (3.7 meters) long and may weigh more than 400 pounds (180 kilograms).

The common dolphin (*Delphinus delphis*) is also a species found worldwide in warm coastal waters and is a frequent inhabitant of the Mediterranean Sea and the Black Sea. Some other species are more restricted in their geographic range. For example, Peale's dolphin (*Lagenorhynchus australis*) is native to cold waters of the Atlantic and Pacific off the southern part of South America. Hector's dolphin (*Cephalorhynchus hectori*) is a small species reaching a length of only 5 feet (1.5 meters) and whose range is limited to the offshore waters of New Zealand.

Dolphins are relatively long-lived, with some individuals living more than 20 years. Most species do not begin to breed until ages of 5 to 8 or more. The female bears a single offspring, called a calf, after a gestation period of 8 to 11 months, depending on the species. As soon as the calf is born, the mother nudges it to the surface for its first breath of air. The young stay with the mothers for at least one and sometimes as long as two years, while continuing to nurse. Most dolphins have their young in the warm months of the year.

The river dolphins are native to South America and southern Asia. The Ganges and Indus dolphins (genus *Platanista*) inhabit the large rivers of the Indian subcontinent: the Ganges, Brahmaputra, and Indus. The whitefin dolphin (*Lipotes vexillifer*), a bluish-gray animal with a white underside, inhabits the Yangtze River of China. The Amazon dolphin (*Inia geoffrensis*) is found in the Orinoco and Amazon Rivers.

River dolphins can be distinguished from ocean-dwelling dolphins by their smaller brains and more limited interactions with each other. Their eyes can detect light but do not form an image. Thus in murky river waters these dolphins must depend solely on sonar and echolocation abilities for finding food (mostly fishes and shrimp) and avoiding objects.

Porpoises

As with dolphins, social interaction among porpoises is common. However, porpoises do not form enormous schools like some of the dolphins, generally remaining in coastal areas in small schools of two to four. Because porpoises do not survive as well in captivity, less is known about their biology and social behavior than that of some dolphins. Porpoises share with dolphins the ability to produce a wide variety of underwater sounds. Porpoises are generally smaller than true dolphins, with few individuals attaining a length of more than 6 feet (1.8 meters).

The harbor porpoise (*Phocoena phocoena*) is one of the most common species. It occurs in the north temperate regions of the Atlantic and Pacific Oceans, being sighted frequently along the coasts of Europe and North America. Harbor porpoises are also noted for "stranding," a phenomenon in which whales leave the water along a beach and, unable to return, eventually die. In some species, such as the pilot whales, several individuals will become stranded at the same time. Harbor porpoises, however, are usually alone.

The Dall's porpoise (*Phocoenoides dalli*) is another common species in the northern Pacific from Japan to California. Dall's porpoises are noted for swimming playfully around ships or small boats.

Dolphin Fish

The name dolphin is also given to an unrelated species: a large fish of open tropical seas. The dolphin fish (*Coryphaena hippurus*) is sometimes called the coryphene or the dorado. It is a shiny golden and blue color with deep blue spots. The colors are brilliant but fade rapidly when the fish is removed from the water. Dolphin fish are an edible game species that may reach lengths of 6 feet (1.8 meters) and weights of more than 100 pounds (45 kilograms).

DOMINIC (1170?–1221). The founder of the Order of Friars Preachers, also called Dominicans, was Domingo de Guzmán. He is now known generally as Saint Dominic. The members of the order were mendicant friars, or traveling preachers. They were not attached to a monastery but based at strategically placed houses in the cities of Europe.

Dominic was born about 1170 in Spain, at Caleruega in Castile. As a member of a religous order, Dominic went to the south of France in 1203 to investigate the threat to the Roman Catholic Church posed by a heretical sect called Albigensians. He proposed to combat the threat by founding an order of wandering preachers. This work began in 1206 and continued through a civil war from 1208 to 1213 that eventually killed all the Albigensians. Dominic's order was formally sanctioned by Pope Honorius III at Rome on

Saint Dominic forgives a sinner, in a painting by the Florentine artist Andrea di Bonaiuti.

SCALA/Art Resource

Dec. 22, 1216. The order's two principal houses were established near the universities of Paris, in France, and Bologna, in Italy, with the stipulation that they set up schools of theology.

Dominic spent the rest of his life in Rome or traveling to the houses of his order. He died at Bologna on Aug. 6, 1221.

DOMINICA. In the Caribbean Sea, lying between Guadeloupe and Martinique, Dominica is an island republic of the Lesser Antilles. It is a mountainous island of volcanic origin covering an area of 290 square miles (750 square kilo-

meters). Its main physical feature is a high, forest-covered mountain range that runs from north to south. Morne Diablotin, in the north, is the highest point at 4,747 feet (1,447 meters). A plain breaks the mountain range at about the center of the chain. The Layou, Pagua, and Castle Bruce rivers all drain the plain. These and the many other rivers and streams on the island are mostly unusable by boats larger than canoes.

There are volcanoes on the island, and, though they are probably now extinct, a number of thermal springs and Boiling Lake in the south are definite signs of continuing volcanic activity. The island soil is rich, and there is dense tropical plant growth and lush rain forests. Dominica has a warm year-round tropical climate with temperatures that range from 78° F (26° C) to 90° F (32° C). Rainfall is very heavy, averaging 250 inches (635 centimeters) in the mountains and 70 inches (178 centimeters) along the coast. Animal life on the island includes 135 species of birds, the iguana, opossum, agouti, boa constrictor, and many species of bat.

Dominica is one of the poorest of the Caribbean nations. Bananas are its main agricultural product and major export. Grapefruit, limes, oranges, and

vegetables are produced. Coconuts, also important to the economy, are used in copra, oils and fats, soap, and detergents. Fruit juices and rum are also produced from local agricultural products. Pumice, which is mined, is the only known mineral resource on the island. There is some livestock raised on the island and a small commercial fishing industry. In addition to bananas, exports include coconut oil and fruit juices. Foods, metals, and manufactured goods are imported. Handicrafts also contribute to the economy, and a local industry produces cigarettes from imported tobacco.

Tourists are attracted to Dominica for the island's rich tropical environment and mild climate. It has excellent swimming, boating and fishing facilities, and an unspoiled wilderness.

There are more than 400 miles (644 kilometers) of paved roads and paths. A deepwater port was completed in 1976 at the capital city of Roseau. A number of steamship services call there. The main airfield is Melville Hall, about 40 miles (64 kilometers) from Roseau.

When Christopher Columbus sighted Dominica in 1493, the island was inhabited by fierce Carib Indians. Because of its steep coastal cliffs, it was one of the last islands to be explored by Europeans. The Indians, French, and British later fought for control of the island, however, and it was awarded to Britain in 1783. Dominica has been under the control of various governments, but it finally became independent in 1978 as the Commonwealth of Dominica. Population (1984 estimate), 74,000.

DOMINICAN REPUBLIC. Located in the Caribbean Sea, the Dominican Republic covers an area of 18,703 square miles (48,440 square kilometers), occupying the eastern portion of Hispaniola, the second largest island of the Antilles. It shares the island with Haiti but the two neighbors have little in common. The inhabitants of Haiti are predominantly black, have French and African cultural roots, and live in an overpopulated and poor environment. In contrast, the population of the Dominican Republic is predominantly mulatto or white, Hispanic in culture, and belongs to a country that suffers from some environmental deterioration but also has areas of lush vegetation and rich farmland.

Land and Climate

The Dominican Republic has the most rugged and complicated terrain on any of the islands of the Antilles. In general terms there are four major mountain systems and three intervening lowlands, lying roughly in an east–west direction.

One of the systems, the Cordillera Septentrional, is located between Montecristi and Nagua across the

This article was contributed by Gustavo A. Antonini, Professor of Geography, Center for Latin American Studies, University of Florida, Gainesville.

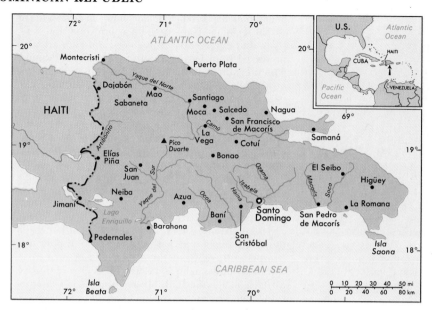

northern coast, and only small areas of coastal plain are found squeezed between the hills and the Atlantic Ocean. The principal mountain system is the Cordillera Central, which runs across the middle of the country from northern Haiti almost to Santo Domingo. Here there are more than 20 mountains with heights greater than 6,500 feet (2,000 meters),

Facts About the Dominican Republic

Official Name: Dominican Republic.

Capital: Santo Domingo.

Area: 18,703 square miles (48,442 square kilometers).

Population (1982 estimate): 5,752,500; 307.6 persons per square mile (118.8 persons per square kilometer); 52 percent urban, 48 percent rural.

Major Language: Spanish (official).

Major Religion: Roman Catholic.

Literacy: 70 percent.

Highest Peak: Pico Duarte.

Major Rivers: Isabela, Macorís, Ozama, Soco, Yaque del Norte, Yaque del Sur.

Form of Government: Republic.

Head of State and Government: President.

Legislature: National Congress.

Voting Qualifications: Citizens who are 18 years old, excluding members of the armed forces and the police, may vote.

Political Divisions: 26 provinces.

Major Cities (1981 census): Santo Domingo 1,313,172, Santiago 278,638, La Romana 91,571, San Pedro de Macorís 78,562, San Francisco de Macorís 64,906.

Chief Manufactured and Mined Products: Refined sugar, textiles, pharmaceuticals, beer, molasses, cement, bauxite, silver, gold, nickel.

Chief Agricultural Products: *Crops*—sugarcane, coffee, tobacco, cocoa, rice, potatoes, beans, cassavas, bananas (plantains). *Livestock*—cattle, goats, horses, donkeys.

Flag: *Colors*—blue, red, and white. The state flag also has the national coat of arms at the center (*see* Flags of the World).

Monetary Unit: 1 Dominican Republic peso = 100 centavos.

including the highest peak in the Antilles called Pico Duarte at 10,130 feet (3,087 meters). The Cordillera Central has a maximum width of 50 miles (80 kilometers) but makes up more than one third of the country. Two smaller mountain systems called Sierra de Neiba and Sierra de Baoruco are in the southwest.

These four mountain systems fix the limits of three lowlands. Between the Cordillera Septentrional and the Cordillera Central is the Cibao Valley. It contains areas of flat land that are particularly fertile to the east of the city of Santiago in a region called the Vega Real. It is well known for producing bananas, cacao, and rice. The San Juan Valley lies between the Cordillera Central and the Sierra de Neiba. This valley also has excellent soil and, with irrigation, has become a major rice-growing region. Farther to the south, between the Sierra de Neiba and the Sierra de Baoruco, is the Enriquillo Basin, which has a drier climate and contains the salty Lago Enriquillo 130 feet (40 meters) below sea level.

The only extensive coastal plain is in the southeast. Called the Caribbean coastal plain, it is the principal sugar cane and beef producing area.

Although the country is at tropical latitudes, the trade winds, the surrounding ocean, and high elevations combine in some areas to produce a climate that is far from typical of the tropics. In fact, frost is common on the highest peaks of the Cordillera Central. In most areas, however, temperatures are moderately high and vary little from season to season. Rainfall is normally greatest on the mountain slopes over which the easterly trade winds blow and decreases on the opposite slopes and in the major valleys.

Plant and Animal Life

The Dominican Republic once had many pine, hardwood, and mixed pine–hardwood forests. But hurricanes, fire, uncontrolled cutting, and conversion to agriculture have destroyed most of this woodland. Only 14 percent of the country still had hardwood forests in 1980. These are concentrated in the dry southwest and northwest and are being rapidly degraded by charcoal manufacturers and by goats that graze on seedlings. Pine forests remain in the higher and least accessible parts but now cover less than 10 percent of the nation. The country imports $30 million more wood products than it exports annually.

Its wide variety of topographic and climatic conditions has given the Dominican Republic the richest plant life in the Antilles. About 36 percent of the approximately 5,600 species are thought to be native. Over 125 plant species are threatened or in danger of extinction, including many kinds of orchids. A total of 139 resident and 90 migratory bird species have been identified. Serious habitat destruction, hunting, and the introduction of such species as the mongoose and rabbit, however, have reduced most native populations.

People

Most inhabitants live in the central part of the country, especially in the Cibao Valley and the Santo Domingo region. In the west along the Haiti border, population is sparse. The annual rate of growth is high at 2.6 percent. At this rate, population doubles in 27 years. Poverty has forced many people to leave the countryside and move into the towns, especially to the capital city, Santo Domingo. The urban population now exceeds the rural, and it is increasingly difficult for the new urban dwellers to find employment. Thousands of Dominicans have chosen to leave the country, particularly to go to the United States.

Although mulattos are most numerous, power has historically been in the hands of Dominican whites. They dominate business, finance, the prestigious professions, government, and high society. Mulattos are the majority in the military officer corps, the provincial towns, the less prestigious professions, and among lower- to middle-level government officials. Almost everyone speaks Spanish and is Roman Catholic. The church is influential on some issues—education, divorce, birth control—but its overall influence has diminished with time.

Economy

The economy is still dominated by agriculture, with 56 percent of the country used for crops or pasture. Small farmers produce staple foods, especially bananas (plantains), yucas, beans, and sweet potatoes. Although they make up the bulk of the rural population, these farmers have little land and they are too poor to apply the best farming practices. As a result their incomes remain low, and many migrate to urban areas in search of a better way of life. Foodstuffs are imported to make up the ever-increasing shortage in the nation's food production. Large farmers own the most fertile land and concentrate on crops for export, particularly sugar cane, coffee, cocoa, and tobacco; they also raise beef cattle.

Sunpath Enterprises—CLICK/Chicago

Fort Diego Columbus, built from 1510 to 1514, stands at the mouth of the Ozama River in the city of Santo Domingo.

There is growing concern about farming hillsides, especially by small farmers who cut down the forest and grow their crops without using conservation techniques that would protect against rapid soil erosion. To make things worse, much of the eroded soil is transported by rain into rivers that carry it into expensive reservoirs built for water supply, irrigation, and hydroelectric energy systems.

Agricultural products account for two thirds of export earnings. The rest comes largely from minerals, especially bauxite, nickel, and gold. The Dominican Republic is among the top ten gold-producing countries of the world and has the largest single gold mine in the Western Hemisphere. The income from the export of these metals is about equal to the amount spent on imported petroleum. Most of the remaining imports are manufactured goods such as machinery, chemicals, and foodstuffs.

In recent years the government has made great efforts to improve the economy by stimulating the tourist industry. More than 500,000 tourists visit the country each year to enjoy the warm climate, attractive beaches, and the capital city.

History and Government

Christopher Columbus' brother Bartholomew founded Santo Domingo in 1496. This makes it the oldest permanently occupied town in the Americas. At that time there were more than a million native inhabitants on the island, but within 50 years most had died of starvation, overwork in the gold mines, and epidemics of European diseases.

The gold that could be obtained using 16th-century mining techniques was exhausted by 1530, and Spain lost interest in her Santo Domingo colony soon afterward with the discoveries of Mexico and Peru. The Spaniards who remained on the island turned to cultivating sugar cane, using black slaves imported from Africa.

In 1697 Spain ceded the western third of Hispaniola to France. By the end of the 18th century, the new French possession known as Saint Domingue was one of the world's richest colonies, producing vast quantities of sugar and cotton. It had 524,000 inhabitants, of whom 88 percent were African slaves. Santo Domingo, with twice the territory of its neighbor, had barely one fifth the population, and its economic growth was slow.

France gained control in 1795 of the whole island, but slave uprisings in the west led in 1804 to the creation there of Haiti, the world's first black republic. In 1814 Spain again got control of the eastern part of the island, but the Dominicans declared independence in 1821. Soon afterward the Haitians invaded the Dominican Republic and ruled it by force for 22 years. This occupation is often considered the cause of an antagonism that still separates Dominicans from Haitians. One favorable consequence of Haitian rule, however, was the freeing of slaves.

Unhappily, liberation from the Haitians did little to bring peace and economic progress. During the rest of the 19th century, the Dominican Republic suffered scores of revolutions, more armed invasions from Haiti, and another period of Spanish domination from 1861 to 1865. Money was borrowed recklessly by corrupt governments, and by 1916 the country was in political and economic chaos. World War I was in progress, and the United States decided to occupy the Dominican Republic to restore order and protect approaches to the Panama Canal. This occupation lasted for eight years, and, though there was opposition to it, the enforced political stability permitted major social and economic advances.

In 1930, however, there was another revolution, and the country fell into the hands of a dictator, General Rafael Leonidas Trujillo Molina. For nearly 31 years, until his assassination in 1961, Trujillo headed a ruthless police state (*see* Trujillo Molina). At the cost of political freedom, the Dominican Republic had another period of imposed stability that, combined with favorable sugar prices, stimulated impressive economic growth. Five years of political turmoil after Trujillo's death led in 1965 to another intervention by the United States, which was concerned about the possibility of a Cuban-style communist takeover.

Since then the political scene has been relatively orderly with freely-elected presidents. The best known is Joaquín Balaguer, who was in power from 1966 to 1978. Much wealth has been generated, but as always it has been unequally distributed. The bulk of the population remains poor and undernourished, caught in a low standard of living.

In the 1980s the low price of sugar in the world market brought on a series of economic crises. Under Salvador Jorge Blanco, who was elected president in 1982, the government instituted an austerity program. Such measures as wage controls and the removal of food subsidies led to rioting in many cities in 1984.

For further reading, see 'The Dominican Republic: a Caribbean Crucible' by H.J. Wiarda and M.J. Kryzanek, published in 1982; 'The Dominican Republic' by I. Bell (1981); and 'The Dominican Republic: Country Environmental Profile', published in 1981 by USAID. Population (1984 estimate), 6,075,000.

DOMINOES. The game of dominoes was apparently invented in Italy or France in the 18th century. It is now played, in a variety of ways, in most countries of the world. The usual set consists of 28 dominoes—flat, rectangular blocks made of bone, wood, or plastic. The faces of 27 of the divided pieces (sometimes called bones) have varied combinations of dots or dots and blanks. The highest count is the double 6. The lowest is the double blank.

Block and draw. Block, the simplest form of the game, is usually played by two persons. The dominoes are laid face down and mixed. The person who is to lead, or "set," is chosen by drawing to see who gets the highest domino. The pieces used in the draw are returned to the pack. Each player then draws seven dominoes and sets them so that his opponent cannot see the dots, or spots.

Beginning with the set, each person plays one domino in turn. He must match the open end of a domino already played. If he is "blocked," his opponent goes on until a domino is placed that the blocked player can match. The game ends when one player "dominoes" (goes out) or when both players are blocked. The winner is the one who dominoes or who has the fewest spots on his remaining pieces. His score is the number of spots on his opponent's unplayed dominoes. A game may be 50 or 100 points.

Draw is similar to block except that when a player is blocked he draws from the reserve until he can play. The last two pieces in the stock, or boneyard, may not be drawn.

All Fives, or Muggins. In this game each player draws five dominoes. The aim is to play so the spots on the ends total 5 or a multiple of 5. For example, if the total is 8, 2 can be added to make 10 (2 points) or 3 can be subtracted to make 5 (1 point). When a player has no domino that matches an end, he draws until he gets one he can use. If he cannot score, he tries to play a domino that will make it difficult for his opponent to score.

The player who dominoes adds to his score the number of fives on his opponent's unplayed domi-

The dominoes are numbered in order of play. When B is played, the two threes in A are ends. With C at the left of A, the ends are six and four. The best-scoring dominoes are the fives and the blanks.

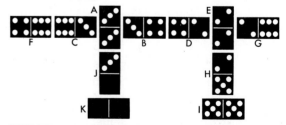

MUGGINS, THE ALL FIVES DOMINOES GAME

A. 3-3, no score (3+3)
B. 3-4, 2 points for two fives (4+3+3=10)
C. 3-6, 2 points (6+4)
D. 4-2, no score (2+6)
E. 2-2, 2 points (2+2+6)
F. 6-4, no score (4+2+2)
G. 2-6, 2 points (6+4)
H. 2-5, 3 points (5+6+4)
I. 5-5, 4 points (5+5+6+4)
J. 3-0, 4 points (4+6+5+5)
K. 0-0, 4 points (4+6+5+5)

noes. For example, 12 would be 2 points and 27 would be 5. A game is usually 61 points.

Matador. The aim of matador is to make sevens. Instead of placing matched ends together, a player puts 5 next to 2, 6 to 1, 3 to 4, and so on. Since the highest number of spots is 6, a blank blocks an end unless someone puts up a "matador." This is either a piece whose spots total 7 exactly or a double blank, which requires another matador to be played next to it. Matadors may also be played in the ordinary way.

Each player begins with seven tiles. The player may draw when he wishes, except that he must draw from the boneyard when blocked. If a player dominoes, his score is the number of spots on his opponent's remaining pieces. If the game is blocked, the winner is the one with the fewest spots. This number is subtracted from his opponent's total.

DONATELLO (1386?–1466). One of the towering figures of the Italian Renaissance, Donatello was the greatest sculptor of the 15th century. He influenced both sculpture and painting throughout that century and beyond.

Donato (Donatello is a diminutive form, just as Kenny is for Kenneth) di Niccolò di Betto Bardi was born in Florence about 1386. He probably learned stone carving from one of the sculptors working on the Florence cathedral in about 1400. Between 1404 and 1407 he worked in the workshop of the Gothic sculptor Lorenzo Ghiberti, who had won the competition to create some bronze doors for the cathedral baptistery. Donatello created two marble statues in a new style for the church of Or San Michele in about 1415. In these statues, 'Saint Mark' and 'Saint George', for the first time since Roman classicism, the human body was shown as a functioning figure with a human personality—in sharp contrast with medieval art. Donatello's well-known statue 'Zuccone' ("pumpkin" because of its bald head) of 1425 for the campanile, or bell tower, of the cathedral is a further development of the style.

For the base of 'St. George' Donatello invented a new kind of relief, or sculpture raised from a flat surface, called *schiacciato,* meaning "flattened out." The carving was extremely shallow with details executed to catch the light in a pictorial manner rather than deeply carved figures against relatively plain backgrounds.

Donatello also worked in bronze, beginning in about 1423. The most important bronze works were 'David', the first large-scale, free-standing nude statue of the Renaissance; 'Gattamelata' in Padua, the first bronze equestrian, or man-mounted-on-horse, statue to commemorate a non-ruler and the model for all subsequent equestrian monuments; and twin bronze pulpits for the Medici church of San Lorenzo in Florence, just before his death there on Dec. 13, 1466. In the late 1440s Donatello also executed a complex high altar for Padua's church of San Antonio containing seven life-size bronze statues, 21 bronze reliefs, and a large limestone relief.

DONIZETTI, Gaetano (1797–1848). Italian composer Gaetano Donizetti's works represent a transitional stage in operatic development between Rossini and Verdi. His 75 operas made him one of the most prolific of 19th-century Italian opera composers.

Donizetti was born on Nov. 29, 1797, in Bergamo in Lombardy, Italy. He began his musical studies with a Bavarian priest. His first success was 'Enrico di Borgogna', performed in Venice in 1818, and during the next 12 years he composed at least 31 operas. After his 'Anna Bolena' was produced in Milan in 1830, his fame spread across Europe and to the United States. His next success came two years later with the comedy 'The Elixir of Love'. He went to Paris but did not have great success there. He returned to Naples for the production of his tragic masterpiece, 'Lucia di Lammermoor', in 1835.

Donizetti was engaged to compose an opera for La Scala opera house in Milan. The work, 'Maria Padilla', was produced in 1841.

Donizetti was married in 1828, but his wife died in 1837 following the stillbirth of a son, their third child not to survive birth. Donizetti died on April 8, 1848, in Bergamo. By 1914 his operas were overshadowed by those of Verdi and Wagner, though his popularity was revived in the 1950s. His operas include 'Lucrezia Borgia', produced in 1833, 'The Daughter of the Regiment' (1840), 'La Favorite' (1840), 'Don Pasquale' (1843), and 'Dom Sébastien, roi de Portugal' (1843).

DON JUAN LEGEND. Kept alive in plays, novels, and poems, the Don Juan legend centers around a fictitious character who is generally regarded as a symbol of libertinism. Libertinism is immoral behavior that is not restrained by conscience or conventions. The legend tells how Don Juan seduced a girl of noble family and then killed her father when he sought revenge. Later Don Juan saw a ghost of the father and flippantly invited it to dinner. The ghost arrived to foreshadow Don Juan's own death.

Don Juan was first given literary personality in the 1630 tragic drama 'The Seducer of Seville' by the Spanish dramatist Tirso de Molina. In this version the drama is heightened by Don Juan's attractive qualities—his lively character, arrogant courage, and sense of humor. The drama's power comes from its rapid pace. There is growing tension as Don Juan's enemies hound him to self-destruction. He refuses to repent and falls to eternal damnation. Through Tirso's version, Don Juan became a universal figure, comparable to Hamlet and Don Quixote.

In the 17th century the Don Juan story was incorporated into the repertoire of strolling Italian players who carried the legend to France. By the 19th century many foreign versions of the Don Juan legend existed. Some of these musical and literary works include Mozart's opera 'Don Giovanni', produced in 1787, Lord Byron's satiric poem 'Don Juan' (1819–24), and George Bernard Shaw's drama 'Man and Superman' (performed in 1907), including the well-known third act, 'Don Juan in Hell'.

John Donne

Courtesy of the National Portrait
Gallery, London

DONNE, John (1572–1631). The clergyman John
Donne was one of the most gifted poets in English
literature. His work had great influence on poets of
the 17th and 20th centuries.

Donne was born in London to wealthy parents.
He was raised as a Roman Catholic, unusual in that
England was almost totally Protestant at the time.
He was educated at Oxford, Cambridge, and Lincoln's
Inn, where he studied law. After graduating he be-
came an adventurer, keen of wit and sharp of pen.
During this period he wrote his 'Satires' and most
of the lusty, cynical verses that make up his 'Songs
and Sonnets'.

In his mid-20s Donne went abroad in foreign service to the Azores, Spain, and Italy. On his return to
England he served Sir Thomas Egerton, Lord Keeper
of the Great Seal. But when Donne eloped with Anne
More, Lady Egerton's niece, his employer turned
against him. In the decade that followed, Donne en-
dured poverty and unemployment.

His religious faith was shaken during this time,
and he was converted to the Church of England. He
became an Anglican clergyman in 1615, and James
I made him his chaplain. In 1621 Donne became
dean of Saint Paul's Cathedral in London and began
writing the sermons and "devotions" that made him
one of the best-known and respected preachers of his
time. He continued to write verse, but of a religious
nature, that was published as 'Divine Poems'.

Some of his essays and sermons were published
during his lifetime. Most of his poetry, though written
much earlier, was published by his son after his death
on March 31, 1631, in London.

DON RIVER. A historic waterway of Russia, the
Don River flows through Soviet Europe. It begins
south of Moscow in the small reservoir of Shat near
the city of Novomoskovsk. It flows from the central
Russian uplands in a generally southerly direction
until it enters the Gulf of Taganrog in the Sea of Azov.

The major waterways feeding the Don are the Kra-
sivaya Mecha, Sosna, Chir, and Donets on its right
bank and the Voronezh, Khoper, and Manych on the
left. In its upper part the Don flows through a narrow
valley along the eastern edge of the central Russian
heights. The valley widens to about 4 miles (6 kilometers) farther down the Don. The Don finally flows into
the Tsimlyansk Reservoir. The reservoir has raised

the level of the river by 80 feet (25 meters), made the
lower part of the river a major transportation artery,
and evened out its annual flow.

The river is fed primarily by snow. An extensive
network of canals in the lower part of the Don provides
irrigation to surrounding rich farm and timber land.
The river carries cargoes of lumber, grain, building
materials, and other bulk freight and provides valuable fishes, including pike, perch, carp, and sturgeon.
Its largest ports are Kalach-na-Donu, Tsimlyansk, and
Rostov-na-Donu.

DORÉ, Gustave (1832–83). Critic Théophile Gau-
tier said that nobody could create better "all the
monsters of fantasy" than the French artist Gustave
Doré. Doré is known for his highly imaginative book
illustrations.

Paul-Gustave Doré was born on Jan. 6, 1832, in
Strasbourg, France. By his early teens he had already
had some of his artwork published. In 1847 he went
to Paris and from 1848 to 1851 drew cartoons for
the weekly magazine *Journal pour Rire*. He also
published books of his ink drawings. Although he
wanted to be a great painter, and he sculpted as
well, Doré's success came from his illustrations in
famous books, for which he used a wood-engraving
process. Some of the best of these were 'Works of
Rabelais', published in 1854, 'Droll Stories' of Balzac
(1855), a Bible (1866), Dante's 'Inferno' (1861), and
Cervantes' 'Don Quixote' (1863). His 1862 drawings
to accompany the fairy tales of Charles Perrault are
still in publication today.

'Don Quixote' was painted by Gustave Doré in about 1863.

The Metropolitan Museum of Art, New York

Many of Doré's drawings were of fascinating, imaginary scenes from myth and legend. He often used religious or historical themes for his paintings, but he did not seem to bring these subjects to life as well as he did the creatures of imagination. Doré died in Paris on Jan. 23, 1883.

DORMOUSE. The little night creature called the dormouse lives in Europe. It has a long furry tail and is related to both the mouse and the squirrel. It lives in trees and bushes, feeding on nuts and berries. It sits erect on its haunches, like a squirrel, when eating.

The dormouse stores food for use during the winter. When cold weather comes, it curls up in its nest and sleeps. On warm days it is likely to wake, eat, and fall asleep again. Its name means "sleeping mouse." Dormice are sometimes tamed and kept as pets. They belong to the family Gliridae, order Rodentia. In the United States the common white-footed mouse is often called a dormouse.

DORTMUND, West Germany. A major transportation and industrial center of the Ruhr region, Dortmund is in North Rhine–Westphalia state. Although there is much industry, Dortmund remains green with about half of its area covered by farms, parks, and forests. There are extensive port facilities at the head of the Dortmund–Ems Canal.

Dortmund is one of Europe's largest producers of beer. Steel and coal are also major products. There is a large wholesale fruit and vegetable market. Several bridge-building firms that operate worldwide are headquartered in the city, and there are also machinery factories.

Dortmund has many educational institutions, including the Max Planck Institute for Industrial Physiology and for the Physiology of Nutrition, the Institute for Spectrochemistry and Spectroanalysis, and Münster University's Social Research Institute. The University of Dortmund was founded in 1966. There are also schools for social studies, journalistic research, mountaineering, mining, teacher training, and adult education. The Museum of the History of Culture and Art is housed in a building that was once a monastery. It houses the "Dortmund treasure," a collection of more than 400 gold coins.

Westfalenhalle, or Westphalia Hall, which was built in 1952, is one of Europe's largest facilities, and it is used for conventions, exhibitions, and sporting events. The Municipal Theater has three main houses for concerts, plays, and operas. In addition to Westfalenhalle, a synagogue built in 1956 is another notable example of modern architecture in Dortmund. In contrast there are three churches that date from the 12th to the 14th century.

Dortmund was known as Throtmanni when a name was first recorded in 885. It became a free imperial city in 1220 and later joined the Hanseatic League, medieval northern European cities that joined to promote commerce. By the 14th century it had become extremely prosperous through trading. Its prosperity

Archiv fur Kunst und Geschichte

The Marienkirche, left, and the Reinoldikirche, right, flank the city center square of Dortmund, West Germany.

declined after the Thirty Years' War, which ended in 1648, and it lost its imperial rights in 1803. Its population was then only about 4,000. With the development of coal mining and iron-ore mining in the 19th century, and the completion of the Dortmund–Ems canal in 1899, Dortmund grew rapidly. Population (1983 estimate), 599,521.

DOS PASSOS, John (1896–1970). The American author Dos Passos was a social historian who championed the underdog. He was also the creator of a fresh and original technique in novel writing.

John Roderigo Dos Passos was born on Jan. 14, 1896, in Chicago, Ill. His father, also named John, was a lawyer who had been a drummer boy in the Civil War. The Dos Passos family traveled in many countries, including England where for a time John attended school.

Dos Passos entered Harvard University in 1912 with the vague intention of becoming an architect. He was graduated *cum laude* in 1916, still with no definite ambition to be a writer. Soon after graduation he went to Spain to study architecture. Early in 1917, during World War I, he joined the ambulance service of the Allies. When the United States entered the war, Dos Passos enlisted in the Medical Corps.

After the war he traveled widely, writing for newspapers and magazines. His wartime experience gave Dos Passos the inspiration and subject matter for his first novel, 'One Man's Initiation—1917', published in England in 1920. In 1921 he published 'Three Soldiers', which was well received by both critics and the public. It is a violent protest against war.

'Manhattan Transfer' (1925) was a turning point in Dos Passos' writing career. In this novel he used several innovations in technique. One device is the telling of many separate stories simultaneously in a sort of impressionistic effort to capture the pace and atmosphere of big-city life.

Dos Passos became increasingly interested in social and political issues and more and more concerned with the problems of poor people. For a time he supported leftist causes. Later, however, he became disillusioned with Communism as a method for social reform.

His most important works are 'U.S.A.', a trilogy of 'The 42nd Parallel' (1930), 'Nineteen Nineteen' (1932), and 'The Big Money' (1936). In these novels Dos Passos used some of the literary devices he had introduced in 'Manhattan Transfer'. Intermingled with the stories are sketches of prominent people who were living during the period covered. He also used newspaper headlines and bits from popular songs to recreate the mood of the time.

Another trilogy, 'District of Columbia', was made up of 'Adventures of a Young Man' (1939), 'Number One' (1943), and 'The Grand Design' (1949). His growing conservatism was evident in these works. He also published poems, essays, plays, and travel books. He was married twice and had one daughter. Dos Passos died in Baltimore, Md., on Sept. 29, 1970.

DOSTOEVSKI, Fedor. (1821–81).

The Russian writer Dostoevski is regarded as one of the world's great novelists. In Russia he was surpassed only by Leo Tolstoi.

Fedor Mikhailovich Dostoevski was born on Nov. 11, 1821, in a Moscow hospital where his father was a physician. At 13 Fedor was sent to a Moscow boarding school, then to a military engineering school in Saint Petersburg, now Leningrad. He obtained an army commission when he was graduated but resigned at 22 to become a writer.

Dostoevski had joined a group of about 20 who were studying French socialist theories. After the 1848 revolutions in Western Europe, Czar Nicholas I decided to round up all revolutionaries. In April 1849 Dostoevski's group was imprisoned. In December a faked death sentence was read to them, and they were led to execution. When they thought they had only a minute to live, the real sentence was read. The youths were taken in chains to Omsk in Siberia. There, Dostoevski said, they were "packed in like herrings in a barrel" with murderers and other criminals. He read and reread the New Testament, the only book he had, and built a mystical creed, identifying Christ with the common people of Russia. He had great sympathy for the criminals.

As a child Dostoevski suffered from mild epilepsy, and it grew worse in prison. After four years in prison, he was sent as a private to a military station in Siberia. There in 1857 he met and married Marie Isaeva, a sickly and hysterical widow who brought him no happiness.

In 1860 Dostoevski was back in St. Petersburg. The next year he began to publish a literary journal that was soon suppressed, though he had by now lost in-

Fedor Dostoevski

terest in socialism. In 1862 he visited Western Europe and hated the industrialism he saw there. Dostoevski had been separated from his wife but visited her in Moscow before her death in 1864. In 1867 he married his young stenographer, Anna Snitkina. He died on Feb. 9, 1881, in St. Petersburg.

The Novels

Not all of Dostoevski's novels are great, but those that are are unsurpassed in their excellence of plot, characterization, and social description. Dostoevski himself best defined his intent when he said: "I portray all the depths of the human soul." He also portrayed a profound devotion to the New Testament Christianity that he learned during his Siberian exile.

His two earliest novels, 'Poor Folk' and 'The Double', both published in 1846, were minor efforts, but 'Poor Folk' was the first Russian social novel. It is a narration of the tragic futility of the life of the poor.

It was 18 years after these works that he wrote the first of his masterpieces, 'Notes from the Underground' (1864). In it Dostoevski created the antihero, a type of fictional character that became prominent in 20th-century novels. The antihero of 'Notes' is a nameless individual whose self-analysis reveals a person for whom all truth and morality are relative, a man torn by conflict between reason and his will. In some ways 'Notes' serves as an introduction to the great novels of the next 16 years: 'Crime and Punishment' (1866), 'The Idiot' (1869), 'The Possessed' (1872), and 'The Brothers Karamazov' (1880), considered by many critics to be the finest novel ever written.

At their simplest level, both 'Crime and Punishment' and 'The Brothers Karamazov' are ingenious murder mysteries, but they are much more. The first is a social novel whose main character, Raskolnikov, is an intellectual rebel against society. His struggles with good and evil lead him to conclude that the murder he commits is justified by his humanitarian goals. In 'The Brothers Karamazov' it is the extravagant father who is killed. Through the conflict of three very different brothers—Ivan, Dmitri, and Alyosha—Dostoevski probes the nature of moral and actual guilt. And in so doing he clarifies the meaning of Christianity and the search for faith.

'The Idiot' is the story of Prince Myshkin, whose faith and personality are symbolic of Christ. 'The Possessed' is an action-packed novel about a Moscow student's murder by fellow revolutionaries. The story reflects Dostoevski's own opposition to revolution and his devotion to the Russia of the Czars and to the Russian Orthodox faith.

DOUALA, Cameroon. The chief port of the African nation of Cameroon, Douala is on the southeastern shore of the Wouri River estuary and west of the capital city of Yaoundé. It is the capital of Littoral province and of Wouri department.

Douala's deepwater port handles most of Cameroon's overseas trade. There are special installations to handle timber products, bananas, gasoline, and bauxite, as well as fishing facilities. Douala is one of the major industrial centers of central Africa. It has breweries, textile factories, and palm oil, soap, and food-processing plants. Building materials, metalwork, plastics, glass, paper, bicycles, and timber products are also produced. Other businesses include boat and ship repairing and radio assembly.

The city is connected by road to all major towns in Cameroon and has railroad links to Kumba, Nkongsamba, Yaoundé, and Ngaoundéré. It is also served by an international airport. The 5,900-foot (1,800-meter) Wouri Bridge joins Douala with the banana port of Bonabéri and carries road and rail traffic to western Cameroon.

There is a mixture of traditional, colonial, and modern architecture in Douala. A branch of the University of Yaoundé and several commercial, agricultural, and industrial schools are also in the city. A museum and a handicraft center create and preserve Cameroonian art.

The Duala peoples are traditionally said to have migrated to the Wouri River estuary at about the end of the 17th century. By 1800 they controlled trade with the Europeans. Several German firms had established themselves in the region by the 1860s. An 1884 treaty led to a German protectorate of which Douala was the capital from 1901 to 1916. It again served as the capital of Cameroon from 1940 to 1946. Population (1981 estimate), 636,980.

DOUBLEDAY, Abner (1819–93). The man often credited with inventing baseball was a United States Army officer named Abner Doubleday. He was born on June 26, 1819, in Ballston Spa, N.Y. He graduated from the military academy at West Point in 1842 and was an artillery officer in the Mexican War from 1846 to 1848 and in the Seminole War in Florida from 1856 to 1858. He also happened to be at Fort Sumter in South Carolina when the first shots of the American Civil War were fired. He fought in several major battles of the war and became a colonel in 1867. He retired from the army in 1873 and settled at Mendham, N.J., where he died on Jan. 26, 1893.

Although his role in originating baseball has been discredited, his name became permanently tied to the game as a result of his formulation of its basic rules in 1839 at Cooperstown, N.Y. Cooperstown was subsequently chosen as the site of the National Baseball Hall of Fame and Museum.

DOUGLAS, Stephen (1813–61). The author of the Kansas-Nebraska Act of 1854 was Stephen Douglas, a United States senator from 1847 until his death. He also gained national fame from a series of debates with Abraham Lincoln (*see* Lincoln-Douglas Debates).

Stephen Arnold Douglas was born on April 23, 1813, at Brandon, Vt. At 20 he moved to Illinois. There he practiced law and entered politics. In 1843 he became one of the youngest members of the House of Representatives.

Douglas' Kansas-Nebraska Act provided that the people in these territories should decide whether the territories would join the Union as slave or as free states. The act was opposed by the antislavery leaders. Among these was Abraham Lincoln. In 1858 he ran against Douglas for the senatorship from Illinois, basing his campaign on the Kansas-Nebraska issue. Douglas won the senatorship. In the debate at Freeport, Ill., however, he was led to declare that any territory could by "unfriendly legislation" exclude slavery. This statement antagonized the South.

When the national Democratic convention met in 1860, the Southern delegates bolted the party rather than support Douglas for president. At a separate convention they named John C. Breckinridge as their candidate. The Northern Democrats nominated Douglas. The split in the party made the election of Lincoln, the Republican candidate, a foregone conclusion.

Douglas now devoted his energy to opposing secession and loyally pledged his support to Lincoln and the Union. This work was cut short by his death from typhoid fever on June 6, 1861, in Chicago. (*See also* Kansas-Nebraska Act; Lincoln, Abraham.)

DOUGLAS, William O. (1898–1980). For more than 36 years William O. Douglas served as an associate justice of the United States Supreme Court, the longest time served on record. Known as a champion of civil liberties and the rights of minorities, he was also a naturalist who wrote on conservation as well as history, politics, and foreign relations.

William Orville Douglas was born on Oct. 16, 1898, in Maine, Minn., and grew up in California and Washington. As a youth, he fell ill with polio, but he escaped permanent paralysis, and a self-imposed program of exercise left him with a lifelong love of the outdoors.

Douglas received his law degree from Columbia University in New York City in 1925. He joined a Wall Street law firm but in 1927 became an assistant professor at Columbia's law school and the next year at Yale University's law school. He was at Yale until his appointment to the Supreme Court in 1939.

At Yale Douglas became known for his studies in bankruptcy, working also with the Department of Commerce. In 1934 he directed a related study for the Securities and Exchange Commission (SEC) and was named to the commission in 1936 and chairman the following year.

When he succeeded Justice Louis Brandeis on the Supreme Court, Douglas was thought to be pro-business, but he became known for his absolutist interpretation of the guarantees of freedom in the Bill of Rights. His opposition to any form of censorship made him a frequent target of political conservatives and religious fundamentalists.

Often in dissent in the years before the more liberal court led by Chief Justice Earl Warren, Douglas faced impeachment charges, or formal charges of official misconduct, in the early 1950s, when he granted a stay of execution to Julius and Ethel Rosenberg who had been convicted of passing atomic secrets to the Soviet Union. Anti-Douglas feelings climaxed in the late 1960s and early 1970s, when his criticism of United States conduct in Southeast Asia and his fourth marriage, to a woman 45 years his junior, subjected him to further attempts at impeachment.

Douglas suffered a stroke at the end of 1974 and retired from the court late the next year. He died in Washington, D.C., on Jan. 19, 1980.

DOUGLAS-HOME, Alec (born 1903).

Britain's 44th prime minister, Alec Douglas-Home, gave up his ancient titles to become prime minister in 1963. Ill health had forced Harold Macmillan to resign the post.

Alexander Frederick Douglas-Home was born on July 2, 1903, in London, England. Always called Alec, he was the eldest son of Charles C.A. Douglas-Home and Lilian, daughter of the 4th earl of Durham.

Alec was educated at Eton and Oxford. When his father succeeded to the earldom of Home in 1918, Alec became Lord Dunglas. In 1931 he was elected to the House of Commons. In 1936 he married Elizabeth Hester. They had one son and three daughters.

During World War II Lord Dunglas served with the Lanarkshire Yeomanry until he was stricken with spinal tuberculosis. In 1943 he returned to Parliament. He lost his seat in the Labour Party victory of 1945 but regained it in 1950.

When his father died in 1951, he became the 14th earl of Home and gave up his seat in the House of Commons to take his hereditary place in the House of Lords. He became prime minister in October 1963. Renouncing his peerage in order to lead the Conservative party in the House of Commons, he became Sir Douglas-Home. His government lasted until October 1964, when Harold Wilson, leader of the Labour party, succeeded him. From 1970 to 1974 Douglas-Home was foreign secretary in the Conservative Cabinet of Edward Heath. After Wilson returned to power, Douglas-Home retired from politics.

Frederick Douglass

Courtesy of the Holt-Messer Collection, Schlesinger Library, Radcliffe College, Cambridge, Mass.

DOUGLASS, Frederick (1817–95).

An escaped slave, Frederick Douglass became one of the foremost black abolitionists and civil rights leaders in the United States. His powerful speeches, newspaper articles, and books awakened whites to the evils of slavery and inspired blacks in their struggle for freedom and equality.

Frederick Douglass was born Frederick Augustus Washington Bailey in Talbot County, Md., sometime in February 1817. His father was an unknown white man; his mother, Harriet Bailey, was a slave. He was separated from her and raised by her elderly parents.

At 7, Frederick was sent to his master, Captain Aaron Anthony, at a nearby plantation. There he first met a brother and two sisters. He later recalled sadly that "slavery had made us strangers."

When he was 8, Frederick became a servant to Hugh Auld, a relative of Captain Anthony who lived in Baltimore, Md. Frederick persuaded Auld's wife to teach him to read. But Auld believed slaves should not be educated and stopped the lessons. White playmates helped Frederick, and he soon learned to read well. A book of speeches denouncing slavery and oppression deepened his hatred of slavery.

In 1833 Frederick was sent to work for Auld's brother, Thomas, at a plantation near Saint Michael's, Md. Frederick's pride angered his new master, who placed him in the hands of a "slave breaker" in an effort to "tame" him. One day the two fought, and Frederick emerged victorious. Sometime later he wrote that the fight had been a turning point in his life. "I was nothing before—I was a man now."

In 1835 Frederick was put to work at a farm near Thomas Auld's plantation. In the following year he and other slaves plotted to escape to the North. Their plan was discovered, and they were jailed. Frederick was released and sent back to Baltimore, where he became a ship's caulker. Once, he was attacked by white workers who resented the competition of slave laborers. They went unpunished because the testimony of black witnesses would not be admitted as evidence in a court. For a while in 1838 Hugh Auld allowed Frederick to find his own jobs and to keep part of his wages.

On Sept. 3, 1838, Frederick escaped from slavery. With identification borrowed from a free black seaman, he traveled to New York City. In less than a day he was a free man. Soon after, he sent for Anna Murray, a free black woman from Baltimore. They were married and settled in New Bedford, Mass. There he took the name Frederick Douglass.

Antislavery Campaigns

Douglass read the *Liberator*, an antislavery newspaper published by the white abolitionist William Lloyd Garrison. He eagerly attended antislavery meetings. In 1841 at an antislavery convention, Douglass described his slave life in a moving speech that began his career as an abolitionist.

Douglass became an agent of the Massachusetts Anti-Slavery Society and in this capacity lectured to large assemblies. Soon he became unhappy with merely retelling his memories of slave life. He later said, "It did not entirely satisfy me to *narrate* wrongs—I felt like *denouncing* them." In 1841 Douglass campaigned in Rhode Island against a proposed new state constitution that would deny blacks the right to vote. In 1843 he traveled through the East and Middle West to address a series of antislavery assemblies known as the "One Hundred Conventions."

In his travels, Douglass was sometimes attacked by proslavery mobs and often met discrimination. Once, he refused to leave his train seat for a segregated car and had to be forcibly removed.

Many listeners were so impressed by Douglass' appearance and personality that they could not believe he had ever been a slave. He had never revealed his

Frederick Douglass sought the support of British audiences for reforms like temperance as well as the abolition of slavery.

Frederick Douglass escaped to the North in 1838. In New York, friendly blacks hid him from fugitive slave hunters.

former name or the name of his master. To dispel doubts about his past, he published an autobiography in 1845, 'The Narrative of the Life of Frederick Douglass: an American Slave'. Fearful that it might lead to his reenslavement, Douglass fled to Great Britain, where he lectured to arouse support for the antislavery movement in the United States. English Quakers raised money to purchase his freedom, and in 1847 he returned home, now legally free.

That year, Douglass founded a new antislavery newspaper, *The North Star*—later renamed *Frederick Douglass's Paper*—in Rochester, N. Y. Unlike Garrison, he had come to believe that political action rather than moral persuasion would bring about the abolition of slavery. Douglass also resented Garrison's view that blacks did not have the ability to lead the antislavery movement. By 1853, he had broken with Garrison and become a strong and independent abolitionist.

While in Rochester, Douglass directed the city's branch of the "underground railroad," which smuggled escaped slaves into Canada. For years he worked to end racial segregation in Rochester's public schools. Douglass hoped that blacks would no longer be employed only as servants and laborers. He proposed that schools be established to train them to become skilled craftsmen.

In 1859 Douglass refused to join the white abolitionist John Brown in his attempt to seize arms for a slave revolt from the federal arsenal at Harpers Ferry, W. Va. (*see* Brown; Harpers Ferry). But Douglass did not reject violence as a weapon against slavery. He believed that "it can never be wrong for the imbruted and whip-scarred slaves, or their friends, to hunt, harass, and even strike down the traffickers in human flesh." Douglass was accused of helping Brown and was again forced to flee to England.

In the spring of 1860 he returned to the United States and began campaigning to elect Gerrit Smith, an abolitionist, as president. Later he came out in support of Abraham Lincoln, the successful Republican candidate. When the Civil War began, in 1861, Douglass urged that it be fought to abolish slavery. He applauded President Lincoln's final Emancipation Proclamation of 1863, which freed slaves in the rebellious states, but expressed his disappointment that not all slaves had been freed. Douglass urged the Union army to use black troops. In 1863 he helped form two black regiments. Black troops in the Union army were given lower wages and fewer chances for promotion than white soldiers. Douglass met with Lincoln to request equal treatment for them.

Civil Rights Advocate

After the Civil War, Douglass held several federal offices. In the District of Columbia he was appointed to the legislative council in 1871, United States marshal in 1877, and recorder of deeds in 1881. From 1889 to 1891 he served as minister to Haiti.

Douglass fought for passage of the 15th amendment to the Constitution—ratified in 1870—which gave blacks the right to vote. Later he saw that Southern blacks had returned to virtual slavery under a farming system called sharecropping. He urged that the federal government grant land to blacks.

Douglass earnestly supported women's rights. In 1848, at the first women's rights convention in the United States, he had demanded that women be allowed to vote. On the day of his death—Feb. 20, 1895, at Anacostia Heights, D.C.—Douglass attended a convention for women's suffrage.

Douglass proclaimed his beliefs in justice for the oppressed in *The North Star:* "Right is of no Sex— Truth is of no Color. . . ." He wanted blacks to lead the struggle for civil rights. The year he died, he urged a black student to "Agitate! Agitate! Agitate!"

Douglass' first wife died in 1882. They had five children. He married Helen Pitts, a white woman, in 1884. His 'Narrative' appeared in expanded editions as 'My Bondage and My Freedom' in 1855 and as 'The Life and Times of Frederick Douglass' in 1881.

DOVER, Del. The capital city of Delaware is Dover. Located on the Saint Jones River at a widening of the river called Silver Lake, it is about 35 miles (56 kilometers) south of Wilmington.

The countryside around Dover is fertile, and much farm produce is brought to the city to be shipped to surrounding and distant markets. Several canning and packing plants are located here. The city's manufactured products

include building materials, paints, rubber products, and perfumes.

In 1683 William Penn ordered that a new county seat be established at the present site of Dover. A courthouse and a prison were built there before 1697, but the town was not actually laid out until 1717. In 1777 Dover replaced New Castle as the capital of Delaware.

The historic State House was built between 1787 and 1792. This fine old building was first used as a county courthouse and a state capitol. It served both purposes until 1873, when the Kent County courthouse was erected. It still houses offices of many of the state departments. The mansion of John Dickinson, "penman of the Revolution," dates from 1740. The Delaware State Museum was built as a church in 1790. Other fine old colonial buildings on or near the Green are Christ Church and the Ridgely House. Legislative Hall, to the east of the Green, was completed in 1933. It is now the capitol.

Near Dover is Delaware State College, established for blacks in 1891. Wesley College lies within the city. Dover's city-owned utilities include an electric plant. Its government is a council-manager form. Population (1980 census), 23,512.

DOVER, England. The most important port of the English Channel, Dover is located at the foot of chalk cliffs on the Strait of Dover 65 miles (105 kilometers) southeast of London. The name Dover originally meant "the waters" or " the stream." Nearby is Shakespeare Cliff, where the first coal in the County of Kent was discovered in 1822. Dover is separated from France, at Calais, by only 22 miles (35 kilometers). On bright days the French coast can be seen.

A pre-Roman settlement was located on Dover's site, and, as Dubris, it served Roman traffic to the European mainland. In the 4th century AD there was a fort guarding the Saxon Shore. Dover Castle towers on the chalk cliffs some 375 feet (114 meters) above the sea. It was used as a fortress in Norman times. It includes a Roman lighthouse, the Saxon Church of Saint Mary in Castro, remains of the Saxon stronghold, and a massive Norman fortress. Dover is the chief of the Cinque Ports, a confederation of five English Channel ports formed in the 11th century to furnish ships and men for the king.

The city fought off the French in the naval battle of Dover, which was fought in 1217. During World War I it was a submarine base, and in World War II it was bombarded by planes and shelled by long-range German guns from the French coast. It was also used as the main port to receive troops and equipment in the evacuation of Dunkirk.

The harbor at Dover was rebuilt and was then improved after the end of World War II. Dover is Bri-

Dover Castle stands atop the famous "white cliffs" of Dover. The city can be seen behind and to the left of the castle and in front of the hills.

© 1962 by Charles E. Rotkin from 'Europe: An Aerial Close-up', Lippincott

tain's foremost passenger ship port and the principal cross-channel ferry port. There are light industries, a military base, and a sizable tourist business. Population (1981 preliminary), 32,843.

DOYLE, Conan (1859–1930). A British physician who turned to writing, Conan Doyle thought he would be remembered for his historical novels. His fame, however, rests on his creation of the master detective of fiction, the incomparable Sherlock Holmes. (*See also* Detective Story.)

Arthur Conan Doyle was born in Edinburgh, Scotland, on May 22, 1859. He was the oldest son of Charles Doyle, an artist. His parents were Irish Roman Catholics, and he received his early education in a Jesuit school, Stonyhurst. Later he got a medical degree at Edinburgh University. He started practice as a family physician in Southsea, England. His in-

Sir Arthur
Conan Doyle

Courtesy of the National
Portrait Gallery, London

come was small, and he began writing stories to make ends meet. In 1891 he decided to give up medicine to concentrate on his writing.

Conan Doyle was knighted in 1902 for his pamphlet justifying England's part in the Boer War, in which he served at a field hospital. He was married twice. The death of his son Kingsley in World War I intensified his interest in psychic phenomena, and in later years he wrote and lectured on spiritualism. He died in Sussex on July 7, 1930.

'A Study in Scarlet', published in 1887, introduced Holmes and his friend Doctor John Watson. The second Holmes story was 'The Sign of Four' (1890). In 1891 Doyle began a series for *Strand* magazine called 'The Adventures of Sherlock Holmes'.

Sherlock Holmes has become known to movie and television audiences as a tall and lean, pipe-smoking, violin-playing detective. He lived at 221 Baker Street in London, where he was often visited by his friend Doctor John Watson, an associate in the many adventures. And according to Doyle, it was Watson who recorded the Holmes stories for posterity.

Conan Doyle said he modeled Holmes after one of his teachers in Edinburgh, Dr. Joseph Bell. Bell could glance at a corpse on the anatomy table and deduce that the man had been a left-handed shoemaker. "It is all very well to say that a man is clever," Conan Doyle wrote, "but the reader wants to see examples of it—such examples as Bell gave us every day in the wards." The author eventually became bored with Holmes and "killed" him. Readers' protests made him change his mind, and the next story told how the detective had miraculously survived the death struggle on the edge of a precipice. Stories dealing with Holmes's exploits continued to appear almost to the end of Doyle's life.

The brave Saint George is shown slaying the dragon with his magic sword. This is one of the most famous of all dragon legends.

DRAGON. According to a legend of the Middle Ages there once lived in a distant pagan land a dreadful monster called a dragon. The flapping of its great batlike wings could be heard for miles around. With a single blow of its terrible claws it could fell an ox. From its nostrils came clouds of smoke and flame that brought death to those who breathed it.

Every year a young girl was offered to it to prevent it from rushing upon the city and destroying all the inhabitants. One year the lot fell to Princess Sabra, daughter of the king. She was saved by the valiant Saint George, youngest and bravest of the seven champions of Christendom. With his magic sword Ascalon, he wounded the monster so badly that the princess was able to put her sash about its head and lead it to the marketplace of the town. There Saint George slew it with one blow. Won over to the Christian faith by this deed of its champion, the people were baptized.

Other Dragon Legends

This is but one of the many dragon stories told in the lore of different countries (see Perseus; Siegfried). Before the time of Columbus and the age of discovery sailors refused to venture into unknown seas for fear of encountering dragons and other monsters of the deep. Old maps show the uncharted seas filled with strange creatures having wings, horns, and claws of such enormous size that they could crush a ship. The dragons of Chinese and Japanese myth and art were reptiles with batlike wings and claws and were supposed to spread disease and death among the people. For ages the dragon was the emblem of the former imperial house of China.

These superstitions may have been based on the fact that mammoth reptiles roamed the prehistoric world. Dinosaurs lived in the ages before man appeared on

earth. However, there may have been some reptiles of great size at the time of the primitive cavemen of Europe. Such beasts would easily give rise to legends of monsters such as the dragons (see Reptiles).

In the East Indies certain small lizards, seven or eight inches long, are known as "dragons." They are about the color of tree bark. The skin along their sides between the legs spreads out into a kind of parachute, enabling them to fly among the branches of the trees in which they live. There are about 20 species, all harmless.

DRAGONFLY. Among the most beautiful and useful of all insects is the dragonfly. It has thin silvery wings. Its body may be steel blue, purple, green, or copper. The dragonfly eats mosquitoes, flies, and other insects harmful to man.

The dragonfly lives on or near the water. It is a quick-darting insect that flies swiftly from place to place. Sometimes it changes its direction so quickly in mid-flight that its sudden movement is hard to follow with the eye. It can also hover over a lake or stream as it looks for food.

The dragonfly's wings are from two to five inches long. The body is about three inches long. Its six legs are far forward and close together. The dragonfly can curve its legs to form a basket. It uses this basket to scoop insects from the air. Then it puts them into its jaws. These jaws have strong teeth.

Two great eyes cover most of the head. Each eye has from 20,000 to 25,000 tiny eyes joined together. With these big eyes it can see its prey easily.

Dragonflies and Damsel Flies

There are two large groups of these insects—the dragonflies themselves and the damsel flies. The dragonfly darts with the speed of an express train. Some can fly 60 miles an hour. The two rear wings are larger than the front pair. They are held outspread when the insect lands. The damsel fly is more slender. It flies more slowly and lazily. The wings are the same size. When the insect rests, the

A dragonfly nymph (left) climbs up a plant stem. The skin splits open (right) and the adult insect works its way out.

wings come together over the back, like a butterfly's.

The dragonfly begins life as a water insect. Then it is called a nymph. The mother lays her eggs in the water. As she flits over the pond again and again she dips under water to wash off the eggs. Some species lay their eggs in long strings on water plants. Such a string may have 100,000 eggs.

The damsel fly cuts a slit in the stems of water plants. Then she puts her eggs in the opening. She uses a part of her body called an *ovipositor* to do this. (The word "ovipositor" means "egg depositor.") Sometimes the damsel fly goes under water and walks about looking for a good cradle. The male may go with the female on this trip.

Life Cycle of the Nymphs

The nymphs hatch out of the eggs in one to four weeks. They are half an inch to nearly two inches long. They are flat, dark creatures and have long legs. They hide under rocks and in the mud. There they wait to jump on a careless insect or even a small fish. These nymphs are as fierce in the water as the grown flies are in the air. They have a strange way of catching their prey. The underlip has joints. It is very long, with a pair of hooks at the tip. They shoot this lip forward and catch the insect on the hooks. When they are not using the underlip they fold it over the face like a mask.

The dragonfly nymph breathes by drawing water into the back part of its intestine. Tiny air tubes take out the oxygen. The nymph then pushes out the water in quick spurts. In this way it drives itself forward, like a jet-propelled airplane. The damsel-fly nymph has three leaflike gills at the end of its body. These gills take in oxygen from the water.

As the nymphs grow they shed their skins 10 to 15 times. They live from one to four years as nymphs. The length of their lives depends upon the species. In winter they sleep in the stream bed. The following spring the life cycle begins once again. When they reach the adult stage, dragonflies live only a few months.

When the dragonfly lands its wings are held outspread. Pictured here is a damsel fly. When it rests its wings come together over the back, like a butterfly's.

Dragonflies are members of the order *Odonata*. The dragonflies proper belong to the suborder *Anisoptera* (from two Greek words meaning "unequal wings"). The damsel flies belong to the suborder *Zygoptera* ("yoke wings"). There are about 2,500 species scattered over the world. North America has about 300 species. One common dragonfly is known as the mosquito hawk (*Anax junius*). It is bright green, with clear wings about two inches long. The "ten spot skimmer" (*Libellula pulchella*) has three blackish-brown and two white spots on each wing. Only the male has the white spots. The ruby-spot (*Hetaerina americana*) is a common damsel fly. Its head and upper body are coppery red. The abdomen is green. The male has a ruby-red spot at the base of the wings. In the female the wing is yellowish brown. The black-wing (*Calopteryx maculata*) is also common.

In the first two pictures the dragonfly is shown freeing itself of the cast nymph skin. It then rests for a time while the wings dry and expand. At last it flies off, and an ugly insect has been transformed into a beautiful one.

Sir Francis Drake in a painting by an unknown artist at the National Portrait Gallery, London.

DRAKE, Francis (1545–96). The first Englishman to sail around the world was Sir Francis Drake. He also took a leading part in defeating the Great Armada sent by Spain to invade England.

Born near Tavistock, in Devonshire, Drake grew up in a seafaring atmosphere. While still a boy he worked as a sailor. When he was 20 he sailed with his cousin, Sir John Hawkins, to Guinea on the west coast of Africa to obtain slaves. He rose to command a ship under Hawkins and was with him when Spaniards attacked the fleet off the port of Veracruz in Mexico. All but two of the English ships were destroyed in this battle, and Drake lost nearly everything he possessed (*see* Hawkins). Drake never forgave the Spanish for their treachery on this occasion or for their cruel treatment of their English prisoners. He devoted the rest of his life to a relentless war against Spain.

Drake gathered together his own band of adventurers and made three profitable voyages to the New World, plundering Spanish settlements and destroying Spanish ships. In 1572 he made a daring march across the Isthmus of Panama. From a high tree he caught his first glimpse of the Pacific Ocean.

Drake's great voyage around the world, from 1577 to 1580, had the secret financial support of Queen Elizabeth I and the war party in her council. They hoped it would end the Spanish monopoly of the profitable trade in the Pacific. Drake set out sailing with five ships. He intended to pass through the Strait of Magellan, near the southern tip of South America, and then explore the waters he had seen from the Isthmus of Panama. When the straits were passed, Drake's ship, the *Golden Hind,* pushed on alone, the other vessels having either turned back or been lost. As he went up the coast, he plundered Spanish settlements in Chile and Peru and captured treasure ships bound for Panama.

Drake then sailed northward and claimed the California coast in the name of his queen. To avoid meeting the angered Spaniards by returning the way he came, he determined to return home by sailing

around the world, as Ferdinand Magellan had done (*see* Magellan). He crossed the Pacific and Indian oceans and reached the Atlantic by sailing around the southern tip of Africa. He reached England in November 1580, nearly three years after he set out. He was warmly acclaimed. Elizabeth shared the treasure he brought on his ship, which was "literally ballasted with silver." She honored him by dining on board his ship and by raising him to knighthood, though she knew this would infuriate the Spaniards.

In the war with Spain that broke out in 1585, Drake won his crowning honors. After once more carrying death and destruction to Spanish settlements in the West Indies, he led a daring expedition into the port of Cadiz, Spain. Here he destroyed so many vessels that for a whole year the Spaniards had to delay the expedition they were preparing for the invasion of England. Drake returned home in triumph.

When the Spanish Armada finally did come sailing up the English Channel in 1588, Drake, as vice-admiral of the English fleet, played a chief part in the week-long running fight that drove off the Spaniards (*see* Armada, Spanish). During this fight Drake encountered a fine galleon commanded by Don Pedro de Valdez. Don Pedro was one of the leading promoters of the idea of dispatching the Armada to England. Yet when he and his men learned that their opponent was the daring El Draque ("the dragon") they surrendered at once.

Some eight years later, on a final expedition against the Spaniards in the West Indies, Drake became ill and died on board his ship in January 1596. More than any other of England's bold privateers, he had helped to set England on the way to becoming the mistress of the seas.

Sir Francis Drake catches his first glimpse of the Pacific Ocean while perched in a tree on the Isthmus of Panama. From that moment his great hope was to sail on that nearly uncharted body of water.

DRAMA

DRAMA. Everyone enjoys a good show. A parade down Main Street, a circus under the "big top," a variety program on the high-school stage—all these delight their audiences. One kind of show that most of us like is a *drama*, or *play*. Plays may be seen "live" on the stage only. They are also enjoyed when reproduced in the movies, on the radio, or on television.

In the theater, under the spell of a fascinating play, we forget ourselves and enter the lives of the characters. We laugh at their antics or come near to tears over their troubles. We are swept along by their adventures or stirred by their discovery of love. The actors bring the play to life. While the curtain is up the play seems real and true.

What Is Drama?

Drama comes from Greek words meaning "to do" or "to act." A play is a story acted out. It shows people going through some eventful period in their lives, seriously or humorously. The speech and action recreate the flow of human life. A play comes fully to life only on the stage. On the stage it combines many arts—those of the author, director, actor, designer, and others.

A playwright may instruct or entertain or he may do both. His attitude toward his subject may be serious or light or a combination of the two. His story may be *intensive*—a small area of life may be explored thoroughly. It may be *extensive*—free, wide ranging, and largely on the surface.

A dramatist starts with characters. These people must be full, rich, interesting, and different enough from each other so that in one way or another they conflict. From this conflict comes the play.

The play has a *beginning*, which tells the audience what took place before the curtain went up and leads into the present action. The *middle* carries the action forward, amid trouble and complications. In the *end* the conflict is resolved, and the play comes to a satisfactory, but not necessarily a happy, conclusion.

One of the most important elements of a play is the plot—what happens and why. The *simple plot* is a direct chain of events. The *complex plot* has an ending different from what the audience expects, although clues to this ending are planted along the way. The *compound plot* is made up of two plots working together.

Comedy and Tragedy

In a strict sense, plays are classified as being either tragedies or comedies. The broad difference between

Hamlet, prince of Denmark, learns from his mother that his father is dead and she has remarried, in 'Hamlet'.

the two is in the ending. Comedies end happily. Tragedies end on an unhappy note. Why do people enjoy watching tragedy?

Aristotle, the ancient Greek philosopher, offered one answer to this question in his *katharsis* theory. The tragedy, he said, acts as a purge. It arouses our pity for the stricken one and our terror that we ourselves may be struck down. As the play closes we are washed clean of these emotions and we feel better for the experience.

A *classical tragedy* tells of a high and noble person who falls because of a "tragic flaw," a weakness in his own character. A *domestic tragedy* concerns the lives of ordinary people brought low by circumstances

Clytemnestra pleads for understanding as she explains why she murdered her husband in Aeschylus' 'Agamemnon'.

American National Theatre and Academy

The French comic dramatist Molière satirized "humanity-hating" types of people in 'The Misanthrope'.

Alix Jeffry

Doctor Faustus makes a pact with the devil in Christopher Marlowe's 'The Tragical Historie of Doctor Faustus'.

beyond their control. Domestic tragedy may be *realistic*—seemingly true to life—or *naturalistic*—realistic and on the seamy side of life.

A *romantic comedy* is a love story. The main characters are lovers; the secondary characters are comic. In the end the lovers are always united. *Farce* is comedy at its broadest. Much fun and horseplay enliven the action. The *comedy of manners*, or *artificial comedy*, is subtle, witty, and often mocking. *Sentimental comedy* mixes sentimental emotion with its humor. *Melodrama* is not funny at all, but it does include comic relief and has a happy ending. It depends upon physical action rather than upon character probing. Tragic or comic, the action of the play comes from conflict of characters—how the stage people react to each other. These reactions make the play.

Drama in Ancient Times

Primitive men acted out their stories of hunting and fighting. They were the first playwrights as well as the first actors. Early religious rituals were dramatic in form. In ancient Egypt the crowning of the pharaoh was celebrated by a play telling of his divine birth. Pharaohs ordered resurrection plays to be performed above their tombs after their deaths.

Ancient Greece was the birthplace of the drama of the Western World. By the 5th century B.C. dramas were presented at religious festivals twice a year. These grew out of the worship of the god Dionysus. Choruses of men were dressed in goatskins to represent *satyrs*—beings who were half man and half goat, attending Dionysus. Tragedy gets its name from the costumes and recitations of the chorus—*tragos* (goat) and *ode* (song).

At the Greater Dionysian festival three contests were held for dramatists. One was in comedy, one in tragedy, and one in the dithyramb (an elaborate choral ode sung by a chorus of 50 singers). From the contests came some of the world's greatest dramatists. Little is known of them, and only a few plays survive. Those that remain are magnificent.

Aeschylus (525–456 B.C.) wrote about 90 tragedies; only seven are known. An early play was 'The Suppliants'. In it the chorus, a group of 15 singers who remain on-stage, is most prominent. In 'The Seven Against Thebes' the tragic hero first appears. 'Oresteia' is a fully developed play. Aeschylus was the first to use a second actor on the stage.

Sophocles (496–406 B.C.) wrote about 125 tragedies. Only seven are left. His plays are calm and nobly tragic, expressing the "golden mean" of Greek philosophy. Sophocles was the first dramatist to use a third actor. Perhaps his greatest play is 'Antigone', which retells, in part, the ancient, tragic Oedipus legend.

Of the approximately 90 plays of Euripides (480–406 B.C.), 18 remain. His tragedies are about men, not gods. He explores the sorrow and suffering in human existence as few writers since have done. One of his best plays is 'Trojan Women'.

Aristophanes (448?–385? B.C.) was the funniest Greek comic dramatist. 'The Clouds' ridicules the philosopher Socrates, and 'The Birds' makes fun of Euripides. The comedies of Menander (342–291? B.C.) are kind and sympathetic but rarely humorous in a boisterous sense. Only one complete play still exists. (*See also* Greek Literature.)

Rome copied Greece, but not very well. There was much dramatic activity but few notable dramatists. Plautus (254?–184 B.C.) and Terence (185?–159? B.C.) followed Menander's pattern in comedy. Seneca's (3? B.C.–A.D. 65) nine tragedies were written to be read. Most of them are impossible to stage. (*See also* Latin Literature.)

Drama Rediscovered in the Middle Ages

In the late Roman Empire the drama was almost forgotten. People preferred the bloody fights of gladiators with wild beasts and the low clowning of entertainers. Then the rising power of the Christian church was thrown against all such entertainment. The theater was banned for nearly a thousand years.

During the Middle Ages life centered around the cathedral. The priests had to teach an uneducated people the Bible stories. So they introduced small playlets into their church services. The first of these was the 'Quem quaeritis', acted out by the priests at Easter. It had only three Latin lines:

> Whom do ye seek in the sepulchre?
> Jesus of Nazareth who was crucified, O Heavenly One!
> He is not there: He has risen as He said. Go, announce
>   that he has arisen from the sepulchre.

This was the beginning of drama in the modern world.

Because so few people understood Latin, more and more of their own language was used. Finally, the plays were considered too unreligious to be acted in the church. They were moved to the cathedral steps and yard. Here began the elaborate Mystery Cycles which told stories from the Bible in dramatic form. Later new religious dramas were found in the lives of the saints. These were the Miracle Plays (*see* Miracle Plays). Next to come were the Morality Plays, which dealt with abstract virtues and vices.

Drama of the Renaissance

In the Golden Age of Spain two playwrights won immortality. They were Lope Félix de Vega Carpio (1562–1635) and Pedro Calderón de la Barca (1600–1681). Lope was immensely prolific. He wrote about 2,200 long and short plays—romances, religious dramas, historical plays, tragedies, and comedies. More than 500 have survived. Perhaps his greatest is 'The Sheep Well', about a peasant village which revolts against its ruling nobleman. About 120 plays by Calderón survive. 'Life Is a Dream' is his best-known work. It tells of a young prince who finally overcomes a curse and becomes a good king.

The Elizabethan Age in England showered the world with a burst of brilliant playwrights (*see* Elizabeth I). The age was ushered in by such dramatists as John Lyly (1554?–1606), who wrote 'Endimion, the Man in the Moon'; Thomas Kyd (1558–94), author of 'The Spanish Tragedy'; and Robert Greene (1560?–92), writer of 'Friar Bacon and Friar Bungay'. The greatest of these early Elizabethans was Christopher Marlowe (1564–93). He wrote the first notable Elizabethan plays. His best is 'Doctor Faustus', in which Faustus sells his soul to the devil in exchange for years of power on earth (*see* Faust Legend).

William Shakespeare (1564–1616) is the acknowledged master of drama not only for his age but for all time. In tragedy, comedy, tragicomedy (or "bitter comedy"), and historical (or chronicle) drama, he is superb. His plays are alive and glowing, filled with characters whom real people admire and envy. His plots are filled with action; his dramas play even better than they read. Above all, his genius penetrates the human heart and mind and shows man as he is, in all his misery and glory.

Sir Anthony Absolute kisses Lydia Languish as Julia watches. Good and gentle fun highlights Richard Brinsley Sheridan's 18th-century comedy 'The Rivals'.

Of his tragedies, 'Hamlet' is the favorite, with several others nearly as popular. Perhaps his most successful comedy is 'A Midsummer Night's Dream'. 'The Tempest' is his most famous tragicomedy. 'Richard III' and 'Henry V' are histories that have been made into motion pictures. In all these, Shakespeare demonstrates the humanity of his characters, the believableness of his plots, and the magic and music of his language. (*See also* Shakespeare.)

After Shakespeare came lesser men, good playwrights but failing to measure up to the master. Ben Jonson (1573?–1637) used the *comedy of humors* in 'Vol-

The restless and envious Hedda drives her former admirer Lövborg to suicide in Henrik Ibsen's masterful character drama 'Hedda Gabler'.
Friedman-Abeles

DRAMA

The Rodgers and Hammerstein musical 'Carousel' was adapted from Molnár's 'Liliom', a romantic fantasy.

Synge, in his 'The Playboy of the Western World', flavored a romantic folktale with realism and humor.

pone', 'The Alchemist', and others. "Humors" were eccentricities, and Jonson had much fun with them (*see* Jonson). Thomas Dekker (1570?–1641), whose happiness was not soured by years of adversity, wrote sunny comedies, especially 'The Shoemaker's Holiday'. The plays of Thomas Middleton (1570?–1627) were roaring farces about middle-class life. 'A Chaste Maid in Cheapside' is one of his best. John Webster (1580?–1625?) wrote two great tragedies—'The Duchess of Malfi' and 'The White Devil'. Webster excelled in scenes of horror and of pathos.

The 17th Century in France and England

Classical tragedy was revived in France during the 1600's. The Unities—of *time*, 24 hours or less; of *place*, a single scene; of *action*, a single plot—described by Aristotle were obeyed. The works of two French tragic dramatists still live. Pierre Corneille (1606–84) wrote 'The Cid', about a medieval Spanish hero, and 'Oedipe', about legendary Greek characters (*see* Corneille). Jean Baptiste Racine (1639–99) also wrote of legendary ancients, but with more humanity than Corneille. Among his plays are 'Andromaque' and 'Phèdre' (*see* Racine).

Molière (1622–73), whose real name was Jean-Baptiste Poquelin, ranks second only to Shakespeare. His specialty was comedy, and such plays as 'Tartuffe' and 'The Misanthrope' show his comic genius. Molière aimed barbed shafts at snobbery. He hit his target and made the whole French nation laugh (*see* Molière).

In England, in 1642, the Puritans closed the theaters. In 1660, when Charles II was restored to the throne, the theaters were reopened. The Restoration was a period of busy theater activity rather than dramatic productivity. The Restoration playwrights developed the *comedy of manners*. This was a sophisticated, witty comedy which amused the intellect but did not warm the heart.

Sir George Etherege (1635?–91) wrote the frivolous 'The Man of Mode, or, Sir Fopling Flutter'. William

Wycherley (1640?–1716) was the author of 'The Country Wife' and 'The Plain Dealer'. Both are acid and sardonic. The finest Restoration dramatist was William Congreve (1670–1729). In four comedies, all written before he was 30, he created a world completely gay and completely unreal. His best play, 'The Way of the World', was his last. John Dryden (1631–1700), author of many tragedies and comedies, stands a little outside the main stream of Restoration comic activity (*see* Dryden).

English Sentimentality and German Romanticism

Restoration sophistication lasted only a little while. In England the 18th century opened on a sentimental note in drama. The comic emphasis was on warmth, kindliness, and agreeableness rather than on wit. Tragedy was equally sentimental. The age saw the beginning of *bourgeois*, or *domestic*, tragedy. The central tragic character was no longer a man of high purpose caught in the web of his one fatal weakness. He was now a poor creature suffering and dying be-

Chekhov's 'Three Sisters' portrays the frustrations of three women from the provinces who dream of going to Moscow.

244

By courtesy of The American Shakespeare Festival Theatre (above only)

Pure fun characterizes Oscar Wilde's 'The Importance of Being Earnest'. It is a comic confusion of names and identities.

cause of a fate he did not understand and could not control.

Oliver Goldsmith (1728–74), jack of all writing trades, wrote an amusing farce 'She Stoops to Conquer' (*see* Goldsmith). The two major comedies of Richard Brinsley Sheridan (1751–1816) were 'The Rivals' and 'The School for Scandal'. They combine sentiment and wit to offer great entertainment. A historically important tragic dramatist was George Lillo (1693–1739). 'George Barnwell, or, The London Merchant' is about a weak young man who succumbs to an evil woman and murders his uncle. This was the first true domestic tragedy in English.

In Germany, Gotthold Ephraim Lessing (1729–81) revived a theater suffocated by classicism. As dramatic critic and playwright he effected great reforms. Friedrich von Schiller (1759–1805) was the first German romantic playwright. His best play is 'Wallenstein', although 'William Tell' is better known (*see* Schiller). Johann Wolfgang von Goethe (1749–1832) is the greatest of all German writers. 'Faust', begun

when Goethe was young and finished only on his last birthday, is a dramatic distillation of his whole philosophy. It is almost unplayable, but it makes magnificent reading (*see* Goethe).

The Beginning of Modern Drama

Modern drama starts with Henrik Ibsen (1828–1906), the earliest and still one of the greatest of modern playwrights. In such plays as 'Peer Gynt', 'A Doll's House', 'Ghosts', and 'Hedda Gabler', this Norwegian dramatist put people into dramatic situations with strongly plotted conclusions. His plays are mainly realistic but they always have overtones of great poetry (*see* Ibsen).

More immediately successful than Ibsen was his fellow Norwegian Björnstjerne Björnson (1832–1910). His best play is 'Beyond Our Power' (*see* Björnson). August Strindberg (1849–1912), of Sweden, was first realist and later surrealist. His keen sense of social psychology produced 'The Father'; his later madness resulted in 'The Ghost Sonata'.

The early modern playwrights in France stressed both an extreme naturalism and an extreme romanticism. Émile Zola (1840–1902) dramatized his own novel 'Thérèse Raquin' as the first real naturalistic "slice of life" play (*see* Zola). Count Maurice Maeterlinck (1862–1949), a Belgian, wrote of the long ago and far away in 'Pelléas and Mélisande' (*see* Maeterlinck). Edmond Rostand (1868–1918) was rousingly romantic in 'Cyrano de Bergerac'. In Italy Luigi Pirandello (1867–1936) did well in 'Right You Are If You Think You Are' and rose to great heights in 'Six Characters in Search of an Author'.

The first great modern German dramatist was Gerhart Hauptmann (1862–1946). He struck home with 'The Weavers', a play that combined naturalistic technique with a flaming social issue. His repressed romanticism finally awoke in 'The Sunken Bell'. Frank Wedekind (1864–1918) brought an obsession with naturalism to such plays as 'Awakening of Spring' and 'Earth Spirit'. Ernst Toller (1893–1939) wrote a

O'Casey's 'Juno and the Paycock' is a realistic portrayal of Irish slum life, with comic overtones.
Vandamm

In Shaw's 'The Devil's Disciple', people under stress make surprising discoveries about themselves.
By courtesy of The American Shakespeare Festival Theatre

Alec Guinness (left) played the psychiatrist-seer in T. S. Eliot's verse drama 'The Cocktail Party'. O'Neill's 'Long Day's Jour- ney into Night' (center) is autobiographical. Thornton Wilder's 'Our Town' (right) is the history of a fictitious small town.

massive study of revolution in 'Man and the Masses'.

The Austrian Arthur Schnitzler (1862–1931), a doctor by profession, probed dramatic problems with psychoanalytic tools. His 'Anatol' series is still popular. Ferenc Molnár (1878–1952) was Hungary's leading playwright. His most famous drama, 'Liliom', was adapted by two Americans, Richard Rodgers and Oscar Hammerstein II, as the musical play and movie 'Carousel'. Karel Capek (1890–1938), a Czech, created a great stir with the symbolic 'R.U.R.' (abbreviation of "Rossum's Universal Robots").

The Drama in Czarist Russia

The plays of 19th-century Russian dramatists are strong character studies. Their plots are weak and inconclusive. Often the situation at the end is the same as it was in the beginning. The characters recognize the need for growth and change; they make tentative gestures toward achieving it; but in the end they fall back on their old ways. This is the Russian play formula, repeated time after time. In the hands of the masters it showed the strengths and weaknesses of the Russian character.

The first notable Russian dramatist was Nikolai Gogol (1809–52). He won his reputation with 'The Inspector-General', a merry satire on village corruption. Ivan Turgenev (1818–83), a great Russian novelist, wrote one memorable play, 'A Month in the Country' (see Turgenev). Count Leo Tolstoi (1828–1910), world-famous as a novelist, wrote 'Power of Darkness' and 'Redemption' to express his fundamentalist religious views (see Tolstoi).

The greatest Russian playwright was Anton Chekhov (1860–1904). In such plays as 'The Sea Gull', 'The Cherry Orchard', 'Three Sisters', and 'Uncle Vanya', he set his characters against a background of changing times. The tragedy is that the characters cannot change too. Their only solution is to live as best they can. Chekhov's plays well illustrate the general trend of Russian drama to stress character analysis rather than plot and action. Leonid Andreev

(1871–1919), mystic and fatalist, wrote 'He Who Gets Slapped', which continues to arouse interest. Maksim Gorki (1868–1936), in 'The Lower Depths', offered a starkly naturalistic, revolutionary drama.

The Irish Renaissance

Many great playwrights helped bring about the Irish Renaissance in literature. Its aim was to revive the old Celtic language and stories. The rebirth began in the 1880's, and its first notable dramatist was William Butler Yeats (1865–1939). His 'Deirdre' and 'Cathleen ni Houlihan' were poetic re-creations of Irish legends and patriotic themes. (See also Yeats.)

The genius of this group was John Millington Synge (1871–1909). Synge's first play was 'In the Shadow of the Glen', which told of the family troubles of a peasant woman. It was followed by 'Riders to the Sea', a tragedy, and 'The Playboy of the Western World', his finest play. This is the story of a young man who boasts of having murdered his father. The old man appears unexpectedly and deflates his son.

The last great writer of the Irish Renaissance was Sean O'Casey (1880–1964). His 'Juno and the Paycock' mixes comedy and tragedy. 'The Plough and the Stars' is a tragic moment of the real-life Easter Rebellion in Ireland in 1916. 'Purple Dust' is a comedy. (See also Irish Literature.)

English Drama

Modern British drama began as a revolt against the prevailing smugness of the Victorian Era. The real evils and tragedies of English life were hidden from view by the self-satisfied attitudes of the upper classes. The dramatic revolt started slowly but soon gained speed.

Henry Arthur Jones (1851–1929) was the first notable playwright of this movement. 'Michael and His Lost Angel' deals with religious hypocrisy. Arthur Wing Pinero (1855–1934) wrote 'The Second Mrs. Tanqueray', a tragedy about a woman who cannot escape her past. Oscar Wilde (1856–1900), the wittiest

Vandamm Studios

Dan McCoy—Black Star

Vandamm Studios

Sherwood's 'Abe Lincoln in Illinois' (left) dramatizes the issues of the Civil War. Williams' 'The Glass Menagerie' (center) is a tragedy of escapism and self-delusion. Inge's 'Come Back, Little Sheba' (right) ends in abandoned dreams.

man of his day, wrote one play that has remained alive, the polished, superficial, but still delightful 'The Importance of Being Earnest'.

The long lifetime of one of the greatest of modern playwrights spanned this era. George Bernard Shaw (1856–1950) excelled in the world of ideas. He could make a host of contrary notions acceptable by the brilliance of his presentation. His galaxy is large. 'Candida', 'The Devil's Disciple', 'Caesar and Cleopatra', 'Man and Superman', 'Major Barbara', 'The Doctor's Dilemma', 'Androcles and the Lion', 'Pygmalion' (and its musical version, 'My Fair Lady'), 'The Apple Cart', and 'Saint Joan' are some of his witty and thought-provoking plays. Shaw's lengthy prefaces to his dramas explain and enhance the ideas in the plays. (See also Shaw.)

Sir James M. Barrie (1860–1937) combined sentiment with skillful playmaking in 'Peter Pan' and 'What Every Woman Knows' (see Barrie). John Galsworthy (1867–1933) was for a time England's leading tragic dramatist. His 'Justice' is a harsh condemnation of law untempered by mercy (see Galsworthy). W. Somerset Maugham (1874–1965) wrote drama as well as fiction. His best plays are 'The Circle' and 'The Constant Wife' (see Maugham). Noël Coward (1899–1973) wrote sophisticated comedy in 'Private Lives' and 'Design for Living' (see Coward).

The American-born T. S. Eliot (1888–1965) projected poetic genius into blank verse dramas of high order. 'Murder in the Cathedral', 'The Cocktail Party', and 'The Confidential Clerk' are plays that conceal deep meaning beneath surface simplicity (see Eliot, T. S.). Christopher Fry (born 1907) also used verse effectively in 'The Lady's Not for Burning' and 'A Sleep of Prisoners' (see Fry, Christopher).

John Boynton Priestley (1894–1984) combined the careers of novelist and playwright. 'Dangerous Corner' was his first of about 40 successful plays. Robert Cedric Sherriff (1896–1975) wrote 'Journey's End', a memorable play about English soldiers in World War I trenches. Terence Rattigan (1911–77) won his first commercial success with 'French Without Tears'. This was followed by such long-run hits as 'The Winslow Boy', 'The Browning Version', and 'The Deep Blue Sea'. Peter Ustinov (born 1921)—actor, producer, and playwright—made his name known with 'The Love of Four Colonels', a delightful romantic comedy. (See also English Literature.)

Modern French Plays

French drama today follows no set pattern. Each playwright has an individual story to tell and chooses whatever style, realistic or symbolic, is best suited to the story. For example, Jean Giraudoux (1882–1944) used symbolism and fantasy in 'Amphitryon 38' and 'Tiger at the Gates', both set in ancient Greece; 'The Madwoman of Chaillot', about a group of varied Parisian characters; and 'Ondine', an "adult fairy tale." Realism marked the plays of Jean-Paul Sartre (1905–80). Among them are 'The Flies', 'No Exit', and 'The Respectful Prostitute'.

Jean Cocteau (1889–1963), master of many arts, wrote in many styles. 'The Eagle Has Two Heads' is a classic tragedy of the widowed queen of Bavaria and her young lover (see Cocteau). Jean Anouilh (born 1910) used the ancient Greek legend of Oedipus in 'Antigone', the Joan of Arc story in 'The Lark', and a modern background for 'Waltz of the Toreadors'.

Drama in the United States

Not until the 1880s did noteworthy drama begin to appear in the United States. Before that time there was a fair amount of theatrical activity. The first play written by an American and performed by a professional company was 'The Prince of Parthia' (produced 1767) by Thomas Godfrey (1736–63). The first play by an American on an American theme was 'The Contrast' (1787) by Royall Tyler (1757–1826). George Aiken (1830–76) dramatized Harriet Beecher Stowe's 'Uncle Tom's Cabin' in 1852. Dion Boucicault (1820–90), Irish by birth, wrote many stirring melodramas, among them 'The Octoroon'.

247

Wide World

Howard Atlee

Both Arthur Miller's 'Death of a Salesman' (left) and Edward Albee's 'A Delicate Balance' (right) explore, each in its own way, man's growing sense of isolation and estrangement from his fellowmen in modern times.

Several playwrights of the late 19th and early 20th centuries prepared the way for modern realistic drama. James A. Herne (1839–1901) wrote 'Margaret Fleming', an honest treatment of a wife's reaction to her husband's adultery. 'The New York Idea' by Langdon Mitchell (1862–1935) takes an irreverent attitude toward marriage. 'The Nigger' by Edward Sheldon (1886–1946) anticipates the racial problem plays of later years.

Around 1920 American drama became a major literary form, thanks largely to Eugene O'Neill (1888–1953), America's greatest playwright. O'Neill broke with theatrical conventions to experiment with a variety of techniques. 'Beyond the Horizon' and 'Desire Under the Elms' are powerful, realistic dramas, using the language of ordinary people. 'The Emperor Jones' is a romantic drama about the destruction of a self-made black dictator. 'The Hairy Ape' and 'The Great God Brown' are symbolist dramas. Characters in 'Strange Interlude' make heavy use of asides and soliloquies to reveal their thoughts. 'Marco Millions' is a satire on big business. 'Mourning Becomes Electra' is a New England version of the classical Greek tragedy 'Oresteia'. (See also O'Neill.)

Other playwrights who made a significant contribution to American drama in the 1920s include Elmer Rice (1892–1967), whose 'The Adding Machine' is a study of a regimented mind in a regimented society. 'Street Scene', also by Rice, pictures life in a New York City slum. George Kelly (1887–1974) wrote 'Craig's Wife', an unflattering portrait of the American middle-class woman. Maxwell Anderson (1888–1959), who later became known for his verse dramas, collaborated with Laurence Stallings (1894–1968) on 'What Price Glory?', an antiheroic play about World War I (see Anderson, Maxwell). Sidney Howard (1891–1939) wrote 'They Knew What They Wanted', his masterpiece about a mail-order bride.

During the 1930s Sidney Kingsley (born 1906) captured the mood of the depression years with 'Dead End', a vivid study of slum life, and Clifford Odets (1906–63) dramatized the struggles of working-class people with 'Waiting for Lefty', 'Awake and Sing', and 'Golden Boy'. Lillian Hellman (1905–84) wrote her first plays on poisoned human relationships— 'The Children's Hour' and 'The Little Foxes' (see Hellman). Irwin Shaw (1913–84) combined social protest and fantasy in 'Bury the Dead'. During the decade Robert E. Sherwood (1896–1955) wrote two of his best works, 'Idiot's Delight' and 'Abe Lincoln in Illinois'. Thornton Wilder (1897–1975) developed new dramatic techniques in that most American of plays, 'Our Town'. William Saroyan (1908–81) wrote 'The Time of Your Life', a unique blend of sentiment and fantasy. Outstanding comedies were written by S. N. Behrman (1893–1973) ('No Time for Comedy') and Philip Barry (1896–1949) ('The Philadelphia Story'). George S. Kaufman (1889–1961) collaborated with Moss Hart (1904–61) on the comedies 'You Can't Take It with You' and 'The Man Who Came to Dinner'.

In the 1940s and 1950s the American stage was dominated by two major dramatists, Arthur Miller (born 1915) and Tennessee Williams (1911–83). 'Death of a Salesman', the tragedy of an ordinary man destroyed by false values, is Miller's masterpiece. Two of Williams' finest psychological dramas are 'The Glass Menagerie' and 'A Streetcar Named Desire'. An important playwright of the 1950s was William Inge (1913–73), whose dramas of neglected small-town people include 'Come Back, Little Sheba', 'Picnic', 'Bus Stop', and 'The Dark at the Top of the Stairs'. Plays by William Branch (born 1927), Louis Peterson (born 1922), and Lorraine Hansberry (1930–65) reflected the increased racial consciousness of the 1950s. Branch's 'A Medal for Willie' deals with the effect of a soldier's death on his family. Peterson's 'Take a Giant Step' explores the problems of an adolescent boy. Lorraine Hansberry's 'A Raisin in the Sun' dramatizes the dreams and conflicts of a black family in a multiracial society.

Much of the theatrical experimentation and excitement of the 1960s took shape in off-Broadway and "little" theaters. There were attempts to break down the distinction between audience and performers. Some plays took nonplay forms. Language taboos and subject-matter taboos were often abandoned.

Many dramatists made significant contributions to the American theater. Probably the most successful and productive of them was Neil Simon, whose comedies ran on Broadway almost continuously from 1961. He is best known for 'The Odd Couple' (1965) about two newly-divorced men who share an apartment in New York City. This comedy later became both a motion picture and a television series. In 1984 the script was rewritten for two women to play the leads. Among Simon's other plays were 'Come Blow Your Horn' (1961), 'Barefoot in the Park' (1963), 'Last of the Red Hot Lovers' (1969), 'The Sunshine Boys' (1972), 'California Suite' (1976),. 'They're Playing Our Song' (1979), 'Brighton Beach Memoirs' (1983), and 'Biloxi Blues' (1985).

Among the more serious dramatists were Edward Albee, Arthur Kopit, Sam Shepard, David Rabe, David Mamet, and Lanford Wilson. Albee did several plays for off-Broadway productions, but his first great success on Broadway was 'Who's Afraid of Virginia Woolf?' (1962). This was followed by 'Tiny Alice' (1964), 'A Delicate Balance' (1967), 'All Over' (1971), 'The Lady from Dubuque' (1980), and 'The Man Who Had Three Arms' (1983).

Kopit first became prominent with 'Oh Dad, Poor Dad, Mama's Hung You in the Closet and I'm Feeling So Sad' (1962). Later plays included 'Wings' (1978) and 'Secrets of the Rich' (1978). Shepard and Rabe also worked as off-Broadway playwrights before gaining national reputations. Shepard's plays include 'The Tooth of Crime' (1974), 'Angel City' (1976), and 'True West' (1981). Rabe's work started as a protest against the Vietnam War: 'The Basic Training of Pavlo Hummel' (1971), 'Sticks and Bones' (1971), and 'Streamers' (1976). On a different theme he wrote 'In the Boom Boom Room' (1975) about a female go-go dancer. 'Hurly Burly' appeared in 1984.

David Mamet worked in experimental theater in Chicago, where he founded the Saint Nicholas Theater Company in 1973. Among his plays were 'American Buffalo' (1977), 'Lakeboat' (1981), and 'Glengarry Glen Ross' (1983). Lanford Wilson, a founder of New York's Circle Repertory Theatre, was best known for his 'The Hot 1 Baltimore' (1973) about a group of social misfits waiting for the hotel in which they live to be demolished. Some of his other plays were 'The Mound Builders' (1975), 'Talley's Folly' (1979), and 'Angels Fall' (1983).

Two other American dramatists became known through the production of single award-winning plays. Harvey Fierstein wrote and starred in 'Torch Song Trilogy' (1981), and Bernard Pomerance achieved success with 'The Elephant Man' (1979).

There were several successful black dramatists in the years after 1960. Some of the more prominent black playwrights were LeRoi Jones (Imamu Amiri Baraka), Ed Bullins, Douglas Turner Ward, Lonne Elder III, and Joseph A. Walker. Jones stressed black separatism in 'The Toilet' (1964), 'Dutchman' (1964), and 'Slave Ship' (1969). The plays of Ed Bullins included 'The Electronic Nigger' (1968), 'Clara's Ole Man' (1965), 'The Pig Pen' (1970), and 'Daddy' (1977). Ward, artistic director for the Negro Ensemble Company, wrote 'Day of Absence' (1965) and 'Brotherhood' (1970). Elder was known primarily for 'Ceremonies in Dark Old Men' (1969). Walker was very successful with 'The River Niger' (1973).

Later British Drama

The many fine British dramatists with works presented after 1960 included Harold Pinter, Edward Bond, Joe Orton, David Storey, Tom Stoppard, Peter Nichols, Peter Shaffer, Alan Ayckbourn, Michael Frayn, Trevor Griffiths, Howard Brenton, Howard Barker, David Hare, and Stephen Poliakoff. Pinter's first play was 'The Room' (1957). Later works include 'No Man's Land' (1975), 'The Hot House' (1980), and 'Family Voices' (1981). Bond, one of the more controversial authors, wrote 'Saved' (1965), 'Bingo' (1974), and 'The Restoration' (1981). Orton wrote strange and sensational plots in 'Entertaining Mister Sloane' (1964), 'Loot' (1966), and 'What the Butler Saw' (produced in 1969). David Storey's best-known works were 'The Changing Room' (1971) and 'Mother's Day' (1976).

The reputation of Tom Stoppard was established in both England and the United States with 'Rosenkrantz and Guildenstern Are Dead' (1967). Later plays included 'Travesties' (1974) and 'Night and Day' (1978). Peter Nichols had his first success with 'A Day in the Death of Joe Egg' (1967), followed by 'The National Health' (1969), 'Passion Play' (1980), and others. Peter Shaffer had a number of successful plays in the 1950s and 1960s, but he is remembered more for 'Equus' (1973) and 'Amadeus' (1979), both of which later became motion pictures.

Alan Ayckbourn wrote comedic farces, beginning with 'How the Other Half Loves' (1969). Perhaps the most successful comedy writer was Michael Frayn, whose 'Noises Off' (1981) was well received in both London and New York City.

Trevor Griffiths' best-known play was 'Comedians' (1975). Howard Brenton wrote 'Christie in Love' (1969) and 'Sore Throats' (1979). Howard Barker staged 'Cheek' (1970) and 'No End of Blame' (1981). David Hare made his debut with 'Slag' (1970), followed by 'Teeth 'n' Smiles' (1975) and 'Plenty' (1978). Stephen Poliakoff began with 'City Sugar' (1976) and continued with 'American Days' (1979) and 'The Summer Party' (1980).

BIBLIOGRAPHY FOR DRAMA

Brockett, O.G. History of the Theater, 4th ed. (Allyn, 1981).
Reiter, Seymour. World Theater (Horizon, 1973).
Watson, George. Drama: an Introduction (St. Martin, 1984).
Weiss, S.A. Drama in the Modern World (Heath, 1974).

Tiepolo, Giovanni Battista
(1696–1770), Italian.
THE REST ON THE FLIGHT INTO EGYPT.
Pen and brown wash. 16⅞ in. x 11⅜ in.
Fogg Art Museum, Harvard University, Cambridge, Mass.

DRAWING

DRAWING. Drawing uses a kind of universal language. The word "draw" means to drag a pointed instrument such as a pen, pencil, or brush over a smooth surface, leaving behind the marks of its passage. The scribbles of children are drawings as truly as are the sketches of the masters. Children make marks on surfaces long before they learn to write. It is easy to understand, therefore, that drawing is the most fundamental of the arts and is closely related to all the others. Writing itself is simply the drawing of letters, which are symbols for sounds.

Although drawings differ in quality, they have a common purpose—to give visible form to an idea and the artist's feeling about it. As an art form, drawing is the translation of the idea and the emotion into a form that can be seen and felt by others.

The same definition applies to painting (*see* Painting). The difference lies in the materials and in the method used. A painting usually begins to take form

as a drawing. The drawing may give a better understanding of the artist's feeling about the subject than the final work. Drawings are often more spontaneous and less labored than paintings. A great drawing not only reveals the technical skill of its creator—it also communicates to the observer the intense emotion of the artist at the time the work was created.

Two Personal Approaches to Drawing

This personal feeling is clearly seen in the work of Giovanni Battista Tiepolo, a Venetian who lived in the 18th century. His pen and brown-wash drawing 'The Rest on the Flight into Egypt' shows the artist's light-hearted approach to a serious religious subject. The drawing is full of the sunny brightness found in the work of the Venetians.

Tiepolo achieved his effect through the brilliant handling of the untouched highlights on the figures of Mary, Joseph, and the Child. The swift, curving pen lines, combined with transparent wash and sharp, stabbing dark areas, throw the figures into a dazzling light. The composition is filled with warmth. For the emotional effect he wishes to convey, it is not necessary to give detail. His knowledge of space proportion and foreshortening were faultless.

In striking contrast is the wash drawing 'Interior' (next page), by Fernand Léger, a French artist of the 20th century. Léger composed drawings with mechanical precision. This picture is almost divided vertically through the center. On the left side a figure has been analyzed and drawn in geometric forms. The dark semicircle in the right center foreground is repeated in the arch and in the lines of the steplike construction on the right. The artist organized and executed his design with deliberate care. The planes of the drawing suggest pieces of machinery.

As a follower of the Cubist school, Léger reduced natural forms to geometrical shapes. His style permitted him to break down objects and reassemble them in his own way to get the effect he wanted.

In addition to the way in which they feel about their subjects, artists reflect in their drawing their individual approaches to techniques and tools.

Line Drawings

Pure line is the simplest technical approach to drawing. In *line drawings,* form is usually expressed by line only. There is no attempt to distinguish between light and dark. Master draftsmen have discovered that understatement, or the skillful use of a few lines, has usually resulted in a better drawing. Relative distance forward and backward is frequently achieved by emphasizing the width or depth of certain lines, particularly those closest to the observer.

Line drawing was used in Asiatic, Egyptian, and early Greek art, and its influence can be traced through Byzantine and medieval work, particularly in those areas where the Asiatic influence was strong. Such a drawing is the Persian pen sketch 'Camel with Driver'. In this composition the animal is drawn in rounded outline. Only a few evidences of textural

Léger, Fernand
(1881–1955), French.
INTERIOR.
Wash drawing. 11 in. x 9 in.
Galérie Louise Leiris, Paris, France.

treatment are found on its head, tail, and forelegs. The camel driver is treated in the same way.

Form Drawings

Form and shadow may be shown in a drawing by means of a series of lines or crossing lines in many different directions. Such lines, known as hatch and cross-hatch lines, together with sharply accented high lights, were used by such masters as Rembrandt.

Most artists have used combinations of line and form techniques. The drawings of Michelangelo, however, represent pure form drawings. His 'Studies for the Libyan Sibyl' (on a later page), a superb drawing in red chalk, stresses the modeling of the figure. Notice the powerful handling of the muscles of the back and arms, shown in broad masses. This drawing makes one feel the roundness of the figure.

Perspective and foreshortening have been used by some artists to give depth to their drawings. Objects in the distance usually are made smaller, and the receding edges of forms seem to converge at one or more vanishing points (see Perspective). Other artists abstract the essential features of a form without in any way representing it in an imitative style. Still others use drawing to produce emotional effects. Short, jagged lines might indicate intense anger; broad curves might signify contentment.

The Tools of Drawing

The character of a drawing is also conditioned by the tools the artist uses in its development and by the material on which he draws. Most drawings are done on paper, which may vary in weight, surface texture, and color. Smooth papers are usually used for fine pen and pencil drawings. Rough surfaces are desirable for dry brush drawings. As we have observed in the 'Dancer Bending Forward', colored papers may be used to give tonal background to a chalk or charcoal sketch.

Pen and *ink* have been used by artists since ancient times. During the Middle Ages the quill pen was popular. Drawing pens of varying width are widely used by artists of modern times. Black

India ink and other kinds and colors are used today. The Chinese liked to use brush and ink, and this combination is still common.

Pencils did not come into general use until after 1800. Now many different sizes and shapes, together with a wide range of hard and soft lead, are available. *Chalk* and *charcoal* were known to the artists of ancient times. Both can be rubbed into the surface of a paper in developing tonal effects, as we have seen in the drawings of Degas and Michelangelo. They are limited in use because they smear easily. *Crayons*

CAMEL WITH DRIVER.
16th century, Persian.
Pen drawing.

Prehistoric Caves.
30,000 to 17,000 B.C.
THE STAG FRIEZE. 15 ft. x 3 ft.
From 'The Lascaux Cave
Paintings', by Fernand Windels.
Viking Press.

have the advantage of color. *Pastel* colors are made of finely ground crayon pigment with a small quantity of gum or resin to hold the particles together. Pastel allows soft effects in a full range of colors.

Original drawings may usually be seen only in museums and art galleries. They are known to the public chiefly through *prints*. A print is one of many impressions, or reproductions, of an original drawing. The original may be drawn on stone (a lithograph), on a metal plate (an engraving or etching), or on wood (a woodcut).

Prehistoric and Ancient Drawings

The oldest drawings of which we have any record are those on the walls of caves in which Stone Age men lived (*see* Man). The first of these caves was discovered in 1879 at Altamira, in northern Spain. The most recent was found during World War II at Lascaux in southern France. 'The Stag Frieze', from one of the Lascaux caves, shows early man's ability to draw ani-

mal figures with a few lines and to have a complete grasp of the form.

Ancient Egyptian writing developed from drawings which represented objects and events (*see* Egypt, Ancient, subhead "Three Ways of Writing"). Each picture symbol, which included birds, fruit, and flower forms, was drawn in outline with great restraint. It was stylized and stiff and in sharp contrast to the realistic drawings of the cave men.

Greek art is known to us through beautiful vases. The one shown on this page is a cylix, a two-handled drinking cup with a shallow bowl set on a stem and foot. Notice the decorative way in which the human figures are drawn to fill the space. The directness and dignity of the outlines in this vase painting give us some idea of the Greek artist's concern with problems of proportion and figure composition.

Fifteenth-century Italy produced some of the world's greatest artists (*see* Renaissance). One of these was Sandro Botticelli (*bŏt-ĭ-chĕl'ĭ*) of Florence. His

Douris
(about 470 B.C.), Greek.
VOTING OF THE
GREEK CHIEFS.
Painted on a cylix.

Botticelli, Sandro, or Alessandro di
(1444?–1510), Italian.
ABUNDANCE.
Pen and wash. 12½ in. x 10¼ in.
British Museum, London, England.

'Abundance' is a fine pen and wash drawing, which is accented with white. It shows Botticelli's use of line to create an emotional effect. The central figure seems to advance with a flutter of draperies. The movements of the body and the masses of hair are repeated in the curving lines of the horn of plenty. The whole drawing is marked by lightness, grace, and rhythm.

Among the greatest artists of the Renaissance were Leonardo da Vinci, Raphael, and Michelangelo (*see* Leonardo da Vinci; Michelangelo; Raphael). Michelangelo was both painter and sculptor. Many of his drawings are studies of the human body. A page is shown here from one of his notebooks with sketches for the Libyan Sibyl, later painted on the ceiling of the Sistine Chapel, in the Vatican in Rome.

Artists of Northern Europe

The medieval and Renaissance artists of Germany did their best work in engraving, woodcutting, and drawing. Between the mid-15th and mid-16th centuries, they surpassed all other artists in these fields. It is known that the prints of Martin Schongauer served as inspiration for Raphael and that they were admired by Michelangelo. They were distinguished by exquisite precision of detail.

The greatest of the German artists was Albrecht Dürer (*see* Dürer). In the pen and ink drawing 'The Lamentation' (next page) is an example of his intensive use of religious subject matter. Many of his engravings and woodcuts are characterized by great detail. In the execution of 'The Lamentation', however, details are subordinated to the design of the drawing as a whole. Vertical lines dominate the composition—in the cross, the ladder, the upraised arms of the figure on the left. The crowded figures form a triangle, sloping upward from a wide base to a point at the cross and ladder. Skillful use of light and shade gives the figures depth and roundness.

Hans Holbein the Younger was the last of the important German Renaissance artists (*see* Holbein). In Flanders, Peter Paul Rubens combined Italian influence with the native Flemish style (*see* Rubens).

Holland produced the great Rembrandt van Rijn (*see* Rembrandt). He depicts everyday activities with simplicity and sincerity. In his drawing of 'Saskia with Her Child' (next page) the sway of the figure is

Michelangelo Buonarroti
(1475–1564), Italian.
STUDIES FOR THE LIBYAN SIBYL.
Red chalk. 11⅜ in. x 8⅜ in.
Metropolitan Museum of Art, New York, N. Y.

Dürer, Albrecht (1471–1528), German.
THE LAMENTATION.
Pen and ink. 11⅜ in. x 8¼ in.
Meta and Paul J. Sachs Collection, Fogg Art Museum,
Harvard University, Cambridge, Mass.

emphasized in the sweeping folds of the dress and in the way in which the child is clasped in the young mother's arms. Rembrandt's drawings always reveal his concern with problems of light, shade, and space. As in most of his work, the shadows are luminous, and unessential details are omitted.

Artists of the 18th and 19th Centuries

The most famous artist of 18th-century France was Jean Antoine Watteau. His sketchbooks are filled with exquisite drawings of details of human figures, animals, and landscapes. England's greatest 18th-century artist was William Hogarth (*see* Hogarth). In Spain, Francisco Goya became famous for his drawings of the horrors of war and the vices of the Spanish court.

Honoré Daumier, French artist of the 19th century, was deeply influenced by Goya, and like the Spaniard he satirized the evils of his day. Both men were indebted to Rembrandt for their sharp contrasts of light and shade, and to Michelangelo for their handling of form.

Paul Cézanne is regarded as the father of modern painting. He concentrated on the form of things and stressed the idea that natural forms are basically geometric. This analysis was carried further by the Cubists, who attempted to show all sides of an object at the same time (*see* Cézanne).

20th-Century Drawings

The drawings of the 20th century seem to reflect the restlessness, the motion, and the scientific progress of the modern age. Some of them are characterized by free line. Others, like those of Léger, reduce life to geometrical forms (*cubism*).

X-ray techniques, in which one can see the inside and outside of forms at the same time, have produced drawings unlike those of any other period. Artists who are concerned with *expressionism* attempt to record the emotional feeling of a scene rather than its realistic appearance. The *surrealists* are interested in the subconscious mind and in the interpretation of psychoanalytic problems.

A comparison of three drawings of heads illustrates the continuous searching of the 20th-century artist for new ways to communicate ideas. In the 'Head of a Girl with Braids', we have a decorative ink

Rembrandt Harmenszoon van Rijn
(1606–1669), Dutch.
SASKIA WITH HER CHILD.
Pen and wash. 7⅜ in. x 5⅛ in.
Pierpont Morgan Library, New York, N. Y.

Matisse, Henri (1869–1955), French.
HEAD OF A GIRL WITH BRAIDS.
Ink drawing. 22⅛ in. x 14¾ in.
Art Institute of Chicago,
Chicago, Ill.

drawing by the French artist Henri Matisse (mȧ-tēs'). His mastery of line is evident in the simple treatment of the hair, the sweep of the shoulder, and the contour of the face. The entire composition is rhythmic. Because only essential strokes have been used, the drawing is crisp and uncluttered.

Pablo Picasso, a Spanish artist who worked in France for many years, experimented with many different techniques. One of these involves superimposing transparent planes one on top of the other in order to show several sides of an object at the same time. This approach to drawing also makes the subject look like it is rotating slowly. In the 'Head of a Woman', Picasso has gone a step further. He has eliminated the superimposed planes and has drawn a double head in line alone. Because of the displacement of the features this head seems to move up, down, and around. The drawing implies psychological as well as physical changes, since the expression also continues to vary.

'Old Man Figuring', an etching by Paul Klee (klā), looks at first glance like a simple outline drawing overlaid with horizontal lines. It is at once whimsical and sophisticated. As the old man scratches

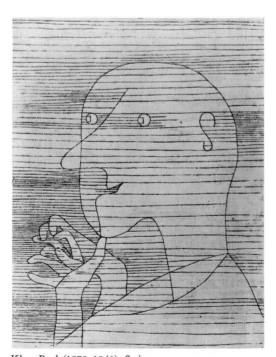

Klee, Paul (1879–1940), Swiss.
OLD MAN FIGURING.
Etching. 11¾ in. x 9⅜ in.
Museum of Modern Art, New York, N. Y.

Picasso, Pablo (1881–1973), Spanish.
HEAD OF A WOMAN.
Pen and ink on brownish-gray paper. 10⅝ in. x 8¼ in.
Museum of Modern Art, New York, N. Y.

255

Wu Chên
(1280–1354), Chinese.
BAMBOO IN THE WIND.
Brush drawing. $29\frac{5}{8}$ in. x $21\frac{3}{8}$ in.
Museum of Fine Arts, Boston, Mass.

his chin with curving fingers, his eyes peer out with a look of wonder from behind irregularly spaced horizontal lines. Klee's approach to drawing is both a unique and a personal one. Often it is concerned with mental processes.

The Drawings of China and Japan

Oriental drawings show a masterly use of line. This can be seen in the way Wu Chên, a 14th-century Chinese artist, rendered the main stalk and branches in 'Bamboo in the Wind'. The lettering on the right side of this piece reminds us of the close relationship that exists in the Orient between the arts of writing, printing, and drawing.

Japanese prints have become well known to the Western world. Best known of the Japanese artists are Hokusai and Hiroshige, who worked in the 19th century. (For pictures in color, see Japan, section "Culture.") A Japanese-American, Yasuo Kuniyoshi, produced fine drawings in the United States. One of these is the 'Dream', an ink sketch in which the blend of Oriental and modern feeling is at once apparent. Unlike other present-day artists, Kuniyoshi never used abstract symbols. The animal, the plant forms, and even the figure soaring upward in the 'Dream' can all be easily identified.

Drawing and Commercial Art

Drawing is the backbone of commercial art, a field that continues to gain in importance wherever eye appeal is thought to be significant in selling products. In commercial work, drawing is used by the fashion artist, the illustrator, the layout person, and the designer. 'Compton's Encyclopedia' uses commercial artists to illustrate many of its articles (see, for example, Digestive System).

The comic strips and political drawings in newspapers are called cartoons. Animated cartoons are produced by filming hundreds of drawings one after another (see Cartoons; Motion Pictures).

A caricature is a political cartoon that exaggerates a situation or a person's characteristics. It has proved a powerful weapon in politics. Among famous caricaturists of modern times were Sir John Tenniel of England and Thomas Nast of America. The latter broke up the powerful Tweed Ring by means of his drawings (see Tammany Hall; Nast. See also Arts, The; Mechanical Drawing; Painting.)

Yasuo Kuniyoshi
(1893–1953), American.
DREAM.
Ink drawing. 13 in. x 19 in.
Collection of Mrs. Edith Gregor Halpert,
Downtown Gallery, New York, N. Y.

DREAMS. During sleep the mind often seems to contain a stage on which unfolds a story or sequence of events. These episodes are what are most commonly called dreams. They are illusions or hallucinations of real experiences. What type of reality they express is difficult to decipher.

Meaning. What dreams signify has puzzled mankind for thousands of years. In the ancient world dreams were often considered prophetic. Homer's 'Iliad' contains a passage in which King Agamemnon is visited in a dream by a messenger of Zeus to prescribe the king's future actions. The Old Testament is filled with accounts of prophetic dreams, the most famous of which is the account of Joseph in the book of Genesis (*see* Folklore). In some cultures dreams are considered a reflection of reality, a means to convey the truth about one's life that cannot be seen in day-to-day living.

Dreams have also been viewed as nothing more than extensions of the waking state, a carryover into sleep of what a person has thought about or experienced while awake. One of the best-known modern theories of dreams was set forth by Sigmund Freud in his book 'The Interpretation of Dreams', which was published in 1899. He asserted that the feelings and wishes that are repressed in wakeful thought, particularly those associated with sex and hostility, are released in dreams.

All the conflicting notions about the nature of dreams lead to no definite conclusions. It is perhaps best to agree with the French writer Michel de Montaigne that "Dreams are the true interpreters of our inclinations, but art is required to sort them out."

Physiology of dreaming. The state of the body during sleep continues to be carefully studied. In 1953 it was discovered that while dreaming an individual experiences a burst of rapid eye movements (REM), active brain waves, and an increased rate of breathing. In newborn infants this dream state takes up about 50 percent of the sleep period. This declines until about age 10 and stabilizes at 25 percent through young adulthood to age 60. After that there is a slight decline among the elderly.

Dream states have been observed in many mammals, including dogs, monkeys, elephants, rats, and opossums. Surgical studies of mammal brains indicate that the dream state involves an area within the brain stem known as the pontine tegmentum. Dreaming itself seems to be associated with a hormone called norepinephrine, or noradrenaline (*see* Hormones). The order and length of dreaming and nondreaming periods during sleep appear to be regular, and there seem to be associations between these patterns and the emotional state of the individual before going to sleep.

DREDGE AND POWER SHOVEL. Digging soil from the bottoms of lakes, rivers, and other bodies of water is called dredging. Dredges, which are mounted on floats, are used to do such work to deepen, widen, or straighten channels in rivers, harbors, or bays; to build dikes and levees; and to prepare foundations for bridges, lighthouses, and other structures. Dredging is also used to dig mineral deposits, diamonds, and marine life of commercial value from river bottoms and soils deposited by rivers. Power shovels are used to dig up dry land.

Dredges

There are two types of dredge: the mechanically operated and hydraulically operated. Mechanical dredges, which are similar to land-based excavating machines, were the first to be developed and can be classified as dipper, grapple, or ladder dredges.

The most common is the dipper dredge. The typical American dredge, it is widely used for river improvement and in digging drainage canals. It consists of a hoisting engine with a swinging crane. A boom hangs from the crane end with a great thrusting shovel, or dipper. Vertical rods called spuds are lowered into the lake or river bed to steady the dredge. The boom lowers the dipper to the bottom. A cable draws the dipper forward into the material to be raised. When the dipper is full, it is lifted clear of the water and swung around to the desired position for dumping. The bottom of the dipper is hinged. Pulling a cable attached to a latch lets the bottom open, and the load drops out. The dipper dredge can even rip through soft rock without blasting. The usual dipper holds from one half to 6 cubic yards (11 cubic meters), or about 15 tons, to each dipperful.

The clamshell grapple dredge has a grab bucket composed of two great scoops, hinged at the top, which can be closed like a clamshell. The open bucket

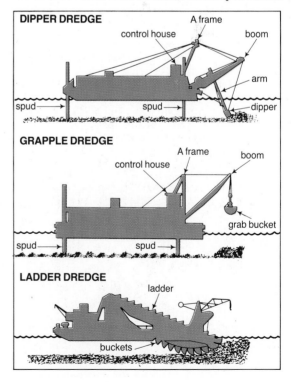

DIPPER DREDGE — control house, A frame, boom, arm, spud, spud, dipper

GRAPPLE DREDGE — control house, A frame, boom, grab bucket, spud, spud

LADDER DREDGE — ladder, buckets

is lowered from the end of a crane. The two halves are then closed, and the filled bucket is raised by means of wire ropes. An orange-peel grapple dredge has a bucket made of three or four triangular blades with sharp tips. The tips bite under the material to be raised. Grapple dredges are operated in deep water.

The operation of dipper and grapple dredges is intermittent, while a ladder dredge digs trenches and other narrow cuts continuously. It uses sharp-edged buckets carried on an endless chain or wheel. The assembly makes a first cut to the desired depth. Then a power plant draws it along, and it continues the cut as it moves.

Mechanical dredges are unable to transport materials for long distances. They are not self-propelled and are low in productivity. Their advantage lies in their usefulness in dredging in restricted locations such as ditches and jetties, and they can be equipped with devices to treat and drain water from dredged material in mining operations.

There are three basic types of hydraulically operated dredges—dustpan, hydraulic cutterhead, and self-propelled hopper dredges. The self-propelled dustpan dredge, which resembles a large vacuum cleaner or dustpan, consists of a dredge pump that draws a mixture of water and the material to be dredged—called the dredging spoil—through a suction pipe and pumps it to a disposal area through a floating pipeline. The suction heads are outfitted with high-velocity water jets for softening the bottom, but they cannot cut through hard or compacted material. They are suitable only for dredging soft materials.

The hydraulic cutterhead dredge is similar to a dustpan dredge but is equipped with a rotating cutter at the end of the suction pipe. It can be used effectively in all types of alluvial materials and compacted deposits such as clay and hardpan. Larger cutterhead dredges are also used to cut through and remove soft rock materials without blasting.

A self-propelled hopper dredge has a molded ship's hull and functions similarly to plain suction-type dredges like dustpan dredges. The bottom material is sucked up by dredge pumps through a dragarm, and the mixture of water and dredging spoil is then deposited in storage compartments called hoppers.

After filling the hoppers, the dredge proceeds to a disposal site to empty the hoppers through bottom doors or by pumping the water-spoil mixture through a pipeline. After emptying the hopper, the hopper dredge returns to the dredging area.

Power Shovels

Power shovels use a dipper and a power plant set on a turntable, which, in turn, is mounted on a caterpillar tread. With the turntable, the operator can dig in one spot, lift the dug up material, swing the scoop, and dump the material into a waiting truck or railroad car. The capacity of dippers normally ranges from 1 to 20 cubic yards (.75 to 15 cubic meters), though much larger units with a capacity of up to 200 cubic yards (150 cubic meters) are used in mining operations. Power shovels driven by gasoline or diesel engines or by electric motors have almost entirely replaced earlier steam shovels.

Another type of earth-moving machine is the bulldozer, which is basically a tractor equipped with a front-mounted curved blade or mold board. Bulldozers are versatile and are used for various earth-moving operations such as clearing land and pushing soil and rocks from place to place. The volume of soil or rock that can be moved by one push is up to 20 cubic yards (15 cubic meters) for a large bulldozer. A crawler tractor-type bulldozer can clear brush from more than 3 acres (1.2 hectares) in one hour.

A specialized machine called a ladder trencher, or ditcher, is effective for opening trenches for utility lines, telephone cables, drainage and sewer lines, and the like. It consists of two main components: a crawler, or rubber-tired carrier, and a digging mechanism. Depending on the soil condition and the depth of the trench to be excavated, the trencher can move at a speed of up to 2 miles (3.2 kilometers) per hour. It has a long boom, and an endless chain rotates along the boom. Buckets or clamshells attached to this chain dig at the bottom of the trench, bring up excavated material, and unload it onto a conveyer while the machine moves slowly along. The width of the excavated trench ranges between 18 and 60 inches (46 and 152 centimeters). Ladder trenches can be used for digging depths of up to 20 feet (6 meters).

Another machine with a wide radius of action uses a dragline, which is a lifting crane with a drag bucket. A long boom flings out the bucket on the line and drops it into the material to be excavated. The machine then pulls in the line, drawing in the bucket until it is filled, lifts it, and swings it with the crane boom to dump the material wherever desired. The size of the scoop is normally between $\frac{1}{2}$ and 3 cubic yards (.38 and 2.3 cubic meters). A clamshell is a modified lift crane with the hook replaced by a clam bucket. It is suitable for raising loose material such as the removal of silt from bottoms of rivers, lakes, or harbors. It is also used to unload ore, coal, and crushed stone (see Coal). Draglines and clamshells are land-based machines that are similar to dipper and clamshell dredges.

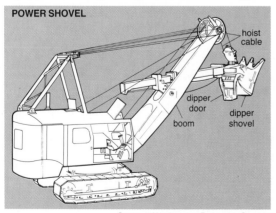

POWER SHOVEL

hoist cable

dipper door

dipper shovel

boom

Courtesy of Northwestern Engineering Company

Devices that carry buckets on an endless chain are used to unload sand or gravel from ships and barges. The unloading of grain is normally carried out by large suction heads or dustpans. The loading of grain silos and the unloading of ships' holds take place with these giant vacuum cleaners.

DRED SCOTT DECISION. Dred Scott was a black slave who belonged to an officer in the United States Army. His master had taken him from the slave state of Missouri to the free state of Illinois and then to Minnesota, which had been declared a free territory by the Missouri Compromise of 1820 (*see* Missouri Compromise).

When his master was ordered back to Missouri by the Army, Scott went with him. After his master died, however, Scott sued, claiming that he was no longer a slave because he had lived on free soil. The case was carried to the United States Supreme Court. In 1857 a majority of the court (seven out of nine), through the opinion of Chief Justice Roger B. Taney, declared that Scott was still a slave and not a citizen and so had no constitutional right to sue in a federal court. The decision further held that Congress had no power to prohibit slavery in the territories and that the Missouri Compromise therefore was unconstitutional.

President James Buchanan urged all the people to accept the decision as final, but antislavery leaders in the North refused and continued their agitation against slavery. By convincing many Northerners that Southern slaveholders were determined to rule the nation, the Dred Scott decision greatly widened the gap between the North and the South and helped bring on the Civil War (*see* Civil War, American).

DREISER, Theodore (1871–1945). With the novel 'Sister Carrie', author Theodore Dreiser so shocked his publisher that he tried not to issue the book. Even then, in 1900, it was published only in an altered form. A similar fate was to greet most of Dreiser's novels, until in 1925 his 'An American Tragedy' was published to wide critical and popular acclaim.

Dreiser was born in Terre Haute, Ind., on Aug. 27, 1871. He was the 12th of 13 children in a poverty-stricken family. His formal education was meager, but he finished a year at the University of Indiana before he went to New York City to become a journalist in 1894. Supported by his prosperous composer brother Paul (who spelled his name Dresser), he wrote magazine articles. Distressed over the hostile reception of his 'Sister Carrie', he had a nervous breakdown. His next novel, 'Jennie Gerhardt' (1911), was likewise condemned because, like 'Sister Carrie', it was a story of unconventional sexual relationships. Critics and public alike objected to Dreiser's "naturalism," his view of people as victims of blind forces and their own uncontrolled passions.

Dreiser's next two novels, 'The Financier' (1912) and 'The Titan' (1914), were based on the exploits of the American transportation magnate Charles Tyson Yerkes. When these books were also unsuccessful,

Dreiser turned from the novel to other forms of writing for the next ten years. The publication of 'An American Tragedy', based on a famous murder case, was his first financial success. After this novel the quality and quantity of his work fell sharply. His last two novels, 'The Bulwark' (1946) and 'The Stoic' (1947), were published after his death. Dreiser died in Hollywood, Calif., on Dec. 28, 1945.

DRESDEN, East Germany. The third largest city of East Germany and, historically, one of the cultural centers of Europe, Dresden was almost totally destroyed by British and American bombers during World War II.

Dresden is in southeastern East Germany, and the Elbe River runs through it. Its boundaries extend to the hills that mark the limits of the Elbe Basin. The heart of the old city, on the south side of a bend in the river, has been reconstructed since the war. The Zwinger, built for one of the electors of Saxony in the early 18th century, is a museum and was also, in its early days, a scene for royal festivities. Its collection of paintings was removed for safekeeping during World War II and was returned in 1956. Near the Zwinger is the Opera House designed by Gottfried Semper in the mid-19th century. The Opera House, associated with such composers as Carl Maria von Weber, Richard Wagner, and Richard Strauss, was reopened after reconstruction was completed in 1985. To the east of the Opera House is the New Market Square. The Kreuzkirche, the oldest church in the city, is on the Old Market Square. Prager Strasse, once a major shopping street, is now a pedestrian mall.

Nearby coal fields led to the industrialization of Dresden in the late 19th century. Manufactured products include precision and optical instruments, radio and electrical equipment, hydroelectric generators, and X-ray and photographic equipment. Flowers and shrubs are grown for export. The world-famous Dresden china is made at nearby Meissen.

Though not the cultural giant it once was, Dresden still has a professional theater, an opera company, and a symphony orchestra. The Technical University is the main institution of higher education. The Central Institute for Nuclear Physics and the German Museum of Hygiene are also in Dresden.

Dresden's origins extend to at least the early 1200s, when the Margrave of Meissen built a castle near a fishing village. In 1489 it became the residence and capital of the Albertine line of Wettin rulers. The city burned in 1491 and was heavily damaged in the Seven Years' War in the 18th century and again during the Napoleonic wars. The World War II bombing raids of Feb. 13 and 14, 1945, created a fire storm effect that killed 35,000 to 135,000 residents. Population (1983 estimate), 521,786.

By courtesy of (left) Lehnert & Landrock, Cairo; (center) SCALA New York; (right) Chuzeville—Musée du Louvre, Paris

The figures on the throne of Tutankhamen (left) show styles of Egyptian royal dress as worn in about 1350 B.C. Both sexes of ancient Greece wore simple, draped garments like those of the bronze charioteer (center) and the figurine (right).

DRESS

DRESS. The word *dress* is closely related to the word *clothing*, yet the two words are used in somewhat different ways. A man wearing a handsomely tailored suit is referred to as well dressed. The Eskimo survives the Arctic winter because he is well clothed. People clothe themselves out of necessity, but they dress out of a desire to look attractive. (*See also* Clothing; Dress Design; Fashion.)

Throughout history, many factors have affected the manner in which people dress. In early civilizations, climate and the raw materials that were available were important in influencing what styles of dress were adopted. Later, advances in technology brought new tools and clothing materials that made new styles possible (*see* Textiles).

Ancient Egypt

Present styles of Western dress evolved gradually from the garments worn by the people of ancient civilizations. The people of Egypt's Old Kingdom (which began about 2700 B.C.) wore very few clothes. The men's sole garment, the *schenti*, or loincloth, was wrapped about the hips and held in place by a belt. The women wore only a straight, narrow skirt that hung from below the breasts to the feet. It was suspended either from a single strap that crossed over one shoulder or from a pair of straps, one over each shoulder. Both men's and women's garments were made of cotton or linen and were usually white.

By about 950 B.C., other garments had been added. Men wore several skirts over their short loincloths. Each skirt was shorter than the one directly under it. The introduction of these skirts was followed by the introduction of a tunic that was seamed at the side and was so woven as to be almost transparent. Women also wore the tunic, usually with a cape that was knotted at the breast.

In ancient Egypt it was fashionable for both men and women to shave their heads. For protection against the sun, the rich wore wigs and the poor wore skullcaps. The women of ancient Egypt used cosmetics lavishly. They perfumed their wigs and rubbed their bodies with fragrant oils. They decorated their eyes with green and black kohl, a cosmetic with an antimony or soot base, and painted their lips red.

The Aegean Islands

While the Egyptian empire was flourishing, the island of Crete was also the site of a well-developed civilization. The curved silhouette of Cretan dress echoed the spiral motif characteristic of Cretan art.

Cretan men wore only a short loincloth. It was fastened at the waist by a wide belt. This was tightly cinched to give the effect of a very small waist and round, full hips. Women's clothing was designed to produce the same results. It consisted of a long, full, multitiered skirt and a small jacket. The skirt was brightly colored and patterned. The jacket covered only the back and arms.

Ancient Greece

In ancient Greece both men and women wore the *chiton*, a draped garment that was sewn up one side and fastened at the shoulder by a clasp or buckle. The woman's garment fell to the ankles; the man's usually reached only to the knees. The chiton was made of wool, cotton, linen, or silk.

Two types of chitons were worn in ancient Greece. The *Doric chiton* was folded over at the top and held at the waist by a tied belt. The *Ionic chiton*, made of a lighter material, was closely pleated and had wide false sleeves. In time, the differences between the chitons began to disappear as the Doric was made of a lighter material and the Ionic lost its sleeves.

People of ancient Rome, wearing togas and pallae, parade across a processional frieze (left) that was finished in 9 B.C. A detail from a tomb decorated in about 1450 B.C. (above) records the typical dress of a Cretan woman.

Women wore the *peplos* over the chiton. The peplos was a rectangular cloth that was fastened at the shoulders and held in place by a high belt. Men wore either the *chlamys*, a short cloak that was folded over the shoulders, or the *himation*, a large, loosely draped cloak that was fastened over one shoulder.

The Roman Empire

Dress was one of the many elements of Greek culture that the Romans absorbed after they conquered Greece in the 2d century B.C. The Roman woman's costume looked much like its Greek counterpart. The tunic, worn indoors, was based on the Greek chiton. Over the tunic the woman wore the *stola*—a long, straight robe of linen or lightweight wool. It was either left to hang straight or bloused over a belt. The *palla*, a cloak, was draped over the stola.

Roman men also wore a tunic; however, only the workman or the slave appeared in it in public. The Roman citizen wore a *toga* over his tunic. The toga has been regarded as the masterpiece of draped garments. Its surface was unbroken, and it required no fastening with pins or buckles. The toga was a semicircular length of wool cloth that was draped according to an exact prescription. First the wearer arranged the toga in folds parallel to the straight edge of the fabric. Then he placed one end of the fabric over his left shoulder from the rear and brought the rest of the fabric across his back and under his right arm. Next he brought the length over his chest and his left arm and shoulder, thus securing

the first end. The second end hung down his back.

The color of the toga or its border identified the Roman's position in society. Ordinary citizens wore a white toga. Magistrates, priests, and upper-class boys wore a purple-bordered toga. Emperors wore an embroidered purple toga over a gold-embroidered tunic.

The Byzantine Era

When the Roman Empire was divided in the 4th century A.D., Byzantium, later named Constantinople and known today as Istanbul, became the capital of the eastern part. The dress worn by the people of Byzantium bore traces of the influence of Greece, Rome, and the Orient. Their drapery, derived from Roman dress, displayed the lush fabrics of the East— heavy silks, damasks, and brocades.

Christianity also had an effect on Byzantine dress. In keeping with its teachings, the men and women of Byzantium concealed their bodies entirely. Both sexes wore long, straight, sleeved tunics made of silk or linen and bound at the waist with a belt that was often heavily encrusted with jewels.

Over the tunic, Byzantine bishops and priests wore the *dalmatica*, a wide garment with many folds. Byzantine women wore a stola or a palla over the tunic. These outer garments were fastened at the shoulder with a jeweled clasp. The men's garments were usually made of a solid-color fabric, while the women's garments were patterned.

The principal feature that distinguished Byzantine garments was the incorporation of jewels and precious metals. Silk and gold threads used in Byzantine garments made them look very different from those of Greece and Rome even though they were essentially the same. Precious gems were used also in rings, bracelets, brooches, buckles, and earrings.

This article was reviewed by James Laver, whose works on dress include 'Style in Costume', 'The Shape of Things: Dress', and 'Modesty in Dress'.

261

Early Byzantine court dress is pictured in a mosaic that was probably completed during the 6th century. Byzantine garments were traditionally ornamented with gems and precious metals and were frequently woven with silk and gold threads.

The Romanesque Period

The word *Romanesque* has often been used to describe the styles of dress, art, and architecture that prevailed during the early Middle Ages. Romanesque dress departed from Byzantine dress in one important way—men's clothing was quite distinct from women's.

Men's clothing consisted of leggings, a tunic, and a cloak. The leggings, which had evolved from the trousers worn by the Germanic tribes, were held up by a belt at the waist and were supported by bands wound around the legs. The tunic, also belted, was wide and loose, with long sleeves. Warriors wore a tunic made of *chain mail*, or small metal links, that was slit up the front and back of the skirt to permit greater freedom of movement. The cloak was fastened at the shoulder by a brooch.

Women wore three basic garments—a woolen tunic, a cloak fastened with a brooch, and a kerchief as a head covering. The colors of these garments were usually bright and solid. The hooded cloak also came into widespread use during the period. It was worn by clerics, religious pilgrims, and shepherds. All Romanesque garments tended to follow the natural lines of the body. They were not designed to emphasize either height or breadth.

The Gothic Period

During the late Middle Ages, known as the Gothic period, the manner of dress made a complete break with tradition. A new male costume came into use consisting of pointed shoes, tight hose, and a short tunic—tight-fitting, buttoned down the front, and belted around the hips. This garment was first known as a *gipon* and later as a *doublet*. In the last quarter of the 14th century another garment came into use that was first known as a *houppelande* and later as a *gown*. Often it reached to the ankles, but it was also worn knee-length. The sleeves of the gown were usually wide at the wrists, and the edges were often *dagged*, or cut in fancy shapes.

The hood achieved its greatest popularity in the 15th century, when it was lengthened into the *liripipe* —a long, narrow band at the crown. Men began to wear hats with brims that projected in a peak over the forehead, and parti-colored garments became fashionable.

Women's dress at this period showed even more drastic changes. Instead of all-enveloping garments that concealed the shape of the figure, women began to constrict the waist by means of stiffening in the bodice and to wear a low-cut neckline, or *décolletage*, that revealed the throat and part of the breasts.

Women also changed their headdress. A veil was frilled to form an arch around the face, or the hair was worn in two wide sections covered with latticework attached to a fillet on top of the head. In the 1400's many elaborate forms of headdress developed. There were horned headdresses and heart-shaped headdresses.

In the second half of the 15th century, up to about 1485, the most unusual form was the butterfly headdress, which consisted of a veil of diaphanous material supported on a wire frame and often reaching enormous proportions. Other varieties were the turban

Robert Doisneau—Rapho Guillumette

Giraudon

The Normans and Saxons shown in the Bayeux tapestry (above) wear the tunics and leggings characteristic of Romanesque dress. The tapestry was embroidered during the 11th century. An illumination for a 15th-century French prayer book (right) shows men and women in dress typical of the late Gothic era, when clothing had voluminous sleeves and lavish trimming.

headdress, the cap in the shape of an inverted flower-pot, and, in France, the *hennin*, or steeple headdress.

The Renaissance

Patterned fabrics, usually velvets and brocades, were more popular than materials of a single color from about 1480 to 1510. During this period of the Renaissance, Italian styles dominated European fashion. Men's garments became shorter and wider, with lower necklines. Women's skirts also became shorter, and the long, trailing gown disappeared.

From about 1510 to 1550 Germanic dress had the greatest influence on European fashion. A short, square look characterized menswear. With brief, wide gowns, men wore hose and short breeches that were padded for added fullness. They also wore broad-toed shoes and wide-brimmed caps. Women's clothing also emphasized breadth. Skirts were voluminous and pleated or were topped with a pleated apron. The neckline was finished with a standing collar.

The German Renaissance was also marked by the development of a unique method of ornamentation known as *slashing*. Two layers of cloth were placed one over the other. The outer was then slashed to reveal the contrasting inner one. Slashing was used extensively in men's and women's gowns, shoes, and caps.

From about 1550 to 1600 the Renaissance was dominated by Spanish fashions. The costumes worn during this period were influenced more by geometric shapes than by the contours of the body. The human form was considered as two basic platforms—hips and shoulders. While clothing was constructed to fit the wearer, on the outside it was padded and shaped to show a completely different form. Dark silks and velvets were the most popular fabrics, for they were effective backdrops for precious stones and jewelry. During this period a person's wealth was gauged by

the value of the gems sewn onto his clothing.

In men's dress the short gown was replaced by a short cloak. The cloak was worn with *trunk hose*, or short breeches, padded with horsehair. Knitted stockings were developed at this time, and their close adherence to the legs contrasted with the padded body. Spanish influence is seen in devices for expanding women's skirts, sometimes to extraordinary dimensions. The earliest of these was known as the *Spanish farthingale*. It consisted of an underskirt suspended by means of hoops growing wider toward the hem, a curious anticipation of the crinoline of the 19th century. The *French farthingale*, worn at court in the 1560's and by almost every woman after 1580, was shaped like a drum. The skirt was draped horizontally over it and then fell vertically to the ground. The *roll farthingale* consisted of a padded bolster worn around the hips.

The *ruff*—a pleated, heavily starched collar worn by men and women alike—is also identified with the Spanish Renaissance. It began as a small collar but reached great proportions by the 17th century.

The Baroque Era

The artist Michelangelo is often credited with fathering the baroque style of art and architecture. During this era the continuous straight lines of the Renaissance gave way to intricate curves. The whirling motion of the baroque style was particularly striking in men's dress. Lace and ribbon were used unsparingly to decorate men's costumes in the early part of the era. They were especially evident in military dress—on the cuffs, the collar, and the wide sash that was tied around the waist.

Typical menswear during the mid-17th century consisted of a vestlike doublet with elbow-length sleeves. The doublet was worn over a shirt whose

263

'The Ambassadors' (left), a painting by the German artist Hans Holbein the Younger, portrays members of the northern European middle class during the first half of the 16th century. Puffed sleeves, wide shoulders, and hats with brims were used to create a general appearance of breadth and weight during the Renaissance. Spanish court dress of the mid-17th century is shown in the portrait of the Infanta Maria Theresa (above), painted by the Spanish artist Diego y Velasquez. The wide skirts and lace trim contributed to an illusion of movement in baroque costume.

sleeves extended below those of the doublet. Breeches with wide legs hung to the knees and were trimmed with as much as 140 yards of silk ribbon.

During the late 17th century the long jacket appeared. Although at first cut rather loosely, it was soon fitted more closely to the body. The doublet was lengthened to become a knee-length waistcoat. Narrow breeches replaced the wide kind that had been worn earlier. A *cravat* made of lace or lace-edged linen was tied at the neck. From that time on, the necktie has played an important role in menswear.

The baroque wig best exemplified the prevailing quest for ornamentation and dignity. Toward the end of the 17th century, false hair became more popular than natural hair. Men's wigs were usually brown or black and fell over the shoulders in unruly masses of curls, often reaching to the waist in back. Women's coiffures were styled similarly but were even more elaborate. The hair on the crown of the wig was arranged in a high headdress that resembled a row of organ pipes, and curls fell over the forehead. The back of the head supported a starched lace cap.

The headdress was supposed to help create a long, slender silhouette. Other devices included the tight corset, which held the body rigid, and the train. The restraints imposed by both were well suited to the formality of life during the baroque era.

The 18th Century

The baroque tradition of dress reached its culmination in France during the mid-18th century. The discovery of Chinese art by the West led to a preoccupation with delicate ornamentation and decoration. Chinese motifs, such as bellflowers and canopies, appeared as decorative touches on gowns. Soft pastel

colors were borrowed from Chinese paintings for use in men's and women's garments.

The dress worn by both men and women was directed toward establishing a conelike silhouette. Women's tightly corseted torsos terminated in huge skirts that, though falling straight at the front and back, were extended at the sides so that at the hem they were up to 12 feet across. These great skirts forced the ladies of the day to pass sideways through most doorways. Men's coats and waistcoats were narrow at the shoulders and stiffened at the hem to hold them out from the body.

Men, as well as women, used cosmetics heavily during the mid-18th century. The effect was not a natural one, however, as complexions were made to resemble porcelain. The face was stark white, with lips of bright red.

By 1774, the year Louis XVI ascended the French throne, French fashions had literally reached new heights. Women were wearing elaborate coiffures that were almost as tall as they were. The hair was pulled up over pads and cushions, and false hair was added for even greater height. Coiffures also utilized almost every kind of decoration imaginable—from feathers to blown glass to model ships.

The English fashions that predominated during the late 18th century were in marked contrast to the French ones that preceded them. The clothing Englishmen wore then was very similar to men's clothing today. Wool in bolder, darker colors replaced the pastel silks and satins that had previously been used. The coat, which was often double-breasted, was relatively loose and comfortable. It was worn with a short, square-cut waistcoat and breeches or *culottes* (knee breeches). Pantaloons of a knitted material

The romantic mood created by the clothing worn during the 18th century is captured in the painting 'Conversation in a Park' (above), attributed to the English artist Thomas Gainsborough. By the end of the 18th century, women's clothing had taken on a simplicity of style, as shown in the portrait (right) of Mademoiselle Rivière by the French painter Jean Ingres.

later replaced the culottes and usually were tucked into leather riding boots.

Women's clothing styles were often derived from menswear. The woman of the late 18th century wore a high-crowned man's hat on her head and a man's *redingote*, or riding coat. Women's dresses usually were made entirely of white fabric.

During the last few years of the 18th century, fashions were greatly influenced by the French Revolution—the most lasting effect being the substitution of long trousers for culottes by revolutionaries who wanted to distinguish themselves from the aristocrats. Those who wore trousers called themselves *sans-culottes*—literally, "without culottes."

Women's clothing in France also took on a new simplicity following the revolution. A ban on silks and velvets brought about the use of cottons and linens in dresses. Along with other aristocratic frivolities, the high-heeled shoe disappeared. It was replaced by a soft, flat slipper of cloth or kid, which was cut low and laced across the instep.

A fascination with Greek and Roman dress had a marked effect on women's clothing. Dresses of sheer cottons, such as muslin or batiste, flowed from a bodice, often ending in a train. These dresses, known as *chemises*, were usually sleeveless or short-sleeved.

While the fashionable female imitated Greek or Roman dress, her male counterpart adopted an exaggeration of the Englishman's costume. His hair was worn ragged and fell over the ears. Neckcloths cov-

ered his throat and the end of his chin. His coat—worn with tight trousers—had wide lapels and collar.

The 19th Century

At the beginning of the 19th century, the passion for ancient motifs in women's dress was on the wane. This was partly a result of the ban on the importation of Indian cotton muslin that Napoleon had imposed in an effort to revive the French silk industry. With only heavier materials available, clothing styles were forced to change. The train again vanished, and short, puffed sleeves appeared. Dresses were still white, though usually worn with colorful shawls. Skirts were shorter, leaving the feet exposed.

In menswear, breeches and riding boots had been replaced by long, wide trousers by 1815. In England during the early 19th century, men's clothing was dominated by the influence of George Bryan (Beau) Brummell, who popularized the complicated cravat and the idea of simple but well-tailored garments.

In the middle of the century there was a revival of 18th-century French fashions, with undulating curves determining the shape of men's and women's garments. Men wore trousers that were cut to add breadth to their hips. The trousers were topped by a narrow-waisted coat or overcoat.

Women took on the hourglass silhouette. The waist was restricted by a corset, while seven or eight petticoats buoyed out the skirt. The fullness at the hem was balanced by an exaggerated fullness at the breast.

265

Dresses had fitted bodices and trumpet-shaped skirts at the end of the 19th century, as shown in an illustration (above) done by the English artist Aubrey Beardsley for 'The Yellow Book'. In the 'Portrait of Madame Matisse' (right), by the French painter Henri Matisse, the subject wears the loosely cut style of dress popular during World War I.

Later in the period, a *crinoline*, or hooped underskirt, replaced the petticoats.

During the last quarter of the 19th century the crinoline, which had evolved from a round to an oval shape, disappeared. It was replaced by the *bustle*, a pad or frame worn below the waist at the back, over which the overskirt was draped. While the bustle was in vogue, the fullness of the skirt was concentrated at the back, the front falling straight.

A new corset compressed the abdomen and gave the women who wore it an S-shaped, somewhat sway-backed posture. This garment provided the foundation for the most popular dress of the day, which had a high neck, fitted bodice, and trumpet-shaped skirt. Women also adopted a man-tailored three-piece suit that could be mass-produced. The focal point of this costume was a blouse with a frilly front.

Unsuccessful efforts had been made to reform the 19th-century costume of women, largely on the ground that it was hazardous to health. In 1851 Amelia Bloomer of Seneca Falls, N. Y., designed a revolutionary costume consisting of a jacket and a short skirt worn over long, baggy trousers gathered at the ankles. Although her costume was not adopted for general wear, the pants—called *bloomers*—were worn by women for gymnastic and other physical exercises through the turn of the century. Amelia Bloomer's efforts were followed by those of doctors who wanted to put an end to the corset, but their attempts to inject reason into fashion met with failure.

The 20th Century

During the 19th century, artisans staged a revolt against the products of industry by designing hand-

made decorative items to camouflage machine-made objects. During the 20th century, however, they began to accept machine-made products on their own merits. In the first two decades of the century a popular artistic point of view was that an object achieved beauty by fulfilling its purpose.

This idea was incorporated into the design of women's clothing at about the time of World War I. Dresses took on the lines of the Japanese *kimono*—a wide-sleeved, loose-fitting garment. As dresses and coats fell loosely about the body, the corset practically disappeared. In the 1920's, the straight line established the shape of dresses—and hemlines began to climb. By 1925, women's dresses had become short, sleeveless tubes, belted at the hips. They reached to the knee, revealing legs clad in light-colored silk stockings. Although the length of the skirts has since varied from mid-calf in 1947 to several inches above the knee during the late 1960's, it has remained relatively short since the 1920's.

Another innovation was the widespread adoption of trousers by women. The bloomers of the preceding century evolved into lounging pajamas during the 1920's and 1930's. From the 1930's, slacks were worn

266

During the 1920's, hemlines climbed above the knee, and men wore long raccoon coats, as illustrated in this drawing (above) by the American cartoonist John Held, Jr. Hemlines rose again during the 1960's, and the minidress became popular, as shown in the American artist Wayne Thiebaud's painting 'Girl in White Boots' (right).

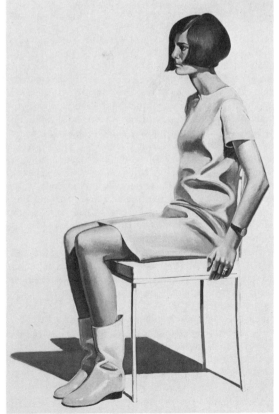

for many leisure activities, and pantsuits became widely acceptable for office and formal wear by 1970.

Styles in menswear did not change drastically during the first half of the 20th century. During the 1960s, however, a new interest in men's fashions, sometimes called the Peacock Revolution, got under way in Great Britain. There, small shops sold menswear in bright colors and flamboyant styles. From the young men attracted to these shops, the trend spread to older men. By the end of the 1960s, men's fashions were borrowing freely from women's. Men wore necklaces, fur coats, and print trousers. Many styles, known as "unisex" fashions, were being designed for wear by either men or women.

For the "Annie Hall" look (borrowed from a 1977 motion picture), women used outsized articles of men's clothing to create their own free-form outfits. In the 1980s this loose, overscaled shape was popularized by Japanese designers, and softened versions of menswear began to dominate women's styles.

BIBLIOGRAPHY FOR DRESS

Black, J.A. and Garland, Madge. A history of Fashion, rev. ed. (Morrow, 1980).

Hill, M.H. and Bucknell, P.A. Evolution of Fashion: Pattern and Cut from 1066–1930, rev. ed. (Drama Book, n.d.).

Wilcox, R.T. The Mode in Costume (Scribner, 1983).

By courtesy of Allan Stone Gallery, Collection Sabol

DRESS DESIGN

The experienced dress designer's final sketches—often skillfully simple in execution—convey the total conception of each garment's line, form, color, and texture.

DRESS DESIGN. Like architecture, interior design, and sculpture, dress design is a visual art that deals with three-dimensional forms. Dress designing is a specialized, competitive, and somewhat glamorous field. The designer must be able to create clothing that is both fashionable and functional. The finished garment has to fit the body of the wearer, be suitable for certain activities, and be relatively durable. (*See also* Arts, The; Design; Fashion.)

Dress design was a profession as early as the 1600's. One of the first well-known designers was Rose Bertin, a French milliner who served Marie Antoinette. She encouraged the queen's interest in dress fashions and designed her gowns. During the French Revolution Mademoiselle Bertin fled to England, where she continued to influence women's fashions.

Women dominated dress design until the last half of the 19th century. The first man to make a name in dress design was Charles Frederick Worth, an English tailor who became the *couturier*, or designer, of the empress Eugénie, consort of Napoleon III. In 1858 he opened a *salon*, or fashion house, in Paris, France. His clients included not only Eugénie and her court but also well-known actresses and other women who could afford his services. Worth was the first designer to show dresses made of fabrics of his own choosing. Previously, dressmakers had used fabrics provided by their patrons. He was also the first to display his designs on live *mannequins*, or models.

Largely because of Worth, dress design became one of France's most important industries. In 1868 he helped found the Chambre Syndicale de la Couture Parisienne. Today this trade association works to preserve France's dominance in the field of dress design. It sets the dates for the showing of each new fashion collection, usually in January and June, and directs a school that trains young people for careers in the French *couture*, or fashion, *houses*.

The Dress Designer Today

The position, degree of influence, and fame of the modern dress designer depends largely on where he lives and works. In Paris the system of *haute couture*, or high fashion, is dominated by a relatively small group of designers, most of whom own fashion houses and employ assistants, seamstresses, and marketing personnel. The great Paris designers of the 20th century include Christian Dior, Gabrielle "Coco" Chanel, Balenciaga, Yves Saint Laurent, André Courreges, Pierre Cardin, and Marc Bohan.

People from all over the world attend the Paris showings. The audiences are made up of manufacturers' representatives, buyers from retail stores, and private customers. Up to 200 new designs may be displayed at a showing. Private customers and retail buyers are charged much less for a particular

These Mondrian-inspired dresses by French designer Saint Laurent have the same length, fullness, and cut, but the creative placement of vertical and horizontal lines and dramatic blocks of color provides each with different emphasis.

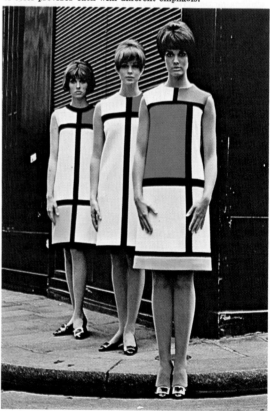

The fabric is so important to dress design that it is frequently selected even before preliminary sketches for a new design are begun. Although most fashion houses maintain a stockroom with bolts of materials available at all times for custom tailoring, the ready-to-wear manufacturer selects the fabrics that he wishes to order in great quantities from the latest samples, or swatches, provided by textile supply houses.

design than is the manufacturer who plans to produce it on a large scale and sell copies at a lower price.

Until recently French designers did not produce ready-to-wear apparel. Instead, each customer selected one of the new designs and chose a fabric for it. The dress was then made to her measurements at the designer's fashion house. During the late 1960s, however, most Paris designers had begun to show ready-to-wear apparel in boutiques, or small specialty shops, in addition to their couture collections.

In the United States dress designers work somewhat differently from the French. Few of the thousands of firms in the United States that manufacture clothing are owned or controlled by their designers. Also, most of the successful American dress designers usually create only ready-to-wear apparel.

Until World War II most American dress designers worked anonymously in garment factories. During that war, when Paris was occupied by German troops, French designers lost their influence on fashion, and American designers began to achieve recognition. Beginning in 1943 Coty American Fashion Critics' Awards were given to influential designers such as Norman Norell and Geoffrey Beene. Some designers—for example, Perry Ellis and Ralph Lauren—won citations for both women's fashion and menswear. After similar awards were established by the Council of Fashion Designers of America in 1985, the Coty awards were ended.

Elements of Dress Design

Of the many elements of dress design—including texture, line, and form—that of *color* is perhaps the most complex. Three characteristics—hue, value, and saturation—help identify a color. Hue locates the color in its position on the spectrum. Blue and orange are both hues. Value refers to the amount of light a color reflects. Pink and crimson are two values of the hue red. Saturation describes the degree of purity of a color. Lemon yellow, for example, is purer than beige. (*See also* Color.)

Color has a great effect on the other elements in dress design. Two colors with different values create a definite line if placed next to each other. For that reason, a designer who wants to call attention to the lines of a navy-blue blazer might trim the lapels in white. Two intense colors of opposite hues can produce an unpleasant vibrating sensation. This might make it difficult to focus the eyes on a herringbone-patterned fabric of pink and chartreuse.

Colors can also affect the wearer's complexion. A magenta worn next to the face might make the skin appear greenish, while a blue green might give it a rosy cast. Colors, like clothing styles, go in and out of fashion. Red, white, and blue may be popular one season—only to be replaced by plum, moss green, and clay a few months later. There is usually enough variety in fashionable colors, however, to allow almost every woman to choose a color that she likes and that flatters her.

Texture refers to both the look and feel of a fabric.

> This article was reviewed by Sharon Harris, fashion designer and guest fashion-design critic, The Art Institute of Chicago.

DRESS DESIGN

From the designer's final sketch, a sample garment is made up in muslin (right). When approved, it is taken apart, and its pieces are used as a pattern (below, top). If more than one garment is to be produced, however, a paper pattern is cut from the flat muslin pieces. The paper pattern is placed over a number of layers of fabric, and the cutter then uses an electric knife that enables him to cut through all of the layers at one time (below, bottom).

Joseph Janowicz—Compton's Encyclopedia

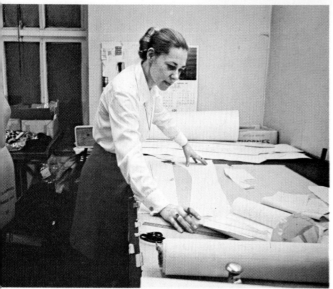

Fabrics can be rated by an almost infinite number of textural qualities. For example, a fabric can be either crisp or limp, heavy or light, nubby or smooth, dull or shiny. A fabric's texture determines many things about a garment, such as its resistance to wear, its ability to hold a given shape, and how much light it will reflect. Many textures may be used in a single costume. What textures are compatible is largely a matter of prevailing fashions.

Line can be created in a variety of ways. The use of a fabric with a pattern, contrasting trim, or two colors with different values can emphasize or define lines. Some popular modern dresses have used both trim and color to create horizontal and vertical lines. The length, fullness, and cut of a dress are also important in determining line.

The lines of a dress outline its *form*, or shape. Three basic forms are involved in dress design—the shape of the body, the shape of the dress, and the shape of the individual parts of the dress. In the course of time, dress designs have often superimposed geometric forms upon the natural shape of the body. During the 19th century, for example, corsets and bustles forced the body to conform with the swaybacked, S-shaped dress in fashion. The most attractive dresses, however, are usually those that harmonize with the natural proportions of the body.

Each of the elements in dress design is strongly related to the others. The process of dress design requires a knowledge of all of these elements or at least the ability to use them effectively.

The Process of Designing a Dress

The dress designer, whether employed by a fashion house or a ready-to-wear manufacturer, goes through a number of steps in creating a collection. He may begin with a conception of the design and may then make several sketches from which a final sketch evolves. However, while this is usually true for French designers, American designers frequently choose or are given a specific fabric with which to work and then make their sketches with this fabric in mind.

After the design is approved, it is made up in muslin. Darts and seams are put into the muslin

SOME CREATIVE DRESS DESIGNERS

Some prominent persons are not included below because they are covered in the main text of this article or in other articles in Compton's Encyclopedia (see Fact-Index).

Adrian, Gilbert (1903–59). American. Created the glamorous screen images of such stars as Norma Shearer, Joan Crawford, Greta Garbo, and Jean Harlow. Innovations: broad-shouldered suits, 'Letty Lynton' sleeves, unorthodox use of fabrics.

Balenciaga, Cristóbal (1895–1972). Spanish. Called the "designer's designer" and "prophet of the silhouette." Noted for elegant ball gowns. Innovations: "sack" dresses, shortened coat sleeves, patterned tights, plastic rainwear.

Burrows, Stephen (born 1943). American. First successful black designer. Popularized avant-garde sportswear. Innovations: "lettuce" hems, asymmetrical necklines, zigzag seams.

Chanel, Gabrielle (1883–1971). French. Introduced casual styles in high-fashion circles. Her "poor girl" look liberated clothes from clutter and confinement. Innovations: chemise dresses, braid-trimmed collarless cardigans, costume jewelry, turtleneck sweaters, the "little black dress."

Courrèges, André (born 1923). French. Noted for futuristic, youth-oriented styles. White became his trademark. Innovations: "paper doll" coats, vinyl trim, hip-hugger pants, short boots.

Dior, Christian (1905–57). French. Built the first international fashion empire of licensed accessories. Innovations: 1947's New Look, built-in corseting, geometric silhouettes.

Ellis, Perry (born 1940). American. Called the "king of slouch." Exaggerated scale and proportion in sportswear ensembles. Innovations: dimple sleeves, open-pocket-seamed skirts and culottes, hand-knit peplum sweaters, tailored ruffles, blueboys.

Gernreich, Rudi (1922–85). Austrian-American. Famed for offbeat fashions like topless swimsuits and see-through tops. A former dancer, he introduced leotards and stretch knits to street dress. Innovations: miniskirts, colored stockings.

Kenzo (born 1939). Japanese. His oversized, layered *Jungle Jap* outfits were widely copied. Innovations: tabards, leg warmers, drawstring pants, fold-over waistbands, balloon dresses.

Klein, Anne (1923–74). American. Pioneered sophisticated styles in junior sizes and the "total look" in misses' clothes. Innovations: interchangeable separates, designer activewear.

Lauren, Ralph (born 1939). American. Originated the "American prairie" look and, for movies, the 'Great Gatsby' and 'Annie Hall' looks. Innovations: Fair Isle sweaters, tartan scarves.

McCardell, Claire (1905–58). American. Her *Pieces* playclothes were the forerunner of related separates. Innovations: the Popover, the Monastic, jumpsuits, hooded sweaters.

Norell, Norman (1900–72). American. Called the "dean of American fashion." Pioneered use of fine designer techniques in ready-to-wear clothing. Innovations: divided skirts, sailor's middy.

Rabanne, Paco (born 1934). Spanish. Advocate of welded pop art sculpture as clothing. Innovations: use of plastic discs, aluminum, paper, mesh, fluorescent and neon colors.

Rhodes, Zandra (born 1940). British. Exponent of the "punk" look. Innovations: hand-screened fabrics for "mod" styles, pin-attached sleeves, raw pinked edges, elasticized pull-up hems.

Saint Laurent, Yves (born 1936). French. Originator of almost every major fashion trend since the 1950s. Innovations: pantsuits, cropped topcoats, maxiskirts, many looks—"little girl," "chic beatnik," "Mondrian," "rich peasant."

Schiaparelli, Elsa (1896–1973). Italian-French. Creator of shocking pink. Combined eccentricity with simplicity. Innovations: unusually colored furs, padded shoulders, "shortie" coats.

garment as it is molded on a model or a dressmaker's dummy. It is then examined for line and form. At this stage, many American manufacturers require that the garment be judged by such economic criteria as yardage requirements and difficulty of construction.

If a garment is slated for mass production, the muslin prototype is taken apart, and its sections are used to cut a flat pattern. From such patterns it is possible to cut through hundreds of layers of fabric at one time. The ready-to-wear manufacturer often saves pattern pieces, since some of them can be reused if a design is repeated with only slight modifications. No separate patterns are used for custom-made garments, as the finished dress is made directly from the unstitched muslin model. If a woman makes her own clothing at home, she usually buys a commercially made paper pattern in a standard size.

After the muslin garment is approved and the pattern made, a copy of the dress is produced in the intended fabric. If the fabric has not yet been selected at this point, it is chosen in a texture and color that will convey the lines of the design. In the fashion house, the model who will wear the design in the showing is selected, and the sample garment is tailored especially for her. In the ready-to-wear house, a few copies are made for the season's showing and for salesmen to display to retailers. If the dress is accepted by both the retail buyers and the salesmen, it is graded into many sizes and mass-produced in the factory.

The Relationship of Dress Design to Fashion

The success of a particular dress design determines whether or not it will become a fashion. The extent and duration of fashion cycles have been influenced by changes in technology. When articles of clothing had to be handmade, fashions often lasted for decades (see Dress). The mass-production of dresses in the same design, however, has greatly reduced the amount of time it takes for a design to reach a large number of people. The mass media—television, motion pictures, magazines, and newspapers—are also important in spreading fashions throughout the world. Thus, designs can go in and out of fashion much more quickly. (See also Fashion.)

In recent years it has become almost impossible to single out one style as the prevailing fashion. So many designs are brought before the public at the same time that many different fashions can exist simultaneously. A woman might own an ankle-length skirt, a knee-length skirt, and jeans and be fashionable wearing any one of them. (See also Clothing.)

BIBLIOGRAPHY FOR DRESS DESIGN

Bailey, M.J. Those Glorious Years: the Great Hollywood Costume Designs of the Thirties (Citadel, 1982).

Jarnow, J.A. Inside the Fashion Business, 3rd ed. (Wiley, 1981).

Kopp, Ernestine and others. Designing Apparel Through the Flat Pattern, 5th ed. (Fairchild, 1981).

Tate, S.L. and Shafer, Mona. Inside Fashion Design, 2nd ed. (Harper, 1983).

DREYFUS CASE

DREYFUS CASE. The trial started on Dec. 19, 1894, and lasted four days. The accused was French Army Captain Alfred Dreyfus, who was charged with passing military secrets to Colonel Max von Schwartzkoppen, German military attaché in Paris. The evidence was a single piece of paper listing secret documents that had been turned over to the Germans. The handwriting on the document was declared to be that of Capt. Dreyfus.

The trial was the most explosive affair ever to disrupt the French Third Republic. Austria and France were, at the time, the two most anti-Semitic nations in Europe, and Dreyfus was a Jew. The Dreyfus affair set off a wave of intense anti-Semitism in France that lasted for decades. And it did much more. In the words of journalist–historian William L. Shirer: "For the next twelve years France would be torn by strife over the rights and wrongs of the case. . . . Families were torn asunder, old friendships destroyed, duels fought, governments overthrown, careers ruined."

Why so much turmoil? Dreyfus was innocent. But the army and many political leaders were determined to convict him. He was indeed convicted and sentenced to imprisonment on Devil's Island, the French penal colony off the coast of South America. Even before the trial he had been convicted by the press in a wave of popular hysteria against traitors in general and Jews in particular.

The minister of war, General Auguste Mercier, demanded a conviction. One of his underlings, Major Hubert Henry, knew the evidence was weak. To improve the army's case, he created a number of forged documents, purportedly in Dreyfus' handwriting. He also swore in court that he had been told by an unimpeachable source that Dreyfus was guilty. Thus the army captain was convicted on the basis of forged evidence and false testimony.

Truth Emerges

Slowly the truth of the case began to emerge. It met the furious opposition of those who wanted the case kept closed—the army, most of the press, and the government. In March 1896, through the diligence of Maj. Georges Picquart, an application for promotion made by Maj. Ferdinand Walsin Esterhazy was discovered to be in handwriting that matched that on the documents list that had helped convict Dreyfus. And Esterhazy was known to have been in regular communication with the Germans.

Once the truth began circulating, there arose a furious opposition to reopening the case. Then, on Jan. 13, 1898, there appeared in the Paris newspaper *L'Aurore* one of the most famous political documents ever published: novelist Émile Zola's open letter entitled 'J' Accuse' ('I Accuse'), asserting that the army had framed Dreyfus. This letter was the turning point in the affair. Major Henry confessed to the forgeries and committed suicide. Esterhazy was tried but found innocent at the insistence of the army. The High Court of Appeals ordered a new trial for Dreyfus and threw out the evidence on which he had been convicted. The new trial was held in the summer of 1899, and again Dreyfus was convicted, so determined was the army not to appear wrong. He was nevertheless pardoned by the president of France and released from military prison in September.

Exoneration

In July 1906 the High Court of Appeals set aside the second conviction. Dreyfus was readmitted to the army and promoted to major. Picquart, who had become an outcast in the military establishment, was rehabilitated as well. He was made a brigadier general and two years later became minister of war.

So complicated were the maneuverings in this case that the whole truth has never emerged. But new evidence came to light years later. Colonel Schwartzkoppen died in 1917. In 1931 his private papers were published. They revealed that it had indeed been Esterhazy who was the spy for the Germans. The German colonel had kept silent because it served his purpose to have France in turmoil. He also wanted to keep receiving information from Esterhazy.

DROUGHT. The rains did not come. But the winds blew. And on millions of acres of American farmland, from North Dakota to Texas and from Colorado to Missouri, the topsoil was carried away. It was the Dust Bowl of the early 1930s, the worst drought in American history, and it drove more than half the region's population away.

The Dust Bowl was an example of what is called unpredictable drought, the abnormal failure of rainfall in an area where rainfall is normally adequate. Such droughts usually do not affect a very large area and generally occur in regions that are scientifically classified as humid or subhumid.

There are three other types of drought: permanent, seasonal, and invisible. Permanent drought characterizes the driest climates, such as the arid parts of the American Southwest or East Africa: the latter region experienced its most severe drought of the century in the 1980s. In such regions agriculture is impossible without permanent irrigation (*see* Irrigation).

Seasonal drought occurs in climates that have well-defined rainy and dry seasons. Such regions are said to have tropical or subtropical climates (*see* Climate, section "Classification of Climates"). Many of these regions lie near the Equator: the Indian subcontinent, Southeast Asia, and portions of Africa, Central America, and South America. Southern California and Southern Australia are also subject to seasonal droughts. For agriculture to be successful, planting must be adjusted so growth will take place in the rainy season.

Invisible drought occurs in summer when high temperatures induce high rates of evaporation. Even frequent showers cannot replace the lost water.

Drought is the most serious hazard to agriculture in many places. Apart from affecting crops, it also depletes soil moisture, lowers the underground water supply, and reduces stream flow, limiting irrigation.

DRUGS

A laboratory technician in a germ-free suit supervises the production of an antihepatitis vaccine.

Hank Morgan—Rainbow

DRUGS. Physicians use special chemical compounds to diagnose, prevent, or treat certain kinds of diseases. These compounds are drugs. A more scientific name for them is pharmaceuticals. (*See also* Anesthesia; Antibiotic; Antiseptic; Antitoxin; Disease; Medicine; Pharmacy; Vaccines.)

As far back as history can be traced, including Egyptian hieroglyphics, there are references to medicinal drugs recommended for various ailments. However, until the 20th century, only a few of the drugs mentioned or used really worked. Those that did work were based on "discovery"—the accidental observation revealing that certain plant substances would ease pain or help cure an illness. In 1776, for example, English botanist and physician William Withering learned that an herbal tea made by an old farm woman was effective in treating dropsy, or excess water in the tissues, which is caused by the inability of the heart to pump strongly enough. He found that one ingredient of the tea, which was made with leaves of the foxglove plant, strengthened the heart's pumping ability. The drug made from the foxglove plant is now known as digitalis.

While finding drugs through discovery did yield a few important vaccines and medicines, it was not until the 20th century with its new method—inventing drugs—that science made it possible to treat, cure, or prevent a host of diseases that once afflicted human beings. To invent a useful drug it was first necessary to understand far more about how the body worked, why disease occurred, and why and how certain chemicals acted in the body. This last field of study and research is called pharmacology.

Where Drugs Come From

Drugs are obtained from many different sources. Some come from plants, while others come from animals or minerals. Since plant and animal tissues are not the same from one organism to another, one of the first problems pharmacologists had to solve was that of uniform dosage. For example, belladonna is a drug that is sometimes used to treat stomach cramps. It comes from a plant called nightshade (*see* Nightshade). All nightshade plants, however, do not contain the same amount of belladonna. Physicians could not know whether the doses of belladonna that they prescribed were too strong or too weak. To solve this problem, researchers assumed that only a certain part of the crude drug had the ability to act on the body. This they called the active principle, and they set themselves the task of finding and standardizing this active principle.

Eventually the active principles of various crude drugs were isolated. These could be measured. Certain quantities could thus be put into powders, tablets, capsules, and other medicinal vehicles. The important point is that the doctor now knew exactly how much of a given drug he or she was prescribing and could tell within reason what effects the prescription would have on a patient.

Today most drugs are no longer derived by isolating and purifying crude plants or tissues. Instead they are synthesized, or made, in chemical laboratories (*see* Chemistry). For example, when the drug cortisone was discovered, it was produced at great cost from the adrenal glands of dead animals. Later, scientists learned how to make it from the bile of slaughtered oxen at somewhat less cost. Still later it was synthesized from a variety of easily available plants. The synthetic drugs that duplicate the active principles of plants, animals, or minerals are superior to natural substances because they contain only the active principles, with impurities and other useless substances eliminated.

Biologicals. Some substances derived from animal sources and used as drugs are not obtained from dead animals. Biologicals are such substances. They are made in a live animal's body. Tetanus toxoid, which is used to immunize persons against tetanus, or lockjaw, is such a biological (*see* Disease, "How the Body Fights Disease"). The biological is made in this way: A small quantity of tetanus organisms is injected into

273

a horse. Tetanus organisms produce tetanus toxin within the animal's body. A sample of the horse's blood is then drawn. The tetanus toxin contained in the blood is chemically treated to render it harmless. However, this "poisonless" toxin, or toxoid, retains the power to stimulate in a person's blood the formation of antibodies against tetanus toxin. Thus it can be injected into a person to immunize him against the tetanus disease.

Synthetics. A number of synthetic drugs are not duplicates of natural substances. Just as the invention of drugs was an enormous advance over the time when drugs could be found only through accidental discovery, science now is capable of designing entirely new drugs.

One way by which new drugs are designed is by modifying the molecular structure of other drugs. Such modified drugs, called analogues, are often more effective, cause fewer side effects, and can be produced more cheaply than the original drug. Thus, to eliminate some of the serious side effects of cortisone, and to increase its potency, scientists modified its molecular structure to get prednisone, hydrocortisone, and a number of other analogues. While this kind of "molecular manipulation" is an important source of new drugs, there is another way to make new medicines. This recently developed technique involves altering the genetic code of bacteria, thereby turning them into tiny drug manufacturing factories (*see* Genetics). This method can make bacteria do things no natural bacteria are capable of, such as make human growth hormone, insulin, or even a human brain hormone, somatostatin.

How Drugs Act

Drugs act by changing the way some of the cells in the body behave. Although people speak often of the effect of a drug, what one actually sees is a change in the way the body is working. For example, aspirin does not by itself reduce fever. Rather, it temporarily affects the nerve cells in the brain that regulate body temperature. Changing—that is, stimulating or depressing—the normal way a cell or tissue acts is one of the two main ways by which drugs act in the body. Drugs that act in this way are called pharmacodynamic agents. The other way by which drugs act involves destroying or slowing the growth of disease-causing organisms without affecting the body's normal cells. Drugs that act in this way are called chemotherapeutic agents. Antibiotics such as penicillin, streptomycin, tetracycline, and the sulfa drugs are chemotherapeutic agents.

Reactions to Drugs

In order for a chemical to be considered a drug it must have the capacity to affect how the body works—to be biologically active. No substance that has the power to do this is completely safe, and drugs are approved only after they demonstrate that they are relatively safe when used as directed, and when the benefits outweigh their risks. Thus, some very

(Top) Dan McCoy—Rainbow; (above) Courtesy, Abbott Laboratories

A chemist (top) builds a model of a chemical compound—a first step in the design of a new drug. A researcher (above) at a pharmaceutical firm uses a computer to examine models of actual drugs and proposed designs for new drugs.

dangerous drugs are approved because they are necessary to treat serious illness. Digitalis, which causes the heart muscle to contract, is a dangerous drug, but doctors are permitted to use it because it is vital for treating patients whose heart muscle is weak. A drug as potent as digitalis would not be approved to treat such minor ailments as temporary fatigue because the risks outweigh the benefits.

Many persons suffer ill effects from drugs even though they take the drug exactly as directed by the doctor or the label. The human population, unlike a colony of ants or bees, contains a great variety of genetic variation. Drugs are tested on at most a few thousand people. When that same drug is taken by millions, some people may not respond in a predictable way to the drug. A person who has a so-called idiosyncratic response to a particular sedative, for example, may become excited rather than relaxed. Others may be hypersensitive, or extremely sensitive, to certain drugs, suffering reactions that resemble allergies.

A patient may also acquire a tolerance for a certain drug. This means that ever-larger doses are necessary to produce the desired therapeutic effect. Tolerance may lead to habituation, in which the person becomes so dependent upon the drug that he or she becomes addicted to it. Addiction causes severe psychological and physical disturbances when the drug is taken away. Morphine, cocaine, and Benzedrine are common habit-forming drugs. (*See also* Narcotic.) Finally, drugs often have unwanted side effects. These usually cause only minor discomfort such as a skin rash, headache, or drowsiness. Certain drugs,

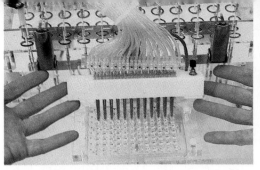
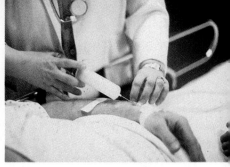

Antibiotic drugs (right) are mass-produced using a pipette cluster. A physician (far right) injects a hospitalized patient with a newly developed drug.

however, can produce serious, even life-threatening adverse reactions. For example, the drug Thalidomide was once called one of the safest sedatives ever developed, but thousands of women in the United Kingdom who took it during pregnancy gave birth to seriously deformed babies. Other adverse reactions stem from mixing drugs. Thus, taking aspirin, which has blood-thinning qualities, for a headache can be very harmful if one is also taking other blood-thinning drugs such as heparin or dicumarol.

Drug Regulation

In the United States the Food and Drug Administration (FDA) regulates the manufacture and sale of medicinal drugs under the terms of the Food, Drug, and Cosmetic Act of 1938. A number of important changes have been made to this law. For example, in 1962 the law required manufacturers to prove that their drugs are effective as well as safe—that they actually work as claimed. Another recent change provides incentives to study and manufacture drugs for "orphan diseases," ailments that strike only a comparatively small number of people.

The FDA regulates both "ethical," or prescription, drugs and "proprietary" drugs, also known as over-the-counter drugs. Ethical drugs can only be obtained with a prescription, while proprietary drugs, which generally treat only the symptoms, not the cause, of an illness, do not require a prescription.

The initials "U.S.P" or "N.F." often appear after the name of a drug. They mean that the drug has been listed in the 'United States Pharmacopeia' or 'National Formulary' and has been prepared according to specific standards. Both are nongovernment publications printed under the direction of medical and pharmaceutical experts who establish standards for the manufacture of drugs.

DRUG ABUSE

Drugs are not always beneficial to their users. In the sense of treating the cause or symptoms of an illness, some drugs have no beneficial use at all. Such drugs act on the nervous system in various ways, and those who use these drugs take them without medical approval and for recreational, not medical, reasons. Often the consequences of recreational drug-taking are harmful both to the individuals who abuse drugs and to the people around them.

In earlier years most of the people who abused drugs either had easy access to medicines or were slum dwellers for whom drugs seemed to provide the only escape from a hopeless existence. In the 1950s more people of all classes and occupations began to use mood-changing drugs without medical supervision, and more kinds of mood-changing drugs became available through both legal and illegal channels. In the early 1970s drug use by United States troops serving in the Vietnam War was widely publicized.

Some mood-changing drugs induce relaxation or sleep. Others induce feelings of exhilaration. All affect the nervous system and all can cause emotional change. A person who is unhappy or dissatisfied may be tempted to change his state of mind by taking such drugs.

The temporary sense of well-being that is produced in this way has no effect on the situation that was making the drug user unhappy. After the effects of the drug have worn off, the user is faced with the same problems that plagued him previously. He may then take another dose of the drug rather than endure the pain and trouble of grappling with them. When this happens, the person is said to have acquired a psychological dependence on the drug. As a result, he may stop maturing. In severe cases, he directs all his energies to getting more of the drug. In less severe cases—particularly dependence on such legal drugs as the nicotine in cigarettes and the caffeine in coffee—the user simply makes taking the drug part of his daily routine. Here the inconvenience of dependency is considered his own problem.

Chemicals from the Opium Poppy

The opium poppy contains a narcotic drug called opium, the raw material for some of the most important and powerful pain-killers medicine can provide. Morphine, codeine, opium itself, and man-made chemicals that resemble opium are prescribed for the relief of extreme pain. But opium can also be converted into the dangerous drug heroin.

The effect of opium-related drugs depends to a certain extent on the user. Pain-free persons may simply feel dizzy and nauseated on first taking an opiate. For most susceptible people, however, a dose of an opiate makes worries seem distant. This carefree feeling may be followed by a period of stupor. A severe depression commonly follows the stupor, and a regular abuser of opiates will want another dose of the drug to ward off this depression.

If a person takes any opiate often enough, his body will very probably develop a strong need for more. This need is called drug dependence, or addiction. The person must take increasing amounts of the drug to duplicate his original experience with it. If he stops taking it, he becomes very ill with a withdrawal

The sources of illicit drugs are many and difficult to control. In South America, a farmer (far left) dries coca leaves before processing them into cocaine. In Turkey, a poppy (left top) oozes sap that will be gathered for opium production. Marijuana (left) is grown illegally on many farms and in remote locations in the United States.

Photographs, Gamma/Liaison

syndrome. Under proper medication the withdrawal syndrome is said to be like influenza, but without such help it can be agonizing. Many drug habits are maintained to avoid this syndrome.

Heroin addiction presents a special danger. Other opiates are obtained illegally from medical supplies. But heroin is not used for medicinal purposes, and the criminals who produce it are not subject to any quality controls. The heroin they peddle is usually contaminated with all sorts of microorganisms. Moreover, the purchaser never knows just how much heroin he is buying. Heroin often kills when an addict buys an unusually pure sample and unintentionally injects an overdose.

Sleep-Inducing Drugs

Several types of chemicals induce sleep and cause intoxication. These chemicals also cause physical and psychological dependence. The group includes ethyl alcohol, barbiturates, and many related sedatives. Alcohol causes special problems because susceptible people can buy it legally.

Barbiturates, also known as "downers," may be prescribed by doctors for insomnia and tension. It is very easy to become addicted to them. People who are psychologically dependent on barbiturates are often as obsessed as heroin users with obtaining their drug. Furthermore, barbiturates cause severe depression. Those taking barbiturates can easily lose track of how many they have taken. This can lead to a fatal overdose. In addition, combining alcohol and barbiturates frequently leads to coma or death (see Coma; Death). Once physical dependence on alcohol or barbiturates has been established, withdrawal without medical help may cause convulsions, delirium, and, unlike withdrawal from the opiates, even death.

Stimulants

Amphetamines, also known as "uppers," "pep," "speed," "bennies," and "whites," produce wakefulness. Medically they are used to cope with sleep disorders, to help control appetite, and to fight depression. They do not cause physical dependence, so withdrawal is not dangerous. But psychological dependence does occur. Many people develop a barbiturate-amphetamine cycle. They need pills to go to sleep and to wake up.

Some people take amphetamines to increase their energy. Fatigue, however, has a biological purpose. It prevents a person from overextending himself and damaging his body by too much activity. Athletes using amphetamines risk heart damage. Amphetamines also impair judgment.

Some people take amphetamines for a carefree feeling similar to that produced by opiates. The high doses they use can increase blood pressure enough to cause sudden death. Another possible result is a severe form of mental illness.

Cocaine

Derived from two species of coca plant, cocaine, like morphine, has mind-altering properties. Cocaine came to the attention of Western medicine because it can kill pain. Later the psychiatrist Sigmund Freud used it to help a physician friend free himself from morphine addiction. While the friend did lose his addiction to morphine, he became dependent on cocaine instead. Since Freud's early experiment a great many people have tried using cocaine under the erroneous impression that it is a safe way to "get high," or to elevate one's mood. There is, however, a growing awareness that it is by no means safe and that cocaine use carries severe consequences, both physical and mental. In addition to physical dependency, high doses can cause convulsions, sleeplessness, exhaustion, hallucinations, severe mental illness such as paranoid delusions, and hyperthermia, or abnormally high body temperature. There are increasing reports of cocaine use among young people being associated with heart attacks that often end in death. At present there is no generally effective way to treat persons addicted to cocaine.

276

Methaqualone

With the street names of "sopors," "ludes," "pillows," "disco biscuits," and "vitamin Q," the most seriously abused drug after marijuana in the United States is methaqualone, or Quāāludes. In high doses it resembles the barbiturates in both symptoms and severity. In low to medium doses it causes a form of intoxication similar to that from alcohol, which includes slowed reflexes and loss of judgment and inhibitions. It has been estimated that in some parts of the United States methaqualone is a contributing factor in 20 percent of fatal car accidents.

Hallucinogens and Marijuana

LSD (lysergic acid diethlamide) is one of the most powerful mind-altering drugs known. Drugs with similar effects are mescaline (found in the mescal cactus), psylocybin (from a Mexican mushroom), and certain drugs from the bark and seeds of other plants. Many more such chemicals can be artificially synthesized. One, responsible for many emergency room admissions, is PCP, which stands for phencyclidine and is known also as "angel dust," "hog," "Sernyl," and "peace pill."

All these drugs are hallucinogens. When a person takes a very small amount of any of them, he may experience great distortions in what he perceives. Users hope that the disorientation will be mystical or pleasurable, but the actual outcome cannot be foreseen. Often the user is terrified or feels that people are plotting to harm him. Some users feel invulnerable or invisible and may be hurt when they try to fly or to walk into heavy traffic. Furthermore, the same distorted feelings may recur days or months later. The use of hallucinogens may push unstable people over the brink into a long-term mental illness.

The flowering tops and leaves of the hemp plant, known scientifically as *Cannabis sativa*, are known as marijuana. Although the exhilarating effects of marijuana have been known since AD 200, very little reliable information about its long-term physical effects is available, other than the fact that heavy, long-term use can damage the lungs and cause mental changes that dull the desire to be productive or competitive, as in sports. Marijuana is not physically addictive. Susceptible people have been known to develop a psychological dependence on it. Chemically, marijuana is usually considered a mild hallucinogen. Legally, it was a narcotic until its reclassification as a dangerous drug in 1970. However, penalties for its possession remained high in many places.

The Legal and Social Response to Drug Abuse

Before 1966 United States laws governing drug abuse were harshly punitive. The first federal drug-control law, enacted in 1914, was the Harrison Narcotic Act, which provided for the punishment of people who handled opium and related drugs illegally. In 1937 similar penalties were applied to the unauthorized handling of marijuana. The penalties

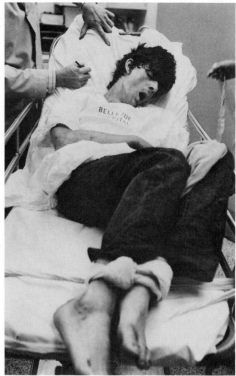

Leonard Freed—Magnum

Withdrawal from the highly addictive drug heroin can be a terrible experience. Sometimes the patient must be restrained.

were increased in 1951 and again in 1956, when a first conviction for the possession of narcotics was made punishable by two to ten years' imprisonment. Penalties for the illicit sale or possession of stimulants, sedatives, and hallucinogens were established in 1965 by the Drug Abuse Control Amendments. These penalties were milder than those for the sale or possession of narcotics and marijuana. The Drug Abuse Control Amendments also set up five schedules, or categories, of drugs subject to special regulation. The most restrictive, Schedule I, covers drugs such as LSD and PCP that have a high potential for abuse, no medical use, and lack of safety even under medical supervision.

The Narcotic Addict Rehabilitation Act of 1966 heralded a change in the legal attitude toward drug abusers. It provided an alternative to prison for abusers charged or convicted of nonviolent federal crimes. They could choose treatment for addiction rather than prosecution or punishment.

Institutions have been established to help drug abusers overcome the habit. Typically, they offer a supportive, drug-free atmosphere where a patient can live with others who have similar problems. The period of residence may last several years. A drug abuser is less likely to relapse if he does not return to the social situation in which he turned to drugs.

DRUM *see* MUSICAL INSTRUMENTS.

Courtesy of the Public Archives of Canada

William Henry Drummond

DRUMMOND, William Henry (1854–1907). The character of the *habitant,* or French-Canadian farmer and backwoodsman, is reflected in the poems of William Henry Drummond. His humorous and sympathetic dialect verses helped create a better understanding between the French-speaking and the English-speaking people of Canada.

William Henry Drummond was born in County Leitrim, Ireland, on April 13, 1854. In 1864 his family moved to Canada.

Drummond was educated at McGill University and at Bishop's University, where he received a medical degree in 1884. For several years Drummond practiced medicine in small communities. He moved to Montreal in 1888. Six years later he married May Harvey. They had four children. In 1895 Drummond was appointed professor of medical jurisprudence at Bishop's University. He died on April 6, 1907, in Cobalt, Ont. His best poems have been included in 'Habitant Poems', selections from his work.

DRUZES. Numbering perhaps about 300,000, the Druzes are a small religious sect scattered in villages throughout Lebanon, Syria, Israel, and Jordan. About half of them live in Syria, more than one third in Lebanon. (*See also* Lebanon, section "History".)

Because of their belief in Allah as the one God, the Druzes are often considered an Islamic group. But their teachings are sufficiently distinctive to set them apart from the Muslim majority of the Middle East (*see* Islam). The God of Islam revealed himself to his Prophet, Muhammad, whose writings were compiled into the Koran. The Druzes believe that their founder, al-Hakim bi-Amrih Allah, which means "ruler by God's command," was actually an incarnation of God—the last and most significant of several such incarnations, or emanations.

Hakim was the sixth caliph of the Fatimid Dynasty in Egypt, and he ruled from 996 until 1021. He had been a persecutor of Jews, Christians, and Muslims within his domain. But for some reason, in 1017, he began promoting toleration for all. In that year he was proclaimed by his followers to be an incarnation of Allah. In 1021 he disappeared. He was probably murdered, but his followers said that he had gone into hiding and would reappear after 1,000 years.

The Druzes cloak their religion in secrecy. Not even all members of the faith are permitted to learn the secret doctrines. Believers are divided into two groups: the sages initiated into the teachings (called *Hakimyah*), and the uninitiated. The sages themselves are divided into grades, the highest being the *ajawid,* meaning "the generous," who alone know the secrets of the *Hakimyah*.

Druzes believe that the number of faithful has been determined from eternity. Hence they believe in transmigration of souls: when a believer dies, his soul enters the body of a newborn infant. All Druzes have the duty to accept the truth about Hakim, deny other religious beliefs, avoid unbelievers, and maintain solidarity and mutual aid with other Druzes.

DRY CLEANING. Garments and other articles that are washed in liquids other than water are said to be dry-cleaned. Most modern dry-cleaning fluids are either petroleum or synthetic solvents.

The two kinds of solvents are used with different equipment. Petroleum types can be used in open washing machines. Synthetic solvents evaporate very quickly in the air. They are used in closed, airtight washing machines.

COMMERCIAL DRY CLEANING

In the dry-cleaning plant, garments and other items are first labeled with a mark or tag. Usually fabrics are examined to see if there are any badly worn or faulty parts. These might not survive the dry-cleaning process without further damage. Such areas cannot always be found by a visual inspection.

Many items are measured before cleaning if the material is thought to be shrinkable. The measurements are marked on the identification tag for the guidance of the finishers.

Items for cleaning are classified and sorted into separate portable hampers according to their fibers. Wool, silk and rayon, cotton and linen, and man-made fibers are some of the most common classifications. The items then are further separated by colors—dark, medium, and light.

Garments make up the bulk of articles that are dry-cleaned. Draperies and fine tablecloths are often dry-cleaned also. Certain fabrics cannot stand up under laundering and must be processed in this way.

Steps in Washing and Drying

After the articles have been sorted, they are agitated in a clear solvent and then in a soapy solvent. Next they are rinsed in a clear solution. A dry-cleaning machine using petroleum solvent contains a perforated metal cylinder, which revolves slowly in a metal shell containing the cleaning substance. The synthetic-solvent machine is sealed airtight and the cleaning fluid is then pumped into it.

Next the items are placed in an extractor. Here centrifugal force removes most of the moisture. If a petroleum solvent is used, the garments are then placed either in a drying tumbler or a drying cabinet. The tumbler consists of a rotating and reversing woven wire cylinder supported and housed within a metal casing. In addition to drying the solvent, it also deodorizes it.

The drying cabinet is used for items that cannot withstand rotary drying action, such as silk or rayon clothing. The drying room must be properly ventilated to remove solvent gases or moisture. This is done by changing the air every few minutes.

Finishing the Article

After drying, most items need finishing. Some garments are pressed whole on special forms inflated with air. The fabric is softened with steam to remove wrinkles and then cooled until it returns to its original shape. Portions of the garment, such as a coat's lining, may be touched up by hand-pressing. Special forms keep draperies and other items in their proper size and shape during cleaning. Modern plants use a variety of equipment to accommodate all types of garments and other articles.

After finishing, trimmings and removable shoulder pads are replaced. These were taken off garments in the check-in, or marking, department. Finally, the article is bagged or boxed for delivery to the customer.

Treating Soiled Materials

Commercial plants separate especially soiled articles so they will not dirty cleaner items processed with them. Articles that are still stained or soiled after dry cleaning are sometimes washed in water. Certain spots or stains may require washing in a soap and water solution to which special agents have been added.

Stubborn spots or stains may need the attention of a "spotter." This worker uses special chemicals and a steam-air spray gun to remove the spots or stains.

REMOVING SPOTS AND STAINS AT HOME

A professional cleaner is best equipped to remove spots and stains on fabrics. Dry cleaning requires a thorough understanding of the type of stain, the properties of the stain removers used, and the characteristics of the fabric.

However, there are methods of removing spots and stains or of preventing them from setting that can be used in the home. Treating the spots and stains promptly is essential. This prevents fiber-attacking chemicals in the stain-forming substance from weakening the fabric. Drying or heat, furthermore, allows the spot to set. It becomes almost impossible to remove.

Nearly all stains will be lightened by rinsing immediately with water at about body temperature. Some spots will become "fixed" by hotter washing.

After flushing out as much of the stain as possible, specific treatments for the type of stain are necessary. Five types of stain removal treatments are described here. In sections B and E more specific treatments are described in detail.

To find out how to remove a certain type of spot or stain, look it up in the Stain Removal Guide in this article. Across from the type of stain may be found one or more letters and numbers. These refer to the stain removal treatments that follow. With these directions and the additional instructions in the Stain Removal Guide, many fabric spots and stains can be treated in the home.

A. Solvent Treatments (Cleaning Fluids)

Oily or greasy materials can be dissolved in solvents such as naphtha, benzine, alcohol, carbon tetrachloride, or prepared cleaning fluids obtainable in retail

---

STAIN REMOVAL GUIDE

Stain	Treatment*	Stain	Treatment*
Adhesive tape	A	Ink—ball-point	E-4 or A (Repeat as necessary)
Airplane glue	E-7 (Test fabric for safety)	Ink—fluid	D and B
Argyrol	E-9 (Rinse thoroughly)	Iron	E-2 (Rinse thoroughly)
Beer	B	Lipstick	A and C (Wash in hot water and soap or detergent)
Blood	E-8 or B†		
Candle wax	E-3 and A	Mildew	B-3 (If fabric cannot be bleached, stains cannot be removed)
Chewing gum	E-3 and A		
Chocolate	E-8 or E-5 and B		
Coffee	E-8 or E-5 and B	Mud	E-1
Crayon	E-3 and A	Mustard	E-10
Dye	B or C	Paint	A (Turpentine is a good solvent)
Fingernail polish	E-7 (Test fabric and colors)	Rust	E-2
Fruit	B or C (Rinse thoroughly)	Shoe polish	A and E-1 and B
Grass	E-6 (Rinse thoroughly)	Tar	A
Grease	A (May need to be repeated)	Tea	B (Rinse thoroughly)

*Letters and numbers are keyed to following pages.
†Where several steps are indicated take them in order given.

markets. All solvents are flammable or give off poisonous fumes. Do not use near open flames or in closed rooms. Ventilate well.

Apply solvents by placing the fabric—stained side down—against an absorbent cloth. Drop solvent on back of stain and tamp with a cloth wet with solvent. Move soiled part to a clean area on the absorbent cloth and repeat until stain has been removed.

B. Bleaching

Colored stains that rinsing does not flush away or that will not come off in washing may require a bleaching (oxidizing) action. This method can be used only on white materials or on colors that will withstand bleaching. Colored fabrics may be tested for fastness by applying the bleach solution to a hidden area such as the inside of a seam or under a hem.

1. A mild bleaching solution can be made by dissolving one tablespoon of sodium perborate bleach in a cup of warm water.
2. Two tablespoons of hydrogen peroxide in a cup of water will bleach stronger stains.
3. A teaspoon of household hypochlorite-type bleach (5 per cent) in a cup of water will bleach some very stubborn stains. Each bottle gives instructions.

In using the bleaching technique, the solution should be applied to the stain and allowed to stand from 15 to 30 minutes. In using any bleach, be sure to rinse thoroughly before drying or pressing.

C. Reducing Agents

On white goods only, some stains that have resisted bleaching treatments may be removed by a material called a "stripper." Color removers sold with household dyes can be used on some dye stains by following the directions on the package. Do not use these on colored fabrics unless the intention is to remove all color from the entire fabric.

D. Hot Soaping Treatment

Many stains respond to a hot washing with a strong soap solution. Where white or fast-color fabrics are concerned, residual oil stains, yellow stains on collar fold lines, and mud stains may be removed by washing in water heated to 160° F (71° C) with a strong solution of soap or detergent. Adding one tablespoon of a compound for automatic dishwashing to a gallon of the soap solution helps.

E. Special Treatments

The following are a number of special treatments for specific types of stains as listed in the Stain Removal Guide.

1. Wash out stain with warm water, rub on a wet bar of soap, scrub with fingers.
2. Sprinkle salt on stain. Apply lemon juice and allow to stand. Place in sun to speed removal or use one teaspoon of oxalic-acid crystals (poison) in a cup of hot water and drop solution on the stain. Rinse thoroughly after 10 minutes.

3. Scrape off excess with dull knife. Apply solvent or cleaning fluid by methods described in section A (Solvent Treatments).
4. Apply liquid detergent (all-purpose, heavy duty), then rinse thoroughly.
5. Soak stain in lukewarm water for an hour. Using three tablespoons of household ammonia to a gallon of water will help soften the stain. Wash thoroughly.
6. Sponge with alcohol. Treat remaining stain with one of the bleaching solutions in section B (Bleaching).
7. Apply acetone or nail-polish remover as described under section A. This cannot be used on cellulose acetate fibers or Arnel. Test by applying polish remover to small clipping from seam. If the clipping softens and feels tacky, do not use this treatment.
8. Apply solution of digester or enzymes (pepsin from drugstore).
9. Apply drop of tincture of iodine (poison). Rinse after one minute. Apply solution of photographer's hypo (sodium thiosulfate), two teaspoons to a cup of hot (140° F; 60° C) water.
10. Soak in warm glycerin for 30 minutes. Work between fingers. Wash in hot suds.

HISTORY OF DRY CLEANING

Dry cleaning as an industry started during the 19th century, in the period from 1825 to 1845. Many different stories reportedly tell of its origin. They all have one thing in common. Some fabric was accidentally saturated with a volatile liquid and, much to everyone's surprise, the material appeared clean after it dried. One such tale tells about a French sailor who accidentally fell into a vat of turpentine. When his soiled uniform dried, it was clean.

Camphene is the liquid most frequently mentioned in all the stories. It is produced from pinene, the main constituent of turpentine. At first this volatile liquid was used only to remove spots from garments that were afterward scoured with water or other cleansing agents. Later it was used for complete cleaning.

New solvents were developed as dry cleaning grew to a recognized industry. Grease solvents derived from petroleum, such as gasoline and naphtha, were used. These are highly flammable, however. They also tend to leave a strong odor that must be removed from the fabric.

Modern Cleaning Solutions

For a while carbon tetrachloride was used as a solvent. It is a nonflammable liquid. It produces poisonous fumes, however, which must be drawn away from the cleaning vats. More recently synthetic solvents such as perchlorethylene have been used. These leave little odor and are not flammable.

Dry-cleaning establishments today may choose between petroleum and synthetic solvents. Some employ both types. Most firms, however, use only one kind. (See also Laundry.)

John Dryden

Courtesy of the National Portrait
Gallery, London

DRYDEN, John (1631–1700). The most important literary figure in England during the last quarter of the 17th century was John Dryden. He wrote plays, poems, essays, and satires of great popularity. His clear and precise style was the model for 18th-century English prose.

John Dryden was born on Aug. 9, 1631, in the village of Aldwincle All Saints in Northamptonshire. He studied at Westminster School and at Trinity College, Cambridge. Lady Elizabeth Howard, sister of one of Dryden's closest friends, became his wife in 1663.

Dryden was short, stout, and red-faced. His friends nicknamed him "poet squab." He was considered to be a modest and generous person. He died in London on May 1, 1700, and was buried in the Poets' Corner of Westminster Abbey.

Dryden's writings contained few high ideals and noble thoughts. His works reflected the age in which he lived. Dryden's career followed the shifting politics of his time. His family supported the Puritan leader Oliver Cromwell. At Cromwell's death in 1658 Dryden wrote his famous work, the 'Heroic Stanzas'. When the monarchy was restored in 1660, Dryden celebrated the return of Charles II in his 'Justice Restored'. Dryden defended the Church of England in 'A Layman's Religion', published in 1683. Later, becoming a Roman Catholic, he praised James II and the Roman Catholic church in 'The Hind and the Panther'.

His plays sought to please the audiences of his time and to win patrons. Few survive today. Though not best remembered as a poet, Dryden established the rhymed heroic couplet as the principal English meter for satire and condensed statement (*see* Poetry).

Dryden's literary criticisms were the first great body of such works in English literature. Here his mastery of style made him supreme. His satires also rank among the finest. 'Mac Flecknoe' is considered one of his best.

Many of Dryden's lines are still quoted. The most famous is "None but the brave deserves the fair." Perhaps his most popular works are the odes 'Alexander's Feast' and 'A Song for St. Cecilia's Day'. (*See also* English Literature.)

DUBLIN, Ireland. The capital and largest city of Ireland, Dublin is only 44 square miles (114 square kilometers) in area but is rich in cultural achievements. It serves as the political, economic, and cultural center of Ireland.

The River Liffey divides the city in half. Its dark waters, known in Irish as *dubh linn,* gave the city its name. Some of the city's most notable buildings face the river. The Four Courts, seat of Ireland's judiciary, and the Custom House are excellent examples of Dublin's late 18th-century architecture. Both buildings were damaged heavily during the Civil War but have been restored. South of the river is Dublin Castle, which was begun in 1204 and almost totally rebuilt in Georgian style in the 18th century. The castle was the seat of English authority in Ireland until 1922. Today it is the site of the inaugurations of Ireland's presidents. Near the castle are Christ Church and Saint Patrick's, Dublin's two Protestant cathedrals. Both date from Dublin's earliest days as a Viking settlement. They were extensively rebuilt by the Anglo-Norman invaders of the late 12th and early 13th centuries and were again rebuilt in the 19th century. Ireland's original Parliament House, now the Bank of Ireland, dates from the 18th century and is also in Georgian style. Today Ireland's Parliament meets in Leinster House, an 18th-century mansion thought by some to be the model for the design of the White House in Washington, D.C.

Maritime trade has always been one of Dublin's most important activities. Dublin is Ireland's largest port and major exporter. It has also developed into the largest manufacturing city in Ireland, though the

O'Connell Bridge, over the River Liffey in central Dublin, is named after the Irish patriot Daniel O'Connell.

Art Resource/EB Inc.

factories, aside from breweries and distilleries, are engaged primarily in light manufactures. The city's most famous business is the Guinness Brewery, founded in 1759 and one of Ireland's largest employers and exporters. Economic planning efforts have attempted to locate manufacturing plants outside Dublin, and the city has had a dwindling share of manufacturing employment since the early 1960s.

Dublin has an illustrious educational and cultural past. Trinity College, or University of Dublin, founded in 1591, has graduated authors Jonathan Swift, Oliver Goldsmith, and Oscar Wilde and British statesman Edmund Burke. Its library houses the 8th-century 'Book of Kells', the famous illuminated, or decorated, gospel book. Dublin was the site of the premiere of Handel's 'Messiah' in 1742. The Royal Dublin Society was founded in 1731, the Royal Irish Academy in 1786, and the Irish Academy of Letters in 1932 by William Butler Yeats and George Bernard Shaw, two Dublin literary giants. Other famous literary figures include Richard Brinsley Sheridan, John Millington Synge, James Joyce, and Samuel Beckett.

The city played a leading role in the revival of Irish language and literature of the late 19th and early 20th centuries (see Irish Literature). Especially noteworthy was the opening of the Abbey Theatre, dedicated to the revival of Irish drama, in 1904. Museums include the National Museum, the National Gallery of Ireland, and the Hugh Lane Municipal Gallery of modern art. North of the river and west of the city center is Phoenix Park, nearly 2,000 acres (800 hectares) with a zoo and a racetrack.

History

Dublin is probably at least 2,000 years old, but real historical evidence for its existence begins about 831 when Norse Vikings established a settlement on the south side of the River Liffey. Their settlement prospered until the Anglo-Norman invasion of 1170, when English control was firmly established.

Until the middle of the 17th century, Dublin remained a small, walled medieval town. When Oliver Cromwell captured it in 1649, it had only 9,000 residents and was in a state of shambles. By the end of the 17th century, however, a remarkable growth began with Protestant refugees from the European continent pouring into Dublin. In the course of the next century, Dublin grew enormously in size and wealth and soon became the second city of the British Empire. This prosperity made Dublin an exciting city for the Protestant Ascendancy, members of the Anglo-Irish aristocracy who had denied basic civil rights to the native Roman Catholics.

In 1800 the Act of Union between England and Ireland abolished the Irish Parliament and drastically reduced Dublin's status. A long decline set in that only began to be reversed after Ireland became independent in 1922.

Dublin is governed by an elected corporation and a salaried manager. Population (1981 census), city, 525,882; metropolitan area, 915,115.

DU BOIS, W. E. B. (1868–1963). For more than 50 years W. E. B. Du Bois, a black editor, historian, and sociologist, was a leader of the civil rights movement in the United States. He helped found the National Association for the Advancement of Colored People (NAACP) and was its outstanding spokesman in the first decades of its existence.

William Edward Burghardt Du Bois was born on Feb. 23, 1868, in Great Barrington, Mass. His parents, Alfred and Mary Burghardt Du Bois, were of African and European ancestry. As a boy, William was sometimes ignored by white townspeople because of his race. As an adult, he usually felt comfortable only among other blacks.

An excellent student, Du Bois graduated from Fisk University in 1888 and from Harvard College in 1890. He traveled in Europe and studied at the University of Berlin. In 1895 he received the Ph.D. degree from Harvard. His dissertation, 'The Suppression of the African Slave Trade', was published in 1896 as the first volume of the Harvard Historical Studies.

After teaching Greek and Latin at Wilberforce University from 1894 to 1896, Du Bois studied Philadelphia's slums. In 'Philadelphia Negro', published in 1899, a pioneering sociological study, he hoped to dispel the ignorance of whites about blacks, which he believed was a cause of racial prejudice. Du Bois taught at Atlanta University from 1897 to 1910 and from 1897 until 1914 directed its annual studies of Negro life.

In 'The Souls of Black Folk' (1903), Du Bois declared that "the problem of the Twentieth Century is the problem of the color-line." He criticized the famous black educator Booker T. Washington for accepting racial discrimination and minimizing the value of college training for blacks. Du Bois felt that blacks needed higher education for leadership. In his essay "The Talented Tenth" he wrote: "The Negro race, like all races, is going to be saved by its exceptional men." (See also Washington, Booker T.)

The split between Washington and Du Bois reflected a bitter division of opinion among black leaders. In 1905, at Niagara Falls, Canada, Du Bois

As editor of the *Crisis*, W. E. B. DuBois, center, publicized black achievements and published black writers and artists.

Milton Meltzer

joined the more militant leaders to demand equal voting rights and educational opportunities for blacks and an end to racial discrimination. But the Niagara Movement declined within a few years, and he then helped form another group, which in 1910 became the National Association for the Advancement of Colored People. He edited the NAACP's journal, the *Crisis,* in which he often wrote that blacks should develop farms, industries, and businesses separate from the white economy. NAACP officials, who desired integration, criticized this opinion, and he resigned as editor in 1934. He returned to Atlanta University, and in 1939 he launched *Phylon,* a new magazine about blacks' lives.

Du Bois was interested in African blacks and led several Pan-African congresses. He was awarded the Spingarn medal in 1920 for his efforts to foster black racial solidarity. Although he clashed with Marcus Garvey, the leader of a "back to Africa" movement, and attacked his scheme for an African empire, he lauded Garvey's racial pride.

In his later years Du Bois came to believe that the United States could not solve its racial problems and that the only world power opposed to racial discrimination was the Soviet Union. He was awarded the Communist-sponsored International Peace prize in 1952 and the Soviet Lenin Peace prize in 1958. Du Bois joined the Communist party of the United States in 1961 and emigrated to Ghana, where he became a citizen, in 1963. He died there on Aug. 27, 1963. He had been married twice, to Nina Gomer and to Shirley Graham, and had two children.

Du Bois was brilliant, proud, and aloof. He once wrote: "My leadership was a leadership of ideas. I never was, nor ever will be, personally popular." Du Bois wrestled with his conflicting desires for both integration and black nationalism. His Pan-African and Communist views removed him from the mainstream of the United States civil rights movement. But he never wavered in his efforts to teach blacks their rights as human beings and pride in their heritage. Among his writings are 'Black Reconstruction' (published in 1935) and 'Dusk of Dawn' (1940).

DUCHAMP, Marcel (1887–1968). One of the leading spirits of 20th-century painting was the French artist Marcel Duchamp. He led the way to pop and op art from his famous cubist 'Nude Descending a Staircase, No. 2', through his "ready-mades," and in the movement called dadaism.

Duchamp was born in Blainville, Normandy, France, on July 28, 1887. He was one of six children, four of whom became artists. He went to Paris in 1904 and began drawing cartoons for comic books. He passed rapidly through the then current trends in painting—postimpressionism, fauvism, and cubism—producing in 1911 'Portrait', his first cubist painting. 'Nude Descending a Staircase, No. 2' was sent to the 28th Salon des Indépendants in 1912 but was refused. The following year Duchamp sent it to the Armory Show in New York City, where it caused

Courtesy of the Philadelphia Museum of Art, Louise and Walter Arensberg Collection

Marcel Duchamp's 'Nude Descending a Staircase, No. 2' when first shown outraged public opinion. Today it is highly regarded.

a scandal. It was considered a mockery of painting itself and marked the end of a serious interest in painting by the artist.

For the next ten years Duchamp spent most of his time on an oil and lead wire construction, 'The Large Glass, or The Bride Stripped Bare by Her Bachelors, Even', which he eventually left unfinished. During that time he also produced his "ready-mades," beginning in 1913 with 'Bicycle Wheel', which was simply an ordinary bicycle wheel. He moved to New York City in 1915 and was received as a famous man. Nevertheless, he still did not paint and devoted himself to the game of chess. He continued to be interested in surrealistic art, creating a coalsack ceiling for a 1938 exhibition in Paris and a rain room for one in 1947.

As artist and anti-artist, Duchamp is considered one of the leading spirits of 20th-century painting. His entirely new attitude toward art and society, far from being negative or nihilistic, led the way to pop art, op art, and many of the other movements developed by younger artists. Not only did he change the visual arts but he also changed the mind of the artist. His 20 or so canvases and glass constructions were sold to close friends and left to the Philadelphia Museum of Art, where almost all his art is assembled. He also created a limited edition of a suitcase. He did 300 of them, each containing reproductions of his works. He died in Neuilly, near Paris, on Oct. 2, 1968.

A Canada goose, with its mate nearby, wards off intruders and defends its nestful of eggs by flapping its wings and honking.

Breck P. Kent—Animals Animals

DUCK, GOOSE, AND SWAN. Of the nearly 150 species of ducks, geese, and swans worldwide, most are strong swimmers with powerful wings for long-distance migrations. They have stout bodies, short legs, webbed feet, and flat bills. These waterfowl characteristically lay eggs that are unspotted and have young that leave the nest and begin feeding themselves soon after hatching. The fossil record of the family extends back more than 80 million years to the late Mesozoic era. The largest waterfowl are the swans and the smallest are the ducks. Geese are intermediate in size.

Ducks

Ducks are found throughout the world from the Arctic regions to South America, Africa, and Australia. Some species, for example the pink-headed duck of India, are very rare. Some, such as the Labrador duck, have become extinct in recent years, whereas others occur in large numbers. Because of their long migrations south during the winter, some species range over large portions of the northern continents. About 40 species of ducks are found in North America.

Ducks are well adapted for cold conditions. Their outer coat of closely packed feathers is made waterproof by oil from a gland near the tail, which is a trait characteristic of all waterfowl. Beneath the coat of feathers is a thick inner layer of soft, fluffy feathers called down. Ducks' webbed feet are able to withstand icy waters because blood is shunted away from them during extreme cold.

The male, called the drake, has showy plumage during the breeding season while the female is more muted in appearance. A brightly colored wing patch, called the speculum, is present in both sexes of some species. A duck's legs are set far back on the body, providing an advantage in swimming. However, the positioning of the legs makes a duck extremely awkward when walking on land. In short flights some ducks have been recorded at speeds greater than 70 miles (112 kilometers) per hour.

Most ducks nest on the ground, near water, in depressions lined with plants and with down from the birds' own breasts. The down, with its excellent insulating properties, is used to cover the eggs when the female is away from the nest. After the breeding season, ducks molt, or shed their feathers. At this time they cannot fly because they lose all of their wing quills at once. Most other birds lose only one quill at a time from each wing.

Ducks are classified in various ways by scientists, but a common grouping is based on habits and food. Two major groups are the diving ducks and the surface-feeding, or dabbling, ducks. The dabbling ducks live in marshes, shallow ponds, and slow-moving streams. They dive very little. Instead, they feed by "tipping up" with the head down, feet and tail in the air, and probing the mud bottoms for shellfish and insect larvae. Some swim around in the water eating surface plants and aquatic insects.

Mallards are the most common of the dabbling ducks. They are found throughout the Northern Hemisphere. The drake has a glossy green head and a white ring around the neck. The back is gray-brown, the breast rich chestnut, the underparts grayish-white. The speculum is purple. The female mallard is a mottled brown.

The blue-winged, green-winged, and cinnamon teals, the smallest of the dabbling ducks, are highly prized as food by hunters. One of the most colorful ducks in the world is the male of the wood duck, a dabbler of the eastern United States. Wood ducks lay their eggs in tree cavities. A close relative is the mandarin duck of Asia. Other dabblers are the shovelers, widgeons, and black duck. Another duck popular among hunters is the pintail. It is widely distributed but very wary, and it ranges throughout the Northern Hemisphere and winters as far south as Central America and the West Indies.

Diving ducks live on the open waters of large lakes and seacoasts. They dive for their food of fishes, shellfish, and water plants. They feed by day and spend the night on the water far from shore. Some species migrate as far south as Central America during the winter.

The canvasback is a common diving duck sought by hunters. It is so named because of its compact, grayish-colored back that resembles coarse canvas. The head and neck are red-brown. The redhead is a closely related species. Other common diving ducks are the scaups, ring-necked duck, goldeneyes, and the old squaw.

Eiders are beautifully patterned ducks native to northern Europe and North America. They are especially valued for their down. Commercial eiderdown is taken from the nest that the female lines during nesting. Eider ducks remain far north during winter, primarily in marine coastal areas. Scoters are also coastal diving ducks that winter along both the Atlantic and Pacific.

Mergansers are fish-eating ducks that are placed in a separate subfamily from other divers. They differ from all other ducks in having a long, narrow, cylindrical bill with saw-tooth edges. The red-breasted merganser, a common species in coastal and large lake areas of the United States during winter, is also found in China and Africa. The beautiful hooded merganser winters throughout much of North America.

Some types of ducks have been domesticated and are raised commercially as food and for their eggs and down. Domesticated ducks are hardy and comparatively resistant to parasites and diseases. They require simple housing and thrive even without water to swim in. New York is the largest producer of domesticated ducks in the United States. Most New York duck farms are on Long Island where millions of ducks are produced each year.

Geese

Geese have heavier bodies and longer necks than ducks. Unlike ducks, male and female geese are similar in appearance during all seasons. The male goose is called a gander. The juvenile is called a gosling. Geese are found throughout the world and include the pied goose of Australia, the rare Hawaiian goose, and the red-breasted goose of Siberia.

The several varieties of Canada geese are the best-known wild geese in North America. These large birds average about 36 inches (92 centimeters) in length, are gray-brown above, and have a black head and neck. A prominent white patch runs under the chin and up both cheeks. They nest from the northern United States to the Arctic tundra and winter as far south as Mexico. Canada geese mate for life. The female lays four to ten eggs that the male helps incubate. Both parents furiously defend the young, hissing violently and attacking intruders with their strong bills and beating wings.

Among the North American species is the snow goose, a white bird with black wing tips. The blue goose is a gray variety of snow goose with a white head. Both spend the winter in the southern United States, particularly in the Gulf Coast region. The brant is a small goose, closely related to the Canada goose, with a black head, neck, and breast. Brants nest in Arctic areas around the world and spend the winter in saltwater habitats of the Atlantic and Pacific coasts. The greylag is the best known of the European wild geese. These belong to a group known as the gray geese from which many domesticated stocks have been developed.

Geese have been domesticated for centuries. In Europe and Asia, geese have been used successfully as guards because they honk when a trespasser approaches. Goose down is prized as stuffing for pillows and quilts. Quill pens made from goose feathers were used for centuries. Today, some farms specialize in raising geese for market.

Swans

Five of the seven species of swans are solid white in color and make their breeding grounds in Arctic regions. The typical swan nest is a large pile of reeds and water plants. The eggs, averaging about six, are greenish. Young swans are called cygnets. The male is called a cob; the female, a pen. They feed on seeds, roots, small invertebrates, and fish eggs. Swans migrate southward into temperate areas during the winter. They are the most majestic of the waterfowl, being graceful in the air and stately on the water. The common swan of Europe is called the mute swan. Mute swans reach a length of 5 feet (152 centimeters) and a weight of 30 pounds (13.6 kilograms). The plumage is white, the legs black, and the bill orange-red with a black knob on the upper bill, near the eyes.

In North America the family has two native species—the trumpeter swan, largest of North American waterfowl, and the whistling swan. Mute swans have been successfully introduced in the northeastern United States. Swans have many calls, from the high-pitched note of the young birds to the bass notes of the old males.

Two species of swans live in the Southern Hemisphere, the black-necked swan of South America and the black swan of Australia. The black swan is a handsome bird with soot-black plumage and a coral bill. It is the state emblem of Western Australia.

A pair of mallard ducks "tip up" to feed off a lake's bottom. They are the most common dabbling ducks.

S.J. Krasemann—Peter Arnold, Inc.

□ Duck

□ Goose

□ Swan

In this table, lengths are measured from tip of tail to tip of bill. This represents a small selection of ducks, geese, and swans and is not intended to be inclusive.

Wood Duck ■
(Aix sponsa)

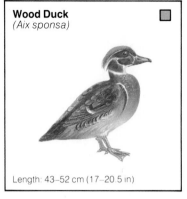

Length: 43–52 cm (17–20.5 in)

Pintail ■
(Anas acuta)

Length: 64–74 cm (25–29 in)

American Wigeon ■
(Anas americana)

Length: 46–58 cm (18–23 in)

Green-winged Teal ■
(Anas crecca)

Length: 32–39 cm (12.5–15.5 in)

Northern Shoveler ■
(Anas clypeata)

Length: 43–51 cm (17–20 in)

Mallard ■
(Anas platyrhynchos)

Length: 52–71 cm (20.5–28 in)

Ring-necked Duck ■
(Aythya collaris)

Length: 37–46 cm (14.5–18 in)

Greater Scaup ■
(Aythya marila)

Length: 39–51 cm (15.5–20 in)

Canvasback Duck ■
(Aythya valisineria)

Length: 50–61 cm (19.5–24 in)

Common Goldeneye ■
(Bucephala clangula)

Length: 41–51 cm (16–20 in)

Surf Scoter ■
(Melanitta perspicillata)

Length: 43–53 cm (17–21 in)

Red-breasted Merganser
(Mergus serrator)

Length: 50–66 cm (19.5–26 in)

Common Eider
(Somateria mollissima)

Length: 58–69 cm (23–27 in)

Greylag Goose
(Anser anser)

Length: 76–89 cm (30–35 in)

Brant
(Branta bernicla)

Length: 58–66 cm (23–26 in)

Canada Goose
(Branta canadensis)

Length: 56–92 cm (22–36 in)

Red-breasted Goose
(Branta ruficollis)

Length: 53–56 cm (21–22 in)

Hawaiian Goose
(Branta sandvicensis)

Length: 58–66 cm (23–26 in)

Lesser Snow Goose
(Chen caerulenscens)

Length: 64–79 cm (25–31 in)

Black Swan
(Cygnus atratus)

Length: 102–127 cm (40–50 in)

Mute Swan
(Cygnus olor)

Length: 147–152 cm (58–60 in)

Trumpeter Swan
(Cygnus buccinator)

Length: 150–180 cm (59–71 in)

Tundra (Whistling) Swan
(Cygnus columbianus)

Length: 119–147 cm (47–58 in)

Conservation

Each year the United States Fish and Wildlife Service and the Canadian Wildlife Service conduct waterfowl surveys in cooperation with state and provincial game departments. The purpose of these surveys is to determine the numbers of each species. Hunting is controlled each year on the basis of the surveys. Hunters are required to purchase a federal duck stamp in addition to a state license to hunt. The money is used to purchase and maintain migratory bird refuges and waterfowl production areas. Ducks Unlimited is a private, non-profit organization of American and Canadian sportsmen with the objective of increasing the number of waterfowl.

Classification

Ducks, geese, and swans belong to the family Anatidae in the order Anseriformes. The waterfowl are taxonomically placed into several subfamilies: swans, Cygninae; geese, Anserinae; whistling ducks of the Americas, Africa, and Asia, Dendrocygninae; dabblers, Anatinae; diving ducks, Aythinae; stiff-tailed ducks, Oxyurinae; and mergansers, Merginae. (*See also* Birds.)

DULUTH, Minn. The busiest American port on the Great Lakes is the harbor shared by Duluth, Minn., and Superior, Wis. It is situated at the western end of Lake Superior (*see* Great Lakes).

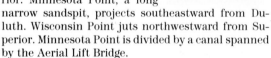

The harbor is well protected from the storms of Lake Superior. Minnesota Point, a long narrow sandspit, projects southeastward from Duluth. Wisconsin Point juts northwestward from Superior. Minnesota Point is divided by a canal spanned by the Aerial Lift Bridge.

The completion of the Saint Lawrence Seaway in 1959 opened the harbor to direct overseas commerce. Facilities include grain elevators, ore loaders, bunker terminals for oil and coal, refrigerated docks, and a container dock. Grains, iron ore, refined petroleum products, other liquids, and refrigerated commodities are the main products shipped out. Coal, grain, and crude petroleum are shipped in from other Great Lakes ports. Six railways and the interstate highway system provide connecting transport, and Duluth's airport lies 12 miles (19 kilometers) away. The harbor is usually icebound from early December to mid-April. The cold waters of Lake Superior keep the city's summer temperatures reasonably low.

Duluth's chief manufactures include iron and steel products, paper and paper products, transportation equipment, textiles, leather, chemicals, processed foods, metal alloys, electronic devices, and washing machines.

From Superior Street, the main thoroughfare, and London Road, Duluth rises on steep hills to the long Skyline Drive on the heights above the city. Among the institutions of higher learning are the College of Saint Scholastica and the University of Minnesota, Duluth. Here also are the Children's Museum and Art Center and the Tweed Art Gallery.

Duluth was named for Daniel Greysolon, sieur du Lhut, a French explorer who reached Lake Superior in 1679. The first permanent settlement was made in 1853. The Duluth ship canal was cut through Minnesota Point in 1871. After 1880 the city grew rapidly with the development of the mining industry. The commission form of government was adopted in 1913. In 1956 it was replaced by the mayor-council form. Population (1980 census), 92,811.

DUMAS, Alexandre (1802–70). The novels and plays of Alexandre Dumas are filled with action and clever talk. Some critics, however, have said that Dumas's work is not good literature because it is sometimes carelessly written and historically inaccurate.

Alexandre Dumas was born on July 24, 1802, in the French town of Villers-Cotterets. His father, who was one of Napoleon's generals, was the son of a French aristocrat and a Haitian black slave. The general died when the boy was about 4. Dumas's mother, who was the daughter of an innkeeper, was unable to give him much education. As a young boy he became a lawyer's messenger. When Dumas was 20, he worked in Paris as a junior clerk. His illegitimate son, called Alexandre Dumas the Younger, was born when Dumas was 22.

After several failures as a playwright, Dumas wrote 'Henri III'. It was produced in Paris in 1829 and was a great success. Dumas became prominent as one of the leaders of the Romantic movement.

In the 1840s Dumas turned nearly all his attention to writing vivid historical novels. The best known are 'The Three Musketeers', published in 1844; 'Twenty Years After' (1845); 'The Count of Monte Cristo' (1845); 'The Viscount Bragelonne' (1850); and 'The Black Tulip' (1850).

Dumas hired collaborators, added material here and there to their work, and changed the plot and characters, giving the works that charm and movement that made his novels popular. Collaborators' names never appeared on the title pages of these works, but this omission was a practice of the day. Dumas earned vast sums, but he spent money faster than he earned it. His wish to be elected to the French Academy was never fulfilled. He died on Dec. 5, 1870.

Alexandre Dumas the Younger (1824–95) as a dramatist achieved a high place in French literature. Unlike his father he was elected to the French Academy, in 1874, and he died a wealthy man. His best-known play, taken from his novel 'La Dame aux camélias' (The Lady of the Camellias), was made famous in America by Sarah Bernhardt under the title 'Camille'. Verdi's opera 'La Traviata' was also taken from the novel. Many of the younger Dumas's plays deal with marriage reforms and morals. He died on Nov. 27, 1895.

DUNCAN, Isadora (1877–1927). One of the first to raise the status of interpretive dance to that of creative art was Isadora Duncan. She was controversial in both her professional and private lives.

Born Angela Duncan on May 26, 1877, in San Francisco, she rejected, even as a child, the rigidity of classical ballet. She sought a more natural way of expressing herself through dance. She had changed her name to Isadora by 1894. Her first public appearances, in Chicago and New York City, were not successful, and she left for Europe at age 21 to seek recognition abroad. Her free-form style was enthusiastically welcomed in England and elsewhere in Europe. Duncan was the first Western dancer to perform barefoot and without tights, preferring a filmy, loosely fitting tunic.

Duncan opened dance schools in France, Germany, Russia, and the United States. Her dance style consisted more of improvisational movements than of strictly defined ones, and they were, therefore, seldom repeated. She danced to the music of the master composers, which was at first criticized but later appreciated. Her considerable influence on modern dance occurred mostly after her death.

Duncan had two children out of wedlock, both of whom were killed in an automobile accident in 1913. In 1922 she married a Russian poet 17 years younger than she. Following a tour of the United States, where they were labeled Bolshevik agents, they returned to Europe. Her husband's increasing mental instability turned him against Duncan, and he returned to the Soviet Union and committed suicide in 1925. Duncan lived the last years of her life in Nice, France. She died tragically there on Sept. 14, 1927, when, while riding in a car, her scarf became entangled in a rear wheel and she was thrown to the ground.

DUNEDIN, New Zealand. Situated in a picturesque setting in southeastern South Island, New Zealand, the port city of Dunedin stands at the head of Otago Harbor beneath steep hills. Its rugged landscape was shaped partly by volcanic outpourings. Dunedin is the fourth largest city in the country.

The city is an industrial center, producing woolens, textiles, home appliances, footwear, furniture, soap, fertilizer, and chemicals. It also has flour milling and ship repair plants, engineering works, and iron and brass foundries. In addition to its excellent port, Dunedin is served by an airport, the Picton–Bluff State Highway, and the South Island Main Trunk Railway to Christchurch.

The city is noted for its green Town Belt, which was planned by the city founders to surround the inner city with 500 acres (200 hectares) of forest. Dunedin's present-day architectural makeup is a combination of Victorian and modern buildings. The University of Otago, founded in 1869, is the oldest university in New Zealand. The Otago Polytechnic Institute is also located in Dunedin. The city is a religious center, having both Roman Catholic and Anglican cathedrals, and is also the home of Knox, Selwyn,

J. Waddington—New Zealand Tourist Office

The first building of the University of Otago at Dunedin was built of bluestone by Scottish immigrants.

and Holy Cross theological colleges. Dunedin has a botanical garden and several museums, including the Dunedin Public Art Gallery, the Otago Museum, and the Theomin Gallery.

Dunedin was founded in 1848 as a Scottish Free church settlement. The site was chosen because of timber resources and farming potential. The discovery of gold in 1861 in central Otago district brought many people and prosperity to the town. During the second half of the 19th century, it was the largest town in New Zealand. It became a borough in 1855 and a city ten years later. Population (1983 estimate), city, 77,500; metropolitan area, 105,600.

DUNHAM, Katherine (born 1910). In 1968, when *Dance Magazine* presented an award to black dancer, choreographer, and anthropologist Katherine Dunham, it called her "the forerunner of the numerous fine contemporary Negro groups now emerging and developing." She was instrumental in changing the status of the black dancer from entertainer to artist.

Dunham was born in Chicago on June 22, 1910. She became interested in dance while in high school and in 1931 opened a dance school to help pay for her education at the University of Chicago, where she received a master's degree and a Ph.D. in anthropology. In 1936 she began 18 months of ethnic dance research in the Caribbean. In 1940 she formed the first all-black concert dance troupe in order to perform 'Tropics and le Jazz Hot', a revue that was based largely on her scholarly research. Dunham's choreography combined black island dances with ballet and theatrical effects, resulting in a unique dance style. Critics applauded her work, and in 1943 she and her company conducted a successful tour. In 1945 the Dunham School of Dance was opened in New York City. Many of its students went on to become noted performers.

289

Katherine Dunham, center, and her all-black dance troupe appeared in 'Tropical Revue' in 1945 and 1946.

Dunham choreographed for the Broadway stage, the opera, and films. She was artistic and technical director for the president of Senegal and an artist-in-residence at Southern Illinois University. Her autobiography, 'A Touch of Innocence', was published in 1959.

DUNKIRK, France. An important commercial seaport, Dunkirk lies in the extreme north of France on the Strait of Dover. In the evacuation of Dunkirk, one of the great actions of World War II, the town was demolished, but much of it had been rebuilt by 1953.

With the German breakthrough in 1940, Belgium had surrendered on May 28. The French flank crumbled before a German advance that swept around the Allied armies in the north. Britain's only army was caught between the sea and the thrust of Hitler's tank units. On the Dunkirk beaches, the British, with some French and Dutch units, stood almost helpless. The small Royal Air Force held off the German planes. From May 29 to June 4, small volunteer craft crossed the channel and evacuated 360,000, or three fourths, of the Allied forces in the face of a terrible artillery bombardment. (*See also* World War II.)

The name Dunkirk (French, *Dunkerque*) means "dune-church." It is said that Saint Eloi founded a small church, or "kirk," here on the sand dunes in the 7th century. In the 10th century it was fortified by Baldwin III, count of Flanders. England held it for four years after 1658, but Charles II, needing money, then sold it to Louis XIV.

Canals and railways link Dunkirk to the rich farmlands, coal mines, and factory centers of France and Belgium. The chief industries are shipbuilding, shipping, fishing, iron founding, refining, and lacemaking. Population (1982 census), 73,618.

DUPLICATING MACHINE. A device for making duplicate copies of a document is a duplicating machine. The major types of duplicating machines are stencil, or mimeograph; hectograph, or spirit duplicator; multilith, or offset lithograph; and photocopying, or xerographic. All duplicating machines require the preparation of a master from which copies are made by a machine. Strictly speaking, duplicating machines are different from photocopying machines, in which copies are made from an original in an exposure–image-forming process.

Mimeograph

The stencil duplicator uses a stencil consisting of a coated fiber sheet through which ink is pressed. Using a typewriter with the ribbon shifted out of the way so that the keys do not strike it, the information to be duplicated is typed on the stencil. The keys cut the coating on the stencil and expose the fiber base, making it possible for ink to pass through it. Corrections can be made by a sealing fluid that permits retyping over the patched error. Handwriting or drawings can be added to the stencil with a hand stylus, or smooth metal point.

In the more common type of stencil duplicator, the stencil is fastened to the ink-saturated surface of a hollow, rotating cylinder. As the cylinder rotates, ink flows through the cuts in the stencil to the sheets of paper fed under the cylinder. Up to 5,000 copies can be made from a single stencil. Stencils may be stored for long periods for reuse.

Spirit Duplicator

The most common type of hectograph uses the so-called spirit process for making a master copy. The spirit method is also called the direct, or fluid, process. The master copy is prepared by typewriter, handwriting, or a computer-printing device that produces a reverse image using a waxy dye. The master sheet is then fastened to a rotating drum. Copy sheets are slightly moistened by an alcohol-based fluid and brought into direct contact with the master sheet. A small amount of the dye on the master sheet transferred to the copy sheets results in finished copies. Multicolor duplication in one operation is possible. Up to 300 copies can be made from one master sheet.

Xerography

The duplication method most widely used by modern office photocopiers is called xerography (from the Greek words meaning dry writing). Although developed in 1937, the process did not become available for commercial use until 1950. Xerography is extremely versatile and can be used to produce copies of all kinds of written, printed, and graphic matter. The basis of the process is photoconductivity, an increase in the ability of certain substances to allow an electric current to flow through them when struck by light. The chemical element selenium, for example, is a poor electrical conductor, but when light is absorbed by some of its electrons and a voltage is applied, these electrons are able to pass more freely from one atom to another. When the light is removed, their mobility falls. Xerography typically uses an aluminum drum coated with a layer of selenium. Light reflected from the surface of the document to be copied is focused on the selenium surface. Negatively charged particles of dry ink—that is, the toner—are sprayed onto the selenium, forming a reverse image of the document on the drum. A sheet of copy paper is passed close to the drum, and a positive electric charge under the sheet attracts the negatively charged ink particles, resulting in the transfer of the image to the copy paper. Heat is then briefly applied to fuse the ink particles to the paper.

Some photocopiers are able to print on both sides of the paper, sort and collate, automatically produce a specified number of copies, and enlarge or reduce the image reproduced from the original.

DU PONT FAMILY. If wealth is any measure of success, the history of the Du Pont family in the United States is one of the great American success stories. An early member of the family founded the E.I. du Pont de Nemours Company in 1801 near Wilmington, Del., as a gunpowder manufacturing plant. Within a century it became the world's largest manufacturer of explosives. In the 20th century the corporation is the nation's largest chemical company. It has, since 1930, introduced such highly profitable synthetic materials as nylon, Lucite, Teflon, Orlon, Dacron, Mylar, and neoprene, synthetic rubber.

Pierre Samuel du Pont de Nemours (1739–1817) was born in Paris and became a prominent economist in the years before the French Revolution began in 1789. To escape the conflicts that followed the revolution he emigrated to the United States with his sons Victor and Eleuthère Irénée in January 1800.

Victor (1767–1827) was attaché to the first French legation to the United States in 1787 and aide-de-camp to Lafayette from 1789 to 1791. Later, after unsuccessful business ventures, he was appointed a director of the Bank of the United States. His son, Samuel Francis (1803–65), became a naval officer, rising to the rank of rear admiral in the Civil War.

It was Eleuthère Irénée du Pont (1771–1834) who started the gunpowder plant that formed the basis of the family fortune. While still living in France he had studied under the great chemist Antoine Lavoisier. He had also worked at a French munitions plant. Seeing the poor quality and high price of American gunpowder, he established his own factory in Delaware. When his gunpowder of greatly superior quality went on the market in 1804, the federal government became his best customer.

After Eleuthère Irénée died, his two sons, Alfred Victor (1798–1856) and Henry (1812–89), ran the company. Henry ran it during the great period of American industrial expansion from 1850 to 1889. One of Henry's sons, Henry Algernon (1838–1926), was, like his father, a West Point graduate. During the Civil War he earned the Medal of Honor. He joined the company in 1878 and, after retiring in 1902, he was elected United States senator from Delaware and served from 1906 to 1917.

After the death of Henry du Pont in 1889, the company was directed by Eugene du Pont (1840–1902), a grandson of the founder. In 1902 it seemed for a while that the company would be sold. Then three cousins—Thomas Coleman du Pont (1863–1930), Alfred Irénée du Pont (1864–1935), and Pierre Samuel du Pont (1870–1954)—took control.

The three cousins soon bought out their leading competitors in the explosives business and turned the Du Pont Company into one of the nation's largest corporations. In 1917, when General Motors seemed about to fail, Pierre bought nearly one fourth of that corporation's stock and reorganized the auto firm. Du Pont retained control of General Motors until 1959, when the federal government forced a divestiture. After World War I the Du Pont Company began developing synthetic products and became a major chemical firm.

Irénée du Pont (1876–1963) followed his brother Pierre as head of the company in 1919 and remained active as a director until 1946. A younger brother, Lammot (1880–1952), took over the company presidency in 1926 and held the post until 1940. He also served as a director of General Motors.

The last member of the family to run the firm was Lammot du Pont Copeland (born 1905), who retired in 1971. Although the company is no longer a family corporation, the Du Ponts still own large amounts of its stock and usually have at least one family member on its board of directors.

DURBAN, South Africa. The chief seaport of South Africa and the largest city of Natal Province, Durban stands at Natal Bay on the Indian Ocean. The harbor is one of the world's major commercial ports, a point of entry for bulk raw materials and industrial equipment. It serves the Witwatersrand industrial region with exports of minerals, coal, sugar, and corn. Petroleum is refined and piped from Durban to Johannesburg. Durban is also the headquarters of South Africa's sugar industry and a center of diversified manufacturing activity.

Durban's civic and business center is on land that rises gently to the Berea, a residential district on a ridge of hills encircling the harbor and beach. The city sprawls over 116 square miles (300 square kilometers) along the coast. The Bluff, made up of hills that separate the landlocked bay from the sea, overlooks the city at the south.

The University of Natal was founded in 1909 for white students; the University of Durban–Westville is primarily for Indian students. There is also a technical college as well as several libraries. There is a local history museum and the Durban Museum and Art Gallery. The city's numerous parks include the Botanic Gardens with an orchid house, Jameson Park and its rose gardens, and Snake Park with a collection of poisonous reptiles.

Durban was settled in 1824 by a band of Cape Colony traders led by F.G. Farewell. The land was granted to the traders by the Zulu king Shaka. The city was named for Sir Benjamin D'Urban, governor of the Cape Colony, in 1835. It became a town in 1854 and a city in 1935. After World War I Durban changed from a Victorian town into a modern metropolis with multistoried buildings, some skyscrapers. With adjacent Pinetown, Durban has a larger Indian than white population. Ntuzuma, Umlazi, and Embumbulu districts immediately to the west have been developed as black commuter suburbs. They are part of the KwaZulu nonindependent black state. Population (1980 preliminary census), city, 505,963; metropolitan area, 960,792.

DÜRER, Albrecht (1471–1528).

The son of an unimportant goldsmith, Albrecht Dürer became known as the "prince of German artists." He was the first to fuse the richness of the Italian Renaissance to the harsher northern European arts of painting, drawing, and engraving.

Albrecht Dürer was born in Nuremberg, Germany, on May 21, 1471. Before being taken into his father's shop to learn goldsmithing, he was sent to school to learn reading and writing. His talent for drawing, however, led his father to send him at 15 to work for and learn from a Nuremberg painter. Upon completing this apprenticeship in 1490, Dürer took the traditional young artist's trip to the art centers of Germany. In 1494, about the time of his marriage to

'Knight, Death and Devil' is one of the best known of the engravings made by the artist Albrecht Dürer.

The Art Institute of Chicago

Agnes Trey, he visited Venice. From that period on the Italian influence was evident in his work.

Back in his home city, Dürer worked at both painting and wood engraving. Paintings were costly, and they could be enjoyed only by the purchaser and his immediate circle. By using the new craft of printing, many copies of an engraving could be made. The reproductions were used largely to educate people in religious and classical history.

In 1507 Dürer made another visit to Venice; he remained there a year and a half. After his return he seems to have renounced painting as an important work, and instead devoted most of his time to engraving on wood and copper. In 1513 and 1514 he completed his three best-known copper engravings: 'Knight, Death and Devil', 'St. Jerome in His Study', and ' Melancholia'.

Dürer also delved into the mathematics of proportion and perspective and during his lifetime published two works on these subjects. He was a friend of Martin Luther and several other leaders of the Reformation. He died in Nuremberg on April 6, 1528. (*See also* Drawing; Painting.)

DURKHEIM, Émile (1858–1917).

A pioneer social scientist, Émile Durkheim established sociology as a separate discipline, or field of study. He was the first to subject the specific events of everyday life to close sociological study and to determine specific scientific methods of examination.

Émile Durkheim was born on April 15, 1858, in Épinal, France. He studied philosophy at the prestigious École Normale Supérieure in Paris. Upon graduation in 1882 he taught in secondary schools until 1887, when he was appointed to a lectureship especially founded for him at the University of Bordeaux. This was the first course of social science officially provided in a French university.

Durkheim's first book, 'The Division of Labor in Society', published in 1893, focused on the problems of new technology and the mechanization of work. This division of labor, according to Durkheim, made workers both more alien to one another, as their jobs were different, and more dependent on one another, as none any longer built the whole of a product. The methods to be used to examine society in this new discipline Durkheim laid out in 'The Rules of Sociological Method' (1895).

His classic 'Suicide' (1897) examines the ties that bind individuals to the society in which they live—and their breakdown. Suicide appeared to be more frequent in societies where individuals are less a part of the life around them, as in modern industrial societies. He distinguished three types of suicide: In egoistic suicide the individual shuts himself off from other human beings. Anomic suicide comes from the belief that the world has fallen apart around one. Altruistic suicide springs from great loyalty to a cause.

In 1902 Durkheim was appointed to the University of Paris, becoming a full professor in 1906. He taught there until his death on Nov. 15, 1917.

DU SABLE, Jean Baptist Point (1745?–1818). The first settler in what is now Chicago was a black man named Jean Baptist Point du Sable. Of French and African parentage, he was probably born in Haiti in about 1745. When he was about 20 he went to New Orleans as a member of a French trading firm. He soon went up the Mississippi River to Saint Louis, then on to the present site of Peoria, Ill., where he married a Potawatomi Indian.

Sometime before 1779 Du Sable settled at the site that would become Chicago and started a trading post. Ultimately he established a prosperous trading business and a farm. He sold the business in May 1800 and moved to St. Charles, Mo., where he died on Aug. 28, 1818. In 1803, near the site of Du Sable's property, the Fort Dearborn settlement was founded. Its name was changed to Chicago in 1830.

DUSE, Eleonora (1859–1924). The Italian actress Eleonora Duse is considered one of the greatest performers of tragedy. Her expressiveness and physical grace made her a legend in her own lifetime.

Duse was born in a railroad car near Vigevano, Italy, in 1859. Most members of her family were actors, and she made her first stage appearance at age 4. At 14 she played Shakespeare's Juliet, but her fame came in 1879 when she played the title role in Émile Zola's 'Thérèse Raquin'. She appeared in plays by modern French dramatists, her acting talent often making their ordinary characters seem fascinating. Actor–manager Cesare Rossi chose her as his leading lady, and they toured South America in 1885. In Italy she formed her own acting group, which toured the United States, Egypt, and Europe. Everywhere she performed, audiences fell in love with her.

In 1894 Duse herself fell in love, with a young poet named Gabriele d'Annunzio. He wrote many plays for her, which provided new outlets for her expressiveness and made d'Annunzio famous, as well. His novel 'The Flame of Life', first published in 1900, is the story of their love.

Duse found her greatest roles in the dramatic plays of Henrik Ibsen. Her triumphs included Nora in 'A Doll's House' and the title role in 'Hedda Gabler'. She seemed to live a part rather than merely act it, and her posture and gestures were different for every role. She wore no makeup; she had the ability to turn pale or blush at will.

In 1909 Duse retired from the stage, mainly because of poor health. Financial difficulties forced her to return to acting in 1921. She died while touring the United States, in Pittsburgh on April 21, 1924.

DÜSSELDORF, West Germany. Located in northwestern West Germany, mostly on the right bank of the Rhine River, Düsseldorf is the capital of North Rhine–Westphalia state. It is also the center of the Rhine–Ruhr industrial area.

The city's chief industry is iron and steel. Its products also include chemicals, glass, textiles and clothing, electrical engineering and precision tools,

Hackmann—ZEFA

Düsseldorf, West Germany, is located on the Rhine River, one of Europe's busiest waterways.

automobiles, paper, and printing presses. Düsseldorf is also a banking and wholesale center and the home of the administrative offices of many businesses.

Düsseldorf boasts Germany's first skyscraper, the Wilhelm-Marx-Haus, built in 1924. There are three harbors on the Rhine, and one of the nation's busiest airfields is at Lohausen.

Among the city's numerous cultural institutions are the Hetjensmuseum of ceramics, the state museum, and the city library, which has a collection of works by the poet Heinrich Heine, a Düsseldorf native. The University of Düsseldorf was founded in 1965. In the nearby Neanderthal Valley is the Feldhofer Cave, where the remains of a prehistoric man were found in 1856.

The Königsallee is a fashionable treelined shopping street. Landmarks include the 13th- to 14th-century church, Saint Lambertuskirche, and the old town hall, completed in 1588. The town historical collection is housed in Castle Jägerhof, which dates from 1763. The remains of the palace of Frederick I are in the northern district of Kaiserwerth.

Düsseldorf dates from 1159. Its name means village on the Düssel, the Düssel being a small tributary of the Rhine River. It was chartered in 1288 by the count of Berg and was the capital of the duchies of Berg and Jülich from 1511 until it passed to a palatinate, or countship of Palatine, in 1609. From 1805 to 1813 it was the capital of the short-lived Napoleonic grand duchy of Berg. It passed to Prussia in 1815. Düsseldorf became the state capital in 1946. Population (1983 estimate), 583,445.

DUVALIER, François (1907–71). The president of Haiti from 1957 to 1971, François Duvalier was often referred to as "Papa Doc" because he had begun his career as a physician. During his 14 years in power in one of the poorest countries in the world, he used violence and terror to stop all who opposed him.

Duvalier was born on April 14, 1907, at Port-au-Prince, Haiti. He graduated from the University of Haiti's school of medicine in 1934 and served until 1943 as a hospital staff physician. In 1946 the president of Haiti, Dumarsais Estimé, appointed him director general of the National Public Health Service. In this capacity Duvalier conducted a campaign against yaws, an infectious and contagious disease that causes sores on the skin and weakens bones. When Estimé was overthrown by a military coup in 1950, Duvalier went to work for the American Sanitary Mission. At the same time, he attempted to mobilize opposition to the new president, Paul E. Magloire.

Magloire's overthrow in 1956 was followed by a succession of weak governments until Duvalier was elected president in 1957. In order to terrorize and eliminate foes of his regime, he organized a private police force named the Tonton Macoutes. In 1964 he had himself declared president for life. His dictatorial rule isolated Haiti from the rest of the world. The United States cut off financial aid. The Roman Catholic church excommunicated him for harassing priests. Before Duvalier died on April 21, 1971, he designated his 20-year-old son, Jean-Claude Duvalier, called "Baby Doc," to succeed him as president.

DVOŘÁK, Antonín (1841–1904).

A 19th-century Bohemian composer, Dvořák was noted for adapting traditional native folk music into opera, symphony, and piano pieces. His 'From the New World' symphony remains his best-known work. It is thought to be based on the spirituals of black slaves and on other influences Dvořák gained during his years in the United States.

Antonín Dvořák was born on Sept. 8, 1841, in Nelahozeves, near Prague, Czechoslovakia. He was exposed to music in and around his father's inn and as a child became an accomplished violinist playing with amateur musicians at local dances. From 1857 to 1859 he attended an organ school in Prague and for about the next ten years gave music lessons and played the viola in the National Theater.

In 1873 he married Anna Čermáková, and they had six children. A few successful concerts of his works had begun to make his name well-known in Prague. Dvořák received the Austrian State Prize in 1875 for his 'Symphony in E Flat'. A state grant by the Austrian government brought him into contact with Johannes Brahms, who gave him valuable technical advice and also recommended Dvořák to his publisher, Fritz Simrock. It was Simrock's publication of his 'Moravian Duets' in 1876 and 'Slavonic Dances' in 1878 that first attracted worldwide attention to Dvořák and to his country's music. From the praise of leading critics, instrumentalists, and conductors, Dvořák's fame spread abroad, and in 1892 he was made the director of the National Conservatory of Music in New York City. Dvořák missed Bohemia and returned in 1895. During the final years of his life he composed several string quartets and symphonic poems and his last three operas. He was director of the Prague Conservatory from 1901 until he died of Bright's disease on May 1, 1904, in Prague.

DWARF AND GIANT.

Human growth is an intricate process controlled by a number of factors, including heredity, the growth plates of the bones, and hormones produced by the pituitary and the thyroid glands. Certain diseases, injuries, and genetic defects can cause a hormonal imbalance or ineffectiveness resulting in dwarfism or gigantism (see Hormones).

An adult who is much shorter than normal is said to suffer from dwarfism. Traditionally, those with normal proportions of body and limbs were called midgets and those who were disproportioned were called dwarfs. Both terms are now considered insulting and "little people" is the preferred term.

Dwarfism is associated with disturbances in the bone-producing cells of the epiphyseal cartilage, or growth plates, of the bones. The disturbance may result from inadequate levels of growth hormones acting on healthy growth plates, or it may result from adequate or inadequate levels of hormones acting on dysfunctioning growth plates.

Hormonal dwarfism occurs when inadequate amounts of pituitary growth hormone or thyroid hormones are produced. Lack of growth hormone results in normal body proportions and a delicate, doll-like appearance. When insufficient thyroid hormones are produced before birth and during infancy, cretinism, or dwarfism with mental retardation, results. A lack of thyroid hormones that begins later in childhood causes shortness, but intelligence is normal. Hormonal dwarfism can be treated with hormone injections or tablets.

Achondroplastic dwarfism results from a genetic defect of the cartilage cells, but it affects only some of the cartilage in the body, such as the spine or the limbs. Sufferers from this condition typically have a normal size trunk with a painful, curved spine, a relatively large head, and short arms and legs. Hypochondroplastic dwarfism is similar except that the head is a normal size.

Disease can also cause dwarfism. Heart, kidney, and brain diseases can cause growth to be retarded, but correction of the disease, when it is possible, usually corrects the lack of growth. Malnutrition and lack of proper emotional care can also cause dwarfism.

A person who grows much taller than normal is said to suffer from gigantism. In gigantism that begins in childhood, normal ossification, or hardening of the bones, is prevented by the overproduction of growth hormone. Bone growth is therefore abnormally rapid. Usually the cause is unknown, though sometimes a pituitary tumor is found. Treatment consists of X-ray therapy to decrease the activity of the pituitary. A tumor is removed surgically.

The second type of gigantism is called acromegaly, which occurs in some adults over the age of 30. This is also caused by excessive amounts of growth hormone. It is often the result of a tumor growing in the pituitary, but sometimes the cause is unknown. The condition causes the bones of the face, feet, and hands to grow longer. If the cause is a tumor, treatment consists of surgical removal.

(Left) Emil Muench—Ostman Agency; (center) Tom McHugh—Photo Researchers; (right) courtesy CIBA-GEIGY Corp., photo J. Olson

For centuries, natural dyes have been obtained from plants, animals, and minerals. Dried stigmas of the saffron flower (left) produce the color yellow. Certain shellfish, such as the *Purpura haemastoma* (center), secrete fluids that are made into purple dyes. Today a large number of dyes are made artificially from chemicals, especially from petroleum (right).

DYE. Any substance, usually a complex organic compound, that is intensely colored and is used to color other materials is called a dye. Dyes are to some degree absorbed by the material they color. Another type of coloring agent, pigments, are not absorbed. About 75 percent of all dyes are used to color clothing or other textiles. Smaller amounts are used in coloring paper, leather, typewriter ribbons and ink, shoe polish, plastics, food coloring, and many other items.

Today nearly all dyes are made from compounds obtained from petroleum or coal. These dyes are called synthetic dyes—as opposed to natural dyes, obtained from animal, vegetable, and mineral sources, which were used exclusively in the past. The robes of Roman emperors, for example, were dyed with Tyrian purple, which was extracted from a Mediterranean shellfish. The dye called indigo blue came from the leaves of the woad plant. Yellow and red dyes were obtained from certain thistles. American Indians found various dyes in western desert plants. In Mexico a scarlet dye, cochineal, was obtained from dried insects. One mineral source, an iron oxide, is still the principal constituent of rouge.

Dyes may be classified in two unrelated ways. The dyer, for example, classifies dyes according to the procedure used to put the dye on the cloth. The chemist, however, is more interested in the structure of the molecules that make up the dye. Knowing this structure, the chemist can hope to synthesize new dyes. This is a classification by molecular architecture.

Dyeing Procedures

One method used to put dye on cloth is to dip the cloth into a vat containing a water solution of the dye. Indigo, which has a colorless soluble form, is a vat dye that develops the insoluble blue color when it is exposed to oxygen from the air. Oxygen may be introduced into this type of dye by a chemical reagent, a process that gives a more uniform color. The blue coats of American colonial soldiers during the American Revolution were supplied by French dyers using indigo.

Mordant dyeing is a second method. The mordant, a wet metallic hydroxide, usually of tin, chromium, iron, or aluminum, is put on the cloth in one operation. Then the dye—for example, alizarin—when added to the mordanted cloth combines with the mordant so that the color is formed in the cloth. In the case of alizarin with aluminum hydroxide as the mordant, a dye called turkey red is formed. Originally alizarin was obtained from the madder plant and used to make the "Redcoats" of British soldiers. Other mordants with the same dye give different colors.

A few dyes can be applied directly. Congo red, for example, will stick to cotton just by immersing the cotton in a hot solution of the dye. Unfortunately, Congo red turns blue in the presence of acids so it is not practical in air that is polluted with suspended acids, which is common in most modern cities and industrial areas.

Batik dyeing of cotton and silk fabrics originated in Java in ancient times. In this process a wax made of paraffin and beeswax is melted and the liquid wax brushed or blown onto the parts of the fabric not to be dyed. The dye of lightest color is then applied to the unwaxed portion in a cold bath, or at least in a bath not hot enough to melt the wax. The fabric is then washed and dried. The wax can then be removed with a solvent or by ironing the fabric between blotting papers. The masking and dyeing process is repeated with darker colors until the desired colors and designs complete the batik. (*See also* Batik.)

When a fabric is woven with more than one kind of yarn—for example, nylon and polyester—one thread may be dyed by a particular dye while the one next to it is not. The use of appropriate dyes then makes interesting color patterns possible by dipping the cloth in turn into different dye baths to color the mixed threads separately.

Attention has recently been given to using solvents other than water (for example, dry cleaning solvents) to impregnate cloth with dyes. Such solvents are easy to recover and minimize pollution since water solutions are not recovered and are usually released into streams or other bodies of water. Other advantages include rapid wetting of the cloth, speed in dyeing, and less swelling in the fabrics.

Fast and Fugitive Dyes

A dye that retains its color when the cloth is exposed to conditions of its use is called a "fast" dye. Such conditions include exposure to sunlight, washing, cleaning, exposure to acids and alkalies, and hot pressing. An evening gown that retains its true color after it is cleaned but which fades if placed in the sunlight, an improper condition of use, is still said to have a fast color. A dye that fades in a fabric used under proper conditions is called a fugitive dye.

Dyes that are fast for silk or wool may prove fugitive when used with cotton or synthetic fibers. The reverse will also often be true. Dyes must be matched with the proper fabric and the proper method of dyeing.

Why Dyes Have Color

The chemical architecture of the molecules of dye determine the color that the dye will impart to the cloth. The heart of the dye is the chromophore, the color bearer. The common chromophoric groups are the following arrangements of atoms where the dashes represent chemical bonds:

$$-NO_2 \quad -NO \quad -N=N- \quad \underset{\underset{O}{|}}{-N=N-}$$

$$-C=C-C=N= \quad -C=C-C=O$$

and combinations of these groups. C, N, and O represent carbon, nitrogen, and oxygen atoms. The atoms of a chromophore in combination vibrate at the same rate as the corresponding waves of light of the same color in a spectrum and reflect that color to the eye. The nitro group, NO_2, for example, tends to give a yellow color to a molecule.

However, a chromophore is not enough to make a dye. Other helping groups, called auxochromes, intensify the color if they are present along with a chromophore. Some examples are $-OH$, $-NH_2$, and $-NH-CH_3$ (H represents the hydrogen atom). Finally the dye needs still other groups to make the dye at least partly soluble. The solubilizing groups are generally acidic, $-SO_3H$ and $-CO_2H$, and basic, $-NH_2$ and $-NHCH_3$ (S represents sulfur). The auxochromes and solubilizing groups also help to make the dye cling to the cloth. The acidic and basic groups are especially effective in dyeing silk and wool because their counterparts exist in these fabrics. That is, acidic groups in the dye bind to basic groups in the silk or wool and vice versa.

History of Synthetic Dyes

Dyes from nature were used of necessity until an accidental discovery in 1856 launched the synthetic dye industry. An 18-year-old chemistry student, William H. Perkin, working in August Wilhelm von Hofmann's laboratory in London attempted to syn-

thesize quinine and instead discovered how to make mauveine, a purple dye. Perkin was experimenting with a compound called aniline in a possible first step in the pathway to quinine. He obtained a black tarry mess, but when he removed it from the flask with alcohol he observed a purple color in the dilute solution. When he dipped a piece of silk into this mixture, the silk was dyed a reddish purple. This experiment set the stage for the dye industry. Through the help of his father, Perkin started a factory for making synthetic mauveine near London in 1857.

At least 7,500 dyes are recognized now, and thousands of patents have been granted in various countries for the synthesis and application of dyes. Reports of new dyes are published every two weeks.

Linda Matlow—Pix International

Bob Dylan, in concert

DYLAN, Bob (born 1941). "He sounds like a sheep in pain," said one critic of American singer–songwriter Bob Dylan. Yet with his complex, literary lyrics that were studied as poetry by some scholars Dylan changed popular music and won a wide following.

He was born Robert Zimmerman in Duluth, Minn., on May 24, 1941, and as an adult changed his name to Dylan. He originally sang in imitation of folksinger Woody Guthrie, and in the 1960s Dylan's songs like 'Blowin' in the Wind' were popularized by movements against war and social injustice. In 1965 Dylan adopted amplified instruments and began the folk rock form; in 1968 he introduced country and western flavor to his songs; and in the 1970s he turned to gospel music. These changes sometimes upset his fans, but by 1984 Dylan was wooing audiences old and new with concerts that featured a combination of his styles.

DYNAMITE *see* EXPLOSIVE.

DYSPROSIUM *see* PERIODIC TABLE.

The letter D

may have started as a picture sign of a door, as in Egyptian hieroglyphic writing (1). The earliest form of the sign in the Semitic writings is unknown. About 1000 B.C., in Byblos and in other Phoenician and Canaanite centers, the sign was given a linear form (2), the source of all later forms. In the Semitic languages the sign was called *daleth*, meaning ''door.''

The Greeks changed the Semitic name to *delta*. They retained the Phoenician form of the sign (3). In an Italian colony of Greeks from Khalkis (or Chalcis), the letter was made with a slight curve (4). This shape led to the rounded form found in the Latin writing (5). From Latin the capital letter came unchanged into English. In Greek handwriting the triangle of the capital letter was given a projection upward. During Roman times the triangle was gradually rounded (6).

Dab, fish. *see in index* Flounder

Dabbling duck, surface-feeding duck D-284

Dabchick. *see in index* Pied-billed grebe

Daboia, or **Russell's viper** V-328

Da capo, music, *table* M-566a

Dacca. *see in index* Dhaka

Dace, freshwater fish of the family Cyprinidae D-2. *see also in index* Minnow

Dachau, West Germany, town 11 mi (18 km) n.w. of Munich; site of notorious Nazi concentration camp; pop. 32,349, *map* G-115

Dachshund, dog, *picture* D-199

Dacia, ancient country of central Europe; present Hungary and Romania R-318, *map* R-242

Dacko, David, president of Central African Republic (1960-66, 1979-81) C-252

Dacron, a strong chemical fiber used to make knitting yarns, knitwear, and fabrics for men's and women's clothing; nonabsorbent, resists wrinkling, retains a crease well; is woollike in staple form P-228 synthetic fibers F-73

Dactyl (from Greek *daktylos,* "finger," because of fancied resemblance to three joints of finger, one long, two short), poetic foot P-405

Da Cunha, Euclydes (1866-1909), Brazilian writer L-70

Dadaism, a movement in art and literature based on deliberate irrationality and negation of traditional artistic values; began in 1916
Duchamp's paintings D-283
French literature F-397

Daddy longlegs, or **harvestman,** spiderlike arachnid with small body and unusually long legs S-387 eyes N-60c

Dadra and Nagar Haveli, union territory of India, near w. coast; area 189 sq mi (490 sq km); cap. Silvassa; formerly Portuguese possession; pop. 74,165.

Dadswell, Lyndon, Australian sculptor A-802

Daedalus, Greek mythology D-2
airplane history A-199
Icarus, *picture* M-577
Minoan culture A-62

Daemen College. *see in index* Rosary Hill College

Daffodil N-14
Netherlands N-137, *picture* F-223

Da Gama, Vasco. *see in index* Gama

Daggerboard, sailboat B-328

Daggers S-546

Dagnan-Bouveret, Pascal Adolphe Jean (1852-1929), French painter, born in Paris;

pupil of Gérôme; noted for pictures of peasants; an excellent colorist ('The Conscripts'; 'The Consecrated Bread').

Dagö, Estonian S.S.R. *see in index* Hiiumaa

Dagon, a Semitic god, worshiped by Philistines when they settled in Canaan; origin uncertain; little known of cult of the god.

Daguerre, Louis-Jacques-Mandé (1789-1851), French painter and physicist D-2
photography P-298, *picture* P-300

Daguerreotypy, an early photographic process, using silver-coated copper plates P-298, D-2

Dagyr, John Adam (died 1806), Welsh shoemaker in American Colonies S-179

Da Hingon. *see in index* Great Khingan Mountains

Dahnã, ad-, Arabian desert, 30 by 400 mi (50 by 640 km) A-521, S-52b, *map* A-522

Dahl, Anders D. (1751–89), Swedish botanist and friend of Linné, under whom he studied; the dahlia is named for him.

Dahlgren, John Adolf (1809–70), admiral, born in Philadelphia, Pa.; blockaded Charleston during Civil War; inventor of smoothbore Dahlgren gun.

Dahlia, flower of the family Compositae D-3, G-21

Dahomey. *see in index* Benin, People's Republic of

Dail Eireann, name formerly applied to Irish Republican Parliament, now to lower house (House of Representatives) of Ireland's legislature.

'Daily News', newspaper founded by Charles Dickens D-137

Daimler, Gottlieb (1834–1900), German inventor and power automobile builder, born in Württemberg A-858, T-246, *profile* A-856
internal-combustion engine I-252

Daingerfield, Elliott (1859–1932), figure and landscape painter, born in Harpers Ferry, W.Va. ('Slumbering Fog', 'The Child of Mary'; mural paintings in Church of St. Mary the Virgin, New York, N.Y.).

Dairen, (Chinese **Talien**), People's Republic of China, seaport in Liaoning Province; in municipality of Lüta with Port Arthur; pop. 3,086,000, *map* M-84
Lüda L-328

Dairying Industry D-3. *see also in index* Butter; Cheese; Ice cream; Milk; Milk production and marketing; names of countries and states
cattle. *see in index* Cattle

farming produce F-25
machinery F-35
cheese production, *picture* W-203
cream separator, *picture* N-190

Daisy (Chrysanthemum leucanthemum), flower of Compositae family D-8
oxeye, *picture* F-224

Dakar, Senegal, capital and port, on Atlantic Ocean, at tip of Cape Verde; pop. 798,800 D-8
Senegal S-108b

Dakhla, formerly **Villa Cisneros,** Western Sahara, port on Rio de Oro Bay, the Atlantic coast; fisheries; pop. 6,532

Dakota, Indian confederacy. *see in index* Sioux

Dakota River. *see in index* James River

Dakota State College, Madison, S.D.; chartered 1881; formerly called General Beadle State College; liberal arts, education.

Dakota Wesleyan University, Mitchell, S.D.; affiliated with United Methodist church; established 1885; liberal arts, music, and teacher education.

Daladier, Édouard (1884–1970), French statesman, born in Carpentras, near Avignon; member Chamber of Deputies, elected by Radical Socialists, 1919–40; in cabinet most of this period; premier 1933, 1934, and from 1938 until invasion of France in 1940; imprisoned and tried by Vichy regime; interned in Germany 1943–45; member National Assembly 1946–58.

Dalai Lama, ruler of Tibet T-173
Buddhist god incarnation, *picture* S-78

Dalasis, monetary unit of Gambia, *table* M-428

Dalcroze, Émile Jaques-. *see in index* Jaques-Dalcroze

Dale, Sir Henry Hallett (1875–1968), English physiologist, born in London. *see also in index* Nobel Prizewinners, *table*

Dale, Richard (1756–1826), U.S. naval officer, born in Norfolk County, Va.; brilliant service with John Paul Jones on the 'Bonhomme Richard' and other ships; first to board the 'Serapis'; in merchant service to East Indies 1783–94; captain in first U.S. Navy N-104

Dale, Samuel (1772–1841), pioneer and soldier, born in Rockbridge County, Va.; frontier boyhood fitted "Big Sam" for job of government scout; fought in local Indian outbreaks; elected to first General Assembly of Alabama 1817; state made him brigadier general and named Dale County for him.

Dalecarlia ("the valleys"), picturesque forested region in Sweden; iron ore, also copper, silver, lead.

D'Alembert, Jean le Rond. *see in index* Alembert, Jean le Rond d'

Dalén, (Nils) Gustaf (1869–1937), Swedish engineer, born in Stenstorp, near Skövde; noted for invention of automatic flasher and sun valve, used in Dalén light, and of safe method for bottling acetylene gas; Dalén light, automatically enabled at dusk and extinguished at sunrise, used in unmanned lighthouses and other beacons; was blinded by an explosion during an experiment in 1912 but continued active. *see also in index* Nobel Prizewinners, *table*

Daley, Richard J. (1902–76), U.S. mayor of Chicago from 1955 to 1976, and prominent Democratic Party politician D-8
Chicago C-316

Dalgliesh, Alice (1893–1979), U.S. author and editor of children's books, born on island of Trinidad; to U.S. 1911, became citizen 1928 ('America Travels'; 'The Columbus Story'; 'The Fourth of July Story'; 'America Begins'; 'Adam and the Golden Cock') R-105
illustration from 'A Book for Jennifer,' *picture* N-161

Dalhousie, George Ramsay, 9th earl of (1770–1838), British soldier, one of Wellington's generals in Peninsular War and at Waterloo; lieutenant governor of Nova Scotia 1816–20; governor-general of Canada 1820–28; founded Dalhousie College.

Dalhousie, James Ramsay, 10th earl and first marquis of (1812–60), one of the builders of British Indian Empire; governor-general 1849–56; annexed Punjab and other native states; established imperial telegraph and postal systems; built first railroad, completed Ganges Canal, and many other public works.

Dalhousie, N.B., Canada, port town in n., at mouth of Restigouche River, 22 km (14 mi) n.e. of Campbellton; newsprint milling, lumbering, fishing, pop. 6,255, *map* N-163

Dalhousie University, Halifax, N.S., Canada; founded as Dalhousie College in 1818 by the 9th earl of Dalhousie, became a university 1841; arts and sciences (including commerce, education, engineering, music, nursing, pharmacy), dentistry, law, medicine; graduate studies N-373f

Dali, Salvador (born 1904), Spanish painter D-9
motion pictures M-523
'Persistence of Memory, The' P-60

Dalin, Olof von (1708–63), Swedish journalist, poet, and historian; tutor 1750–56 to crown prince (later Gustavus III); inspired by Addison, Swift, and Pope, introduced English influence into Swedish literature ('History of the Swedish Kingdom'; 'The Story of the Horse', satirical poem; 'Swedish Liberty', epic).

Dallas, Alexander James (1759–1817), born on island of Jamaica; U.S. secretary of treasury 1814–16 under Madison; found government bankrupt, left surplus of $20,000,000; Henry Adams says he "fixed the financial system in a firm groove for twenty years."

Dallas, George Mifflin (1792–1864), statesman, son of Alexander J., born in Philadelphia, Pa.; served as U.S. senator, attorney general of Pennsylvania, minister to Russia, minister to England 1856–61; Dallas, Tex., named for him
elected vice-president P-438

Dallas, Tex., 2d largest city of state; pop. 904,078 D-9, T-113, *map* U-41
Southern Methodist University, *picture* U-204 zoo, *picture* Z-361c

'Dallas', television show D-11

Dallas, University of, Irving, Tex.; Roman Catholic; opened 1956; liberal arts and teacher education; graduate program D-10

Dallas Baptist College, Dallas, Tex.; chartered 1898; present name adopted 1965; liberal arts, education, nursing, theology D-10

Dallas Market Center and World Trade Center, building complex, Dallas Tex. D-10

Dalles, or **dells,** river rapids in a gorge or canyon; term used also for a rocky-walled gorge Wisconsin River, *picture* W-196

Dalles, The, Ore., port on Columbia River, 82 mi (132 km) e. of Portland; cherries, fruit and grain crops, livestock; fruit packing; aluminum; site of The Dalles Dam; pop. 10,820, *map* O-193

Dalles Dam, The, Oregon and Washington, on Columbia River; built of concrete and earth; 300 ft (90 m) high; 8,875 ft (2705 m) long O-481, *maps* O-480, 493, W-39, 52

Dallin, Cyrus Edwin (1861–1944), sculptor, born in Springville, Utah; known for monumental statues of Indians with lean, starkly impressive figures ('Appeal to the Great Spirit'), *picture* U-226

Dalling and Bulwer, William Henry Lytton Earle Bulwer, Baron, better known as Sir Henry Lytton (1801–72), English diplomat, born in London; served in

Dallis / Daniels

Constantinople (now Istanbul), Turkey; Madrid, Spain; Florence, Italy; Washington, D.C; concluded Clayton-Bulwer Treaty with U.S.

Dallis grass, a perennial grass (*Paspalum dilatatum*) used for pasture in southern U.S.; native to South America; grows on low ground, prairie or marsh; silky hairs on spikelets of the one-sided flower clusters; also called water grass, paspalum, and water paspalum.

Dall's porpoise D-224

Dalmatia, Yugoslavia, region bordering Adriatic Sea; 12,732 sq km (4916 sq mi) Y-350

Dalmatian, dog, *picture* D-206

Dalmatians, Slavic people S-214

Dalmatica, garment D-261

Dalou, Jules (1838–1902), French sculptor, born in Paris; during the Commune of Paris (1871), took refuge in England and was influential in development of English sculpture; monumental works, including 'The Triumph of the Republic' in the Place de la Nation, Paris.

Dalriada, name of two ancient Gaelic kingdoms, one in Northern Ireland (in County Antrim) and the other in Scotland (in Argyllshire); united with n. kingdom of Picts A.D. 843.

Dal River, Swedish **Dalälven,** central Sweden, rises on Norwegian frontier, flows s.e. and n.e. 400 km (250 mi); enters Gulf of Bothnia, *map* S-524

Dalton, John (1766–1844), English chemist and physicist, born in Eaglesfield, near Cockermouth; mathematics and physics teacher at Manchester 1793–99
- chemistry C-301
- Daltonism (color blindness) E-370
- law of gases G-37

Dalton, Ga., city 75 mi (120 km) n.w. of Atlanta; dairying, poultry, cotton, grain area; tufted carpets and other textiles, wood products; headquarters of Gen. Joseph E. Johnston, defending Atlanta 1863–64; pop. 20,743, *map* G-92

Dalton's law, concerning gases G-37

Daly, John Augustin (1838–99), dramatist and theatrical manager, born in Plymouth, N.C.; organized Shakespearean company headed by Ada Rehan; managed John Drew, Fanny Davenport, Maude Adams.

Daly, Marcus (1842–1900), miner, born in Ireland; came to New York about 1856; made fortune in West; called "copper king" M-462

Daly, Thomas Augustine (1871–1948), poet and journalist, born in Philadelphia, Pa.; associate editor 'Philadelphia Record' 1918–29; columnist 'Philadelphia Evening Bulletin' after 1929 ('McAroni Medleys').

Daly City, Calif., residential city just s. of San Francisco; dairy and truck farms, flowers; merged with old town of Colma 1936; pop. 78,519.

Dam, (Carl Peter) Henrik (1895–1976), Danish biochemist, born in Copenhagen; taught at University of Copenhagen 1923–41; discovered vitamin K (first announced 1935); lectured in U.S. and Canada 1940–41, 1949; did research in U.S. 1942–45; returned to Copenhagen 1946 to serve as professor of biochemistry and head of biology department (now department of biochemistry and nutrition) at Polytechnic Institute, emeritus 1965. *see also in index* Nobel Prizewinners, *table*

Dam, zoology and animal husbandry, a mother animal; used particularly of mammals; in contrast to "sire," a father animal
- cattle C-224

Dam, engineering D-11. *see table* following. *see also in index* Dike; Levee; Waterpower; and individual dams by name
- Akosombo, Ghana G-121
- Aswan, Egypt E-108
  - Aswan High Dam A-662, A-732, N-290
- barrage
  - Indus P-78
  - Nile E-110
- beaver's life-style B-121
- Bonneville. *see in index* Bonneville Dam
- Buffalo Bill, Wyo. W-318, *maps* W-326, *picture* W-316
- Daniel Johnson, Canada Q-9e
- Davis, Ariz.–Nev., *maps* N-144, 157, *picture* N-155
- Denison, Okla.–Tex. T-112, *maps* O-435, T-128, *picture* O-434
- Dnieper. *see in index* Dnieper Dam
- Elephant Butte. *see in index* Elephant Butte Dam
- Falcon, Tex.–Mexico R-209, T-112, *map* T-129, *picture* T-116
- flood cause F-182, *table* F-181
- flood control E-51, F-184, M-392
- Fort Peck, Mont. M-458, *maps* M-414, 460, 471
- Gallipolis, Ohio–W.Va., *picture* O-412
- Garrison, N.D. M-413, N-341
- Gatun, Panama P-91
- Grand Coulee. *see in index* Grand Coulee Dam
- Heart Butte, N.D., *map* N-340, *picture* N-343
- Hoover. *see in index* Hoover Dam
- Hungry Horse, Mont., *map* M-460
- irrigation dams I-354
- Kuybyshev, Russia, *picture* V-383
- Madden, Panama P-91, *map* P-90
- Mississippi River M-392
- Missouri River M-413.
  - Pick-Sloan plan on Missouri River M-414
- Norris, Tenn., *maps* T-97, 100, *picture* T-83
- Ohio River O-432
- Owen Falls. *see in index* Owen Falls Dam
- Owyhee, Ore., *map* O-493
- Roosevelt. *see in index* Theodore Roosevelt Dam
- St. Lawrence Seaway S-20, *picture* U-51
- spillway, *picture* U-91
- Tennessee Valley Authority T-99, *diagram* T-100
- tidal W-77a
- Waikato River, N.Z. N-276
- Wheeler, Ala., *map* T-100
- Wilson (Muscle Shoals), Ala. A-208, *map* T-100

Daman, or **Damão,** India. *see in index* Goa, Daman, and Diu

Damanhur, or **Hermopolis Parva,** Lower Egypt, railroad center 38 mi (61 km) s.e. of Alexandria; textiles; ancient Timenhor (town of Horus) pop. 126,100.

Damascus, or **Esh Sham,** Syria, capital and chief city; pop. 1,202,000 D-18
- Islam M-421
- medieval banner, *picture* M-294
- metalwork M-308
- modern city, *picture* S-550

Damask, a reversible, figured fabric, named for Damascus, where it was first woven in silk; now woven also in linen, rayon, cotton, wool, or combinations; flatter than brocade; table damask and drapery and upholstery damask are two types
- Damascus D-18

Damask rose R-294

Damavand, Mount, highest point (18,934 ft; 5770 m) in Iran, in Elburz Range, n.e. of Tehran; permanently snow-capped volcanic cone.

'Dame aux camélias, La'. *see in index* 'Camille'

Dame's violet. *see in index* Sweet rocket

Damien, Father Joseph de Veuster (1840–89), Belgian priest, born in Tremeloo, near Brussels; missionary to lepers of Molokai, Hawaiian Islands; organized sanitation, schools, industry, and worship; died of leprosy, *picture* H-66
- Statuary Hall, *table* S-437a

Damietta, Egypt, port city, trade center on branch of Nile, 100 mi (160 km) n.e. of Cairo; ancient city bulwark of Egypt against Crusaders; pop. 77,200, *map* E-109

Dammar, resin R-158

Damocles (4th century B.C.), courtier of Dionysius, ruler of Syracuse (Sicily), who taught him the uncertainty of a king's life by seating him under a sword that hung by a single horsehair; hence the expression "sword of Damocles" to denote uncertainty and danger.

Damon and Pythias, Latin story of friendship D-19

Dampier, William (1652–1715), English adventurer and explorer, born in East Coker, near Yeovil; took part in buccaneering expeditions along coast of South and Central America (1679–81); commanded an expedition to the South Seas (1699–1701); discoveries include Dampier Archipelago and Dampier Strait
- Australian exploration A-815

Dampier Archipelago, group of high rocky islands off n.w. coast of Australia; chief islands include Enderby, Legendre, Dolphin, Rosmary, Lewis, and Delambre, *map* A-820

Damping-off, fatal disease of young plants caused by parasitic fungi; controlled by sterilization of soil and plant seeds, and minimization of moisture.

Damrosch, Leopold (1832–85), American musician, born in Germany; founder of German opera in New York, N.Y.; father of Walter Damrosch
- Damrosch, Walter D-19

Damrosch, Walter (Johannes) (1862–1950), American musician D-19
- operas O-464a

Damselfish, fish, member of the family Pomacentridae; found along coral reefs F-128

Damsel fly, insect, member of the family Odonata D-238

Damson plum P-392

Dan, one of the 12 tribes of Israel, named for the first of two sons born to Jacob (also called Israel) and Bilhah (Gen. xxx, 6).

Dan, ancient town in n. Palestine, at head of the Jordan; settled by descendants of Dan; "from Dan to Beersheba," from one end of Palestine to the other.

Dana, Charles Anderson (1819–97), journalist, born in Hinsdale, N.H.; member of Brook Farm; associated with Greeley as editor of 'New York Tribune'; assistant secretary of war during Civil War; later editor of 'New York Sun', on which he impressed his strong, concise style; an important influence in development of American journalism.

Dana, Francis (1743–1811), jurist, born in Charlestown, Mass.; member Continental Congress 1776–78, 1784–85; chief justice Massachusetts Supreme Court 1791–1806.
- envoy to Russia A-35

Dana, James Dwight (1813–95), geologist, mineralogist, and zoologist D-19

Dana, John Cotton (1856–1929), librarian, born in Woodstock, Vt.; introduced radical innovations in libraries; emphasized book service rather than storage; founded first business department and first picture collection; head Newark (N.J.) library 1902–29; founded Newark museum.

Dana, Richard Henry, Jr. (1815–82), jurist and author, grandson of Francis Dana, born in Cambridge, Mass.; wrote 'Two Years Before the Mast', classic sea story; later distinguished as jurist and international lawyer; 'Autobiographical Sketch (1815–1842)' published 1953 G-172

Dana, William H. (born 1930), engineer and test pilot, born Pasadena, Calif.; NASA research pilot in projects including X-15 and lifting body programs.

Dana College, Blair, Neb.; affiliated with American Lutheran church; founded 1884; arts and sciences, business administration, music, and teacher education.

Danaë, Greek mythology, mother of Perseus P-210

Danaides, Greek mythology, the 50 daughters of Danaüs, king of Libya, doomed to fill sieves with water throughout eternity for killing their husbands at their father's command.

Da Nang, or **Tourane,** Vietnam, port city on South China Sea; air base; pop. 492,194 V-323

Danbury, Conn., city 20 mi (30 km) n.w. of Bridgeport; diversified manufacture; Western Connecticut State College; Federal Correctional Institute; settled 1684; pop. 60,470.

Dance D-20. *see also in index* Ballet
- ancient, *picture* E-122
- art forms A-661
- Astaire's choreographed movies A-705
- ballet B-32
- bibliography H-182
- children. *see in index* Children
- folk dance F-255
  - American Indians I-118, *picture* I-130
  - Bali, *picture* E-42
  - Hawaii, hula H-57
  - India I-72, *picture* I-73
  - Indonesia I-160
  - New Zealand N-277
  - Russia R-332g, *picture* B-30
  - Scotland, *picture* S-70
  - Slavic, *picture* S-215
  - Thailand, *picture* T-144
  - Tibet, *picture* T-172
- Muse M-550
- musical comedy M-567a
- suite C-268

Dance of death, medieval rite D-26

Dance Theatre of Harlem, first all-black ballet company D-29

'Dancer with a Fan', painting by Degas, *picture* D-65

'Dancing Master, The', work by Pierre Rameau D-27

Dandelion (*Taraxacum officinale*), flowering herb of composite family D-32, *picture* W-92a
- flower classification F-218

Dandie Dinmont terrier, dog, *picture* D-203

Dandruff, skin disorder that affects the scalp H-5

Dane, Clemence, pen name of Winifred Ashton (1887?–1965), English writer; first novel, 'Regiment of Women', published 1917 (other novels: 'Broome Stages', 'The Flower Girls'; dramas: 'A Bill of Divorcement', inspired by English divorce law, and 'Will Shakespeare', in blank verse).

Danegeld, a tax levied in England 10th to 12th centuries; originated as a tribute to the Danes.

Danelaw, or **Danelagh,** territory in e. England ceded to Danes by Alfred the Great E-231

Danes, a Teutonic people living in Denmark S-52g
- invasion of England E-231

Danger Cave culture, prehistoric Indians I-144

'Dangling Man', work by Bellow B-157

Daniel, Hebrew prophet, central figure of the Book of Daniel; explained Nebuchadnezzar's dreams; interpreted handwriting on the wall seen by Belshazzar P-508, *picture* P-509
- folklore F-263

Daniel, Saint Antoine (1601–48), Canadian Jesuit missionary, born in Dieppe, France; went to Canada with Samuel de Champlain 1633; worked among the Hurons and established school for Indian boys; murdered by Iroquois.

Daniel, Samuel (1562–1619), English poet and historian, born near Taunton; his verse praised for grace and tender feeling (sonnet series to Delia; 'Complaynt of Rosamond'; prose history of England) E-273

'Daniel Deronda', George Eliot's last novel; story of a young Jew, reared a Christian, unaware of his Jewish ancestry, who returns to his own people E-182

Daniel Johnson Dam, Quebec, Canada, on Manicouagan River Q-9e

Daniell, John Frederick (1790–1845), English physicist born in London; inventor of a primary electric (Daniell) cell still in use, of a pyrometer, and other instruments B-108

Daniell cell, for generating electric current B-108, *picture* B-107

Daniels, Jonathan Worth (born 1902), author, son of Josephus Daniels, born in Raleigh, N.C.; editor 'Raleigh News and Observer';

DAMS AND RESERVOIRS IMPORTANT IN THE WORLD

Name	Location	Type*	Purpose†	Year Completed‡	Height in Feet	Length in Feet	Material in Dam (Cubic Yards)	Reservoir Capacity (Billions of Gallons)
HIGHEST DAMS								
Rogunsky	Soviet Union	E	P-I	UC	1,066	2,506	81,096,000	3,091
Nurek	Soviet Union	E	P-I	UC	1,040	2,390	75,864,000	2,745
Grande Dixence	Switzerland	CG	P	1962	935	2,280	7,792,000	106
Inguri	Soviet Union	A	P-I-FC	UC	892	2,513	4,967,000	261
Vaiont	Italy	A	...	1961	858	624	460,000	...
Mica	Canada	ER	P-FC	1974	794	2,600	42,000,000	6,517
Sayano-Shushenskaya	Soviet Union	A	P-N	UC	794	3,504	11,916,000	8,261
Chicoasen	Mexico	ER	P	UC	787	1,568	15,700,000	439
Patia	Colombia	R	P-I-FC-WS	UC	787	1,804	30,869,000	4,993
Chivor	Colombia	ER	P	1977	778	919	14,126,000	215
Mauvoisin	Switzerland	CA	P	1957	777	1,706	2,655,000	48
Oroville	California	E	P-I-FC-WS	1968	770	6,920	78,008,000	1,153
Chirkeyskaya	Soviet Union	A	P-I-FC-WS	1975	764	1,109	1,602,000	734
Bhakra	India	CG	P-I	1963	742	1,700	5,400,000	2,607
Hoover (formerly Boulder)	Arizona-Nevada	CAG	P-I-FC-RR	1936	726	1,244	4,400,000	9,696
Contra	Switzerland	A	P	1965	722	1,246	861,000	23
Mratinje	Yugoslavia	A	P	1975	722	879	971,000	232
Dworshak	Idaho	G	P-FC-RP	1972	717	3,287	6,500,000	1,125
Glen Canyon	Arizona	CAG	P	1964	710	1,560	4,901,000	8,798
Toktogul	Soviet Union	A	P-I	1977	705	1,476	4,186,000	5,148
Daniel Johnson	Canada	CM	P-I	1968	703	4,311	2,950,000	37,473
Auburn	California	A	P-I	UC	700	4,000	6,000,000	758
Luzzone	Switzerland	CA	P	1963	682	1,738	1,739,000	23
Keban	Turkey	ERG	P	1974	679	3,881	20,900,000	8,182
Mohammed-Reza Shah Pahlavi (formerly Dez)	Iran	CA	P-I	1963	666	696	647,000	882
Almendra	Spain	AG	P	1970	662	1,860	2,188,000	700
Kölnbrein	Austria	A	P	1978	656	2,054	1,995,000	53
Reza Shah Kabir	Iran	A	P-I	1975	656	1,247	1,570,000	766
New Bullard's Bar	California	A	P-I-FC-RP	1970	637	2,200	2,700,000	557
New Melones	California	ER	P-I-FC-RP	1975	625	1,600	15,970,000	782
Swift	Washington	E	P	1958	610	2,100	15,800,000	246
LARGEST DAMS								
New Cornelia Tailings	Arizona	E	M	1973	98	35,600	274,026,000	6
Tarbela	Pakistan	ER	P-I	1976	470	9,000	159,200,000	3,617
Fort Peck	Montana	H	P-I-FC-N	1940	250	21,026	125,612,000	6,234
Guri (final stage)	Venezuela	ERG	P	UC	531	30,853	101,819,000	36,720
Yacyreta-Apipe	Argentina and Paraguay	EG	P-I-WS-RP	UC	108	164,000	95,063,000	4,464
Oahe	South Dakota	E	P-I-FC-N	1963	245	9,300	92,008,000	7,687
Oosterschelde	The Netherlands	E	FC-WS	UC	148			
Mangla	Pakistan	E	P-I	1967	380	11,000	85,872,000	1,678
Gardiner	Canada	E	P-I-WS	1968	223	16,700	85,743,000	2,607
Afsluitdijk	The Netherlands	E	FC-WS	1932	62	10,500	82,927,000	1,585
Rogunsky	Soviet Union	E	P-I	UC	1,066	2,506	81,096,000	3,091
Oroville	California	E	P-I-FC-WS	1968	770	6,920	78,008,000	1,153
San Luis	California	E	P-I	1967	382	18,600	77,666,000	664
Nurek	Soviet Union	E	P-I	UC	1,040	2,390	75,864,000	2,745
Garrison	North Dakota	E	P-I-FC-N	1956	203	11,300	66,506,000	7,925
Cochiti	New Mexico	E	FC-RP	1975	253	26,891	64,631,000	167
Tabka	Syria	E	P-I-FC	1975	197	14,764	60,168,000	3,698
Kiev	Soviet Union	EG	P-N	1964	72	177,448	57,552,000	984
Aswan High	Egypt	ER	P-I-RP	1970	364	12,565	57,203,000	44,642
Bennett	Canada	E	P	1967	600	6,700	57,203,000	18,575
Tucurui	Brazil	EG	P-N-WS	UC	282	13,779	56,244,000	8,982
Mission Trailings #2	Arizona	E	...	1973	128	...	52,435	15
Fort Randall	South Dakota	E	P-I-FC-N	1956	165	10,700	50,205,000	1,858
Kaney	Soviet Union	E	P	1974	82	52,950	49,520,000	692
Itumbiara	Brazil	EG	...	UC	328	21,981	47,088,000	4,499
DAMS WITH GREATEST RESERVOIRS								
Owen Falls	Uganda	CG	P-I	1954	100	2,725	...	54,091
Bratsk	Soviet Union	ECG	P-N-WS	1964	410	16,864	18,283,000	44,713
Aswan High	Egypt	ER	P-I-RP	1970	364	12,565	57,203,000	44,642
Kariba Gorge	Zambia and Rhodesia	CA	P	1959	420	2,025	1,350,000	42,361
Akosombo	Ghana	R	P	1965	463	2,100	10,400,000	39,102
Daniel Johnson	Canada	CM	P	1968	703	4,311	2,950,000	37,473
Guri (final stage)	Venezuela	ERG	P	UC	531	30,853	101,819,000	36,720
Krasnoyarsk	Soviet Union	CG	P-FC-N	1972	407	3,493	5,685,000	19,364
Bennett	Canada	E	P	1967	600	6,700	57,203,000	18,575
Zeyskaya	Soviet Union	B	P-I-FC	1975	369	2,343	3,139,000	18,069

*A—Arch B—Slab and Buttress C—Concrete E—Rolled Earth Fill G—Gravity H—Hydraulic Earth Fill
M—Multiple Arch R—Rock Fill S—Stone Masonry
†FC—Flood Control I—Irrigation M—Mining N—Navigation P—Power RP—Recreation Purposes
RR—River Regulation WS—Water Supply
‡UC—Under Construction

Daniels / Darwin

administrative assistant to President Roosevelt 1943–45 ('A Southerner Discovers New England'; 'The Man of Independence', life of Harry S. Truman; 'The End of Innocence', about Washington, D.C., during Woodrow Wilson's administration; 'Prince of Carpetbaggers', Civil War Reconstruction period; 'Stonewall Jackson').

Daniels, Josephus (1862–1948), journalist and Democratic leader, born in Washington, N.C.; editor 'Raleigh (N.C.) News and Observer' after 1894; secretary of navy 1913–21; ambassador to Mexico 1933–41 ('Our Navy at War'; 'Wilson Era'; 'Shirt-Sleeve Diplomat') *pictures* N-334, R-263

Danilova, Alexandra (born 1907), American ballerina, born in Peterhov, Russia; in U.S. after 1934; member Russian State Ballet 1922–24, later with Diaghilev ballet, Col. de Basil's Ballet Russe, Ballet Russe de Monte Carlo.

Danio, any of several species of tropical fish belonging to family Cyprinidae.

Danish language and literature S-52g. *see also in index* Scandinavian languages; Scandinavian literature

Danish modern, furniture style F-462

Dannay, Frederic. *see in index* Queen, Ellery

Dannecker, Johann Heinrich von (1758–1841), German sculptor, born in Württemberg; friend of Schiller; his work a constant struggle between classic and naturalistic schools S-89

D'Annunzio, Gabriele, prince of Montenevoso (1863–1938), Italian novelist, dramatist, and poet, born at Pescara, on Adriatic, of Dalmatian stock; given title of prince 1924 in recognition of patriotic services I-377
  Duse, Eleonora D-293
  seizure of Fiume R-207

'Danse macabre', work by Saint-Saëns M-560

Dante, or **Dante Alighieri,** (1265–1321), greatest Italian poet D-32
  angel and demon portrayal A-414
  Henry VII H-135
  Italian literature I-376, I-385
  portraits by Giotto G-127

Dantès, Edmond, hero of Alexandre Dumas's 'Count of Monte Cristo'; sailor who, condemned through conspiracy to life imprisonment, escapes, gains buried treasure, and returns to dazzle Paris as the fabulously wealthy count of Monte Cristo and to mete out special punishments to his foes.

Danton, Georges Jacques (1759–94), French revolutionary leader D-33
  French Revolution F-403
  Jacobins J-11
  Robespierre R-223

Dantzig, Tobias (1884–1956), U.S. mathematician, born in Shavli, Russia; to U.S. 1910, citizen 1917; professor mathematics University of Maryland 1926–46 ('Number, the Language of Science').

Danube River, ancient **Ister,** 2d longest river of Europe; measures 2820 km (1750 mi), from s.w. West Germany to the Black Sea C-33, *maps* B-825, E-334, G-99a, P-212, W-253
  Austria A-826
  Carpathian Mountains C-173
  Hungary H-274

Danube sheatfish, or **wels** (*Silurus glanis*), catfish C-220

Danvers, Mass., about 4 mi (6 km) n.w. of Salem; baby shoes, leather, electronic, and plastic products; state mental hospital; birthplace of Israel Putnam; home of John Greenleaf Whittier; pop. of township 26,151, *map* M-160
  witchcraft persecutions W-209

Danville, Ill., city on Vermilion River, in e. part of state, about 75 mi (120 km) n. of Decatur; aerosol, metal, and electrical products; hydraulic-lift trucks, apparel; home of Joseph G. Cannon, long-time Republican leader; veterans hospital nearby; pop. 38,985, *map* U-41

Danville, Ky., city about 32 mi (52 km) s.w. of Lexington; tobacco and livestock center; clothing, shoes, glass products; Kentucky School for the Deaf; Centre College of Kentucky; pop. 12,942.

Danville, Va., city near s. boundary, on Dan River, 58 mi (93 km) s.e. of Roanoke; tobacco market; tobacco processing; textile products, hosiery; Stratford College; pop. 45,642, *maps* V-331, 348, U-41

'Danza de los arcos', Mexican folkdance, *picture* F-257

Danzig, Polish **Gdansk,** Poland, a Baltic seaport on the Vistula River; pop. 364,285, *maps* E-334, P-414

Daphne, nymph in Greek mythology; pursued by Apollo, she prayed to be saved from his advances and was turned into a laurel tree L-88
  opera O-460

Daphne, a genus of plants, chiefly shrubs, of the mezereum family, native to Eurasia; some are evergreen, with uncut leaves; fragrant white, lilac, or greenish tubular flowers in clusters; juice of some used in medicine.

'Daphnis and Chloe', Greek pastoral romance by Longus; Daphnis, a boy, and Chloe, a girl, found by shepherds, grow up together, come to love each other, and in the end are happily married; basis for ballet by Ravel.

Dapsang. *see in index* K2

DAR. *see in index* Daughters of the American Revolution

Daras, Battle of, Byzantine Empire defeats Persians in 528 B-534

D'Arblay, Frances. *see in index* Burney, Fanny

Darby, Pa., borough on Darby Creek, just w. of Philadelphia; textile mills; metal and wood products; one of oldest boroughs in state, settled 1660 pop. 13,729, *map* P-185

Darby, Abraham, English engineer B-445

Darby and Joan, John Darby (died 1730) and his wife, Joan, originals of hero and heroine of Henry Woodfall's ballad 'Darby and Joan' or 'The Happy Old Couple'.

Dardanelles, or **Hellespont,** narrow stait separating Europe from Asia D-35, *maps* G-221, E-335, T-299
  Alexander, *map* M-7
  Hero and Leander H-146
  Xerxes' bridge of ships P-215
  World War I W-254

Dare, Virginia (1587–?), first child born of English parents in America N-327

Dar el Beida, Morocco. *see in index* Casablanca

Dar es-Salaam, Tanzania, capital and seaport on Indian Ocean; pop. of greater city 769,445, region 851,522 D-35, T-16–17

Dargomyzhski, Aleksandr Sergeevich (1813–69), Russian composer, born in Tula, Russia; associated with Glinka as a leader of Russian national school; composed for orchestra and stage; influenced by Wagner ('Esmeralda'; 'The Stone Guest'; 'The Mermaid') M-560

Dari, Persian dialect A-89

Darien, Conn., residential community on Long Island Sound, in s.w. of state; incorporated 1820; pop. of township 20,411.

Darien, Gulf of, gulf of Caribbean Sea between Colombia and Republic of Panama.

Darien, Isthmus of, old name for Isthmus of Panama. *see in index* Panama, Isthmus of

Darien Scheme, unsuccessful attempt to establish Scottish colony on Isthmus of Panama (Darien) and attain a free trade route to the Pacific, headed by William Paterson; settlement begun 1698; Spanish opposition, starvation, and disease led to abandonment of project 1700.

Darío, Rubén (1867–1916), Nicaraguan poet D-35, L-69, *picture* L-72
  Jiménez J-118
  monument M-81, *picture* N-283

Darius I, the Great, surnamed Hystaspes (550–486 B.C.), king of Persia D-36, P-211
  audience hall, *picture* I-308
  Behistun Rock carvings A-537, *picture* P-214

Darius II (died 404 B.C.), king of Persia, son of Artaxerxes I; ruled 423–404 B.C.; a weak ruler; many uprisings during his reign.

Darius III (380?–330 B.C.), last king of the ancient Persian Empire; ruled six years; brave and handsome A-279, P-212

Darjeeling, India, health resort in n. West Bengal state; produces quinine; famous for mountain scenery; sanatorium for British soldiers in 19th century; pop. 42,873 I-82, *picture* I-77

Dark, Eleanor (born 1901), Australian novelist with flair for psychological analysis, born in Sydney (historical novels about Australia 'The Timeless Land' and 'Storm of Time').

Dark Ages, history H-160, W-247, *Reference-Outline* M-304. *see also in index* Middle Ages

Dark chocolate, sweet made with cocoa butter, chocolate liquor and finely powdered sugar C-394

Dark horse, American politics, a term applied to a comparatively unknown man brought forward in a nominating convention as a compromise candidate; Presidents Polk, Pierce, Hayes, Garfield, and Harding were dark horses.

Dark-line, or **absorption, spectrum** S-371, *diagram* S-372

Darkling beetle, any beetle of the family Tenebrionidae, which includes meal worms, flour beetles, and many other species occurring under stones, in dead wood, fungi, and dry vegetable products; most species are black or brown.

'Darkness at Noon', by Arthur Koestler R-111i

Darkroom. *see in index* Photography, darkroom techniques in

Dark stars S-412

Darlan, Jean Louis Xavier François (1881–1942), French naval officer and political leader, born in Nérac; commander in chief French naval forces 1939; vice-premier 1941–42; first in line of succession to chief of state of Vichy government; made head of land, sea, and air forces April 1942; deserted Vichy government to become chief of state for Allies in North Africa; assassinated.

Darley, Felix Octavius Carr (1822–88), illustrator and historical painter, born in Philadelphia, Pa.; illustrated Irving's 'Sketch Book' and Lossing's 'History of the United States'; made notable banknote vignettes; published 'Sketches Abroad with Pen and Pencil'.
  'Legend of Sleepy Hollow, The' A-346

Darley, George (1795–1846), Irish poet, born in Dublin; best known for fairy opera 'Sylvia' and for poem 'Nepenthe'.

Darley Arabian, horse, foundation sire of Thoroughbred Horse H-232e, *list* H-232a

Darling, Esther Birdsall (1879–1965), author, born in Marietta, Ohio; lived in Nome, Alaska, 1907–17; bred Alaskan sled dogs ('Baldy of Nome'; 'Navarre of the North').

Darling, Grace Horsley (1815–42), English heroine, born in Bamborough, near Alnwick.

Darling, Jay Norwood (J. N. Ding) (1876–1962), cartoonist, born in Norwood, Mich.; cartoonist 'New York Tribune' (later 'New York Herald Tribune') 1917–49; won Pulitzer prize for cartoons 1923 and 1942.

Darling Range, low mountains in w. Australia, running parallel with s.w. coast for nearly 400 km (250 mi); highest peak Mount Cooke, 580 m (1,910 ft).

Darling River, Australia, rises in Queensland, flows s.w. through New South Wales, joins Murray; length 1870 km (1160 mi) A-769

Darlington, England, city 29 km (18 mi) s. of Durham; iron and steel manufactures and locomotive works; Stockton and Darlington Railway opened 1825 pop. 84,700, *map* G-199h

Darmstadt, West Germany, manufacturing and railroad city 30 km (20 mi) s. of Frankfurt; pop. 141,224, *map* G-115
  Holbein's 'Madonna' H-201

Darnel. *see in index* Rye grass; Tare

Darning needle. *see in index* Dragonfly

Darnley, Henry Stuart, Lord (1545?–67), Scottish noble, 2d husband of Mary, queen of Scots, born in Temple Newsam, Yorkshire M-122

Darrow, Clarence Seward (1857–1938), U.S. lawyer D-36, R-271. *see also in index* Scopes trial
  'Clarence Darrow for the Defense' R-111j

D'Arsonval, Jacques Arsène. *see in index* Arsonval, Jacques Arsène d'

D'Arsonval galvanometer E-147
  instrumentation I-230

D'Artagnan. *see in index* Artagnan, Charles d'

Darter, a group of small freshwater fishes of the perch family found only in America; brilliantly colored; has no air bladder.

Darter, a waterbird of the family Anhingidae found in Asia, Africa, Australia, and the s. U.S.; American species. (*Anhinga anhinga*) also called the snakebird or water turkey; like cormorant in habits.

Dartford, England, picturesque market town of Kent, about 25 km (15 mi) s.e. of London; one of first paper mills in England (1590); traversed by Roman road, Watling Street; pop. 46,280, *map* G-199h

Dart leader, atmospheric discharge L-207, *diagram* L-208

Dartmoor, rugged tableland in s.w. Devon, England; 50 sq km (20 sq mi); height 621 m (2039 ft), *map* B-341

Dartmoor Prison, near Princetown, in w. Dartmoor, England; built 1809 for French captives during Napoleonic Wars; American prisoners of war also held here during War of 1812; at end of war delayed release of prisoners brought on rebellion (April 1815) in which several Americans were killed; later used for convicts and, in World War I, for conscientious objectors.

Dartmouth, England, seaport in Devon, near mouth of Dart River; here Crusaders embarked for Holy Land 1190; Britannia Royal Naval College; pop. 7,190, *map* G-199h

Dartmouth, Mass., 7 mi (11 km) s.w. of New Bedford; settled 1650, incorporated 1664; fisheries; pop. of township 23,966, *map* M-161

Dartmouth, N.S., Canada, industrial and residential city on Halifax Harbor, opposite city of Halifax; pop. 65,341 (1976 census) N-373

Dartmouth College, Hanover, N.H.; private control; formerly for men; chartered 1769; arts and sciences; graduate school of medicine, civil engineering, business administration; originated as Indian school at Lebanon, Conn. U-207

Dartmouth College Case, famous case decided by U.S. Supreme Court 1819; legislature of New Hampshire tried to alter charter of Dartmouth College; decision was that charter was a contract which, according to Constitution, no state could alter, *list* S-518b
  Webster, Daniel W-91

Darts, game D-37

Darwen, England, municipal borough 31 km (19 mi) n.w. of Manchester; cotton goods, paper, fireclay products; pop. 28,500, *map* G-199h

Darwin, Charles Robert (1809–82), English biologist D-37
  animal experimentation A-449
  cats and red clover N-76
  atoll formation P-13
  biogeography B-217
  biological concepts B-229
  botany and evolution B-380
  civilization's progress C-467
  Darwin, Australia D-39

Darwin / Davies

evolutionary theory. *see in index* Darwinism
Galápagos visit G-4
Huxley H-282
interdependency E-46

Darwin, Erasmus (1731–1802), English physician, naturalist, poet; grandfather of Charles Darwin.

Darwin, Sir Francis (1848–1925), English botanist, born in Down, Kent; son of Charles Darwin; was assistant to his father; later became distinguished through his work in physiology of plants.

Darwin, Sir George Howard (1845–1912), English geologist and astronomer, born in Down, Kent; son of Charles Darwin.

Darwin, Sir Horace (1851–1928), English scientist and inventor, born in Down, Kent; son of Charles Darwin; designed instruments for recording earthquake shocks, for measuring growth of small plants.

Darwin, Leonard (1850–1943), English economist, son of Charles Darwin; served in Royal Engineers 1871–90, winning rank of major; wrote on bimetallism and municipal trade.

Darwin, Australia, seaport, capital of Northern Territory; air and naval base; pop. 56,482 (1981 census) D-39, A-773, N-355

Darwinism, evolutionary theory of Charles Darwin E-345, G-4,43b. *see also in index* Darwin, Charles
effect on zoology Z-365
Lamarck's theories superseded L-25

Daryainoor, diamond, *picture* D-129

Das, Chitta Ranjan (1870–1925), Indian nationalist leader, born in Calcutta; active in Swaraj movement; first mayor of Calcutta 1924.

Dasent, Sir George Webbe (1817–96), English author, born in island of St. Vincent, British West Indies; his translations of Scandinavian folklore especially appealing to children ('Gisli the Outlaw') S-472

Dash, mark of punctuation P-534

Dashboard. *see in index* Instrument panel

Dasheen, a broad-leaved plant of the arum family, a variety of Polynesian taro (*Colocasia esculenta*); cultivated chiefly for its edible bulbs, which resemble the potato in food quality; introduced into the United States from Puerto Rico, grown commercially in the South.

Da Silva, Antonio José (1705-39), Brazilian writer L-72

Dasyure, marsupial, genus *Dasyurus,* found in Australia; lives in trees; carnivorous; size of small house cat, snout pointed, fur short and spotted, tail long and bushy; habits like those of weasel C-213.

Data, material processed by a computer C-627

Data bank, or **data base,** collection of information C-627

Data processing, operations involving computers and certain other devices whereby unorganized information is handled, organized according to preplanned procedure, stored, and presented for use C-627
telemetry T-54. *see also in index* Telemetry

Date line, international, *maps* T-179, P-4–5

Date palm, tree P-81, *picture* P-82

Dates, fruit of date palm F-430
characteristics B-178

Dating, radiocarbon M-73

Dating, radiometric G-62

Datta, Michael Madhusudan (1824-73), English dramatist
Indian literature I-108

Datura, a genus of annual or perennial plants, shrubs, and trees of the nightshade family, found in most parts of the world; includes jimsonweed, or thorn apple, and angel's trumpet; horn of plenty (*D. metel*) has large flowers, 18 cm (7 in.) long, white within, violet outside, trumpet-shaped, fragrant, sometimes with several trumpets, one within another.

Daubigny, Charles François (1817–78), French landscape painter and etcher of Barbizon School, born in Paris; first pictures realistic landscapes; later work shows influence of impressionism.

Da'ud, Ibn (died 910), Islamic author I-365

Daudet, Alphonse (1840–97), French novelist D-40, F-397

Daudet, Léon (1867–1942), French literary critic, novelist, and polemical writer, born in Paris; son of Alphonse Daudet; a leader of Royalist party and one of founders of its organ, 'Action Française'; most of his work reflects his vehement personality; his 'Souvenirs' depicts with gentle irony modern political and literary life.

Daugavpils, also **Dvinsk,** Latvian S.S.R., city in s.e.; railroad center; linen and flax; sawmills; pop. 101,000, *maps* E-335, R-344, 348

Daugherty, Harry Micajah (1860–1941), lawyer, born in Washington Court House, Ohio; served as campaign manager for President Harding and as U.S. attorney general in his administration H-29

Daugherty, James Henry (1889–1974), illustrator and author, born in Asheville, N.C.; illustrated Washington Irving's 'Knickerbocker's History of New York' and other books; wrote and illustrated children's books ('Daniel Boone', awarded Newbery Medal 1940; 'Abraham Lincoln'; 'Of Courage Undaunted'; 'Marcus and Narcissa Whitman'; 'William Blake') R-107

Daughters of the American Revolution (DAR) P-140
Harrison, Caroline Scott W-148

Daughters of the Confederacy, United, patriotic organization composed of female relatives and descendants of Confederate Civil War veterans; founded 1894 at Nashville, Tenn.

Daughters of the Founders and Patriots of America P-140

Daughters of the King, a religious organization of women and girls in the Anglican church corresponding to the Brotherhood of St. Andrew; senior and junior departments; founded 1885 in New York, N.Y.; chapters in England, Canada.

Daughters of the Revolution P-140

D'Aulnoy, or **D'Aunoy,** comtesse. *see in index* Aulnoy

Daumet, Pierre Jérôme Honoré (1826–1911), French architect, born in Paris; noted for restoring monuments of French architecture (Palais de Justice, Paris; Château de Chantilly).

Daumier, Honoré (1808–79), French caricaturist, painter, and sculptor D-40
drawing D-254
painting P-50

Dauphin, title of obscure origin; probably at first a proper name; borne first by Guigue IV (died 1142), dauphin of Viennois; the territory held by the Dauphin became known as Dauphiné; after 1364 title given to eldest son of French king, Dauphiné having become crown land
Charles VII C-277

Dauphin, Man., Canada, town on Vermilion River, 235 km (145 mi) n.w. of Winnipeg; grain elevators, flour mills; just n. of Ridge Mountain National Park; pop. 8,971, *map* M-89i

Dauphiné, former province in s.e. France; cap. Grenoble; site of Dauphiné Alps, range with greatest height (4103 m; 13,462 ft).

Dausset, Jean (born 1916), French biologist. *see also in index* Nobel Prizewinners, *table*

Davao, Philippines, port city on Gulf of Davao, s.e. coast of Mindanao; capital of Davao province; trade in abaca and copra; pop. 278,600, with suburbs; P-257a, *maps* P-4, P-253c, 261d

Daveluy, Paule (born 1919), French-Canadian author, born in Ville-Marie, s.w. Que.; won Canadian Books of the Year for Children award 1960 for 'L'Été Enchanté' and 1963 for 'Drôle d'Automne'.

Davenant, Sir William (1606–68), poet and playwright, born in Oxford, England; knighted 1643 by Charles I for fighting at siege of Gloucester; imprisoned, 1650–52; freed, it is said, through influence of Milton, whom he in turn helped after Restoration; buried in Westminster Abbey ('The Wits', comedy; 'Gondibert', epic poem) P-402

Davenport, Charles Benedict (1866–1944), biologist, born in Stamford, Conn.; after 1904 director Carnegie Institution laboratory for experimental evolution at Cold Spring Harbor, N.Y.; made important contributions to the study of genetics.

Davenport, Edward Loomis (1816–77), actor, born in Boston, Mass.; father of Fanny Davenport; known for characters from Shakespeare and Dickens (Brutus in 'Julius Caesar'; Bill Sikes in 'Oliver Twist').

Davenport, Fanny Lily Gypsy (1850–98), American actress, born in London, England; starred in comic and tragic roles under management of Augustin Daly; greatest success in 'Fedora', 'Tosca', and 'Cleopatra'.

Davenport, Homer Calvin (1867–1912), caricaturist, born in Silverton, Ore.; remembered for his political cartoons; originated brutish giants to represent trusts and the dollar-marked suit of Mark Hanna
McKinley cartoon, *picture* S-364

Davenport, John (1597–1670), Puritan divine, born in Coventry, England; left England after ecclesiastical disagreements; one of founders of New Haven, Conn., where he was minister for 30 years N-185.

Davenport, Thomas (1802–51), inventor, born in Williamstown, Vt. S-488, *pictures* V-291, 296

Davenport, Ia., city in e. part of state, on Mississippi River, opposite Rock Island, Ill. (these two cities, with neighboring Moline and East Moline, Ill., known together as the Quad Cities); farm machinery, aluminum rolling, electronic equipment, metal products; meat-packing; St. Ambrose College and Marycrest College; pop. 103,264 I-290, *maps* I-294, U-41

Davey, John (1846–1923), American tree surgeon, born in Somersetshire, England; called "Father of Tree Surgery"; founded Davey Tree Expert Co. T-259

David, Saint (544?–601?), patron saint of Wales, born probably in Cardiganshire; as primate of South Wales, moved seat of church government from Caerlon to Menevia; founded numerous churches.

David, king of Israel (about 1000 B.C.) D-40
Bethlehem B-179
Judaism J-149
Michelangelo M-265
Ruth R-365

David I (1084–1153), king of Scotland 1123–53, son of Malcolm Canmore and Saint Margaret of England; called "Maker of Scotland"; reformed courts, established many towns; promoted trade, shipping, and manufactures.

David II (1324–71), king of Scotland, crowned 1331 at death of father, Robert Bruce; began to rule 1341; weak and inefficient.

David, Edgeworth (Tannatt William Edgeworth David) (1858–1934), Australian explorer, born near Cardiff, Wales; geology professor University of Sydney 1891–1924; one of two members of Shackleton's expedition 1907–09 who located south magnetic pole.

David, Edward E(mil), Jr. (born 1925), electrical engineer, born in Wilmington, N.C.; director of Office of Science and Technology 1971–.

David, Félicien César (1810–76), French composer, born in Cadenet, near Avignon; called "the musical Orientalist"; wandered for years in East; wrote vivid pieces, including symphonic ode, 'The Desert'; oratorio, 'Moses on Sinai'; operas, 'Herculaneum' and 'Lalla Rookh'.

David, Gerard (1460?–1523), Dutch painter who lived in Bruges, Flanders; last great Flemish primitive painter.

David, Jacques-Louis (1748–1825), French painter D-41
sculptural history S-89

David, Pierre Jean (1788–1856), French sculptor; called David d'Angers from his birthplace of Angers, to distinguish him from the painter David; noted for naturalistic portrait busts and medallions (portraits of Washington, Lafayette, Jefferson, Goethe; medallion of Napoleon).

David, House of, dwindling communal religious colony in Benton Harbor, Mich.; founded 1903 by Benjamin Franklin Purnell (King Ben) (1861–1927); not associated with any other sect; in 1930 community split into House of David and Israelite City of David; members do not smoke, drink, or eat meat, and males wear beards

David, Star of. *see in index* Star of David

'David', statue by Donatello D-229

'David', statue by Michelangelo M-265

'David Balfour', by Robert Louis Stevenson, sequel to 'Kidnapped' S-446

'David Copperfield', novel by Charles Dickens N-376, D-134, *picture* D-136

'David Harum', novel by Edward Noyes Westcott (1847–98); hero a shrewd horse trader and humorous homely philosopher.

David Lipscomb College, Nashville, Tenn.; affiliated with Church of Christ; founded 1891; liberal arts and teacher education; quarter system.

Davidson, Jo (1883–1952), sculptor, born in New York, N.Y.; known for his portraits of famous people (Pershing, Clemenceau, Will Rogers, F.D. Roosevelt, John D. Rockefeller, George Bernard Shaw)
sculpture, *picture* O-442

Davidson, John (1857–1909), British poet, born in Barrhead, Scotland; deeply pessimistic, best known for ballads; wrote 'Bruce', 'Scaramouch in Naxos', fantastic plays; 'Fleet Street Eclogues'; 'Earl Lavender'.

Davidson, Randall Thomas, first **baron of Lambeth** (1848–1930), English divine, born in Edinburgh, Scotland; bishop of Rochester 1891–95; bishop of Winchester 1895–1903; archbishop of Canterbury 1903–28.

Davidson College, Davidson, N.C.; affiliated with Presbyterian church, U.S.; for men; founded 1837; liberal arts and sciences.

Davies, Arthur Bowen (1862–1928), artist of great versatility, born in Utica, N.Y.; best known as a painter; a sensitive dreamer and a mystic; for a time work showed influence of cubism; designed tapestries for Gobelin industry in France ('Maya, Mirror of Illusions'; 'Afterthoughts of Earth').

Davies, Sir John (1569–1626), English poet and statesman, born in Tisbury, near Shaftesbury; attorney general for Ireland 1609–19; speaker Irish Parliament 1613–19 (poems: 'Orchestra' and 'Nosce Teipsum').

Davies, Sir Louis Henry (1845–1924), Canadian statesman and jurist, born in Charlottetown, P.E.I.; premier Prince Edward Island 1876–82; Liberal in House of Commons 1882–1901, when he became judge of Supreme Court; minister of marine and fisheries 1896–1901.

Davies, Mary Carolyn, writer, born in Sprague, Wash.; best known for musical, wistful, sentimental verses ('Drums in Our Street', 'Youth Riding', 'Penny Show').

Davies, Robertson (born 1913), Canadian novelist,

Davies / Day

playwright, and theater critic, born in Thamesville, Ont. ('Fifth Business', novel)

Davies, Rodger Paul, U.S. ambassador to Cyprus A-704

Davies, William Henry (1871–1940), British poet, born in Newport, Monmouthshire, England, of Welsh parentage; was tramp and peddler in the U.S. and England for several years; published first book of verse at 34 ('The Soul's Destroyer'); 'The Autobiography of a Super-tramp' is account of early wanderings; in his 'Collected Poems' are lyrics of great simplicity and charm.

Dávila, Pedrarias, or **Pedro Arias de Avila** (1440?–1530), Spanish governor in Central America, born in Segovia, Spain; governed Darien (Panama) and adjacent lands 1514–26; extended tyrannical rule by founding colonies; executed Balboa for insubordination; transferred to Nicaragua 1526 D-117
  Panama P-86

Da Vinci, Leonardo. *see in index* Leonardo da Vinci

Davis, Arthur Hoey, pseudonym Steele Rudd (1868–1935), Australian humorist, born in Drayton, near Toowoomba, Queensland (stories of rural life, 'On Our Selection') A-797

Davis, Benjamin O(liver), Jr. (born 1912), U.S. Air Force officer, born in Washington, D.C.; father was first black general in U.S. Army; World War II combat pilot; became first black major general in Air Force 1959; director of airpower and organization, Air Force, 1961–65; chief of staff U.S. and UN forces in Korea 1965–66; with U.S. Department of Transportation as director of civil aviation security 1970–71 and as assistant secretary for environment, safety, and consumer affairs 1971–75 B-295

Davis, Bette (born 1908), actress, born in Lowell, Mass.; christened Ruth Elizabeth; after short, successful career on stage, entered motion pictures 1931; twice won Academy award, for 'Dangerous' (1935) and 'Jezebel' (1938); also starred in 'Of Human Bondage', 'Now, Voyager', and 'All About Eve'; autobiography, 'The Lonely Life'.

Davis, David (1815–86), jurist, born in Cecil County, Md.; justice U.S. Supreme Court 1862–77; U.S. senator 1877–83.

Davis, Dorothy Salisbury (born 1916), writer D-119

Davis, Dwight Filley (1879–1945), Republican statesman, born in St. Louis, Mo.; officer, World War I; secretary of war 1925–29; governor-general of Philippines 1929–32; established Davis Cup T-102

Davis, Elmer (Holmes) (1890–1958), writer, journalist, and news analyst (radio and television), born in Aurora, Ind.; on staff 'The New York Times' 1914–24; director Office of War Information 1942–45 (essays: 'But We Were Born Free'; novels and short stories) R-277

Davis, George (1820–96), lawyer and statesman, born in New Hanover County, N.C.; attorney general Confederate States of America 1864–65.

Davis, Glenn (born 1924), U.S. football halfback F-298

Davis, Henry Winter (1817–65), statesman, born in Annapolis, Md.; as Whig member of Congress from Maryland 1855–61, 1863–65, opposed Lincoln's policies and urged stringent reconstruction.

Davis, James John (1873–1947), public official, born in Wales; came to U.S. 1881; worked in steel mills; secretary of labor under Harding, Coolidge, Hoover; U.S. senator from Pennsylvania 1930–44; director general Loyal Order of Moose 1906–47, founder of Mooseheart Home and School.

Davis, Jefferson (1808–89), president of the Confederate States of America C-642, *picture* M-384
  Civil War C-473
  Davis, Varina D-43
  Greeley G-236
  Lee, Robert E. L-115
  presidential oath M-475
  Statuary Hall, *table* S-437b
  Stone Mountain, *picture* G-82
  White Houses of the Confederacy R-205

Davis, or **Davys, John** (1550?–1605), English navigator and Arctic explorer, born in Sandridge, near Dartmouth; discovered Davis Strait 1587 A-332
  cross-staff, *picture* N-91
  Falkland Islands explorations F-14

Davis, John William (1873–1955), lawyer and diplomat, born in Clarksburg, W.Va.; member of Congress 1911–13; solicitor general U.S. 1913–18; ambassador to Great Britain 1918–21; Democratic nominee for presidency 1924, *picture* W-122

Davis, Marguerite (1887–1967), biochemist, born in Racine, Wis. V-357

Davis, Mary Gould (1882–1956), writer of children's stories, born in Bangor, Me.; supervisor of storytelling, New York Public Library, 1922–44; editor of Books for Young People 'Saturday Review of Literature' (later 'Saturday Review') 1944–53 ('A Baker's Dozen'; 'The Truce of the Wolf'; 'Girl's Book of Verse') S-464, 481c

Davis, Miles (born 1926), U.S. trumpeter and composer D-43, J-86
  Coltrane, John C-587

Davis, Norman Hezekiah (1878–1944), statesman, born in Bedford County, Tenn.; financial adviser to government during and after World War I; assistant secretary of treasury 1919–20; undersecretary of state 1920–21; member League of Nations Financial Commission; national chairman of American Red Cross 1938–44; prominent Democrat.

Davis, Owen (1874–1956), playwright, born in Portland, Me.; nearly 200 plays; dramatized Edith Wharton's 'Ethan Frome' ('Nellie, the Beautiful Cloak Model'; 'Icebound', Pulitzer prize play 1923; 'The Nervous Wreck').

Davis, Richard Harding (1864–1916), novelist and journalist, born in Philadelphia, Pa.; war correspondent in Spanish-American, Boer, Russo-Japanese wars and World War I ('Soldiers of Fortune'; 'Van Bibber and Others'; 'The Bar Sinister').

Davis, Sam (1842–63), Confederate hero, born near Smyrna, Tenn.; hanged at Pulaski, Tenn., when captured inside Federal lines with military information; asked to betray source of information, he answered: "If I had a thousand lives to live I would lose them all before I would betray my friends or the confidence of my informer"; his statue on Capitol grounds, Nashville
  home, *picture* T-83

Davis, Sammy, Jr. (born 1925), singer, actor, and dancer; born in New York, N.Y.; star of theater, movies, and television; won 1968 Spingarn medal for civil rights work.

Davis, Stuart (1894–1964), painter, lithographer, and writer on art, born in Philadelphia, Pa.; influenced by modern art.
  'Summer Landscape' P-26, *picture* P-27

Davis, Thomas Osborne (1814–45), Irish author I-327

Davis, Varina (1826–1906), first lady of the Confederate States of America D-43

Davis, William Grenville (born 1929), Canadian public official, born in Brampton, Ont., n.w. of Toronto; premier of Ontario 1971–.

Davis, William Hammatt (1879–1964), lawyer and arbitrator, born in Bangor, Me.; administrator and national compliance director NRA 1933–34; chairman National Defense Mediation Board 1941–42; chairman National War Labor Board 1942–45; director Office of Economic Stabilization 1945; on patent advisory panel AEC 1947–57.

Davis, William Morris (1850–1934), geographer and geologist, born in Philadelphia, Pa.; on faculty Harvard University 1876–1912, became professor of geology ('The Coral Reef Problem').

Davis, Calif., city 15 mi (25 km) w. of Sacramento; in agricultural area; cannery; University of California at Davis; incorporated 1917; pop. 36,640.

Davis, Mount, Pennsylvania. *see in index* Negro Mountains

Davis and Elkins College, Elkins, W.Va.; Protestant interdenominational; opened 1904; arts and sciences, teacher education.

Davis Cup, awarded annually to nation winning men's tennis team championship; cup donated 1900 by Dwight F. Davis, American statesman B-366, T-102

Davis Dam, Arizona and Nevada, on the Colorado River, *maps* N-144, *picture* N-155
  Lake Mead N.R.A. N-40a

Davison, Frederic Ellis (born 1917), U.S. Army officer, born in Washington D.C.; commissioned 1941; served in all-black infantry unit in Italy, World War II; made brigadier general while on active duty in Vietnam 1968, third black to hold rank of general.

Davisson, Clinton Joseph (1881–1958), physicist, born in Bloomington, Ill.; member of technical staff of Bell Telephone Laboratories P-307. *see also in index* Nobel Prizewinners, *table*

Davis Strait, between Greenland and Baffin Island; width 180 to 500 mi (290 to 800 km); ice blocks late fall and winter navigation; discovered by John Davis 1587, *map* N-308

Davitt, Michael (1846–1906), Irish political leader, of great force and bitter earnestness, born in Straide, County Mayo; had impoverished childhood; maimed in mill accident; jailed for helping arm Irish nationalists; helped found Irish Land League 1879; often member of Parliament; ardent "home ruler" but opposed Parnell.

Davos Platz, Switzerland, winter resort S-542, *map* S-537

Davout, Louis Nicolas, duke of Auerstädt and prince of Eckmühl (1770–1823), one of Napoleon's marshals, born in Annoux, n.-central France; won brilliant victories at Auerstädt and Eckmühl; turned tide at Wagram; minister of war during "100 days" H-14

Davy, Humphry (1778–1829), English scientist D-43
  arc light E-157
  chemical elements discovery
    magnesium M-45
    potassium and sodium S-247
  Faraday's apprenticeship F-24
  tanning materials L-110

Davy Jones, sailors' colloquial name for the spirit of the sea; "Davy Jones's locker" means the bottom of the sea; perhaps came from "duffy," meaning a ghost, and Jonah, who was swallowed by the whale.

Davys, John. *see in index* Davis, John

Dawes, Charles G(ates) (1865–1951), Republican statesman, born in Marietta, Ohio; U.S. comptroller of currency 1897–1901; organizer and official, trust companies and banks from 1902; U.S. brigadier general, on military board of allied supply 1918–19; first director S. Bureau of the Budget 1921–22; served as vice-president of U.S. 1925–29; ambassador to Britain 1929–32; president Reconstruction Finance Corporation 1932 ('The Banking System of the United States'). *see also in index* Nobel Prizewinners, *table*
  German reparations W-265

Dawes, Henry Laurens (1816–1903), legislator, born in Cummington, Mass.; Republican representative from Massachusetts 1857–73; U.S. senator 1875–83; gave much attention to legislation for Indians; chairman "Dawes" Commission to Five Civilized Tribes 1893–1903.

Dawes, William (1745–99), American patriot, born in Boston, Mass.; ancestor of Charles Gates Dawes R-161
  Lexington and Concord Battle L-144

Dawes Plan, for German reparations payments G-105, W-265

Dawn, morning twilight T-311

Dawn men, or **First Europeans,** *pictures* M-77, S-57c

Dawson, George Mercer (1849–1901), Canadian geologist, born in Pictou, N.S.; son of Sir John William Dawson; director Geological Survey of Canada 1895–1901; Dawson, Yukon, named for him.

Dawson, Sir John William (1820–99), Canadian geologist, born in Pictou, N.S.; father of George Mercer Dawson; professor of geology and principal of McGill University 1855–93; his studies were largely responsible for development of Nova Scotia coal mines; opposed Darwinism.

Dawson, Simon James (1820–1902), Canadian civil engineer and statesman, born in Scotland; aided settlement of the Northwest by exploring country between Lake Superior and the Saskatchewan River; represented Ontario in Canadian House of Commons 1878–91.

Dawson, William Levi (1886–1970), public official and lawyer, born in Albany, Ga.; Chicago alderman 1933–39; U.S. congressman (Democrat) from Illinois 1943–70.

Dawson, Y.T., Canada, on Yukon River; center of Klondike region; capital of Yukon Territory 1898–1951; pop. at time of gold rush 20,000, now 762 Y-352
  Klondike gold rush, *picture* M-18
  national historic sites, *map* N-24b
  Palace Grand Theatre N-24d

Dawson Creek, Canada, city 480 km (300 mi) n.w. of Edmonton, Alta.; oil refining and grain elevators; s. point of Alaska Highway; pop 11,373

Day, Arthur L(ouis) (1869–1960), physicist, born in Brookfield, Mass.; director Geophysical Laboratory, Carnegie Institution of Washington, 1907–36.
  geyser theory G-120

Day, Benjamin (1838–1916), American printer; inventor about 1879 of process for shading plates for printing illustrations and maps, known as the Benday, or Ben Day, process.

Day, Clarence Shepard (1874–1935), writer, born in New York, N.Y.; refusing to enter father's brokerage business, joined Navy; contracted arthritis; after years of invalidism took up writing ('God and My Father'; 'The Best of Clarence Day').
  'Life with Father' R-112a

Day, J(ames) Edward (1914–67), lawyer and government official, born in Jacksonville, Ill.; Illinois insurance commissioner 1950–53; joined Prudential Insurance Company of America 1953, vice-president 1957–61; U.S. postmaster general 1961–63; Democrat.

Day, Stephen (sometimes spelled **Daye**) (1594?–1668), American pioneer printer, born in London, England; set up first printing press in American Colonies 1639 at Cambridge, Mass.; printed 'Freeman's Oath', 'Psalms', almanacs, official documents; town granted him 300 acres (120 hectares) for "being the first that set upon printing."

Dayaks, peoples of Borneo B-368

Dayan, Moshe (1915–81), Israeli general and statesman D-44

Day and night T-178
  calendar C-30
  equinox E-282
  international date line I-253, *diagram* I-254, *maps* P-4, T-179
  planetary motion A-710
  polar regions A-572
  Sabbath S-1
  twilight and dawn T-311

Day care, supervision of children to free mothers for work or other activities;

Deccan / De Havilland

Deccan, or **Dekkan,** (the South), the whole peninsula of India s. of the Narbada River
agriculture, *picture* I-67
India I-63

Deceleration S-345

December, 12th month of year
birthdays of famous persons. *see in index* Birthdays, *table*

Decembrist uprising, unsuccessful revolt of Russian revolutionaries Dec. 1825 against Nicholas I N-283

Decemvirs, (ten men), Roman commission appointed 451 B.C. to draw up laws R-243

Decentralization of industry
Russia R-327
urban population U-108

Deception Bay, mouth of Columbia River O-483

Deception Island, volcanic island in Antarctic Ocean, one of South Shetland Islands; deep lake and hot springs; base for Hearst-Wilkins expedition 1928–29.

Decibel, one tenth of a bel; unit of measure of loudness of sounds to normal human ears; because the power of the ear to distinguish differences in loudness decreases as volume increases, the bel scale is made logarithmic; each unit is 10 times the preceding one; thus a barely audible whisper measures one bel (10 decibels) and a speeding express train about 10 bels (100 decibels), though the train generates 10 billion times as much sound energy; in practice, measurements are made with a special sound meter (acoustimeter) containing numerous electrical circuits whose aggregate sensitivity to pitch and loudness corresponds to that of the human ear P-441e, S-260

Deciduous plants, those which shed their leaves periodically T-252
shrubs S-187

Deciduous teeth T-48, *chart* T-49

Decigram, metric unit of weight (1.543 grains).

Decimals, or **decimal fractions,** arithmetic. *see also in index* Fractions, Common and Decimal
percentage equivalents P-198
subtraction S-500

Decimal system, or **base-ten system** N-379
abacus A-4
arithmetic A-590
Jefferson's adoption for coinage J-92
weights and measures M-236

Decimeter, unit of metric system (10 cm; 3.937 in.), *diagram* W-95

Decimus Junius Juvenalis. *see in index* Juvenal

Decius (201–251), Roman emperor; cruelly persecuted Christians; killed in Thrace in battle against Goths C-401

Decius Mus, Publius, name of three Roman consuls who, according to legend, died for country—the father in the Samnite war (340 B.C.), his son in battle of Sentinum (295 B.C.), his grandson in battle of Ausculum (279 B.C.).

Decker, George H(enry) (born 1902), U.S. Army officer, born in Catskill, N.Y.; became 4-star general 1956; commander of UN forces in Korea 1957–59; Army vice-chief of staff 1959–60, chief of staff 1960–62.

Decker, Thomas. *see in index* Dekker

Declaration of Human Rights, Universal, United Nations U-23

Declaration of Independence D-53. *Reference-Outline* U-197a
drafting committee, *picture* R-162
civil rights C-468
Continental Congress C-692
foundation of civil rights A-10
Jefferson's contribution J-89
labor law development L-4
Locke influences L-278
original draft, *picture* U-143
signers A-38, H-16
Statue of Liberty L-148

Declaration of London (1909), code of rules to govern naval warfare and blockade adopted by the London Naval Conference of 1908–9, in which Great Britain, Germany, France, U.S., Austria-Hungary, Italy, Russia, Spain, Netherlands, and Japan participated B-312

Declaration of Paris, agreement signed 1856 by France, Great Britain, Austria, Prussia, Russia, Turkey, and Sardinia; result of dispute during Crimean War between France and England over treatment of property at sea B-312

Declaration of the Rights of Man
Bill of Rights B-195
French Revolution F-402

Declination, astronomy A-719, S-416
navigation N-88

Declination, compass, also called **variation,** error in magnetic compass due to irregularities in earth's magnetic field C-622, D-161

'Decline and Fall of the Roman Empire', famous history by Edward Gibbon, published 1776–88.

'Decline of the West, The', by Oswald Spengler S-377, C-467

Decoder. *see in index* Receiver

Decompression, explosive S-346a

Decompression sickness, or **aeroembolism,** aerospace medicine A-81

Decompression sickness, or **bends,** or **caisson disease,** physiological problem associated with underwater diving; results from differences in underwater pressure D-188, C-18, H-131

Decoration Day. *see in index* Memorial Day

Decorations, of honor
United States M-110, U-6

Decorative arts D-59. *see also in index* specific art forms, such as Fashion; Interior Design; Pottery

De Coverley, Sir Roger. *see in index* Coverley, Sir Roger de

Decuma, Roman mythology
Fates F-44

Dede Agach, now **Alexandroúpolis,** city, Greece; pop. 22,995, *map* G-213

Dedham, Mass., residential township 10 mi (16 km) s.w. of Boston, on Charles River; paper products; founded 1636, Fairbanks House, built 1636; pop. 25,298, *map* M-160

Deduction, logic P-264
paragraph pattern R-103d

Deductive reasoning L-284

De Duve, Christian (born 1917), Belgian biochemist, born in Thames Ditton, near London, England; co-winner of 1974 Nobel prize for cell structure research; discovered lysosomes; professor University of Louvain 1951, Rockefeller University 1962. *see also in index* Nobel Prizewinners, *table*

Dee, river in Scotland famous for salmon and spectacular scenery; has source in Cairngorm Mountains, flows 140 km (87 mi) to North Sea at Aberdeen, *map* G-199g

Dee, river in Wales and England, 110 km (70 mi) long; rises in n. Wales, flows n.e. past town of Chester into Irish Sea, *map* G-199h

Dee, cyclotron, *diagram* N-377e

Deed of Surrender, (1869), Canada; Northwest Territories purchased by Canada from the Hudson's Bay Company C-101

Deeping, (George) Warwick (1877–1950), English novelist, born in Southend, Essex; gave up medicine for literature; work sympathetically portrays human character ('Sorrel and Son').

Deep mining. *see in index* Underground mining

Deep-sea deposits O-397a, M-340

Deep-sea diving. *see in index* Diving, deep-sea

Deep Sea Drilling Project
frontier exploration F-427

Deep-sea life D-59
fish F-128, O-395c, *picture* F-131

Deep Space Network (DSN), stations to track spacecraft S-343b

Deep-space probe. *see in index* Probe

Deep tillage, or **stubble mulching,** method of plowing to conserve the land C-674
farm machinery F-32

Deer D-61
antlers H-229
buckskin L-109
ecology E-54, N-76
fawn, *picture* P-511
feeding in winter A-39, *pictures* G-51, M-358
hoof H-216
parasite, *picture* P-115
ruminant R-318
species
moose M-486
reindeer R-139

Deer dance, of Pueblo Indians, *picture* N-216

Deere, John (1804–86), inventor, born in Rutland, Vt.; after much experimenting, made first steel plowshare in his small shop in Illinois; became one of great plow manufacturers I-195, *picture* V-296

Deerfield, Ill., residential village 25 mi (40 km) n.w. of Chicago; incorporated 1903; Trinity College pop. 17,430.
playground, *picture* H-99

Deerfield, Mass., 33 mi (53 km) n. of Springfield, on Connecticut River; scene of Deerfield Massacre of 1704; pop. of township 4517, *map* M-160

Deerfield Beach, Fla., town 12 mi (19 km) n. of Fort Lauderdale, on Atlantic Ocean; incorporated 1925; pop. 39,193.

Deerfly, insect related to but smaller than the horsefly; female inflicts painful bites on animals and humans in area of the forehead or in back of the neck.

Deergrass. *see in index* Meadow beauty

Deer Lake, Newf., Canada, town on Deer Lake and Humber River, 47 km (29 mi) n.e. of Corner Brook; supplies hydroelectric power for paper mills in area; pop. 4,289, *map* N-165l

Deer mouse. *see in index* White-footed mouse

Deer Park, N.Y., residential community 35 mi (55 km) e. of New York, N.Y., in Suffolk County; aircraft instruments laboratory; pop. 32,274, *map* N-260

Deer Park, Tex., city 30 mi (50 km) e. of Houston; chemicals; oil refining; annual rodeo, pop. 12,773, *map* T-128

'Deerslayer, The', novel by James Fenimore Cooper A-346

De facto, Latin term meaning "actual, based on fact," applied to a form of government that exercises governing power without internationally recognized legal authority; distinguished from *de jure* government, which exercises power by legal right in international law I-255
legal definition, *table* L-92

Defarge, Madame Thérèse, in 'A Tale of Two Cities', by Charles Dickens, an old woman, wife of a wine seller, who knits incessantly as she counts the heads that fall in the French Revolution.

'Defence of Fort McHenry'. *see in index* 'Star-Spangled Banner'

Defendant, in law L-95

Defender of the Faith, title borne by English rulers H-138

Defender of the Holy Sepulcher, title borne by Godfrey of Bouillon during his rule of Jerusalem following the First Crusade C-787

Defenders of Wildlife H-269

Defense, Department of, United States U-159, *list* U-156. *see also in index* Air Force, Department of the; Army, Department of the; Navy, Department of the
guided missiles and rockets G-255
U.S. government U-159

Defense Advanced Research Projects Agency, United States A-77

Defense Intelligence Agency (DIA) I-237

Defense mechanism, psychology, device used unconsciously to ward off problems one cannot resolve
illness E-200
immaturity M-174
repression P-519

Defense program, United States U-188
World War I, W-176
World War II, W-269
Roosevelt, Franklin D. R-274

Defenses, animal. *see in index* Animals

Defense Transportation, Office of (ODT), United States R-277

Defiance, Ohio, city on Maumee River, 50 mi (80 km) s.w. of Toledo; castings, screw machine products, radio and television parts, dairy products; Defiance College; Fort Defiance built here 1794 by Anthony Wayne; pop. 16,801, *map* O-428

Defiance College, Defiance, Ohio; private control, related to United Church of Christ; chartered 1850; arts and sciences, business administration, Christian education, medical technology, music, teacher education.

Deficiency diseases. *see in index* Disease, human

Definite proportions, law of, or **law of definite composition,** chemistry

Deflation, in economics
inflation I-200

Defoe, Daniel (1661?–1731), English novelist and journalist D-64, E-260
English literature N-376
'Robinson Crusoe' R-111c

De Forest, John William (1826–1906), novelist and Civil War soldier, born in Humphreysville (Seymour), Conn.; realistic novel 'Miss Ravenel's Conversion from Secession to Loyalty' published 1867, republished 1939 ('The Wetherel Affair'; 'Honest John Vane'; 'A Lover's Revolt').

De Forest, Lee (1873–1961), American inventor; pioneer in radio D-64, E-169, I-275, *table* I-273
radar R-29

De Forest, Robert Weeks (1848–1931), lawyer and civic leader, born in New York, N.Y.; president Charity Organization Society, Russell Sage Foundation, and Metropolitan Museum of Art.

Deformation, metal F-317

'De Formato Foetu', work by Fabricius F-5

Defregger, Franz von (1835–1921), Austrian painter, born in Stronach, Tyrol; sympathetic portrayal of peasant life ('The Zither Player'; 'Before the Dance').

Degas, (Hilaire Germain) Edgar (1834–1917), French impressionist "painter of dancers" D-65, P-53
Cassatt C-197

De Gasperi, Alcide. *see in index* Gasperi

De Gaulle, Charles (André Joseph Marie) (1890–1970), French army officer and statesman D-66
France F-358, 364
Malraux M-70
Place Charles de Gaulle P-117, *map* P-120, *picture* P-118

De Geer, Gerard, Baron (1858–1943), Swedish geologist, at University of Stockholm 1897–1924
Ice Age I-9
varves A-536

Degeneration, biology
parasites P-113
penguins P-160

Degerminator, milling process
flour F-215

Degree, subdivision or unit
geometry G-69
standard time T-178
temperature T-158

Degree, music, *table* M-566a

Degrees, academic U-204

De Havilland, Sir Geoffrey (1882–1965), English airplane designer and manufacturer, born in Buckinghamshire; uncle of Joan Fontaine and Olivia de Havilland; in 1920 formed and became technical director of De Havilland Aircraft Company, Ltd., noteworthy for contributions to both military and civilian aviation, including the Comet, first jet airliner in commercial service I-195

De Havilland, Olivia (Mary) (born 1916), American actress, born in Tokyo, Japan, of British parents; sister of Joan Fontaine; in motion pictures since 1935; won Academy

De Havilland / Delius

award for role in 'To Each His Own' (1946) and in 'The Heiress' (1949); also starred in 'Hold Back the Dawn' and 'Snake Pit'; on stage in 'Romeo and Juliet' and 'Candida'.

De Havilland Comet, British aircraft J-111, *picture* J-110

Dehmel, Richard (1863–1920), German lyric poet and dramatist, born in Wendisch-Hermsdorf; school of Liliencron; called a hedonistic Nietzschean; thought by many the foremost poet of his time ('Michel Michael'; 'Collected Works'; 'Selected Letters').

Dehn, Adolf (Arthur) (1895–1968), American painter and lithographer.
- 'Spring in Central Park' P-61, *picture* P-63

Dehumidifier N-106, R-363

Dehydrated food F-281
- meat M-192b
- prune P-516

Deianira, wife of Hercules H-144

'Dei delitte e delle pene'. *see in index* 'Crimes and Punishments'

Deimos, satellite of Mars S-52

Deiphobus, Greek mythology, son of Priam and Hecuba, brother of Hector; married Helen after death of Paris; she later betrayed him to Menelaus, who killed him H-122

Deirdre, Celtic myth, beautiful woman fated to cause misfortune; heroine of Cuchulain Cycle and dramas by, Yeats, James Stephens, and Synge S-473

Deir el-Bahri, temple at Thebes, Egypt, *picture* E-124

Deism, religious movement about 1688–1790; advocated natural religion based on reason rather than revelation; believed God was apart from human affairs; followers included B. Franklin, T. Jefferson, J.J. Rousseau, and Voltaire
- Paine, Thomas P-21

De Jong, Meindert (born 1910), American writer of children's books, born in Wierum, Netherlands; to U.S. 1918, citizen 1924 ('Smoke Above the Land'; 'Shadrach'; 'The Wheel on the School', 1955 Newbery medal; 'The Little Cow and the Turtle'; 'Along Came a Dog'; 'Mighty Ones'; 'The Singing Hill'; 'Far Out the Long Canal'; 'Puppy Summer'; 'Journey from Peppermint Street'; 'A Horse Came Running'; 'The Easter Cat'); received Regina Medal of the Catholic Library Association 1972 R-110

De jure, Latin term meaning "by right"; recognition of a nation's lawful sovereignty, *table* L-92

'De jure belli ac pacis' ('On the Law of War and Peace') (pub. 1625), work by Grotius I-255

Dekagram, unit in metric system (0.353 oz.)

De Kalb, Johann (1721–80), German-French soldier D-67

De Kalb, Ill., city 58 mi (93 km) w. of Chicago, in farm and livestock area; hybrid seed corn, canned vegetables; electrical products; Northern Illinois University; pop. 33,099.

Dekameter, unit in metric system (1000 cm; 393.7 in.)

Dekkan, India. *see in index* Deccan

Dekker, or **Decker, Thomas** (1570?–1641), English dramatist, pamphleteer, and poet, born in London; pictured London life of shop and tavern; collaborated with Ben Jonson and others ('Old Fortunatus') E-273

De Kooning, Willem (born 1904), abstract expressionist painter D-68, P-65

De Koven, Reginald (1859–1920), composer, born in Middletown, Conn.; studied in Europe; founded and conducted Washington Symphony Orchestra; music critic for New York publications O-464a

De Kruif, Paul (Henry) (1890–1971), author, born in Zeeland, Mich.; bacteriologist University of Michigan 1912–17; associate in pathology Rockefeller Institute 1920–22; resigned to write popular accounts of great biological and medical discoveries and the men who made them ('Microbe Hunters'; 'Hunger Fighters'; 'Seven Iron Men'; 'Men Against Death'; 'Man Against Insanity') R-112e

Delacroix, Eugène, in full **Ferdinand-Victor-Eugène Delacroix** (1798–1863), French painter D-68

Delafield, E. M., pen name of Mrs. Edmée Elizabeth Monica de la Pasture Dashwood (1890–1943), English novelist; wrote with humorous irony ('Zella Sees Herself'; 'The Way Things Are'; 'Turn Back the Leaves'; 'The Provincial Lady in America'; 'Late and Soon').

Delagoa Bay, inlet of Indian Ocean in Mozambique, in s.e. Africa; fine harbor; discovered by António do Campo on Vasco da Gama's expedition 1502.

Delahanty, Edward J. (Big Ed) (1867–1903), baseball outfielder, second and first baseman, born in Cleveland, Ohio; played for Philadelphia, N.L., 1888–1901, and Washington, A.L., 1902–3; one of game's great sluggers; hit 4 home runs and a single in one game 1896; only player to lead both leagues in hitting, N.L. 1899 and A.L. 1902.

Delaine Merino, breed of merino sheep developed in the United States, from which a fine strong wool is derived for garment fabric.

De la Mare, Walter (John) (1873–1956), English poet and novelist D-69, E-270
- children's books R-110, S-464

Delambre, Jean Baptiste Joseph (1749–1822), French astronomer; constructed tables of the motion of Uranus, Jupiter, and Saturn, and new solar tables; became perpetual secretary of the mathematical section of the Institute of France 1803; his writings include a history of astronomy.

Deland, Margaret(ta Wade Campbell) (1857–1945), novelist and short-story writer, born in Allegheny (now part of Pittsburgh), Pa. ('John Ward, Preacher'; 'Old Chester Tales'; 'The Kays'; 'New Friends in Old Chester'; 'Vehement Flame').

De Land, Fla., city 20 mi (30 km) s.w. of Daytona Beach; citrus fruit; lumber; dairying; hypodermic needles; electronics; Stetson University; pop. 15,354.

Delano, Calif., city in San Joaquin Valley, 30 mi (50 km) n.w. of Bakersfield; irrigation equipment, farm machinery; wine; incorporated 1915; pop. 16,491.

Delany, Martin Robinson (1812–85), physician, born in Charles Town, Va. (now in West Virginia); he formed National Emigration Convention 1854 to aid black people's return to Africa; first black to attain rank of major in U.S. Army during Civil War.

De la Ramée, Marie Louise, pen name Ouida, (1839–1908), English novelist, born in Bury Saint Edmunds; romantic, highly colored novels ('Under Two Flags'; 'Held in Bondage'), and children's stories ('The Nürnberg Stove'; 'A Dog of Flanders').

De la Roche, Mazo (1885–1961), Canadian writer, born in Toronto, Ont.; known for her series of novels about the Whiteoaks, Canadian family; series includes 'Jalna', 'Renny's Daughter', 'Variable Winds at Jalna'; autobiography, 'Ringing the Changes' C-122, *picture* C-123

Delaroche, Paul, real name Hippolyte Delaroche (1797–1856), French historical and portrait painter, born in Paris ('The Princes in the Tower').

Delaunay, Robert (1885–1941), French abstract painter D-69

De Laval, Carl Gustaf Patrik (1845–1913), Swedish inventor, engineer; first built industrial plants; after 1877 devoted himself to inventions; invented a continuous centrifugal cream separator, the first successful steam turbine, a steam motor, and a flexible shaft for high-speed turbines.

Delaware, or **De la Warr,** or **De la Ware, Thomas West, Baron** (1577–1618), British soldier and administrator; colonial governor of Virginia 1609–18 D-70

Delaware, or **Lenni-Lenape,** confederation of Indian tribes; formerly lived in New Jersey, Pennsylvania, and Delaware I-149, *map* I-136, *table* I-138
- Delaware D-72
- New Jersey N-188
- Penn's treaties P-162

Delaware, 2d smallest state of U.S., in Middle Atlantic group; 2057 sq mi (5328 sq km); cap. Dover; pop. 595,225 D-70, *maps* U-41, 50
- cities. *see also in index* cities listed below and other cities by name
  - Wilmington W-169
- history
  - Civil War C-473
- Middle Atlantic region U-49, *map* U-50, *pictures* U-52, *Reference-Outline* U-133
- population density, *chart* P-261b
- state symbols
  - American holly H-202
  - blue hen chicken P-483
  - flag, *picture* F-159
  - name, *table* S-428
  - peach blossom P-145, *picture* S-427
- Statuary Hall, *table* S-437b

Delaware, Ohio, city on Olentangy River, 23 mi (37 km) n. of Columbus; truck bodies, air conditioners, rubber goods, stoves; Ohio Wesleyan University; pop. 15,008, *map* O-428
- birthplace of Rutherford B. Hayes H-78

Delaware, breed of poultry P-482

Delaware, University of, Newark, Del.; state control; arts and sciences, agriculture, business and economics, education, engineering, home economics and nursing; graduate studies D-74, *picture* D-79

Delaware and Chesapeake Canal. *see in index* Chesapeake and Delaware Canal

Delaware and Hudson Canal, extended from Honesdale, Pa., to the Hudson River at Kingston, N.Y.; built 1825–28.
- trial trip of early locomotive R-73

Delaware and Raritan Canal, N.J., abandoned canal between New Brunswick and Bordentown, connecting Delaware and Raritan rivers; 42 mi (68 km) long; completed 1834; important waterway in mid-19th century N-191

Delaware Aqueduct system, New York A-520, *table* T-292

Delaware Bay, estuary of Delaware River N-193, P-173

Delaware grape G-177

Delaware Memorial Bridge, Delaware River D-73, *picture* D-84

Delaware River, e. U.S. (280 mi; 450 km) D-86, *maps* N-188, 202, P-165, U-50
- aqueduct A-520
  - Philadelphia P-251a, *picture* P-168
  - Morrisville, *picture* P-167
  - Washington's crossing M-110, R-171, *picture* N-195

Delaware River Basin Compact, U.S. government project D-86

Delaware State College, Dover, Del.; established 1891 as land grant college for Negroes, interracial after 1950; liberal arts, teacher education D-74, D-236

Delaware Valley College of Science and Agriculture, Doylestown, Pa.; private control; for men; established 1896; science and agriculture.

Delaware Water Gap
- Delaware D-86
- New Jersey N-187, *maps* N-202, P-185

Delaware Water Gap National Recreation Area, Pennsylvania and New Jersey N-35, *map* N-30

Delbrück, Hans (1848–1929), German historian, born in Bergen, island of Rügen; editor 'Prussian Yearbooks'; opposed submarine policy in World War I on tactical grounds; member of delegation to peace conference ('History of Warfare in Relation to Political History')

Delbrück, Max (1906–81), American biologist, born in Berlin, Germany; to U.S. 1937, became citizen 1945; professor California Institute of Technology 1947–77. *see also in index* Nobel Prizewinners, *table*

Delcassé, Théophile (1852–1923), French statesman, born in Pamiers, France; instrumental in cementing Triple Entente and strengthening French alliance with Russia; minister for foreign affairs 1898–1905, 1914–15; minister of the navy 1911–13; ambassador to Russia 1913.

Del City, Okla., city 5 mi (8 km) s.e. of Oklahoma City; factories make oil drilling rigs, cable, paint; near Tinker Air Force Base; pop. 28,424, *map* O-447

Deledda, Grazia (1875–1936), Italian novelist, born in Nuoro, Sardinia, of humble family; her novels depict vividly the primitive life of Sardinian peasants ('Elias Portulu'; 'The Flight into Egypt'; 'The Flower of Life'; 'The Mother'; 'Reeds in the Wind'; 'Ashes') I-377. *see also in index* Nobel Prizewinners, *table*

De Lee, Joseph Bolivar (1869–1942), obstetrician, born in Cold Springs, N.Y.; professor Northwestern University 1897–1929 and University of Chicago 1929–36; founded Chicago Lying-In Hospital 1895 and Chicago Maternity Center 1932 ('Principles and Practice of Obstetrics').

Delegates
- national convention P-431, *picture* P-432

De Leon, Daniel (1852–1914), American socialist, born on island of Curaçao; came to U.S. about 1874; joined Socialist Labor party 1890; helped form Industrial Workers of the World 1905.

Delft, Netherlands, city 8 km (5 mi) s.e. of The Hague; famous for Delft ceramics; produces yeast, spirits, cables, leather goods; pop. 72,291 P-474, *map* N-133
- Vermeer V-238

Delftware, pottery P-474, *picture* N-136

Delgado, José Matías (1768–1833), Salvadoran priest and national hero; led revolt against colonial rule 1811; resisted incorporation with Mexico 1822–23.

Delhi, India, metropolitan area and union territory; 578 sq mi (1497 sq km); includes New Delhi, seat of present national government, and nearby sites of numerous former capital cities; pop. 5,350,928 D-86. *see also in index* New Delhi; Old Delhi
- India I-70

Delian League G-223

Delibes, (Clément Philibert) Léo (1836–91), French composer, born in Saint-Germain-du-Val, near La Flèche; work light, graceful; excelled in ballet music ('Sylvia', 'Coppelia'), also operettas and opera ('Lakmé').

Delibes, Miguel (born 1920), Spanish writer S-366, *picture* S-367

'Delicate Balance, A,' work by Albee A-260

'Delight of Him Who Wishes to Traverse the Regions of the World, The', work by al-Idrisi
- Islamic literature I-366

Delicious apple, variety of apple A-509, *picture* A-510

Delilah, Philistine woman loved by Samson, whose downfall she caused by having his strength-giving hair cut off (Judg. xvi).

Delinquency, Juvenile. *see in index* Juvenile delinquency

Delinquent children. *see in index* Juvenile delinquency

De L'Isle, William Philip Sidney, first **Viscount** (born 1909), British statesman; secretary of state for air 1951–55; governor-general of Australia 1961–65.

Delius, Frederick (1862–1934), English composer of German descent, born in Bradford; studied in Leipzig, Germany,

Delivery / Denmark

and afterward lived in France; in later life, when blind and paralyzed, won great triumph in England; choral works ('A Mass of Life'; 'Sea Drift'), songs, operas, orchestral works, chamber music.

Delivery room, hospital H-241a

Dell, Floyd, (1887–1969), author, born in Barry, Ill.; left high school to become a reporter; literary editor 'Chicago Evening Post' 1911–13; associate editor 'The Masses' 1914–17, 'The Liberator' 1918–24 (novels: 'Moon-Calf', 'Janet March', 'Love in the Machine Age'; one-act plays)
  Anderson, Sherwood A-408

'Della Famiglia', or **'On the Family',** work by Alberti A-271

Della Robbia, Andrea (1435?–1525?), Italian artist, nephew and pupil of Luca della Robbia D-89, S-86, P-474

Della Robbia, Giovanni (1469–1529), Italian artist, son of Andrea della Robbia D-89

Della Robbia, Girolamo (1488–1566), Italian artist, son of Andrea della Robbia D-89

Della Robbia, Luca (1400?–1482), Italian sculptor, earliest and greatest of Della Robbias D-88, S-86, P-474
  Madonna and the angels, *picture* P-474
  Plato and Aristotle, *picture* P-264
  singing boys S-86, *picture* S-85

Dello Joio, Norman (born 1913), composer and pianist, born in New York, N.Y.; refused career in professional baseball for one in music (ballet: 'On Stage'; choral work: 'Western Star', based on S. V. Benét's poem; orchestral works: 'Sinfonietta', 'Magnificat', 'Variations, Chaconne and Finale', and 'Meditations on Ecclesiastes', awarded 1957 Pulitzer prize in music).

Dells. *see in index* Dalles

Dells of the Wisconsin River, *picture* W-196
  snake dance, *picture* W-203

Delmarva Peninsula, e. U.S., e. of Chesapeake Bay
  Chesapeake Bay C-304
  Delaware D-71
  Virginia V-330

Del Monaco, Mario (1915–1982), Italian operatic tenor, born in Florence; American debut with San Francisco Opera Company 1950; member Metropolitan Opera Company, New York, N.Y., *picture* O-466

Delmonico, Lorenzo, (1813–81), Swiss-born American restauranteur D-89

De Long, George Washington (1844–81), Arctic explorer, born in New York, N.Y.; died of starvation on 'Jeanette' Expedition. *see also in index* 'Jeannette' Expedition

Delos, Greek island in Aegean; smallest but most famous of Cyclades; birthplace of Apollo, *map* G-221
  treasury of Delian League G-223

Delphi, Greece, seat of famous oracle on Mt. Parnassus D-89, *maps* G-213, 221
  oracle A-506, T-159

Delphinium. *see in index* Larkspur

Delphinus, also called **Job's Coffin,** a constellation, *chart* S-420

Delray Beach, Fla., city 16 mi (26 km) s. of West Palm Beach; resort; flower farming; gladioli festival held each year; pop. 34,325.

Del Rio, Tex., city 156 mi (251 km) w. of San Antonio; livestock, especially sheep and goats; site of Amistad Dam between U.S. and Mexico nearby; Laughlin Air Force Base e. of city; pop. 30,034, *maps* T-129, U-40

Delsarte, François Alexandre Nicolas Chéri (1811–71), French musician, born near Cambrai; taught singing and declamation; used system of physical exercises based on relaxation.

Delta, earth deposited by rivers at mouth D-90
  coastal land formations B-112, E-24, *diagram* R-210
  Ganges G-16
  Hwang H-282
  Mekong M-217, V-317, V-321
  Mississippi M-390
  Niger N-287
  Nile E-108, N-290
  Orinoco O-505
  Po P-400
  Rhine, Meuse, and Scheldt N-133

Delta Epsilon Sigma, national college honor society, founded at Washington, D.C., 1939 to recognize scholarship among students and graduates of Catholic colleges.

Delta metal B-410

'Delta Queen', steamboat
  Cincinnati, *picture* C-415

Delta State College, since 1974 **Delta State University,** Cleveland, Miss.; opened 1925; arts and sciences, business administration, and education; graduate studies.

Deltoid muscle, *picture* M-550

Deluge. *see in index* Flood legends

'De Magnete', Gilbert's treatise on magnetism, published 1600 E-153

Demand, economics. *see in index* Supply and demand

Demarcation, Line of. *see in index* Line of Demarcation

Demarçay, Eugène Anatole (1852–1904), French chemist, born in Paris; discovered europium; gave spectroscopic proof of discovery of radium.

'De materia medica', work by Dioscorides
  botany B-380

De Maupassant, Guy. *see in index* Maupassant

Demeter (Roman **Ceres**), Greek goddess of agriculture and marriage M-575, R-176, S-52a

Demetrius. *see in index* Dmitri

Demetrius I (337–283 B.C.), son of Antigonus Cyclops, one of Alexander's generals; called Poliorcetes ("besieger") because he besieged Rhodes with elaborate machinery 305–304 B.C.; won control of Macedonia and Greece, seizing throne 294 B.C.; expelled by Pyrrhus and died a prisoner of Seleucus.

De Mille, Agnes (George) (born 1908), U.S. dancer and choreographer D-91, *profile* B-36
  dance D-30

De Mille, Cecil B(lount) (1881–1959), motion-picture producer, born in Ashfield, Mass.; presented his first film, 'The Squaw Man', in Hollywood, Calif., 1913; produced Lux Radio Theater 1936–45; his screen productions include 'The King of Kings', 'The Sign of the Cross', 'Cleopatra', and 'The Greatest Show on Earth' (Academy award winner for best film of 1952); 'Autobiography'
  directing D-155
  'Ten Commandments' M-522

Deming, N.M., village about 80 mi (130 km) n.w. of El Paso, Tex.; farming, ranching; plastics, luggage, tools; tourist trade; health resort; pop. 9964, *map* N-221

Demo, social protest in Japan
  influence on government policy J-35

Democracy, government by the people; in its pure form, exercised by them directly; in a representative democracy or republic, through their chosen representatives D-91, G-163
  ancient Greece G-223, W-245, C-461
    Solon's laws S-255
  Canada's self-government C-97
  citizenship C-438
  civil rights C-469
  constitution C-683
  England M-45, P-131b
  French Revolution F-402
  Germany G-105
  parliament P-129
  Philippines P-255
  Rousseau's influence R-299b
  Switzerland S-543
  United States
    American Colonies R-162, U-170
    cities C-458
    frontier movement F-424
    jury system J-158
    labor law development L-4
    literature A-343
    Penn's contribution P-162
    political parties P-431

Democratic-Farmer-Labor party, Minnesota M-353

Democratic party (United States) P-432. *see also in index* names of presidents
  Civil War C-477, U-183
  free silver M-19
  Hayes-Tilden controversy H-80
  Jackson's foundation J-9
  Jefferson's principles J-93
  labor movements L-10
  Lincoln-Douglas debate L-220
  Roosevelt, Franklin D. R-272
  speakers of the House of Representatives. *see in index* Representatives, House of, *subhead* speaker
  symbol, *picture* P-431
  Tammany Hall T-13
    Nast cartoons N-15b
  tariff policy T-24
  presidents, *table* P-495a
  vice-presidents, *table* V-310

Democratic People's Republic of Korea. *see in index* Korea

Democratic-Republican party (Jeffersonian) P-432, *Reference-Outline* U-197b
  Jefferson's role J-93
  presidents, *table* P-495a

Democratic Republic of the Congo. *see in index* Zaire, Republic of

Democratic Republic of Vietnam. *see in index* Vietnam, North

'Democratic Vistas', work by Whitman.

Democritus (5th century B.C.), Greek philosopher; called Aristotle of 5th century, also ineptly styled the Laughing Philosopher, as Heraclitus was the Weeping Philosopher.

De Molay, Order of, nonsectarian secret organization of young men between the ages of 14 and 21, founded in 1919 at Kansas City, Mo., and named in honor of the martyred Jacques de Molay, last grand master of the Knights Templars; order is governed by a Grand Council of Freemasons, and the chapters are sponsored by Masonic bodies.

Demon, supernatural being representing evil spirits A-414
  folk medicine F-271

Demonstrations
  Philippines P-255, *picture* P-261a
  United States P-143d, U-196
    civil rights B-296, M-331
    peace march, *pictures* P-143b
  Vietnam, South V-322
    women's rights, *pictures* W-213, 215b

Demonstrative pronoun P-508

De Morgan, William Frend (1839–1917), English novelist, born in London; for 30 years an artist-potter; known for his brilliant blue and green glazes; began to write at 65; excelled in naturalness of dialogue; characters often more important than plot; best novels: 'Joseph Vance', 'Alice-for-Short', 'Somehow Good'.

Demosthenes (about 383–322 B.C.), most famous Greek orator D-96, G-235

Demotic writing (Egyptian) E-125
  ancient writing W-306b
  archaeology A-536

Dempsey, Jack, or **William Harrison Dempsey** (1895–1983), U.S. heavyweight boxer D-96
  heavyweight champion B-391, *picture* B-392

Dempster, Arthur Jeffrey (1886–1950), U.S. physicist, born in Toronto, Ont., Canada; to U.S. 1914, citizen 1918; professor University of Chicago 1919–50.

Demuth, Charles (1883–1935), painter, born in Lancaster, Pa.; expert draftsman; noted for paintings of fruits, flowers, buildings; precise line, luminous color, emphasis on planes; cubistic technique in later work.

Denain, France, town 10 km (6 mi) s.w. of Valenciennes; victory of French over allies under Prince Eugène 1712; pop. 27,840.

Denali, or **Traleika,** also **Bulshaia,** native names for Mt. McKinley. *see in index* McKinley, Mount

Denarius, Roman coin P-188

Denatured alcohol A-275

Denby, Edwin (1870–1929), lawyer and Cabinet official, born in Evansville, Ind.; secretary of navy under Harding and Coolidge 1921–24, resigned as result of Teapot Dome scandal; in World War I, enlisted in Marines as private, rose to major; Democratic representative from Michigan 1905–11
  oil scandals H-32

Dendera, Egypt, village in Upper Egypt, on the left bank of the Nile, opposite Kena; seat of the beautiful temple of Hathor, built in the first century B.C.

Dendrite, branched process from a nerve cell N-129, *diagram* N-130a

Dendrochronology B-381

Dendrology, science of trees A-536, T-259

Deneb, star of the first magnitude in the constellation of Cygnus S-414, *chart* S-419

Denfeld, Louis Emil (1891–1972), U.S. Navy officer, born in Westboro, Mass.; in World Wars I and II; assistant chief Bureau of Naval Personnel 1942–45, chief 1945–47; chief of naval operations 1947–49; retired as admiral 1950.

Dengue, disease M-498

Deng Xiaoping (born 1904), Chinese Communist leader D-96, C-376, *picture* C-377

Denier, unit of weight for yarns.

Deniker, Joseph (1852–1918), French anthropologist, born in Astrakhan', Russia; wrote 'Races of Man' and other important ethnological and zoological works.

Denim, heavy cotton twilled fabric, usually colored; coarser weaves are used for overalls, etc.; finer, for drapery and upholstery; name comes from French town of Nîmes ("serge de Nîmes").

Denis, Saint (Latin **Dionysius**), apostle to the Gauls (A.D. 250?), first bishop of Paris, martyr and a patron saint of France; legend says he ran carrying his head in his hand after he was beheaded for his faith by order of the Roman governor; abbey near Paris burial place of many of the kings of France; festival Oct. 9.

Denis, Maurice (1870–1943), French artist, born in Granville; influenced by Gauguin; noted for murals that show influence of 15th-century Italian fresco painters; excelled in religious arts.

Denison, George Taylor (1839–1925), Canadian soldier and author, born in Toronto, Ont.; lieutenant colonel; in active military service in 1866 during Fenian raids and in 1885 during Riel Rebellion ('A History of Cavalry'; 'Soldiering in Canada'; 'The Struggle for Imperial Unity'; 'Fenian Raid at Fort Erie').

Denison, Tex., industrial city 70 mi (110 km) n. of Dallas; in rich farming section; railroad division point; cotton mills; food processing, wood creosoting; mattresses, work garments; birthplace of Dwight D. Eisenhower; Lake Texoma nearby; pop. 23,884, *maps* T-128, U-40

Denison Dam, Oklahoma and Texas, on the Red River; forms Lake Texoma T-112, *maps* O-435, O-447, T-111, 128, *picture* O-434

Denison University, Granville, Ohio; private control; formerly Baptist; established 1831; liberal arts and sciences, music C-595

Denmark, one of the three Scandinavian countries of n.w. Europe; 43,043 sq km (16,619 sq mi); cap. Copenhagen; pop. 5,013,412 D-97, *Fact Summary* E-327, *map* E-334. For a list of rulers of Denmark, *see table* following
  cities. *see in index* Copenhagen and other cities by name
  arts
    folk art F-254
    porcelain P-476
  church and state issue C-409
  education A-52
    illiteracy P-450
    social studies, *picture* S-241b
  flag, *picture* F-164
  Greenland G-237
  history S-52g
    invasion of England E-231
    Napoleonic Wars N-127

De re aedeficatoria / Detergents

agriculture; pop. 877,620, *map* E-218

'De re aedeficatoria' ('Ten Books on Architecture'), work by Alberti A-271

'De Remedüs Utriusque Fortunae', work by Petrarch, *picture* L-77

'De Re Metallica', by Georgius Agricola, translated into English by Mr. and Mrs. Herbert Hoover H-219

Derennes, Charles (1882–1930), French writer, born in Villeneuve-sur-Lot, near Agen; noted for detailed descriptions of animal life ('Life of the Bat')

'De rerum natura', poem by Lucretius L-77

Derivative, mathematics C-24

Derived intelligence quotient
intelligence tests I-241

Derleth, August (1909–71), writer, born in Sauk City, Wis.; famous for regional stories of Wisconsin (Sac Prairie Saga: 'Wisconsin Earth', 'Sac Prairie People', 'Place of Hawks', 'Walden West'); writer of mystery stories and editor of science fiction anthologies.

Dermaptera, order of insects consisting of the earwigs.

Dermatitis. *see in index* Eczema

Dermatology S-61g, *table* M-212c

Dermis, or **derma,** inner layer of the skin S-210d, *diagram* S-211
pressure end organs T-218

Dermoid cyst, type of cyst C-811

Dermoptera, order of mammals, the flying lemurs, *list* M-71

Dermot MacMurrough (1110?–71), Irish ruler, king of Leinster, pivot of first English intervention in Ireland (1135–71); dethroned because he had carried off another chieftain's wife; sought aid of Henry II; compiled 'Book of Leinster'

Dern, George Henry (1872–1936), public official, born in Dodge County, Neb.; governor of Utah 1925–32; secretary of war 1933–36; prominent Democrat, *picture* R-268

Derne, or **Derna,** Libya, Mediterranean coast city and resort; products include honey, bananas, wool, corn, soap, and flour; pop. 15,218, *picture* L-188

Derome, Nicolas-Denis, called Derome the Younger (1731–91), most important of French family of bookbinders; his work was uneven, but best is highly prized by collectors; developed dentelle (lacework style of gilding); his nephew Alexis Pierre Bradel, called Bradel-Derome the Elder, succeeded him.

Derozio, Henry (1809-31), English author
Indian literature I-108

Derrick, a boom or frame rigged with pulleys for lifting heavy weights. *see also in index* Crane
machinery function C-760
oil well P-235, *diagram* P-237, *pictures* O-441, T-123
sulfur field, *picture* S-509

Derringer, pistol of large bore with a short barrel.

Derry, N.H., 9 mi (15 km) s.e. of Manchester; shoes, books, wood products; set off from Londonderry 1827; pop. of township 18,875, *map* N-183

Derry, Northern Ireland. *see in index* Londonderry

Derthick, Lawrence G(ridley) (born 1905), educator and government official, born in Hazel Green, Ky.; superintendent of schools Chattanooga, Tenn., 1942–56; U.S. commissioner of education 1956–61.

Deruta, central Italy, small village near the Tiber River and 9 mi (15 km) s. of Perugia, famous for maiolica ware; also produces wrought-iron wares.

Dervish, member of Mohammedan religious fraternity living in a monastery or wandering as a beggar; others include howling dervishes and whirling, or dancing, dervishes
Jalal ud-din Rumi J-17

Derwent River, Cumberland, England, flows into Irish Sea; expands into Derwentwater, a small oval lake in s. Cumberland noted for its scenic charm.

Derzhavin, Gavriil Romanovich (1743–1816), Russian poet, born near Kazan R-359–60

De Sabata, Victor (1892–1967), Italian composer and conductor, born in Trieste, Italy; director La Scala Opera, Milan, Italy; guest conductor Pittsburgh Symphony 1948.

Desai, Morarji (born 1896), Indian political leader, born in Gujarat; prime minister 1977–79 I-80

Desalinization, removal of salt from water E-17, O-395a, W-71
solar energy S-516

Desargues, Gérard (1593–1662), French mathematician, born in Lyons; helped found modern geometry; developed Desargues theorem of involutions and transversals.

Descant, musically decorative treble part superimposed above the melody; usually sung by the sopranos while the tenors carry the melody M-556

Descartes, René (1596–1650), French philosopher and mathematician D-104
air experiments A-148
exponential notation A-595
French literature F-395
solar system origin E-27

'Descent from the Cross, The', fresco by Giotto P-29

'Descent of Man, The', work by Charles Darwin D-39

Deschanel, Paul Eugène Louis (1856–1922), French statesman, orator, and writer, born in Brussels, Belgium; Liberal leader; president of France 1920.

Deschutes River, Ore., rises in Cascade Range; flows n. 250 mi (400 km) to Columbia River O-480, *maps* O-493, U-90

'Description de l'Égypte', work by Fourier F-336

Desdemona, heroine of Shakespeare's 'Othello' O-506

Desegregation, removal of racial bars N-293g, E-132, 133
bus N-126c

Deseret, State of, name given by Mormons to their settlement in present Utah; one of nicknames of Utah U-219. *see also in index* Utah

Desert D-104
Africa, *map* S-15. *see also* Libyan Desert; Sahara
Egypt E-109
Kalahari B-280, S-263, *map* S-264
Niger N-285
animals M-433
addax S-16
ostrich, or camel bird O-505d
Asia, *maps* A-618, 636, 637, R-323. *see also in index* Gobi, The; Taklamakan
Afghanistan A-89
Iran I-305
Pakistan P-77
Russia R-324, *map* R-344
Saudi Arabia A-469, S-52b
climate, *table* W-238
Europe E-309
mirage M-370
oasis. *see in index* Oasis
Latin America L-60
nomads N-295
North America, *map* N-312
United States U-84, *picture* U-31. *see also in index* Death Valley; Mojave Desert
Great Salt Lake Desert U-216, *maps* U-80, U-217, 232
High Desert, *map* O-480
Painted Desert A-597, N-43
plant adaptation N-60, P-363, *picture* 362
cactus C-12
grasslands G-192
mesquite M-227
sagebrush S-14, *picture* E-47
soil S-253, *maps* G-61, S-252
South America S-272
transportation, *pictures* P-543, W-239

Desertas, group of three uninhabited islands in the Madeiras (Chão, Bugio, and Deserta Grande); rabbits and wild goats, *map* P-455

Desert candle. *see in index* Eremurus

Desert flat, or **llano,** desert formation D-105

Desert iguana, lizard, *picture* L-273

Desertion
citizenship loss
marriage M-117

Desert terrarium N-73

Desert tortoise, *picture* T-216
aestivates and hibernates H-152

De Seversky, Alexander P. *see in index* Seversky

Desiderio da Settignano (1428–64), Italian sculptor in marble, wood, and terra-cotta; named for birthplace, Settignano, near Florence S-86

Desiderius, last king of the Lombards (ruled 756–774); hostile to Charlemagne when latter repudiated his wife, Desiderius' daughter; supported claims of Charlemagne's nephews to Frankish kingdom; attacked pope's territory and was captured by Charlemagne.

Design D-107 *see also in index* Architecture; Arts; Carving; Clothing; Drawing; Enameling; Furniture; Glass; Jewelry and gems; Metalwork; Painting; Porcelain and chinaware; Sculpture; Tapestry; Textiles; Woodworking and wood carving
airplane, *diagram* S-168
Breuer, Marcel B-434
decorative arts D-59
dress design D-268
Egyptian, *pictures* P-28, S-78
Fuller, Buckminster F-446
furniture F-452
Greek and Roman, *pictures* G-227, R-245
illuminated manuscripts. *see in index* Illuminated manuscripts
industrial design I-169
interior design I-243
knife, fork, and spoon K-257
lotus T-138
Oriental rugs R-314, *picture* R-312
posters. *see in index* Posters
quilts Q-17
ship S-169, *picture* S-177
stage setting T-151, *picture* T-153
streamlining S-486
United States coins M-367
vocational opportunities V-365
wallpaper W-4

Desk, furniture F-457

Desk-Fax, facsimile machine T-53

Desman, name of two species of aquatic, insect-eating animals closely related to moles; one species, Russian desman, lives in s.e. Europe and w. Asia; head and body about 25 cm (10 in.) long, tail 18 cm (7 in.); fur reddish brown above, grayish white with silvery sheen below; tail laterally compressed almost entire length; scientific name *Desmana moschata;* the other species, Pyrenean desman, lives in Spain and France; about 25 cm (10 in.) long (half of this is tail); chestnut above, silver gray below, flanks brownish gray; last quarter of tail laterally compressed; scientific name *Galemys pyrenaicus*
furs, *table* F-464

De Smet, Pierre Jean (1801–73), Jesuit missionary, born in Termonde, Belgium; came to U.S. 1821 and entered the Jesuit order at Baltimore, Md.; first mission 1838 at site of Council Bluffs, Iowa, among Potawatomi; began his work in the Far West 1840; known as "Blackrobe" among the Indians, he made peace between tribes and between Indian and white man; mediated "Mormon War" and Yakima Indian War; in 1868 visited and pacified Sitting Bull, despite the latter's oath to kill the first white man to appear in his camp I-20

Desmids, minute one-cell freshwater algae; bright green in color; divided into symmetrical halves; order Desmidiacead, *picture* L-269

Des Moines, Ia., state capital and largest city; pop. 191,506 D-117, I-290, *picture* I-297, *maps* I-294, U-41

Des Moines River, rises in s.w. Minnesota and flows 450 mi (720 km) s.e. through Iowa to Mississippi River; hydroelectric power source D-117, *maps* M-363, 395, U-70

Desmoulins, (Lucie Simplice) Camille (Benoit) (1760–94), French journalist, born in Guise, near Saint-Quentin; his crying "to arms" as the news of Necker's dismissal reached the Paris crowds (1789) initiated French Revolution; became alienated from Jacobins; guillotined; his wife, Lucile, guillotined a week later.

Desolation (Spanish **Desolación) Island,** an island of Tierra del Fuego, belonging to Chile, near w. end of Strait of Magellan; name also of Kerguelen Island, *map* S-299

De Soto, Hernando (1500?–1542), Spanish explorer of s.e. U.S. and discoverer of Mississippi River D-117, A-331
Florida, *picture* U-130
Georgia G-83
route, *map* U-176

De Soto National Memorial, Florida N-35

Despenser, Hugh le (1262–1326), English peer; leader of Barons' party opposing Edward II; almost alone opposed execution of Piers Gaveston; later himself chief adviser and favorite of king; arrogance and rapacity of his son **Hugh the Younger** (died 1326) largely responsible for their fall and hanging.

Despiau, Charles (1874–1946), French sculptor, born in Mont-de-Marsan, near Bordeaux; portrait busts of women S-91

Des Plaines, Ill., city 17 mi (27 km) n.w. of Chicago, on Des Plaines River; electrical products; industrial research; Chicago-O'Hare International Airport nearby; pop. 53,568.

Des Plaines River, s.e. Wisconsin and n.e. Illinois; joins Kankakee to form Illinois River; length 150 mi (240 km); part of course used by Illinois Waterway.

Desrochers, (Joseph) Alfred (Houle) (born 1901), Canadian poet, born near Sherbrooke, Que.

Desrosiers, Léo-Paul (1896–1967), Canadian novelist, born in Berthierville, Que.

Dessalines, Jean Jacques (1758–1806), Jean Jacques I, emperor of Haiti (1804–6), black slave, insurrectionist general under Toussaint L'Ouverture and tyrannical despot, born in Grande Rivière, near Cap Haitien, Haiti; assassinated H-7
Christophe, Henry C-407

De Stijl ("the style"), art N-138
magazine M-425a

Destin, Fla., community on Choctawhatchee Bay, 5 mi (8 km) e. of Fort Walton Beach; pop. 3,600
Gulf Coast, *picture* G-259a

Destinn, Emmy (Ema Kittl) (1878–1930), Bohemian operatic soprano, born in Prague (now Czechoslovakia); debut 1898 at Berlin; gained world fame; created title role in Puccini's 'The Girl of the Golden West'.

Destroyer, naval vessel N-98, V-322, *pictures* N-93, 103, W-256, *table* N-96

Destroying angel, poisonous mushroom. *see in index* Amanita

Destructive distillation, chemical process
coal-tar products C-527

Détaille, Jean Baptiste Édouard (1848–1912), French painter, born in Paris; renowned paintings of military subjects ('Defense of Campigny'; 'Movement of Troops').

Detection, radio R-60

'Detective Comics', comic books C-190

Detectives, police division P-427

Detective story, literature D-118
Poe P-401

Detector, radio, device for rectifying high-frequency currents in radio receivers R-47

Détente, normalization of relations between U.S. and U.S.S.R. B-435
Kissinger K-251

Deterding, Sir Henri Wilhelm August (1866–1939), Dutch oil magnate, born in Amsterdam; supported the Nazi movement in Germany.

Detergents, cleansing agents G-42, S-231
laundry L-84

Determiner / Dewey

water pollution W-71

Determiner, grammar N-372, P-508, *list* G-167

Determinism, the philosophical doctrine that ethical choices are determined, or prescribed, by mental, physical, and environmental causes; opposed to free will.

Detmold, West Germany, town at edge of Teutoburger Wald, 76 km (47 mi) s.w. of Hanover; nearby was erected a colossal statue of Hermann, or Arminius, who defeated Romans A.D. 9; pop. 63,266, *map* G-114

Detonation. *see in index* Explosion

Detroit, Mich., largest city of state, on Detroit River; "automobile capital of the world"; pop. 1,203,339, D-120, *maps* M-270, 276, U-41, *inset* M-285
history
Ford, Henry F-305
War of 1812 C-96, *picture* W-13
housing H-251
Michigan M-268
museums and art galleries
Flannagan's 'Frog' S-92
Puppet Theater P-536
Rivera's fresco P-67a, *picture* P-67b
natural-gas pipelines G-41
newspapers N-232
population growth, *graphs* G-187
zoo Z-361a, *picture* M-280

Detroit, University of, Detroit, Mich.; Roman Catholic; founded by Jesuits 1877; arts and sciences, architecture, business administration, dentistry, education, engineering, general studies, law; graduate school D-122

Detroit Automobile Company, automobile industry corporation, Detroit, Mich.; organized 1899
Ford's partnership F-305

Detroit Institute of Technology, Detroit, Mich.; private control; established 1891; liberal arts, business administration, engineering

Detroit Lakes, Minn., resort town, 48 mi (77 km) e. of Fargo, N.D., on Detroit Lake and near many lakes; pop. 7,106, *map* M-362

Detroit River, connecting Lake St. Clair and Lake Erie D-120, *map* G-203, M-274

Detroit-Windsor Tunnel, Detroit, Mich., and Windsor, Ont., Canada; a mile (1.6 kilometers) long, 80 ft (24 m) beneath Detroit River; completed 1930, *table* T-292

Dett, Robert Nathaniel (1882–1943), U.S. pianist and composer, born in Drummondsville, Ont., Canada; organized Hampton Institute Choir ('Magnolia Suite'; 'The Chariot Jubilee'; 'In the Bottoms'; 'America the Beautiful'); published 'Dett Collection of Negro Spirituals'.

Dettingen, West Germany, village of Bavaria, on Main River; decisive victory of Allies under George II of England over French under Duc de Noailles, June 27, 1743; pop. 3619.

Deucalion, figure in Greek mythology who built an ark to survive a flood sent by Zeus; with wife Pyrrha, repopulated world by casting stones that turned into humans M-574

Deurne, Belgium, industrial and residential suburb just e. of Antwerp; parks; sports palace; pop. 68,703.

Deuterium H-287, M-166, N-378, *diagrams* R-65
oxide W-68a
plasma P-380

Deuteromycetes, group of fungi.

Deuteron, nucleus of deuterium atom N-378

Deuteronomy, the 5th book of the Bible; contains last injunction of Moses to the Jews and the account of his death.
Judaism's basic creed J-147

Deutsch, Babette (born 1895), writer, born in New York, N.Y.; married Avrahm Yarmolinsky, with whom she translated Russian and German poetry; her poems include 'Fire for the Night', 'Animal, Vegetable, Mineral', 'I Often Wish' ('Poetry in Our Time', criticism; 'Poetry Handbook'; for younger readers: 'Heroes of the Kalevala', 'Walt Whitman, Builder for America') R-111c, S-480
'More Tales of Faraway Folk' S-480, *pictures* S-473, 475, 478

Deutsche mark. *see in index* Mark

Deutscher Werkbund, German association of craftsmen; founded in Munich 1907 A-565

'Deutschland, Deutschland über Alles', national anthem of the Federal Republic of Germany N-53

De Valera, Eamon (1882–1975), Irish political leader D-124, I-322

De Valois, Dame Ninette, or **Edrus Stannus** (born 1898), Irish dancer, teacher, choreographer, and ballet director, born in Ireland; debut in London 1914, later soloist with Diaghilev ballet; her ballet school, established in London 1931, developed into the Royal Ballet ('Come Dance with Me', autobiography) D-24

Devaluation of currency, reduction of the legal value of a currency; usually by reducing the amount of gold represented by the monetary unit
gold prices G-150a
Mexican peso M-256
pound sterling E-250
United States R-270, M-429, N-293g

Devanagari script, writing India I-67

Developer, housing H-249

Developing. *see in index* Photography

Developmental psychology, or **genetic psychology** P-522

Development banks
international trade I-268

Deventer, Netherlands, city on IJssel River; famous for "Deventer koek," a honey cake; pop. 54,669.

DeVere, Aubrey Thomas (1814–1902), Irish poet, born in Curragh Chase, near Limerick; inspired by Greek spirit and by Irish legends ('Irish Odes'; 'Legends of St. Patrick'; 'Legends of the Saxon Saints').

Devereux, James P(atrick) S(innott) (born 1904), U.S. Marine Corps officer, born in Washington, D.C.; joined Marines as a private in 1923, retired 1948; congressman from Maryland 1951–59
defense of Wake Island W-2

Devereux, Robert. *see in index* Essex

Devers, Jacob Loucks (1887–1979), U.S. Army officer, born in York, Pa.; graduated West Point; commander U.S. armored forces 1941–43; Allied deputy commander in Mediterranean theater 1943–44; chief of Allied forces invading s. France Aug. 1944–45; chief of U.S. Army field forces 1946–49.

Devi, Hindu mythology, Siva's wife; dual nature, one gentle, one violent; when gentle, known as Devi, or Rhambha, Hindu Venus; when turbulent, as Durga or Kali, a black goddess of murder, death, and plague.

Deviation, compass C-622, D-161

Devil, Christian and Jewish theology, a fallen angel or evil spirit, especially Lucifer or Satan
angel and demon beliefs A-414
Faust legend F-49
"Old Deluder Satan Act" E-84
'Paradise Lost', *picture* E-253
witchcraft W-209

Devil chasers, New Guinea, *picture* M-39

Devilfish, or **sea devil,** various marine animals
giant squid. *see in index* Giant squid
octopus O-402
ray S-206

Devil-in-a-bush, flower. *see in index* Nigella

Deville, Henri Étienne Sainte-Claire. *see in index* Sainte-Claire Deville

Devil's Advocate, popular name for Promoter of the Faith, an ecclesiastic of the Roman Catholic church, who, during process of canonization, must offer all possible objections against the candidate for sainthood. *see also in index* Canonization

Devil's-darning-needle. *see in index* Dragonfly

Devil's-grass Q-1

Devil's Island, Atlantic, 8 mi. off coast of French Guiana A-337, G-250

Devils Lake, N.D., city near lake of same name, 85 mi (140 km) w. of Grand Forks; farming and livestock center; resort; state school for deaf; Sully Hill National Game Preserve, pop. 7442, *maps* N-353, U-40

Devils Lake, salt lake in North Dakota N-340,N-353

Devil's-paintbrush. *see in index* Hawkweed

Devils Postpile National Monument, California N-35, *map* N-30

Devil's rearhorse, mantis M-91b

Devil's Road, Organ Pipe Cactus N. Mon., Ariz. N-42

Devils Tower National Monument, Wyoming N-35, *maps* N-30, W-327, *picture* W-325

'Devil to Pay in the Backlands, The', work by Guimarães
Latin American literature L-71

Devil worshipers, various peoples who fear and worship the devil on the theory that the powers of evil must be placated.

Devine, Edward Thomas (1867–1948), sociologist and educator, born in Union, Ia.; editor 'Charities', later 'The Survey', 1897–1912 ('The Normal Life'; 'Social Work').

De Vinne, Theodore Low (1828–1914), printer, born in Stamford, Conn.; fought for simplified typefaces; designed Renner type; helped design Century Roman; De Vinne type named for him; wrote 8 books on printing.

Devlin, Bernadette Josephine (born 1947), North Irish political leader, born in Cookstown, County Tyrone; led first great Catholic civil rights demonstration 1968; member of British Parliament from N. Ireland 1969–74; jailed four months for political activities 1970; author of 'The Price of My Soul'.

Devolution, War of (1667–68), waged by Louis XIV of France for possession of Franche-Comté and part of the Spanish Netherlands; he claimed territory in name of his wife, Maria Theresa, daughter of Philip IV of Spain, although she had renounced her rights at time of her marriage; Louis insisted that under the old law of Brabant, property of a deceased father "devolves" to the children of the first marriage, that is, to Maria Theresa rather than to Charles II of Spain; war halted by intervention of triple alliance of England, Sweden, and Holland; by the peace of Aix-la-Chapelle (1668), France retained captured towns of Charleroi and Lille but gave Franche-Comté back to Spain.

Devon, or **Devonshire,** county in s.w. peninsula of England; 6765 sq km (2612 sq mi); cap. Exeter; contains granite tableland of Dartmoor; dairying, agriculture, mining, fisheries; pop. 823,751 E-219, *map* E-218, *picture* E-224
shell sand S-36

Devon, breed of cattle; cows and bulls rather small; oxen grow to great size and are prized for work.

Devonian period, geology (Age of Fishes) B-461, G-63, P-487, *chart* G-64, *pictures* A-460, P-488
Australia A-774

Devonport, England, fortified port on promontory in s.w. Devon; part of Plymouth; military and naval station; large dockyard, *map* G-199h

Devonshire, Elizabeth, duchess of (1759–1824), one of the two beautiful duchesses of Devonshire painted by Gainsborough; Elizabeth's portrait was the famous "Stolen Duchess," lost 25 years.

Devonshire, Spencer Compton Cavendish, 8th **duke of** (1833–1908), English statesman, prominent in Victorian era; a Liberal but opposed Gladstone's Home Rule policy; leader of Liberal Unionists.

Devonshire, Victor Christian William Cavendish, 9th **duke of** (1868–1938), nephew of 8th duke; was 17 years in House of Commons before succeeding to title; was treasurer of His Majesty's household, financial secretary to the treasury, and civil lord of the Admiralty; governor-general of Canada 1916–21; colonial secretary 1922–24.

Devonshire, county in England. *see in index* Devon

De Voto, Bernard Augustine (1897–1955), writer, born in Ogden, Utah; taught English at Northwestern University 1922–27 and Harvard 1929–36; editor 'The Easy Chair', 'Harper's Magazine', after 1935; editor 'The Saturday Review of Literature' 1936–38 ('Mark Twain at Work'; trilogy on America's expansion: 'The Course of Empire', 'The Year of Decision: 1846', 'Across the Wide Missouri', 1947 Pulitzer prize; essays: 'The Easy Chair'), *picture* U-226
writing W-311

De Vries, Hugo (1848–1935), Dutch botanist, born in Haarlem; professor University of Amsterdam; inaugurated plan for studying evolution.

De Vries, Peter (born 1910), writer and editor, born in Chicago, Ill.; with 'Poetry' magazine 1938–44, 'The New Yorker' after 1944; elected to National Institute of Arts and Letters 1969 (novels: 'The Tunnel of Love', 'The Blood of the Lamb', 'Cat's Pajamas & Witch's Milk').

Dew, moisture condensed from air
cloud C-515
dew point H-289, W-85a
fog F-246

Dewar, Sir James (1842–1923), British physicist and chemist, born in Kincardine, Scotland; professor Cambridge University, and Royal Institution of London; joint inventor of "cordite" with Sir Frederick Abel; noted for work on liquefaction of gases and researches on temperatures near absolute zero; produced liquid oxygen in quantity; invented Dewar flask, original thermos bottle.

Dewberry
hybrids R-94

Dewclaw, a vestigial toe of a dog D-194, *picture* D-195

Dewdney, Edgar (1835–1916), Canadian civil engineer and statesman, born in Devonshire, England; came to British Columbia 1859 and became a surveyor; lieutenant governor of the Northwest Territories 1881; minister of the interior 1888–92; lieutenant governor of British Columbia 1892–97.

De Wet, Christiaan Rudolph (1854–1922), Boer general, born in Orange Free State, Union of South Africa; commander Orange Free State forces in Boer War 1899–1902; led rebellion against South African government at outbreak of war 1914; defeated, imprisoned for six months.

Dewey, Charles Melville (1849–1937), landscape painter, born in Lowville, N.Y.; favored early morning and evening effects.

Dewey, George (1837–1917), U.S. naval commander D-124, S-364, *picture* V-296
grave N-20

Dewey, John (1859–1952), U.S. philosopher, psychologist, and educator D-124, V-296
civil rights C-468
functional psychology P-520
influence on education, S-240 *table* E-90

Dewey, Melvil (1851–1931), librarian, born in Adams Center, N.Y.; founder of the 'Library Journal' and one of the founders of the American Library Association; inventor of decimal classification.

Dewey, Thomas E(dmund) (1902–71), lawyer, born in Owosso, Mich.; special prosecutor of racketeering gangs in New York, N.Y., 1935–37; district attorney of New York County 1937–42; governor of New York 1942–54; Republican

Dicksee / Dinar

Dicksee, Sir Francis Bernard (Frank) (1853–1928), English painter, born in London; president Royal Academy 1924–28; won success with 'Harmony'; also painted many landscapes and notable portraits of women.

Dickson, Robert George Brian (born 1916), Canadian jurist, born in Yorkton, Sask.; created queen's counsel 1953; justice Manitoba Court of Appeal 1967–73; justice Supreme Court of Canada 1973–.

Dickson, William (1769–1846), Canadian lawyer, soldier, and colonizer, born in Dumfries, Scotland; came to Canada in 1792; served in Canadian militia in War of 1812; appointed to Legislative Council of Upper Canada 1815; engaged in colonization of Dumfries township, Upper Canada 1827–36.

Dicotyledoneae, or **dicotyledons,** also **dicots,** subclass of plants P-360, S-108, T-259

Dictating machine.
- Edison's machine, *picture* E-73

Dictatorship. *see also in index* Totalitarian state
- ancient
  - Roman plebeians R-244
- basis of force W-247
- democracy D-94
- Franco, Francisco F-376
- modern E-323, G-164, *Reference-Outline* E-340
- Communism. *see also in index* Communism
- Latin America L-67, S-291
- Nazism. *see in index* Nazism
- parliaments P-129

Dictionary R-125
- Hebrew, Saadia ben Joseph S-1
- Johnson, Samuel J-136, R-126
- libraries L-161
- sample entry, *picture* R-126
- selected list R-127
- Webster, Noah W-91

'Dictionary of American Biography', biographical dictionary B-223

'Dictionary of National Biography', biographical dictionary B-223

'Dictionnaire historique et critique', work by Bayle B-223

Dictograph, device used for interoffice communication; in each office is a box containing a transmitter and receiver activated by simple controls.

Didactic poetry P-407

Diderot, Denis (1713–84), French writer, critic, and philosopher D-138
- French literature F-396
- reference books R-124

Didion, Joan (born 1934), U.S. author A-362

Didgeridoo, musical instrument A-795

Didiscus. *see in index* Trachymene

Dido, or **Elissa,** legendary Carthaginian queen
- Aeneas A-63
- Carthage C-185

'Dido and Aeneas', opera by Henry Purcell O-464

Didot, scholarly family of French printers and publishers; greatest since the Estiennes; founded by **François** (1689–1757); his son **François Ambroise** (1730–1804) first used vellum paper; **Pierre** (1761–1853) published beautiful editions of French and Latin classics; **Firmin** (1764–1836) invented stereotyping; **Henri** (1765–1852) designed microscopic types; **Ambroise Firmin** (1790–1876), famous as collector of old manuscripts, brought the family's publishing business to its peak.

Didrikson, Babe. *see in index* Zaharias

Die, metal stamp or mold D-139
- coinmaking M-367
- embossing E-191
- forging F-317
  - zinc castings Z-355
- plastics molding P-382, *picture* P-383
- shoemaking, *picture* S-180
- teaspoon making, *picture* S-204
- wiremaking W-190

Diedrichs, Otto von (1843–1918), German admiral, remembered for attempt (frustrated by Commodore George Dewey and a British admiral) to ignore Dewey's blockade of Manila 1898.

Diefenbaker, John G(eorge) (1895–1979), Canadian statesman C-105, D-140
- Eisenhower E-135
- Pearson P-150
- Trans-Canada Highway T-232

Diegueños, American Indian people of Yuman stock in whose territory in s. California was established San Diego Mission, whence their name.

Dielectric, substance that resists electric spark discharges
- electric condensers E-152

Dielman, Frederick (1847–1935), American artist, born in Hanover, Germany; noted for genre, historical, and mural paintings; designed mosaic panels 'Law' and 'History' in Library of Congress.

Diels, Otto (Paul Hermann) (1876–1954), German chemist, born in Hamburg.

Diem, Ngo Dinh. *see in index* Ngo Dinh Diem

Diemer, Walter, creator of bubble gum C-307

Dienbienphu, Vietnam, town in n.w., V-319, *map* V-321

Dienbienphu, Battle of, Vietnamese history D-140

Diencephalon, or **between brain** B-400

Dieppe, France, seaport and summer resort on English Channel, 170 km (105 mi) n.w. of Paris; destroyed by English and Dutch 1694; occupied by Germans 1870–71 and 1940, liberated by Allies 1944; pop. 29,829.

Dies, Martin (born 1901), lawyer, U.S. congressman, born in Colorado, Tex.; member of the United States House of Representatives 1931–44; chairman of House committee to investigate Un-American Activities 1938–44; prominent Democrat.

Diesel, Rudolf (1858–1913), German engineer, born in Paris, France; known for first commercially successful oil-fuel engine, which bears his name D-140
- internal-combustion engine I-252

Diesel engine D-141, T-236.
- automobile power plant A-860
- farm machinery F-31
- internal-combustion I-252
- locomotives L-279, R-78
- motorboats M-532
- motor ships S-167, *diagram* S-172
- submarines S-493, *diagram* S-495a
- trucks T-271

Diesinking, manufacturing process
- die and diemaking D-139

'Dies Irae' ('day of wrath'), name generally given to a 13th-century hymn on the Last Judgment; used in Roman Catholic church liturgy.

Dieskau, Ludwig August, Baron (1701–67), German soldier, born in Saxony; joined French army and in 1755 sent to Canada as commander in chief of French colonial troops; defeated and taken prisoner by English at Lake George, N.Y.

Diesterweg, Friedrich Adolf Wilhelm (1790–1866), German educator and author, born in Siegen, Westphalia, Prussia; follower of Pestalozzi; stressed value of self-activity in education.

Diet, formal assembly or meeting; name often applied to legislative assemblies of central and n. European countries; also the formal meeting of councillors of Holy Roman Empire. *see also in index* Reichstag
- Bonn G-110, *picture* G-111
- Japanese, J-34, *diagram* J-35, *map* T-192, *picture* T-194
- Spires (1529) R-134

Diet, nutrition F-275
- diabetes D-126

Dietetics F-278, H-206
- hospitals H-241a, *picture* H-241b

Dietitian F-279, H-206, *picture* H-205

Dietrich, Marlene (born 1901), U.S. actress, born in Berlin, Germany; to U.S. 1930 (citizen 1939) after success in German motion picture 'Blue Angel' ('Shanghai Express'; 'Song of Songs'; 'Destry Rides Again'; 'A Foreign Affair').

Dietrich of Bern, name under which Theodoric the Great appears in the 'Nibelungenlied' and other heroic German legends. *see in index* Theodoric the Great

Difference, subtraction S-497

Differential, device that can produce multiple motions from one motion or combine several motions into one; permits automobile wheels to turn at different speeds.
- automobile A-852

Differential calculus, mathematics C-22
- Fermat's invention F-55

Diffraction, bending of radiant energy rays when passing an obstacle.
- electrons P-307
- light structure L-200
- X rays A-237, B-237, S-254, 374

Diffraction grating spectroscope S-372

Diffrient, Niels (born 1928), U.S. industrial designer I-171

Diffusion, physical science
- cell process C-238
- porometer, *picture* B-231

Digambara, sect of Jainism J-14

'Digest', or **'Pandects',** legal work J-161

Digestive system D-142
- cattle R-318
- earthworm A-389, E-32
- frog F-407
- human A-391
  - chewing and drinking H-87
  - glands G-134
  - liver L-261
  - pancreas H-227, *diagram* H-225
  - nutritive reflexes R-132
  - stomach S-454
  - enzymes E-281, *table* E-281
  - pepsin P-197b
  - X-ray studies X-331, *picture* X-330

Digestive tract. *see in index* Alimentary canal

Diggers, Indians who lived in the deserts of western United States; they ate roots and lived in caves and grass huts.

Digger wasp W-58

Digit, single numerical figure N-379
- addition A-590

Digital calculator, device that performs arithmetic operations C-19

Digital computer C-628

Digital instruments I-230

Digitalis, drug M-215a. *see also in index* Foxglove
- heart treatment D-273

Dihigo, Martin (El Maestro) (1905–71), baseball player, born in Matanzas, Cuba; pitcher, outfielder, infielder for Negro, Latin American leagues 1923–50.

Dijon, France, historic city in e., former capital of Burgundy; various manufactures; mustard, wine; university; fine churches; occupied by Germans in 1870 and in 1940; pop. 143,120, *map* E-334

Dika nut, seed of the wild mango, of West Africa; source of oil; ground into an acidy paste and combined with spices for *dika bread,* a food staple of some Africans.

Dike, embankment, usually to protect lowlands from floods D-146. *see also in index* Levee
- dams D-15
- flooding F-182
- Hwang Ho, China H-282
- irrigation I-355
- levees R-211
- Mississippi River M-390
- Netherlands N-133
- New Brunswick N-162d
- seawalls G-7

Diligenti quintuplets (born July 15, 1943), children of Franco and Ana María Diligenti, born in Buenos Aires, Argentina; combined weight at birth about 4.5 kilograms (10 pounds); two boys (Franco and Carlos Alberto) and three girls (María Ester, María Fernanda, and María Cristina) M-524a

Dill, plant of parsley family S-379

Dillard University, New Orleans, La.; private control; formed 1930 by merger of New Orleans University (Methodist-related) and Straight College (Congregational), both founded 1869; liberal arts, education, *map* N-223b

Dillenius, or **Dillen, Johann Jakob** (1687–1747), German botanist, born in Darmstadt; in 1728 became first professor of botany at Oxford University ('Historia Muscorum', book on mosses).

Dillon, C(larence) Douglas (born 1909), U.S. government official and banker, born in Geneva, Switzerland, of American parents; ambassador to France 1953–57; undersecretary of state for economic affairs 1958–61; secretary of the treasury 1961–65; chairman Rockefeller Foundation 1972.

Dillon, George (1906–68), poet, born in Jacksonville, Fla.; associate editor of 'Poetry', a magazine of verse, while student at University of Chicago; Pulitzer prize for poetry 1931; Guggenheim fellowship 1932–33; editor of 'Poetry' 1937–49 ('Boy in the Wind'; 'The Flowering Stone').

Dillon, John (1851–1927), Irish Nationalist political leader, born in Dublin; worked to abolish British rule in Ireland; often in prison; member of Parliament more than 30 years.

Dillon, Leo (born 1933), artist, born Brooklyn, N.Y. and **Dillon, Diane** (Claire Sorber) (born 1933), artist, born in Glendale, Calif.; illustrators of children's books; awarded Caldecott medals for 'Why Mosquitoes Buzz in People's Ears' (1976) and 'Ashanti to Zulu' (1977).

Dilwara Temple, Mount Abu, India, *picture* J-14

Di Maggio, Joseph Paul (Joe) (born 1914), baseball outfielder, born in Martinez, Calif.; played for New York, A.L., 1936–42, 1946–51; led A.L. in batting 1939 and 1940; set major-league record 1941 by hitting safely in 56 consecutive games; hit 361 home runs; lifetime batting average of .325; played in 10 World Series, including 51 games; chosen A.L.'s most valuable player 1939, 1941, and 1947 B-93

Dime, U.S. coin worth 10 cents, or 1/10 of a dollar; term once meant the tenth part, the tithe paid as church or state dues; Wycliffe's Bible translation reads, "He gave him dymes of alle thingis" M-367, *picture* M-425b

Dimeter, line in poetry P-405

Diminuendo, music, *table* M-566a

Dimitrov, Georgi (1882–1949), Communist official, born in Bulgaria; tried for complicity in setting fire to Reichstag 1933; defied Goering and found not guilty; secretary general of Communist International (Comintern) 1935–43; premier of Bulgaria 1946–49.

Dimity, fine cotton fabric with corded stripes or bars; name first applied to heavy fabric of same type made in Spain for bed hangings.

Dimnet, Ernest (1866–1954), French abbé, canon of Cambrai Cathedral, born in Trélon; popular in U.S. as lecturer ('The Brontë Sisters'; 'The Art of Thinking'; 'What We Live By'; 'My Old World', 'My New World', autobiography).

Dimond, Anthony J(oseph) (1881–1953), lawyer and political leader, born in Palatine Bridge, N.Y.; to Alaska as prospector 1904; delegate to U.S. Congress 1933–45; judge U.S. district court, Anchorage, after 1945; champion of Alaskan statehood.

Dimorphotheca, genus of annual and perennial plants and shrubs of the composite family; native to s. Africa; flowers yellow, purple, or white rays with contrasting centers; they close toward sundown; also called Cape marigold or African daisy.

Dinan, city, France, *picture* F-348

Dinant, town in Belgium on Meuse River, 77 km (48 mi) s.e. of Brussels; once noted for copperware; sacked by Burgundians 1466, by French 1554, 1675; captured and burned by Germans Aug. 23, 1914; pop. 6851.

Dinar, monetary unit of Algeria, Bahrain, Iraq, Jordan, Kuwait, Libya, People's Democratic Republic of Yemen, Tunisia,

Dinaric / Discrimination

Yugoslavia; medieval gold coin of Arabia and other Moslem lands worth about $4.50, *table* M-428

Dinaric Alps, mountains in w. Yugoslavia; highest point Dinara (1831 m; 6008 ft).

D'Indy, Vincent. *see in index* Indy

Diners Club, credit card
consumer credit C-762

Dinesen, Isak. *see in index* Blixen Finecke, Baroness Karen

Ding Dong School. *see in index* Horwich, Frances R(appaport)

Dingley, Nelson, Jr. (1832–99), statesman and journalist, born in Durham, Me.; editor and publisher 'Lewiston (Me.) Journal'; member of Congress (Republican) 1881–99; framed protective Dingley Tariff Act of 1897.

Dingley Tariff Act (1897) T-25
McKinley's enactment M-19

Dingo, Australian wild dog A-781, D-212
domestication A-454

Dinka, group of people in the Sudan along the White Nile River; a tall people, with skins almost blue black S-502

Dinkelsbühl, West Germany, town in Bavaria, on Wörnitz River, 71 km (44 mi) s.w. of Nuremberg; contains medieval walls and towers, also the German House, example of German Renaissance wooden architecture; founded 10th century; free imperial city 1351–1802; pop. 8892, *map* G-115

Dinking machine.
shoemaking, *picture* S-181

Dinoflagellates, algae C-715

Dinosaur, extinct reptile
evolution G-65a, R-153
fossils F-323
prehistoric animals A-461, P-488, *picture* P-487
size comparison, *picture* W-130

Dinosaur National Monument, Utah and Colorado N-35, *maps* C-583, N-30, U-232, *picture* C-577
fossil discovery, *pictures* G-62, F-322

Dinwiddie, Robert (1693–1770), British colonial official, born near Glasgow, Scotland; lieutenant governor of Virginia 1752–58; supported French and Indian War
Washington, George W-20

Diocese, district or churches presided over by a bishop; in Roman times was a civil division of territory, but as the early church developed along the same territorial divisions, the word gradually became ecclesiastical A-417

Diocletian (245–313), Roman emperor (284–305), able soldier and energetic ruler, under whom a memorable persecution of Christians took place R-248
baths R-255, *map* R-251
military reforms A-637
persecutes Christians C-401

Diode, type of vacuum tube E-169
rectifying alternating current E-164
schematic diagram R-56

Diodorus Siculus (died about 20 B.C.), Greek historian of time of Julius Caesar and Augustus; of his 'Historical Library', history of world in 40 books, only parts remain.

Dioecious flower F-219

Diogenes (412–323 B.C.), Greek Cynic philosopher D-147

Diomedeidae, the albatross family of birds. *see in index* Albatross

Diomede Islands, two islands in Bering Strait, between Asia and N. America A-571, *maps* U-39, 94

Diomedes, Greek mythology, king of Thrace H-143

Diomedes, one of Greek heroes of Trojan War.

Dionne quintuplets (born 1934), daughters of Oliva and Elzire Dionne, born May 28 at Callander, Ont., Canada; combined weight at birth about 6 kilograms (13 pounds); names Annette, Cecile, Emilie (died 1954), Marie (died 1970), Yvonne; first known quints to live over one hour; Allan R. Dafoe (1883–1943) attending physician; made king's wards by Ontario government 1935, returned to father 1944 M-542a

Dionysia, ancient Greek religious festival A-87

Dionysius, the Elder (432?–367 B.C.), tyrant of Syracuse; cruel despot
Damon and Pythias D-19
Plato P-384

Dionysius Thrax (fl. *c.* 120 BC) Greek grammarian
linguistics contribution L-229

Dionysus, Greek mythology D-147
dance D-22
drama D-242
Midas M-293
Praxiteles' statue 'Hermes with the Infant Dionysus' G-229, S-83
theater A-26, *picture* T-152

Diophantus (fl. 350?–400?), Greek mathematician; six volumes of his 13-volume 'Arithmetica' now known; founded algebra with letters as symbols for operations; solved only equations using whole numbers and their powers A-293

Diopside, transparent to opaque calcium-magnesium silicate; the transparent green variety is cut as a gem; also colorless, gray, or yellow M-336

'Dioptrice', work by Kepler K-229

Dior, Christian (Ernest) (1905–57), French fashion designer, born in Granville, Normandy; established salon in Paris 1946 and one in New York, N.Y., 1948; noted as creator of "new look"
dress design D-271

Diorama, representation of a scene, usually for use in museums and expositions, in which background is a painting and foreground is three-dimensional; the two blend together and give appearance of reality D-148
primitive man, *picture* M-77

Diorite, very hard igneous rock composed chiefly of feldspar and hornblende; usually smaller than masses of granite.
use E-122, G-59

Dioscorides, Pedanius (1st century A.D.), Greek physician, born in Anazarbus, Cilicia; as physician to Roman armies, collected information on plants in many countries ('De Materia Medica' for 15 centuries the authority in botany and medicine).

Dioscuri, "Sons of Zeus," name given to Castor and Pollux. *see in index* Castor and Pollux

Dioxin, or **tetrachlorodioxin,** chemical J-175

Dip, geology, term used to denote inclination of strata of rocks; the angle between the greatest slope of a specific surface and the horizontal plane.

Dip, of compass needle, deviation from horizontal caused by alignment with magnetic lines of force turning to or from horizontal, especially near the magnetic poles. *see also in index* Dipping needle

Diphros, Greek stool
description F-455

Diphtheria, contagious disease A-495
Behring, Emil von M-215c
cause, *picture* D-170
infectious disease, *table* D-171
Schick test S-52h
vaccine V-250

Diphthong, two vowel sounds forming one speech sound and pronounced in one syllable P-268a

Diplodocus, prehistoric reptile R-155, *picture* P-489

Diplomacy D-149

Diplomat D-149
papal P-100, V-270

Diplopia, or **double vision** E-370

Dipole, antenna
radio R-53
television T-71

Dipole, chemical compound in solution S-256

Dipole, magnet M-47

Dipper. *see in index* Big Dipper; Little Dipper

Dipper, or **water ouzel,** perching bird of the family Cinclidae about the size of a robin, with slaty gray plumage and short square tail, which it carries erect like a wren; frequents rapid streams and lakes of Old and New World, dipping and diving into water for its food; the species found in the Rocky Mountain region is *Cinclus mexicanus unicolor*.

Dipper dredge machine for digging soil from bottoms of bodies of water D-257

Dipping, flag display, *list* F-149

Dipping needle, magnetic needle used for measuring the direction of the lines of magnetism of the earth at different places; it is similar to a compass but turns about a horizontal axis instead of a vertical one. *see also in index* Dip

Dipping vat, sunken tank filled with a chemical solution C-231

Diprotodon, extinct giant marsupial allied to kangaroo; fossils in Australia; size of rhinoceros.

Dipsacaceae. *see in index* Teasel family

Dipsy sinker, fishing F-140

Diptera, order of two-winged insects F-243

Dipterocarp, tree P-259b

Dirac, Paul Adrien Maurice (1902–84), English physicist, born in Bristol; professor of mathematics Cambridge University 1932–68 ('Principles of Quantum Mechanics') D-152, A-752
antimatter theory M-172
ether concept E-292
physics P-308

Direct-color photography. *see in index* Color photography

Direct current. *see in index* Electric current.

Direct democracy D-95

Directing, of a dramatic work D-152

Directional gyro, aircraft navigation, *picture* C-623

Direction finder, radio, *picture* R-55

Directions D-156. *see also in index* Latitude and Longitude
biological clocks B-226
compass, magnetic C-621

Direct lithography, printing L-258

Direct-mail advertising A-59

Direct object, grammar S-110

Director, of a dramatic work D-152
motion pictures M-508
play T-149

'Director, The'. *see in index* 'The Gentleman and Cabinet Maker's Director'.

Directorate, interlocking M-450

Directory, committee of 5 which governed France 1795–99, succeeding the Convention
French Revolution F-404
Napoleon N-10
Talleyrand T-13
'XYZ' Affair X-334

Directory, reference book
biographical R-130
libraries L-162

Direct primary P-496

Direct reduction, metalworking I-338

Direct response, merchandising A-59

Directrix, geometry G-69, *diagram* G-70

Dire Dawa, Ethiopia, town on Addis Ababa-Djibouti railroad; trade in coffee, hides; pop. 50,733, *map* E-294

Dirges, songs of praise and sorrow A-120

Dirham, monetary unit of Morocco, *table* M-428

Dirigible, balloon that can be steered A-154. *see also in index* Balloon and Airship design and operation B-38

Dirksen, Everett M(cKinley) (1896–1969), political leader, born in Pekin, Ill.; U.S. congressman (Republican) from Illinois 1933–49; U.S. senator 1951–69, minority leader 1959–69; eloquent speaker; recording, 'The Gallant Men'.

Disability, inability to perform an activity because of some physical or mental disorder; a disabled person is not necessarily handicapped D-163

Disabled American Veterans, organization founded for veterans of World War I, now open to all U.S. veterans injured in war duty; chartered by Congress as official voice of disabled veterans; prime objective is rehabilitation and care of such veterans; national headquarters, Cincinnati, Ohio P-140

Disaccharide, any of several sugars having the formula $(C_{12}H_{22}O_{11})$ and differing in structure of molecule; all can be split into two simple sugars (monosaccharides) S-508
carbohydrate division C-155

Disappointment, Cape, n. headland of Columbia River mouth in Washington; named by Capt. John Meares in 1788 when he searched in vain for the hidden mouth of the river O-483, *maps* U-40, W-52

Disarmament, reduction of naval and military strength of nations by international agreement D-163, P-143b, N-105
Cold War C-545
Hague Peace Conferences H-4
London Naval Conference and Treaty P-18, P-143c, N-105
nuclear control treaties
nonproliferation P-144
space U-27
test ban T-251
United Nations U-23
Washington Conference H-31, P-18

Disassembly line, meat industry M-192

Disasters.
airship explosions B-43
earthquakes, *list* E-32. *see also in index* Earthquake
fires
Hamburg, West Germany H-14
insurance I-235
Moscow, Russia M-493a
Ottawa, Ont., Canada O-510
Rome, ancient N-128
San Francisco, Calif. S-44
Seattle, Wash. S-103b
Smyrna, Turkey S-221
hospital procedures H-241b
marine accidents
'Thresher' N-89
'Titanic' I-8, S-177d
volcanic eruptions V-380
Etna, Mount E-303
Paricutin V-383
Pelée, Mont V-380
Vesuvius, Mount V-305
Pompeii P-442

Disc, phonograph. *see in index* Record, phonograph

Disciples of Christ, or **Christian Church,** frequently known as Campbellites, Christian religious denomination, founded in early 19th century in United States by Thomas and Alexander Campbell; seeks restoration of apostolic Christianity D-164

Disciplinary approach, social studies S-241, 238

Discipline, academic. *see in index* disciplines by name, as Mathematics; Sociology

Discipline of children. *see in index* Child training

Disclimax, ecology E-50

'Discobolus'. *see in index* Discus Thrower

Discomfort Index. *see in index* Temperature-Humidity Index

Discordia, Roman mythology, goddess of discord, corresponding to Greek Eris T-265

Discount, bank
central bank C-260
Federal Reserve System F-51
percentage P-200

Discount stores C-513

'Discourse of a Northwest Passage', work by Gilbert A-332

Discoverers, American satellites used for military and space research; first launch 1959, *table* S-344

'Discovery', Captain Scott's ship S-72

'Discovery', Hudson's ship H-264

'Discovery', one of ships in which Jamestown colonists sailed to America.

'Discovery', space shuttle S-347

'Discovery, Settlement, and Present State of Kentucky, The', work by Filson
Boone B-365

Discrimination, racial A-497. *see also in index* Apartheid; black Americans; Minorities; Prejudice; Segregation; South Africa

Djibouti / Dole

Greek and Roman mythology, the lotus-eaters' island; pop. 62,445.
Djibouti, Republic of, formerly **Afars and Issas, Territory of the (French Somaliland),** nation in e. Africa on Gulf of Aden; formerly a French territory; independent 1977; 8900 sq mi (23,050 sq km); cap. Djibouti; pop. 323,000 D-190, *map* E-294
flag, *picture* F-164
money, *table* M-428
Djibouti, Djibouti, capital and port; pop. 130,000 D-190, E-294
Djibouti, monetary unit, *table* M-428
Djilas, Milovan (born 1911), Yugoslav political leader, born in Montenegro; vice-president and head of parliament of Yugoslavia under Tito; left Communist party 1954; arrested for anti-Communist statements and writings; imprisoned 1956–61, 1962–67 ('The New Class'; 'Conversations with Stalin'; 'Montenegro').
Djokjakarta, Indonesia, city in s.-central Java; ancient temples of Borobudur and Prambanan; pop. 500,000, *map* E-36
Djoser, or **Zoser,** king of Egypt (2700 B.C.) E-119
Dmitri, or **Demetrius,** Russian pretender who appeared 1603 and took name of heir to the throne, who had been secretly killed by the usurping czar Boris Godunov; reigned ably until his murder 1606 R-352
DNA (deoxyribonucleic acid), found in cell nucleus B-199, C-239
biophysics research B-237
Franklin's research F-385
heredity H-144
embryology E-195
genetics G-43c
virus, *picture* D-166
Dnepr, or **Dnieper River,** river of s.w. U.S.S.R.; length 1400 mi (2250 km) D-190, *maps* E-335, R-322, W-253
Russian history R-351
Dnepr Dam, U.S.S.R., on Dnieper River, 320 km (200 mi) from its mouth, at Zaporozh'ye, Ukrainian S.S.R.; concrete dam with 3 locks; generates 660,000 kilowatts (900,000 horsepower); construction directed by American engineers and cost about $110,000,000 D-191, K-231
Dnepropetrovsk, U.S.S.R, city in the Ukrainian S.S.R., 400 km (250 mi) n.e. of Odessa; iron and steel products; flour; timber depot; pop. 863,000, *maps* E-335, R-344
Dnestr, or **Dniester River,** river of s.w. U.S.S.R; length 839 mi (1,350 km) D-191, *maps* E-335, R-322
Doan, Charles A(ustin) (born 1896), physician, born in Nelsonville, Ohio; specialist in blood diseases; professor of medicine and director of medical research Ohio State University 1930–44, dean 1944–61.
Doane College, Crete, Neb.; affiliated with United Church of Christ; established 1872; liberal arts, teacher education.
Dobby, weaving F-5, *picture* T-133
Dobell, Bertram (1842–1914), English bookseller and poet, born in Battle; arranged publication of James Thomson's 'The City of Dreadful Night'; identified and edited poetry of Thomas Traherne.
Döbereiner, Johann Wolfgang (1780–1849), German chemist, born in near Hof, Bavaria; invented Döbereiner's lamp, ignited by action of hydrogen on platinum sponge and widely used before prevalence of sulfur match; discovered furfural; in chemistry, classified similar elements in groups of three (Döbereiner's triads).
Doberman pinscher, dog D-193, *picture* D-201
Dobie, J(ames) Frank (1888–1964), author and educator, born in Live Oak County, Tex.; professor of English University of Texas 1933–47; popular, authoritative legends of Southwest ('Coronado's Children'; 'Tales of the Mustangs'; 'The Longhorns'; 'Cow People'); awarded Presidential Medal of Freedom 1964, *picture* T-124a
Dobrovolsky, Georgi T. (1928–71), Soviet cosmonaut, born in Odessa; chosen for space program 1963; flight commander Soyuz II, in which he and two others died as craft was reentering earth's atmosphere, *table* S-348
Dobruja, farming district in s.e. Europe, on Black Sea R-316
Dobrynin, Anatoli Fedorovich (born 1919?), Soviet diplomat, born in Ukraine; Soviet embassy staff to U.S. 1952–55; UN undersecretary 1957–60; ambassador to U.S. 1962–.
Dobson, (Henry) Austin (1840–1921), English poet and essayist, born in Plymouth; graceful use of French verse forms ('At the Sign of the Lyre') E-275
Dobsonian Telescope A-731
Dobzhansky, Theodosius (1900–75), Russian-American scientist D-191
Dock, George (1860–1951), physician, born in Hopewell, Pa.; professor of medicine University of Michigan, Tulane and Washington universities; contributed to pathology of hookworm, malaria, and dysentery.
Dock, coarse weedy herbs of genus *Rumex* of buckwheat family; 0.6 to 1.2 m (2 to 4 ft) high; small greenish flowers in panicles; leaves long, lance-shaped *picture* W-92b
Dock, space for a ship between two adjoining piers or wharves; in U.S. often called a slip; also an enclosed place for ships, with gates to maintain desired water level regardless of tides H-25. *see also in index* Port
amphibious transport dock N-99
dry dock S-171, *pictures* N-162c, R-269
ore dock, *picture* W-195
Docking. *see in index* Rendezvous and docking
Dock Street Theater, Charleston, S.C. C-280
Doctor, university degree E-100a, U-204
Doctor, medical. *see in index* Medicine; Physician
Doctor bird, Jamaican name for hummingbird J-17
'Dr. Breen's Practice', work by Howells A-352
'Doctor Faustus, The Tragical History of', play by Marlowe. *see in index* 'D. Faustus, The Tragicall History of'
Doctorfish, fish of the genus *Teuthis*, with knifelike movable spine on each side of tail; also known as surgeonfish, lancet, barberfish, or tang; lives in warm seas.
Doctors' Commons, formerly a self-governing teaching body of practitioners of canon and civil law
Dickens' position D-134
Doctrine of the Faith, Congregation for the, Roman Catholic church P-100
Documentary, photography and motion pictures M-528
acting history A-26
Lange, Dorothea L-29
Documentation, assembling and coding of recorded information for maximum accessibility to users
antiques A-494
report writing R-151b
Dodd, William Edward (1869–1940), historian and diplomat, born near Clayton, N.C.; professor University of Chicago 1908–33; ambassador to Germany 1933–37 ('Woodrow Wilson and His Work').
Dodder, leafless parasitic plant introduced into U.S. from Europe with clover seeds; now a rapidly growing pest P-114, *pictures* P-363a
Doddridge, Philip (1702–51), English nonconformist clergyman, born in London; wrote hymns; gave Bibles to poor.
Dodds, Johnny (1892–1940), jazz clarinetist, born in New Orleans, La.; self-taught; played with Joseph Oliver; inspired other clarinetists.
Dodecagon, geometry G-69
Dodecahedron, geometry G-72
Dodecanese, Greek island group chiefly in s.e. Aegean Sea, off Turkey; 2680 sq km (1035 sq mi); pop. 121,017, *map* G-213
Dodge, Grace Hoadley (1856–1914), social worker, born in New York, N.Y.; organized 1884 the Industrial Education Association to introduce industrial education into public schools; helped found Teachers College of Columbia University 1889.
Dodge, Grenville Mellen (1831–1916), civil engineer and Union general in Civil War, born in Danvers, Mass.; chief engineer Union Pacific Railroad 1866–70; Republican representative from Iowa 1867–69.
Dodge, John F. (1864–1920), and his brother **Horace E.** (1868–1920), early automobile manufacturers; after working as machinists and manufacturers of automobile parts, started their own automobile manufacturing company A-859
Dodge, Mary (Elizabeth) Mapes (1831–1905), editor and writer for children, born in New York, N.Y. ('Hans Brinker, or The Silver Skates'; 'The Land of Pluck').
DODGE, artificial satellite, *table* S-344
Dodge City, Kan., city on Arkansas River, about 150 mi (240 km) w. of Wichita; cattle market and wheat terminal; dairy and other food products; farm equipment; Saint Mary of the Plains College; annual rodeo; pop. 18,001 K-177
Dodgem, amusement park ride A-384
Dodgson, Charles Lutwidge. *see in index* Carroll, Lewis
Dodo, extinct bird B-276.
Dodoma, Tanzania D-35
Dodona, Greece, city of ancient oracle, *map* G-221
Dodsley, Robert (1703–64), English author and publisher, birthplace probably Mansfield; suggested, published, and helped finance Johnson's 'Dictionary'.
'Dodsworth', work by Lewis L-142
Doe, John. *see in index* John Doe
Doe, female, especially adult, of deer, antelope, hare, and most other mammals of which the male is known as a buck deer D-61
Doenitz, Karl (1891–1980), German submarine expert, born in Grünau, near Berlin; made commander in chief of German navy 1943; succeeding Hitler, was Führer May 1945; imprisoned for war crimes 1946–56; wrote 'Memoirs'.
Doering, William von Eggers (born 1917), chemist, born in Fort Worth, Tex.; first to synthesize quinine (1944), with R. B. Woodward; professor chemistry Yale University 1952–67, Harvard University 1967–.
Dog, animal belonging to the family Canidae D-192. *see also in index* dogs by name
anatomy
reflexes R-132
senses S-218, S-260
teeth, *picture* T-48
bibliography H-190
disease P-138, V-251
domestication A-454, *pictures* M-78, S-57d
Eskimo travel E-287
food and feeding, *picture* V-243
fur, *tables* F-464, 465
hunting breeds, *picture* H-278
lifespan A-126, *chart* A-423
myth and legend
Argos O-409
Cerberus H-2, H-143
pet care P-243
related species. *see in index* Jackal; Wolf
test of life L-264
training *picture* V-243
police work, *picture* P-428
space travel S-345
whistle S-260
Dogbane, spreading, milky-juiced herb (*Apocynum androsaemifolium*) with erect branching stem; opposite, oval leaves; small bell-shaped flowers, white or pink; plant believed poisonous to dogs.
Dogbane family, or **Apocynaceae,** family of plants and trees, native chiefly to tropics, including the dogbane, oleander, crape jasmine, star jasmine, periwinkle, amsonia, and Indian hemp.
Dogberry, Shakespeare's 'Much Ado About Nothing', constable, type of official stupidity. *see also in index* 'Much Ado About Nothing'
Doge, elective duke or chief magistrate of the city-republics of Venice and Genoa during Middle Ages V-278
Doge's Palace, Venice, Italy V-277
Dogfish. *see in index* Bowfin
Dogfish, or **grayfish,** shark S-144
Dogger Bank, extensive sandbank in North Sea N-362
Dogie, cattle ranching cowboys, *picture* C-753
Dog mushroom, *picture* M-553
Dog racing, sport D-214, *picture* D-207
Dogrib, Indian people that lives in Northwest Territories, Canada, *map* I-136, *table* I-138
Dog salmon, chum salmon, or **keta salmon,** fish of the family Salmonidae S-28
Dog Star, or **Sirius** S-413
Dog tooth. *see in index* Cuspid
Dogtooth violet, also called **adder's-tongue, trout lily,** or **fawn lily** F-240, *picture* F-232
Dogwood, shrub or tree.
flowering, *picture* M-402
state flower, *pictures* S-427, N-330
Dogwood family, or **Cornaceae,** family of shrubs and trees, including the dogwood, golddust tree, and cornelian cherry. *see also in index* Dogwood
Dohnányi, Ernö (Ernst von Dohnányi) (1877–1960), Hungarian composer, born in Pressburg, now Bratislava, Czechoslovakia; symphonies, piano pieces, string quartets, songs, and operas ('The Tenor').
Doisy, Edward Adelbert (born 1893), biochemist, born in Hume, Ill.; professor of biochemistry St. Louis University School of Medicine 1923–65; isolated theelin, female sex hormone, 1929. *see also in index* Nobel Prizewinners, *table*
Do it yourself. *see in index* Hobby
Dolbear, Amos Anderson (1837–1910), inventor and physicist, born in Norwich, Conn.; made valuable studies and inventions regarding the writing telegraph, electric gyroscope, magnetotelephone, wireless telegraphy, and electric waves as applied to photography; announced convertibility of sound into electricity 1873.
Dolce, music, *table* M-566a
'Dolce vita, La', or **'The Sweet Life'** motion picture, F-53, M-525
Dolci, Carlo (1616–86), Italian painter, born in Florence; small religious paintings pleasing in color ('Christ Blessing the Bread and Wine'; 'St. Cecilia').
Doldrums, or **belt of calms** W-179, *diagrams* E-21, W-180
daily thundershowers R-88
Dole, James Drummond (1877–1958), industrialist, born in Boston, Mass.; to Hawaii 1900; organized Hawaiian Pineapple Co., Ltd. 1901 (now Dole Co., it is world's chief producer of pineapples); president and general manager 1901–32, chairman of board 1932–48, *picture* H-66
Dole, Nathan Haskell (1852–1935), U.S. author, editor, and translator, born in Chelsea, Mass.; original works include 'Young Folks' History of Russia', 'Famous Composers', 'The Hawthorne Tree and Other Poems', 'Omar, the Tent Maker', 'The Pilgrims'; edited and translated many Russian, French, Italian, Spanish, German works.
Dole, Robert J. (born 1923), public official, born in Russell, Kan.; member (Republican) Kansas legislature 1951–53; U.S. Congressman from Kansas 1961–69; senator 1969–; chairman Republican National Committee 1971–72; vice-presidential candidate 1976
Ford's 1976 candidacy F-305

Dole / Dooley

Dole, Sanford Ballard (1844–1926), American jurist and political leader D-214
Hawaii H-60
Liliuokalani L-209

Dole, government allowance to unemployed E-248

Dolichocephaly (long-headedness), ethnology R-25, *picture* R-27

Dolichonyx, oryzivorus. *see in index* Bobolink

Dolin, Anton, real name Patrick Healey-Kay (born 1904), English dancer and choreographer, born in Sussex; with Diaghilev ballet 1923–25, 1928–29, later with Sadler's Wells Ballet (London), Markova-Dolin Ballet, and Ballet Theatre; ballets created include 'Bluebeard', 'Camille', 'Romantic Age'; author of 'Ballet Go Round', autobiography, and 'Alicia Markova, Her Life and Art'.

Doll. D-215
bibliography H-186
Egyptian, *picture* E-121
Greece, *picture* G-222
Indian, American I-117
puppets and marionettes. *see in index* Puppets and marionettes

Dollar, monetary unit of nations; U.S. dollar equals 1/38 of troy oz (0.93 gram) of gold; besides United States, nations on dollar system include Australia, Bahamas, Barbados, Belize, Canada, Fiji, Guyana, Jamaica, Liberia, Malaysia, New Zealand, Singapore, Trinidad and Tobago, and Zimbabwe, *table* M-428
foreign exchange F-307
name's origin C-540
United States R-270
devaluation G-153, N-293g
mint H-83, M-367
money M-427, R-168

Dollar diplomacy, U.S. government policy to promote citizens' commercial interests in foreign countries by peaceful means.
Wilson W-175

Dollarfish. *see in index* Butterfish

Doll Collectors of America, organization founded in 1935 D-215

Dollfuss, Engelbert (1892–1934), Austrian statesman, born near Sankt Pölten of peasant stock; as chancellor 1932–34, defied Austrian Nazis; assassinated A-827, *list* A-704

Dollhouse D-222, *picture* D-215

Dollond, John (1706–61), English optician, born in London; constructed achromatic lenses for telescopes by combining crown and flint glasses T-63

'Doll's House, A', a drama by Henrik Ibsen concerning Nora, a wife who demands a right to her own ideals and individuality; when first produced, in 1879, caused a stir.

Dolly, platform on wheels for moving heavy materials, *picture* R-73

Dolly Varden trout T-269

Dolmens, Stone Age monuments S-455

Dolmetsch, Arnold (1858–1940), French connoisseur and collector of musical instruments, born in Le Mans P-316

Dolomite, form of limestone; used as a building stone and for furnace linings, refractories, and in metallurgical processes M-335, N-281, *tables* M-229, O-497

Dolomites (from mineral dolomite), limestone mountains in e. Alps; highest peak, Marmolada (3342 m; 10,964 ft), in n. Italy; tourists, mountain climbing T-322
Italy, *picture* I-384

Dolores, Mission, San Francisco, Calif.; founded 1776 by Father Junípero Serra; interior decorated with paintings done by Indians and a hand-carved altar covered with gold leaf, brought from Mexico 1870 K-247

Dolores Hidalgo, Mexico, city 40 km (25 mi) n.e. of Guanajuato; farming center; here in 1810 a Roman Catholic priest, Miguel Hidalgo y Costilla, began Mexico's revolt against Spain; pop. 12,311 H-155–6

Dolphin, sea mammal related to whale D-223, *picture* A-426. *see also in index* Porpoise

Dolphin fish, or **coryphene,** or **dorado,** edible game fish D-224

Dolton, Ill., village 18 mi (29 km) s. of Chicago; glass and metal products; incorporated 1892; pop. 24,766.

Dom, Portuguese for Spanish Don. *see in index* Don

Doma Cathedral, Riga, Latvian S.S.R., *picture* L-83

Domagk, Gerhard (Johannes Paul) (1895–1964), German physician and research chemist, born in Lagow, Brandenburg A-491

Domain, mathematics A-297

Domain, magnetic M-49a

Domain, public. *see in index* Lands, public

'Dombey and Son', novel by Charles Dickens D-137, *picture* D-136

Dome, building, cupped roof or ceiling, usually hemispherical B-497. *see also in index* Arch; Vault
Astrodome, Houston, Tex. H-261, *pictures* T-123
Byzantine A-549, B-536
Capitol, U.S. W-30, *picture* U-154
Dome of the Rock. *see in index* Dome of the Rock
Fuller, Buckminster F-446
geodesic. *see in index* Geodesic domes
Georgian, *picture* N-162e
Pro Football Hall of Fame, *picture* O-424
St. Peter's M-266, V-268
Taj Mahal, *picture* T-11

Domenichino, Zampiere (1581–1641), Italian painter, born in Bologna; pupil of the Carracci; excelled in religious frescoes; one of earliest landscape painters ('Communion of St. Jerome'; 'Scourging of St. Andrew'; 'The Guardian Angel').

Domenico, Saint. *see in index* Dominic, Saint

Dome of the Rock, also called **Mosque of Omar,** Jerusalem, built over rock supposed by Jews to be scene of the sacrifice of Isaac, and, by Moslems, of the Prophet's ascension J-100, *picture* J-99
Israel, *picture* I-370

Domesday Book, or **Doomsday Book,** William I's statistical record of England W-163

Domestic animals. *see in index* Animals, domestic

Domestic science. *see in index* Home economics

Domestic system. *see in index* Homework, industrial

Domestic tragedy, drama concerning the lives of ordinary people D-241

Domett, Alfred (1811–87), English poet and colonial statesman, born in London; prime minister of New Zealand 1862–71 ('Ranolf and Amohia').

Dominant, music M-566

Dominant trait, heredity H-144, *list* G-43b

Dominguez, Francisco Atanasio, 18th-century Spanish missionary and explorer
explorations C-586, U-219, *map* U-176

Dominic, or **Saint Dominic** (1170–1221), founder of Order of Friars Preachers, or Dominicans D-224

Dominica, island republic, West Indies; formerly British state; became independent 1978; 300 sq mi (780 sq km); cap. Roseau; limes, bananas, oranges, coconuts, cacao, vanilla; pop. 74,000 D-225, W-108
Commonwealth membership C-602

Dominican College, Houston, Tex.; Roman Catholic; for women; established 1946; closed 1974.

Dominican College of San Rafael, San Rafael, Calif.; Roman Catholic; chartered 1890; liberal arts, education; graduate school.

Dominican Republic, formerly **Santo Domingo,** the eastern two thirds of the island of Hispaniola; area 18,816 sq mi (48,733 sq km); cap. Santo Domingo; pop. 6,075,000 (1984 est.) D-225, *maps* W-104, N-309
Caribbean literature C-166
Columbus C-594
hospital H-239
flag, *picture* F-164
money, *table* M-428
national anthem, *table* N-52
OAS O-504
railroad mileage, *table* R-85
United States G-173, R-286

Dominicans, or **Black Friars,** or **Order of Friars Preachers,** religious order of Roman Catholic Church established in 1216 by Saint Dominic M-446, D-224

Dominion Day, Canadian national holiday C-100

Dominions, British. colonialism and imperialism C-556
Statute of Westminster E-249

Dominique, breed of poultry P-482

Dominoes, game D-228

Domitian (A.D. 51–96), Roman emperor (A.D. 81–96), murdered for his cruelties; the Apostle John was banished to Patmos probably during his reign R-247
Bible B-184
Epictetus banished E-282
persecutes Christians C-401

Dom João IV. *see in index* Joao IV

Dom Pedro I and II. *see in index* Pedro I and II

Domrémy-la-Pucelle France, village in n.e., on Meuse River; preserves house in which Joan of Arc was born; pop. 184.

Domus Aurea, or **Golden House,** Roman palace built by the emperor Nero A-548

Don, Spanish title of respect; derived from Latin *dominus,* "a lord"; name also applied to masters and fellows at English universities. For names preceded by Don, such as Don Carlos, *see in index* individual names, such as Carlos

Donaldson, Jesse Monroe (1885–1970), public official, born near Shelbyville, Ill.; from job as letter carrier in 1908, advanced to the position of U.S. postmaster general (1947–53).

Donatello (1386?–1466), Italian sculptor D-229, S-85
Alberti A-271
'Saint Peter', statue, *picture* P-225
singing gallery S-86

Donati's comet, discovered by Giovanni Donati 1858; 72,000,000 km (45,000,000 mi) long by 16,000,000 km (10,000,000 mi) wide; orbit about 2040 years.

Donatus, Aelius (fl. mid-4th century), Roman grammarian L-230

Don Bosco College, Newton, N.J.; Roman Catholic; for men; founded 1928; liberal arts, theology.

Doncaster, England, city in Yorkshire, 50 km (30 mi) s. of York, between Don and Trent rivers; coal mining, locomotive works; Roman and Norman remains; pop. 84,050, *map* G-199h

Donck, Adriaen Van der. *see in index* Van der Donck

Donegal, Ireland, extreme n.w. county of island of Ireland; 4830 sq km (1865 sq mi); cap. Lifford; agriculture, fisheries, woolen manufactures; pop. 108,549
fairy stories S-481b

Donelson, Emily (died 1836), White House hostess for President Jackson W-145

Donetsk, formerly **Stalino,** U.S.S.R., city of e. Ukrainian S.S.R.; industrial and educational center; pop. 879,000 U-2, *maps* E-335, R-344, 349

Donets River, s.w. European Russia; flows s.e. 1080 km (670 mi) to join Don River; navigable 255 km (140 mi) above mouth, *maps* E-335, R-344, 349
basin, K-230, U-2

'Don Giovanni', Mozart's opera, of which Don Giovanni (Don Juan) is hero; first presented at Prague 1787 O-464d

Doniphan, Alexander William (1808–87), soldier, born in Mason County, Ky.; led Missouri troops in the Mexican War.

Donizetti, Gaetano (1797–1848), Italian composer D-229
opera O-465

Donjon, or **Keep,** or **Dungeon,** castle structure C-199

Don Juan legend, or **Don Giovanni legend,** Spanish legend of a libertine man; subject of many works D-229
Byron poem B-401, E-264
motion picture M-523
Mozart opera O-464d
Spanish literature B-384, S-365a

Donkey. *see in index* Ass

Donleavy, J(ames) P(atrick) (born 1926), author, born in Brooklyn, N.Y. (novels: 'The Ginger Man', 'The Onion Eaters'; play: 'Fairy Tales of New York'; short stories: 'Meet My Maker the Mad Molecule').

Donnay, Charles Maurice (1859–1945), French dramatist and essayist, born in Paris; wrote of social problems; brilliant memoirs; elected to French Academy 1907.

Donn-Byrne, Brian Oswald. *see in index* Byrne, Donn

Donne, John (1573–1631), English metaphysical poet D-230
English literature E-259

Donnelly, Ignatius (1831–1901), writer and political leader, born in Philadelphia, Pa.; U.S. congressman from Minnesota 1863–69; wrote 'Great Cryptogram', trying to prove Bacon wrote Shakespeare's works.

Donner, Frederic G(arrett) (born 1902), business executive, born in Three Oaks, Mich.; joined financial staff of General Motors Corporation 1926, director 1942–, chairman of the board and chief executive officer 1958–67; director COMSAT 1968–.

Donner party, party of immigrants to California led by George Donner; were trapped in snow in Sierras 1846–47 and underwent terrible suffering; three rescue parties were sent to their camp (on what is now Donner Lake).
cannibalism C-139

Donner Pass, highway and railway pass, altitude 7135 ft (2175 m), just w. of Donner Lake, where tragedy befell Donner party, in Sierras of California, near Nevada border and n.w. of Lake Tahoe; U.S. Weather Bureau observatory.

Donnybrook, part of the city of Dublin, Ireland; known for its annual fair, started 1204 and abolished 1855 because of fights and debauchery.

Donora, Pa., borough on Monongahela River, about 20 mi (30 km) s. of Pittsburgh; in agricultural area; fiber partitions, chemicals; pipe fabrication; founded 1901; pop. 7524, *map* P-184

Donoso, José (born 1924), Chilean writer
Latin American literature L-70

Donovan, Art(hur) (born 1925), football tackle, born in New York, N.Y.; played for Baltimore Colts 1950, 1953–61, New York Yanks 1951, and Dallas Texans 1952.

Donovan, Raymond J. (born 1930), businessman and public official, born in Bayonne, N.J.; executive of Schiavone Construction Co. 1959–81; U.S. secretary of labor 1981–.

'Don Quixote de la Mancha', romance by Cervantes C-261
illustrations by Dore D-230
Spanish literature S-365a, L-243

Don River, s. U.S.S.R., rises in Lake Tula, flows s.e. and s.w. 2130 km (1325 mi) into Sea of Azov D-230, R-323, *maps* E-335, R-322, W-253
Volga-Don Canal V-383

Don River, or **Dun River,** Yorkshire, England; rises on moor near Penistone; navigable for 63 km (39 mi) below Sheffield S-148, *map* G-199h

"Don't count your chickens before they're hatched" F-3

Doodlebug
ant lion larva A-495. *see also in index* Ant lion

Dooley, Mr., humorous Irish-American saloonkeeper, created by Finley Peter Dunne. *see also in index* Dunne, Finley Peter

Dooley, Thomas A(nthony) (1927–61), physician, born

Doolittle / Douglas, Stephen

in St. Louis, Mo.; as U.S. Navy doctor, organized care of refugees from Communist Vietnam 1954; medical missionary in s.e. Asia 1956–60; described his experiences in 'Deliver Us from Evil', 'The Edge of Tomorrow', and 'The Night They Burned the Mountain'. *see also in index* MEDICO
'Night They Burned the Mountain, The' R-111h

Doolittle, Hilda (H. D.) (1886–1961), poet, born in Bethlehem, Pa., one of best of imagist school; verses of clear, delicate beauty with classical atmosphere ('Sea Garden'; 'Walls Do Not Fall'; 'By Avon River'; 'Helen in Egypt').

Doolittle, James H(arold) (born 1896), aviator, born in Alameda, Calif.; U.S. Army 1917–30, 1940–45; led air forces in invasion of Tunisia; made commander of N. W. African Strategic Air Force Feb. 1943 and of 8th U.S. Air Force (Britain) Dec. 1943, transferred to Pacific 1945; a vice-president of Shell Oil Corp. 1946–58, a director 1946–67; chairman National Advisory Committee for Aeronautics 1956–58 A-205
World War II W-272

Doomsday Book. *see in index* Domesday Book

Doon, river of Ayrshire, Scotland, flowing n.w. 50 km (30 mi) into Firth of Clyde; immortalized by Burns ('The Banks o' Doon').

Door
Ghiberti's bronze doors G-123, S-85, *picture* R-147
lock and key L-277
painting tips, *picture* P-76

Doorbell E-151, *diagram* E-150
transformer T-233

Doorn, Netherlands, village near Utrecht; retreat of Kaiser William II of Germany after his abdication; pop. 7148.

Doornik, Belgium. *see in index* Tournai

Door Peninsula, Wisconsin, bounded on n.w. by Green Bay G-204

Dope, cellulose acetate solution
synthetic fibers F-72

Doppler effect, law in physics discovered by Christian Doppler (1803–53); applied to sound, light, and radar from moving sources A-721, S-260, S-373, U-201, *diagram* S-261

Doppler system, radar R-32
mining surveying M-339

Dorado, or **coryphene,** or **dolphin fish,** edible game fish D-224

Dorado, El. *see in index* El Dorado

Dorati, Antal (born 1906), U.S. orchestral conductor, born in Budapest, Hungary; musical director Ballet Theatre 1941–45; conductor Dallas Symphony Orchestra 1945–49, Minneapolis Symphony Orchestra 1949–60.

Dorcas, or **Tabitha,** disciple of Jesus at Joppa, a woman "full of good works" (whence the "Dorcas societies" of the church); raised from the dead by Peter (Acts ix, 36–40).

Dorchester, Guy Carleton, Baron. *see in index* Carleton

Dorchester, England, capital of Dorsetshire; Roman remains; one of the towns on the circuit of Jeffreys' "Bloody Assizes" after the Monmouth Rebellion; 292 were sentenced to death here in 1685, pop. 13,660, *map* G-199h

Dorchester Heights National Historic Site, Boston, Mass. N-35

Dordogne River, s.-central France; 490 km (305 mi) long; unites with Garonne to form Gironde, *map* E-334

Dordrecht, or **Dort,** Netherlands, port on island formed by Merwede and three other rivers, 19 km (12 mi) s.e. of Rotterdam; shipbuilding; heavy machinery, chemicals, food products; first assembly of independent states of Holland 1572; Synod of Dort (1618–19) upheld Calvinism pop. 80,714, *map* N-133

Dordt College, Sioux Center, Iowa; Christian Reformed church; founded 1955; liberal arts, business, education.

Doré, (Paul) Gustave (1832–83), French painter and illustrator D-230
folklore, *pictures* F-260, 262
'Paradise Lost', *picture* E-253

Doria, Andrea (1468–1560), Genoese admiral and patriot, soldier of fortune under Francis I of France and Emperor Charles V; drove French from Genoa, set up republic, became perpetual censor.

Dorians, one of four great branches of Greek people; took name from Dorus, son of Hellen; came from n. or n.w. and invaded Corinth, then Crete; Spartans always regarded as representatives of unmixed Dorian blood A-62, G-221

Doric, dialect in ancient Greece G-236

Doric architecture A-546, *pictures* A-547

Doric chiton, draped garment D-260

Dorion, Sir Antoine Aimé (1818–91), Canadian statesman and jurist, born near Trois-Rivières, Que.; held several Cabinet positions; one of leaders of French-Canadian Liberals during Confederation; chief justice of province of Quebec 1874–91.

Doris, small state in n.-central part of ancient Greece, s. of Thessaly; reputedly cradle of Dorian branch of Greek people, *map* G-221

Dorking, breed of poultry P-482, *picture* P-481

Dormont, Pa., residential borough, s.w. suburb of Pittsburgh; settled about 1790, incorporated 1909, pop. 11,275, *map* P-184

Dormouse, small Old World squirrellike rodent D-231. *see also in index* White-footed mouse

Doronicum, or **leopard's-bane,** genus of perennial plants of the composite family, native to Eurasia; hairy leaves have long petioles (stems); flowers solitary, yellow, daisylike, borne high above foliage.

Dorothea, Saint, virgin supposedly martyred under Diocletian in Cappadocia; patroness of gardeners; festival Feb. 6.

Dorothea, heroine of Goethe's 'Hermann und Dorothea', a simple story of German small-town life (1798) G-148

Dörpfeld, Wilhelm (1853–1940), German archaeologist, born in Barmen; aided Heinrich Schliemann in excavation of Troy.

Dorr, Rheta Childe (1872–1948), writer and suffragist, born in Omaha, Neb.; wrote 'What 8 Million Women Want' in behalf of women's rights; in 'Drink-Coercion or Control', she described Scandinavian liquor laws; also wrote a biography of Susan B. Anthony.

Dorr, Thomas Wilson (1805–54), lawyer and political reformer, born in Providence, R.I.; led action to widen suffrage in R.I., *picture* R-190
Rhode Island R-184, *picture* T-314

Dorrit, Little. *see in index* 'Little Dorrit'

Dorsal fin, fish anatomy, *diagram* F-125, *picture* F-126

D'Orsay, Alfred Guillaume Gabriel, Count (1801–52), French dandy and wit, born in Paris; friend of Byron and of countess of Blessington; skillful amateur painter and sculptor.

Dorset, Thomas Sackville, first **earl of** (1536–1608), English statesman and poet, one of leading advisers of Queen Elizabeth I; carried death warrant to Mary, queen of Scots; author of 'Induction', introductory poem to 'Mirror for Magistrates', of which he was part author, probably most important work between Chaucer and Spenser; helped write 'Gorboduc', first English tragedy.

Dorset, or **Dorsetshire,** England, county on English Channel; 2520 sq km (973 sq mi); cap. Dorchester; agriculture, stock raising; stone quarrying; pop. 313,460, *map* E-218

Dorset, breed of sheep S-147

'Dorsetshire', British cruiser S-177h

Dorsey, George Amos (1868–1931), anthropologist, writer, and lecturer, born in Hebron, Ohio; curator of anthropology Field Museum of Natural History, Chicago, Ill., 1898–1915; professor of anthropology University of Chicago 1898–1915; made expeditions to many countries ('Why We Behave Like Human Beings').

Dorsey, Thomas Francis (Tommy) (1905–56), trombonist and bandleader, born near Mahanoy City, Pa.; was coleader of orchestra with brother **James Francis** (Jimmy) (1904–57), saxophonist, clarinetist, and bandleader, born in Shenandoah, Pa.; severed connections 1935, Jimmy kept their band, Tommy organized his own 1936, merged 1953.

Dort, Netherlands. *see in index* Dordrecht

Dortmund, or **Throtmanni,** West Germany, city 119 km (73 mi) n.e. of Cologne, in center of coal basin; first mentioned in 899; later a Hanseatic leader, pop. 648,883 D-231, *maps* G-99a, E-334, *picture* G-100

Dorus. *see in index* Dorians

Dory, fish. *see in index* John Dory

Dory, boat B-324

'Doryphorus', statue by Polyclitus G-228

Doshisha University, Kyoto, Japan K-312

Dos Passos, John (Roderigo) (1896–1970), American writer D-231, A-359

Dōst Mohammad Khān (1826–1863), ruler of Afghanistan A-91

Dostoevski, Fedor (1821–81), Russian novelist D-232, R-360, *picture* R-359
'Crime and Punishment' N-376, R-112c

Dothan, Ala., city near s.e. corner of state, 96 mi (154 km) s.e. of Montgomery; hosiery, lumber and wood products, clothing, wheel toys, peanut and cottonseed products; annual National Peanut Festival pop. 48,750, *map* U-41

Dot map M-101, *map* M-102

Dou, Gerard. *see in index* Douw, Gerard

Douai, France, manufacturing town 29 km (18 mi) s. of Lille; captured by Germans in 1914 and 1940; pop. 47,347.

Douala, city, Cameroon; (1980 estimate) pop. 636,980 D-233

Douaumont, fortified hill and village near Verdun, France V-282

Double bass, or **bass viol,** or **contrabass,** musical instrument V-327, *diagram* M-570, *picture* M-569
Koussevitzky K-302

Double Bubble, chewing gum C-307

Doubleday, Abner (1819–93), U.S. Army officer D-233
baseball B-94, *picture* B-96

Double Eagle, balloon ocean crossings B-44

Double exposure, photography, *picture* P-283
motion pictures M-519, *picture* M-522

Double flat, music M-564

'Double Helix, The', by James D. Watson R-112f

Double jeopardy, legal term; prosecution of an individual more than once for the same offense C-775

Double knit, ribbed cloth with twice-knitted look obtained by knitting interlocking loops with two needles; usually made of acrylic or wool; used for clothing K-260

Double-reduced tin I-347

Double refraction, light by crystals, the breaking up of a beam of unpolarized light into two polarized beams
cell analysis B-237

Double sharp, music M-564

Double stars. *see in index* Binary stars

Double sugar. *see in index* Disaccharide

Doublet, or **gipon,** garment D-262

Doublet, imitation gem with a genuine top J-113

Doublet, lens P-284

Double vision E-370

Doubling, or **duplation,** multiplication technique A-593

Doubs River, 430 km (270 mi) long, in e. France, rises in Jura Mts., flows n.e. into Switzerland, loops w. into France, and finally flows s.w. into Saône River, *map* S-537

Doubt, River of, Brazil. *see in index* Roosevelt River

Doubting Thomas A-507

Dough, bread B-429

Dougherty, Denis J(oseph), Cardinal (1865–1951), Roman Catholic prelate, born in Ashland, Pa.; was first American bishop of Philippine Islands; archbishop of Philadelphia after 1918; created cardinal 1921.

Dougherty, Paul (1877–1947), painter, born in Brooklyn, N.Y., brother of Walter Hampden; known for marines which portray the sea in both calm and storm ('Land and Sea'; 'Sun and Mist'; 'Storm Quiet').

Dougherty, Walter Hampden. *see in index* Hampden, Walter

Doughty, Sir Arthur George (1860–1936), Canadian historian and archivist, born in Maidenhead, Berkshire, England; went to Canada 1886 ('Quebec of Yesteryear'; 'Canada and Its Provinces', edited with Adam Shortt).

Doughty, Charles Montagu (1843–1926), English traveler, poet, and scientist, born in Suffolk; lifelong student of geology, archaeology, and English of Chaucer and Spenser; lived for many years among Arabs ('Travels in Arabia Deserta'; 'Dawn in Britain', epic in 6 vols.).

Doughty, Thomas (1793–1856), pioneer in American landscape painting, born in Philadelphia, Pa.; self-taught; works characterized by predominance of brown tones; member of Hudson River School.

Douglas, Scottish family famous in history, song, and legend; an earl of Douglas fell fighting against "Hotspur" Percy at Otterburn 1388; Douglas of Lochleven was jailer of Mary, queen of Scots 1567–68.

Douglas, David (1798–1834), botanist, born in Scone, Scotland; explored in California, Oregon, and British Columbia from 1823 to 1832; the Douglas fir and several plants named in his honor; killed in Hawaiian Islands.

Douglas, Donald W(ills) (1892–1981), engineer and aircraft manufacturer, born in Brooklyn, N.Y.; with Glenn L. Martin Co. 1915–20; in 1920 founded Douglas Co., incorporated as Douglas Aircraft Co. 1928.

Douglas, Sir James (1286–1330), noble of famous Scottish family; known as "the Good" and also as "Black Douglas" (because of his frequent raids on English border).

Douglas, Sir James (1803–77), Canadian statesman, born in British Guiana; governor Vancouver Island 1851–63, British Columbia 1858–64; founded in 1843, on present site of Victoria, B.C., the first Hudson's Bay Company post on Vancouver Island
Canada C-99

Douglas, James H(enderson) (born 1899), lawyer and government official, born in Cedar Rapids, Iowa; undersecretary of the air force 1953–57, secretary 1957–59; deputy secretary of defense 1959–61.

Douglas, Lloyd C(assel) (1877–1951), author and clergyman, born in Columbia City, Ind.; ordained Lutheran minister 1903; began writing novels on spiritual regeneration in modern living 1929 ('Magnificent Obsession'; 'Green Light'; 'Disputed Passage'; 'The Robe'; 'Big Fisherman').

Douglas, Stephen Arnold (1813–61), U.S statesman D-233
Civil War C-472
Kansas-Nebraska Act K-189
Lincoln-Douglas debates L-219

Douglas, Thomas / Drake, Joseph

Douglas, Thomas Clement (born 1904), Canadian political leader, born in Falkirk, Scotland; member of House of Commons 1935–44; premier of Saskatchewan 1944–61; head of New Democratic party 1961–71.

Douglas, William O(rville) (1898–1980), jurist, born in Maine, Minn. D-234, *picture* W-50

Douglas, Ariz., city in s.e. corner, on Mexican border, just n. of Agua Prieta, Mexico; copper smelting; electronics; agriculture and cattle raising; pop. 13,058, *map* U-40

Douglas, Ga., city 35 mi (55 km) n.w. of Waycross; farm and timber region; mobile homes and garment industries; poultry raising; incorporated 1858; pop. 10,980, *map* G-93

Douglas, Isle of Man, capital, on s.e. coast of island; seaport and resort area; automobile races; pop. 19,517, *map* G-199h

Douglas, Mount, s. Montana, just n. of Yellowstone National Park; 11,300 ft (3440 m), *map* M-470

Douglas fir, evergreen tree (*Pseudo-tsuga taxifolia*) of pine family, sometimes called Douglas spruce; pyramid-shaped crown; leaves blue green, 2 cm (¾ in.) to 4 cm (1½ in.) long, two white bands on underside; cones, drooping with prominent bracts, grow to 9 cm (3½ in.); wood red brown to yellow brown; also known in lumber trade as larch, fir, Oregon pine; tree named for David Douglas F-92, W-49, *picture* F-314, *table* W-218
- shipbuilding S-165
- state tree, *picture* O-486

Douglas-Home, Sir Alec (Alexander Frederick Douglas-Home) (born 1903), British political leader D-234, E-251

Douglass, Andrew Ellicott (1867–1962), climatologist and astronomer, born in Windsor, Vt.; professor after 1906 and director 1918–38 of Steward Observatory, University of Arizona; author of 'Climatic Cycles and Tree Growth'
- tree-ring record A-536

Douglass, Frederick (1817–95), U.S. antislavery orator and journalist, D-234, *pictures* N-124, M-136
- North Star B-291, *list* B-299
- women's rights W-215c

Douglas spruce. *see in index* Douglas fir

Douhet, Giulio (1869–1930), Italian general, born in Caserta, near Naples; advocated "lightning war" with emphasis upon ruthless use of air power to crush resistance; author of 'Il Dominio dell'aria' (The Dominion of the Air) A-156

Doukhobors, or **Dukhobors,** religious sect, founded in Russia middle 18th century; emigrated to Canada in large numbers; name means "spirit wrestlers"; now call themselves "Christians of the Universal Brotherhood."

Doumer, Paul (1857–1932), 13th president of Third Republic of France, born in Aurillac; in French politics and statecraft from 1887; in Chamber of Deputies 26 years; finance minister under Briand; elected president 1931, assassinated by Russian fanatic May 1932.

Doumergue, Gaston (1863–1937), 12th president of Third Republic of France (1924–31), born in Aigues-Vives, near Nîmes; lawyer at age of 22; president French Senate 1923–24; retired 1931; reinstated as prime minister Feb. to Nov. 1934.

Doum palm, or **Egyptian doum palm,** tree (*Hyphaene thebaica*) of the palm family, native to Nile region; grows 6 to 9 m (20 to 30 ft); usually forked with leaves 65 to 75 cm (25 to 30 in.) long; fruit oval, yellow orange with fibrous center that tastes like gingerbread; common name is gingerbread tree.

Douro, (Spanish **Duero**), river rising in n. Spain and flowing w. through Portugal to Atlantic; 780 km (485 mi) P-455, S-350, *maps* E-334, P-455, S-350

Douw, or **Dou,** or **Dow, Gerard** (1613–80), Dutch portrait and genre painter, pupil of Rembrandt; pictures done with utmost exactness ('Woman Sick of the Dropsy'; 'The Evening School'; 'Young Mother').

Dove, name applied to various pigeons P-323. *see also in index* Rock dove
- birds, B-255, *picture* B-246

'Dove and the Ant, The', fable, *table* F-4

Dover, Robert (1575–1641), English captain and attorney; founded and directed the Cotswold games as a protest against the Puritanism of his day; games comprised wrestling, jumping, gymnastics, rural dances.

Dover, Del., state capital, 35 mi (55 km) s. of Wilmington; pop. 23,512 D-236, *map* U-41
- Delaware D-72, *picture* D-79

Dover, England, ancient **Dubris,** port on English Channel; pop. 35,640 D-236, *map* G-199h

Dover, N.H., city on Cocheco River, 6 mi (10 km) n.w. of Portsmouth; electronic devices, printing presses, business machines, molded plastic products, wood products, shoes; settled 1623; pop. 22,377 N-170, *map* N-183

Dover, N.J., town 20 mi (30 km) w. of Paterson; knit goods, metal products, clothing; government munitions depot nearby; pop. 14,681, *map* N-202

Dover, Ohio, city 2 mi (3 km) n.w. of New Philadelphia, on the Tuscarawas River; products include steel, chemicals, bricks, tile, cheese, and cattle feed; pop. 11,516, *map* O-428

Dover, Strait of, channel connecting North Sea with English Channel and separating England and France; 30 to 43 km (20 to 27 mi) wide.

Dover, Treaty of (1670), treaty between England and France C-2

Dover Castle, castle, Dover, England D-236, *picture* D-237

Dover sole, fish F-175

Doves Press, noted English printers.

Dovetail joint, used in cabinetmaking C-175

Dow, Charles Henry. *see in index* Dow-Jones Average

Dow, Gerard. *see in index* Douw

Dow, Neal (1804–97), temperance orator, born in Portland, Me.; author of Maine prohibition law; Prohibition presidential nominee 1880.

Dowager, widow with a dower; especially designates widow of titled person to distinguish her from wife of her husband's heir who has same title, as queen dowager.

Dowden, Edward (1843–1913), Irish educator and literary critic, born in Cork; noted Shakespearean scholar; professor of English literature University of Dublin 1867 until death ('Shakespeare, His Mind and Art'; 'Poems'; 'Shakespeare Primer'; 'Life of Shelley').

Dowel, pin of wood or metal for holding two parts together.

Dower, law
- legal definition, *table* L-92

Dowie, John Alexander (1848–1907), U.S religious leader, born in Edinburgh, Scotland; self-styled "Elijah the Restorer"; preached "faith healing"; founded Christian Catholic church 1901 at Zion City, Ill.

Dowitcher, shorebird of family Scolopacidae; the dowitcher (*Limnodromus griseus*) is about 27 cm (10½ in.) long; ranges from Arctic regions of North America to n. South America.

Dow-Jones Average, index of relative prices of 30 selected industrial stocks, 20 railroad stocks, and 15 utility stocks; used to express general level of stock market prices; developed by Charles Henry Dow (1851–1902) and Edward D. Jones (1856–1920)
- stocks S-452

Dowling College, Oakdale, N.Y.; private control; founded 1959, chartered 1968; located on former William K. Vanderbilt estate; liberal arts; graduate study.

Down, county of Northern Ireland, in easternmost part of island of Ireland; land area 2466 sq km (952 sq mi); pop. 286,631.

Down, direction D-157

Down, football F-297

Down, plumage, *picture* P-480
- bird B-242
- duck D-284
- feather F-50
- goose D-285

Downers Grove, Ill., village 22 mi (35 km) s.w. of Chicago; bearings and other metal products, bakery products; George Williams College; pop. 39,274.

Downes, (Edwin) Olin (1886–1955), music critic, born in Evanston, Ill.; on 'Boston Post' 1906–24, afterwards on 'New York Times'; lecturer and writer on musical theory, history, and appreciation ('Symphonic Masterpieces'; 'A Treasury of American Song', with Elie Siegmeister; 'Olin Downes on Music').

Downey, Stephen W. (1839–1902), public official, born Westernport, Md.; to Territory of Wyoming 1869 as lawyer; member Wyoming territorial and state legislatures; Republican congressman 1879–81; in 1886 sponsored bill creating University of Wyoming (opened 1887), *picture* W-324

Downey, Calif., city 9 mi (15 km) s.e. of Los Angeles; products include aircraft, missiles, electronics, metal goods, soap, chemicals, and plastics; pop. 82,602.

Downing, Andrew Jackson (1815–52), landscape gardener, born in Newburgh, N.Y.; planned landscaping for U.S. Capitol and White House; wrote books on horticulture A-562

Downing Street, popular name for the British government; so called because both Foreign Office and the official residence of the prime minister are there in London.

Down payment, financing
- consumer credit C-762
- house H-245, *list* H-257

Downs, system of chalk hills in s.e. England; North Downs in Surrey and Kent, South in Sussex; latter feeding ground for famous Southdown sheep E-219

Down's syndrome. *see in index* Mongolism

Downstage, theater T-149, *diagram* T-150

Down under, term used to designate the Antipodes—Australia, New Zealand, and the like; for example, the man from down under.

Downy mildews M-314

Downy woodpecker W-223

Dowser. *see in index* Divining rod

Dowson, Ernest Christopher (1867–1900), English poet, born in Lee, near London; hypersensitive, ill with tuberculosis, and addicted to drugs and drink, lived lonely, unhappy life; best known for musical and delicate lyrics often colored with sadness; most famous poem popularly known as 'Cynara'.

Doyle, Sir Arthur Conan (1859–1930), British novelist D-237
- English literature E-274, S-184, D-118

DPs. *see in index* Displaced persons

Dracaena, genus of perennial plants of lily family, native to the tropics; used as foliage plants because of broad or sword-shaped, varicolored leaves; dragon tree (*D. draco*) of Canary Islands grows to 20 m (60 ft); its dried juice supposed to resemble dragon's blood.

Drachenfels, "dragon's rock," mountain in West Germany, 16 km (10 mi) s.e. of Bonn, on the Rhine River, 1065 ft. high; medieval ruins on its crest.

Drachma, monetary unit of Greece; historic value about 2 cents; coined in copper-nickel; in ancient Greece, silver coin worth 9 to 17 cents, *table* M-428

Drachmann, Holger Henrik Herholdt (1846–1908), Danish poet, dramatist, and short-story writer, born in Copenhagen ('Tendrils and Roses'; 'Once upon a Time' and 'Wayland the Smith', plays; 'The Sacred Five', autobiographical).

Draco (7th century B.C.), compiler of first written code of Athenian laws; penalties so harsh that any unduly severe laws are called "Draconian" G-223, L-91

Draco, northern constellation, *charts* S-416, 418

'Dracula', novel by Bram Stoker F-262

Dracut, Mass., community situated 3 mi (5 km) n. of Lowell; incorporated 1702; pop. of township 21,249, *map* M-161

Draft
- military conscription. *see in index* Conscription
- ship, *diagram* S-176

Draft animals, animals used for drawing loads. *see in index* Transportation, *subhead* animal power

Draft horses, or **heavy horses,** for pulling loads H-232e

Drafting. *see in index* Mechanical drawing

Drafting machine, mechanical drawing instrument M-199, *picture* M-196

Drag, cattle driving C-754

Drag, fishing, *list* F-146

Drag, speeding object
- airplane A-180
  - brake parachute P-109a
  - exterior ballistics B-37
  - streamlining S-486

Draga (Mme. Draga Mashin) (1867–1903), queen of King Alexander I (Obrenovich) of Serbia; formerly lady in waiting to his mother, Queen Natalie; assassinated with king by group which opposed the marriage.

Dragline, earth-moving machine D-258

Dragon, breed of pigeons P-324

Dragon, mythological animal D-238
- Chinese, *pictures* A-457
- folklore F-260
- St. George G-74, *picture* G-143
- Siegfried and Fafnir S-192a

Dragon, name of two kinds of lizard.

Dragon Boat Festival, list F-66

Dragonfly, or **devil's-darning-needle,** or **horse stinger,** insect, member of the Odonata family D-238
- fossil, *picture* G-63

Dragon's blood, reddish-brown resin G-263, P-275

Dragon ship N-356

Dragon tree. *see in index* Dracaena

Dragoon bird. *see in index* Umbrella bird

Drag race A-874

Drainage, land. *see in index* Irrigation and reclamation

Drainage, plumbing P-393

Drainage Canal, Chicago. *see in index* Chicago Sanitary and Ship Canal

Drainage canal C-126

Drainage systems, or **drainage basins** W-79. *see also in index* rivers by name
- United States U-34, *map* U-32

Drake, Edwin Laurentine (1819–80), pioneer oil producer, born in Greenville, N.Y.; first to produce oil by drilling to its source P-232

Drake, Francis (1545–96), English explorer and privateer D-240
- California C-40
- raids Armada fleet A-627
- St. Augustine, Florida S-16b
- San Juan, Puerto Rico P-530
- voyages A-332, *maps* A-297, M-37

Drake, Joseph Rodman (1795–1820), poet, born in New York, N.Y.; often used signature "Croaker" ('The Culprit Fay'; 'The American Flag'); subject of Fitz-Greene Halleck's eulogy

Green be the turf above thee,
Friend of my better days!
None knew thee but to love thee,

Drake / Drought

Nor named thee but to praise.
Drake, male duck D-284
Drakensberg, mountain range in s.e. Africa S-263, *map* S-264
Lesotho L-137
Natal N-16
Drake University, Des Moines, Iowa; private control; opened 1881; liberal arts, business administration, education, fine arts, journalism, law, pharmacy; graduate division.
Drama D-241, L-243. *see also in index* Motion pictures; Opera; Theater; *also* chief dramatists by name
acting A-24
arts A-662
American A-356
English E-254, *pictures* E-255, 257
Elizabethan S-135
German G-96b
Passion play O-390
Greek G-233
Italian literature I-378
Latin literature L-76
Scandinavian S-52g
Spanish S-365a
ballet B-32
hobbies H-183
medieval. *see in index* Miracle play; Morality; Mystery play
music drama M-559, W-2
opera O-460
orchestra O-477
pageant P-20
puppets and marionettes P-535
television, *picture* T-67
theaters T-148, *pictures* T-152, 153
Drama bharata natya, Indian dance D-30
Dramamine, proprietary name for Dimenhydrinate, an antihistamine drug used to relieve nausea and motion sickness.
Dramatic poetry, poetry P-407
Drammen, Norway, seaport at mouth of Drammen River, on arm of Oslofjord; pop. 31,312, *maps* N-365, E-334
Draper, Henry (1837–82), scientist, born in Prince Edward County, Va.; son of John William Draper; known for proving presence of oxygen in sun and for spectral photography
catalog of stars S-414
Draper, John William (1811–82), U.S. scientist, born near Liverpool, England; helped found medical school of New York University; renowned for researches in photochemistry, spectrum analysis, and radiant energy; made portrait photography possible through improvements on Daguerre's process; his sons **Henry** (1837–82) and **John Christopher** (1835–85) were also scientists of note.
Draper, Ruth (1884–1956), monologist, born in New York, N.Y., granddaughter of Charles A. Dana; international reputation for vivid character sketches, which she wrote.
Draperies. *see in index* Curtains and draperies
Draught beer, alcoholic beverage B-132
Draughts. *see in index* Checkers
Drava River, German **Drau,** rising in the Tyrol, flows s.e. between Hungary and Yugoslavia, joining Danube River after 720 km (450 mi), *map* E-334
Dravidian languages L-42, *diagram* L-44
India I-67, I-106
Dravidians, people of India
Asian language patterns A-683
classification, *chart* R-26
Drawbridge, bridge that can be partly or wholly raised or lowered or moved to one side
bascule bridge B-442
Drawers, furniture F-453
Drawing D-250. *see also in index* Painting
bibliography H-182
ink I-206
mechanical drawing M-196, V-367, *pictures* V-362, 368
pens P-157
perspective P-220
police sketches, *chart* P-428
prehistoric H-236, *pictures* M-77, H-236
Drawing, metalworking operation T-207
Drawing, process in manufacture of synthetic and natural fibers F-74
cotton manufacturing C-740
Drawing board M-196
Draw loom S-392
Draw poker. *see in index* poker
Drayton, Michael (1563–1631), English poet, born in Hartshill, near Nuneaton; work scholarly and varied ('Poly-Olbion'; 'The Ballad of Agincourt'; 'Nimphidia, the Court of Faery').
'Dreadnought', battleship N-105
'Dream', drawing by Kuniyoshi D-256
Dreamland Park, Coney Island, N.Y. A-385
'Dream of the Red Chamber,' novel by Ts'ao Chan C-390
Dreams illusions or hallucinations of real experiences which occur during sleep D-257, S-217
psychoanalysis P-518
'Dream Songs', work by Berryman A-364
Drebbel, Cornelis van (1572–1634), Dutch inventor, born in Alkmaar; some of his inventions so unusual he gained reputation as sorcerer; among them were new fabric dyeing processes and a compound microscope
submarine S-493
Dredge, machine for digging soil from bottoms of bodies of water D-257
fishing F-134
mining M-340
gold G-150b
tin, *picture* E-41
oyster dredge O-519, *pictures* O-517, M-135
Panama Canal dredge, *picture* P-87
Dredging spoil, mixture of water and the material to be dredged D-258
Dred Scott decision, (1857) United States Supreme Court decision D-259, U-147
Buchanan's administration B-476
Lincoln-Douglas debates L-226
portrait of Dred Scott, *picture* M-406
slavery territory issue B-291, C-472
trial site, *picture* S-21
Dreiser, Paul. *see in index* Dresser, Paul
Dreiser, Theodore (1871–1945), U.S. author D-259, A-352
Anderson, Sherwood A-408
Indiana state song W-1
Drepanum, Sicily. *see in index* Trapani
Dresden, East Germany, city of Saxony, on Elbe River; pop. 521,786 D-259, *maps* G-99a, 115, E-334
Dresden china, or **Dresden ware** P-475
Dresden Codex, astronomical records written by the Mayas A-729
Dresden Green, diamond, *picture* D-129
Dress D-260. *see also in index* Clothing; Clothing industry; Fabrics; Sewing; Textiles
design D-268
fashion F-39
Dressage, horse, *list* H-232a
Dress design D-268
fashion F-39
Dresser, or **Dreiser, Paul** (1857–1911), songwriter, born in Terre Haute, Ind.; brother of Theodore Dreiser ('The Blue and the Gray'; 'On the Banks of the Wabash, Far Away', Indiana state song) W-1
Dressing, ore M-228, M-343, O-498
gold G-150c
Dressler, Marie, real name Leila Koerber (1873–1934), actress, born in Cobourg, Ont., Canada; joined Joe Weber as comedienne 1906; Academy award for 'Min and Bill' (1931); in many motion pictures, including 'Tugboat Annie'.
Dressmaking S-120
patterns G-31
Dress rehearsal, of theatrical production T-150
Dreux, France, town 55 km (35 mi) s.w. of Paris; Huguenots defeated here by Roman Catholics under duke of Guise 1562; taken by Germans 1870, 1940; pop. 28,156.
Drevet, Pierre (1663–1738), French engraver, born in Loire, near Vienne E-279
Drevet, Pierre Imbert (1697–1739), French engraver, born in Paris; son and pupil of Pierre Drevet; specialized in portrait engraving, often working on plates with his father.
Drew, Charles R(ichard) (1904–50), medical scientist, surgeon, born in Washington, D.C.; head of surgery department Howard University 1941–50; blood-plasma authority; organized blood banks early World War II; Spingarn medal 1944.
Drew, Daniel (1797–1879), capitalist and stock speculator, born in Carmel, N.Y.; early associate of Jim Fisk and Jay Gould; founder of Drew Theological Seminary.
Drew, Georgiana. *see in index* Barrymore, Georgiana
Drew, John (1853–1927), actor, born in Philadelphia, Pa.; son of John Drew, Irish-American comedian; famed as Petruchio in 'The Taming of the Shrew' and Charles Surface in 'School for Scandal'.
Drew Ali, Muslim leader B-307
Drew University, Madison, N.J.; independent control, affiliated with United Methodist church; founded 1866; liberal arts, theology; graduate school; offers special semester on United Nations.
Drexel, Anthony Joseph (1826–93), banker, born in Philadelphia, Pa.; founder of Drexel Institute of Art, Science, and Industry, Philadelphia; son of Francis M. Drexel, founder of Philadelphia banking house.
Drexel, Mary Katharine (1858?–1955), Roman Catholic nun, born in Philadelphia, Pa.; founded (1889) Sisters of the Blessed Sacrament for Indians and Colored People.
Drexel University, Philadelphia, Pa.; private control; founded 1891 as Drexel Institute of Art, Science, and Industry; humanities and social science, business administration, engineering, home economics, library science, and science; graduate studies; quarter system; off-campus center at Baltimore, Md. U-208, *map* P-251b
Dreyfus, Alfred (1859–1935), French military officer, born in Mulhouse; center of case that convulsed French political life 1894–99; later cleared of treason charge, restored to his rank 1906, and promoted D-272. *see also in index* Dreyfus Case
Devil's Island G-250
France, Anatole F-341
Jaurès support J-83
Zola's defense Z-356
Dreyfus Case, (began Dec. 19, 1894), France, trial of Alfred Dreyfus who was charged with passing military secrets to Germany; began wave of anti-Semitism D-272. *see also in index* Dreyfus, Alfred
Dreyfuss, Henry (1904–72), U.S. industrial designer I-169, 174
Dribble, sports
basketball B-97
soccer S-232
Dried food. *see in index* Dehydrated food
Drift, slow-moving ocean current. *see in index* Ocean currents
Drift, continental E-27, G-65a
Drift, glacial. *see in index* Glacial drift
'Drifters' (1929), documentary film M-529
'Drifting Cloud, The', or **'Ukigumo',** novel by Shimei Futabatei J-82
Drift mine M-341
coal mining C-521, *diagram* C-520
Drill, marine snail
oyster drill O-518, S-222
Drill, w. African baboon M-441
Drill, instrument for boring holes T-200, *diagram* T-204, *pictures* T-199
bow drill, *pictures* U-95, T-199
cordless drill, *picture* M-533
mining M-339
oil well P-235, *diagram* P-237, *picture* P-239
pneumatic P-398
prehistoric, *picture* M-75
push drill T-200, *picture* T-198
Drill, or **drilling,** stout, twilled cotton material used for army uniforms, hunting and work clothes, pockets, shoe linings, and bookbinding; khaki-colored drill is called khaki.
Drill press, machine tool T-204, *pictures* T-200
Drill ship, vessel for marine research
frontier exploration F-427
Drin, longest river in Albania A-257
Drinker's respirator. *see in index* Iron lung
Drinks, alcohol A-276
Drinkwater, John (1882–1937), English poet, dramatist, and critic, born in Leytonstone, near London: was one of the promoters of the Pilgrim Players (later the Birmingham Repertory Theatre) and managed and produced for them ('Abraham Lincoln', 'Oliver Cromwell', plays; 'New Poems'; 'The Pilgrim of Eternity', life of Byron; 'Inheritance', autobiography) E-275
Drip irrigation, or **trickle irrigation** I-355
Driscoll, John Leo (Paddy) (1896–1968), football halfback and coach, born in Evanston, Ill.; halfback and coach 1919–31, 1941–64, Chicago Cardinals and Chicago Bears.
Driskill Mountain, n.w. Louisiana; highest point in state (535 ft; 165 m) L-309, *map* L-310
Drive, sports
golf, *diagram* G-155a
tennis T-102, *pictures* T-103
Driver ant, or **army ant,** or **legionary ant,** insect of the family Formicidae A-468
Driver's license S-5
Driver training, automobile A-492, 863, S-5
Drive shaft, mechanics
automobile A-852, *picture* A-851
Droeshout, Martin (1601–?), English engraver, born in London; most active 1620–51; engraved portrait of Shakespeare appeared in 1623
portrait of Shakespeare S-132, *picture* S-135
Drogheda, Ireland, seaport on Boyne River, 43 km (27 mi) n. of Dublin; Poynings' Law, or Statute of Drogheda, which placed Irish legislature completely under England's control, was passed here in 1494; captured by Cromwell 1649; taken by William III 1690 after battle of the Boyne; pop. 17,908, *map* G-199h
Drogue parachute S-346c
Dromedary, or **Arabian camel** (*Camelus dromedarius*), one-humped camel of the Camelidae family C-62, *picture* W-239
Drôme River, s.e. France; rises in Dauphiné Pre-Alps and flows into Rhone River 19 km (12 mi) s.w. of Valence; 120 km (75 mi) long.
Dromio, each of the twins in Shakespeare's 'Comedy of Errors'; slaves of two brothers, also twins, each named Antipholus.
Drone airplane, pilotless plane A-160, G-252, *picture* A-163
Drone bee B-126
Drood, Edwin. *see in index* 'Mystery of Edwin Drood, The'
Dropmore, attractive garden perennial (*Anchusa italica*) of the borage family, with blue flowers resembling forget-me-nots.
Drop-off, fishing, *list* F-146
Dropper, fishing, *list* F-146
Dropping mercury electrode Q-5
Dropsie University, Philadelphia, Pa.; nonsectarian; established 1907; Hebrew and Semitic studies, education; graduate study; Middle East institute.
Dropsy, term sometimes used for edema, an abnormal accumulation of body fluids M-215b
Drosophila, fruit fly G-43c, I-227
Drought, or **drouth,** long period of dryness, often in cycles; menaces crops, animals, and people; has driven starving hordes to attack and seize

Drowned / Duccio

moist lands; combated by contour plowing and by planting drought-resistant crops D-272
  anticyclones W-85
  Brazil L-60
  Chad C-263
  farming F-29
  flood control F-185
  wheat production W-135

Drowned coasts and valleys, formed when coastline subsides below sea level, permitting sea to cover land; estuaries of rivers so flooded are called "drowned valleys," and a coastline is called a "drowned coast" R-211, I-5, E-310

Drowning
  lifesaving techniques F-119, S-535

Drug abuse N-15, O-471, *pictures* H-100
  crime C-771
  drug addiction D-275
  juvenile delinquency J-163

Drug Abuse Control Amendments, penalties for illicit sale or possession of stimulants, sedatives, and hallucinogens D-277

Drug Abuse Office and Treatment Act, United States N-15

Drug Enforcement Administration, United States N-15, U-160

Drug laws. *see in index* Food and drug laws

Drugs, or **pharmaceuticals,** special chemical compounds D-273
  advertising A-59
  alcoholism A-276
  amnesia A-373
  anesthetics A-412. *see also in index* Anesthetics
  animal experimentation A-448
  antidotes P-410
  antihistimine A-492
  antitoxins
    Behring M-215c
    snakebite S-227
  arthritis A-650
  bioethical decisions B-214
  brain research B-400
  fatigue F-46
  hallucinogens. *see also in index* LSD; Peyote
    marijuana H-133
    narcotics A-48, N-15. *see also in index* Narcotics
    opiates O-471, P-446
  history M-215
  hormone manufacture H-229
  immunosuppressive S-519c
  industry P-248a
  pharmacy P-248a
  regulation N-15
    Food and Drug Administration F-274, P-538
  sources
    animal, *list* M-192
    bionics B-234
    plants P-377
  stimulants T-44, W-236
    caffeine C-535
  sulfa O-504
  therapy D-169

Drugstore beetle B-118, 140

Druids, priestly class among ancient Celts
  autumn festival H-12
  Celts C-242

Drum, any of a number of fishes belonging, with the croakers, to the family Sciaenidae; red drum (*Sciaenops ocellata*), called channel bass on Middle Atlantic coast and redfish in Texas, reaches weight of 35 kg (75 lbs); only member found exclusively in fresh water is the freshwater drum (*Aplodinotus grunniens*), also called gaspergou and sheepshead. *see also in index* Croaker

Drum, musical instrument M-568, *pictures* M-569
  bands B-55
  Garfield Cadets, *picture* B-57
  Mexican fiesta, *picture* M-246

Drumcliff Churchyard, County Sligo, Ireland, *picture* I-322

Drumheller, Alta., Canada, Red Deer River, 108 km (67 mi) n.e. of Calgary; coal mines, oil and gas fields in area; dinosaur bones found nearby, pop. 6508.

Drumlin, oval clay hill of glacial origin; common in w. New York, New England, and s. Wisconsin; Bunker Hill is a drumlin G-132
  Ice Age formation I-6

Drummond, Sir George Gordon (1772–1854), British soldier, born in Quebec, Canada; commanded British at Lundy's Lane, War of 1812; made general 1825.

Drummond, Henry (1851–97), Scottish religious writer and scientist, born in Stirling ('Natural Law in the Spiritual World'; 'The Ascent of Man').

Drummond, Sir Jack Cecil (1891–1952), English biochemist; professor of biochemistry University of London 1922–45; scientific adviser British ministry of food 1939–46.

Drummond, William (1585–1649), Scottish poet and historian, born near Edinburgh ('Flowers of Sion'; 'The Cypresse Grove').

Drummond, William Henry, (1854-1907) Canadian poet D-278

Drummond, Lake, s.e. Virginia, in center of Dismal Swamp; about 6 mi (10 km) in diameter; linked by Dismal Swamp Canal with Chesapeake Bay, *map* V-349

Drummond lights, or **calcium lights,** or **limelights** L-210

'Drums along the Mohawk', work by Edmonds A-358

'Drum-Taps', work by Whitman A-350

Drupe, fleshy fruit containing a stony seed covering, such as a peach F-465

Drury, Allen Stuart (born 1918), author, born in Houston, Tex.; on staff 'The New York Times' 1954–59; Washington correspondent 'Reader's Digest' 1959–63 ('Advise and Consent', awarded 1960 Pulitzer prize; 'A Shade of Difference'; 'Capable of Honor'; 'The Throne of Saturn').

Drury College, Springfield, Mo.; founded 1873; private control; arts and sciences, art, music, and teacher education; graduate studies.

Drury Lane Theatre, London, England L-288, T-156
  Garrick, *picture* G-34

Druzes, or **Druses,** religious sect of Syria and Lebanon combining elements of Islam, Christianity, and Judaism, founded by Hakim, 6th Fatimite caliph in 11th century; teaches belief in one God, who has appeared many times on earth, the last incarnation as D-278
  Hakim L-112, S-550
  Islam I-362
  Israel I-370

Dryad, or **Hamadryad,** mythology, a wood nymph F-12, N-386

Dryasdust, antiquary invented by Scott as figure in novels; the name, made more famous by Carlyle, is applied to a tiresome writer.

Dry battery, or **cell.** *see in index* Electric battery and cell

Dry bulk, cargo T-236

Dry cleaning D-278, L-85

Dry continental climate
  climate classification C-501

Dryden, Hugh L(atimer) (1898–1965), physicist, born in Pocomoke City, Md.; with National Bureau of Standards 1918–47, associate director 1946–47; director National Advisory Committee for Aeronautics 1949–58; deputy administrator NASA 1958–65; Presidential Certificate of Merit 1948 for developing missile used against Japanese in World War II; posthumously awarded National Medal of Science 1966.

Dryden, John (1631–1700), English poet, critic, essayist D-281
  English literature E-259
  poet laureate P-402

Dry dock H-26, S-171, *pictures* N-162c, R-269, S-171

Dryer, laundry L-84, *picture* L-87

Dry farming
  Spain S-351
  United States U-77
    Montana M-459
    Wyoming W-316

Dry fly, fly rod lure, *picture* F-142

Drygalski, Erich von (1865–1949), German polar explorer, geophysicist, and geographer; born in Königsberg, East Prussia, *table* P-422

Dry Ice, solidified carbon dioxide, trade name R-137
  snow S-228
  sublimation S-254f, M-168

Drying food. *see in index* Dehydrated food

Drying oils P-73–4

Dry measure, *tables* W-96

Dry-plate photography P-299

Dry-point etching E-280

Dry subtropical climate
  climate classification C-500

Dry Tortugas, group of 10 coral keys in Gulf of Mexico, 70 mi (110 km) w. of Key West; included in Florida; during Civil War, Fort Jefferson was Federal prison; Carnegie Institution set up marine biology laboratory 1904; nearby are commercially important shrimp beds, discovered 1949
  Fort Jefferson N. Mon. N-36, *map* N-30

Dry walls, or **plasterboard** B-494

Dry-wood termites T-106

Dry yeast Y-338

DSN, or **Deep Space Network** S-343b

Dual Alliance of 1891, union formed between France and Russia by a secret treaty to offset Triple Alliance (Germany, Austria, Italy); with entrance of Great Britain (1907) became Triple Entente.

Dualism, philosophy, *list* P-265

Dual Monarchy (Austria-Hungary). *see in index* Austria-Hungary

Dual-purpose cattle. *see in index* cattle

Duane, William John (1780–1865), American lawyer, born in County Tipperary, Ireland; came to Philadelphia when a child; appointed secretary of the treasury 1833 by President Jackson but replaced by Ralph B. Taney as result of quarrel over Bank of the United States; executor and director of Girard College 1831–65.

Duars plain, region in Bhutan B-180

Duarte, Calif., city 18 mi (29 km) n.e. of Los Angeles; electronic components, chemicals, wood products; pop. 16,766.

Duarte, Pico, mountain in Dominican Republic D-226

Dubai, United Arab Emirates, capital of the sheikhdom of Dubai and port, on Persian Gulf; commercial center and airport; pop. 55,000.

Du Barry, Marie Jeanne Bécu, Comtesse (1743–93), French adventuress, born in Vaucouleurs; followed Mme. de Pompadour as favorite of King Louis XV, over whom she had absolute influence; beheaded by revolutionists
  Petit Trianon V-303

Dubbing, motion pictures M-512

Dubček, Alexander (born 1921), Czech political leader, born in Uhrovec; joined Communist party 1939, first secretary 1968–69 C-816

Du Bellay, Jean. *see in index* Bellay, Jean du

Dubhe, star, *chart* S-422

Dubinsky, David (1892–1982), U.S. labor leader, born in Brest-Litovsk, Poland (now U.S.S.R.); an officer of International Ladies' Garment Workers' Union 1921–66, president 1932–66.
  labor movements L-10

Dublin, county on e. coast of Ireland, in province of Leinster; area 922 sq km (356 sq mi); industries, farms, fisheries; pop. 795,047, *map* I-283

Dublin, Ga., city 47 mi (76 km) s.e. of Macon, on Oconee River; farming and lumbering area; meat-packing; plywood, furniture, cottonseed and peanut oils, textiles; U.S. Navy hospital; pop. 16,083, *map* G-92

Dublin, Gaelic **Baile Atha Cliath,** Republic of Ireland, capital; pop. of greater city, 650,153 D-281, I-317, *pictures* I-319, 321, *map* G-199h
  National Botanic Garden, *table* B-379

Dublin, University of, or **Trinity College,** founded 1591; arts and sciences, divinity, law, medicine, engineering; open to women; fine library and manuscripts I-321, U-209

Dublin Castle, castle, Dublin, Ireland D-281

'Dubliners', work by Joyce J-144

'Dublin University Magazine', Irish literary publication I-327

Dubois, Clément François Théodore (1837–1924), French organist and composer, born in Rosnay, near Argentan.

Dubois, Eugène (1858–1941), Dutch anatomist and surgeon; on Java discovered bones of *Pithecanthropus erectus.*

Du Bois, Guy Pène (1884–1958), artist and writer on art, born in Brooklyn, N.Y., of Creole ancestry; landscape and figure compositions; advocate of realism.

Dubois, Paul (1829–1905), French sculptor and painter; his greatest work, in Renaissance spirit, is tomb of General Lamoricière at Nantes; also noteworthy are statues of Joan of Arc at Reims and Montmorency at Chantilly; painted only portraits.

Du Bois, W(illiam) E(dward) B(urghardt) (1868–1963), U.S. social leader D-282, N-126a, W-16
  NAACP B-293

Du Bois, William Pène (born 1916), author-illustrator of children's books, born in Nutley, N.J., son of Guy Pène du Bois ('Flying Locomotive', 'The Great Geppy', 'Lazy Tommy Pumpkinhead', 'The Horse in the Camel Suit', and the 'Otto' series; illustrated 'The Mousewife', by Rumer Godden).

Du Bois, Pa., industrial city 80 mi (130 km) n.e. of Pittsburgh; in coal region; railroad shops; gas meters, metal products, electronic equipment; Gateway Fair; pop. 9290, *map* P-184

Dubos, René Jules (1901–82), U.S. bacteriologist, born in France; professor Harvard Medical School 1942–44, The Rockefeller University 1957–71; 1969 Pulitzer prize in general nonfiction for 'So Human an Animal' shared with Norman Mailer S-64h

DuBridge, Lee Alvin (born 1901), educator and physicist, born in Terre Haute, Ind.; director radiation laboratory Massachusetts Institute of Technology 1940–45; president California Institute of Technology 1946–69; science adviser to U.S. president 1969–70; wrote 'Introduction to Space'.

Dubrovnik (Italian **Ragusa**), Yugoslavia, Adriatic port of Dalmatia, 61 km (38 mi) n.w. of Kotor; center of Serbian culture 15th to 17th centuries; pop. 55,000, *map* E-334

Dubuque, Julien (1762–1810), Canadian trader, born in St. Pierre les Brecquets, Que.; first white settler of Iowa; in 1788 secured permission from Fox Indians to work lead mines on Iowa side of Mississippi River; put old Indians and squaws to work in mines; died bankrupt; buried by Indians with the honors given a chief I-293, *picture* I-295

Dubuque, Iowa, city separated from Illinois and Wisconsin by Mississippi River; pin lead and zinc region; meat-packing, woodworking; construction and industrial equipment, furniture, farm machinery, plumbing supplies; Clarke College, Loras College, University of Dubuque; pop. 62,321, *map* U-41

Dubuque, University of, Dubuque, Iowa; affiliated with United Presbyterian Church in the U.S.A.; founded 1852; liberal arts, teacher education, and theology; graduate studies.

Ducat, gold coin formerly used in various countries of Europe; still used by Netherlands and other countries for foreign trade; historic value about $3.90, silver ducat worth about half this; first coined by Roger II of Sicily about 1150; coined by Venice, where it became known as *zecchino* ("sequin").

Duccio di Buoninsegna (about 1260–1320), Italian painter, born in Siena; founder of Sienese school of painting; influenced by Byzantine art; his great altarpiece painted for the Siena cathedral is still preserved.

Dummer / Duquesne

Robert Burns, pop. 28,149, *map* G-199g

Dummer, Jeremiah (1645–1718), silversmith and engraver, born in Newbury, Mass.; examples of work in colonial silver collections of Metropolitan Museum of Art, New York, N.Y., and Museum of Fine Arts, Boston, Mass.

Dumont, Gabriel (1838–1906), Canadian rebel, born in Assiniboia; took part in Northwest rebellion of 1885 as adjutant general of rebel forces; escaped to United States.

Dumont, N.J., borough in Bergen County, 16 mi (26 km) n.e. of Jersey City; cement industry; clothing; pop. 18,334, *map* N-202

Dumont d'Urville, Jules Sébastien César (1790–1842), French navigator, born in Condé-sur-Noireau, near Saint-Lô; explored and charted in the South Atlantic, South Pacific, and Antarctic, *table* P-422

Dumouriez, Charles François (1739–1823), French general, born in Cambrai; distinguished himself in French Revolution; had notable part in victories at Valmy, France, and at Jemappes, Belgium; suffered defeat at Neerwinden, Belgium, 1793, then denounced as traitor; died an exile in England.

Dun & Bradstreet, Inc., formerly **Mercantile Agency,** credit agency supplying to subscribers reports on the antecedents, character, capacity, capital, and credit of businessmen throughout the world; main office New York, N.Y.; grew from company formed 1841 by Louis Tappan; present name 1933.
credit rating C-763

Dunant, Jean Henri (1828–1910), Swiss author and philanthropist, born in Geneva; founder of Red Cross Society R-117

Dunbar, Paul Laurence (1872–1906), writer, born in Dayton, Ohio; best known for poetry, much of it in dialect; home in Dayton has been made a public shrine ('Lyrics of Lowly Life'; 'Lyrics of the Hearthside'; 'Complete Poems') N-126a, *pictures* N-124, O-426
literary contribution B-293, 301

Dunbar, William (1460?–1520?), Scottish poet; Sir Walter Scott said that he is "unrivaled by any which Scotland has produced"; disciple of Chaucer but with wider humor and less gentle satire ('Two Married Women and the Widow'; 'The Dance of the Seven Deadly Sins').

Dunbar, Scotland, resort town on Firth of Forth, 40 km (25 mi) e. of Edinburgh; historic old castle; Cromwell defeated Scottish Covenanters here 1650; pop. 4,460, *map* G-199g

Dunbarton College of Holy Cross, Washington, D.C.; Roman Catholic; for women; founded 1935; closed 1973.

Duncan (died 1040), Scottish king murdered by Macbeth; Shakespeare based his version of 'Macbeth' on Holinshed, who pictured Duncan as kind and honorable, but earlier historians disagree with this.

Duncan, Charles W. (born 1926), public official, born in Houston, Tex.; deputy secretary of defense 1977–79; secretary of energy 1979–81.

Duncan, Isadora (1877–1927), U.S. dancer D-289
dance D-29
Russian literature R-360a

Duncan, Okla., city 72 mi (116 km) s.w. of Oklahoma City; oil-field equipment, petroleum products; pop. 22,517, *map* O-446

Duncanville, Tex., town 11 mi (18 km) s.w. of Dallas; dairy farming; cotton; athletic equipment; pop. 27,781, *map* T-128

Dunce cap, *picture* E-83

'Dunciad, The', satiric poem by Alexander Pope P-445, E-261

Dundalk, Md., urban community just s.e. of Baltimore; steel manufacturing; large marine terminal of the Port of Baltimore; pop. 71,293, *map* M-139

Dundee, Scotland, seaport on Firth of Tay, 58 km (36 mi) n.e. of Edinburgh; chief linen and jute manufactures in Great Britain; shipbuilding; marmalade; three churches (Town Churches) under one roof; pop. 181,950, *maps* G-199g, S-67

Dundonald, earl of. *see in index* Cochrane, Thomas

Dundreary, Lord, caricature of a British nobleman in Tom Taylor's comedy 'Our American Cousin'; made famous by Edward A. Sothern; revived by his son Edward H. Sothern; at a performance of this play Lincoln was shot.

Dundy, Elmer, American politician A-385

Dune, sand. *see in index* Sand dune

Dunedin, New Zealand, important seaport on s.e. coast of South Island; woolen manufactures, gold mining; Otago University; pop. 105,600 D-289, N-275, *maps* N-277e, P-4

Dune dwellers M-432

Dunfermline, Scotland, in county of Fife, 26 km (16 mi) n.w. of Edinburgh; damask table linen; birthplace of Charles I and Andrew Carnegie; burial place of Robert Bruce; pop. 50,305, *map* G-199g

Dung beetle, or **tumblebug** B-120, 140, *pictures* B-138

Dungeon, or **Keep,** or **Donjon,** castle structure C-199

Dunguaire Castle, near Galway Bay, Ireland, *picture* I-317

Dunham, Bertha Mabel (1881–1957), Canadian author and librarian, born near Harriston, Ont.; won Canadian Book of the Year for Children award 1948 for 'Kristli's Trees'
books for adults include 'Toward Sodom', 'Trail of the King's Men', 'Grand River', 'Trail of the Conestoga'.

Dunham, Katherine (born 1910), U.S. dancer, choreographer, and anthropologist D-289

Dunkers, or **Dunkards,** name for German Baptist Brethren, the oldest body being Church of the Brethren (Conservative Dunkers); originated in Germany in early 18th century, but leaders soon moved to U.S.; practices similar to those of Quakers and Mennonites; advocate baptism by immersion, nonresistance, plain attire; refuse to take oaths
Pennsylvania P-166, *picture* P-173

Dunkirk (French **Dunkerque**), France, seaport on the Strait of Dover; pop. 73,618 D-290
World War II W-268, *pictures* W-269, 287

Dunkirk, N.Y., industrial city 37 mi (60 km) s.w. of Buffalo, on Lake Erie; in heart of grape belt; stainless steel, tool steel, foundry and metal products, textiles, grape juice and other food products; fine harbor; pop. 15,310, *map* N-260

Dun Laoghaire, formerly **Kingstown,** Ireland, seaport and resort on s. shore of Dublin Bay, 11 km (7 mi) s.e. of Dublin; pop. 51,772, *map* G-199h

Dunlap, William (1766–1839), playwright, painter, and author, born in Perth Amboy, N.J.; first professional dramatist of U.S.; helped found National Academy of Design; wrote histories of theater and arts of design in U.S.

Dunlin, shorebird of family Scolopacidae; the dunlin (*Erolia alpina*) is 20–23 cm (8–9 in.) long, rusty red above, with black patch across belly in summer plumage; in winter, gray above, grayish breast; stout long bill, with downward droop at tip; bird known in U.S. as red-backed sandpiper; nests across n. part of world; winters along Gulf of Mexico, Africa, India.

Dunlop, John Boyd (1840–1921), Scottish inventor and veterinary surgeon, born in Dreghorn, near Irvine; invented pneumatic bicycle tire; wrote 'History of the Pneumatic Tyre'.

Dunlop, John T. (born 1914), educator, labor mediator, public official, born in Placerville, Calif.; professor Harvard University 1950–; director Cost of Living Council 1973–74; U.S. secretary of labor 1975–76.

Dunmore, John Murray, 4th **earl of** (1732–1809), English colonial administrator; governor of New York 1770; governor of Virginia 1771–76; governor of Bahamas 1787–96.

Dunmore, Pa., industrial borough 2 mi (3 km) e. of Scranton; in anthracite-mining district; brick, stone, apparel; pop. 16,781, *map* P-185

Dunne, Finley Peter (1867–1936), journalist and humorist, born in Chicago, Ill.; famous for creation of "Mr. Dooley" ('Mr. Dooley in Peace and in War'; 'Mr. Dooley's Philosophy'; 'Mr. Dooley Remembers: the Informal Memoirs of Finley Peter Dunne', edited by Philip Dunne).

Dunning, John Ray (1907–75), nuclear physicist, born in Shelby, Neb.; with Columbia University from 1929 (professor from 1946, dean of engineering from 1950); pioneer in neutron research; a leader in developing atomic bomb; split uranium atom at Columbia University 1939; experimented with separation of U-235.

Dun River, England. *see in index* Don River

Dunsany, Edward John Moreton Drax Plunkett, 18th **Baron** (1878–1957), Irish story writer, dramatist, and poet, born in London, England; fantastic and imaginative work (plays: 'Plays of Gods and Men', 'Plays of Near and Far'; autobiography: 'Patches of Sunlight'; short stories: 'The Book of Wonder', 'The Sword of Welleran and Other Tales of Enchantment'; novel: 'Guerrilla') E-270

Dunsmore, John Ward (1856–1945), artist, born near Cincinnati, Ohio; known for historical subjects; work represented in National Academy of Design, New York, N.Y., and Art Museum, Cincinnati.

Dunsmuir, James (1851–1920), Canadian statesman and capitalist, born in Fort Vancouver, Wash., near Portland, Ore.; prime minister of British Columbia and president of the council 1900–2; lieutenant governor of British Columbia 1906–9.

Duns Scotus, John, also known as Doctor Subtilis (1265?–1308), Scottish theologian and philosopher, born at Duns; one of the greatest of the scholastics; celebrated opponent of doctrines of Thomas Aquinas; the bigoted stand Duns Scotus' followers, Duns men, took against classicism of Renaissance gave rise to use of his name in form of "dunce" to mean pedant and later ignoramus
Scholasticism P-265

Duns Scotus College, Southfield, Mich.; Roman Catholic; for men; founded 1930; Franciscan Friars seminary.

Dunstable, John (1370?–1453), English musician, born in Dunstable; one of earliest composers to use counterpoint.

Dunstan, Saint (925?–988), abbot of Glastonbury, archbishop of Canterbury, and adviser to kings Edmund I and Edgar of England; first of a long line of English ecclesiastical statesmen; festival May 19.

Duntroon, Australian military college M-320

Duodecimal system, or **base-twelve system** N-379b
multiplication table N-379c

Duodenum, the first portion of the small intestine S-455, *diagram* S-454
digestive system D-144, *diagram* D-143

Duomo, Italian word for cathedral. *see in index* Cathedral

Duotone, special method of making printing reproductions from black and white photographs or drawings to add depth and interest by two-color printing; the dot pattern of the two printing plates, made much as in four-color printing, retains the same range of dark and light areas so that the darker areas take on more color and heighten contrasts.

Dupatta, Pakistani scarf P-78

Duplation, or **doubling** A-593

Dupleix, Joseph François, Marquis (1697–1763), greatest French governor in India but failed to maintain French rule there; recalled to France 1754 and died in obscurity and want.

Duplessis, Joseph Sifrède, French artist
Franklin's portrait, *picture* F-385

'Duplex, The', work by Bullins A-363

Duplicate bridge. *see in index* Contract bridge

Duplicating machine, appliance for making multiple copies of typewritten or handwritten pages D-290. *see also in index* Addressograph; Flexowriter; Mimeograph; Multigraph
printing P-503

Du Pont, Éleuthère Irénée (1771–1834), U.S. industrialist, born in Paris, France; younger son of Pierre Samuel du Pont de Nemours; learned gunpowder making from Antoine Lavoisier; in 1802 founded near Wilmington, Del., a powder plant which became great chemical corporation, E.I. du Pont de Nemours & Company, Inc.; the firm was continued by his descendants: **Alfred Victor du Pont** (1798–1856), senior partner 1834–50. **Henry du Pont** (1812–89), head of the firm 1850–89. **(Thomas) Coleman du Pont** (1863–1930), president of the company 1902–15; U.S. senator 1921–22 and 1925–28. **Pierre Samuel du Pont** (1870–1954), president of the company 1915–19. **Irénée du Pont** (1876–1963), president of the company 1919–26. **Lammot du Pont** (1880–1952), president of the company 1926–40, chairman of the board 1940–48. Henry's son **Henry Algernon du Pont** (1838–1926), commanded Artillery in Civil War and was U.S. senator 1906–17. **Lammot du Pont Copeland** (born 1905), great-great-grandson of the founder, president of the company 1962–67, chairman 1968–71 D-291
Delaware D-76

Du Pont, Samuel Francis (1803–65), U.S. Navy officer, born in Bergen Point, N.J.; served in Mexican War and as Union rear admiral in Civil War; his father, **Victor Marie** (1767–1827), was elder son of Pierre Samuel du Pont de Nemours.

Du Pont de Nemours, Pierre Samuel (1739–1817), French statesman and political economist, born in Paris; imprisoned and property confiscated in French Revolution; emigrated to U.S. with family 1789; returned to France 1802, fled again to U.S. 1815; his sons Victor Marie and Éleuthère Irénée, founders of the two American branches of the family, dropped the "de Nemours" D-291

Du Pont de Nemours, E.I., & Company, Inc., world's largest maker of chemical products; headquarters, Wilmington, Del. D-291, W-169, *pictures* D-73, 81

Dupré, Jules (1812–89), French landscape painter, born in Nantes; member of the Barbizon School.

Dupré, Marcel (1886–1971), French organist, born in Rouen; brilliant record, Paris Conservatoire; phenomenal memory brought him wide acclaim; toured U.S. 1948.

Duquesne, Pa., iron and steel manufacturing city 10 mi (16 km) s.e. of Pittsburgh, on Monongahela River; pop. 10,094, *map* P-184

Duquesne University, Pittsburgh, Pa.; Roman Catholic; founded 1878; arts and sciences, business administration, education, law, music, nursing, pharmacy; graduate school; Institute of African Affairs, *map* P-345b

Duquesnoy / Duvoisin

Duquesnoy, François, also called **François Flamand** (1594?–1643), Flemish sculptor; skilled in portrayal of children in ivory, terra-cotta, bronze, and marble.

Duralumin, alloy of aluminum with copper, magnesium, manganese, and trace quantities of iron and silicon; resistant to corrosion.

Dura mater, the outermost of three membranes, or meninges, which cover the brain and spinal cord; tough and fibrous; name from Latin, meaning "hard mother."

Durance River, France, rises in French Alps, flows 345 km (215 mi) to Rhone.

Durand, Asher Brown (1796–1886), portrait and landscape painter and engraver, born in South Orange, N.J.; one of the founders of the National Academy of Design.

Durand, Ruth Sawyer. *see in index* Sawyer, Ruth

Durang, John, American dancer B-35

Durango, state in n. Mexico; 119,647 sq km (46,196 sq mi); pop. 1,121,925 (1976 est.); cap. Durango; several mining districts; united with Chihuahua until 1823, *map* M-260d

Durango, Colo., city and port in s.w., on Animas River, about 135 mi (215 km) s.e. of Grand Junction; pop. 11,426

Durango, Mexico, capital of state of Durango; altitude 1890 m (6,200 ft);center of agricultural, mining, and lumbering district; pop. 191,034, M-250, *map* M-260d

Durant, William Crapo (1861–1947) organized General Motors Corporation in 1908, *profile* A-856

Durant, Will(iam James) (1885–1981), historian and author, born in North Adams, Mass.; director Labor Temple School, New York, N.Y., 1914–27 ('The Story of Philosophy'); with his wife, **Ariel Durant** (Ida Kaufman Durant) (1898–1981), he wrote 'The Story of Civilization', the 10th volume 'Rousseau and Revolution' winning Pulitzer prize 1968, 11th and final volume 'The Age of Napoleon' 1975.

Durant, Okla., city 45 mi (70 km) s.e. of Ardmore; trade center of farming and livestock region; peanut processing; resort area; Southeastern State College; pop. 11,972, *maps* O-447, U-41

Durante, Jimmy, real name James Francis Durante (1893–1980), comedian, born in New York, N.Y.; called "Schnozzola" because of large nose; on stage, screen, radio, and television (plays: 'Strike Me Pink', 'Red, Hot and Blue', 'Stars in Your Eyes'; films: 'Get-Rich-Quick Wallingford', 'Music for Millions', 'Two Sisters from Boston').

Duranty, Walter (1884–1957), English journalist, born in Liverpool; in U.S. after 1949; best known for 'I Write as I Please', about his experiences as Moscow correspondent for 'New York Times'; wrote other reports on U.S.S.R., including 'USSR: the Story of Soviet Russia' and 'Stalin & Co.'

Durazzo, Albania. *see in index* Durrës

Durban, South Africa, chief seaport of Natal Province, on Indian Ocean; resort area; automobile assembling; chemicals, textiles; pop. 960,792 (1980 est.) D-291, N-16, *map* S-264

Durbar, historic British India, a court of Indian princes, held either for affairs of state or for receiving distinguished visitors.

Durendal, sword of Roland R-238

Dürer, Albrecht (1471–1528), German painter and engraver D-292, P-38
- 'Christ before Pilate', engraving, *picture* A-664
- drawing D-253, *picture* D-254
- 'Four Apostles' P-38, *picture* P-39
- Great Horse, engraving, *picture* H-236
- 'Holy Anthony, The', engraving, *picture* E-277
- method of engraving E-278
- Nuremberg, *picture* E-277

Durga. *see in index* Devi

'Durgesanandini', work by Bankim Chandra Chatterjee
- Indian literature I-108

Durham. *see in index* milking Shorthorn; shorthorn

Durham, John George Lambton, first **earl of** (1792–1840), English statesman, born in London; famous governor-general of Canada 1838 C-98

Durham, maritime county of n.e. England; 2630 sq km (1015 sq mi); industries include shipbuilding, ironworking, coal; pottery, paper, and glass; pop. 1,515,643, *map* E-218

Durham, England, county seat of Durham County, in n.e., on Wear River; university; cathedral; castle built by William the Conqueror; pop. 25,780, *map* G-199g

Durham, N.C., city in n.-central part of state, 20 mi (30 km) n.w. of Raleigh; industrial, educational, medical center; North Carolina Central University; pop. 100,538 N-325, *maps* N-336, 328, U-41

Durham, N.H., 30 mi (50 km) e. of Concord; pop. of township 10,652, *map* N-183

Durham report, Canadian history C-98. *see also in index* Durham, John George Lambton

Durham Station, N.C., battleground of Civil War near Durham, scene of Johnston's surrender to Sherman April 26, 1865; end of the war.

Durian, tall forest tree (*Durio zibethinus*) resembling the elm; grown in East Indies.

Durkheim, Émile (1858–1917), French sociologist D-292

Durkin, Martin P(atrick) (1894–1955), labor official, born in Chicago, Ill.; Illinois state director of labor 1933–41; president United Association of Journeymen and Apprentices of the Plumbing and Pipe Fitting Industry of the United States and Canada (A.F.L.) 1943–52 and after Sept. 1953; U.S. secretary of labor Jan.–Sept. 1953.

Duroc-Jersey, coarse, sturdy breed of hog H-197, *picture* H-198

Durovernum, England. *see in index* Canterbury

Durra, variety of grain sorghum native to Asia and n. Africa; introduced into U.S. as early as 1804; of slight economic importance
- millet M-325

Durrell, Lawrence (George) (born 1912), British novelist and poet, born in India; served in foreign press service at Athens, Greece, and at Cairo and Alexandria, Egypt (Alexandria Quartet: 'Justine', 'Balthazar', 'Mountolive', 'Clea').

Dürrenmatt, Friedrich (born 1921), Swiss author, born near Bern; novels and dramas important in contemporary German literature G-97

Durrës, (Italian **Durazzo**), Albania, seaport, formerly the capital; exports cheese, olive oil, cereal grains, tobacco; scene of important historical events since ancient times; pop. 39,946, *map* E-344

Dur Sharrukin ("City of Sargon"), Assyrian city near present village of Khorsabad, Iraq, close to modern Mosul; remains of Assyrian art found in 1843–55.

Durston, Hannah. *see in index* Dustin

Durum wheat W-132, *picture* W-134

Duruy, Jean Victor (1811–94), French historian and educator, born in Paris; minister of education 1863–69; wrote histories of France, Rome, Greece.

Duryea, Charles Edgar (1861–1938), born near Canton, Ill., and brother **James Frank** (1869–1967), born Washburn, Ill., automobile manufacturers, *profile* A-856, *picture* H-40

Du Sable, Jean Baptist Point, trader and first settler on site of Chicago, Ill. D-293, C-317

Du Sable Museum of African-American History, Chicago, Ill. landmark, *list* B-299

Duse, Eleonora (1859–1924), Italian actress D-293, A-27

Dushan, Stephen (Stephen Nemanya IX) (1308?–55), ruler of Serbia S-113

Dushanbe, formerly **Stalinabad,** Tadzhik S.S.R., capital; textile center; Tadzhik State University; pop. 374,000, *maps* R-322, 344

'Dusk', relief sculpture by Lachaise L-17

Dusky salamander S-25

Düsseldorf, West Germany, industrial city and port on Rhine River, 35 km (22 mi) n.w. of Cologne; in Ruhr-Rhineland industrial area; banking center; art, music, and educational city; pop. 583,445 D-293, *maps* G-99a, E-334
- Neanderthal man M-80

Dust, fine, dry particles of matter
- explosions E-361
  - prevention S-6
- fog formation F-246
- ice formation I-5
- solar system S-254d
  - Mars P-353
  - nebula N-123, *picture* U-202
- storms E-55
  - volcanic V-378

Dust Bowl, United States D-272
- Colorado C-568
- documentary film M-529
- soil conservation C-673, E-52, U-77

Dust-cloud hypothesis, theory of solar system's formation P-355

Duster, machine F-33

Dustin (Dustan, Duston, or **Durston), Hannah** (1657–?), heroine, born in Haverhill, Mass.; captured in Indian raid on Haverhill, March 1697; escaped after killing her captors with the aid of two other prisoners.

Dustpan dredge, machine for digging soil from bottoms of bodies of water D-258

Dusty miller, common name for several plants, especially *Lychnis coronaria* and species of artemisia, cineraria, and centaurea; one plant (*Centaurea cineraria*) has yellow or purple flowers; plants named for white, flourlike appearance of leaves and stems.

Dutch art
- delft pottery P-474
- painting N-137, P-31, *pictures* G-257, N-139, P-33

Dutch Borneo. *see in index* Borneo, Indonesian

Dutch cheese, or **Cottage cheese,** or **Pot cheese,** or **Smearcase** C-289

Dutch clover C-410

Dutch colonial architecture, *picture* S-266

Dutch East India Company, also called **United East India Company,** trading company established in 1602; had a monopoly of trade with East Indies E-43, I-271
- American exploration A-333
- colonies in South Africa S-266
- Hudson H-264, N-248
- Jakarta J-16

Dutch East Indies, or **Netherlands Indies.** *see in index* Indonesia

Dutch elm disease, fatal disease of elm trees, caused by fungus *Ceratostomella ulmi;* carried chiefly by European elm bark beetle; fungus spreads through the sapwood, destroying tree's circulatory system; diseased branches and trees must be removed and burned; first appeared in e. United States 1930 in a shipment of elm logs from Netherlands; spread rapidly w., in many communities killing almost every elm; powerful new insecticides, injected into healthy trees, have been found effective in controlling the disease. *see also in index* Elm bark beetle
- DDT use E-54
- fungi F-450

Dutch Guiana. *see in index* Surinam

Dutch Harbor, Alaska, village on small island in Aleutians; pop. 5; U.S. naval base set up in World War II, *map* U-39

Dutch in America
- architecture, *picture* N-248
- colonial government N-248
- Connecticut C-653
- Delaware D-75
- explorations H-264
- Irving I-358
- New Jersey N-193
- New York N-241, 248
- Pennsylvania P-173, 166

Dutch language N-135
- linguistic analysis L-230

'Dutchman, The', work by Baraka A-363

Dutchman's-breeches, spring wildflower (*Dicentra cucullaria*) of the n. and e. U.S.; named from shape of cream-colored blossoms, which cluster from stalks growing directly from root F-231, *picture* F-233

Dutchman's log, early method of calculating ship speed L-283

Dutchman's-pipe, or **pipe vine,** climbing shrub (*Aristolochia macrophylla*) of birthwort family; alternate heart-shaped leaves and brownish purple, pipe-shaped flowers; vine may climb to height of 9 m (30 ft); native both in temperate and warm regions.

Dutch metal, malleable brass containing approximately 76 to 80 percent copper and 20 to 24 percent zinc; rolled into thin sheets and used as imitation gold leaf.

Dutch Netherlands, or **United Provinces** N-139. For history, *see in index* Netherlands

Dutch Reformed church. *see in index* Reformed churches

Dutch West India Company, established 1621 with monopoly of trade on American and African coasts N-248
- commercial traders A-335, Y-343
- Delaware D-75
- New Amsterdam N-248
- Stuyvesant S-492

Dutch West Indies. *see in index* Netherlands Antilles

Dutt, Romesh Chunder (1848-1909), English author
- Indian literature I-108

Duty (customs) T-22. *see also in index* Tariff

Duun, Olav (1876–1939), Norwegian novelist, born on Fosnaes Island; taught in folk schools; 'The People of Juvik', six-volume cycle, traces history of a Norwegian peasant family from beginning of 19th century to the early 20th century.

Duval, Claude (1643–70), French highwayman in England, born in Domfront, Normandy; famous for daring and politeness; robbed "gentlemen of their purses and ladies of their hearts"; hanged at Tyburn.

Duvalier, François (1907–71), Haitian political leader D-293, H-8

Duvalier, Jean-Claude, (born 1951) president of Haiti from 1971; succeeded his father, François Duvalier, as president for life thus becoming the world's youngest president D-294

Duveneck, Frank (1848–1919), painter, etcher, and sculptor, born in Covington, Ky.; studied at Munich, Germany; taught at Cincinnati (Ohio) Art Academy; work bold and vigorous.

Duvetyn, duvetine, or **duvetyne,** soft fabric with a twill weave and velvety nap; originally made from woolen yarns, now from combinations of wool, spun silk, rayon, and cotton.

Du Vigneaud, Vincent (1901–78), biochemist, born in Chicago, Ill.; professor and head of biochemistry department, medical school, George Washington University, 1932–38; professor of biochemistry, medical college, Cornell University, 1938–67; professor of chemistry, Cornell University, 1967–75. *see also in index* Nobel Prizewinners, *table*
- vitamin H discovery V-358

Duvoisin, Roger (Antoine) (1904–80), American author-illustrator of children's books, born in Geneva, Switzerland; came to U.S. 1927 as textile designer, became citizen 1938; illustrated A. Tresselt's 'White Snow, Bright Snow' (1948 Caldecott medal) and 'Hide and Seek Fog'; wrote and illustrated 'And There Was America', 'They Put Out to Sea', 'A for the Ark', 'Two Lonely Ducks', 'The House of Four Seasons', 'Veronica', 'Lonely Veronica', 'Veronica's Smile' R-107

Duxbury, Mass., old town on Massachusetts Bay, 30 mi (50 km) s.e. of Boston; settled by Miles Standish, William Brewster, and John Alden 1631; pop. of township 11,807 S-410, *map* M-161
  Standish house, *picture* P-396

Dvina River. *see in index* Northern Dvina River; Western Dvina River

Dvinsk, Latvian S.S.R. *see in index* Daugavpils

Dvořák, Antonín (1841–1904), Bohemian composer and conductor D-294, M-559, *picture* M-560

Dwarf, adult who is much shorter than normal who has the condition known as dwarfism; the terms 'midget' and 'dwarf' have been used traditionally, but both terms are now considered insulting and 'little people' is the preferred term D-294, H-225
  folklore F-12
    'Gulliver's Travels' G-260, S-532, *picture* S-532
  Tom Thumb. *see in index* Tom Thumb

Dwarfism, growth disorder in humans which causes shortness of stature D-294

Dwarf cornel, or **bunchberry,** herb (*Cornus canadensis*) of the family Cornaceae, *picture* P-511

Dwarfed trees. *see in index* Bonsai

Dwarf gourami, fish A-463

Dwarf juniper, or **common juniper** J-157

Dwellings. *see in index* Architecture; Shelter

Dwiggins, William Addison (1880–1956), typographer, book designer and illustrator, born in Martinsville, Ohio; skilled in combining type and hand-drawn designs ('Layout in Advertising'; 'Form Letters–Illustrator to Author').

Dwight, John (1637 or 1640–1703), English potter, birthplace probably Oxfordshire P-474

Dwight, Jonathan (1858–1929), ornithologist, born in New York, N.Y; assistant surgeon, department laryngology, Vanderbilt Clinic, 1894–1904; president Linnaean Society 21 years; also president of the American Ornithologists' Union ('Gulls of the World'; 'Plumages and Molts of the Passerine Birds of New York'; 'A Study of the Scoters of the World').

Dwight, Theodore William (1822–92), jurist and educator, born in Catskill, N.Y.; famous law teacher and founder of law school at Columbia University; writer on law subjects; active in political and social (chiefly prison) reform.

Dwight, Timothy (1752–1817), clergyman and educator, born in Northampton, Mass.; president Yale College 1795–1817; able teacher and writer on religion and politics.

Dwight, Timothy (1828–1916), clergyman and educator, born in Norwich, Conn.; namesake of grandfather; president Yale College 1886–99; on American committee for the revision of the English Bible 1873–85.

Dworshak Dam, Idaho, on North Fork of Clearwater River I-21

Dyaks, people in Borneo E-40

Dyce, William (1806–64), British painter, born in Aberdeen, Scotland; belonged to Pre-Raphaelite school; paintings were of religious and Arthurian themes.

Dyck, Christopher van (17th century), Dutch type designer; types are considered more beautiful than Garamond's but historically not so important because they introduced no new influence T-318

Dy-Dee Baby, doll D-221

Dye D-295
  aniline N-292
  batik method B-106
  cloth, *picture* W-120
    wool W-228, *picture* W-232
    yarn, *picture* T-134
  colors C-561
  furs F-466
  molybdenum compounds M-425
  tamarind T-13
  toad secretion T-187
  X-ray examinations X-331

Dyer, Mary (died 1660), Quaker martyr; emigrated about 1635 from England to Massachusetts colony; driven out because of her sympathy with the tolerant religious views of Anne Hutchinson; became a Quaker and persisted in returning to Massachusetts despite two decrees of banishment; was finally hanged on Boston Common.

Dyersburg, Tenn., city in n.w. part of state, 18 mi (29 km) e. of Mississippi River; cotton and wool textiles, cottonseed oil; food processing; pop. 15,856, *maps* T-78, 96

Dyewood. *see in index* Brazilwood

'Dying Gaul', or **'Dying Gladiator',** famous Greek statue G-230

'Dying Swan', ballet by Fokine F-246

Dyke. *see in index* Dike

Dyke College, Cleveland, Ohio; private control; founded 1848; business administration.

Dykes, John Bacchus (1823–76), English clergyman, born in Hull; noted composer of hymn tunes ('Holy, Holy, Holy', words by Reginald Heber; 'Jesus, Lover of My Soul', words by Charles Wesley).

Dykstra, Clarence Addison (1883–1950), educator, born in Cleveland, Ohio; president University of Wisconsin 1937–44; director Selective Service (Army draft) 1940–41; chairman Defense Mediation Board 1941; provost University of California at Los Angeles after Nov. 1944.

Dylan, Bob, (born 1941), U.S. singer D-296

Dymaxion car, automobile designed by Buckminster Fuller F-446

Dynamic psychology P-519

Dynamics, mechanics of matter in motion M-206. *see also in index* Mechanics

Leibniz L-122

Dynamite E-361
  Nobel N-294

Dynamite tree. *see in index* Sandbox tree

Dynamo, electric generator. *see in index* Electric generator

Dynamometer, apparatus for measuring power P-483

'Dynasty of Raghu', epic poem by Kalidasa K-167

Dyne, the centimeter-gram-second (C.G.S.) system, a force which can accelerate a mass of one gram one centimeter a second every second.

D'Youville College, Buffalo, N.Y.; Roman Catholic; founded 1908; arts and sciences, nursing, and teacher education.

Dysentery, intestinal disease amoebic dysentery A-375 bacillary dysentery V-251

Dyslexia, reading problem R-103e, *picture* R-103f

Dyspepsia, or **indigestion,** digestive disorder.

Dysphasia. *see in index* Aphasia

Dysprosium (Dy), rare chemical element, *table* P-483

Dzershinski Square, Khar'Kov, U.S.S.R., *picture* K-231

Dzhugashvili, Iosif Vissarionovich, real name of Joseph Stalin S-402

Dzibilchaltun, Yucatán Y-349, *map* M-260e
  archaeology A-533